HOWELL D. CHICKERING, JR.

Beowulf

Howell D. Chickering, Jr., is the G. Armour Craig Professor of Language and Literature at Amherst College. His critical essays, chiefly on medieval English poetry, have appeared in such journals as *The Chaucer Review*, *Journal of English and Germanic Philology*, *Journal of Medieval and Renaissance Studies*, *The Kenyon Review*, *Philological Quarterly*, *PMLA*, *Speculum*, and *Viator.*

Beowulf

Beowulf

A DUAL-LANGUAGE EDITION

Translated and with an Introduction and Commentary by

HOWELL D. CHICKERING, JR.

Anchor Books

A DIVISION OF RANDOM HOUSE, INC.

NEW YORK

ANCHOR BOOKS EDITIONS, 1977, 1989, 2006

Copyright © 1977, 2006 by Howell D. Chickering, Jr.

Library of Congress Cataloging-in-Publication Data
Beowulf : a dual-language edition.
Bibliography: p.
I. Chickering, Howell D.
PR1583.C48
829.3
72-21250

Anchor ISBN-10: 1-4000-9622-7
Anchor ISBN-13: 978-1-4000-9622-0

www.anchorbooks.com

Printed in the United States of America

To Kate, Julie, and Ben

Contents

Preface

This book is meant to make *Beowulf* available as poetry to readers who have not studied Old English (Anglo-Saxon) before and to those who have only a rudimentary knowledge of it. The text, translation, and commentary are designed for flexible use, from a rapid reading of the translation to a literary study of the Old English poem.

Beowulf is the first great heroic poem in English literature. Usually this important fact is not obvious to the general reader when he reads the poem in Modern English. Invariably it seems quaint. The trouble is that *Beowulf* is so rich in meaning that no single transla-tion, however excellent, can make all or even most of its poetry come across. Thus in this presentation I have chosen to keep the original text always on view. The facing translation gives its gist (one man's version) and the commentary offers background information necessary for understanding. This method does not bring out every meaning of the original—poetry being the ornery, delightful thing it is—but if the reader will use these two aids alongside the Old English, he can experience its poetic power first hand.

One insurmountable problem with any free-standing translation of *Beowulf* is that the greatness of the original depends importantly on the clangor and magnificence of the language, the very sound of its sense. It cannot be duplicated in any other words. Of course, this goes for all poetry in translation, but here it is a larger drawback than usual, because *Beowulf* was composed to be heard aloud, prob-ably recited by a bard before a company of men. Its art, based on traditional oral poetry, is highly sophisticated in diction and sound texture. Any real encounter with this poem must include an appre-ciation of how it sounds and some idea of "how it goes" in the original. A dual-language edition seems the best way to make these features evident to the general reader. But even the dual-language approach is useless unless the sound comes alive on the reader's tongue while he has the sense clearly in mind. I have therefore included a Guide to Reading Aloud. By using this Guide and the facing translation, the reader should be able to read the Old English text aloud with adequate comprehension and a fair sense of its rhythmic power. One ought to read aloud frequently, in fact—at times, even declaim it—in order to capture the energy and sonority that make *Beowulf* a permanent delight.

My translation takes a few liberties from time to time, but for the most part it gives the plain sense of the original or, when a literal translation would be unclear, the intended meaning as I see it. By not trying to imitate the alliteration and other audible features of the facing original, I was able to concentrate on reproducing (so far as possible) the poetic ordering of parts, sentence by sentence. The punctuation and the facing lines do not correspond exactly, due to differences between Old and Modern English, but the translation keeps pace with the original every five lines. The nuances of meaning lost by this approach, and alternative translations of difficult phrases, are mentioned in the notes frequently enough, I think, to confirm the truth of E. T. Donaldson's observation that "the *Beowulf* poet (along with most great poets) forges a complex style that simultaneously discloses differing aspects of the same situation; lacking his vision and his language (not to mention his talent), we tend to emphasize one aspect at the expense of the other." [1]

The verse form of the translation is the best solution I could find to the problem of keeping a sense of poetry alive when one is reading only the Modern English. It seemed to me that if the language of a translation were clear enough and the sound of the original immediately available, then the prose sense could work within a framework of lines—the ghost of a poetic form, as it were—to let the reader feel still in touch with poetry. Not even the professional Beowulfian can easily imagine a prose version back into poetry, and a sense of *lines* seemed indispensable to give the casual reader a fair sense of the form and pace of the original. But what sort of lines?

---

[1] E. Talbot Donaldson, *Beowulf: A New Prose Translation* (New York: W. W. Norton & Co., 1966), p. xiii.

After some experiment and study of other translations, I concluded that the form of the original is best conveyed by a four-stress line with a heavy caesura, using alliteration and assonance only sparingly. The problem is one of tact. Alliteration is a key element in Old English metrics and almost unavoidable in translations of *Beowulf*, but long stretches of it in Modern English will stupefy the most ardent reader. My verse form derives instead from the stress pattern in the Old English line, which is an equally basic element in the metrical scheme. The translation is not a metrical imitation, however. The stresses follow the natural emphasis of the Modern English sense, sometimes with five beats in a line instead of four.

The translation has few other pretensions to literary form. I have not hesitated to use blind references and parataxis to give some inkling of the craggy sentence structure of the original, which probably was "difficult" at points even for the Anglo-Saxon audience. As for the flamboyant, highly connotative vocabulary of the Old English —properly the despair of any translator—it is usually subdued by other literary effects, notably by ironic understatement and a severe economy of meter. Thus I felt I could leave the more complex connotations for the commentary as long as the translation did not sound overblown. I have tried to keep the facing version always one step lower in pitch than the original. There is a truly heroic restraint in the Old English lines that is felt continually as one reads along. Of all the different aspects of the poem, this restraint seemed most important for a facing translation, since it would indicate the presence of further poetic qualities in the original.

Even with a previous knowledge of Old English, it is very hard to read through the original for the first time and feel you have absorbed it all. Large poetic forces seem to be at work, imperfectly understood. This pleasant difficulty is complicated by the fact that the literal meaning is often in doubt and the significance of many passages is hotly debated by critics. Thus a serious effort to present the whole poem should really include alternative translations and some indication of the range of possible interpretations. Most translations do not present this side of the poem, and with some reason. The poet tells a good story superlatively well, and his basic design, which joins a meditation on mortality to the events of the hero's life, comes through clearly even in prose. Recent scholarship has clarified much, but it can be argued that too many questions remain for anyone but specialists to bother to scrutinize the poem closely. On the other hand, you can say that if a poem is worth reading at all, it is worth reading attentively. Much of the literary and cultural context of *Beowulf* is now lost to us or can be understood only by knowing a certain amount of lore. Some interpretation is necessary if one wants to understand the poem on its own terms. Therefore, besides alternative translations and critical remarks, the commentary contains background information and discussions of difficult questions. The notes are limited to what I thought would abet literary understanding and are selective rather than comprehensive. Even so, it is likely they will be too voluminous for some readers. As a student and teacher of Old English, I know only too well how annotation can deaden the very things it was meant to illuminate. I will be happy indeed if this presentation of *Beowulf*, used roughly or gently, brings the reader to that point of rereading and savoring which every great poem deserves.

Acknowledgments

For permission to use their manuscript facsimiles I am indebted to the Council of the Early English Text Society and to the publishing house of Rosenkilde and Bagger, Copenhagen. I wish to thank the Trustees of Amherst College for a Ford Foundation Trustee-Faculty Fellowship in 1969–70 which enabled me to work on this book. I also thank Presidents Calvin H. Plimpton and John William Ward and Dean Prosser Gifford for generous subsidies toward its preparation.

It is a pleasure to acknowledge help of many kinds from Charles Adams, Willis Barnstone, Saul Brody, Frederic Cheyette, Howell D. Chickering, Sr., Rowland Collins, Benjamin DeMott, Eugene Eoyang, Valdemaro Fioravanti, John M. Hill, Kemp Malone, Floyd Merritt, William Pritchard, Georgie Remer, Michael Simpson, William Strachan, and R. H. Turcotte. My *Beowulf* classes at Amherst College and the University of Colorado helped me sharpen my sense of how to present the poem to a modern audience. Among many students I thank especially Stephen Belcher, Martin Bickman, Alan Blum, David Greenlie, Michael Millikin, and Kemp Roelofs. For truly expert assistance in typing the manuscript I thank Colin Hasse and Irene Morrissey. I am grateful also to Sharon Livesey, who read a penultimate draft of the translation against the original and made many valuable criticisms. Professor Edward B. Irving, Jr., of the University of Pennsylvania very kindly read the entire book in manuscript, and I owe him special thanks for saving me from both the clumsy and the embarrassing. I also thank Professor John M. Hill of the United States Naval Academy for his invaluable assistance in proofreading the Old English text. Professor Mary Blockley of Smith College collaborated in preparing the appendix of glosses, for which I thank her most gratefully. Errors and inadequacies that remain are my own.

I am grateful to Anchor Books for allowing me to add an After-word nearly thirty years after the first edition of this book. I thank Susan Raymond-Fic for her assistance in preparing the accompanying Section IV of the Bibliography, and my colleagues Fredric L. Cheyette of Amherst College, Craig R. Davis of Smith College, Stephen J. Harris of the University of Massachusetts at Amherst, and John M. Hill of the United States Naval Academy for reading drafts of the Afterword and making helpful suggestions. I also thank Sara Jane Moss, my favorite general reader, for her good ear and uxorial attention to my tone.

Introduction

Beowulf is written in the unrhymed four-beat alliterative meter of Old English poetry. It is the longest surviving poem in Old English, containing 3,182 lines. Roman numerals divide the poem into an introduction and forty-three sections, or fitts. They are of unequal length and their numbering is a bit confused. While these sections often match the logical breaks in the narrative, they do not reveal a clear division into chapters or cantos. The fitts may be a later scribal addition and not the work of the poet, who remains anonymous. The poetic structure of *Beowulf* is a good deal more intricate than the fitt divisions indicate, or than the story itself. But the story comes first.

SUMMARY

Part I

Lines 1–836. The poem opens, as it is to end, with a funeral: the sea burial of Scyld, the founder of the Danish royal line. The first fifty lines are the epitome of a hero's career, combining loss with triumph. Then the main narrative begins. King Hrothgar of Denmark has long been afflicted by a huge demon, Grendel, who nightly kills and eats the warriors in the king's great hall, Heorot. Beowulf, a prince of the Geats, a tribe located in southeastern Sweden, hears of the trouble in Denmark and journeys there with his troop of men to win his fame by challenging the giant monster. He is the strongest man of his time, with the force of thirty men in

1

his hand-grip. His reception at Hrothgar's court is described at length. On the night of his arrival Grendel attacks again, but God favors Beowulf, who conquers Grendel barehanded, ripping off the monster's arm at the shoulder.

Lines 837–1250. The next morning there is general rejoicing. Heroic tales of Sigemund and Heremod are told in Beowulf's honor. At the royal banquet that evening Hrothgar gives him sumptuous gifts. A bard sings the lay of the Finnsburh episode. The juxtaposition of this tragic feud from the Danish past with the present festivities allows the poet to hint that the Danish royal house will soon fall through treachery.

Lines 1251–1650. Later that night Grendel's mother attacks the hall to avenge her son and carries off Hrothgar's chief counselor. Beowulf undertakes to dive to the bottom of the mere, or haunted lake, where she dwells. His second great combat, in her underwater dwelling, is difficult and at first she nearly kills him. He finally manages to slay her, with the help of a strange, magical sword he finds in the mere-hall. He is given up for dead by the onlookers, but when he resurfaces he is carrying Grendel's head, which he has cut off for a trophy. He has now cleansed Denmark of the evil race of monsters.

Lines 1651–1887. When Beowulf announces his deed to the king, Hrothgar warns the young hero of the dangers of pride, in a sermon of exceptional poetic force. The next day, after more gift-giving, Beowulf departs. The old king, who loves him like a son, weeps to see him go.

Lines 1888–2199. Back in Geatland Beowulf reports his doings to his uncle, King Hygelac. He prefaces them with an account of the state of Denmark, which he foresees will soon be attacked by a neighboring tribe, the Heathobards. Beowulf tells of a proposed peace settlement, in which Hrothgar has given his daughter in marriage to Ingeld, the king of the Heathobards. In Beowulf's opinion the peace will not last long. Then he gives his beloved chieftain Hygelac the gifts he received from Hrothgar, and Hygelac rewards him even more magnificently, giving him treasure and lands.

Here ends the story of Beowulf's youth, or Part I as it is often called, two thirds through the poem. Part II, his final combat in old age, occupies the last thousand lines of the poem. It brings to har-

vest the tragic anticipations of the old heroic stories in the interlaced
episodes of Part I. As the action gets underway, the atmosphere is
heavy with an elegiac sense of loss and impending doom.

Part II

Lines 2200–2541. After the death of Hygelac and his son, due
to their poor judgment as war-leaders, Beowulf comes to the Geatish
throne. He rules peacefully for fifty years, until a robber disturbs a
sleeping dragon that guards a treasure hidden in a grave-mound. The
dragon awakes and flies flaming through the night, burning down
houses. Beowulf goes with his troop to the mouth of the dragon's
cave, where he meditates at length on the tumultuous and bloody
history of the royal house of the Geats and their bitter feuds with
the Swedes. He declares heroically that he will meet the dragon in
single combat and bids his men stand aside.

Lines 2542–2723. When Beowulf resists the dragon's first charge,
he is engulfed in flames. All his men flee in terror except one young
warrior, his kinsman Wiglaf, who rushes through the flames to
Beowulf's aid. In the dragon's second charge, Beowulf strikes the
dragon's head, and his sword breaks from the overpowering strength
of his grip. In the third attack, the dragon bites Beowulf through the
neck. Then Wiglaf thrusts his sword through the dragon's soft under-
belly, and the flames abate. Beowulf finishes off the dragon with his
knife, but it is plain that he has received his death-wound.

Lines 2724–2891. Beowulf bids Wiglaf bring him the treasure
from the dragon's hoard, so that he may see it before he dies. He
rejoices that he has ruled well and can die with a good conscience,
laments that he leaves no heirs, and gives Wiglaf orders for his
burial-mound. He dies, and Wiglaf grieves. The cowardly troops now
return and receive the full measure of Wiglaf's scorn.

Lines 2892–3182. Wiglaf sends a messenger with the news of
Beowulf's death to the king's stronghold. The messenger's speech to
the king's council is an epic prophecy of the doom of the Geats at
the hands of their enemies now that their protector is dead. Beowulf
is cremated on a great pyre, and the treasure and his ashes are buried
together in a monumental barrow on a headland by the sea.

STYLE

Diction

To appreciate the poetry that tells this story, it is helpful to know something about its literary conventions. Often they differ sharply from what we expect to find in modern poetry. The Old English term for the poet was *scop* 'the maker,' from the verb *scieppan* 'to shape, to make.' Apparently the poet's shaping activity was not consciously regarded as invention or as due to inspiration. Old English poetry always describes the bard's activity as "to exchange words," "to tie words together," "to find one word bound truly to another." Such phrases indicate that the Old English poet composed, whether aloud or in writing, by drawing on a commonly shared pool of poetic diction. He would "tie" pairs of half-lines together by their stressed alliteration, often with some additional semantic or syntactic connection between the stressed words. (For a description of the verse form, see the Guide to Reading Aloud.)

These half-lines were in fact metrical formulas, and they lend a special decorum to the diction of *Beowulf*. The audience (and the poet) could take a primal satisfaction in the way traditionally corresponding phrases were joined, like to like, across the caesura. *Eorl* 'noble' or *æþeling* 'prince' in the first half-line would almost irresistibly suggest that *ellen* 'courage, valor' should receive the alliterating stress in the second half-line. To hear this expectation fulfilled created a strong aesthetic sense of "rightness." This binding together of complementary words creates hundreds of pairs that are used over and over, such as *hālig/heofon* 'holy'/'heaven,' *dryhten/duguð* 'lord'/'troop,' and *fyren/fēond* 'sin'/'enemy.' Apparently Old English poets and their audiences thought of these alliterating pairs not only as metrical equivalents but also as corresponding in meaning. This does not mean that the poets could only select standard patterns, or that the diction forced them to make trite associations across the caesura. The better Old English poets had developed the art of adjusting their formulas to the precise context of the narrative. They were hardly ever forced to choose one word over another simply to meet the demands of alliteration. In addition, there was the further pleasure of surprising yet not entirely thwarting the listener's expectations by the use of contrastive pairs. Examples are *ēadig/earm* 'happy'/'wretched' or *wearm/winter* 'warm/winter.' Again and again in *Beowulf* such dictional contrasts point up the larger meaning of the action.

Alliterative contrast is prominent, for instance, in line 119: *swefan æfter symble—   sorge ne cūðon* 'sleeping after feast—   they knew not sorrow.' Such dictional undercurrents of narrative irony can be extended for several lines, as in the swift narrative transition to sorrow after joy when the poet first introduces Grendel in lines 99–101. There the alliterating words gain in drama and thematic meaning because "blessedly" is matched with the evil "one" (100). The poet uses the same motif of sorrow-after-joy again, with even the same formula of *oð ðæt ān ongan* 'until one began,' when he introduces the dragon two thousand lines later (2209–11). When heard aloud, these lines send a shiver up the spine. They boldly assert a sudden change and seem to imply that there is a violent instability abroad in the world. They have this quality of palpability because the poet brought to full life the innately contrastive properties of the alliterative line. The verse form itself seems to enact the impending change in events.

Vocabulary

The lexicon of *Beowulf* is loaded with synonyms and partial synonyms: there are more than thirty different words for "king" alone. It is a "word-hoard" indeed, with some four thousand vocabulary entries for a little more than three thousand lines. Many of these words—in fact, a third of the whole vocabulary—are compounds. Often they are different combinations of the same compound elements, adapted to a particular context. Their referents are usually the recognizable furniture of the heroic world—the hero, his companions, and his adversaries. But while "the sea" or "a battle" are familiar and simple concepts, when roughly fifty different poetic compounds are used for each, the sheer abundance of appropriate names elevates the concepts to the epic level. On the average, there is a nominal or adjectival compound every other line and a new compound in every third line. A large number of these compounds are far removed from the ordinary Old English prose vocabulary, and many of the most interesting are unique to *Beowulf*. The author was by far the most gifted Old English poet in his verbal inventiveness.

Naming

Naming is basic to all poetry, but perhaps most so to Germanic alliterative verse, which has its presumed origins in magic and ritual. The runes of the native Old English alphabet were originally the secret names for things, and a knowledge of them gave powers to men. The stressed, alliterating words in *Beowulf* are usually nouns and adjectives, and the heavy nominalism of the poetic lexicon was doubtless inherited. However, the poet utilized it more fully than other Old English poets. In the act of making compounds, he also made kennings and variations. The kenning, originally an Old Norse term, is a descriptive name or poetical periphrasis, like *helm-berend* 'the helmet-bearing one' for a warrior; or *hron-rād* 'the whale's pasture' for the sea; or *hilde-lēoma* 'battle-flame' for a sword. This last example is about as imagistic as this sort of metaphorical naming ever becomes in Anglo-Saxon hands. The Old Norse skalds took the kenning to extravagant lengths, but poetic appellations in Old English are usually either transparent equivalents for the literal word or variations upon a previously stated term. Once a sword was called a *sweord*, then the "battle-flame" just cited might come next, to be followed by *gūð-bill* 'war-sword.' This interplay of naming has a metaphorical value in itself, but *Beowulf*, like most Old English poetry, lacks many direct metaphors that boldly substitute one thing or quality for another unlike it. Similes are rare, too, and when they occur in *Beowulf* they command special thematic attention, as when the strange sword from the mere melts away "like an icicle when God unwinds the bonds of frost" (1605 ff.). The similes have a studied quality, and usually occur at moments of reflection during the aftermath of events.

The poet was also fond of intentional ambiguity or double meaning, as in *wæl-fylle* 'slaughter-fall' 125, where the second element *-fyll* can suggest "feast" or "fill" as well as "a fall in battle." A poet who could show the cool-eyed wit of naming Grendel the "hall-guard" of the Danes was hardly the man to overlook the right opportunities for such word play. Very likely he also intended thematic significance for many of the names of his characters. Hrothgar's hall is named after his royal emblem, *Heorot* 'hart, stag.' "Wolf" and "Boar" are the names of two especially thuggish young warriors who appear late in the poem. *Hyge-lāc,* most recently etymologized as "instability of thought," goes on a disastrously misjudged raid to Frisia. By contrast his queen, *Hygd* 'thought, mind,' stays at home, and when he dies she wisely offers the kingdom to Beowulf. Hygelac's name already existed when the poet began his poem, but he probably invented the name Hygd to bring out its significance by contrast. Another character, Unferth, has been plausibly explained as a quasi-allegorical figure named "Strife," from "un + peace." His lineage almost sounds like a moral equation: Sword's Legacy (*Ecg-lāf*) sires Mar-Peace (*Un-ferð*). Alternatively, *Unferð* might be taken as "foolish" or "poor-spirited." Not all of these thrusts of etymological wit are certain, but there are enough overly appropriate proper names in *Beowulf* to conclude that the poet commanded this learned mode of signification.

Variation

The technique of variation has been called "the very soul of Old English poetical style," and it is highly developed in *Beowulf.* "Variation" is basically a double or multiple statement of one concept or term in which each restatement suggests a new aspect, be it a more general attribute or a more specific one. The simplest form of variation is an epithet following a name. More complex variations may run to five or more restatements, as in the names for God in lines 180 ff. or for Hrothgar in 350 ff. Usually variations are cast in grammatically parallel form, as in 2132–33: "I did heroic deeds, risked my life, performed glorious feats." In addition to slowing the narrative pace, variation raises into high relief those aspects of the action the poet wishes to emphasize. In any poetry that depends on formulas, there will be a strong artistic pressure to vary the formulas, but this should not mislead us into thinking that variation is merely ornamentation. In the *Beowulf* poet's hands, it is an analytic instrument. He will usually break an event into its separate components and present them as a series of pictures, like a tapestry. This verbal

splitting and recombining of ordinary perceptions to create some-
thing new is a sign of true poetry and is related to the larger cyclical
structure of the poem.

Syntax

As we listen to the poem aloud, we can hear that the poet's basic
method is to hang a notion, a referent, in the air and then to rewrite
it in its several simultaneous aspects. This is basically the method
of recurrence-with-elaboration (Joan Blomfield's term) and there
must be a grammatical device to carry along the nouns and adjectives
that will elaborate the concept. In addition to parallelism, the Old
English poetic style uses parataxis (lack of subordinating connec-
tives) to create a forward-leaning sentence that can tolerate an in-
definite number of additions before its close. This sort of "free
grammatical space" can be seen in the paratactic lines 2132–33
translated above. In that variation many more than three clauses
might have been added. They might have been complementary,
balancing each other, or they might have been contrastive. We may
justly feel that the second clause has an air of subordination about
it, as though it meant "*when* I risked my life." Perhaps the poet, in
recitation, inflected his half-lines so as to give his listeners a sense
of higher and lower grammatical importance.

We can't always know how to interpret the parataxis. In line
2390b we encounter the half-line *þæt wæs gōd cyning* 'he was a good
king.' This comes at the end of a verse paragraph describing how
the Swedish king Onela took vengeance upon Hygelac's son. After
he killed him, Onela left the Geatish throne in Beowulf's hands.
Who was the good king, Beowulf or Onela? The words lying quiet
on the page without grammatical connection will not resolve the
question. We have to look to the narrative context for an answer.
More usually, as in lines 6–11, parallel constructions and syntactic
subordinations permit a lengthy yet elaborately controlled variation
upon a simple idea.

The poet makes syntax itself into a dramatic instrument when he
describes combats. Temporal and causal sequences are ordered so
as to bring us right up close to the most violent actions. An example
is when the doors of Heorot burst apart upon Grendel's entry, and
we see the result before the cause. A more complicated example

occurs in lines 1269–74, where the dual factors by which Beowulf conquers Grendel—his own strength and God's help—are arranged in a syntactic microcosm of the Boethian universe of the poem. Beowulf's strength is given him by God, in a subordinate clause that falls between his two sources of power, which are expressed in paratactic parallel clauses. Their duality is maintained throughout the long sentence. Its final clause stating the results of these dual factors even has both parallel clauses for antecedents.

Litotes

The poem's style has a deliberate pace, slowly building up telling details, to gain both depth and immediacy. At the same time, the poet will make sharp juxtapositions of contrasting themes, moods, or episodes that throw his own viewpoint into the foreground. One of his most attractive forms of verbal irony, and one general to the Old English heroic style, is litotes, or deliberately steep understatement, often couched in the negative. A good example is the interjected comment in lines 1506–9, the most frightening point in Beowulf's fight with Grendel's mother:

> Bær þā sēo brim-wylf,   þā hēo tō botme cōm,
> hringa þengel   tō hofe sīnum,
> swā hē ne mihte,   —nō hē þæs mōdig wæs—
> wæpna gewealden

> Then the angry sea-wolf   swam to the bottom,
> carried to her den   the lord of those rings,
> clutched him so hard   he might not draw sword,
> —no matter how brave—

Literally the interjection translates as "he was not at all spirited about that" and we can well imagine that Beowulf felt a good bit less than swell. A sharp incongruity like this can wrest a grin from us even at the direst points in the action. Here it invites our sympathy for the hero's distress—even as we smile, we share his grim doggedness. At other points, litotes seems aimed at an abstract laughter generated by the heroic code. For example, after Beowulf has dismembered Grendel and delivered his victory speech, "then was

Ecglaf's son [Unferth] the more silent about [his own] war-works."
The pregnant comparative means that the obstreperous Unferth was
shamed into complete silence and possibly even moved to open ad-
miration of Beowulf's great deed. However litotes is applied (and in
the dragon fight this device is hardly humorous), its tense under-
statement, the assertion by near silence, is best understood as a form
of heroic irony.

General Features of Style

The poet creates wide-ranging effects through litotes. Not all are
sad. He is jovial in his treatment of Beowulf's exchanges with the
Danish coast-guard and Unferth, and in the comic psychology with
which he presents Grendel's last trip to Heorot. The latter episode
is done from the fumbling loser's point of view and would be openly
hilarious if we were not also caught up in the terror and excitement
of the fight itself. Throughout Part I, the poet offers crisp, bright
images of the heroic world. There is a sparkling glitter both from
the waves of the ocean and the armor of warriors marching on the
beach. Simple images bring the familiar to fresh life, and we feel,
through the poet's own ease and vigor, much of the youthful high
spirits of Beowulf himself. Yet there is always room in this style for
acute contrasts, darkenings of mood, ironic undercurrents. Thus
when Part II takes on a more elegiac character, we are impressed
not only by the vivid rendering of poignant situations and the poet's
capacity for expressing deep feeling directly; we also recognize and
admire the sustained dignity of a style that has given him such scope.
As the modern scholar-poet Gwyn Jones has it, he touches the harp
both in joy and in sorrow, and with as much variety of effect and
orchestration of parts as in a nineteenth-century opera.

Having sought to find, in a Modern English translation, some sort
of equivalent for the poet's maneuvers of style, I discover, oddly,
that I have lost respect for certain lines and have gained admiration
for others. It cannot be said that the poetry itself is, line by line,
even or smooth. As one would expect from the diction and devices
described above, it is various, a whole landscape filled with heights
and flats. Its language is always marvelous when it is focused on the
concrete, which includes states of feeling as well as objects and
actions. Yet how flat and loose the language can become when ad-

monishing a character or thinking out a thought. The generalizations in the poem seem to come from the stylistic world of homily and gnome, the action and speeches from earlier heroic verse. The sequential transitions—not the poetic juxtapositions, that is, but the familiar "and then . . . and then"—show many of the seams and joints found in later Middle English minstrel verse. Yet to acknowledge these deficiencies is not to derogate *Beowulf*. It has fewer faults of style than *Paradise Lost*. And its successes are enormous. While the style is slow, open, and massive in the larger structure of its verse paragraphs, line by line it is like the poems of Gerard Manley Hopkins: packed, crowded, ornate, abrupt. The poet loved words for their own sake, their malleability, their playful likeness to each other (a bear bears beer on a bier). He displays an almost sinful luxury in the ceremonious variety of his always just epithets. At the same time there is an easy, flexible economy in his narration. The poet was obsessed with the instrumentality of language, rather than the simple referential function of words. This lack of machine-finish, the visible texture of the verse, its comfortable irregularities (phrases from G. T. Shepherd) are indications of the strength of his exploratory imagination. It is not too far-fetched a comparison to say that the *Beowulf* poet is like Shakespeare in his daring exploration of the interrelationships between words and actions. As often as he is puzzling, he is also astonishing.

These are qualities of style evident in the study. To declaim the whole poem aloud before an audience, however, as I and my students have done, is to discover a whole set of further characteristics. Aloud, the style is like a big, clean, strong horse that can go at a collected trot or a slow canter for hours at a time. The disposition of the parts of a sentence, which in the study of the poem may seem analytic and abstract, is governed chiefly by the alliterative emphasis when heard aloud. Concepts that are not stressed by the alliterating words are not important in the rush of the telling. The poem goes very speedily when said aloud, and the corrupt spots matter very little as the whole design emerges rapidly. How gorgeous, and how natural, it must have sounded in its own day! Our group of declaimers included both male and female voices, older and younger. Our voices were of all timbres, varied in confidence at public speaking and in correctness of pronunciation. We took turns declaiming without regard to the age or sex of the characters speaking. I discovered how *durable* the poem's speaking style is, how hospitable to a variety of dramatic interpretations. Almost all the nuances of intonation that we could introduce into our voices seemed plausible. Moreover, we could hear that the poet had adapted the voices of his characters to their natures and settings. Our own performances showed us that *their* performances were governed mainly by the narrative and thematic contexts in which they spoke and acted.

To declaim Part II, so problematic a section in today's interpretations of the poem's meaning, was to discover that the poet had made extra room for side remarks, had given himself even more space than usual. This suggests to me that we should take his own remarks there more seriously in determining his intent and perhaps should look less for implicit symbols. The verse is so swift in Part II that it is no wonder that conflicts of meaning remain unresolved. Yet that very swiftness helps emphasize the poet's own parallels and contrasts. The reference to Hygelac's raid at 2355 ff., since it is in the poet's own voice, seems to declare the more plainly that it is central to Beowulf's final disaster. Later one seems to hear a silent parallel between Hygelac's breast-treasure and the dragon's treasure. Similarly, the reference (by Beowulf) to the guiltless, unavengeable death of the Geatish prince Hæthcyn seems an obvious parallel or foreshadowing of Beowulf's own death. Declamation also shows the daring directness with which the poet has Wiglaf express his feelings of loyalty when he rushes through the fiery breath of the dragon to aid Beowulf (2663–68). Heard aloud, his speech is frankly sentimental.

Declamation can also bring a new viewpoint to Wiglaf's long final speech (3077–109) after the Messenger's prophecy. "Often many must suffer for the will of one," Wiglaf begins, and since he speaks right after the poet's own acknowledgment of the curse on the gold, we are inclined to hear it as criticism of Beowulf. But to hear the whole thirty-line speech aloud is to hear a restorative motion traced through Wiglaf's voice. It is a speech that balances the Messenger's declaration of doom against a movement into ritual praise of the hero and a declaration that all was done rightly in the final fight and will be done fittingly in the final burial. All in all, the style of the poem, as it is available to the ear, discloses a stable set of Christian and heroic attitudes and feelings, and an emphasis on action and feeling over ideas. I conclude from the experience of listening—

though such a conclusion has no historical validity—that while the poet may have known some exegetical commentaries or Latin poems, they are not the basis of his poetic idea. If anything, the hypothesis that the poet composed extemporaneously by oral formulas is made newly attractive when one listens to the poem.

NARRATIVE TECHNIQUE

Repetition

Poetry that comes from oral traditions has certain special narrative techniques peculiar to it, and *Beowulf* is no exception. The most comprehensive analysis to date was made by the late James Notopoulos, a Harvard classicist, in his essay "Studies in Early Greek Oral Poetry." He lists as typical the use of a prologue announcing the themes of the poem; foreshadowings and flashbacks; summaries and recapitulations; verbal repetitions; the use of grammatical particles to link one narrative unit to another (*swā* and *þā* in OE.); and the use of divine intention to integrate an episodic story. Only this last device is not clearly present in Beowulf, although we might say that the poet's philosophical viewpoint on this transitory, violent life will serve the same function.

One type of verbal repetition in *Beowulf* is "ring-composition" (Notopoulos' term). This entails the use of a leit-motif word such as *hand* at the outset of an episode, and then, after occasionally weaving the word into the texture of the narrative itself, its prominent reintroduction at the end of the episode. It is a form of "binding" like alliteration in the line, only on the level of narrative coherence. Apparently the poet felt a certain artistic propriety in using the same words when the same subject was in view. Beyond decorum, however, he also wanted to emphasize key images by repetition. Whenever a reader feels he is in the presence of a word with thematic force, it will almost always have been repeated from another context. The rhythm of the narrative repetitions themselves gives the poem's story line the effect of wave upon wave, as new effects are piled up within parallel narrative frameworks.

Sometimes the poet's emphasis upon incremental repetition results in minor temporal confusion. Both the Danes' journey to the mere and Hrothgar's speech of thanksgiving in front of Heorot are described as taking place at the same time (836, 917). This can be explained as the poet's attempt to render two simultaneous events (see Sisam, *Structure,* pp. 31–32). It can be claimed that this is primitive narrative that lacked any technical device to show that they were contemporaneous, but a more cogent explanation turns on the poet's need for repetition. The phrase *ðā wæs on morgen* might be better seen as the "binding" words in a ring-composition whose prime significance is the interposed allusions to Sigemund and Heremod. This technique is not primitive; it is simply oral. And the poet's ability to show more than one thing at a time is fully demonstrated by his mixing of the languages of action and psychology in the Grendel fight and his depiction of the reactions of dramatic audiences while each of Beowulf's three great fights is going on.

Narrative repetitions have a further effect: they are like a basal rhythm, a long chant going on at a half-conscious level. They move the presentation of the poem out of our ordinary sequential chronology and toward its own time. This quality of incantation does not rule out our responding to other qualities in the narrative depiction, but it makes them all seem the more equivalent to each other and the more subject to the poet's own world-view. In this respect, the fictional world of *Beowulf* is no less sophisticated than the self-enclosed cyclical space-time of a novel by Samuel Beckett.

Conventional Themes

In addition to dictional formulas, Old English poets used certain stock themes or type-scenes to help pattern their storytelling. The latter are simply defined as stereotyped sequences of details which are conventionally used whenever certain types of events are to be told. For instance, whenever a hero lands on a beach, as Beowulf does in coming and going from Denmark, there will be some allusion to brightness or light. The sun will shine, or the cliffs will glisten in the sunlight. This applies even when the story of the swimming contest between Beowulf and Breca is told by the hero: as he makes his landfall, the sun shines from the east. Another theme is the Beasts of Battle—wolf, eagle, and raven—who foreshadow carnage on the battlefield. They are used throughout Old English battle poetry for a variety of effects ranging from the mysterious to the elegiac to the tensely frightening. In *Beowulf*, however, the poet holds off using this strong theme till almost the very end, despite the many battles between men, as well as between men and monsters. He could have used it in the Finn Episode, the Ingeld-Freawaru Episode, or in the several accounts of the wars with Onela and Ongentheow, the Swedish kings: while not obligatory, it would have been appropriate. But he saves it until nearly the end, when the Messenger is giving his prophecy of future war for the Geats. Then he brings it in with chilling effect to reinforce the likely outcome of a new Swedish attack. These narrative themes—others include "bed after banquet" and "joy after sorrow"—have a strength that can only be gained by artistic convention. They inevitably carry forceful associations in their train, much like the forceful emphasis built up by the alliterative pattern of the line itself. They satisfyingly map out, for poet and listeners alike, what is about to be told. In addition, they free the poet to think more carefully about the finer texture of his verbal effects and about how he will interrelate one episode to another.

Dramatic Audience

Characterization in *Beowulf* is limited by the diction and style. Characters do not converse; they deliver formal speeches in the epic style. Within a speech of thirty or fifty lines, however, the poet finds ample room to dramatize a character's attitudes—toward himself, his subject, and his audience. Beowulf's responses to the Danish coast-guard, to Unferth, and to Hrothgar early in the poem are all excellent and subtle examples of this side of the poet's art. One of his favorite narrative techniques is to show the meaning of events by giving us the reaction of the dramatic audience inside the poem to them. For example, the Danes are horrified when they first hear Grendel's "victory-less song" while he struggles with Beowulf. Their terrified reaction to his yowling measures its enormous loudness as no direct statement could. As a descriptive device, this is common to epic. But the *Beowulf* poet puts the dramatic audience to an even better use: he shows us the exact gap between the actuality of the event and the Danes' understanding of it—they *should* be overjoyed to hear that scream. In fact, he uses a dramatic audience to show the misapprehension of ordinary men during each of the hero's three monster-fights.

Point of View

Whether the dramatic audience is an individual, like Wiglaf listening to Beowulf's dying words, or a whole company of men, like the Danes outside Heorot, we feel that there is a living scene before us, characters who move about freely in a world of known and habitable space. They respond to one another, and they often leave things unsaid. As they move within this epic space, the characters become as credible as those in a realistic novel, though of course neither their actions nor speeches are at all realistic or novelistic. At times it is difficult to know how far to press this sense of fictive life in the poem. Beowulf reports to Hygelac that a feud will soon break out between the Danes and Heathobards, even after the peace-weaving marriage of Hrothgar's daughter Freawaru to Ingeld the Heathobard. This is commonly offered as a sterling example of Beowulf's prescience and good judgment, his fitness to become king later. But what does it say of Hygelac, the dramatic listener who hears it? Since he is later to die as the result of an arrogant raid into Frisia, pursuing the war ethic into the ground, we might expect that his response to Beowulf would matter to the poet. Apparently it did not.

When Beowulf reports his first two contests to Hygelac (2000–162), he recapitulates what the poet's audience already knows, with some variant details. Even after we allow for the added details, such as Grendel's huge glove made of dragon-skins, as due to the oral-formulaic habit of never recomposing the same scene exactly the same way, we still must decide what artistic force the passage has, measured against the rest of *Beowulf*. Many critics feel that here the poet falls short. One way to salvage Beowulf's recapitulation is to see it as what the two fights meant to Beowulf himself, how it appeared from his point of view. The awkward repetitions in his retelling have been claimed as the only means available to the poet for exploring the psychology of his hero from within. However, Beowulf's viewpoint is really no more than an abbreviated version of the viewpoint the poet already has created during the contexts of each fight. Our modern modes of analyzing character will not easily apply.

Narrative "point of view" as we understand it today, however, is fully under control in *Beowulf*, and it is manipulated in a manner that several critics have compared to modern cinematic technique. The technique of "cutting" from one aspect of a situation to another —perhaps most fully and successfully worked out in the Grendel fight—may have come to the poet as a further extension of the technique of variation. He also shows the ability to manipulate point of view so that he forces us to participate actively in the scenes he describes, rather than holding them at a distance for aesthetic appreciation. In the powerful description of Grendel's mere, syntax, image, and simile pull us deeper and deeper into the uncanny scene until we too seem to blink, blear-eyed, before the smoky waters.

The narrative techniques of epic poetry can be compared to photography in other respects. When we take a moment to reflect on our mental pictures of the story, we find that scenery and symbol have merged; the locales and the heroic actions performed in them cannot be easily pulled apart. Moreover, behind the focus on individual characters moving about in the foreground, there is the vista of the ordinary world in the distance, undistorted by the hyperbole of the heroic code. The moments when the Geats anchor their newly tarred ship after landing on the Danish coast, or when they stack their spears outside Heorot like a bristling haycock, are visualized with the simple naturalness and authority of a Robert Flaherty or Cartier-Bresson. Epic narration always has these sharp glimpses of the usual world which illuminate ordinary, repeated experiences.

Composition by Context

Since *Beowulf* was composed to be heard aloud, the immediate field of attention is limited to what the audience can hold in mind at one time. The present moment has supremacy in the listener's consciousness. Perhaps this is one reason why modern readers of the poem find it so hard to give a satisfactory account of how the poem is unified. The limit of our aural attention is like the rectangular frame of a camera or the circle of light from a flashlight moving down the page. We cannot go beyond it; it has to move if we are to see the next thing that happens. The limitation of an immediate rhetorical effect seems to have been in the poet's mind when he constructed his scenes. They are often a series of "stills" or a slow "pan" of the near foreground. Yet the poet also has a flexibility in his narrative viewpoint that goes beyond this comparison. Scyld's rise to power and the closing lament for Beowulf are told at a remote distance from the events themselves, and they gain a mythic force from this distance. The poet's penchant for generalizing upon his story, and for juxtaposing one episode against another, further reveals his intense interest in the *context* in which events take place.

This constant stress on situation is distinctive not only to *Beowulf* but to Germanic epic generally. (It has recently been emphasized by J. M. Evans as a technique in the OE. *Genesis B.*) A narrator's comments upon events are bound to give historical perspective and psychological depth to the action. But the *Beowulf* poet takes this narrative method into new fields. He is forever "resetting" the context in which we have just seen the heroic action performed. Beowulf's conquest of Grendel, for instance, is first seen in terms of Sigemund, then Heremod; after the celebration in the hall, it is seen anew in terms of the Finnsburh Episode, and then it is related to the future treachery of Hrothulf at the Danish court, which is also reinforced by the Finn story itself.

The changing of contexts thus gives Beowulf's splendidly successful first fight the status of a metaphor: it is a brilliant achievement but it is to be followed by a renewal of dark terror. "Nothing gold can stay" (Robert Frost). A desire to enlarge the context seems to have been the controlling principle behind almost all of the poet's interweavings of other stories around the narrative core of Beowulf's three fights. Through the dramatic ironies of the stories, he invites us to consider the somber shadows of human unknowing that surround the bright center of epic vitality. This suggests that his very movement from context to context, the poetic act of resetting, should itself be taken as a metaphor. The largest example of this is the change in mode and tone between Parts I and II. It is as though each provided the setting in which to see the other half of the hero's story—a pair of hinged mirrors.

It has been argued that such shifts and juxtapositions show a high degree of formal abstraction in the poetics of *Beowulf*, or one might say in its noetics. It is clear the poet and his audience were deeply interested in contemplating a thing from every angle; hence the non-synchronic and additive style of narration, and the conception of poetic unity based on the perception of thematic pattern. But I think it is moot, frankly, whether the poet was interested in abstract form for its own sake. If we wish to describe the structure of the poem in formal terms, it will behoove us to be sharply aware of the degree to which criticism imposes its own metaphors upon the poem. It is also worth remembering that there is no other poem in Old English, or in any other language, that has the same sort of structure as *Beowulf*. It is a "sport," one of a kind.

STRUCTURE

Interlace Structure

One of the more popular critical views today sees the art of juxtaposition in *Beowulf* as comparable to the intricate interlacings of zoomorphic ornaments in Anglo-Saxon art. This has been argued by John Leyerle in two innovative essays, and Eamon Carrigan has worked out the view more extensively in a monograph (see Bibliography). Leyerle takes the phrase *wordum wrixlan* 'to exchange [or weave] words' as referring to the interlayering of narrative episodes. He suggests that even the technique of variation itself could be defined as a form of interlace. This interweaving idea is well known in later French chivalric romances, where it is called *entrelacement*, but we have no clear evidence that it was part of Anglo-Saxon critical terminology. The closest anyone has come, so far, is the distinction between "natural" and "artificial" order in the *Scholia Vindobonensia,* an eighth-century work of the school of Alcuin. In Leyerle's definition the "interlace structure" of *Beowulf* does not mean, as in the French romances, the interweaving of two whole narratives. Rather, it is largely confined to anticipation (especially in Part II) and to shifts of viewpoint (especially in Part I). The meaning of the whole pattern is hard to see, however, unless one turns it into an abstract statement, which the poet very rightly never does. Consequently, it is by a leap of intuition that Leyerle perceives that the major theme of *Beowulf* is the fatal contradiction at the core of heroic society. To wit: the heroic code exalts the indomitable will of the hero as an individual, but as a king it is his duty to act for the common good of society and not for his own glory. Therefore when Beowulf undertakes his great struggle with the dragon he is in fact engaging in an imprudent action which, far from saving his people, will lead to the destruction of the Geats. This view (first advanced briefly by J. R. R. Tolkien in 1953) would indict Beowulf for the very flaw that Hrothgar warned him against, *ofer-hygd* 'excessive pride.' Elsewhere in Old English poetry this quality is something of a virtuous vice, especially in the *Battle of Maldon*. Criticism of both poems has been stymied by the fact that each poet appears to enter a positive ethical judgment about his hero's noble daring, even though his losing the battle will seal the fate of those around him.

To single out this theme as *the* abstract pattern offered by the interlace design is perhaps a little tendentious. The hero can be criticized on sheerly moral grounds, as we will see in some of the Christian readings of the poem. One could as well point to other interlaced threads. For instance, all the digressions deal with stories that concern treachery or violence. Stanley Kahrl has recently accepted Leyerle's view of the structure, without going so far as to indict the hero, and he has pointed out that "feud" (OE. *fæhð*) is a term pervasively woven into the fabric of the poem in virtually every context: all conflicts, of any sort, are seen as feuds. Thus Cain's feud with God, Grendel's with the Danes, although both are causeless in the terms of Anglo-Saxon society. "Feud" might as well be the main "interlaced" theme.

The tragedy of a world in which human solutions to violence always lead to further violence is an important part of the moral perspective of the poem. But I question whether a visual analogy can characterize the poem's structure. In Anglo-Saxon art, the zoomorphic vines and fantastically elongated animals which occur in jewelry, manuscript illustrations, and carved stone crosses are almost always ornamental. If the visual interlace has any symbolism, it is obscure. Almost certainly it is non-narrative art. Why then should we think that a poet who had something to say, a meaning to make clear, would want to borrow the template for his over-all design from an ornamental plaiting motif? This metaphor for the structure of the poem is especially useful in pointing to the supremacy of the poem's own organization over chronological sequence, but there is no reason why we should turn the non-chronological into spatial. Even with its peculiar static and cyclical structure, *Beowulf*, like all poetry, remains temporal art.

Magnetic Structure

True it is that most of the materials woven round the hero's exploits state similar themes. Instability in the affairs of men, tragedy after triumph: again and again these themes loom out at us. Tribal enmity always sweeps aside attempts to compromise, it seems, so that after the vivid precedents of the Finnsburh and Heathobard stories, the outbreak of war between the Swedes and Geats is felt to be all the more inevitable. Joan Blomfield has characterized the structure of the poem by pointing out that these apparently scattered materials, disconnected in time and space, are grouped in a wide sweep around the hero's character. In fact they *are* his character: they are the comparisons and contrasts by which we may arrive at a just appreciation of his nature. This essentially is the metaphor of a magnet. The life of the hero draws many other disparate but significant stories toward it like iron filings to a magnet. The pattern they make will be the whole subject of the poem. It is the tension between the center and the circumference that allows the poet in Part II to move away from the mythical into the sorrowfully real and to give his hero a death of distressing poignancy.

Binary Structure

This magnetic structure—by which, for instance, we are led sadly to compare Wealhtheow's misplaced trust in Hrothulf to Hygd's trust in Beowulf—can be described less metaphorically as "repetition with variation" (Blomfield again) or as "contrast within parallels." The noblest manifesto for this latter view of the poem's structure was issued by J. R. R. Tolkien: "*Beowulf* itself is like a line of its own verse written large, a balance of two great blocks, A + B: like two of its parallel sentences with a single subject but no expressed conjunction. Youth + Age; he rose—fell. It may not be, at large or in detail, fluid or musical, but it is strong to stand: tough builder's work of true stone." In another place Tolkien wrote that the structure of the poem "is essentially a balance, an opposition of ends and beginnings. In its simplest terms, it is a contrasted descrip- of two moments in a great life, rising and setting; an elaboration the ancient and intensely moving contrast between youth and age, irst achievement and final death." Tolkien regarded this balance between Parts I and II as "a simple and *static* structure, solid and strong."[1]

Tolkien's account of the poem's architecture has much to recommend it and has permeated criticism of the poem so deeply that we find it hard not to think of Parts I and II as givens. This view is grounded upon the technique of silent juxtaposition found so frequently in the poem, and "A + B" is also a good description of the tonal change that so confounds the classification of the poem by any single genre or mood. Recently Jerome Mandel has attempted to work out this principle of contrast-within-parallels as a favored structuring of poetic meanings throughout the Old English corpus—extending Tolkien's observation about *Beowulf* to *The Wanderer*, *Deor*, and *The Dream of the Rood*. But one may remain slightly uneasy about a theory of structure that moves wholesale from the metrical unit to the whole, claiming a full analogy. It may be a fallacy to see the part in the whole or as governing the whole.

A further objection to this view of the poetic structure is that it is not really so much "A plus B" as "A becomes B." There are references in Part I to Hygelac's raid as early as lines 1202–14, although following Tolkien's scheme we might not expect them. And then there is the statistical middle of the poem, which encompasses both the fight with Grendel's mother and Hrothgar's sermon. In preference to a static binary structure, other critics have seen the poem as dynamic and tripartite.

Tripartite Structure

This view usually sees an increase in the significance of the hero, and in the difficulty of his victories, during the three successive monster-fights. The metaphor here might be the ladder or any other image of linear sequence. The only problem with this commonsensical view, which is indisputably true, is that it does not account for the interlarding of the episodic material or the important poetic principle of contrast. Usually proponents of the "three-act structure" see *Beowulf* not in the either-or position that Leyerle and Tolkien find

[1] J. R. R. Tolkien, in *Beowulf and the Finnesburg Fragment: A Translation into Modern English Prose*, trans. John R. Clark Hall, rev. ed. by C. L. Wrenn (London: Allen & Unwin, 1950), p. xlii; *PBA* 22 (1936), p. 271.

him, but as evolving, through three stages, from the ideal warrior to the ideal sovereign. L. L. Schücking and Robert Kaske have argued this view at length.

CRITICAL INTERPRETATIONS

If the structure of the poem can so readily be made to account for Beowulf's virtues, we may inquire more closely what they are. Professor Kaske would take the entire poem to be built around the virtues of *sapientia* and *fortitudo,* wisdom and courage. Beowulf is gifted with *fortitudo* in the first part of the poem, and it is tested by his fights with the Grendel family. The ideal of kingship, however, requires not only that a king be strong—as was Scyld the Dane, the paradigm announced in the prologue—but also that he be wise and concerned for the good of his people. Since his groundbreaking article on the role of these familiar medieval conceptual formulas in the digressive design of the poem, Kaske has taken one step toward the position that Beowulf's virtues may be valued differently in the two different contexts of his heroic youth and kingly age. Hrothgar's sermon (crucial in this interpretation) is a psychological analysis of the loss of *sapientia* in the strong man, while his own lack of strength is indicated by the futility of his attempts to make peace with the Heathobards. Here Hrothgar's *sapientia* is limited by his loss of *fortitudo.* He is, Kaske says, no longer at his best when facing decisions involving violence. While this is certainly the case, there are other explanations equally good. To farm out the theme of the poem to two Latin abstractions may be, at best, more helpful in seeing the whole climate of thought in which the poet lived than the whole truth about Beowulf. Kaske calls Grendel a perversion of *fortitudo* governed by *malitia,* or malice—all action without reflection, while the Danes are all reflection without action. This is to move not to the text, where nothing is so neat (it is after all Hengest the Dane who takes the bloodiest vengeance), but onto an intellectual checkerboard, a level of abstraction where such terms can be moved about at will.

This is a common move in the thinking of critics who are committed to making clear the world of Christianity that they think surrounds the poem. Such attempts are interesting because often the

critics' own motions of mind are like those of the Church Fathers
whom they use as authorities. The movement of thought toward
abstraction is, in any case, very strong in many believing Christians'
minds—witness Tolkien in 1936 asserting that the Dragon is a figure
for *malitia*. And literary constructions, then as now (Joyce's *Ulysses*),
often stand on abstract footings. Kaske asserts that Beowulf does
in fact live up to the double ideal (*Critical Approaches*, pp. 22 ff.).
He claims that there is an implicit equation between Beowulf's life
and Christ's. The meaning of the parallel is that Beowulf is not a
God-man, but a man like ourselves, and his death is not going to
save anyone. To some degree this is a satisfying interpretation. But
there is a notorious absence of any explicit references to Christ in
Beowulf. How then can one protect this parallel, which many other
readers have also seen, from the charge of false analogy? Kaske's
own defense is that an implicit analogy of almost any kind between
Beowulf and Christ might account for the lack of reference. This is
like Leyerle's assumption that no explicit statement of the meaning of
the interlace design is possible if its implicit poetic effect is to be
fully confirmed in the actual experiencing of the poem. These argu-
ments set their own conclusions beyond proof. If only there were
another way to prove the poem's total intention!

The practice of giving an abstract name to a recurrent theme
in the poem, and then weaving the name itself into one's own
scheme, is a common way to conceive the thematic structure of
the whole poem. For instance, John Gardner has recently offered, as
a parallel for the three-part structure of the poem, the three terms
in Fulgentius' exposition of Vergil: valor, wisdom, and glory. The
allegoresis involved in his analysis leads him to conclude that the
Christological Beowulf of the poem's deepest level redeems what
would have been, before the coming of Christianity to the Anglo-
Saxons, the tragedy of Beowulf the good man. The trouble with such
critical operations upon the poem is that the assumption which en-
ables the critic to do his interpreting, the very perspective on which
the Christian reading rests, is not examined. One strategy of this
sort of criticism is to focus on images apart from the literal context
in which they appear. This allows Allen Cabaniss in "*Beowulf* and
the Liturgy" to make an analogy in which Beowulf's dive into the
mere is a figure for Christian baptism and to associate the lapse of
time during his dive with Christ's death and resurrection. Even more

unguarded exercises of this method are made by Father McNamee in *"Beowulf*—An Allegory of Salvation?" and by Lewis Nicholson, who goes between the literal meaining and possible Christian symbols in such a free-floating manner that the funeral rites of Scyld become "an elaborate and impressive *figura* of Christian baptism." Unguarded though these critical arguments may be, however, they have the important feature of being responsible to a real historical context. They refuse to subject the poem to modern un-medieval values and preconceptions.

An attractive Christian interpretation of the poem that emphasizes the particular historical contexts possible for the poet's thought is now available in Margaret Goldsmith's book *The Mode and Meaning of Beowulf*" (1970). Her approach is based on Anglo-Saxon literary and ecclesiastical parallels and turns less on the relation of the poem's images and actions to scriptural antecedents, or the assumption of a one-to-one pattern of correspondences with something unstated, and more on the "anagogy" of the poem: that is, the analysis, in conventional patristic terms, of the moral causes and effects upon the hero. By this approach Professor Goldsmith is able to generate both a cogent argument for Beowulf's actions occurring in the same "thought-world" (her term) as the Lives of Sts. Anthony and Guthlac and an argument for Beowulf succumbing, although with every good intention, to the vice of avarice when he seeks to acquire the hoard in his final fight. Her thesis is that *Beowulf* is a simple allegory of the soul in which the values of the heroic world are examined against the history of all mankind from Genesis to Apocalypse. She finds no plain meaning, but by putting Hrothgar's sermon with the poet's ambivalent treatment of the hoard, she can see *Beowulf* as a moral allegory whose Christian teaching proceeds, so far as it does, by irony. Many of her textual points are strikingly apt, but when she focuses on the dragon fight, she succumbs to the same abstract-pattern syndrome as other Christological interpreters of the poem, be they proponents of Beowulf as an analogue of Christ or Beowulf as a doomed man. Goldsmith adds a psychological twist: the dragon is a figure of *malitia* primarily in that he is an externalization of Beowulf's own sinful nature. The literal Beowulf fighting the literal dragon, when seen as a moral abstraction, becomes an externalized expression of his own soul fighting his own sinful nature. Without the salvation of Our Redeemer, even the most valiant hero is bound to lose this battle. Unfortunately, although the concept of externalization appears in OE. Christian poems based on patristic psychology such as *The Wanderer* and *The Seafarer,* there is no intrinsic need to assume it exists in *Beowulf.*

Professor Goldsmith's argument that the poem criticizes the moral quality of Beowulf's actions was formulated in different terms by Leyerle, as we have seen, and also by Eric G. Stanley. Lines 2819–20 explicitly state that Beowulf is not beyond God's grace, but it is not stated—explicitly or implicitly—that he will ever find it. "Heaven swallowed the smoke," the poet says at the conclusion of Beowulf's cremation. What could be more ambiguous? Stanley's interpretation has the virtue of keeping alive the sense of lexical ambiguity in those passages crucial for the evaluation of Beowulf's conduct. He is also careful to show how a sense of Beowulf's insufficiency gets stated at the end of the poem, so that we have the tragedy of a hero with flaws, of a heathen without hope. In Stanley's view, "though the poet presents the heroic ideal of his people lovingly, he presents it as ultimately unavailing and therefore not worth ambition. Perhaps there is a hint even that Beowulf, being a pagan too eager in the hour of his death for posthumous fame and the sight of gold—what else *can* pagans think about when they die?—will not, for all his virtues, be saved from everlasting damnation in hell. . . . What is implied is that the poet is aware of the fact that the pagan heroic ideal stands in conflict with the ascetic ideal of Christianity, as it was known in the English monasteries of the poet's time. By the standards of that higher ideal the heroic ideal is insufficient" (Stanley, *C & B,* p. 139).

On the other hand, we might interpret this collocation of values in the poem with a different, yet still medieval, emphasis. Medieval tragedy has been defined as the view that all human good is transitory; its loss inevitable and painful. Hence the higher the hero, the more painful the loss. The villain is not the hero's motive but the human condition itself. (See Larry D. Benson's excellent discussion in *TSL* 11 [1966], cited in the Bibliography.) The medieval tragic hero is apt to be an exemplar, and medieval tragedy asks two contradictory attitudes of the reader: sincerely admiring and yet just as sincerely rejecting worldly ideals. We moderns insist on choosing and subordinating one to the other. Perhaps the *Beowulf* poet did not. There are hints throughout Part II that run both ways. I myself am

inclined to take the view, recently urged by T. A. Shippey and
Stanley B. Greenfield, that the poet was aware of the tension that
his ending created and that he did not wish to resolve it unambiguously.

This interpretation may yield too modern a poem, but I think
we can see signs of this binocular vision well before the end. Beowulf
does not reply to Hrothgar's sermon. Does he understand how forcefully it might apply to himself? He is still only a young warrior.
Notice further that Hrothgar does not reach an exordium that indicts
or persuades Beowulf, as sermons usually do, but instead he uses
his own case as a Boethian example of misfortune outlived. Yet
Beowulf is to reveal in his report to Hygelac that a new disaster will
shortly befall Hrothgar. Not *all* his misfortunes have been outlived.
How far, then, should we press the meaning of his sermon when it
is undercut by dramatic irony? Again, when we try to analyze the
poet's treatment of the hoard, we find that its different contexts
give the hoard a contrariety of functions that makes any attempt
at an overarching signification unconvincing. Gold plays a positive
and necessary part in the heroic action of the poem: it is the reward
for valor and the signal of a man's moral worth. Being generous with
gold is praised throughout the poem, just as hoarding it is always
vilified. The curse on the dragon's gold is followed quickly by a
highly obscure passage which may have been meant to exonerate
Beowulf from any charge of covetousness (3074–75). Even when
critics try to give the hoard a specifically Christian meaning, there
is no resolution. Professor Goldsmith can see the hoard as an image
of cupidity, but Charles Donahue, in his "Reconsideration" article,
can regard it as the means by which Beowulf advances toward Christian charity. Though it may appear a dodge to those who yearn for a
definitive interpretation of the poem's meaning and the final attitude
we should take toward Beowulf, it is probably wisest to say, with
T. A. Shippey, that the two attitudes of admiring and criticizing the
heroic ideal remain combined throughout the ending.

Finally, the poem has a further meaning which is acted out by
the reader himself as he goes through his gyrations of puzzled interpretation and reinterpretation. And that is, as Bolton has noted,[2]

---

[2] C. L. Wrenn, ed., *Beowulf*, 3rd ed. rev. by W. F. Bolton (London: Harrap, 1973), p. 88.

the indeterminacy of human knowledge itself. The poet's belief in the limits of our knowledge is revealed by his heavily contextual treatment of all the actions and by their deliberately opaque interrelatedness. The poem seems to say that human beings can know "the truth" only within the immediate context of their own experience. Thus the precise relationships between the parts of the poem seem always to escape us. Probably this was intentional. Because of its multiformity of structure and attitude, the meanings of the poem have been overdetermined. *Beowulf* suggests more than it asserts.

Guide to Reading Aloud

The Verse Form

Old English poetry is accentual and alliterative verse. Its meter is defined by its stress patterns, not by vowel length or number of syllables. The Old English poetic line has two halves, divided by a sharp pause, or caesura. There are two beats to each half-line. Thus there are four beats to the line. The alliteration of the whole line is determined by the first heavily stressed syllable of the second half-line. This third stress will alliterate with either or both of the two stresses in the first half-line. The third stress is the key sound that locks the two half-lines together. The fourth stress does not usually alliterate.[1] Naturally there must be at least four syllables in each half-line so that two stresses can be made. A varying number of unaccented syllables surrounding the stresses is permitted. Lines 4–7 of *Beowulf* illustrate these features:

C Oft SCyld SCēfing   SCeaþena þrēatum,   A

A Monegum Mǣgþum   Meodo-setla oftēah;   E

A Ēgsode Eorlas,   syððan AErest wearð   B

A Fēasceaft Funden;   hē þæs Frōfre gebād   B

---

[1] This is the basic form. There can be "enriched" alliteration on all four stresses, as in line 2261, and criss-cross patterns such as A B • B A, but these are ornamental additions.

29

[Often Scyld Scefing   seized mead-benches
from enemy troops,   from many a clan;
he terrified warriors,   even though first he was found
a waif, helpless.   For that came a remedy]

The markings ∕ , ＼ , and ∪ indicate heavy stress, half stress, and
weak stress. The alliterating sounds are capitalized in bold face. It
should be noted that any initial vowel can alliterate with any other.

The letters in the margins above identify the metrical type of each
half-line. While there are variations within each type, basically there
are only six stress patterns used throughout Old English poetry. This
classification was made by the German scholar Eduard Sievers in
the late nineteenth century. There are more than six thousand half-
lines in *Beowulf*, and they all fall into one of the following types
of stress pattern:

Type		*OE. Examples*	*Mod. Eng. Examples*
A	∕∪∕∪	fēasceaft funden	knights in armor
B	∪∪∕∪∕	syð∂an ǣrest wear∂	on the roaring sea
C	∪∕∕∪	oft Scyld Scēfing	on high mountains
Da	∕∕∖∪	þēod-cyninga	bright archangels
Db	∕∕∪∖	blǣd wīde sprang	bold brazenfaced
E	∕∪∖∪∪∕	meodo-setla oftēah	high-crested helms

If we substitute these Modern English examples (devised by J. R. R.
Tolkien) in the OE. quotation above, we can see that the half-line
patterns make up whole lines of roughly equal weight, no matter
what types are used in any given line:

C   on high mountains   knights in their armor   A

A   knights in armor   high-crested helms   E

A   knights in armor   on the roaring sea   B

A   knights in armor   on the roaring sea   B

The conventions of the verse form in *Beowulf* do not permit long
runs of the same stress patterns, and the last two lines here are close
to the limit of metrical repetition. Nor are there usually two half-
lines of the same type within a single line. Instead, different types

are joined together in each line, to meet the needs of meaning and syntax and to create a harmonious variety from half-lines of similar length. Roughly 40 per cent of the half-lines are Type A.

A great deal of unnecessary technical fuss can be made over Sievers' types. It helps to notice the similarity between Types A and D and what we normally call trochaic feet; between Type B and our traditional iambics; and the fact that Type C [∪ / / ∪] is the inside-out version of Type E [/ ∪ ∪ /]. The metrical types are best understood as selections from the wide variety of normal stress patterns found within any given two-beat utterance of spoken English prose. The stress patterns of Old English verse differ from the patterns in Old English prose chiefly in two respects: their stresses are clearer, and they have fewer unstressed syllables. The stresses are clearer because they are louder and higher. In normal speech, when a speaker emphasizes a word or syllable, he raises its stress by raising his voice in pitch and volume. In Old English verse, it is the artifice of alliteration—coming on top of the natural heavy stress— that produces the "overstressed" effect. This gives a formal rhythm to the line, so that it sounds rather like chanting to a 4/8 musical tempo.

This regularity of timing was not taken into account by Sievers, whose method of scansion, if practiced scrupulously, leads to an ungainly drawling or hurrying up of some half-lines. The rhythm and tempo of Old English verse during recitation have been explained by another theory worked out mainly by Andreas Heusler and John Pope. This system takes the musical concept of the measure as its basis and states that four isochronous (equally timed) measures are found in all lines. When a normal enunciation of the syllables in the half-line does not fill the measure, Pope has suggested that the harp would be struck to fill in the "rest" in the verbal music. From the description of the scop's performance at the hall-feast in lines 89–90 and elsewhere, it is clear that the harp, or more exactly, the Germanic round lyre,[2] was used in the recitation of Old English verse. Whether it was used only to fill rests or used

---

[2] See Myrtle and Rupert Bruce-Mitford, "The Sutton Hoo Lyre, *Beowulf*, and the Origins of the Frame Harp" in Rupert Bruce-Mitford, *Aspects of Anglo-Saxon Archaeology* (London: Gollancz, 1974), pp. 188–97 and plate 40.

continuously and whether chords or single notes were struck are still matters for conjecture.

The isochronous theory is especially attractive as an explanation for the "hypermetric" verses found occasionally in Old English verse. Examples of such "long lines" occur in lines 1163–68, 1705–7, and 2995–96 of *Beowulf*. They are like Sievers' usual half-line types, but with extra unaccented syllables and roughly twice the length of ordinary verses. They are explained in Pope's theory as a doubling of the regular 4/8 measure, filling out the same time interval but in 4/4 tempo.

Attempts to combine the two systems of scansion have often been made, and new analyses of Old English meter have recently been offered from other points of view as well.[3] But the endeavor to find a comprehensive theory of Old English meter is rather like trying to account for all the variations upon iambic pentameter throughout the history of later English poetry. Paull F. Baum, a scholar of great good sense, was well nigh irrefutable when he said the *Beowulf* is roughly isochronous and roughly trochaic (Types A and D). If the reader remembers these two points and lets his voice follow the natural flow of the sense, he can scan the poem easily and can gain a clear sense of how the alliterative meter reinforces poetic meaning.

Aids to Scansion and Recitation

Alliteration. To find the alliteration of a given line, look at the first large word in the second half-line. Very likely (but not always) it will be the third stress and the key to the alliteration. Check to see if its initial consonant is matched by a stressed word or words in the first half-line. If its initial letter is a vowel, look for any other initial vowels in the first half-line.

Stress. All Old English words normally have the heavy stress on the first syllable of the root. Thus root syllables receive the alliterating stresses. To find the root of a word, the following rules are helpful. (1) Compounds: the first element of a compound receives the heavy stress, and the second element receives a half stress.

---

[3] See, for instance, Samuel J. Keyser, "Old English Prosody," *College English* 30 (1969), 331–65; 31 (1969), 71–80; Robert D. Stevick, *Suprasegmentals, Meter and the Manuscript of "Beowulf"* (The Hague: Mouton, 1968).

Examples: *mán-cỳnn, hrón-rãde, geár-dàgum*. (2) Prefixes: since they come before the root, prefixes need to be recognized and given weak stress. The following are the most frequent: *ā-, æt-, an-, be-, bī, for-, ge-, ofer-, on-, tō, un-, wið-*. The noun and verb prefix *ge-* is especially common and is never stressed. Sometimes a prefix that changes the meaning of a word (e.g., *un-*) will receive a strong stress. (3) Finally, if there is no prefix, the first syllable of a word will be the root. Division into syllables follows the same rules as Modern English.

Parts of Speech. The alliterating stresses fall most often on nouns, then on adjectives, then verbs. Once the student of Old English begins to recognize these parts of speech—and the general reader can see the ancestors of many Modern English words, even without learning Old English—the task of getting the stress right is greatly simplified. Verbs frequently come at the end of the second half-line, receiving the non-alliterating fourth stress. When they come earlier in a clause they do not take a heavy stress even if they could alliterate. For example:

weorod wæs on wynne 'the troop was in joy'   (2014)

Here *wæs* might even take only a light stress, depending on how fast the reader is reciting. The other parts of speech—adverbs, pronouns, conjunctions—all take light stress, with the exception that if they are out of their natural word order in the sentence, they may be given heavy stress:

Ic *mínne* can
glǽdne Hróþulf (1180–81a)
'I know [this about]   *my* noble Hrothulf'

Rhetorical emphasis can also elevate pronouns and adverbs to heavy stress:

on *þǽm* dǽge *þysses* līfes 'in *that* day   of *this* life' (197)
gǽst *inne* swǽf   'the guest slept *within*'   (1800b)

But as a general rule, expect nouns and adjectives to receive the alliteration and the heavy stresses.

Grammatical Formulas. Some half-line types are naturally filled by certain grammatical units. For instance, Type Da will exactly accommodate the genitive plural of a compound present participle used as a noun:

brim-líþendra '·of the sea-traveling (ones)'
ymb-sittendra 'of the (ones) sitting round,' i.e., neighbors

Type A [/ ∪ / ∪] fits a number of especially common grammatical patterns in the plural:

adjective + noun: láðe gýstas 'hateful strangers'
subject + verb: beornas féollon 'the warriors fell'
object + verb: gáras bǽron 'spears they bore'
infinitive + verb: wealdan mostón 'to wield they were able'
noun + adjective: wíges georne 'for war eager'

(Examples adapted from Bruce Mitchell.[4]) Once the reader recognizes such grammatical combinations, he will also know how to stress the words.

Recitation. Tastes will differ according to the prosodical persuasion of one's teacher. It is possible to read *Beowulf* aloud as a sort of quick and lively rhythmical prose, without pausing noticeably between half-lines. At the other extreme, some readers prefer a heavy bardic chant, like Vachel Lindsay's *The Congo* at half speed. I think an intermediate pace is best, somewhat slower than ordinary conversation but not so slow as Presidential oratory. The alliterating stresses should come out clearly, strongly, and regularly, with pauses between half-lines as the punctuation indicates.

The stress and intonation of the Modern English sense make the best guide to the recitation of the original. The reader should feel free to introduce tonal nuances, changes of speed, prolongations for emphasis, and rhetorical pauses. A poem that was meant to be said aloud invites dramatic interpretation. The beginner should not be shy about experimenting, so long as he sees clearly where the alliterating stresses fall and how they mold the meaning of the sentences.

---

[4] *Beowulf*, trans. Kevin Crossley-Holland, introd. Bruce Mitchell (New York: Farrar, Straus & Giroux, 1968), p. 24.

Old English Pronunciation

All the letters in Old English regularly represent their sounds and must be pronounced. This includes letters now silent in their Modern English descendants, as in *wrītan* 'to write' where the *w* is pronounced as well as the *r*.

Vowels	Mod. Eng. Equivalents	OE. Examples
a	not	nama 'name'
ā	father	stān 'stone'
æ	that, hat	þæt 'that'
ǣ	Dad, mad	dǣd 'deed'
e	set, help, egg	helpan 'to help'
ē	they, hate	hē 'he'
i	pit, hit	hit 'it'
ī	mean, machine	hīe 'they'
o	ought	holm 'sea,' god 'God'
ō	goad	gōd 'good'
u	put, full	full 'full'
ū	rude	nū 'now'
y	as in Fr. *tu*	fyllan 'to fill'
ȳ	as in Ger. *grün*, Fr. *lune*	lȳtel 'little'

Diphthongs

In OE. diphthongs the first vowel is always stressed more heavily than the second, and the two vowels form a single syllable. The first vowel is pronounced as it appears in the chart above. The sound of the second vowel is reduced to the schwa [ə] of Mod. Eng. *but*. The principal diphthongs in *Beowulf* are:

ea   eald 'old,' wearð 'became'
ēa   ēast 'east,' scēap 'sheep'
eo   eorl 'nobleman,' heorte 'heart'
ēo   dēop 'deep,' bēor 'beer'

Consonants

Most of the consonants are pronounced as in Modern English.

Since all letters in OE. represent sounds, double consonants should
be enunciated twice, as in *biddan* 'to pray,' pronounced as though
it were Mod. Eng. "bid-don."

Consonants that are pronounced differently:
1. *sc* is like *sh* in Mod. Eng. *ship*: OE. scip 'ship'
2. *cg* is like *dg* in Mod. Eng. *edge*: OE. ecg 'edge'
3. *h* at the beginning of a word is aspirated as in Mod. Eng.
    house. Thus OE. hūs 'house.' Otherwise *h* is pronounced like
    Ger. *ch* in *ach* or *ich*. Thus OE. niht 'night' sounds like Ger.
    nicht.
4. *c* usually has the sound of *k*, and *g* is usually the hard *g* of
    God. (This means that *-ing* sounds like "ingk.") However, it
    is crucial to pay attention to the following rule:

    Before or after *i* or *e*, and after *æ*, *c* has the sound of *ch*
    as in *child*, and *g* has the sound of *y* as in *yet*.

    These palatalized pronunciations occur just as frequently as
    do the hard *g* and *k* sounds. Examples:

    dæg 'day,' pronounced roughly "dæy"
    cild 'child,' pronounced "chilled"
    micel 'great,' pronounced "mitchel"
    ic 'I,' pronounced "itch"
    spræc 'speech,' pronounced "sprætch"
    ge- the prefix, always pronounced "yuh" or "yeh"
    hefig 'heavy,' pronounced roughly "heavy"
    giefu 'gift,' pronounced roughly "yivoo"

    Exceptions to this rule can be recognized by the pronunciation
    of their Mod. Eng. descendants: OE. bæc 'back,' cēne 'keen.'
5. Two letters peculiar to OE. are þ (thorn) and ð (eth) which
    interchangeably represent the *th* sound. Both letters can have
    either the voiceless sound of Mod. Eng. *thin* or the voiced
    sound of Mod. Eng. *other*.
6. The same is true for the letters *s* and *f*. When they are voiced,
    they sound like *z* and *v*. To know when to voice them, the
    best short rule to follow is this:

Usually keep these consonants voiceless, but whenever
f, s, þ or ð occurs between two vowels, then voice it as
v, z, or the *th* sound in *other.*
If one of the immediately adjacent letters is a voiced con-
sonant (*l, r, m, n*), treat that consonant as if a vowel under
this rule and voice the middle consonant. Example: *māþm*
'treasure.' Additionally, *of* and *is,* when in their usual un-
stressed positions, are voiced as *ov* and *iz.* The intervocalic
rule holds only for single consonants. Whenever one of these
three consonants—*f, s,* or *þ/ð*—is doubled, it becomes voice-
less. Examples: OE. *lǣssan* 'less,' *oððe* 'or.' Examples of
intervocalic voicing of *f, s,* and *þ/ð:*

gelēafa 'belief'
Scēfing
hlāford 'lord'
egesa 'terror'
ālȳsan 'to loosen'
duguðe 'troop'
geoguþe 'youth'

Practice Selection

To practice the pronunciation of Old English before beginning
Beowulf, the reader may wish to try the following Late West Saxon
version of the Lord's Prayer. The sense and cadence are the same
as in Modern English. Voiced *f, s,* and *þ* are italicized. Palatalized
c and *g* are indicated by *ċ* and *ġ.*

Fæder ūre,
þū þe eart on heo*f*onum,
sī þīn nama ġehalgod.
Tōbecume þīn rīċe.
Gewur*þe* ðīn willa on eorðan swā swā on heo*f*onum.
Ūrne ġedæġhwāmlīcan hlāf syle ūs tō dæġ.
And for*ġ*y*f* ūs ūre gyltas, swā swā wē for*ġ*y*f*ad ūrum gyltendum.
And ne ġelǣd þū ūs on costnunge,
ac ālȳs ūs o*f* y*f*ele. Sō*þ*līċe.[5]

[5] Adapted from Robert J. Kispert, *Old English: An Introduction* (New York: Holt, Rinehart and Winston, 1971), p. 19.

Further Help

The Guide above is necessarily brief and does not cover every case. For those who wish to learn Old English on their own, the following texts are recommended. Each combines a presentation of the grammar with selected readings:

Henry Sweet, *Anglo-Saxon Primer,* revised by Norman Davis, 9th ed. (Oxford: Clarendon Press, 1953).

Bruce Mitchell and Fred C. Robinson, *A Guide to Old English: Revised with Texts and Glossary* (Oxford: Basil Blackwell, 1982, distributed in North America by University of Toronto Press).

Frederic G. Cassidy and Richard N. Ringler, *Bright's Old English Grammar and Reader,* 3rd ed. (New York: Holt, Rinehart and Winston, 1971).

Robert J. Kispert, *Old English: An Introduction* (New York: Holt, Rinehart and Winston, 1971).

Also useful to students of Old English are:

John R. Clark-Hall, *A Concise Anglo-Saxon Dictionary,* ed. with supplement by Herbert D. Meritt, 4th ed. (Cambridge: Cambridge University Press, 1962).

Stephen A. Barney, with the assistance of Ellen Wertheimer and David Stevens, *Word-Hoard: An Introduction to Old English Vocabulary* (New Haven and London: Yale University Press, 1977).

The following LP record provides a fine example of pronunciation and recitation:

Jess B. Bessinger, Jr., "*Beowulf, Cædmon's Hymn* and Other Old English Poems Read in Old English," Caedmon Records, TC 1161 (1962). Also available as Caedmon tape cassette SWC 1161.

Note: The Glosses to Select Passages are keyed to the grammars in Sweet and Mitchell-Robinson.

Beowulf

Textual Note

The poem has been printed with the long vowels marked and the nominal compounds hyphenated for easy pronunciation. The punctuation of the facing translation does not always correspond to the Old English. Common scribal abbreviations have been silently expanded. The only Old English characters used are æ, þ, and ð.

To ascertain the text, I have used the facsimiles and commentary in Kemp Malone, *The Nowell Codex,* Early English Manuscripts in Facsimile, XII (Copenhagen, Baltimore, and London: Rosenkilde and Bagger, 1963); *The Thorkelin Transcripts,* EEMF, I (Copenhagen, Baltimore, and London: Rosenkilde and Bagger, 1951); and Julius Zupitza, *Beowulf (Facsimile),* 2nd ed., with new collotype photographs, introduction by Norman Davis, Early English Text Society, No. 245 (London: Oxford University Press, 1959). The studies of the ultra-violet photographs of the MS. by A. H. Smith, John Pope, and Norman Davis, and Kemp Malone's articles on the Thorkelin transcripts have also been consulted.[1] I have not examined the MS. at first hand. To determine punctuation and preferred emendations I have compared the editions of Klaeber, Dobbie, Wrenn, and Wrenn-Bolton. On occasion I have also consulted Else von Schaubert's

---

[1] A. H. Smith, "The Photography of Manuscripts," *London Medieval Studies* 1 (1937–39), 179–207; John C. Pope, *The Rhythm of Beowulf,* 2nd ed. (New Haven: Yale University Press, 1966), pp. xxiv–xxviii; Davis, in his edition of Zupitza's facsimile, pp. v–xiii; Malone, *PMLA* 64 (1949), 1190–218, and *SN* 14 (1942), 25–30.

revision of the Heyne-Schücking *Beowulf*, 18th ed. (Paderborn: Ferdinand Schöningh, 1963); Johannes Hoops's *Beowulfstudien* and *Kommentar zum "Beowulf"* (both Heidelberg: C. Winter, 1932); and Tilman Westphalen's *Beowulf 3150–55: Textkritik und Editionsgeschichte* (Munich: Fink, 1967).

All letters in the OE. text that were once legible but now lost or difficult to read are indicated by italics. Each ellipsis point in the text or notes indicates a letter completely lost. Emendations and additions are italicized and appear in brackets. Emendations made by the omission of letters are indicated only in the notes. A slash in the notes indicates the end of a line of writing in the MS. My aim has been a readable poetic text that also shows the present condition of the MS. and something of our extraordinary dependence on earlier scholarship for the "received text." The reader should be able to see at a glance which Old English letters depend on the Thorkelin transcripts or on expert paleographic examination and which MS. forms are most often emended.

The italicized letters cover many problems, even under the relatively simple rubric of "once legible but now lost or difficult to read." First, this has meant italics for all the readings recorded only in the Thorkelin Transcripts A and B (1787) or by such early transcribers as Wanley (1705), Conybeare (1826), and Kemble (1830). Secondly, there are those letters still extant which have deteriorated so much since the earliest editions that they can only be ascertained by first-hand examination. Sometimes even the expert eyes of Zupitza and Malone needed the confirmation of the Thorkelin readings to decipher a letter that was covered or partly lost. (Examples: *þ* 383b, *m* 385b, *i* 386b, *a* 401b.) At other times their readings depended on the context of surrounding letters. For instance, in *self* 920 "the *l* is badly damaged but recognizable; if it stood alone it wouldn't be" (Malone, in correspondence). Therefore in both the notes and the text I have italicized, as being difficult to read, those letters where it seemed to me, from the experts' commentary, that they had had some doubt. Finally, some letters depend on deduction rather than ocular proof. An example is *wide-ferhð* 702, reported by Thorkelin A and B as *ride-ferhð*. All we have to go on are the transcripts and our knowledge of the kinds of copying errors the transcribers typically made (here *r* for *w*). In a case like this, I use the letter which in all probability the transcriber had in mind. It will be obvious to the specialist that these procedures rely heavily on the textual scholarship of Kemp Malone, and indeed my whole attempt to report lost and difficult letters would be impossible without his work. The italics in the text are not meant to replace his several exceedingly detailed and exact descriptions. In addition, scribal self-corrections, to which Malone paid scrupulous attention, are not ordinarily noted in the present text. My purpose is simply to give a convenient indication of difficult readings.

In the emendations I have followed a moderately conservative policy and usually print the MS. readings whenever possible. For the corrupt spots, there is simply no way of confirming editorial conjectures. And while some words and grammar can be corrected, the spelling and dialect of the original text cannot be reconstructed from our single late copy.[2] Many of my emendations coincide with W. F. Bolton's revision of Wrenn's edition (3rd ed., 1973), a standard modern text. I have also taken to heart the warning of Kenneth Sisam, who made a good case against an unthinking acceptance of the text of the existing MS. To use excessive caution on a late version that has presumably gone through many copies, Sisam argued, not only encourages overstrained interpretations of MS. readings, but also inhibits intelligent conjecture.[3] In addition, Fred C. Robinson has noted several places where a long-accepted emendation does not remove a crux but merely creates a different one. In such cases it can be beneficial to examine the MS. form anew.[4] To keep the page clean, I have limited the textual footnotes

---

[2] The argument against conjectural emendation is best stated by R. W. Chambers in his revision of *Beowulf and the Finnsburg Fragment*, ed. A. J. Wyatt (Cambridge: Cambridge University Press, 1914), pp. xxiii–xxviii.

[3] Kenneth Sisam, "The Authority of Old English Poetical Manuscripts," *Studies in the History of Old English Literature* (London: Oxford University Press, 1953), pp. 29–44, and *The Structure of "Beowulf"* (London: Oxford University Press, 1965), pp. 67–71.

[4] Fred C. Robinson, "Two Non-Cruces in *Beowulf*," *TSL* 11 (1966), 151–60.

to the MS. forms of emended words, with occasional brief explanations. Only the first known emendator is credited. Full lists of the many different emendations that have been proposed may be found in Klaeber and Dobbie.

List of Bibliographical Abbreviations Used in
the Textual Footnotes

Bugge
    Sophus Bugge, "Spredte iagttagelser vedkommende de oldengelske digte om *Beowulf* og *Waldere*," *Tidskrift for Philologi og Paedagogik* 8 (1868–69), 40–78, 287–307; "Zum *Beowulf*," *ZDP* 4 (1873), 192–224; "Studien über das Beowulfepos," *PBB* 12 (1887), 1–112, 360–75.

Chambers
    R. W. Chambers, ed., *Beowulf*, 3rd ed. Cambridge: Cambridge University Press, 1933.

Conybeare
    John J. Conybeare, *Illustrations of Anglo-Saxon Poetry*, ed. William D. Conybeare. London: Harding and Lepard, 1826.

Cosijn
    Peter J. Cosijn, *Aanteekeningen den "Beowulf."* Leiden: Brill, 1891–92.

Davis
    Norman Davis, introductory note in Zupitza, cited below.

Dobbie
    Elliott Van Kirk Dobbie, ed., *Beowulf and Judith*. The Anglo-Saxon Poetic Records, IV. New York: Columbia University Press, 1953.

Ettmüller
    Ernst M. L. Ettmüller, *Engla and Seaxna Scopas and Boceras*. Quedlinburg and Leipzig: Basse, 1850.

Grein
    Christian W. M. Grein, ed., *Beowulf*. Cassel and Göttingen: Wigand, 1867.

Grundtvig
    N. S. F. Grundtvig's Danish translation, *Bjowulf's Drape*. Copenhagen: Seidelin, 1820.

Heyne
    Moritz Heyne, ed., *Beowulf*, 4th ed. Paderborn: F. Schöningh, 1879.

Holthausen
  Ferdinand Holthausen, ed., *Beowulf,* 7th ed. Heidelberg: C. Winter, 1938.
Kaluza
  Max Kaluza, *Der altenglische Vers: eine metrische Untersuchung,* Pt. II: *Die Metrik des Beowulfliedes.* Berlin: Felber, 1894.
Kemble
  John M. Kemble, *The Anglo-Saxon Poems of Beowulf, The Traveller's Song, and The Battle of Finnesburh,* 2nd ed. London: W. Pickering, 1835–37.
Klaeber
  Frederick Klaeber, ed., *Beowulf and the Fight at Finnsburg,* 3rd ed. Boston: D. C. Heath, 1950.
Kluge
  Friedrich Kluge, "Zum *Beowulf,*" *PBB* 9 (1884), 187–92; and his contributions in Alfred Holder, ed. *Beowulf,* Vol. IIa: *Berichtigter Text mit knappem Apparat und Wörterbuch,* 2nd ed. Freiburg and Tübingen: Mohr, 1899.
Malone, *NC*
  Kemp Malone, ed., *The Nowell Codex.* Early English Manuscripts in Facsimile, XII. Copenhagen, Baltimore, and London: Rosenkilde and Bagger, 1963.
Pope
  John C. Pope, *The Rhythm of Beowulf,* 2nd ed. New Haven: Yale University Press, 1966.
Rieger
  Max Rieger, *Alt- und angelsächsisches Lesebuch.* Giessen: Ricker, 1861; "Zum *Beowulf,*" *ZDP* 3 (1871), 381–416; "Die alt- und angelsächsische Verskunst," *ZDP* 7 (1876), 1–64.
Sedgefield
  W. J. Sedgefield, ed., *Beowulf,* 3rd ed. Manchester: Manchester University Press, 1935.
Schücking
  Levin L. Schücking's revision of the 8th ed. of Moritz Heyne's *Beowulf.* Paderborn: Schöningh, 1908.
Smith
  A. H. Smith, "The Photography of Manuscripts," *London Medieval Studies* 1 (1937–39), 179–207.
Thorkelin
  Grímur Jónsson Thorkelin, ed., *De Danorum Rebus Gestis Secul. III et IV. Poema Danicum Dialecto Anglosaxonica.* Copenhagen: Rangel, 1815.

Thorkelin A and B

Kemp Malone, ed., *The Thorkelin Transcripts*. Early English Manuscripts in Facsimile, I. Copenhagen, Baltimore, and London: Rosenkilde and Bagger, 1951.

Thorpe

Benjamin Thorpe, *The Anglo-Saxon Poems of Beowulf, The Scop or Gleeman's Tale, and The Fight at Finnesburg*, 2nd ed. London: J. R. Smith, 1875.

Trautmann

Moritz Trautmann, ed., *Das Beowulflied*. Bonn: Hanstein, 1904.

von Schaubert

Else von Schaubert's revision of the Heyne-Schücking *Beowulf*, 18th ed. Paderborn: F. Schöningh, 1963.

Wrenn

C. L. Wrenn, ed., *Beowulf with the Finnesburg Fragment*, 2nd ed. London: Harrap, 1958.

Wrenn-Bolton

C. L. Wrenn, ed., *Beowulf with the Finnesburg Fragment*, 3rd ed., rev. by W. F. Bolton. London: Harrap, 1973.

Zupitza

Julius Zupitza, ed., *Beowulf (Facsimile)*, 2nd ed., with new collotype photographs, introd. by Norman Davis. Early English Text Society, No. 245. London: Oxford University Press, 1959.

Text and Translation

Hwæt! Wē Gār-Dena   in geār-dagum,
þēod-cyninga,   þrym gefrūnon,
hū ðā æþelingas   ellen fremedon!
    Oft Scyld Scēfing   sceaþena þrēatum
5 monegum mægþum   meodo-setla oftēah;
egsode eorl[as]   syððan ærest wearð
fēasceaft funden;   hē þæs frōfre gebād,
wēox under wolcnum,   weorð-myndum þāh,
oðþæt him æghwylc   þāra ymb-sittendra
10 ofer hron-rāde   hȳran scolde,
gomban gyldan.   Þæt wæs gōd cyning!
Ðǣm eafera wæs   æfter cenned
geong in geardum,   þone God sende
folce tō frōfre;   fyren-ðearfe ongeat
15 þæt hīe ær drugon   aldor-[lē]ase
lange hwīle;   him þæs Līf-frēa,
wuldres Wealdend,   worold-āre forgeaf:
[Bēow] wæs brēme   —blǣd wīde sprang—
Scyldes eafera,   Scede-landum in.
20 Swā sceal [geong g]uma   gōde gewyrcean,
fromum feoh-giftum   on fæder [bea]rme,
þæt hine on ylde   eft gewunigen
wil-gesīþas,   þonne wīg cume,
lēode gelǣsten;   lof-dǣdum sceal
25 in mægþa gehwǣre   man geþēon.

6a   MS. eorl: em. Kemble.
15b   MS. aldor..ase: em. Grundtvig.
18a   The MS. reads "Beowulf" here and 53; see Commentary, p. 278.
20a   MS. ....uma: em. Grein.
21b   MS. ...rme: em. Chambers.

Listen! We have heard   of the glory of the Spear-
                                                    Danes
in the old days,   the kings of tribes—
how noble princes   showed great courage!
    Often Scyld Scefing   seized mead-benches
5 from enemy troops,   from many a clan;
he terrified warriors,   even though first he was found
a waif, helpless.   For that came a remedy,
he grew under heaven,   prospered in honors
until every last one   of the bordering nations
10 beyond the whale-road   had to heed him,
pay him tribute.   He was a good king!
A son was born him,   a glorious heir,
young in the courtyards,   whom God had sent
to comfort the people   —well had He seen
15 the sinful distress   they suffered earlier,
leaderless for long.   Therefore the Life-lord,
the Ruler of glory,   granted earthly honor:
[Beow] was famed   —his name spread far—
"Scyld's son,"   through all the Northern lands.
20 So ought a [young] man,   in his father's household,
treasure up the future   by his goods and goodness,
by splendid bestowals,   so that later in life
his chosen men   stand by him in turn,
his retainers serve him   when war comes.
25 By such generosity   any man prospers.

Him ðā Scyld gewāt   tō gescæp-hwīle
fela-hrōr fēran   on Frēan wǣre.
Hī hyne þā ætbǣron   tō brimes faroðe,
swǣse gesīþas,   swā hē selfa bæd
30   þenden wordum wēold   wine Scyldinga;
lēof land-fruma   lange āhte.
Þǣr æt hȳðe stōd   hringed-stefna,
īsig ond ūt-fūs,   æþelinges fær.
Ālēdon þā   lēofne þēoden,
35   bēaga bryttan,   on bearm scipes,
mǣrne be mæste.   Þǣr wæs mādma fela
of feor-wegum,   frætwa, gelǣded;
ne hȳrde ic cȳmlīcor   cēol gegyrwan
hilde-wǣpnum   ond heaðo-wǣdum,
40   billum ond byrnum;   him on bearme læg
mādma mænigo,   þā him mid scoldon
on flōdes æht   feor gewītan.
Nalæs hī hine lǣssan   lācum tēodan,
þēod-gestrēonum,   þon þā dydon,
45   þe hine æt frum-sceafte   forð onsendon
ænne ofer ȳðe   umbor-wesende.
Þā gȳt hī him āsetton   segen *ge*[*l*]denne
hēah ofer hēafod,   lēton holm bera*n*,
gēafon on gār-secg;   him wæs geōmor sefa,
50   murnende mōd.   Men ne cunnon
secgan tō sōðe,   sele-rǣden[*d*]e,
hæleð under heofen*um*,   hwā þǣm hlæste onfēng.

I   Ðā wæs on burgum   [*Bēow*] Scyldinga
lēo*f* lēod-cyning   longe þrāge
55   folcum gefrǣge   —fæder ellor hwearf
aldor of earde—   oþþæt him eft onwōc
hēah Healfdene;   hēold þenden lifde,
gamol ond gūð-rēouw,   glǣde Scyldingas.
Ðǣm fēower bearn   forð-gerīmed

47b   MS. *ge*.denne: em. Malone, *NC*, p. 50.
51b   MS. sele rædenne: em. Kemble.
53b   See note to 18a.

        Scyld then departed   at the appointed time,
still very strong,   into the keeping of the Lord.
His own dear comrades   carried his body
to the sea's current,   as he himself had ordered,
30 great Scylding lord,   when he still gave commands;
the nation's dear leader   had ruled a long time.
There at the harbor   stood the ring-carved prow,
the noble's vessel,   icy, sea-ready.
They laid down the king   they had dearly loved,
35 their tall ring-giver,   in the center of the ship,
the mighty by the mast.   Great treasure was there,
bright gold and silver,   gems from far lands.
I have not heard   of a ship so decked
with better war-dress,   weapons of battle,
40 swords and mail-shirts;   on his breast there lay
heaps of jewels   that were to drift away,
brilliant, with him,   far on the power of the flood.
No lesser gifts   did they provide him
—the wealth of a nation—   than those at his start
45 who set him adrift   when only a child,
friendless and cold,   alone on the waves.
High over his head   his men also set
his standard, gold-flagged,   then let the waves lap,
gave him to the sea   with grieving hearts,
50 mourned deep in mind.   Men cannot say,
wise men in hall   nor warriors in the field,
not truly, who   received that cargo.
I   Then in the strongholds   [Beow] the Scylding
was king of all Denmark,   beloved by his people,
55 famous a long time   —his noble father
having passed away---   had a son in his turn,
Healfdene the great,   who, while he lived,
aged, war-fierce,   ruled lordly Scyldings.
From Healfdene are numbered   four children in all;

60 in worold wōcun,   weoroda ræswa[n],
     Heorogār ond Hrōðgār   ond Hālga til;
     hȳrde ic þæt [*Ȳrse   wæs On*]elan cwēn,
     Heaðo-Scilfingas   heals-gebedda.

     Þā wæs Hrōðgāre   here-spēd gyfen,
65 wīges weorð-mynd,   þæt him his wine-māgas
     georne hȳrdon   oððþæt sēo geogoð gewēox
     mago-driht micel.   Him on mōd be-arn
     þæt heal-reced   hātan wolde,
     medo-ærn micel   men gewyrcean,
70 þone y*ldo be*arn   æfre gefrūnon
     ond þǣr on innan   eall *g*edǣlan
     geongum ond ealdum,   swylc him God *s*ealde,
     būton folc-scare   ond feorum gumena.
     Ðā ic wīde gefrægn   weorc gebannan
75 manigre mægþe   geond þisne middan-geard,
     folc-stede frætwan.   Him on fyrste gelomp,
     ædre mid yldum,   þæt hit wearð eal-gearo,
     heal-ærna mǣst;   scōp him Heort naman,
     sē þe his wordes geweald   wīde hæfde.
80 Hē bēot ne ālēh,   bēagas dǣlde,
     sinc æt symle.   Sele hlīfade
     hēah ond horn-gēap,   heaðo-wylma bād,
     lāðan līges;   ne wæs hit lenge þā gēn
     þæt se [*e*]cg-hete   aþum-swerian
85 æfter wæl-nīðe   wæcnan scolde.
     Ðā se ellen-gǣst   earfoðlīce
     þrāge geþolode,   sē þe in þȳstrum bād,
     þæt hē dōgora gehwām   drēam gehȳrde
     hlūdne in healle;   þǣr wæs hearpan swēg,
90 swutol sang scopes.   Sægde, sē þe cūþe

60b MS. ræswa: em. Kemble.

62 Scribal omission but no gap in MS. Em. follows Grundtvig, Bugge, and
M. G. Clarke, *Sidelights on Teutonic History during the Migration Period*
(Cambridge: Cambridge University Press, 1911), pp. 82 ff.

70a Usually em. þon[*n*]e 'than' but I follow Robinson, *TSL* 11 (1966),
151–55.

84a MS. secg hete: em. Grein, but see R. P. Tripp, *ELN* 18 (1980), 81–86.

60 from the leader of armies   they woke to the world,
Heorogar, Hrothgar,   and Halga the good;
it is told that [Yrse   was Onela's] queen,
bed-companion   of the Battle-Scylfing.
    Then Hrothgar was given   victory in battle,
65 such honor in war   that the men of his house
eagerly served him,   while younger kinsmen
grew into strength.   It came to his mind
that he would command   a royal building,
a gabled mead-hall   fashioned by craftsmen,
70 which the sons of men   should hear of forever,
and there within   he would share out
among young and old   all God had given him,
except common land   and the lives of men.
Then, I have heard,   the work was announced
75 to many peoples   throughout middle-earth,
that they should adorn   this nation's hall.
In due time, yet quickly   it came to be finished,
greatest of hall-buildings.   He, whose word
had power everywhere,   said its name, "Heorot"—
80 he broke no promises,   but dealt out rings,
treasures at his table.   The hall towered high,
cliff-like, horn-gabled,   awaited the war-flames,
malicious burning;   it was still not the time
for the sharp-edged hate   of his sworn son-in-law
85 to rise against Hrothgar   in murderous rage.
    Then the great monster   in the outer darkness
suffered fierce pain,   for each new day
he heard happy laughter   loud in the hall,
the thrum of the harp,   melodious chant,
90 clear song of the scop.   He spoke, who could tell

frumsceaft fīra   feorran reccan,
cwæð þæt se Ælmihtiga   eorðan worh[te],
wlite-beorhtne wang   swā wæter bebūgeð:
gesette sige-hrēþig   sunnan ond mōnan
95 lēoman tō lēohte   land-būendum,
ond gefrætwade   foldan scēatas
leomum ond lēafum;   līf ēac gesceōp
cynna gehwylcum   þāra ðe cwice hwyrfaþ.
Swā ðā driht-guman   drēamum lifdon,
100 ēadiglīce,   oððæt ān ongan
fyrene fre[m]man,   fēond on helle.
Wæs sē grimma gæst   Grendel hāten,
mære mearc-stapa,   sē þe mōras hēold,
fen ond fæsten;   fīfel-cynnes eard
105 won-sælī wer   weardode hwīle,
siþðan him Scyppend   forscrifen hæfde
in Cāines cynne—   þone cwealm gewræc
ēce Drihten   þæs þe hē Ābel slōg.
Ne gefeah hē þære fæhðe,   ac hē hine feor forwræc,
110 Metod for þȳ māne,   man-cynne fram.
Þanon untȳdras   ealle onwōcon,
eotenas ond ylfe   ond orc-nēas,
swylce gī[ga]ntas   þā wið Gode wunnon
lange þrāge;   hē him ðæs lēan forgeald.
115 }
II } Gewāt ðā nēosian   syþðan niht becōm,
hēan hūses,   hū hit Hring-Dene
æfter bēor-þege   gebūn hæfdon;
fand þā ðær inne   æþelinga gedriht
swefan æfter symble—   sorge ne cūðon,
120 wonsceaft wera.   Wiht unhælo,
grim ond grædig,   gearo sōna wæs,
rēoc ond rēþe,   ond on ræste genam

92b   MS. worh..: em. Kremble.
101a MS. fre.man: em. Kemble.
106a MS. scyppen, with "d" added above line in another hand.
107a The "in" appearing in MS. caines altered from "m" by erasure. Cf.
MS. camp 1261b.
113a MS. gi..ntas: em. Thorkelin. See Malone, *PMLA* 64 (1949), 1193.

the beginning of men,   knew our ancient origins,
told how the Almighty   had made the earth,
this bright shining plain   which the waters surround:
He, victory-creative,   set out the brightness
95 of sun and moon   as lamps for earth-dwellers,
adorned the green fields,   the earth, with branches,
shoots, and green leaves;   and life He created,
in each of the species   which live and move.
Thus the brave warriors   lived in hall-joys,
100 blissfully prospering,   until a certain one
began to do evil,   an enemy from Hell.
That murderous spirit   was named Grendel,
huge moor-stalker   who held the wasteland,
fens, and marshes;   unblessed, unhappy,
105 he dwelt for a time   in the lair of the monsters
after the Creator   had outlawed, condemned them
as kinsmen of Cain   —for that murder God
the Eternal took vengeance,   when Cain killed Abel.
No joy that kin-slaughter: the Lord drove him out,
110 far from mankind,   for that unclean killing.
From him sprang every   misbegotten thing,
monsters and elves   and the walking dead,
and also those giants   who fought against God
time and again;   He paid them back in full.
II   When night came on,   Grendel came too,
115 to look round the hall   and see how the Ring-Danes,
after their beer-feast,   had ranged themselves there.
Inside he found   the company of nobles
asleep after banquet—   they knew no sorrow,
120 man's sad lot.   The unholy spirit,
fierce and ravenous,   soon found his war-fury,
savage and reckless,   and snatched up thirty

þrītig þegna;   þanon eft gewāt
hūðe hrēmig   tō hām faran,
125   mid þǣre wæl-fylle   wīca nēosan.
        Ðā wæs on ūhtan   mid ǣr-dæge,
        Grendles gūð-cræft   gumum undyrne;
        þā wæs æfter wiste   wōp ūp āhafen,
        micel morgen-swēg.   Mǣre þēoden,
130   æþeling ǣr-gōd,   unblīðe sæt,
        þolode ðrȳð-swȳð,   þegn-sorge drēah,
        syðþan hīe þæs lāðan   lāst scēawedon
        wergan gāstes.   Wæs þæt gewin tō strang,
        lāð ond longsum.   Næs hit lengra *fyrst*
135   ac ym*b* āne niht   eft *gefremede*
        morð-beala māre   ond nō mearn for*e*,
        fǣhðe ond fyrene;   wæs tō fæst on þām.
        Þ*ā* wæs ēað-fynde   þe him elles hwǣr
        gerūm*l*īcor   ræste [*sōhte*],
140   bed æfter būrum,   ðā hi*m* gebēacnod wæs,
        gesægd sōð*l*īce   sweo*t*olan tācne
        heal-ðegnes hete;   hēold hyne syðþan
        fyr ond fæstor   sē þǣm fēond*e* ætwand.
        Swā rīxode   ond wið rihte wan
145   āna wið eallum,   `oðþæt īdel stōd
        hūsa sēles*t*.   Wæs sēo hwīl micel:
        twelf wintra tīd   torn geþolode
        wine Scyld[*ing*]a,   wēana gehwelcne,
        sīdra sorga;   forðām [*secgum*] wearð,
150   ylda bearnum   undyrne cūð,
        gyddum geōmore,   þætte Grendel wan
        hwīle wið Hrōþgar,   hete-nīðas wæg,
        fyrene ond fǣhðe   fela missēra,
        singāle sæce;   sibbe ne wolde
155   wið man*n*a hwone   mægenes Deniga,
        feorh-bealo feorran,   fēa þingian;

139b   No gap in MS: em. Grein.
148a   MS. scyldenda: em. Grundtvig.
149b   No gap in MS: em. Schücking.

of the sleeping thanes.   From there he returned
to his home in the darkness,   exulting in plunder,
125 took his slaughtered feast   of men to his lair.
    It was in the darkness,   the cold before dawn,
that Grendel's war-strength   was made plain to men.
Then a deep wail   rose up after feasting,
a great cry at dawn.   The famous leader,
130 so long their good king,   sat silent in grief,
the strong man suffered   his loss of thanes,
when they found the tracks   of the monstrous enemy,
the devilish spirit.   Too great was that outrage,
too hateful, long-lasting.   And it was no longer
135 than the following night   he returned to the hall,
slaughtered even more,   and he grieved not at all
for his wicked deeds—   was too deep in sin.
Then it was easy   to find a few men
who [sought] rest elsewhere,   at some slight distance,
140 slept in the outbuildings, once the full hate
of the mighty hall-server   was truly told,
made clear as a beacon   by signs too plain.
Whoever escaped   kept farther away.
    So Grendel held sway,   strove against right,
145 one against many,   till that greatest hall
stood useless, deserted.   The time was long,
the space of twelve winters,   that the Scylding king
endured in torment   all possible cares,
the fullest agony.   And so it was told
150 afar [to men,]   and the sons of men,
through mournful lays,   that Grendel had fought
long against Hrothgar,   driven by hate,
had committed crimes   for many seasons,
a relentless feud.   He wanted no peace
155 with any of the men   in the Danish host,
to put off his killing,   settle it by payment;

ně þǣr nǣnig witena   wēnan þorfte
beorhtre bōte   tō ban[an] folmum;
[*ac se*] ǣglǣca   ēhtende wæs,
160 deorc dēaþ-scūa   duguþe ond geogoþe
seomade ond syrede;   sin-nihte hēold
mistige mōras;   men ne cunnon
hwyder hel-rūnan   hwyrftum scrīþað.
    Swā fela fyrena   fēond man-cynnes,
165 atol ān-gengea,   oft gefremede,
heardra hȳnða.   Heorot eardode,
sinc-fāge sel   sweartum nihtum;
nō hē þone gif-stōl   grētan mōste,
māþðum for Metode,   nē his myne wisse.
170 Þæt wæs wrǣc micel   wine Scyldinga,
mōdes brecða.   Monig oft gesæt
rīce tō rūne,   rǣd eahtedon,
hwæt swīð-ferhðum   sēlest wǣre
wið fǣr-gryrum   tō gefremmanne.
175 Hwīlum hīe gehēton   æt hærg-trafum
wīg-weorþunga   wordum bǣdon,
þæt him gāst-bona   gēoce gefremede
wið þēod-þrēaum.   Swylc wæs þēaw hyra,
hǣþenra hyht;   helle gemundon
180 in mōd-sefan,   Metod hīe ne cūþon,
dǣda Dēmend,   ne wiston hīe Drihten God,
nē hīe hūru heofena Helm   herian ne cūþon,
wuldres Waldend.   Wā bið þǣm ðe sceal
þurh slīðne nīð   sāwle bescūfan
185 in fȳres fæþm,   frōfre ne wēnan,
wihte gewendan!   Wēl bið þǣm þe mōt
æfter dēað-dæge   Drihten sēcean
ond tō Fæder fæþmum   freoðo wilnian!
III   Swā ðā mǣl-ceare   maga Healfdenes
190 singāla sēað,   ne mihte snotor hǣleð

158b   MS. banum: em. Kemble.
159a   Loss at edge of MS. restored by Rieger.
175b   MS. hrærg trafum: em. Grundtvig.

    none of the counselors   had any great need
    to look for bright gifts   from his reddened hands.
    [Instead] the monster   was lying in wait,
160 a dark death-shadow,   ambushed and devoured
    both young men and veterans;   in perpetual night
    held the misty moors;   men cannot know
    where whispering demons,   such warlocks glide.
      Many awful sins   against mankind,
165 the solitary fiend   often committed,
    a fearsome shaming;   made his lair in Heorot,
    the jewel-decorated,   in the black nights;
    he could not come near   the gift-throne, the treasure,
    because of God—   he knew not His love.
170 It was great torture   for the lord of the Scyldings,
    a breaking of spirit.   The wise men would sit,
    high-ranking, in council,   considered all plans,
    what might be done   by the bravest men
    against the onslaught.   Little it helped them.
175 At times they prepared   sacrifice in temples,
    war-idol offerings,   said old words aloud,
    that the great soul-slayer   might bring some comfort
    in their country's disaster.   Such was their custom,
    the hope of the heathen;   they remembered Hell
180 in their deepest thoughts.   They knew not the Lord,
    the Judge of our deeds,   were ignorant of God,
    knew not how to worship   our Protector above,
    the King of Glory.   Woe unto him
    who in violent affliction   has to thrust his soul
185 in the fire's embrace,   expects no help,
    no change in his fate!   Well is it with him
    who after his death-day   is allowed to seek
    the Father's welcome,   ask His protection!
III   So Healfdene's son   brooded continually
190 over his sorrows;   the wise man could not

wēan onwendan;   wæs þæt gewin tō swȳð,
lāþ ond longsum,   þe on ða lēode becōm,
nȳd-wracu nīþ-grim,   niht-bealwa mæst.
    Þæt fram hām gefrægn   Higelāces þegn,
195 gōd mid Gēatum,   Grendles dǣda;
sē wæs mon-cynnes   mægenes strengest
on þǣm dæge   þysses līfes,
æþele ond ēacen.   Hēt him ȳð-lidan
gōdne gegyrwan;   cwæð, hē gūð-cyning
200 ofer swan-rāde   sēcean wolde,
mǣrne þēoden,   þā him wæs manna þearf.
Ðone sīð-fæt him   snotere ceorlas
lȳt-hwōn lōgon   *þēah* hē him *lē*of wǣre;
hwetton hige-*rōfne,*   *hǣl* scēawedon.
205 Hæfde se gōda   Gēata lēoda
*ce*mpan gecorone   þāra þe hē cēnoste
findan mihte;   fīf-tȳna sum
sund-wudu sōhte   secg wīsade
lagu-cræftig mon   land-gemyrcu.
210   Fyrst forð gewāt;   flota wæs on ȳðum,
bāt under beorge.   Beornas gearwe
on stefn stigon;   strēamas wundon
sund wið sande;   secgas bǣron
on bearm nacan   beorhte frætwe
215 gūð-searo geatolīc;   guman ūt scufon
weras on wil-sīð   wudu bundenne.
Gewāt þā ofer wǣg-holm   winde gefȳsed
flota fāmī-heals,   fugle gelīcost,
oðþæt ymb ān-tīd,   ōþres dōgores,
220 wunden-stefna   gewaden hæfde,
þæt ðā līðende   land gesāwon,
brim-clifu blīcan,   beorgas stēape,
sīde sæ-næssas;   þā wæs sund liden,
ēoletes æt ende.   Þanon up hraðe
225 Wedera lēode   on wang stigon,

204a "rofne" now entirely gone, but deduced from errors in the Thorkelin
transcripts. See Malone. *PMLA* 64 (1949), 1195.

ward off the trouble.   The strife was too great,
hateful, long-lasting,   that had come to the nation,
cruel spirit's envy,   gigantic night-evil.
  Far off in his homeland   Hygelac's thane,
195 good man of the Geats,   heard about Grendel;
he was the strongest   of all living men
at that time   in this world,
noble and huge.   He ordered made ready
a good wave-rider,   announced he would seek
200 the warrior-king,   famous ruler,
across the swan's riding,   since he needed men.
Against that journey   all sensible men
said not a word,   though he was dear to them,
but encouraged such heart,   observed the omens.
205 The mighty man   had carefully chosen
from tribes of the Geats   champions, battlers,
the best he could find,   the acknowledged brave.
A group of fifteen   he led to his ship;
the sea-skilled man   marched down to the shore.
210 Time passed quickly.   They made all secure.
Then the ship was floating   beneath the cliffs.
Armored warriors   climbed the prow;
the sea-currents eddied;   they carried up weapons,
stored them amidships,   all the bright ornaments,
215 stately battle-dress.   Then the men shoved off,
on a willing journey   in their well-braced ship.
Across open seas,   blown by the wind,
the foamy-necked ship   went like a bird,
till in good time,   the second day out,
220 the curved prow-carving   had gone so far
that the seafaring men   sighted land,
silvery sea-cliffs,   high rocky shores,
broad headlands.   The deep sea was crossed,
their journey at an end.   The troop of Storm-Geats
225 went over the side,   climbed ashore,

sǣ-wudu sǣldon   —syrcan hrysedon,
gūð-gewǣdo—   Gode þancedon
þæs þe him ȳð-lāde   ēaðe wurdon.
    Þā of wealle geseah   weard Scildinga

230 sē þe *holm*-clifu   healdan scolde
beran ofer bolcan   beorhte randas
fyrd-searu fūslicu;   hine fyrwyt bræc
mōd-gehygdum   hwæt þā men wǣron.
Gewāt him þā tō waroðe   wicge rīd*an*

235 þegn Hrōðgāres,   þrymmum cwehte
mægen-wudu mundum,   meþel-wordum frægn:
"Hwæt syndon gē   searo-hæbbendra,
byrnum wer*e*de,   þe þus brontne cēol
ofer lagu-strǣte   lǣdan cwōmon,

240 hider ofer holmas?   [*Ic hwi*]le wæs
ende-sǣta,   ǣg-wearde hēold,
þē on land Dena   lāðra nǣnig
mid scip-herge   sceðþan ne meahte.
Nō hēr cūðlīcor   cuman ongunnon

245 lind-hæbbende,   nē gē lēafnes-word
gūð-fremmendra   gearwe ne wisson,
māga gemēdu.   Nǣfre ic māran geseah
eorla ofer eorþan   ðonne is ēower sum,
secg on searwum;   nis þæt seld-guma

250 wǣpnum geweorðad—   nǣfre him his wlite lēoge,
ǣnlīc ansȳn!   Nū ic ēower sceal
frum-cyn witan,   ǣr gē fyr *heon*an,
lēas-scēaweras,   on land Den*a*
furþur fēran.   Nū gē feor-būend,

255 mere-līðende,   mīn[*n*]e gehȳrað
ānfealdne geþōht: ofost is sēlest
tō gecȳðanne   *h*wanan ēowre cyme syndon."

IIII   Him se yldesta   andswarode,
werodes wīsa,   word-hord onlēac:

240b MS. holmas le wæs: em. Kaluza.
250b Usually em. næf[*n*]e 'unless,' but I follow Robinson, *TSL* 11 (19(
155–57.
255b MS. mine: em. Kemble.

        made their ship fast.   Their chain-mail clanked,
        their bright battle-shirts.   They gave thanks to God
        the wave-road was smooth,   had been easily crossed.
            From high on a wall   the Scylding watchman
230 whose duty it was   to guard the sea-cliffs
        saw glinting shield-bosses   passed hand to hand
        down the gangplank,   an army's war-gear.
        His mind was afire   to know who they were.
        He rode his horse   straight down to the shore,
235 retainer of Hrothgar,   brandished his spear,
        shook the strong wood,   mighty in his hand,
        spoke out stiffly: "Who are you armored men,
        protected by mail,   who thus come sailing
        your high ship   on the sliding wave-roads,
240 overseas to this shore?   [Long have I] held
        the sea-watch in season,   as the king's coast-guard,
        that none of our enemies   might come into Denmark,
        do us harm with an army,   their fleet of ships.
        Never more openly   have warriors landed
245 when carrying shields,   and you have no leave
        from our men of battle,   agreement with kinsmen.
        Never have I seen   a mightier noble,
        a larger man,   than that one among you,
        a warrior in armor.   That's no mere retainer
250 so honored in weapons—   may that noble bearing
        never belie him!   I must know your lineage,
        now, right away,   before you go further,
        spies scouting out   the land of the Danes.
        Now, you far strangers   from across the sea,
255 ocean-travelers,   hear my simple thought:
        haste is needed,   and the sooner the better,
        it is best to be quick   and say whence you come."
IIII   That noblest man   then gave him an answer,
        the leader of the band   unlocked his word-hoard:

260 "Wē synt gum-cynnes   Gēata lēode
    ond Higelāces   heorð-genēatas.
    Wæs mīn fæder   folcum gecȳþed,
    æþele ord-fruma   Ecgþēow hāten;
    gebād wintra worn   ǣr hē on weg hwurfe,
265 gamol of geardum;   hine gearwe geman
    witena wēl-hwylc   wīde geond eorþan.
    Wē þurh holdne hige   hlāford þīnne,
    sunu Healfdenes,   sēcean cwōmon,
    lēod-gebyrgean: wes þū ūs lārena gōd!
270 Habbað wē tō þǣm mǣran   micel ǣrende
    Deniga frēan;   ne sceal þǣr dyrne sum
    wesan, þæs ic wēne.   Þū wāst—gif hit is
    swā wē sōþlīce   secgan hȳrdon—
    þæt mid Scyldingum   sceaðona ic nāt hwylc,
275 dēogol dǣd-hata,   deorcum nihtum
    ēaweð þurh egsan   uncūðne nīð
    hȳnðu ond hrā-fyl.   Ic þæs Hrōðgār mæg
    þurh rūmne sefan   rǣd gelǣran
    hū hē frōd *ond* gōd   fēond oferswȳðeþ,
280 gyf him edwend*an*   ǣfre scolde
    bealuwa bisigu,   bōt eft cuman,
    ond þā cear-wylmas   cōlran wurðaþ;
    oððe ā syþðan   earfoð-þrāge,
    þrēa-nȳd þolað,   þenden þǣr wunað
285 on hēah-stede   hūsa sēlest."
        Weard maþelode,   ðǣr on wicge sæt,
    ombeht unforht: "Ǣghwæþres sceal
    scearp scyld-wiga   gescād witan,
    worda ond worca,   sē þe wēl þenceð.
290 Ic þæt gehȳre,   þæt þis is hold weorod
    frēan Scyldinga.   Gewītaþ forð beran
    wǣpen ond gewǣdu;   ic ēow wīsige.
    Swylce ic magu-þegnas   mīne hāte
    wið fēonda gehwone   flotan ēowerne,
295 nīw-tyrwydne   nacan on sande
    ārum healdan,   oþðæt eft byreð
    ofer lagu-strē*mas*   lēofne mannan

260 "We are of the race   of the Geatish nation,
    sworn hearth-companions   of Hygelac their king.
    My own father   was well known abroad,
    a noble battle-leader,   Ecgtheow by name.
    He saw many winters   before he passed on,
265 old, from our courtyards;   every wise counselor
    throughout the world   remembers him well.
    We come with good heart   to the land of the Danes,
    to seek out your lord,   the son of Healfdene,
    shield of the people: be good in your words.
270 We have a great mission   to the famous king,
    leader of the Danes,   and I too agree
    nothing should be secret.   You are aware
    —if it is indeed   as we have heard told—
    that among the Scyldings   some sort of enemy,
275 mysterious ravager,   in pitch-black night,
    brings terrible malice,   an unknown hatred,
    shame and great slaughter.   From a generous mind
    I can offer Hrothgar   good plan and counsel,
    how, old and good,   he may conquer his enemy,
280 if reversal of fortune   is ever to come to him,
    any exchange   for baleful affliction,
    cooling of care-surges   hot in his heart;
    or else ever afterwards   through years of grief
    he must endure   terrible suffering,
285 so long as that hall   rises high in its place."
        The coast-guard spoke,   sitting on his horse,
    fearless official: "A keen-witted shield-bearer
    who thinks things out carefully   must know the dis-
                                                    tinction
    between words and deeds,   keep the difference clear.
290 I hear you say   that this is a troop
    loyal to the Scylding.   Now then, go forth,
    take your armor and weapons.   I shall be leading you.
    I also shall order   my young comrades
    to guard your ship,   new-tarred on our sand,
295 against any enemies,   to hold it in honor
    till once again,   over sliding seas,
    the coil-necked wood   bears friendly men

    wudu wunden-ha*ls*   *tō* Weder-mearce,
    gōd-fremmendra   swylcum gifeþe bið
300 þæt þone hilde-ræs   hāl gedīgeð."
       Gewiton him þā fēran.   Flota *s*tille bād
    seomode on s[*ā*]le   sīd-fæþmed *s*cip
    on ancre fæst.   Eoforlīc scionon
    ofer hlēor-beran,   gehroden golde;
305 fāh ond fȳr-heard,   ferh-wearde hēold
    gūþ-mōd gr[*i*]mmon.   Guman ōnetton,
    sigon ætsomne,   oþþæt hȳ [*s*]æl timbred,
    geatolīc ond gold-fāh   ongyton mihton,
    þæt wæs fore-mærost   fold-būendum
310 receda under roderum   on þæm se rīca bād;
    līxte se lēoma   ofer landa fela.
    Him þā hilde-dēor   [*h*]of mōdigra
    torht getæhte,   þæt hīe him tō mihton
    gegnum gangan;   gūð-beorna sum
315 wicg gewende,   word æfter cwæð:
    "Mæl is mē tō fēran;   Fæder alwalda
    mid ār-stafum   ēowic gehealde
    sīða gesunde!   Ic tō sæ wille,
    wið *wrā*ð werod   wearde healdan."
       Stræt wæs stān-fāh,   stīg wīsode
320 gumum ætgædere.   Gūð-byrne scān,
    heard, hond-locen,   hring-īren scīr
    song in searwum,   þā hīe tō sele furðum
    in hyra gryre-geatwum   gangan cwōmon.
325 Setton sæ-mēþe   sīde scyldas,
    rondas regn-hearde,   wið þæs recedes weal;
    bugon þā tō bence,   byrnan hringdon,
    gūð-searo gumena.   Gāras stōdon,
    sæ-manna searo,   samod ætgædere,
330 æsc-holt ufan græg;   wæs se īren-þrēat

302a MS. sole: em. Ettmüller.
306a MS. grummon: em. Sedgefield.
307b MS. æl: em. Kemble.
312b MS. of: em. Kemble.
322b MS. hæleþum: em. Grein.

to the Geatish shores—   all of the valiant,
good men of the Weders,   to whom it is given
300 to survive, unharmed,   that rush of battle."
     And so they set off.   Their ship swung calmly,
rode on its ropes,   the wide-beamed ship
fast at anchor.   Boar-figures gleamed
over plated cheek-guards,   inlaid with gold;
305 shining, fire-hardened,   fierce war-masks
guarded their lives.   The warriors hastened,
marched in formation,   until they could see
the gold-laced hall,   the high timbers,
most splendid building   among earth-dwellers
310 under the heavens   —the king lived there—
its gold-hammered roofs   shone over the land.
The battle-worthy guide   showed them the glittering,
brilliant hall   of spirited men,
that they might go straight,   then wheeled his horse
315 back through the troop,   spoke out a word:
"It is time I returned;   the Father all-powerful
in His mercy   keep you safe
through all your ventures.   I am off to the sea
to keep the watch   for enemy marauders."
V⎫
320⎭   The road was stone-paved,   a straight path guided
the men in their ranks.   Bright their war-mail,
hardened, hand-linked;   glistening iron rings
sang in their battle-shirts   as they came marching
straight to that hall,   fearful in war-gear.
325 The sea-weary men   set their broad shields,
spell-hardened rims,   against the high wall,
eased down on benches,   their chain-mail clinking,
fit dress for warriors.   Their spears were stacked,
the seafarers' weapons,   bristling upright,
330 straight ash, gray points.   That iron-fast troop

68 Beowulf

wǣpnum gewurþad.   Þā ðǣr wlonc hæleð
ōret-mecgas   æfter æ[þ]e[l]um frægn:
"Hwanon ferigeað gē   fætte scyldas,
grǣge syrcan   ond grīm-helmas,
335 here-sceafta hēap?   Ic eom Hrōðgāres
ār ond ombiht.   Ne seah ic elþēodige
þus manige men   mōdiglīcran.
Wēn' ic þæt gē for wlenco,   nalles for wrǣc-sīðum,
ac for hige-þrymmum   Hrōðgār sōhton."
340 Him þā ellen-rōf   andswarode,
wlanc Wedera lēod,   word æfter spræc,
heard under helme: "Wē synt Higelāces
bēod-genēatas;   Bēowulf is mīn nama.
Wille ic āsecgan   sunu Healfdenes,
345 mǣrum þēodne   mīn ǣrende,
aldre þīnum,   gif hē ūs geunnan wile
þæt wē hine swā gōdne   grētan mōton."
Wulfgār maþelode;   þæt wæs Wendla lēod,
wæs his mōd-sefa   manegum gecȳðed,
350 wīg ond wīsdōm: "Ic þæs wine Deniga
frēan Scildinga   frīnan wille,
bēaga bryttan,   swā þū bēna eart,
þēoden mǣrne,   ymb þīnne sīð,
ond þē þā andsware   ǣdre gecȳðan,
355 ðe mē se gōda   āgifan þenceð."
Hwearf þā hrædlīce   þǣr Hrōðgār sæt,
eald ond unhār   mid his eorla gedriht;
ēode ellen-rōf   þæt hē for eaxlum gestōd
Deniga frēan: cūþe hē duguðe þēaw.
360 Wulfgār maðelode   tō his wine-drihtne:
"Hēr syndon geferede,   feorran cumene
ofer geofenes begang   Gēata lēode;
þone yldestan   ōret-mecgas
Bēowulf nemnað.   Hȳ bēnan synt,
365 þæt hīe, þēoden mīn,   wið þē mōton

339a MS. *þrymmum* rests only on the self-correction of Thorkelin A. See Malone, *PMLA* 64 (1949), 1196.

was honored in weapons.   Then a haughty noble
asked the picked men   about their descent:
"From where have you carried   those gold-trimmed
                                                          shields,
iron-gray corselets,   and grim mask-helmets,
335 this host of battle-shafts?   I am Hrothgar's
herald and chamberlain,   but never have I seen
so many foreigners   bolder in spirit.
I expect in pride   —scarcely in exile!—
out of high courage   you have come to Hrothgar."
340 Then he was answered   by the valiant warrior;
the Geatish leader   spoke in his turn,
strong in his helmet: "We are Hygelac's
companions in hall.   Beowulf is my name.
I wish to make known   my business here
345 to the son of Healfdene,   famous king,
lord of your lives,   if it please him to grant
that we may approach   his generous self."
Wulfgar made answer   —a prince of the Vendels—
the truth of his character   was known to many,
350 his courage and wisdom: "I shall ask the friend
of all tribes of Danes,   lord of the Scyldings,
great ring-giver,   most noble ruler,
about your arrival,   as you have requested,
and soon will announce,   will return you the answer
355 our king sees fit   to give unto me."
     Then he walked quickly   to where Hrothgar sat,
old, gray-bearded,   surrounded by nobles;
strode up the hall   till he stood face to face
with the Danish king;   he knew the noble custom.
360 Wulfgar addressed   his friend and lord:
"A troop of Geats   has arrived here,
traveling far   across the broad sea.
Battle-veterans,   these soldiers call
their leader Beowulf.   They make the request,
365 my Scylding lord,   that they might exchange

wordum wrixlan,   nō ðū him wearne getēoh
ðīnra gegn-cwida,   glæd-man Hrōðgār:
hȳ on wīg-getāwum   wyrðe þinceað
eorla geæhtlan;   hūru se aldor dēah,
370 sē þǣm heaðo-rincum   hider wīsade."
VI   Hrōðgār maþelode,   helm Scyldinga:
"Ic hine cūðe   cniht-wesende;
wæs his eald-fæder   Ecgþēo hāten,
ðǣm tō hām forgeaf   Hrēþel Gēata
375 āngan dohtor;   is his eafora nū
heard hēr cumen,   sōhte holdne wine!
Ðonne sægdon þæt   sǣ-līþende,
þā ðe gif-sceattas   Gēata fyredon
þyder tō þance,   þæt hē þrītiges
380 manna mægen-cræft   on his *mund*-gripe,
heaþo-rōf, hæbbe.   Hine hālig God
for ār-stafum   ūs onsende
tō West-Denum,   þæs ic wēn hæbbe,
wið Grendles gryre.   *Ic þǣm gōdan sceal*
385 *for his mōd-þræce*   *mādmas bēodan.*
Bēo ðū on ofeste,   hāt *in* gān
sēon sibbe-gedriht   samod ætgædere;
gesaga him ēac wordum   þæt hīe sint wil-cuman
Deniga lēodum."   [*Þā tō dura healle*
390 *Wulfgār ēode,*]   word inne ābēad:
"Ēow hēt secgan   sige-drihten mīn,
aldor Ēast-Dena,   þæt hē ēower æþelu can,
ond gē him syndon   ofer sǣ-wylmas
heard-hicgende,   hider wil-cuman.
395 Nū gē mōton gangan   in ēowrum gūð-getāwum
under here-grīman,   Hrōðgār geseon;
lǣtað hilde-bord   hēr onbidian,

375b MS. eaforan: em. Kemble.
389b–390a No gap in MS: conjectural restoration by Grein as adapted by Wrenn.
395b MS. guð geata wum: em. Ettmüller.
397b Originally MS. onbidina in error for "onbidian," with smudged erasure of "n" after the "di"; thus Malone, *NC*, p. 55. Other scholars see the altered "in" as erased "m" and read "onbīdan."

their words with yours.   Choose among answers
but give no refusal,   Hrothgar my friend:
in battle-dress, weapons,   they appear worthy
of nobles' esteem,   and tall, truly strong,
370 the chief who has led   such soldiers here."
VI   Then Hrothgar spoke,   protector of Scyldings:
"Why, I knew him   when he was only a boy;
his father, now dead,   was named Ecgtheow:
Hrethel of the Geats   gave him a wife,
375 his only daughter.   And so his brave son
has now come here,   seeks a loyal friend!
In fact, the merchants   who used to carry
gifts of coins,   our thanks to the Geats,
380 said he had war-fame,   the strength of thirty
in his mighty hand-grip.   Holy God
in the fullness of mercy   has sent him to us,
to the Danish people,   if I'm not mistaken,
against Grendel's terror.   I must offer this man
385 excellent treasures   for his daring courage.
Now be in haste,   call these men in,
let them meet our nobles,   gathered kinsmen;
say to them also   they are more than welcome
to the Danish nation."   [Then Wulfgar went
390 to the door of the hall,]   spoke from the doorway:
"I am ordered to tell you   our glorious ruler,
king of the East-Danes,   knows your lineage,
and that you good men,   strong battle-hearts
from beyond the sea,   are welcome to him.
395 Now you may enter,   in your battle-armor,
wearing war-masks,   to see Hrothgar;
let shields stay here,   tightened war-wood,

        wudu, wæl-sceaftas,   worda geþinges."
        Ārās þā se rīca,   ymb hine rinc manig,
400   þrýðlīc þegna hēap;   sume þær bidon
        heaðo-rēaf hēoldon   swā him se *hea*rda bebēad.
        Snyredon ætsomn*e*   þā secg wīsode,
        under Heorotes hrōf;   [*ēode hilde-dēor*,]
        he*ard* under helme,   þæt hē on hēoðe gestōd.
405   Bēowulf maðelode   —on him byrne scān,
        sea*ro*-net seowed   smiþes orþancum:
        "Wæs þū, Hrōðgār, hāl!   Ic eom Higelāces
        mǣg ond mago-ðegn;   hæbbe ic mǣrða fela
        ongunnen on geogoþe.   Mē wearð Grendles þing
410   on mīnre ēþel-tyrf   undyrne cūð;
        secgað sǣ-līðend   þæt þæs sele stand*e*,
        reced sēlesta   rinca gehwylcum
        īdel ond unnyt,   siððan ǣfen-lēoht
        under heofenes hādor   beholen weorþeð.
415   Þā mē þæt gelǣrdon   lēode mīne,
        þā sēlestan,   snotere ceorlas,
        þēoden Hrōðgār,   þæt ic þē sōhte,
        forþan hīe mægenes cræft   mīne cūþon,
        selfe ofersāwon   ðā ic of searwum cwōm
420   fāh from fēondum   þær ic fīfe geband
        ȳðde eotena cyn,   ond on ȳðum slōg
        niceras nihtes,   nearo-þearfe drēah,
        wræc *Weder*a nīð   —wēan āhsodon—
        forgrand gr*am*um;   ond nū wið Grendel sceal,
425   wið þām āglǣcan,   āna gehēgan
        ðing wið þyrse.   *Ic* þē nū ðā,
        brego Beorht-Dena,   biddan wille,
        *eod*or Scyldinga,   ānre bēne,
        þæt ðū mē ne forwyrne,   wīgendra hlēo,
430   frēo-wine *f*olca,   nū ic þus feorran cōm,
        þæt ic mōte āna,   [*ond*] mīnra eorla gedryht,
        þes hearda hēap,   Heorot fǣlsian.

_____

403b No gap in MS: conjectural restoration by von Schaubert.
431b "ond" shifted by Kemble from before "þes" in 432.

> your battle-shafts wait   the result of words."
>
> The noble one rose,   and his men with him,
400 a powerful band;   some of them stayed
> to guard the weapons,   as their leader ordered.
> As a troop they marched   under Heorot's roof,
> their chief at the front.   Brave in his helmet,
> [he advanced] till he stood   before the king.
405 Then Beowulf spoke,   in his gleaming mail,
> the ring-net sewn   by a master smith:
> "Hail, Hrothgar,   health ever keep you!
> I am Hygelac's   thane and kinsman;
> mighty the deeds   I have done in my youth.
410 News of Grendel   reached me in Geatland;
> travelers say   that this great building,
> brightest hall,   stands empty, useless
> to all the warriors   when evening light
> fades from the sky,   brightness of heaven.
415 My people advised me,   wise men among us,
> our best counselors,   that I should seek you,
> chieftain Hrothgar,   king of the Danes,
> since they had known   my tested strength;
> they saw themselves   how I came from combat
420 bloodied by enemies   where I crushed down five,
> killed a tribe of giants,   and on the waves at night
> slew water-beasts;   no easy task,
> but I drove out   trouble from Geatland—
> they asked for it,   the enemies I killed.
425 Now, against Grendel,   alone, I shall settle
> this matter, pay back   this giant demon.
> I ask you now,   protector of Scyldings,
> king of the Bright-Danes,   a single favor—
> that you not refuse me,   having come this far,
430 guardian of warriors,   friend of the nations,
> that I be allowed   to cleanse great Heorot,
> alone, with my men,   my noble warriors.

Hæbbe ic ēac geāhsod,   þæt sē æglǣca
for his won-hȳdum   wǣpna ne recceð.
435 Ic þæt þonne forhicge,   swā mē Higelāc sīe,
mīn mon-drihten,   mōdes blīðe,
þæt ic sweord bere   oþðe sīdne scyld,
geolo-rand tō gūþe,   ac ic mid grāpe sceal
fōn wið fēonde   ond ymb feorh sacan,
440 lāð wið lāþum;   ðǣr gelȳfan sceal
Dryhtnes dōme   sē þe hine dēað nimeð.
Wēn' ic þæt hē wille,   gif hē wealdan mōt,
in þǣm gūð-sele   Gēatena lēode
etan unforhte,   swā hē oft dyde,
445 mægen Hrēð-manna.   Nā þū mīnne þearft
hafalan hȳdan,   ac hē mē habban wile
d[r]ēore fāhne,   gif mec dēað nimeð;
byreð blōdig wæl,   byrgean þenceð,
eteð ān-genga   unmurnlīce,
450 mearcað mōr-hopu;   nō ðū ymb mīnes ne þearft
līces feorme   leng sorgian!
Onsend Higelāce,   gif mec hild nime,
beadu-scrūda betst,   þæt mīne brēost wereð,
hrægla sēlest;   þæt is Hrǣdlan lāf,
455 Wēlandes geweorc.   Gǣð ā wyrd swā hīo scel."
VII   Hrōðgār maþelode,   helm Scyldinga:
"F[or gewyr]htum þū,   wine mīn Bēowulf,
ond for ār-stafum   ūsic sōhtest.
Geslōh þīn fæder   fǣhðe mǣste,
460 wearþ hē Heaþolāfe   tō hand-bonan
mid Wilfingum;   ðā hine [w]āra cyn
for here-brōgan   habban ne mihte.
Þanon hē gesōhte   Sūð-Dena folc
ofer ȳða gewealc,   Ār-*Scyld*inga;

443b The third letter of "Gēatena" is "a" altered from "o": Malone, *NC*, p. 56. Wrenn reads "Gēotena" as an Anglian form.

447a MS. deore: em. Kemble.

457a MS. fere fyhtum: em. Trautmann.

461b MS. gara cyn: em. Thorpe, newly supported by Joseph Tuso, *MLQ* 29 (1968), 259–62.

I have heard it said   this evil monster
in his wild recklessness   scorns all weapons.
435 I therefore decline,   that Hygelac my lord
may be pleased to the heart,   to take any sword
or broad-braced shield,   yellow war-wood,
into this combat,   but with my own hand-grip
I will meet this enemy   and fight for life,
440 foe against foe.   Whoever death takes
will have to trust   in the judgment of God.
I expect he will wish,   if he gains control,
to feed unafraid   on Geatish men too,
to eat in the war-hall,   as he often has done,
445 the might of the Hreth-men.   No need then
to cover my face;   he, with his mouth,
will cover enough,   if death takes me;
will carry my body   to a bloody feast,
hardly in mourning,   will dine alone,
450 splash his lair red;   no need for you
to worry any longer   about my burial!
But send back to Hygelac,   if battle takes me,
this excellent war-shirt   shielding my breast,
my finest cloak;   it is Hrethel's heirloom,
455 Weland made it.   Fate will go as it must."
VII   Then Hrothgar replied,   the Scyldings' protector:
"For [our past deeds,]   and out of kindness,
you have now sought us,   Beowulf my friend.
Your father struck up   a mighty feud,
460 slayer of Heatholaf   among the Wylfings,
by his own hand.   Then the treaty-folk
could not harbor him   for fear of war,
and so he traveled   to the land of South-Danes,
over rolling waves   to Honor-Scyldings.

465 ðā ic furþum wēold   folce Deniga
ond on geogoðe hēold   gimme-rīce,
hord-burh hæleþa;   ðā wæs Heregār dēad,
mīn yldra mæg   unlifigende,
bearn Healfdenes;   sē wæs betera ðonne ic!

470 Siððan þā fæhðe   fēo þingode;
sende ic Wylfingum   ofer wæteres hrycg
ealde mādmas;   hē mē āþas swōr.
Sorh is mē tō secganne   on sefan mīnum
gumena ængum,   hwæt mē Grendel hafað

475 hȳnðo on Heorote   mid his hete-þancum,
fær-nīða gefremed;   is mīn flet-werod,
wīg-hēap gewanod;   hīe wyrd forswēop
on Grendles gryre.   God ēaþe mæg
þone dol-sceaðan   dæda getwæfan!

480 Ful oft gebēotedon   bēore druncne
ofer ealo-wæge   ōret-mecgas,
þæt hīe in bēor-sele   bīdan woldon
Grendles gūþe   mid gryrum ecga.
Ðonne wæs þeos medo-heal   on morgen-tīd,

485 driht-sele drēor-fāh,   þonne dæg lixte,
eal benc-þelu   blōde bestȳmed,
heall heoru-drēore;   āhte ic holdra þȳ læs
dēorre duguðe,   þē þā dēað fornam.
Site nū tō symle   ond onsæl meoto,

490 sige-hrēð secgum,   swā þīn sefa hwette."
Þā wæs Gēat-mæcgum   geador ætsomne
on bēor-sele   benc gerȳmed;
þær swīð-ferhþe   sittan ēodon,
þrȳðum dealle.   Þegn nytte behēold,

495 sē þe on handa bær   hroden ealo-wæge,
scencte scīr wered;   scop hwīlum sang
hādor on Heorote;   þær wæs hæleða drēam,
duguð unlȳtel   Dena ond Wedera.

465b MS. deninga: em. Thorpe.

490a MS. secgum from Malone, *NC*, p. 57. The trans. follows J. W. Bright, *MLN* 31 (1916), 217–23. Wrenn reads: on sæl meoto / sige hrēð-secg[a] 'in due time attend to the victories of glorious warriors,' i.e., listen to Danish lays.

465 That was when first I ruled the Danes
   and held, in youth, a gem-rich kingdom,
   bright fort of heroes. Heorogar had died,
   the son of Healfdene, my older brother
   no longer alive; he was better than I!
470 Later I settled the feud by payment;
   I sent to those Wylfings, over the water's ridge,
   fine old treasures; your father swore me oaths.
   It gives me great pain to have to reveal
   to any man what fearful attacks,
475 shame, and disaster Grendel has brought me
   in his persecution. The ranks in my hall,
   my men, are less; fate swept them off
   in Grendel's terror. Yet God may easily
   stop the mad deeds of the foolhardy ravager!
480 Often indeed my warrior thanes
   boasted over ale-horns, bold in their mead,
   that they would meet Grendel's attack
   in the banquet hall with a rush of swords.
   But at dawn this mead-hall was bright in blood,
485 all the bench-planks a running slick,
   the hall red with gore. I had fewer men,
   loyal comrades, after such deaths.
   Now sit at the feast, unbind your thoughts
490 to men, great warrior, as your heart desires."
    Then a bench was cleared, room made in the hall
   for the gathered Weders standing in a troop;
   the courageous men took their seats,
   proud in their strength; a thane did his office,
495 carried in his hands the gold ale-flagons,
   poured bright mead. At times the scop sang,
   bright-voiced in Heorot; there was joy of warriors,
   no small gathering of Geats and Danes.

VIII   Unferð maþelode,   Ecglāfes bearn,
500 þe æt fōtum sæt   frēan Scyldinga,
     onband beadu-rūne—   wæs him Bēowulfes sīð,
     mōdges mere-faran,   micel æfþunca
     forþon þe hē ne ūþe   þæt ænig ōðer man
     æfre mærða þon mā   middan-geardes
505 gehēdde under heofenum   þonne hē sylfa:
     "Eart þū sē Bēowulf,   sē þe wið Brecan wunne,
     on sīdne sæ   ymb sund flite,
     ðær git for wlence   wada cunnedon
     ond for dol-gilpe   on dēop wæter
510 aldrum nēþdon?   Nē inc ænig mon,
     nē lēof nē lāð,   belēan mihte
     sorh-fullne sīð,   þā git on sund rēon;
     þær git ēagor-strēam   earmum þehton,
     mæton mere-stræta   mundum brugdon,
515 glidon ofer gār-secg;   geofon ȳþum wēol,
     wintrys wylm[*um*].   Git on wæteres æht
     seofon niht swuncon;   hē þe æt sunde oferflāt,
     hæfde māre mægen.   Þā hine on morgen-tīd
     on Heaþo-Ræmes   holm up ætbær;
520 ðonon hē gesōhte   swæsne ēþel,
     lēof his lēodum,   lond Brondinga,
     freoðo-burh fægere,   þær hē folc āhte,
     burh ond bēagas.   Bēot eal wið þē
     sunu Bēanstānes   sōð*e* gelæste.
525 Ðonne wēne ic tō þē   wyrsan geþingea
     ðēah þū heaðo-ræsa   gehwær dohte
     grimre gūðe,   gif þū Grendl*es* dearst
     niht-longne fyrst   nēan bī*dan*."
       Bēowulf maþelode,   bearn Ecgþēowes:
530 "Hwæt þū worn fela,   wine mīn Unferð,
     bēore druncen   ymb Brecan spræce,

   499a MS. HVN ferð: em. Rieger, as also in 530, 1165, 1488. Apparently
the scribe succumbed to the analogy of other Germanic names such as Hun-
lafing 1143.

   516a MS. wylm: em. Kluge.

   530b MS. hun ferð.

VIII   Unferth, Ecglaf's son,   rose up to speak,
500 who sat at the feet   of the lord of the Scyldings;
     he unbound a battle-rune—   the journey of Beowulf,
     the brave seafarer,   caused him chagrin,
     for he would not grant   that any other man
     under the heavens   might ever care more
505 for famous deeds   than he himself:
     "Are you the same Beowulf   who challenged Breca
     to a swimming match   on the open sea?
     There out of pride   you both tested sea-ways,
     through foolish boasting   risked lives on the deep.
510 None could dissuade you,   friend nor foe,
     keep either of you   from that hapless trip,
     when you two went swimming   out of the bay,
     your arms embracing   the crests, sea-currents,
     flung out your hands   to measure the sea-roads,
515 the ocean of wind.   The steep seas boiled
     in winter's pourings.   You both toiled seven nights,
     driven by the waves,   and in that swimming
     he overcame you,   had greater strength.
     The sea cast him up   on the Heatho-Ræms' shore;
520 from there at daybreak   he sought his homeland,
     beloved by his people,   came back to the Brondings,
     fair peace-fort   where he had subjects,
     stronghold, and treasures.   The good son of Beanstan
     had truly fulfilled   his whole boast against you.
525 And so at your hand   I expect worse results,
     although you have been   always successful
     in fierce battle-rushes,   if you really dare
     wait here for Grendel   the whole night long."
          Beowulf replied,   the son of Ecgtheow:
530 "What a great deal,   Unferth my friend,
     full of beer,   you have said about Breca,

        sægdest from his sīðe.   Sōð ic talige
        þæt ic mere-strengo   māran āhte,
        earfeþo on ȳþum,   ðonne ænig ōþer man.
535 Wit þæt gecwædon   cniht-wesende
        ond gebēotedon—   wæron bēgen þā git
        on geogoð-fēore—   þæt wit on gār-secg ūt
        aldrum nēðdon   ond þæt geæfndon swā.
        Hæfdon swurd nacod,   þā wit on sund rēon,
540 heard on handa;   wit unc wið hron-fixas
        werian þōhton.   Nō hē wiht fram mē
        flōd-ȳþum feor   flēotan meahte,
        hraþor on holme,   nō ic fram him wolde.
        Ðā wit ætsomne   on sǣ wǣron
545 fīf nihta fyrst,   *oþ*þæt unc flōd tōdrāf
        wado weallende,   wedera cealdost,
        nīpende niht,   ond norþan-*w*ind
        heaðo-grim ondhwearf.   Hrēo wǣron ȳþa,
        wæs mere-fixa   mōd onhrēred;
550 þǣr mē wið lāðum   līc-syrce mīn,
        heard, hond-locen,   helpe gefremede,
        beado-hrægl brōden   on brēostum læg
        golde gegyrwed.   Mē tō grunde tēah
        fāh fēond-scaða,   fæste hæfde
555 grim on grāpe;   hwæþre mē gyfeþe wearð
        þæt ic āglǣcan   orde gerǣhte,
        hilde-bille;   heaþo-rǣs fornam
        mihtig mere-dēor   þurh mīne hand.
VIIII   "Swā mec gelōme   lāð-getēonan
560 þrēatedon þearle.   Ic him þēnode
        dēoran sweorde,   swā hit gedēfe wæs.
        Næs hīe ðǣre fylle   gefēan hæfdon,
        mān-fordǣdlan,   þæt hīe mē þēgon,
        symbel ymb-sǣton   sǣ-grunde nēah;
565 ac on mergenne   mēcum wunde
        be ȳð-lāfe   uppe lǣgon,
        sweo[*r*]*dum* āswefede,   þæt syðþan nā

567a   MS. swe*odum* from Thorkelin A only: em. Kemble.

      told of his deeds.   But to tell the true story,
      I had more sea-strength,   power in swimming,
      and also more hardship,   than any other man.
535 To each otheı we said,   as boys will boast,
      —we both were still young—   that we two alone
      would swim out to sea,   to the open ocean,
      dare risk our lives,   and we did as we said.
      We held naked swords   hard in our hands
540 as we swam on the sea;   thought to protect us
      from whales' tusks.   He could not glide,
      swim farther from me,   away on the surge,
      the heaving waves,   no swifter in water,
      nor would I leave him.   Five nights we swam,
545 together on the ocean,   till it drove us apart
      in its churning, sliding;   that coldest weather
      turned against us,   dark night and water,
      the north wind war-sharp.   Rough were the waves,
      and angry sea-beasts   had been stirred up.
550 Then my body-armor,   hard-linked, hand-joined,
      did me some service   against their attack;
      my chain-metal war-shirt,   worked with gold,
      covered my chest.   A fierce sea-monster
      dragged me down deep,   held me on the bottom
555 in his cruel grip.   However, it was granted
      that my point reached him;   I stabbed as I could
      with my sharp sword,   with battle-thrust killed
      the huge sea-beast   by my own hand.
VIIII   "Again and again   the angry monsters
560 made fierce attacks.   I served them well
      with my noble blade,   as was only fitting.
      Small pleasure they had   in such a sword-feast,
      dark things in the sea   that meant to eat me,
      sit round their banquet   on the deep sea-floor.
565 Instead, in the morning,   they lay on the beach,
      asleep from my sword,   the tide-marks bloodied
      from their deep gashes,   and never again

ymb bront*ne* ford brim-līðende
lāde ne letton. *Lēoht* ēastan cōm,
570 beorht bēacen Godes, brimu swaþredon,
þæt ic sǣ-næssas gesēon mihte
windige weallas. Wyrd oft nereð
unfǣgne eorl, þonne his ellen dēah.
Hwæþere mē gesǣlde, þæt ic mid sweorde ofslōh
575 niceras nigene. Nō ic on niht gefrægn
under heofones hwealf heardran feohtan,
nē on ēg-strēamum earmran mannon;
hwaþere ic fāra feng fēore gedīgde
sīþes wērig. Ðā mec sǣ oþbær,
580 flōd æfter faroðe on Finna land
w[a]du weallendu. Nō ic wiht fram þē
swylcra searo-nīða secgan hȳrde,
billa brōgan. Breca nǣfre gīt
æt heaðo-lāce, nē gehwæþer incer,
585 swā dēorlīce dǣd gefremede
fāgum sweordum —nō ic þæs [*fela*] gylpe—
þēah ðū þīnum brōðrum tō banan wurde,
hēafod-mǣgum; þæs þū in *helle* scealt
werhðo drēogan, þēah þīn *wit duge*.
590 Secge ic þē to sōðe, sunu Ecg*lāfes*,
þæt nǣfre Gre[*n*]del swā fela gryra gefremede,
atol ǣglǣca ealdre þīnum,
hȳnðo Heorote, gif þīn hige wǣre,
sefa swā searo-grim, swā þū self talast;
595 ac hē hafað onfunden þæt hē þā fǣhðe ne þearf,
atole ecg-þræce ēower lēode
swīðe onsittan, Sige-Scyldinga;
nymeð nȳd-bāde, nǣnegum ārað
lēode Deniga, ac hē lust wigeð,
600 swefeð ond s[*nē*]deþ, secce ne wēneþ

581a MS. wudu: em. Grundtvig.
586b No gap in MS: supplied by Grein.
591a MS. gre del: em. Thorkelin.
600a MS. sendeþ: em. Rudolph Imelmann, *ESt* 66 (1932), 324 ff. The
MS. form could mean "sends (to death)."

did they trouble the passage   of seafaring men
across the ocean.   Light came from the east,
570 God's bright beacon,   and the seas calmed,
till I saw at last   the sea-cliffs, headlands,
the windy shore.   So fate often saves
an undoomed man   when his courage holds.
However it was,   I had chanced to kill
575 some nine sea-beasts.   I never have heard
of a harder night-fight   under heaven's vault,
or a man more oppressed   on the ocean streams.
Yet I survived   those clutches and lived,
weary in my venture.   The sea bore me,
580 ocean's current,   lifting walls of water,
to the land of the Lapps.   I never have heard
such struggle, sword-terror,   told about you.
Never in the din   and play of battle
585 did Breca or you   show such courage
with shining blades   —not to boast about it—
though you were a man-slayer,   killed your brothers,
closest kinsmen,   for which you must suffer
damnation in hell,   clever though you are.
590 I'll tell you a truth,   son of Ecglaf:
never would Grendel   have done so much harm,
the awesome monster,   against your own leader,
shameful in Heorot,   if heart and intention,
your great battle-spirit,   were sharp as your words.
595 But he has discovered   he need not dread
too great a feud,   fierce rush of swords,
not from your people,   the 'Victory-Scyldings.'
He exacts his tribute,   has mercy for none
of the Danes he finds,   but hugs his feast-joys,
600 kills and devours,   expects no attack

tō Gār-Denum.   Ac ic him Gēata sceal
eafoð ond ellen   ungeāra nū
gūþe gebēodan.   Gǣþ eft sē þe mōt
tō medo mōdig,   siþþan morgen-lēoht
605 ofer ylda bearn   ōþres dōgores,
sunne swegl-wered   sūþan scīneð!"
    Þā wæs on sālum   sinces brytta,
gamol-feax ond gūð-rōf;   gēoce gelȳfde
*b*rego Beorht-Dena,   gehȳrde on *Bēo*wulfe
610 folces hyrde   fæst-rǣdne geþōht.
    Ðǣr wæs hæleþa hleahto*r*,   hlyn swynsode,
word wǣron wynsume.   Ēode Wealhþēow forð,
cwēn Hrōðgāres   cynna gemyndig;
grētte gold-hroden   guman on healle,
615 ond þā frēolīc wīf   ful gesealde
ǣrest Ēast-Dena   ēþel-wearde;
bæd hine blīðne   æt þǣr*e* bēor-þege,
lēodum lēofne;   hē on lust geþeah
symbel ond sele-ful   sige-rōf kyning.
620 Ymb-ēode þā   ides Helminga
duguþe ond geogoþe   dǣl ǣghwylcne
sinc-fato sealde   oþþæt sǣl ālamp,
þæt hīo Bēowulfe,   bēag-hroden cwēn
mōde geþungen   medo-ful ætbær;
625 grētte Gēata lēod,   Gode þancode
wīs-fæst wordum,   þæs ðe se willa gelamp,
þæt hēo on ænigne   eorl gelȳfde
fyrena frōfre.   Hē þæt ful geþeah,
wæl-rēow wiga,   *æt W*ealhþēon,
630 ond þā gyddode   gūþe gefȳ*sed*;
Bēowulf maþelode,   bearn Ecgþēowes:
"Ic þæt hogode,   þā ic on holm gestāh,
sæ-bāt gesæt   mid mīnra secga gedriht,
þæt ic ānunga   ēowra lēoda
635 willan geworhte,   oþðe on wæl crunge,
fēond-grāpum fæst.   Ic gefremman sceal
eorlīc ellen,   oþðe ende-dæg
on þisse meodu-healle   mīnne gebīdan."
Ðām wīfe þā word   wēl līcodon,

from any Spear-Danes.   But I will soon show him,
this very night,   the courage and strength
of the Geats in combat.   Whoever pleases
may walk brave to mead   once a new day,
605   tomorrow's dawn,   the sun clothed in light
shines from the south   on the sons of men."
     Then the treasure-giver   was greatly pleased,
gray-bearded, battle-famed,   chief of the Bright-Danes;
the nation's shepherd   counted on Beowulf,
610   on the warrior's help,   when he heard such resolve.
There was laughter and noise,   a pleasing din,
the glad words of men.   Wealhtheow came forward,
Hrothgar's queen,   mindful of courtesies;
attired in her gold,   she welcomed the men.
615   The noble lady   gave the first cup,
filled to the brim,   to the king of the Danes,
bade him rejoice   in this mead-serving,
beloved by his people;   he took it happily,
victory-famed king,   the hall-cup and feast.
620   The lady of the Helmings   walked through the hall,
offered the jeweled cup   to veterans and youths,
until the time came   that the courteous queen,
splendid in rings,   excellent in virtues,
came to Beowulf,   brought him the mead.
625   She greeted him well,   gave thanks to God,
wise in her words,   that her wish came to pass,
that she might expect   help against crimes
from any man.   He accepted the cup,
battle-fierce warrior,   from Wealhtheow's hand,
630   then made a speech,   eager for combat—
Beowulf spoke,   Ecgtheow's son:
"I made up my mind,   when I set out to sea,
boarded our ship   with my band of men,
that I would entirely   fulfill the desire
635   of the Danish nation   or else fall slaughtered,
in the grip of the foe.   Tonight I will do
a heroic deed   or else I will serve
my last day of life   here in this mead-hall."
These words well pleased   the royal lady,

640 gilp-cwide Gēates;   ēode gold-hroden
     frēolicu folc-cwēn   tō hire *frēan* sittan.
         Þā wæs eft swā ær   inne on healle
     þrȳð-word sprecen,   ðēod on sǣlum,
     sige-folca swēg,   oþþæt semninga
645 sunu Healfdenes   sēcean wolde
     æfen-ræste;   wiste þǣm āhlǣcan
     tō þǣm hēah-sele   hilde geþinged,
     siððan hīe sunnan lēoht   gesēon meahton,
     oþ ðe nīpende   niht ofer ealle,
650 scadu-helma gesceapu   scrīðan cwōman,
     wan under wolcnum.   Werod eall ārās.
     [*Ge*]grētte þā   guma ōþerne,
     Hrōðgār Bēowulf,   ond him hǣl ābēad,
     wīn-ærnes geweald,   ond þæt word ācwæð:
655 "Nǣfre ic ǣnegum men   ær ālȳfde,
     siþðan ic hond ond rond   hebban mihte,
     ðrȳþ-ærn Dena   būton þē nū ðā.
     Hafa nū ond geheald   hūsa sēlest,
     gemyne mǣrþo,   mægen-ellen cȳð,
660 waca wið wrāþum!   Ne bið þē wilna gād
     gif þū þæt ellen-weorc   aldre gedīgest."
  X   Ðā him Hrōþgār gewāt   mid his hæleþa gedryht,
     eodur Scyldinga   ūt of healle;
     wolde wīg-fruma   Wealhþēo sēcan,
665 cwēn tō gebeddan.   Hæfde Kyning-wuldor
     Grendle tōgēanes,   swā guman gefrungon,
     sele-weard āseted;   sundor-nytte behēold
     ymb aldor Dena,   eoton-weard' ābēad.
     Hūru Gēata lēod   georne truwode
670 mōdgan mægnes,   Metodes hyldo.
     Ðā hē him of dyde   īsern-byrnan
     helm of hafelan,   sealde his hyrsted sweord,
     īrena cyst,   ombiht-þegne,
     ond gehealdan hēt   hilde-geatwe.
675 Gespræc þā se gōda   gylp-worda sum,
     Bēowulf Gēata,   ær hē on bed stige:

652a MS. grette: em. Grundtvig.

640 the boast of the Geat.   The gracious queen,
    her cloak gold-laden,   then sat by her lord.
        Again as before   many words were spoken,
    great noise in the hall,   the company rejoicing,
    a victorious folk,   until, before long,
645 the son of Healfdene   wished to retire,
    take his night's rest.   He knew an attack
    upon his high hall   had been planned by the monster
    ever since dawn,   when first light was seen,
    until darkening night   should cover them all
650 and dark shapes of shadow   come gliding out,
    black under clouds.   The troop all arose.
    Then the old king   addressed the young warrior,
    Hrothgar to Beowulf,   wished him good luck,
    control of the wine-hall,   and spoke these words:
655 "Never before,   since I could lift shield-arm,
    have I entrusted   the hall of the Danes
    to any other man,   except to you now.
    Now hold and guard   this royal house,
    remember fame   and show brave strength,
660 watch for your foe!   A work of such courage
    will have full reward   if you come through alive."

  X   Then Hrothgar went   with his band of men,
    the Scylding king,   out from the hall;
    the great man wanted   to find Wealhtheow,
665 his bed-companion.   The King of Glory
    had now set a hall-guard   brave against Grendel,
    so men had learned;   he did special service
    for the lord of the Danes,   kept giant-watch.
    And the Geatish man   trusted completely
670 in his proud strength   and the favor of God.
    He unlaced his chain-shirt,   iron body-warden,
    undid his helmet,   gave his gold-wrapped sword,
    finest iron,   his gear to a steward,
    bade him look well   to that equipment.
675 Then the good warrior,   Beowulf the Geat,
    made his boast known   before he lay down:

"Nō ic mē an here-wæsmun   hnāgran talige
gūþ-geweorca,   þonne Grendel hine;
forþan ic hine sweorde   swebban nelle,
680 aldre benēotan,   þēah ic eal mæge.
Nāt hē þāra gōda,   þæt hē mē ongēan slēa,
rand gehēawe,   þēah ðe hè rōf sīe
nīþ-geweorca;   ac wit on niht sculon
secge ofersittan,   gif h[ē] gesēcean dear
685 wīg ofer wǣpen,   ond siþðan wītig God
on swā hwæþere hond,   hālig Dryhten
mærðo dēme,   swā him gemet þince."
Hylde hine þā heaþo-dēor,   hlēor-bolster onfēng
eorles andwlitan,   ond hine ymb monig
690 snellīc sæ-rinc   sele-reste gebēah.
Nænig heora þōhte   þæt hē þanon scolde
eft eard-lufan   ǣfre gesēcean,
folc oþðe frēo-burh,   þǣr hē āfēded wæs;
ac hīe hæfdon gefrūnen   þæt hīe ǣr tō fela micles
695 in þǣm wīn-sele   wæl-dēað fornam,
Denigea lēode.   Ac him Dryhten forgeaf
wīg-spēda gewiofu,   Wedera lēodum,
frōfor ond ful*tum,*   *þæt hīe* fēond heora
ðurh ānes cræft   ealle ofercōmon,
700 selfes mihtum.   Sōð is gecýþed,
þæt mihtig God   manna cynnes
weold *wīde*-ferhð.   Cōm on wanre niht
scrīðan sc*eadu*-genge.   Scēotend swǣfon,
þā þæt horn-reced   healdan scoldon,
705 ealle būton ān*um.*   Þæt wæs yldum cūþ,
þæt hīe ne mōste,   þā Meto*d* nolde,
se syn-scaþa   under sceadu bregdan,
ac hē wæccende   wrāþum on andan
bād bolgen-mōd   beadwa geþinges.
710 }   Ðā cōm of mōre   under mist-hleoþum
XI } Grendel gongan,   Godes yrre bær;

684b MS. het: em. Kemble.
702a Edge of MS. entirely gone, but "ride" in Thorkelin A, who made
ninety-six errors of "r" for "w."

"No poorer I hold   my strength in a fight,
my work in battle,   than Grendel does his;
and so I will not   kill him by sword,
680   shear off his life,   though I easily might.
He does not know   the warrior's arts,
how to parry and hew,   cut down a shield,
strong though he be   in his hateful work;
so swords are laid by   if he dare seek battle,
685   tonight no weapons,   and then mighty God,
the Lord wise and holy,   will give war-glory
to whichever side   He thinks the right."
Then he lay down,   the pillow took the cheek
of the battle-brave noble,   and round him many
690   valiant sea-fighters   sank to hall-rest.
None of them thought   he would ever return
from that long hall-floor   to his native land,
the people and home-fort   where he'd been raised,
for each one knew   dark murder had taken
695   too many men   of the Danes already,
killed in the wine-hall.   But the Lord had granted
the men of the Weders   comfort and help,
a weaving of war-luck,   that they overcame
their enemy entirely,   by one man's strength,
700   by his own powers.   It is a known truth
that mighty God   has ruled mankind
throughout far time.   Now in the night
the dark walker came   gliding in shadow;
the bowmen slept   who were to hold
705   the gabled hall   —all but one.
It was known to men   that the demon could not
drag them into shadows   when God did not wish it.
And Beowulf, wakeful,   on watch for the foe,
angrily awaited   the outcome of battle.
710 } Then up from the marsh,   under misty cliffs,
XI } Grendel came walking;   he bore God's wrath.

mynte se mān-scaða   manna cynnes
sumne besyrwan   in sele þām hēan.
Wōd under *wolc*num   tō þæs þe hē wīn-reced,
715 gold-sele gum*e*na,   gearwost wisse,
fǣttum fāhne.   Ne wæs þæt forma sīð
þæt hē Hrōðgāres   hām gesōhte;
nǣfre hē on aldor-dagum   ǣr *ne* siþðan
heardran hǣle,   heal-ðegnas fand.
720 Cōm þā tō recede   rinc sīðian
drēamum bedǣled.   Duru sōna onarn
fȳr-*ben*dum fæst   syþðan hē hire folmum [*ge*]hrān;
onbrǣd þā bealo-hȳdig,   ðā *hē* [*ge*]bolgen wæs,
recedes mūþan.   Raþe æfter þon
725 on fāgne flōr   fēond treddode,
ēode yrre-mōd;   him of ēagum stōd
ligge gelīcost   lēoht unfǣger.
Geseah hē in recede   rinca manige,
swefan sibbe-gedriht   samod ætgædere,
730 mago-rinca hēap.   Þā his mōd āhlōg;
mynte þæt hē gedǣlde,   ǣr þon dæg cwōme,
atol āglǣca,   ānra gehwylces
līf wið līce,   þā him ālumpen wæs
wist-fylle wēn.   Ne wæs *þæt w*yrd þā gēn,
735 þæt hē mā mōste   manna cynnes
ðicgean ofer þā niht.   Þrȳð-swȳð behēold,
mǣg Higelāces,   hū se mān-scaða
under fǣr-gripum   gefaran wolde.
Nē þæt se āglǣca   yldan þōhte,
740 ac hē ge*f*ēng hraðe   forman sīðe
slǣpendn*e* rinc,   slāt unwearnum,
bāt bān-locan,   bl*ō*d ēdrum dranc,
syn-snǣdum swealh;   sōna hæfde
unlyfigendes   eal gefeormod,
745 fē*t* ond folma.   Forð nēar ætstōp,

722b MS. ..hran from Malone, *NC*, p. 59: restored by Zupitza.
723b "he" from Conybeare (1826). MS. ...bolgen, much faded, restored
tentatively by Zupitza and Malone. Norman Davis would restore the whole
passage as "[*þǣr a*]bolgen."

The evil thief planned   to trap some human,
one of man's kind,   in the towering hall.
Under dark skies   he came till he saw

715 the shining wine-hall,   house of gold-giving,
a joy to men,   plated high with gold.
It was not the first time   he had visited Hrothgar;
never in his life,   before or after,
did he find harder luck   or retainers in hall.

720 The evil warrior,   deprived of joys,
came up to the building;   the door burst open,
though bound with iron,   as soon as he touched it,
huge in his blood-lust;   enraged, he ripped open
the mouth of the hall;   quickly rushed in—

725 the monster stepped   on the bright-paved floor,
crazed with evil anger;   from his strange eyes
an ugly light   shone out like fire.
There in the hall   he saw many men—
the band of kinsmen   all sleeping together,

730 a troop of young warriors.   Then his heart laughed;
evil monster,   he thought he would take
the life from each body,   eat them all
before day came;   the gluttonous thought
of a full-bellied feast   was hot upon him.

735 No longer his fate   to feed on mankind,
after that night.   The mighty man,
kinsman of Hygelac,   watched how the killer
would want to move   in sudden attack.
Nor did the monster   think long to delay:

740 he lunged the next moment,   seized a warrior,
gutted him sleeping   —ripped him apart—
bit into muscles,   swilled blood from veins,
tore off gobbets,   in hardly a moment
had eaten him up,   all of the dead man,

745 even hands and feet.   He stepped further in,

nam þā mid handa   hige-þīhtigne
rinc on ræste,   ræhte ongēan
fēond mid folme;   hē onfēng hraþe
inwit-þancum   ond wið earm gesæt.
750 Sōna þæt onfunde   fyrena hyrde,
þæt hē ne mētte   middan-geardes,
eorþan scēatta,   on elran men
mund-gripe māran;   hē on mōde wearð
forht on ferhðe;   nō þȳ ǣr fram meahte.
755 Hyge wæs him hin-fūs,   wolde on heolster flēon,
sēcan dēofla gedræg;   ne wæs his drohtoð þǣr
swylce hē on ealder-dagum   ǣr gemētte.
Gemunde þā se gōda,   mǣg Higelāces,
æfen-sprǣce,   uplang āstōd
760 ond him fæste wiðfēng;   fingras burston;
eoten wæs ūtweard,   eorl furþur stōp.
Mynte se mǣra,   [þ]ǣr hē meahte swā,
wīdre gewindan   ond *on* weg þanon
flēon on fen-hopu;   wiste *h*is fingra geweald
765 on grames grāpum;   *þæt* wæs gēocor sīð
þæt sē hearm-sca*þa*   to Heorute ātēah.
Dryht-sele *d*ynede;   Denum eallum wearð,
ceaster-bū*e*ndum,   cēnra gehwylcum,
eorlum ealu-scerwen.   Yrre wǣron bēgen,
770 rēþe ren-weardas.   Reced hlynsode;
þā wæs wundor micel   þæt se wīn-sele
wiðhæfde heaþo-dēorum,   þæt hē on hrūsan ne fēol,
fǣger fold-bold;   ac hē þæs fæste wæs
innan ond ūtan   īren-bendum
775 searo-þoncum besmiþod.   Þǣr fram sylle ābēag
medu-benc monig,   mīne gefrǣge,
golde geregnad,   þǣr þā graman wunnon.
Þæs ne wēndon ǣr   witan Scyldinga
þæt hit ā mid gemete   manna ænig,
780 [*b*]etlīc ond bān-fāg   tōbrecan meahte,

762b MS. ..*ær* from Thorkelin A: em. Ettmüller.
765b MS. þæt he wæs: em. Grundtvig.
780a MS. het lic: em. Grundtvig.

and caught in his claws   the strong-minded man
where he lay on his bed—   the evil assailant
snatched at him, clutching;   hand met claw,
he sat straight at once,   thrust the arm back.
750 The shepherd of sins   then instantly knew
he had never encountered,   in any region
of this middle-earth,   in any other man,
a stronger hand-grip;   at heart he feared
for his wretched life,   but he could not move.
755 He wanted escape,   to flee to the fen,
join the devils' rout.   Such greeting in hall
he had never met   before in his life.
Then the brave man remembered,   kinsman of Hyge-
                 lac,
his speeches that evening,   rose to his feet
760 and held him close;   fingers snapped;
the giant pulled away,   the noble moved with him.
The ill-famed creature   thought to go elsewhere,
anywhere possible,   away from the hall,
into deep marshes,   felt his fingers
765 in a terrible grip.   An unhappy journey
the evil harmer   had made to Heorot.
The king's hall thundered: to all the Danes,
the city's inhabitants,   to every brave listener
it was a wild mead-sharing.   The grapplers were
                 furious—
770 angry hall-guards.   The building clattered;
it was a great wonder   the mead-hall withstood
those two battle-ragers,   did not crash to earth,
tall-standing house.   But inside and out
good smiths had turned   strong iron bands,
775 made the walls fast.   Many mead-benches
inlaid with gold,   came up from the floor,
so I have heard,   where the fighters crashed.
Before this the wise men,   Scylding counselors,
had not expected   that any warrior
780 could ever destroy it,   splendid, horn-bright,

  listum tōlūcan, nymþe līges fæþm
  swulge on swaþule. Swēg up āstāg
  nīwe geneahhe; Norð-Denum stō*d*
  atelīc egesa, ānra gehwylcum
785 þāra *þe* of wealle wōp gehȳrdon,
  gryre-lēoð *ga*lan Godes andsacan
  sige-lēasne sang, *sār* wānigean
  helle hæfton. Hēold hine fæste,
  sē þe manna wæs mægene str*e*ngest
790 on þǣm dæge þysses līfes.
XII Nolde eorla hlēo ænige þinga
  þo*ne* cwealm-cuman cwicne forlǣtan,
  nē his līf-dagas lēoda ænigum
  nytte tealde. Þǣr genehost brægd
795 eorl Bēowulfes ealde lāfe,
  wolde frēa-drihtnes feorh ealgian,
  mǣres þēodnes, ðǣr hīe meahton swā.
  Hīe þæt ne wiston, þā hīe gewin drugon,
  heard-hicgende hilde-mecgas
800 ond on healfa gehwone hēawan þōhton,
  sāwle sēcan: þone syn-scaðan
  ænig ofer eorþan īrenna cyst,
  gūð-billa nān grētan nolde,
  ac hē sige-wǣpnum *for*sworen hæfde,
805 ecga gehwylcre. Scolde *h*is aldor-gedāl
  on ðǣm dæge þysses *lī*fes
  earmlīc wurðan ond se ellor-gāst
  on fēonda geweald feor sīðian.
  Ðā þæt *o*nfunde sē þe fela ǣror
810 mōdes myrðe *m*anna cynne,
  fyrene gefremede —he *f*āg wið God—
  þæt him se līc-homa lǣstan nolde
  ac hine se mōdega mǣg Hygelāces
  hæfde be honda; wæs gehwæþer ōðrum
815 lifigende lāð. Līc-sār gebād
  atol ǣglǣca; him on eaxle wearð
  syn-dolh sweotol; seonowe onsprungon,
  burston bān-locan. Bēowulfe wearð
  gūð-hrēð gyfeþe; scolde Grendel þonan

       by ordinary means,   pull it down by craft,
       unless licking fire   should swallow it in flames.
       A sound went out,   loud and high,
       raised horrible fear   in Danish hearts,
785 in each of the men   on the palisade wall
       who heard the cry—   God's enemy
       screaming his hate-song,   a victory-less tune,
       the hellish captive   moaning his pain.
       He held him tight,   the strongest man
790 who ever lived   in the days of this life.
XII   The protector of nobles   had no desire
       to let the killer-guest   walk away free,
       nor thought his life   could do the least service
       to any nation.   Beowulf's warriors
795 all drew their swords,   time-tested heirlooms,
       wanted to defend   the life of their comrade,
       their famous chief,   however they could.
       But they did not know,   as they entered the fight,
       hard-minded men,   battle-warriors,
800 meaning to swing   from every side,
       to cut out his soul,   that keen battle-edges,
       best iron in the world,   sharpest blade,
       could not harm him,   the evil demon,
       not touch him at all—   he had bespelled
805 all weapons of battle.   His leave-taking,
       his life's parting   from the days of this world
       was to be painful;   the alien spirit
       was to journey far   in the power of fiends.
       Then he discovered,   who earlier brought
810 trouble of heart   to the race of men
       by his many crimes   —at feud with God—
       that his body-casing   would not keep life:
       that Hygelac's kinsman,   the bold-hearted man,
       had him in hand.   It was hateful to each
815 that the other lived.   The terrible creature
       took a body wound there;   a gaping tear
       opened in his shoulder;   tendons popped,
       muscle slipped the bone.   Glory in battle
       was given to Beowulf;   Grendel fled,

820   feorh-sēoc flēon   under fen-hleoðu,
      sēcean wyn-lēas wīc;   wiste þē geornor,
      þæt his aldres wæs   ende gegongen,
      dōgera dæg-rīm.   Denum eallum wearð
      æfter þām wæl-ræse   willa gelumpen.

825   Hæfde þā gefælsod,   sē þe ær feorran cōm,
      snotor ond swȳð-ferhð,   sele Hrōðgāres,
      genered wið nīðe;   niht-weorce gefeh,
      ellen-mærþum.   Hæfde Ēast-Denum
      Gēat-mecga lēod   gilp gelæsted,

830   swylce oncȳþðe   ealle ge*bētte*,
      inwid-sorge,   þē hīe ær drugon
      ond for *þrēa*-nȳdum   þolian scoldon,
      torn unlȳt*el*.   Þæt wæs tācen sweotol,
      syþðan hilde-dēor   hond ālegde,

835   earm ond eaxle   —þær wæs eal geador
      Grendles grāpe—   under gēapne *hr[ōf]*.

XIII   Ðā wæs on morgen,   mīne gefræge,
      ymb þā gif-healle   gūð-rinc monig;
      fērdon folc-togan   feorran ond nēan

840   geond wīd-wegas   wundor scēawian,
      lāþes lāstas.   Nō his līf-gedāl
      sārlīc þūhte   secga ænegum
      þāra þe tīr-lēases   trode scēawode,
      hū hē wērig-mōd   on weg þanon,

845   nīða ofercumen,   on nicera mere,
      fæge ond geflȳmed   feorh-lāstas bær.
      Ðær wæs on blōde   brim weallende,
      atol ȳða geswing   eal gemenged
      hāton heolfre,   *heo*ro-drēore wēol;

850   dēað-fæge dēog,   siððan *d*rēama lēas
      in fen-freoðo   feorh ālegde,
      *hæþ*ene sāwle;   þær him hel onfēng.
         Þanon *eft* gewiton   eald-gesīðas,
      swylce geong *m*anig   of gomen-wāþe,

855   fram mere mōdge   *m*ēarum rīdan,
      beornas on blancum.   Ðær wæs Bēowulfes

836b   MS. *hr..* from Thorkelin B: em. Grundtvig.

820 wounded, death-sick,   under marshy hills
to his joyless den;   with that huge wound
he knew for certain   his life had ended,
the sum of his days.   The desire of all Danes
had come to pass   in that deadly fight.

825   Thus he had cleansed,   who came from afar,
wise, great-hearted,   Hrothgar's hall,
defended it well.   He rejoiced in his courage,
in his great night-work.   The Geatish man
had kept his boast   to the men of the East-Danes,

830 also had bettered   every distress,
the evil sorrow   they long had suffered
in hardest need   —had had to endure
no small grief.   It was a clear sign
once the brave man   fastened the arm,

835 from hand to shoulder   —there all together
was Grendel's claw—   under the high roof.

XIII   Then, so I've heard,   there were many warriors
round the gift-hall   that fine morning;
chieftains came   from near and far,

840 long distances,   to look at the marvel,
the monster's tracks.   His parting from life
was no cause for grief   to any of the men
who examined the trail   of the conquered one,
saw how, despairing,   he had rushed away,

845 ruined in the fight,   to the lake of monsters,
fleeing, doomed,   in bloody footprints.
There the lake water   boiled with blood,
terrible surgings,   a murky swirl
of hot dark ooze,   deep sword-blood;

850 death-fated, he hid   joyless in the fen,
his dark stronghold,   till he gave up life,
his heathen soul;   there Hell received him.
  Then home again   the tried retainers,
the young men too,   gay as a hunt,

855 came from the mere,   joyful on horseback,
well-mounted warriors.   Beowulf's deed

mærðo mæned;   monig oft gecwæð
þætte sūð nē norð   be sǣm twēonum
ofer eormen-grund   ōþer nǣnig

860   under swegles begong   sēlra nǣre
rond-hæbbendra,   rīces wyrðra.
Nē hīe hūru wine-drihten   wiht ne lōgon,
glædne Hrōðgār,   ac þæt wæs gōd cyning.
   Hwīlum heaþo-rōfe   hlēapan lēton,

865   on geflit faran   fealwe mēaras,
ðǣr him fold-wegas   fǣgere þūhton,
cystum cūðe.   Hwīlum cyninges þegn,
guma gilp-hlæden,   gidda gemyndig,
sē ðe eal-fela   eald-gesegena

870   worn gemunde,   word ōþer fand
sōðe gebunden;   secg eft ongan
sīð Bēowulfes   snyttrum styrian
ond on spēd wrecan   spel gerāde,
wordum wrixlan.   Wēl-hwylc gecwæð

875   þæt hē fram Sigemunde   secgan hȳrde
ellen-*dǣ*dum,   uncūþes fela,
Wælsinges gewin,   *wīde* sīðas,
þāra þe gumena bearn   gearwe ne wiston,
fǣhðe ond fyrena,   būton Fitela *mid* hine,

880   þonne hē swulces hwæt   secgan wol*de*,
ēam his nefan,   swā hīe ā wǣron
æt nīða gehwām   nȳd-gesteallan;
hæfdon eal-fela   eotena cynnes
sweordum gesǣged.   Sigemunde gesprong

885   æfter dēað-dæge   dōm unlȳtel,
syþðan wīges heard   wyrm ācwealde,
hordes hyrde.   Hē under hārne stān,
æþelinges bearn,   āna genēðde
frēcne dǣde,   ne wæs him Fitela mid;

890   hwæþre him gesǣlde,   ðæt þæt swurd þurhwōd
wrǣtlīcne wyrm,   þæt hit on wealle ætstōd,
dryhtlīc īren;   draca morðre swealt.
Hæfde āglǣca   elne gegongen,
þæt hē bēah-hordes   brūcan mōste

895   selfes dōme;   sǣ-bāt gehlēod,

was praised aloud;   many kept saying
that north or south,   between the two seas,
across the whole earth,   no other man
860 under heaven's vault,   of all shield-holders,
could ever be better,   more worthy of kingdoms.
Nor did they find fault   with their lord and friend,
gracious Hrothgar,   that excellent king.
    At times the warriors   made their horses rear,
865 let fine dark steeds   go racing in contest
wherever the footing   was straight and firm,
the paths well known.   At times the scop,
a thane of the king,   glorying in words,
the great old stories,   who remembered them all,
870 one after another,   song upon song,
found new words,   bound them up truly,
began to recite   Beowulf's praise,
a well-made lay   of his glorious deed,
skillfully varied   his matter and style.
875 He sang all he knew   of famous Sigemund,
his feats of courage,   many strange things,
the Wælsing's strife,   far-off journeys,
feuds and crimes   unknown to men,
except to Fitela,   always beside him
880 when he wished to talk,   to speak of such things,
uncle to nephew;   they had always been
battle-companions   in all their hardships;
together they killed   a whole tribe of giants
with their two swords.   No small glory
885 shone for Sigemund   after his death-day:
hardened by wars,   he killed a dragon,
treasure's keeper.   Beneath gray stones
that prince's son   dared go alone,
reckless in courage,   nor was Fitela there;
890 still it was granted   that the sword drove through
the slithering beast   shining in scales,
stood fixed in the wall;   the dragon died
in that terrible thrust.   The fearsome warrior
had bravely gone in   to gain the ring-hoard,
895 take gold at will.   The son of Wæls

bær on bearm scipes   beorhte frætwa,
Wælses eafera;   wyrm hāt gemealt.
   Sē wæs wreccena   wīde mǣrost
ofer wer-þēode,   wīgendra hlēo,
900 ellen-dǣdum   —hē þæs ǣr onðāh—
siððan Heremōdes   hild sweðrode,
eafoð ond ellen;   he mid eotenum wearð
on fēonda geweald   forð forlācen
snūde forsended.   Hine sorh-wylmas
905 lemede tō lange;   hē his lēodum wearð,
eallum æþellingum   tō aldor-ceare.
Swylce oft bemearn   ǣrran mǣlum
swīð-ferhþes sīð   snotor ceorl monig,
sē þe him bealwa tō   bōte gelȳfde,
910 þæt þæt ðēodnes bearn   geþēon scolde,
fæder-æþelum onfōn,   folc gehealdan,
hord ond hlēo-burh,   hæleþa rīce,
ēþel Scyldinga.   Hē þǣr eallum wearð,
mǣg Higelāces,   manna cynne,
915 frēondum gefægra;   hine fyren onwōd.
   Hwīlum flītende   fealwe strǣte
mēarum mǣton.   Ðā wæs morgen-lēoht
scofen ond scynded.   Ēode scealc monig
swīð-hicgende   tō sele þām hēan,
920 searo-wundor sēon;   swylce self cyning
of brȳd-būre,   bēah-horda weard,
tryddode tīr-fæst   getrume micle,
cystum gecȳþed,   ond his cwēn mid him
medo-stigge mæt   mægþa hōse.
XIIII
925   Hrōðgār maþelode—   hē tō healle gēong
stōd on stapole,   geseah stēapne hrōf
golde fāhne   ond Grendles hond:
"Ðisse ansȳne   Alwealdan þanc
lungre gelimpe!   Fela ic lāþes gebād,
930 grynna æt Grendle;   ā mæg God wyrcan

902a MS. earfoð: em. Jacob Grimm, *Andreas und Elene* (Cassel: Wigand
1840), p. 101.

      loaded his boat,   carried bright treasures,
      piled them amidships.   The dragon melted in its heat.
        He was the most famous   hero-adventurer,
      a battle-leader   known to all nations
900 for deeds of bravery   —gained much by courage—
      after the warfare   of Heremod had ended,
      his strength and valor;   among the giants
      he was well betrayed   into enemy hands,
      met a quick end.   His black moods
905 had lasted too long;   he brought to his people
      a lifetime's sorrow,   and death to his nobles.
      In earlier times   many wise men
      had often mourned   over the fortunes
      of that strong-willed man;   had counted on him
910 for relief from afflictions,   trusting the son
      of the king would prosper,   take his father's title,
      protect the nation,   treasure and stronghold,
      kingdom of heroes,   the homeland of Scyldings.
      The dearer by far   was Beowulf now,
915 a friend to all.   Heremod sank in sin.
        Now and then racing,   they paced their horses
      on the sandy road.   By then it was morning,
      long after daybreak.   Many retainers,
      stout-hearted, walked   to the lord's high hall
920 to see the strange marvel.   The king himself
      came stately and gracious   from the queen's chambers,
      guard of the ring-treasure   famed in nobility,
      with his troop of earls,   his queen beside him
      in company of women,   the mead-path procession.
XIIII   Hrothgar spoke,   went up to the hall
925 to stand on the porch,   gazed at the roof,
      steep plated gold,   and Grendel's hand:
      "For this fine sight,   swift thanks to God!
      Many rough visits,   terrible attacks,
930 I suffered from Grendel,   but God can always

wunder æfter wundre,   wuldres Hyrde.
Ðæt wæs ungeāra,   þæt ic ænigra mē
wēana ne wēnde   tō wīdan feore
bōte gebīdan,   þonne blōde fāh
935 hūsa sēlest   heoro-drēorig stōd,
wēa wīd-scofen   witena gehwylc[*um*]
ðāra þe ne wēndon,   þæt hīe wīde-ferhð
lēoda land-geweorc   lāþum beweredon
scuccum ond scinnum.   Nū scealc hafað
940 þurh Drihtnes miht   dæd gefremede,
ðe wē ealle   ǣr ne meahton
snyttrum besyrwan.   Hwæt, *þæt* secgan mæg
efne swā hwylc mægþa,   swā ðone magan cende
æfter gum-cynnum,   gyf hēo gȳt lyfað,
945 þæt hyre Eald-metod   ēste wǣre
bearn-gebyrdo.   Nū ic, Bēowulf, þec,
secg betsta,   *mē* for sunu wylle
frēogan on ferhþe;   heald forð tela
nīwe sibbe.   Ne bið þē [*n*]ænigre gād
950 worolde wilna,   þe ic geweald hæbbe.
Ful oft ic for lǣssan   lēan teohhode,
hord-weorþunge   hnāhran rince,
sǣmran æt sæcce.   Þū þē self hafast
dǣdum gefremed,   þæt þīn [*dōm*] lyfað
955 āwa tō aldre.   Alwalda þec
gōde forgylde,   swā hē nū gȳt dyde!"
   Bēowulf maþelode,   bearn Ecþēowes:
"Wē þæt ellen-weorc   ēstum miclum,
feohtan fremedon,   frēcne genēðdon
960 eafoð uncūþes.   Ūþe ic swīþor,
þæt ðū hine selfne   gesēon mōste
fēond on frætewum   fyl-wērigne!
Ic hi[*ne*] hrædlīce   heardan clammum
on wæl-bedde   wrīþan þōhte,

936b MS. gehwylcne: em. Kemble.
949b MS. ænigre: em. Grein.
954b No gap in MS.; "dōm" supplied by Kemble.
963a MS. him: em. Thorpe.

      do wonder on wonder,   eternal in power.
      It was not long ago   that I did not hope
      to see any change   in all my afflictions
      for the rest of my life,   when shiny with blood
935 this best of houses   stood deep in gore,
      a grief reaching far   into all our hearts,
      for none of my men   saw how to keep
      this work of nations   from monstrous terrors,
      phantom devils.   But now a retainer
940 has brought about   through the might of the Lord
      what we never could,   for all our plans.
      Who bore such a son   into man's world,
      that woman can say,   if living still,
945 that Eternal God   was gracious to her
      at her birth-giving.   Now, my Beowulf,
      best of men,   I will love you like a son,
      cherish you for life.   Keep this new kinship
      deep in your heart.   Nothing I own,
950 of my worldly goods,   would I keep from you.
      Often for less   I have given treasures,
      honorable gifts   to lesser warriors,
      poorer at battle.   But now, by yourself,
      you have done such a deed   that your [fame] is
                                assured,
955 will live forever.   May Almighty God
      reward you with good,   as he has today!"
        Then Beowulf spoke,   the son of Ecgtheow:
      "With willing hearts   we have achieved
      this work of courage,   risked all against
960 that unknown strength.   Yet I wished the more
      that you might have seen   the enemy himself,
      in his scaly harness,   dead in the feast-hall.
      I planned to bind him   in hard clinches,
      tie him on his death-bed   as soon as we met,

965 þæt hē for [*mu*]nd-gripe   mīnum scolde
    licgean līf-bysig,   būtan his līc swice.
    Ic hine ne mihte,   þā Metod nolde,
    gang*es* getwǣman,   nō ic him þæs georne ætfealh,
    feorh-genīðlan;   wæs tō fore-mi*htig*
970 fēond on fēþe.   Hwæþere hē his folme for*lēt*
    tō līf-wraþe   lāst weardian,
    earm ond *ea*xle;   nō þǣr ænige swā þēah
    fēasceaft *gu*ma   frōfre gebohte;
    nō þȳ leng leofa*ð*   lāð-getēona
975 synnum geswenced,   ac hyne sār hafað
    in [*n*]īd-gripe   nearwe befongen,
    balwon bendum;   ðǣr ābīdan sceal
    maga māne fāh   miclan dōmes,
    hū him scīr Metod   scrīfan wille."
980   Ðā wæs swīgra secg,   sunu Eclāfes
    on gylp-sprǣce   gūð-geweorca,
    siþðan æþelingas   eorles cræfte
    ofer hēanne hrōf   hand scēawedon,
    feondes fingras;   foran æghwylc wæs
985 steda nægla gehwylc   stȳle gelīcost,
    hæþenes hand-sporu   hilde-rinces
    egl unhēoru.   Ǣghwylc gecwæð
    þæt him heardra nān   hrīnan wolde
    īren ǣr-gōd,   þæt ðæs āhlæcan
990 blōdge beadu-folme   *on*beran wolde.
XV   Ðā wæs hāten hreþe   Heort innanweard
    folmum gefrætwod;   fela þǣra wæs,
    wera ond wīfa,   þe þæt wīn-reced
    gest-sele gyredon.   Gold-fāg scinon
995 web æfter wāgum,   wundor-sīona fela
    secga gehwylcum   þāra þe on swylc starað.
    Wæs þæt beorhte bold   tōbrocen swīðe,
    eal inneweard   īren-bendum fæst,

965a MS. hand gripe: em. Kemble.
976a MS. mid gripe: em. Klaeber.
986b MS. hilde ends folio 154ʳ and folio 154ᵛ starts with repeated *hi*lde, here deleted.

965   that life might be difficult   once he lay
      fast in my hand-grip,   unless he could vanish.
      I could not keep him   —God did not will it—
      from an early departure;   not firmly enough
      did I welcome my enemy.   Too overpowering
970   was his rude going.   However, he left us
      a visitor's token,   a hand, life-protector,
      the whole arm and shoulder.   The miserable creature
      got little comfort   from that dear gift,
      will live no longer,   ferocious spoiler,
975   loathsome in crimes;   but gaping pain,
      a torturing wound-grip,   has strapped him tight,
      death's open harness,   and dead, he must wait,
      dripping with guilt,   the last great days,
      however bright God   will choose to judge him."
980   Unferth, Ecglaf's son,   was then more silent,
      had no more taunts   about valor in combat
      once all the nobles   had looked at that hand,
      the gigantic fingers,   high on the roof
      through the young earl's strength.   Each socketed nail
985   stood out from the front,   glistened like steel,
      a terrible hand-spike,   heathen's armament,
      a giant war-claw.   All men agreed
      that no hard iron,   though forged as of old,
      could have cut into,   weakened the monster's
990   great battle-talon,   now bloodily severed.
XV   Then the order was given   to furnish again
      the inside of Heorot;   each hand was willing,
      men and women   adorning the guest-house,
      that great wine-hall.   Tapestries gleamed,
995   gold weavings on walls,   marvelous pictures
      shifting in lights   to each who looked at them.
      That shining building   had been badly damaged
      despite iron strapping   inside and out,

heorras tōhlidene;   hrōf āna genæs
1000 ealles ansund,   þē se āglǣca
fyren-dǣdum fāg   on flēam gewand,
aldres orwēna.   Nō þæt ȳðe byð
tō beflēonne,   fremme sē þe wille,
ac ges[ē]can sceal   sāwl-berendra
1005 nȳde genȳdde,   niþða bearna,
grund-būendra   gearwe stōwe,
þǣr his līc-homa   leger-bedde fæst
swefeþ æfter symle.   Þā wæs sǣl ond mǣl
þæt tō healle gang   Healfdenes sunu;
1010 wolde self cyning   symbel þicgan.
Ne gefrǣgen ic þā mǣgþe   māran weorode
ymb hyra sinc-gyfan   sēl gebǣran.
Bugon þā to bence   blǣd-āgande,
fylle gefǣgon;   fægere geþǣgon
1015 medo-ful manig   māgas þāra
swīð-hicgende,   on sele þām hēan,
Hrōðgār ond Hrōþulf.   Heorot innan wæs
frēondum āfylled;   nalles fācen-stafas
Þēod-Scyldingas   þenden fremedon.
1020   Forgeaf þā Bēowulfe .   brand Healfdenes
segen gyldenne   sigores tō lēane,
hroden hil[d]e-cumbor,   helm ond byrnan,
mǣre māðþum-sweord   manige gesāwon
beforan beorn beran.   Bēowulf geþah
1025 ful on flette;   nō hē þǣre feoh-gyfte
for scōtenum   scamigan ðorfte.
Ne gefrǣgn ic frēondlīcor   fēower mādmas
golde gegyrede   gum-manna fela
in ealo-bence   ōðrum gesellan.
1030 Ymb þæs helmes hrōf   hēafod-beorge

1004a MS. ge sacan: em. Kemble.
1022a MS. hilte cumbor: em. Ettmüller.
1026a MS. scotenum: von Schaubert reads as dat. pl. of "scēotend" (warrior). Usually em. sc[ē]oten[d]um.

its hinges sprung open;   the bright roof alone
1000   came through unharmed   when the fiendish outlaw,
red-stained in crimes,   turned back in flight,
despairing of life.   No man escapes
easily from death   —let him try who will—
but all soul-bearers   walking the earth,
1005   each son of man,   driven by need,
must enter his place   made ready from birth,
where the body-covering   deep in its earth-bed
sleeps after feast.   Then came the feast-time
when the son of Healfdene   went to his hall;
1010   the king himself   would share the great meal.
I never have heard   of a greater gathering
who bore themselves better,   grouped round their
                             gold-lord.
Men known for courage   sat down in hall,
rejoiced in the feast-meal;   their famous kinsmen
1015   in courtesy shared   many flagons of mead
under that roof,   the mighty-minded ones,
Hrothgar and Hrothulf.   The inside of Heorot
was filled with good friends;   at that time none
of the princely Scyldings   betrayed each other.
1020   Then Healfdene's sword-son   gave to Beowulf
a golden war-standard,   ensign of victory
with plated ornament,   helmet and mail-shirt,
a jewel-crusted long-sword,   and many saw these
laid before the man.   Beowulf drank
1025   the mead of that hall;   there was no shame
in those sumptuous gifts   before the assembly.
I have not heard   of many great men
who gave to another,   in more open friendship
upon the mead-bench,   four such treasures,
1030   each worked with gold.   The helmet's comb

wīrum bewunden   wala ūtan hēold
þæt him fēla *lāf*   frēcne ne meahton
scūr-heard sceþðan,   þonne scyld-freca
ongēan gramum   gangan *s*colde.

1035 Heht ðā eorla hlēo   eah*ta* mēaras
fǣted-hlēore   on flet tēon
in *u*nder eoderas;   þāra ānum stōd
sadol searwum fāh,   since gewurþad;
þæt wæs hilde-setl   hēah-cyninges,

1040 ðonne sweorda gelāc   sunu Healfdenes
efnan wolde;   nǣfre on ōre læg
wīd-cūþes wīg,   ðonne walu fēollon.
Ond ðā Bēowulfe   bēga gehwæþres
eodor Ingwina   onweald getēah,

1045 wicga on*d* wǣpna;   hēt hine wēl brūcan.
Swā manlīce   mǣre þēoden,
hord-weard hæleþa   heaþo-rǣsas geald
mēarum ond mādmum,   swā hȳ nǣfre man lyhð,
sē þe se*c*gan wile   sōð æfter rihte.

XVI
1050
    Ðā gȳt æghwylcum   eorla drihten
þāra þe mid Bēowulfe   brim-lāde tēah,
on þære medu-bence   māþðum gesealde,
yrfe-lāfe,   ond þone ænne heht
golde forgy*l*dan,   þone ðe Grendel ær

1055 māne ācwealde,   swā hē hyra mā wolde,
nefne him wīti*g* God   wyrd forstōde
ond ðæs mannes mōd.   *Me*tod eallum wēold
gumena cynnes,   swā h*ē* nū gīt dēð.
Forþan bið andgit   æghwǣr sēlest,

1060 ferhðes fore-þanc.   Fela sceal gebīdan
lēofes ond lāþes,   sē þe longe hēr
on ðyssum win-dagum   worolde brūceð.
    Þær wæs sang ond swēg   samod ætgædere
fore Healfdenes   hilde-wīsan,

1065 gomen-wudu grēted   gid oft wrecen,
ðonne heal-gamen   Hrōþgāres scop

1031b MS. walan: em. Ettmüller.
1051b MS. brim leade: em. Kemble.

was an iron tube,   wound with silver wires,
that kept firm head-guard,   so that file-sharp swords,
battle-hardened,   might not harm him
when carrying shield   against the foe.
1035 The protector of warriors   then bade his men
lead in eight horses   with gold-plated trappings
to the floor of the hall;   the first had a saddle
cunningly wrought,   studded with gems.
It had been Hrothgar's,   the king's war-seat,
1040 when Healfdene's son   joined in the sword-play;
valiant at the front,   his warfare was never
less than famous   when the dead were falling.
Entirely to Beowulf   the lord of the Ingwines
gave the ownership   of horses and weapons,
1045 bade use them well.   Manfully, generously,
that famous king,   hoard-guard of heroes,
repaid the battle-rush   with those fine gifts,
such horse and treasure   that no man will fault them
who has the least care   to tell the truth.
XVI }
1050 }   Then, still more,   to those on the mead-bench
who made the sea-journey,   Beowulf's followers,
the lord of warriors   gave each a treasure,
true old heirlooms,   and ordered that gold
be paid for the man   that Grendel killed
1055 before in his sin   —he would have killed more
had not wise God   and Beowulf's courage
changed that fate.   The Lord then ruled
all the race of men,   as He still does now.
Therefore understanding   is always best,
1060 the spirit's forethought.   Much love, much hate,
must he endure   who thinks to live long
here in this world,   in our days of strife.
    There was tumult and song,   melodious noise,
in front of Healfdene's   battle-commander;
1065 the harp was plucked,   good verses chanted
when Hrothgar's scop   in his place on the mead-bench

æfter medo-bence   mænan scolde
[*be*] Finnes eaferum,   ðā hīe se fær begeat:
hæleð Healf-Dena,   Hnæf Scyldinga,
1070 in Frēs-wæle   feallan scolde.
Nē hūru Hildeburh   herian þorfte
Eotena trēowe;   unsynnum wearð
beloren lēofum   æt þām [*l*]i[*n*]d-plegan
bearnum ond brōðrum;   hīe on gebyrd hruron
1075 gāre *w*unde;   þæt wæs geōmuru ides!
Nalles hōlinga   *H*ōces dohtor
metodsceaft bemearn,   *syþ*ðan morgen cōm,
ðā hēo under swegle   gesēon meahte
morþor-bealo māga,   þær hē[*o*] ær mæste hēold
1080 worolde wynne.   Wīg ealle fornam
Finnes þegnas,   nemne fēaum ānum,
þæt hē ne mehte   on þæm meðel-stede
wīg Hengeste   wiht gefeohtan
nē þā wēa-lāfe   wīge forþringan
1085 þēodnes ðegne;   ac hig him geþingo budon
þæt hīe him ōðer flet   eal gerȳmdon,
healle ond hēah-setl,   þæt hīe healfre geweald
wið Eotena bearn   āgan mōston,
ond æt feoh-gyftum   Folcwaldan sunu
1090 dōgra gehwylce   Dene weorþode,
Hengestes hēap   hringum wenede
efne swā swīðe,   sinc-gestrēonum
fǣttan goldes,   swā hē Frēsena cyn
on bēor-sele   byldan wolde.

1068a No gap in MS.: addition by Thorpe. Thus the "fær" (sudden attack) is the triumphant second battle in which the Danes slaughter Finn and his men (1146 ff.). An alternative is to leave the text unemended, with a colon after 1067, and trans. thus: "Along with Finn's sons, when the attack came on them, the hero of the Half-Danes, Hnæf of the Scyldings, had to fall." This way "the attack" is the first battle at night, described in the *Finnsburh Fragment*. See Commentary, p. 323.

1072a The OE. word "Eoten" (giant) is a by-name for the Frisians or more generally for enemies, like "Wederas" (Weathers) for the seafaring Geats or "Scyldingas" (descendants of Scyld) for the Danes.

1073b MS. hild plegan: em. Kemble.

1079b MS. he: em. Thorpe.

came to tell over   the famous hall-sport
[about] Finn's sons   when the attack came on them:
Hnæf of the Scyldings,   hero of the Half-Danes,
1070 had had to fall   in Frisian slaughter.
No need at all   that Hildeburh praise
the faith of the "giants";   guiltless herself,
she lost her loved ones   in that clash of shields,
her son and brother   —they were born to fall,
1075 slain by spear-thrusts.   She knew deep grief.
Not without cause   did Hoc's daughter mourn
the web's short measure   that fated morning
when she saw their bodies,   her murdered kinsmen,
under the skies   where she had known
1080 her greatest joy.   The battle destroyed
all of Finn's thanes,   except a small remnant,
so he could not press   the fight with Hengest
to any end   in that meeting-place,
dislodge by force   the battle's survivors,
1085 the prince's thane.   So they offered terms:
they would give them space   on a fresh bench-floor,
a hall with high throne   of which they should have
half the control   with the sons of giants,
and Folcwalda's son   should honor the Danes
1090 on every day   ring-giving occurred,
should deal out his gifts   to Hengest's men
exactly as often,   as free with his gold,
rich plated treasure,   as when he encouraged
the men of the Frisians   in his drinking-hall.

1095   Ðā hīe getruwedon   on twā healfa
       fæste frioðu-wǣre.   Fin Hengeste
       elne unflitme   āðum benemde
       þæt hē þā wēa-lāfe   weotena dōme
       ārum hēolde,   þæt ðǣr ǣnig mon
1100   wordum nē worcum   wǣre ne brǣce,
       nē þurh inwit-searo   ǣfre gemǣnden
       ðēah hīe hira bēag-gyfan   banan folgedon
       ðēoden-lēase,   þā him swā geþearfod wæs;
       gyf þonne Frȳsna hwylc   frēcnen sprǣ*ce*
1105   ðæs morþor-hētes   myndgiend wǣre,
       þonne hit sweordes ecg   s[*ē*]ðan scolde.

       Āð wæs geæfned,   ond icge gold
       āhæfen of horde.   Here-Scyldinga
       betst beado-rinca   wæs on bǣl gearu.
1110   Æt þǣm āde wæs   ēþ-gesȳne
       swāt-fāh syrce,   swȳn eal-gylden,
       eofer īren-heard,   æþeling manig
       wundum āwyrded;   sume on wæle crungon.
       Hēt ðā Hildeburh   æt Hnæfes āde
1115   hire selfre sunu   sweoloðe befæstan,
       bān-fatu bærnan   ond on bǣl dōn.
       Earme on eaxle   ides gnornode,
       geōmrode giddum.   Gūð-rinc āstāh;
       wand *tō* wolcnum   wæl-fȳra mǣst,
1120   hlynode *for* hlāwe;   hafelan multon,
       bengeato *bu*rston,   ðonne blōd ætspranc,
       lāð-bite līces.   Līg ealle forswealg,
       gǣsta *gī*frost,   þāra ðe þǣr gūð fornam
       bēga folces;   wæs hira blǣd scacen.
XVII⎱
1125⎰   Gewiton him ðā wīgend   wīca nēosian
       frēondum befeallen,   Frȳs-land gesēon,
       hāmas ond hēa-burh.   Hengest ðā gȳt
       wæl-fāgne winter   wunode mid Finne

1106b MS. syððan: em. Klaeber, but see Roger Dahood, *MÆ* 49 (1980), 1–4.
1107b "icge" otherwise unrecorded. Trans. follows James L. Rosier, *PMLA*
81 (1966), 342–46. See also line 2577.

1095 Then, on both sides, they made their pledge
   to this binding truce. Earnestly Finn
   took oath before Hengest to hold in such honor,
   by his counselors' judgment, those sad survivors
   that no man should ever, by word or deed,
1100 break off the truce, nor plotting in malice
   give them any affront, though now they followed
   the lord who had killed their own ring-giver—
   without a leader, out of necessity;
   that if any Frisian, in provocation,
1105 should call to mind the murderous feud,
   the edge of the sword should settle it for good.
    The oath was performed, old native gold
   piled from Finn's hoard. The chief of the War-
                  Scyldings,
   best of warriors, was laid on the pyre.
1110 It was easy to see the blood-crusted chain-shirts,
   gilded boar-helmets, the sheen of gold
   and gore all mingled, great nobles dead
   in their fated wounds. No few had fallen.
   Then Hildeburh ordered her own dead son
1115 placed on the pyre beside his uncle Hnæf,
   their bone-cases burned, given full fire-burial.
   Beside them both the noblewoman wept,
   mourned with songs. The warrior rose up;
   the mighty death-fire spiraled to heaven,
1120 thundered before the mound. Their heads melted,
   their gashes spread open, the blood shot out
   of the body's feud-bites. Fire swallowed up,
   greediest spirit, ate all of both tribes
   whom war had taken. Their glory was gone.
XVII }
1125 } Then Finn's warriors, without those comrades,
   took themselves home, back into Frisia,
   sought their high fort. But Hengest remained
   through the death-stained winter, living with Finn,

[*ea*]l unhlitme;   eard gemunde
1130 þēah þe [*n*]e meahte   on mere drīfan
hringed-stefnan;   holm storme wēol,
won wið winde,   winter ȳþe belēac
īs-gebinde,   oþðæt ōþer cōm
gēar in geardas,   swā nū gȳt dēð,
1135 þā ðe syngāles   sēle bewitiað,
wuldor-torhtan weder.   Ðā wæs winter scacen,
fæger foldan bearm.   Fundode wrecca,
gist of geardum;   hē tō gyrn-wræce
swīðor þōhte   þonne tō sæ-lāde,
1140 gif hē tor*n-ge*mōt   þurhtēon mihte
þæt hē Eote*na* bearn   inne gemunde.
Swā hē ne fo*r*wyrnde   worold-rædenne,
þonne him Hūnlāfing   hilde-lēoman,
billa sēle*st*,   on bearm dyde;
1145 þæs wæron mid Eote*num*   ecge cūðe.
Swylce ferhð-frecan   Fin eft begeat
sweord-bealo slīðen   æt *his* selfes hām,
siþðan grimne gripe   Gūðlāf ond Ōslāf
æfter sæ-sīðe,   sorge mændon,
1150 ætwiton wēana dæl;   ne meahte wæfre mōd
forhabban in hreþre.   Ðā wæs heal hroden
fēonda fēorum,   swilce Fin slægen,
cyning on corþre,   ond sēo cwēn numen.
Scēotend Scyldinga   tō scypon feredon
1155 eal in-gesteald   eorð-cyninges,
swylce hīe æt Finnes hām   findan meahton
sigla, searo-gimma.   Hīe on sæ-lāde
drihtlīce wīf   tō Denum feredon,
læddon *tō* l*ē*odum.   Lēoð wæs āsungen,
1160 glēo-man*nes* gyd.   Gamen eft āstāh,

1128-29 MS. finnel un / hlitme: em. Klaeber.
 1130a MS. he: em. Holthausen.
 1141 Trans. follows Bruce Mitchell, *Neophilologus* 52 (1968), 292-99.
 1151b "hroden" (decorated) often em. "roden" (reddened) to avoid
double alliteration in second half-line.

   stayed without choice; he thought of his homeland
1130 but he could not steer his ring-prowed ship
   on the cold sea; the deep heaved in storms,
   dark under wind; the waves froze
   in chains of shore-ice till the next year came,
   green to the towns, as it still does today;
1135 glory-bright weathers keeping their season,
   forever in order. Winter was gone,
   the lush fields fair. The exile departed,
   the guest, from the court; he thought more of ven-
                 geance,
   total and utter, than departure by sea,
1140 how to drive the matter to a full grief-meeting,
   that the Frisians be deeply remembered by sword.
   So he did not disdain the world-wide custom
   when Hunlaf's son laid the sword in his lap,
   good battle-flame, finest of blades;
1145 its cutting edges were well known to the Frisians.
   And thus in his turn to war-minded Finn
   came fierce sword-evil, in his own home,
   once Guthlaf and Oslaf spoke of their grief
   after the sea-journey, the fierce attack
1150 and their sorry stay. The restless spirit
   would not stay in the breast. The hall was decorated
   with the lives of the foe, a tapestry of blood,
   Finn slain too, the king with his troop,
   and the queen taken. The Scylding warriors
1155 bore to their ship every good heirloom
   they found in the house of the great king Finn,
   gold seals, gem-brooches. Over the sea
   they carried the queen back to the Danes,
   brought her to her people. This lay was sung through,
1160 the story of the scop. The glad noise resumed,

beorhtode *b*enc-swēg,   byrelas sealdon
wīn of *w*under-fatum.   Þā cwōm Wealhþēo forð
gān under gyldnum bēage   þǣr þā gōdan twēgen
sǣton suhterge-fæde*r*an;   þā gȳt wæs hiera sib
    ætgædere,
1165 æghwylc ōðrum trȳwe.   Swylce þǣr Unferþ þyle
æt fōtum sæt frēan Scyldinga;   gehwylc hiora his
    ferhþe trēowde,
þæt hē hæfde mōd micel,   þēah þe hē his māgum nǣre
ār-fæst æt ecga gelācum.   Sprǣc ðā ides Scyldinga:
"Onfōh þissum fulle,   frēo-drihten mīn,
1170 sinces brytta;   þū on sǣlum wes,
gold-wine gumena,   ond tō Gēatum sprǣc
mildum wordum,   swā sceal man dōn;
bēo wið Gēatas glæd,   geofena gemyndig,
nēan ond feorran   þū nū hafast.
1175 Mē man sægde,   þæt *þ*ū ðē for sunu wolde
here-ri[*n*]c hab*b*an.   Heorot is gefælsod
bēah-sele beorh*t*a;   brūc, þenden þū mōte,
manigra *mēd*o,   ond þīnum māgum lǣf
folc ond rīce,   þonne ðū forð scyle,
1180 metodsceaft sēon.   *Ic* mīnne can
glædne Hrōþulf,   þæt hē þā *ge*ogoðe wile
ārum healdan,   gyf þū ǣr þon*ne* hē,
wine Scildinga,   worold oflǣtest;
wēne ic þæt hē mid gōde   gyldan wille
1185 uncran eaferan,   gif hē þæt eal gemon,
hwæ*t* wit tō willan   ond tō worð-myndum
umbor-wesendum ǣr   ārna gefremedon."
Hwearf þā bī bence,   þǣr hyre byre wǣron,
Hrēðrīc ond Hrōðmund,   ond hæleþa bearn,
1190 giogoð ætgædere;   þǣr se gōda sæt,
Bēowulf Gēata   be þǣm gebrōðrum twǣ*m*.
XVIII   Him wæs ful boren   ond frēond-laþu
wordum bewǣgned,   ond wunden gold
ēstum geēawed,   earm-rēade twā,

1165b MS. hun ferþ.
1176a MS. here ric: em. Kemble.
1182b Thorkelin A reads þŏn, presumably in error for abbreviated þoñ.

bright-clanking bench-music;   wine-bearers poured
from fluted silver.   Wealhtheow came forth,
glistening in gold,   to greet the good pair,
uncle and nephew;   their peace was still firm,
1165 each true to the other.   Likewise Unferth,
spokesman at court,   sat at Hrothgar's feet;
all knew his courage,   that he had great spirit,
though he kept his kinsmen   in nothing like honor
when edges met.   Then Wealhtheow spoke:
"Accept this cup,   my noble lord,
1170 gold-giving king;   be filled in your joys,
treasure-friend to all,   and give to the Geats
your kind words,   as is proper for men;
in your generous mind,   be gracious to the Weders,
remembering the gifts   you have from all tribes.
1175 I have been told   you would have this warrior
for your son.   Heorot is cleansed,
bright hall of rings;   use while you may
your gifts from so many,   and leave to your kinsmen
the nation and folk   when you must go forth
1180 to await your judgment.   Full well I know
of my gracious Hrothulf   that he would rule
the young men in honor,   would keep all well,
if you should give up   this world before him.
I expect he will want   to repay our sons
1185 only with good   once he recalls
all we have done   when he was younger
to honor his desires   and his name in the world."
She turned to the bench   where her sons were sitting,
Hrethric, Hrothmund,   and all the young men,
1190 the sons of nobles.   There sat Beowulf,
the Geatish hero,   between the two brothers.
XVIII   A flagon was brought him,   and friendship passed
aloud in words,   and wire-wrought gold
given with a will: two rich arm-bands,

1195   hrægl ond hrin*gas*,   heals-bēaga mǣst
       þāra þe ic on fol*dan*   *ge*frǣgen hǣbbe.
       Nǣnigne ic under sweg*le*   sēlran hȳrde
       hord-mā[ðð]um hǣleþa,   syþðan Hāma ætwǣg
       tō [*þǣ*]re byrhtan *byrig*   Brōsinga mene,
1200   sigle ond sinc-fæt;   searo-nīðas fealh
       Eormenrīces;   gecēas ēcne rǣd.
       Þone hring hæfde   Higelāc Gēa*ta*
       nefa Swertinges,   nȳhstan sīðe,
       siðþan hē under segne   sinc ealgode,
1205   wæl-rēaf werede;   hyne wyrd fornam,
       syþðan hē for wlenco   wēan āhsode,
       fǣhðe tō Frȳsum.   Hē þā frætwe wǣg,
       eorclan-stānas   ofer ȳða ful,
       rīce þēoden;   hē under rande gecranc.
1210   Gehwearf þā in Francna fæþm   feorh cyninges,
       brēost-gewǣdu   ond se bēah somod;
       wyrsan wīg-frecan   wæl rēafeden
       æfter gūð-sceare;   Gēata lēode
       hrēa-wīc hēoldon.   *H*eal swēge onfēng.
1215   Wealhðēo maþelode,   hēo fore þǣm werede sprǣc;
       "Brūc ðisses bēages,   Bēowulf lēofa,
       hyse, mid hǣle,   *ond þ*isses hrægles nēot
       þēo[*d*]-gestrēona,   *ond gebēoh* tela;
       cen þec mid cræfte,   ond þyssum cnyht*um* wes
1220   lāra līðe;   ic þē þæs lēan geman.
       Ha*fast* þū gefēred,   þæt ðē feor ond nēah
       ealne wīde-fer*hþ*   weras ehtigað,
       efne swā sīde   swā sǣ bebū*geð*
       wind-geard, weallas.   Wes, þenden þū lifige,
1225   æ*þeling*, ēadig!   Ic þē an tela
       sinc-gestrēona.   Bēo þū suna mīnum
       dǣdum gedēfe,   drēam-healde*nde*.

1198a   MS. hord mad mum: em. Grein.
1199a   MS. here: em. Ettmüller.
1200b   "fealh" (incurred) usually em. "f[*lēa*]h" (fled) after Heinrich Leo
Über Beowulf (Halle: E. Anton, 1839), p. 44.
1218a   MS. þeo ge streona: em. Grundtvig.

1195   a mail-shirt, and rings,   and the largest gold collar
ever heard of on earth,   so it is told.
No better treasures,   gold gifts to heroes,
were known under heaven   since Hama bore off
to the shining city   the Brosings' necklace,
1200   gem-figured filigree.   He gained the hatred
of Eormanric the Goth;   chose eternal reward.
This collar-ring traveled   on Hygelac's breast
on his final voyage,   nephew of Swerting,
when under the standard   he defended his treasure,
1205   spoils of the kill;   fate took him off
that time he sought trouble,   stirred up a feud,
a fight with the Frisians,   in his pride and daring.
He wore those gold wires,   rarest gem-stones,
across the cup of waves,   a mighty prince.
1210   He fell beneath his shield.   Into Frankish hands
came his life, body-gold,   and the great ringed collar;
lesser warriors   rifled the corpses
after the battle-harvest.   Dead Geats
filled the field.   Now cheers for Beowulf rose.
1215   Then Wealhtheow spoke   before all the company:
"Enjoy this neck-ring,   the treasure of a people,
my dear young Beowulf,   and have good luck
in the use of these war-shirts—   have all success.
Make known your strength,   yet be to these boys
1220   gentle in counsel.   I will not forget you for that.
You have brought it about   that far and near
none but admire you,   and always will,
a sea-broad fame,   walled only by wind.
While you may live,   be happy, O prince!
1225   It is right that I grant you   these jeweled treasures.
Be to my sons   gracious in deeds,
winner of hall-joys,   in your great strength.

Hēr is æghwylc eorl   ōþrum getrȳwe,
mōdes milde,   man-drihtne hol[d];
1230 þegnas syndon geþwǣre,   þēod eal-gearo,
druncne dryht-guman   dōð swā ic bidde."
        Ēode þā tō setle.   Þǣr wæs symbla cyst,
druncon wīn weras;   wyrd ne cūþon,
geōsceaft grim[m]e,   swā hit āgangen wearð
1235 eorla manegum,   syþðan æfen cwōm,
ond him Hrōðgār gewāt   tō hofe sīnum,
rīce tō ræste.   Reced weardode
unrīm eorla,   swā hīe oft ǣr dydon;
benc-þelu beredon;   hit geondbrǣded wearð
1240 beddum ond bolstrum.   Bēor-scealca sum
fūs ond fǣge   flet-ræste gebēag.
Setton him tō hēafdon   hilde-randas
bord-wudu beorhtan.   Þǣr on bence wæs
ofer æþelinge   ȳþ-gesēne
1245 heaþo-stēapa helm,   hringed byrne,
þrec-wudu þrymlīc.   Wæs þēaw hyra
þæt hīe oft wǣron   an wīg gearwe,
gē æt hām gē on herge,   gē gehwæþer þāra
efne swylce mǣla,   swylce hira man-dryhtne
1250 þearf gesǣlde;   wæs sēo þēod tilu.
XVIIII   Sigon þā tō slǣpe.   Sum sāre angeald
æfen-ræste,   swā him ful oft gelamp
siþðan gold-sele   Grendel warode,
unriht æfnde,   oþþæt ende becwōm,
1255 swylt æfter synnum.   Þæt gesȳne wearþ,
wīd-cūþ werum,   þætte wrecend þā gȳt
lifde æfter lāþum,   lange þrāge,
æfter gūð-ceare.   Grendles mōdor,
ides, āglǣc-wīf   yrmþe gemunde,
1260 sē þe wæter-egesan   wunian scolde,
cealde strēamas,   siþðan Ca[in] wearð
tō ecg-banan   āngan brēþer,

1229b MS. heol: em. Thorkelin.
1234a MS. grimne: em. Ettmüller.
1261b MS. camp: em. Grundtvig.

Each noble here   is true to the other,
every kind heart   death-loyal to lord.
1230 The thanes are united,   a nation prepared;
our men, having drunk,   will do as I ask."
     Then she went to her seat.   It was a great feast,
they drank rare wine.   Little they knew
of their long-prepared fate,   as it came again fiercely
1235 to many a noble,   once evening had come
and mighty Hrothgar   retired to his chambers,
the king to his rest.   A great many men
occupied the hall,   as often before,
cleared away bench-planks,   laid out their bedding.
1240 One of those beer-drinkers,   who was soon to die,
lay down to hall-rest   ripe in his fate.
At their heads were placed   their round battle-shields,
bright linden-wood.   Above each noble
you could see his war-helmet   gleaming on the bench,
1245 its high crown,   and his iron ring-coat,
strong-thrusting shaft.   This was their custom,
to be ready for battle   at any time,
at home or out harrying,   whichever occasion
might turn to a time   when their sworn lord
1250 had need of their strength.   They were a good troop.
XVIIII   Then they sank into sleep.   One paid sorely
for that night's rest,   as happened so often
when Grendel had held   the great golden hall,
did sickening crimes,   till the end came
1255 and he died for his sins.   Men came to know
—it was soon plain enough—   his avenger still lived
after that battle,   for a long time,
in hate, war-sorrow.   Grendel's mother,
a monster woman,   kept war-grief
1260 deep in her mind,   dwelt in terrible waters,
icy cold streams,   since Cain raised the sword
against closest kinsman,   put blade to his brother;

fæderen-mǣge;   hē þā fāg gewāt,
morþre gemearcod,   *man*-drēam flēon,
1265 wēsten warode.   Þ*anon* wōc fela
geōsceaft-gāsta;   wæs þǣra Grend*el* sum
heoro-wearh hetelīc,   sē æt Heorote fand
wæccendne wer   wīges bidan.
Þǣr him āglǣca   ætgrǣpe wearð;
1270 hwæþre hē gemunde   mægenes strenge,
gim-fæste gife,   ðe him God sealde,
ond him tō Anwaldan   āre gelȳfde,
frōfre ond fultum;   ðȳ hē þone fēond ofercwōm,
gehnǣgde helle-gāst.   Þā hē hēan gewāt,
1275 drēame bedǣled   dēaþ-wīc sēon,
man-cynnes fēond.   Ond his mōdor þā gȳt
gīfre ond galg-mōd   gegān wolde
sorh-fulne sīð,   sunu [*d*]ēo[ð] wrecan.
     Cōm þā tō Heorote,   ðǣr Hring-Dene
1280 geond þæt sæld swǣfun.   Þā ðǣr sōna wearð
edhwyrft eorlum   siþðan inne fealh
Grendles mōdor.   Wæs se gryre lǣssa
efne swā micle,   swā bið mægþa cræft,
wīg-gryre wīfes,   be wǣpned-men
1285 þonne heoru bunden,   hamere geþuren,
sweord swāte fāh   swīn ofer helme,
ecgum *dyhttig*,   andweard sċireð.
Þā wæs on *healle*   *hea*rd-ecg togen,
sweord ofer setlum,   sīd-rand manig
1290 hafen handa fæst;   helm ne gemunde,
byrnan sīde,   þā hine se brōga angeat.
Hēo wæs on ofste,   wolde ūt þanon,
fēore beorgan,   þā hēo onfunden wæs.
Hraðe hēo æþlinga   ānne hæfde
1295 fæste befangen,   þā hēo tō fenne gang.
Sē wæs Hrōþgāre   hæleþa *lē*ofost
on gesīðes hād   be sǣm twēonum,
rīce rand-wiga,   þone ðe hēo on ræste ābrēat,

1278b MS. þeod: em. Holthausen, but the MS. reading "to avenge the people of her son," i.e., the race of Cain, makes equally good sense.

dripping with that fate,   bright-stained outlawry,
gore-marked by murder,   he fled man's joys,
1265 lived in wastelands.   Out of that deep
and abysm of time   came monsters, spirits.
Grendel was one,   angry battle-demon,
who found at Heorot   a wakeful watchman.
The monster had seized him   there in his hall-bed,
1270 but there he remembered   his greatness of strength,
jewel of a gift   that God had given him,
trusted in the mercy   of the Lord all-powerful,
his comfort and aid;   by these he vanquished
his enemy hall-guest,   shamed the hell-spirit.
1275 Wretched, he fled,   joyless to death-bed,
the foe of mankind.   And now his mother,
still greedy for slaughter,   wanted to visit,
make a grievous journey,   avenge her son's death.
   She came then to Heorot   where Ring-Danes slept
1280 throughout the hall.   And then to the nobles
came reversal of fortune,   once Grendel's mother
reached into the hall.   Terror was the less
by just so much   as the strength of women,
attack of battle-wives,   compared to armed men,
1285 when wrought sword,   forged under hammer,
the iridescent blade,   blood-wet, cuts
through enemy's boar-guard,   an edge ever firm.
Then in the great hall   hard blades were drawn,
swords above benches,   many broad shields
1290 raised high in hand;   none thought of helmet,
of iron garments,   when the fierce attack came.
In a rush she came in,   and left quite as soon,
to save her life,   once they discovered her.
But that one noble   she quickly snatched up,
1295 tight in her clutches,   as she left for the fen.
To Hrothgar that man   was the dearest warrior
he had among liege-men   between the two seas,
a mighty shield-fighter   whom she tore from his bed,

blǣd-fǣstne beorn.　　Næs Bēowulf ðǣr,
1300　ac wæs ōþer in　　ǣr geteohhod
æfter māþðum-gife　　mǣrum Gēate.
Hrēam wearð in Heorote;　　hēo under heolfre genam
cūþe folme;　　cearu wæs genīwod,
geworden in wīcun.　　Ne wæs þæt gewrixle til,
1305　þæt hīe on bā healfa　　bicgan scoldon
frēonda fēorum.　　Þā wæs frōd cyning,
hār hilde-rinc,　　on hrēon mōde
syðþan hē aldor-þegn　　unly*figendne*,
þone dēorestan　　dēadne wisse.
1310　Hra*þe wæs* tō būre　　Bēowulf fetod
sigor-ēadig se*cg*.　　Samod ǣr-dæge
ēode eorla sum,　　æþele cempa,
self mid gesīðum,　　þǣr se snot*era* bād,
hwæþre him Alwalda　　ǣf*re* wille
1315　æfter wēa-spelle　　wyrpe gefremman.
Gang ðā æfter flōre　　fyrd-wyrðe man
mid his hand-scale　　—heal-wudu dynede—
þæt hē þone wīsan　　wordum næg*de*,
frēan Ingwina;　　frægn gif him wǣre,
1320　æfter nēod-laðu[*m*],　　niht getǣse.
XX　　Hrōðgār maþelode,　　helm Scyldinga:
"Ne frīn þū æfter sǣlum;　　sorh is genīwod
Denigea lēodum.　　Dēad is Æschere,
Yrmenlāfes　　yldra brōþor,
1325　mīn rūn-wita　　ond mīn rǣd-bora,
eaxl-gestealla,　　ðonne wē on orlege
hafelan weredon,　　þonne hniton fēþan,
eoferas cnysedan.　　*Swy*[*lc*] *sc*olde eorl wesan,
[*æþeling*] ǣr-gōd,　　swylc *Æschere wæs*!

1302a　MS. oin, with the "i" inserted.
1314a　MS. alf walda: em. Thorpe.
1318b　MS. hnæg, with "de" from Thorkelin A and B: em. Grein.
1320a　MS. neod laðu: em. Ettmüller.
1328b　MS. *swy*..: restored by Thorkelin.
1329a　No gap in MS.: supplied by Grein.

          a man rich in fame.   Beowulf was not there—
1300   the honored Geat   was earlier assigned
          another building   after the gold-giving.
          Shouts came from Heorot;   she had seized in its gore
          the famous claw-arm;   then grief was renewed,
          came again to that building.   No good exchange,
1305   that those on both sides   had to pay with the lives
          of kinsmen and friends.   The gray-bearded king,
          once a great warrior,   was darkened in mind
          when he learned of the death—   his chief thane,
          his nearest man,   no longer alive.

1310   Quickly Beowulf,   victory-blessed man,
          was called to the building.   In the dark before dawn
          the noble champion   came with his men,
          renowned among heroes,   to where the old king
          sat wondering if ever   the Almighty would grant him
1315   a change in fortune   after this news.
          The tall battle-hero   marched through the hall
          with his hand-picked troop   —the floorboards thun-
                                                                        dered—
          till he stood by the king,   spoke face to face
          to the lord of the Ingwines,   asked if he'd passed
1320   an agreeable night   as he had intended.

   XX   Hrothgar made answer,   the Scyldings' protector:
          "Ask not of joy: sorrow has returned
          to the Danish people.   Æschere is dead,
          the elder brother   of Yrmenlaf,
1325   my chief adviser,   my rune-counselor—
          he stood by my shoulder   at shield-wall, the forefront,
          when we guarded our heads   as the armies clashed,
          boar struck boar.   So a man should be,
          good from the start,   as Æschere was.

1330 Wearð him on Heorote   tō hand-banan
     wæl-gǣst wæfre;   ic ne wāt hwæ[d]er
     atol ǣse wlanc   eft-sīðas tēah,
     fylle gefrǣgnod.   Hēo þā fæhðe wræc,
     þe þū gystran niht   Grendel cwealdest
1335 þurh hǣstne hād   heardum clammum,
     forþan hē tō lange   lēode mīne
     wanode ond wyrde.   Hē æt wīge gecrang
     ealdres scyldig,   ond nū ōþer cwōm
     mihtig mān-scaða,   wolde hyre mǣg wrecan,
1340 gē feor hafað   fæhðe gestǣled,
     þæs þe þincean mæg   þegne monegum,
     sē þe æfter sinc-gyfan   on sefan grēoteþ,
     hreþer-bealo hearde;   nū sēo hand *lige*ð,
     sē þe ēow wēl-hwylcra   wilna dohte.
1345   "*Ic* þæt lond-būend,   lēode mīne,
     sele-rǣdende   secgan hȳrde,
     þæt hīe gesāwon   swylce twēgen
     micle mearc-stapan   mōras healdan,
     ellor-gǣstas.   Ðǣra ōðer wæs,
1350 þæs þe hīe gewislīcost   gewitan meahton,
     idese onlīcnæs;   ōðer earm-sceapen
     on weres wæstmum   wræc-lāstas træd,
     næfne hē wæs māra   þonne ænig m*a*n ōðer;
     þone on gēar-dagum   Grendel nem*do*[*n*]
1355 fold-būende;   nō hīe fæder cunnon,
     hwæ*þer* him ænig wæs   ǣr ācenned
     dyrnra gāsta.   Hīe dȳgel lond
     warigeað, wulf-hleoþu,   windi*ge* næssas,
     frēcne fen-gelād,   ðǣr fyrgen-strēam
1360 under næssa genipu   niþer gewīteð,
     flōd under foldan.   Nis þæt feor heonon
     mīl-gemearces,   þæt se mere stan[d]eð;

1331b   MS. hwæþer: em. Grein.
  1333a   Often em. to "fylle gefægnod" (rejoiced in her feast). My trans.
follows Wrenn.
  1354b   MS. nem*dod* from Thorkelin A and B: em. Kemble.
  1362b   MS. stanðeð: em. Thorkelin.

1330 Here within Heorot   a restless corpse-spirit
became his killer.   I do not know
where she went with his body,   flesh-proud, terrible,
infamous in slaughter.   She avenged that feud
in which, last night,   you killed Grendel
1335 with fierce grips,   in your violent strength,
because too long   he had destroyed
my Danish people.   In battle he fell,
life-forfeit in guilt;   now another has come,
mighty in her evil,   would avenge her son,
1340 and too long a way   has she pushed her revenge,
as it may seem   to many of these thanes
who grieve, mind-deep,   for their treasure-giver,
a cruel heart-killing.   Now the hand is vanished
that served your joys   in all right ways.
1345   "I have heard land-holders   among my people,
counselors in hall,   speak of it thus:
they sometimes have seen   two such things,
huge, vague borderers,   walking the moors,
spirits from elsewhere;   so far as any man
1350 might clearly see,   one of them walked
in the likeness of a woman;   the other, misshapen,
stalked marshy wastes   in the tracks of an exile,
except that he was larger   than any other man.
In earlier days   the people of the region
1355 named him Grendel.   They know of no father
from the old time, before them,   among dark spirits.
A secret land they guard,   high wolf-country,
windy cliffs,   a dangerous way
twisting through fens,   where a mountain torrent
1360 plunges down crags   under darkness of hills,
the flood under the earth.   Not far from here,
measured in miles,   lies that fearful lake

ofer þǣm hongiað   hrinde bearwas,
wudu wyrtum fæst   wæter oferhelmað.
1365 Þǣr mæg nihta gehwǣm   nīð-wundor sēon,
fȳr on flōde.   Nō þæs frōd leofað
gumena bearna   þæt þone grund wite.
Ðēah þe hǣð-stapa   hundum geswenced,
heorot hornum trum   holt-wudu sēce,
1370 feorran geflȳmed,   ǣr hē feorh seleð,
aldor on ōfre,   ǣr hē in wille,
hafelan [hȳdan].   Nis þæt hēoru stōw!
Þonon ȳð-geblond   ūp āstīgeð
won tō wolcnum,   þonne wind styreþ
1375 lāð gewidru,   oðþæt lyft drysmaþ,
roderas rēotað.   Nū is se rǣd gelang
eft æt þē ānum.   Eard gīt ne const,
frēcne stōwe,   ðǣr þū findan miht
fela-sinnigne secg;   sēc gif þū dyrre!
1380 Ic þē þā fǣhðe   fēo lēanige,
eald-gestrēonum,   swā ic ǣr dyde,
wundini golde,   gyf þū on weg cymest."
XXI   Bēowulf maþelode,   bearn Ecgþēowes:
"Ne sorga, snotor guma!   Sēlre bið ǣghwǣm
1385 þæt hē his frēond wrece,   þonne hē fela murne.
Ūre ǣghwylc sceal   ende gebīdan
worolde līfes;   wyrce sē þe mōte
dōmes ǣr dēaþe;   þæt bið driht-guman
unlifigendum   æfter sēlest.
1390 Ārīs, rīces weard,   uton hraþe fēran,
Grendles māgan   gang scēawigan.
Ic hit þē gehāte: nō hē on helm losaþ,
nē on foldan fæþm,   nē on fyrgen-holt,
nē on gyfenes grund,   gā þǣr hē wille.
1395 Ðȳs dōgor þū   geþyld hafa

1372a No gap in MS. but insertion mark for verb: supplied by Kemble.
1382a MS. wun / dini from Malone, *NC*, p. 68. Zupitza and Klaeber allow a possible wun / dmi. Thorkelin A: rundmi; Thorkelin B: wund-dini.
1388b MS. driht gumen, with "a" added over the "e."
1391b MS. gang: final "g" added above the line in a different hand.

overhung with roots   that sag and clutch,
frost-bound trees   at the water's edge.
1365 Each night there is seen   a baleful wonder,
strange water-fires.   No man alive,
though old and wise,   knows that mere-bottom.
The strong heath-runner,   chased far by hounds,
the full-horned stag,   may seek a safe cover,
1370 pursued to despair—   still he will sooner
die on the bank   than save his head
and plunge in the mere.   Not a pleasant place!
Tearing waves   start up from that spot,
black against the sky,   while the gloomy wind
1375 stirs awful storms   till the air turns choking,
the heavens weep.   Now again, you alone
are our only help.   You still do not know
the awful place   where you might find
the sin-filled creature;   seek it if you dare!
1380 I will reward   your feud with payments,
most valued treasures,   as I did before,
old twisted gold,   if you live to return."
XXI   Then Beowulf answered,   the son of Ecgtheow:
"Grieve not, wise king!   Better it is
1385 for every man   to avenge his friend
than mourn overmuch.   Each of us must come
to the end of his life: let him who may
win fame before death.   That is the best
memorial for a man   after he is gone.
1390 Arise, guard of kingdoms,   let us go quickly,
and track down the path   of Grendel's kinsman!
I promise you this: he will find no escape
in the depths of the earth,   nor the wooded mountain,
nor the bottom of the sea,   let him go where he will.
1395 Be patient this day   amid all your woes,

wēana gehwylces,   swā ic þē wēne tō."
    Āhlēop ðā se gomela,   Gode þancode,
mihtigan Drihtne,   þæs se man ge*spræc.*
*Þ*ā wæs Hrōðgāre   hors ge*bæted,*
1400 wicg wunden-feax.   Wīsa fengel
geato*līc* gende;   gum-fēþa stōp
lind-hæbbendra.   Lā*stas* wǣron
æfter wald-swaþum   wīde gesȳne,
gang ofer grundas,   gegnum fōr
1405 ofer *myr*can mōr,   mago-þegna bær
þone sēlestan   sāwol-lēasne,
þāra þe mid Hrōðgāre   hām eahtode.
Oferēode þā   æþelinga bearn
stēap stān-hliðo,   stīge nearwe,
1410 enge ān-paðas,   uncūð gelād,
neowle næssas,   nicor-hūsa fela.
Hē fēara sum   beforan gengde
wīsra monna,   wong scēawian,
oþþæt hē fǣringa   fyrgen-bēamas
1415 ofer hārne stān   hleonian funde,
wyn-lēasne wudu;   wæter under stōd
drēorig ond gedrēfed.   Denum eallum wæs,
winum Scyldinga,   weorce on mōde
tō geþolianne,   ðegne monegum,
1420 oncȳð eorla gehwǣm,   syðþan Æscheres
on þām holm-clife   hafelan mētton.
Flōd blōde wēol   —folc tō sǣgon—
hātan heolfre.   Horn stundum song
fū*slīc* f[*yrd*]-lēoð.   Fēþa eal gesæt.
1425   Gesāwon ðā æfter *wætere*   wyrm-cynnes fela,
sellīce sǣ-dracan   *sun*d cunnian,
swylce on næs-hleoðum   nicras *lic*gean,
ðā on undern-mǣl   oft bewitigað
sorh-fulne sīð   on segl-rāde,
1430 wyrmas ond wil-dēor.   Hīe on weg hruron

1424 MS. *f*...: restored by Karl Bouterwek, *ZDA* 11 (1859), 92; "gesæt" corrected in the scribe's hand from "geseah."

as I have good cause   to expect you to be."
    The old king leaped up,   gave thanks to God,
to the mighty Lord,   for Beowulf's words.
Then Hrothgar's horse   with braided mane
1400 was bridled and saddled;   the wise prince rode
in state, magnificent;   his troop went on foot,
shields at the ready.   The creature's tracks
were plainly visible   through the wood-paths,
her trail on the ground;   she had gone straight
1405 toward the dark lands   with the corpse of the best
thane and kinsman,   now unsouled,
of all those who held   the nation with Hrothgar.
Then the troop of nobles   climbed up high
into stony hills,   the steep rock-lands,
1410 through narrow files,   an unknown way,
dangerous cliffs   over water-snakes' caves.
With a few wise counselors   the king rode ahead
to search out the way,   till suddenly he came
upon stunted firs,   gnarled mountain pines
1415 leaning over stones,   cold and gray,
a joyless wood.   The water beneath
was stirred with blood.   To every Dane
it was a wound mind-deep,   cold grief for each
of the Scylding nobles,   many thanes' sorrow,
1420 when they discovered   Æschere's head
sitting on the cliff   beside that water.
The mere welled up   —the men looked on—
in hot heart's blood.   Time and again
the sharp war-horn sang.   The men on foot
1425 all sat down.   They saw strange serpents,
dragonish shapes,   swimming through the water.
Water-beasts, too,   lay curled on the cliff-shelves,
that often slither off   at dark daybreak
to attend men's sorrow   upon the sail-roads,
1430 sea-beasts and serpents.   Away they rushed madly,

bitere ond gebolgne;   bearhtm ongēaton,
gūð-horn galan.   Sumne Gēata lēod
of flān-bogan   fēores getwǣfde,
ȳð-gewinnes,   þæt him on aldre stōd
1435 here-strǣl hearda;   hē on holme wæs
sundes þē sǣnra,   ðe hyne swylt fornam.
Hrǣþe wearð on ȳðum   mid eofer-sprēotum
heoro-hōcyhtum   hearde genearwod,
nīða genǣged   ond on næs togen
1440 wundorlīc wǣg-bora;   weras scēawedon
gryrelicne gist.   Gyrede hine Bēowulf
eorl-gewǣdum,   nalles for ealdre mearn;
scolde here-byrne   hondum gebrōden,
sīd ond searo-fāh,   sund cunnian,
1445 sēo ðe bān-cofan   beorgan cūþe,
þæt him hilde-grāp   hreþre ne mihte,
eorres inwit-feng   aldre gesceþðan;
ac se hwīta helm   *h*afelan werede,
sē þe mere-grundas   men*gan* scolde,
1450 sēcan sund-gebland   since geweor*ð*ad,
befongen frēa-wrāsnum,   swā hine fyrn-dagum
worhte wǣpna smið,   wundrum tēode,
besette swīn-līcum,   þæt hine syðþan nō
brond nē beado-mēcas   bītan ne meahton.
1455 Næs þæt þonne mǣtost   mægen-fultuma,
þæt him on ðearfe lāh   ðyle Hrōðgāres;
wæs þǣm hæft-mēce   Hrunting nama;
þæt wæs ān foran   eald-gestrēona;
ecg wæs īren,   āter-tānum fāh,
1460 āhyrded heaþo-swāte;   nǣfre hit æt hilde ne swāc
manna ǣngum,   þāra þe hit mid mundum bewand,
sē ðe gryre-sīðas   gegān dorste,
folc-stede fāra;   næs þæt forma sīð
þæt hit ellen-weorc   æfnan scolde.
1465 Hūru ne gemunde   mago Ecglāfes,
eafoþes cræftig,   þæt hē ǣr gespræc
wīne druncen,   þā hē þæs wǣpnes onlāh
sēlran sweord-frecan;   selfa ne dorste
under ȳða gewin   aldre genēþan,

thrashing in anger,   when they heard the bright sound,
song of the war-horn.   A Geatish bowman
cut short the life   of one of those swimmers,
the huge serpent dying   as the sharp war-shaft
1435 stood deep in its body;   swam the more slowly
in flight through the water   when death overtook him.
He was quickly assailed   in the water with boar-pikes,
hard hooked blades,   given mighty jabs,
dragged up the cliff,   an awesome thing,
1440 monster from the deep.   The warriors gazed
at the spawn of the waves.   Then Beowulf showed
no care for his life,   put on his armor.
His broad mail-shirt   was to explore the mere,
closely hand-linked,   woven by craft;
1445 it knew how to keep   his bone-house whole,
that the crush of battle   not reach his heart,
nor the hateful thrusts   of enemies, his life.
His shining helmet   protected his head;
soon it would plunge   through heaving waters,
1450 stir up the bottom,   its magnificent head-band
inset with jewels,   as in times long past
a master smith worked it   with his wondrous skill,
set round its boar-plates,   that ever afterwards
no sword or war-ax   could ever bite through it.
1455 Not the least aid   to his strength was the sword
with a long wooden hilt   which Hrothgar's spokesman
now lent him in need,   Hrunting by name.
It was the best   of inherited treasures,
its edge was iron,   gleaming with venom-twigs,
1460 hardened in war-blood;   never in the fray
had it failed any man   who knew how to hold it,
dared undertake   the unwelcome journey
to the enemy's homestead.   It was not the first time
it had to perform   a work of great courage.
1465   The son of Ecglaf,   clever and strong,
could hardly have thought   of his earlier words,
spoken while drinking,   as he gave that weapon
to the better swordsman.   He did not himself
dare risk his life   under clashing waves,

1470   driht-scype drēogan,   þǣr hē dōme forlēas,
       ellen-*mǣrð*um.   Ne wæs þǣm ōðrum swā
       sy*ð*þan hē *h*ine tō gūðe   gegyred hæfde.

XXII   Bēowulf maþelode,   bearn Ecgþēowes:
       "Geþenc nū, se mǣra   maga Healfdenes,
1475   snottra fengel,   nū ic eom sīðes fūs,
       gold-wine gumena,   hwæt wit geō sprǣcon,
       gif ic æt þearfe   þīnre scolde
       aldre linnan,   þæt þū mē ā wǣre
       forð-gewitenum   on fæder stǣle.
1480   Wes þū mund-bora   mīnum mago-þegnum,
       hond-gesellum,   gif mec hild nime;
       swylce þū ðā mādmas,   þe þū mē sealdest,
       Hrōðgar lēofa,   Higelāce onsend.
       Mæg þonne on þǣm golde ongitan   Gēata dryhten,
1485   gesēon sunu Hrǣðles,   þonne hē on þæt sinc starað,
       þæt ic gum-cystum   gōdne funde
       bēaga bryttan,   brēac þonne mōste.
       Ond þū Unferð lǣt   ealde lāfe,
       wrǣtlīc wǣg-sweord,   wīd-cūðne man
1490   heard-ecg habban;   ic mē mid Hruntinge
       dōm gewyrce,   oþðe mec dēað nimeð."
       Æfter þǣm *wordum*   Weder-Gēata lēod
       efste mid elne,   na*las and*sware
       bīdan wolde;   brim-wylm onfēng
1495   *hil*de-rinc.   Ðā wæs hwīl dæges,
       ǣr hē þone grund-wong   ongytan mehte.
       Sōna þæt *on*funde,   sē ðe flōda begong
       heoro-gīfre behēold   hund missēra,
       grim ond grǣdig,   þæt þǣr gumena sum
1500   æl-wihta eard   ufan cunno*de*.
       Grāp þā togēanes;   gūð-rinc gefēng
       at*olan* clommum;   nō þȳ ǣr in gescōd
       hālan līce;   hring ūtan ymb-bearh,
       þæt hēo þone fyrd-hom   ðurhfōn ne mihte,
1505   locene leoðo-syrcan   lāþan fingrum.

1488a MS. hunferð.

1470 test his courage;   he lost fame for that,
       his name for valor.   It was not so with Beowulf,
       once he was dressed,   prepared for battle.

XXII   Beowulf spoke bravely,   Ecgtheow's son:
       "Famed son of Healfdene,   wisest of princes,
1475 remember all well,   now that I am ready,
       gold-friend of warriors,   what we spoke of before,
       that if I lose my life   while at work in your cause,
       you will still be to me   as a father always.
1480 Be shield and protector   of my young men here,
       close battle-comrades,   if this fight claims me;
       and also the treasures   which you have given me,
       beloved Hrothgar,   send back to Hygelac,
       lord of the Geats.   He will understand
1485 when he sees such gold,   the son of Hrethel
       will know full well   that I had found
       a ring-giving lord   of all manly virtues,
       rejoiced in his good   while I was able.
       And be sure that Unferth,   that well-known man,
       has my family treasure,   wonderful wave-sword,
1490 hardened, sharp-edged.   With Hrunting I will find
       a deserving fame   or death will take me!"
          After these words   the man of the Weders
       turned away boldly,   would not wait
       for answer, farewell.   The surging waters
1495 received the warrior.   After that plunge,
       it was most of the day   before he found bottom.
       Soon enough she   who war-thirsty held
       the kingdom of waters   for a hundred winters,
       fierce and kill-greedy,   saw that some human
1500 came to explore   the water-devils' home.
       Then she snatched him up,   seized the good warrior
       in her horrible claws;   but none the sooner
       broke into his body;   he was ringed all around,
       safe from puncture;   her claws could not pierce
1505 his close-linked rings,   rip the locked leather.

Bær þā sēo brim-wyl[f],   þā hēo tō botme cōm,
hringa þengel   tō hofe sīnum,
swā hē ne mihte,   —nō hē þæ[s] mōdig wæs—
wǣpna gewealdan,   ac hine wundra þæs fela
1510 swe[n]cte on sunde,   sǣ-dēor monig
hilde-tūxum   here-syrcan bræc,
ēhton āglǣcan.   Đā se eorl ongeat
þæt hē [*in*] nīð-sele   nāt-hwylcum wæs,
þǣr him nǣnig wæter   wihte ne sceþede,
1515 nē him for hrōf-sele   hrīnan ne mehte
fǣr-gripe flōdes;   *fȳr-lēoht* geseah,
blācne lēoman   beorhte *scīnan*.
      Ongeat þā se gōda   grund-wyrgenne,
*mer*e-wīf mihtig;   mægen-rǣs forgeaf
1520 hilde-*b*ille,   ho[n]d sweng ne oftēah
þæt hire on ha*f*elan   hring-mǣl āgōl
grǣdig gūð-lēoð.   Đā se gist onfand
þæt se beado-lēoma   bītan *n*olde
aldre sceþðan,   ac sēo ecg geswāc
1525 ð*ē*odne æt þearfe;   ðolode ǣr fela
hond-*gem*ōta,   helm oft gescær,
fǣges fyrd-*hræg*l;   ðā wæs forma sīð
dēorum māðme,   *þæt* his dōm ālæg.
      Eft wæs ān-rǣd   nalas elnes *læt*
1530 mǣrða gemyndig   mǣg Hȳlāces.
Wearp ðā wunde[n]-mǣl   wrǣttum gebunden
yrre ōretta,   þæt hit on eorðan læg,
stīð ond stȳl-ecg;   strenge getruwode,
mund-gripe mægenes.   Swā sceal man dōn,
1535 þonne hē æt gūðe   gegān þenceð
longsumne lof,   nā ymb his līf cearað.
Gefēng þā be eaxle   —nalas for fǣhðe mearn—

1506a MS. brim wyl: em. Kemble.
1508b MS. þæm: em. Grundtvig.
1510a MS. swecte: em. Kemble.
1513a No gap in MS.: "in" supplied by Thorpe.
1520b MS. hord swenge: em. Grundtvig and Trautmann.
1531a MS. wundel mæl, with second "l" corrected from "g": em. Kemble.

Then the angry sea-wolf   swam to the bottom,
carried to her den   the lord of those rings,
clutched him so hard   he might not draw sword,
—no matter how brave—   and terrible water-beasts
1510 attacked as they plunged,   strange sea-creatures
with sword-like tusks   thrust at his armor,
monsters tore at him.   The noble prince
then saw he was [in]   some sort of hall,
inhospitable,   where no water reached;
1515 a vaulted roof   kept the rushing flood
from coming down;   he saw firelight,
a flickering blaze,   bright glaring flames.

    Then he saw   the witch of the sea-floor,
towering mere-wife.   He put his whole force
1520 behind his sword-edge,   did not withhold
the two-handed swing;   the sharp ring-patterns
sang hungrily,   whined round her head.
But then he discovered   his battle-flame would not
bite through to kill;   the edge failed its man
1525 at need, though before   in many hand-fights
it often had carved   through strong helmets,
mail-coats of the doomed.   That was the first time
a word could be said   against the great treasure.

    Still he was resolute,   not slow in courage,
1530 remembered his fame,   the kinsman of Hygelac.
The angry champion   threw away the sword,
bejeweled, ring-patterned;   it lay on the ground,
strong, bright-edged.   His own strength he trusted,
the strength of his hand-grip.   So must a man,
1535 if he thinks at battle   to gain any name,
a long-living fame,   care nothing for life.
Then he seized her shoulder   —welcomed that feud—

Gūð-Gēata lēod   Grendles mōdor;
brægd þā beadwe heard,   þā hē gebolgen wæs,
1540 feorh-genīðlan,   þæt hēo on flet gebēah.
Hēo him eft hraþe   hand-lēan forgeald
grimman grāpum,   ond him togēanes fēng;
oferwearp þā wērig-mōd   wigena strengest,
fēþe-cempa,   þæt hē on fylle wearð.

1545 Ofsæt þā þone sele-gy*st*   ond hyre seax getēah,
brād, brūn-ecg;   wolde hire bearn wrecan,
āngan eaferan.   Him on eaxle læg
brēost-net brōden;   þæt gebearh fēore,
wið ord ond wið ecge   ingang forstōd.

1550 Hæfde ðā forsīðod   sunu Ecgþēowes
und*er* gynne grund,   Gēata cempa,
nemne him heaðo-byrne   helpe gefremede,
here-net hearde,   ond hālig God
gewēold wīg-sigor;   wītig Drihten,
1555 rodera Rǣdend,   hit on ryht gescēd
ȳðelīce,   syþðan hē eft āst*ō*d.

XXIII   Geseah ðā on searwum   sige-ēadig bil,
eald sweord eotenisc   ecgum þȳhtig,
wigena weorð-mynd;   þæt [*wæs*] wǣpna cyst,
1560 būton hit wæs māre   ðonne ǣnig mon ōðer
tō beadu-lāce   ætberan meahte,
gōd ond geatolīc,   gīganta geweorc.
Hē gefēng þā fetel-hilt,   freca Scyldinga,
hrēoh ond heoro-grim,   hring-mǣl gebrægd
1565 aldres orwēna,   yrringa *s*lōh
þæt hire wið halse   heard grāpode
bān-hringas bræc;   bil eal ðurhwōd
fǣgne flǣsc-homan;   hēo on flet gecrong,
sweord wæs swātig,   secg weorce gefeh.
1570   Līxte se lēoma,   lēoht inne stōd,
efne swā of hefene   hādre scīneð

1541b Usually em. to "andlēan" (requital, payment) following Rieger,
but see line 2094 and Commentary, p. 336.
1545b MS. seaxe: em. Ettmüller.
1559b No gap in MS.: added by Kemble.

the man of the War-Geats   against Grendel's mother,
combat-hardened,   now that he was battle-furious,
1540   threw his opponent   so she fell to the ground.
Up again quickly,   she gave him hand-payment
with a terrible crush,   again grabbed him tight.
Then that strongest man   of champions afoot
stumbled wearily   so he fell to the ground.
1545   She sat on her hall-guest   and drew her broad knife,
a sharp weapon,   to buy back her son,
her only kinsman.   Across his chest
lay the iron net;   it saved his life
as she hacked and stabbed,   would give her no entry.
1550   The warrior Geat   might have perished then,
Ecgtheow's son,   somewhere under the earth,
had not his war-shirt   given good help,
hard ring-netting,   and holy God
controlled the fight,   the mighty Lord,
1555   Ruler of skies,   decided it rightly,
easily, once   he stood up again.
XXIII   Then he saw among the armor   a victory-bright blade
made by the giants,   an uncracking edge,
an honor for its bearer,   the best of weapons,
1560   but longer and heavier   than any other man
could ever have carried   in the play of war-strokes,
ornamented, burnished,   from Weland's smithy.
The bold Scylding drew it   from its magic scabbard,
savage in battle-lust,   despairing of life,
1565   angrily raised   the shearer of life-threads,
swung hard on her throat,   broke through the spine,
halved the doomed body;   she toppled to the ground:
the sword was blood-wet,   the man rejoiced.
1570   Then the cave-light shone out,   a gleam from within,
even as from heaven   comes the shining light

rodores candel.   Hē æfter recede *w*lāt;
hwearf þā be wealle,   wǣpen hafena*de*
heard be hiltum   Higelāces ðegn,
1575 yrre *ond* ān-rǣd.   Næs sēo ecg fracod
hilde-rince,   ac hē hraþe wolde
Grendle forgyldan   gūð-rǣsa *f*ela
ðāra þe hē geworhte   tō West-Denum
*oft*or micle   ðonne on ænne sīð
1580 þonne hē *Hr*ōðgāres   heorð-genēatas
slōh on sweo*f*ote,   slǣpende frǣt
folces Denigea   fȳf-tȳne men,
ond ōðer swylc   ūt offerede,
lāðlicu lāc.   Hē him þæs lēan forgeald,
1585 rēþe cempa,   tō ðæs þe hē on ræste geseah
gūð-wērigne   Grendel licgan,
aldor-lēasne,   swā him ǣr gescōd
hild æt Heorote.   Hrā wīde sprong,
syþðan hē æfter dēaðe   drepe þrōwade,
1590 heoro-sweng heardne,   ond hine þā hēafde becearf.
Sōna þæt gesāwon   snottre ceorlas,
þā ðe mid Hrōðgāre   on hol*m* *wliton,*
þæt wæs ȳð-geblond   eal gemenged,
brim b*lōde* fāh.   Blonden-feaxe
1595 gomele ymb gōdne   ongeador sprǣcon,
þæt hig þæs æðelinges   eft ne wēndon,
þæt hē sige-hrēðig   sēcean cōme
mǣrne þēoden;   þā ðæs monige gewearð
þæt hine sēo brim-wylf   ābroten hæ*f*de.
1600 Ðā cōm nōn dæges.   Næs ofgēafon
hw*ate* Scyldingas;   gewāt him hām þonon
gold-*wine* gumena.   Gistas sē[*t*]an
mōdes sēoce,   ond o*n* mere staredon;
wīston ond ne wēndon   þæt hīe heora wine-drihten
1605 selfne gesāwon.   Þā þæt sweord ongan
æfter heaþo-swāte   hilde-gicelum,
wīg-bil wanian.   Þæt wæs wundra sum,

1599b MS. abreoten: em. Kemble.
1602a MS. secan: em. Grein.

   of God's candle. He looked through the chamber,
   moved along the wall, raised his weapon,
   single-minded, Hygelac's thane,
1575 still in a fury. Nor was that blade idle,
   useless to the warrior, but quickly he meant
   to repay in full each bloody snatching
   Grendel had made, visiting the West-Danes,
   much more often than just the one time
   when fifteen men of the Danish nation,
1580 Hrothgar's beloved hearth-companions,
   he had killed in their beds, ate them sleeping,
   and another fifteen bore off to his lair,
   a hateful gift. A full reward
   for such sinful crimes the fierce champion
1585 paid him back, for there he saw
   Grendel lying battle-weary,
   armless, lifeless from the hurt he'd received
   in the fight at Heorot. The corpse sprang open
   as he cut deep into it after death,
1590 a firm-handed battle-stroke, and chopped off his head.
    Soon the wise men above who gazed with Hrothgar
   at the turbulent water saw blood drifting up,
   a churning foam; the spreading stain
   was dark, lake-wide. The gray-bearded elders
1595 spoke quietly together about the brave Geat;
   they did not think to see him return,
   said he would not come to seek the king again
   with another victory; it seemed to many
   that the wolfish woman had ripped him to pieces.
1600 Then the ninth hour came. The valiant Scyldings
   gave up the cliff-watch; the gold-friend departed,
   went home with his men. The Geatish visitors
   still sat, heartsick, stared at the mere.
   They wished, without hope, they could see their lord,
1605 their great friend himself. Below, that sword
   had begun to melt in battle-bloody icicles;
   that it melted away was as much a marvel

þæt hit eal gemealt   īse gelīcost,
ðonne forstes bend   Fæder onlæteð,
1610 onwindeð wǣl-rāpas,   sē geweald hafað
sǣla ond mǣla;   þæt is sōð Metod.
Ne nōm hē in þǣm wīcum   Weder-Gēata lēod,
māðm-ǣhta mā,   þēh hē þǣr monige geseah,
būton þone hafelan   ond þā hilt somod,
1615 since fāge;   sweord ǣr gemealt,
forbarn brōden-mǣl;   wæs þæt blōd *tō þæs* hāt,
ǣttren ellor-gǣst,   sē *þǣr inne* swealt.
Sōna wæs on sunde,   sē þe *ǣr* æt sæcce gebād
wīg-hryre wrāðra,   wæter up þurhdēaf;
1620 wǣron ȳð-gebland   eal gefǣlsod,
ēacne eardas,   þā se ellor-*g*āst
oflēt līf-dagas   ond þās lǣnan gesceaft.
Cōm þā tō lande   lid-manna helm
swīð-mōd swymman,   sǣ-lāce gefeah,
1625 mægen-*byr*þenne   þāra þe hē him mid hæfde.
Ēodon him þā tōgēanes,   Gode þancodon,
ðrȳðlīc þegna hēap,   þēodnes gefēgon
þæs þe hī hyne gesundne   gesēon mōston.
Đā wæs of þǣm hrōran   helm ond byrne
1630 lungre ālȳsed.   Lagu drūsade,
wæter under wolcnum,   wæl-drēore fāg.
Fērdon forð þonon   fēþe-lāstum,
ferhþum fægne,   fold-weg mǣton,
cūþe strǣte;   cyning-balde men
1635 from þǣm holm-clife   hafelan bǣron
earfoðlīce   heora ǣghwæþrum
fela-mōdigra;   fēower scoldon
on þǣm wæl-stenge   weorcum geferian
to þǣm gold-sele   Grendles hēafod,
1640 oþðæt semninga   tō sele cōmon
frome, fyrd-hwate   fēower-tyne
Gēata gongan;   gu*m*-dryhten mid
mōdig on gemonge   meod*o*-wongas trǣd.

1617b "ellor" corrected from "ellen" by the same hand; MS. *inne* from Thorkelin B only.

       as ice itself   when the Father unwinds
       the bonds of frost,   loosens the freezing
1610 chains of water,   Who keeps the power
       of times and seasons;   He is the true God.
       The man of the Weders   took nothing more
       from the dark gift-hall,   despite heaped treasure,
       except that head   and the hilt, jewel-bright.
1615 Already the sword   had melted away,
       its blade had burned up;   too hot the blood
       of the poisonous spirit   who had died within.
       And soon he was swimming   who at battle withstood
       the mortal attacks   of two evil creatures,
1620 rose through the waters;   the currents were cleared,
       the broad expanse,   now the alien spirit
       had finished her days   and this fleeting life.
          And thus the man came,   protector of sailors,
       strong swimmer, to land;   rejoiced in the weight
1625 of the great water-booty   he carried with him.
       They clustered around him,   his thanes in their armor,
       gave thanks to God   for return of their prince,
       that they saw him alive,   happy and whole.
       From the mighty man   they took shirt and helmet,
1630 quickly unstrapped him.   The waters subsided,
       the lake beneath clouds   still stained with blood.
       Then they left that place   by the narrow path.
       They marched glad-hearted,   followed the trail,
       reached familiar ground;   brave as kings,
1635 they carried that head   away from the cliff
       —it was hard going   for both pairs of men,
       stout-hearted warriors—   four men it took
       to raise on a war-spear   Grendel's head,
       laboriously guide it   back to the gold-hall.
1640 In marching formation   they came to the hall-door,
       the fourteen Geat-men,   brave, battle-ready,
       and the lord of those men   marched right among them;
       proud with retainers   he came across fields.

Ðā cōm in gān   ealdor ðegna,
1645 dǣd-cēne mon   dōme gewurþad,
hæle hilde-dēor,   Hrōðgār grētan.
Þā wæs be feaxe   on flet boren
Grendles hēafod,   þǣr guman druncon,
egeslīc *for* eorlum   ond þǣre idese mid,
1650 wlite-sēon wrǣtlīce   weras on sāwon.
XXIIII   Bēowulf maþelode,   bearn Ecgþēowe*s*:
"Hwæt, wē þē þās sǣ-lāc,   sunu Healfden*es*,
lēod Scyldinga,   lustum brōhton,
tīres tō tācne,   þe þū hēr tō lōcast.
1655 Ic þæt unsōfte   ealdre gedīgde,
wigge under wætere,   weorc genēþde
earfoðlīce;   ǣtrihte wæs
gūð getwǣfed,   nymðe mec God scylde.
Ne meahte ic æt hilde   mid Hruntinge
1660 wiht gewyrcan,   þēah þæt wǣpen dūge;
ac mē geūðe   ylda Waldend
þæt ic on wāge geseah   wlitig *ha*ngian
eald-sweord ēacen   —oftost wīsode
*w*inigea lēasum—   þæt ic ðȳ wǣpne gebrǣd.
1665 *O*fslōh ðā æt þǣre sæcce,   þā mē sǣl *ā*geald,
hūses hyrdas.   Þā þæt hilde-bil
for*ba*rn, brogden-mǣl,   swā þæt blōd gesprang,
*hā*tost heaþo-swāta.   Ic þæt hilt þanan
fēon*d*um ætferede,   fyren-dǣda wræc,
1670 dēað-*c*wealm Denigea,   swā hit gedēfe wæs.
Ic *hit* þē þonne gehāte,   þæt þū on Heorote mōst
sorh-lēas swefan   mid þīnra secga gedryht
ond þegna gehwylc   þīnra lēoda,
duguðe ond iogoþe,   þæt þū him ondrǣdan ne þearft,
1675 þēoden Scyldinga,   on þā healfe,
aldor-bealu eorlum,   swā þū ǣr dydest."
Ðā wæs gylden hilt   gamelum rince,
hārum hild-fruman   on hand gyfen,
enta ǣr-geweorc;   hit on ǣht gehwearf
1680 æfter dēofla hryre   Denigea frēan,
wundor-smiþa geweorc;   ond þā þās worold ofgeaf
grom-heort guma,   Godes andsaca,

That prince of thanes   then entered the hall,
1645 brave in his deed,   honored in fame,
a man battle-tested,   he greeted Hrothgar.
Then Grendel's head   was dragged by its hair
across the floor to the benches   where warriors drank,
to the nobles and queen,   terrible before them.
1650 All the men stared   at the awesome sight.
XXIIII   Ecgtheow's son   then addressed the king:
"Behold, son of Healfdene,   Scylding leader,
this gift from the sea   we have brought you gladly,
a token of victory,   which you look on here.
1655 Not very easily   did I save my life
in battle under water;   performed this work
with greatest trouble;   at once the fight
was decided against me,   except that God saved me.
In that battle   I could not use Hrunting
1660 though that weapon   is still good,
but the Ruler of men   granted the favor
that I see on the wall   a bright sword hanging,
gigantic heirloom   —most often He guides
the friendless, distressed—   so that I found
1665 the right weapon to draw.   When my chance came
I cut down the monsters,   those hall-guards, with edges;
the wave-sword burned up,   quenched in that blood,
a hot battle-pouring.   From my enemies
I plundered this hilt,   revenged their crimes,
1670 the many Danes killed,   as was only fitting.
Now I can promise you   safe nights in Heorot
without further sorrow,   with the men of your troop,
and each dear retainer   picked from your people,
the youths and the veterans;   you will have no need,
1675 O lord of the Scyldings,   for fear in that matter,
dark man-killing,   as you did before."
Then the strange gold hilt   was placed in the hand
of the gray-bearded king,   wise war-leader,
old work of giants;   after the fall of devils
1680 it came to the hands   of the lord of the Dane-men,
from magic smithies;   once the fierce spirit,
long God's opponent,   guilty creature,

    morðres scyldig,   ond his mōdor ēac;
    on geweald gehwearf   worold-cyninga
1685 ðǣm sēlestan   be sǣm twēonum,
    ðāra þe on Sceden-igge   *sceat*tas dǣlde.
     Hrōðgār maþelode,   hylt scēawode,
    ealde lāfe,   on ðǣm wæs ōr *wri*ten
    fyrn-gewinnes,   syðþan flōd of*slōh*,
1690 gifen gēotende,   gīganta cyn;
    frēcne *ge*fērdon;   þæt wæs fremde þēod
    ēcean Dryh*tne*;   him þæs ende-lēan
    þurh wæteres wylm   Waldend sealde.
    Swā wæs on ðǣm scen*num*   scīran goldes
1695 þurh rūn-stafas   rihte *ge*mearcod,
    geseted ond gesǣd,   hwām þæt sweo*rd* geworht,
    īrena cyst,   ǣrest wǣre,
    wreo*þ*en-hilt ond wyrm-fāh.   Ðā se wīsa spræc,
    *su*nu Healfdenes—   swīgedon ealle:
1700 "Þæt lā mæg secgan,   sē þe sōð ond riht
    fremeð on folce,   feor eal gemon,
    eald eðel-wea*rd*,   þæt ðes eorl wǣre
    geboren betera!   Blǣd *is* ārǣred
    geond wīd-wegas,   wine mīn Bēo*wulf*,
1705 ðīn ofer þēoda gehwylce.   Eal þū hit geþyldum
                   healdest,
    mægen mid mōdes snyttrum.   Ic þē sceal mīne
                   gelǣstan
    frēode, swā wit furðum sprǣcon.   Ðū scealt tō frōfre
                 weorþan
    eal lang-twīdig   lēodum þīnum
    *hæle*ðum tō helpe.   Ne wearð Heremōd *swā*
1710 eaforum Ecgwelan,   Ār-Scyldingum;
    *ne ge*wēox hē him tō willan,   ac tō wæl-fea*lle*
    ond tō dēað-cwalum   Deniga lēodum.
    Brēat *bol*gen-mōd   bēod-genēatas,
    eaxl-ge*st*eallan,   oþþæt hē āna hwearf,
1715 mǣre þēo*den*,   mon-drēamum from,

1686a MS. sce deninge, with second "n" altered to "g" by same hand.

and his murderous mother   had quitted this world,
it came to the power   of the best overlord
1685 between the two seas,   of all world-rulers
in Scandinavia   who gave good treasures.
    Hrothgar spoke,   examined the hilt,
great treasure of old.   There was engraved
the origin of past strife,   when the flood drowned,
1690 the pouring ocean killed   the race of giants.
Terribly they suffered,   were a people strange
to eternal God;   their final payment
the Ruler sent them   by the rushing waters.
On its bright gold facings   there were also runes
1695 set down in order,   engraved, inlaid,
which told for whom   the sword was first worked,
its hair-keen edges,   twisted gold
scrolled in the hilt,   the woven snake-blade.
Then all were quiet.   Wise Hrothgar spoke:
1700 "Now can he say,   who acts in truth
and right for his people,   remembers our past,
old guard of homeland: this prince was born
the better man!   Your glorious name
is raised on high   over every nation,
1705 Beowulf my friend,   your fame spreads far.
Steadily you govern   your strength with wisdom.
I will keep a friend's vows,   as we said before.
You shall become   a help to your people,
a long-lasting hero.   Not so was Heremod
1710 to the sons of Ecgwela,   the Honor-Scyldings;
grew not to their joy,   but killed Danish men
in his own hall, bloodily.   Swollen in heart,
he cut down companions,   raging at table,
till exiled, alone,   a famous prince,
1715 was sent from man's joys,   notoriously bad,

ðēah þe hine *mi*htig God   mægenes wynnum,
eafeþum *st*ēpte,   ofer ealle men
forð gefreme*de*.   Hwæþere him on ferhþe grēow
brēost-*h*ord blōd-rēow;   nallas bēagas geaf
1720 De*n*um æfter dōme;   drēam-lēas gebād,
þæt hē þæs gewinnes   weorc þrōwade,
lēod-bea*l*o longsum.   Ðū þē lær be þon,
gum-cyste ongit!   Ic þis gid be þē
āwræc wintrum frōd.   Wundor is tō secganne,
1725 hū mihtig God   manna cynne
þurh sīdne sefan   snyttru bryttað,
eard ond eorlscipe;   hē āh ealra geweald.
Hwīlum hē on lufan   læteð hworfan
monnes mōd-geþonc   mæran cynnes,
1730 seleð him on ēþle   eorþan wynne
tō healdanne,   hlēo-burh wera,
gedēð him swā gewealdene   worold*e dæ*las,
sīde rīce,   þæt hē his selfa ne *mæg*
for his unsnyttrum   ende geþencean.
1735 Wunað hē on wiste,   nō hine wiht dweleð
ād*l* nē yldo,   nē him inwit-sorh
on sefa[*n*] sweorceð,   nē gesacu ōhwær
ecg-he*te* ēoweð,   ac him eal worold
wendeð on *wil*lan.   Hē þæt wyrse ne con,
XXV   oðþæt him on innan   ofer-hygda dæl
1740   we*axe*ð ond wrīdað,   þonne se weard swefeð,
sāwele hy*rde*;   bið sē slæp tō fæst,
bisgum gebunde*n*,   bona swīðe nēah,
sē þe of flān-boga*n*   fyrenum scēoteð.
1745 Þonne bið on hreþre   under helm drepen
biteran stræle   —him bebeorgan ne con—
wōm wundor-bebodum   wergan gāstes;
þinceð him tō lȳtel   þæt hē lange heold,

1737a MS. sefað from Thorkelin A and B: em. Grundtvig.

1741a MS. we*axe*ð from Grundtvig's examination of the MS. in 1829 (Malone, *NC*, p. 73).

1748b MS. he to lange: Zupitza and Malone claim erasure of this second "tō" in the line as a scribal error. Wrenn sees only discoloration and retains

                    though God had given him   the joys of great strength,
                    had set him, mighty,   above all men.
                    Despite good fortune   his thought grew savage,
                    his heart blood-thirsty;   never a ring
    1720   did he give, for glory,   to the Danish men.
                    Joyless he lived   and unhappy he died,
                    suffering long   for that harm to his people.
                    From this may you learn   a man's true virtues!
                    For your sake I tell it,   wise in my years.
    1725   It is always a wonder   how God the Almighty
                    in His full understanding   deals out to men
                    their wisdom of mind,   their lands, nobility.
                    He rules everything.   Sometimes He lets
                    a high-born heart   travel far in delight,
    1730   gives a man holdings,   joy of his birthright,
                    stronghold of nobles,   puts in his control
                    great tracts of land,   such wide kingdoms
                    that lacking true wisdom   he cannot imagine
                    his rule at an end.   Happily he lives
    1735   from feast to feast.   No thought of harm
                    from illness, age,   or malicious tongues
                    darkens his mind,   nor does conflict anywhere
                    sharpen its blade,   but the whole world
    XXV ⎱ turns to his pleasure.   He knows no worse
    1740 ⎰ until, within him,   his portion of arrogance
                    begins to increase,   when his guardian sleeps,
                    the soul's shepherd.   Too sound is that sleep,
                    bound up in cares;   the killer very near
                    who shoots his bow   with treacherous aim.
    1745   Then he is hit in the heart,   struck under helmet
                    with the bitter arrow,   the dark commands
                    of the wicked demon,   and he knows no defense.
                    Too brief it seems,   that long time he ruled.

"tō" in his text. Either paleographical judgment affects the moral force of the
passage.

gȳtsað grom-hȳdig,   nallas on gylp seleð
1750 fǣdde bēagas,   ond hē þā forð-gesceaft
forgyteð ond forgȳmeð,   þæs þē him ǣr God sealde,
wuldres Waldend,   weorð-mynda dǣl.
Hit on ende-stæf   eft gelimpeð
þæt se līc-homa   *lǣne* gedrēoseð,
1755 fǣge gefealleð;   fēhð oþer *tō*,
sē þe unmurnlīce   mādmas dǣleþ
*eorl*es ǣr-gestrēon,   egesan ne gȳmeð.
Bebeorh þē ðone bealo-nīð,   Bēowulf lēofa,
secg betsta,   ond þē þæt sēlre gecēos,
1760 ēce rǣdas;   *of*er-hȳda ne gȳm,
mǣre cempa!   Nū is þīnes *mægn*es blǣd
āne hwīle;   eft sōna bið
þæt *þec* ādl oððe ecg   eafoþes getwǣfeð,
oððe *fȳr*es feng   oððe flōdes wylm
1765 oððe gripe *mēc*es   oððe gāres fliht
oððe atol yldo,   *oð*ðe ēagena bearhtm
forsiteð ond forsworceð;   semninga bið,
þæt ðeɔ, dryht-guma,   dēað oferswȳðeð.
    "Swā ic Hring-Dena   hund missēra
1770 wēold under wolcnum,   ond hig wigge belēac
manigum mægþa   geond þysne middan-geard,
æscum ond ecgum,   þæt ic mē ænigne
under swegles begong   gesacan ne tealde.
Hwæt mē þæs on ēþle   edwend[e]n cwōm,
1775 gyrn æfter gomene,   seoþðan Grendel wearð,
eald-gewinna   ingenga mīn;
ic þǣre sōcne   singāles wæg
mōd-ceare micle.   Þæs sig Metode þanc,
ēcean *Dryht*ne,   þæs ðe ic on aldre gebād,
1780 þæt ic on *þone* hafelan   heoro-drēorigne
ofer eal*d gew*in   ēagum starige!
Gā nū tō setle,   *sym*bel-wynne drēoh
wīg-geweorþad;   unc sceal worn fela

1750a Often em. fæ[tt]e (Thorpe), but the MS. form is an acceptable variant.
1774b MS. ed wendan: em. Grein.

Angry and covetous,   he gives no rings
1750 to honor his men.   His future state
is forgotten, forsworn,   and so is God's favor,
his portion of honor   from Heaven's hall-ruler.
Then it finally happens,   the body decays,
his life-house fails him,   only a loan;
1755 death-doomed, he falls.   Another succeeds him,
reckless, unmourning,   gives out his gifts,
the noble's old treasures;   heeds not, nor fears.
Guard against   that awful curse,
beloved Beowulf,   finest noble,
1760 and choose the better,   eternal gains.
Turn not to pride,   O brave champion!
Your fame lives now,   in one strong time.
Soon in their turn   sickness or war
will break your strength,   or the grip of fire,
1765 overwhelming wave,   or sword's swing,
a thrown spear,   or hateful old age;
the lights will darken   that were your eyes.
Death overcomes you   all at once, warrior.
   "Thus, fifty winters,   I ruled the Ring-Danes
1770 under these skies   and by my war-strength
kept them safe   from spear and sword
throughout middle-earth—   such rule that no one
under the heavens   was my adversary.
And look, even so,   in my homestead, reversal:
1775 —if joy, then sorrow—   once Grendel became
my nightly invader,   our ancient enemy.
I bore great heart-care,   suffered continually
from his persecution.   Thanks be to God,
the Eternal Lord,   I came through alive,
1780 and today may look   at this huge bloody head
with my own eyes,   after long strife!
Go now to your seat,   enjoy the feast,
honored by your battle.   Many are the treasures

māþma gemǣnra,   siþðan *mor*gen bið."

1785   Gēat wæs glæd-mōd,   gēong sōn*a* tō,
setles nēosan,   swā se snottra heht.
Þ*ā wæs* eft swā ǣr   ellen-rōfum,
flet-sittendum   fægere gereorded
nīowan stefne.   Ni*ht*-helm geswearc

1790 deorc ofer dryht-gu*mum*.   Duguð eal ārās;
wolde blonden-feax   beddes nēosan,
gamela Scylding.   Gēat unigmetes wēl,
rōfne rand-wigan,   restan ly*ste*.
Sōna him sele-þegn   sīðes wērgum,

1795 feorran-cundum   forð wīsade,
sē for andrysnum   ealle beweote[*d*]e
þegnes þearfe,   swylce þȳ dōgore
heaþo-līðende   habban scoldon.

        Reste hine þā rūm-heort;   reced hlīuade
1800 gēap ond gold-fāh;   gæst inne swæf
oþþæt hrefn blaca   heofones wynne
blīð-heort bododade.   *Ðā cōm* beorht scacan
[*scīma ofer sceadwa;*]   scaþan ōnetton,
*wæro*n æþelingas   eft tō lēodum

1805 fūse tō *farenne*;   wolde feor þanon
cuma col*len-*ferhð   cēoles nēosan.
Heht þā se hear*da* *H*runting beran
sunu Ecglāfes,   heht *his* sweord niman,
lēoflīc īren;   sægde him *þæs* lēanes þanc,

1810 cwæð, hē þone gūð-wine   *gō*dne tealde,
wīg-cræftigne,   nales *word*um lōg
mēces ecge;   þæt wæs mōdig secg.
Ond þā sīð-frome,   searwum gearwe
wīgend wǣron;   ēode weorð Denum

1815 æþeling tō yppan,   *þēr* se ōþer wæs,
h[*æ*]le hilde-dēor   Hrōðgār grētte.

1796b   MS. beweotene: em. Grundtvig.
1803a   No gap in MS: conjectural restoration by Klaeber, trans. "the brightness (of dawn) across the shadows."
1805a   MS. *far*ene ne from Thorkelin B: em. Kemble.
1816a   MS. helle: em. Kemble.

     to be divided when morning returns."
1785 Blithe in his heart, the Geat moved at once
     to take his seat as the wise king bade.
     Then again as before, for the courage-famed,
     holders of the hall, a second feast came,
     with as many delights. The protecting dark
1790 came down on the hall-thanes. All the men rose.
     The gray-haired king was ready for bed,
     the aged Scylding. Immeasurably tired,
     ready for sleep, was the great Geat warrior.
     At once a hall-thane led him forth,
1795 weary from his venture; with every courtesy
     tended the needs of the noble foreigner,
     provided such comforts as battle-voyagers
     used to have in those days.
      Then the great-hearted man slept undisturbed.
1800 The hall towered high, golden in darkness.
     The guest slept within till the black raven,
     the blithe-hearted, announced the dawn,
     heaven's joy. Then sunrise came
     and the warriors prepared to return to their people;
1805 the brave visitor would set his sail
     for their far land, hoped soon to see it.
     Then the valiant Geat asked Ecglaf's son
     to carry Hrunting, keep the great sword,
     cherished iron; thanked him for the loan,
1810 said he thought it a good war-friend,
     strong in battle, did not blame its edges.
     Beowulf was noble, generous in spirit.
     And then the travelers were ready to leave,
     equipped in their harness; their Dane-honored prince
1815 marched to the high seat where the other leader
     was sitting in state; the hero saluted him.

XXVI   *Bē*owulf maþelode,   bearn Ecgþēowes:
      "Nū *w*ē sæ-līðend   secgan wyllað,
      feorran cumene,   þæt wē fundiaþ
1820 Higelāc sēcan.   Wǣron hēr tela,
      willum bewenede;   þū ūs wēl dohtest.
      Gif ic þonne on eorþan   ōwihte mæg
      þīnre mōd-lufan   māran tilian,
      gumena dryhten,   ðonne ic gȳt dyde,
1825 gūð-geweorca,   ic bēo gearo sōna.
      Gif ic þæt gefricge   ofer flōda begang
      þæt þec ymb-sittend   egesan þȳwað,
      swā þec hete*nde*   hwīlum dydon,
      ic ðē þūsenda   þegna bri*nge*,
1830 hæleþa tō helpe.   Ic on Higelāce wāt,
      Gēata dryhten,   þēah ðe hē geong sȳ,
      folces hyrde,   þæt hē mec fremman wile
      wordum ond worcum,   þæt ic þē wēl heri*ge*
      ond þē tō gēoce   gār-holt bere,
1835 mægenes fultum,   þǣr ðē bið manna þearf.
      G*if* him þonne Hrēþrīc   tō hofum Gēata
      geþinge[ð], þēodnes bēarn,   hē mæg þǣr *f*ela
      frēonda findan;   feor-cȳþðe bēoð
      sēlran gesōhte   þǣm þe him selfa dea*h*."
1840   Hrōðgār maþelode   him ond andsware:
      "Þē þā word-cwydas   wigtig Drihten
      on sefan sende;   ne hȳrde ic snotorlīcor
      on swā geongum feore   guman þingian.
      Þū eart mægenes strang   ond on mōde frōd,
1845 wīs word-cwida.   Wēn ic talige,
      gif þæt gegangeð,   þæt ðe gār nymeð,
      hild heoru-grimme   Hrēþles eaferan,
      ādl oþðe īren   ealdor ðīnne,
      folces hyrda,   ond þū þīn feorh hafast,
1850 þæt þe Sǣ-Gēatas   sēlran næbben

1833a MS. weordum: em. Thorpe and refined by Dobbie, p. 309.
1836a MS. hreþrinc: em. Grundtvig.
1837a MS. geþinged: em. Grein.

XXVI   Beowulf spoke,   Ecgtheow's son:
         "Now we voyagers,   coming from afar,
         would like to say   that we wish to seek
1820   our Hygelac again.   We have been entertained
         most properly, kindly,   brought every good thing
         we could possibly ask.   You have dealt well with us.
         If ever I can do   anything on earth
         to gain your love more,   lord of warriors,
1825   than my fighting thus far,   I will do it at once.
         If I ever hear,   across the far seas,
         that neighboring peoples   threaten you with battle,
         as enemies have moved   against you before,
         I will bring to your side   a thousand thanes,
1830   warriors to help you.   I know this of Hygelac,
         lord of the Geat-men,   young though he is,
         our nation's shepherd,   that he would support me
         in word and deed,   that I might continue
         to show you honor,   by help of spear-wood
1835   aid you with strength   when you need men.
         If, on the other hand,   Hrethric decides,
         a king's son,   to come to our court,
         he will find only friends.   Distant lands
         are the better sought   by one himself good."
1840   Hrothgar replied,   made a speech in answer:
         "The all-wise Lord   has sent these words
         into your mind.   No man wiser
         have I ever heard speak   so young in years:
         great in your strength,   mature in thought,
1845   and wise in your speeches.   If the son of Hrethel
         should ever be taken   in blood-angry battle,
         sickness, the sword   or spear kill your lord
         and you should still live,   I would fully expect
         the Geats could not choose   a better king
1850   anywhere alive,   a hoard-guard for heroes,

tō gecēosen*ne* cyning ǣnigne,
hord-weard hæleþa, *gyf* þū healdan wylt
māga rīce. Mē þīn *m*ōd-sefa
līcaðˀ leng swā wēl, lēofa Bēowulf.
1855 Hafast þū gefēred þæt þām folcum *s*ceal,
Gēata lēodum ond Gār-Denum,
sib gemǣn[*e*], ond sacu restan,
inwit-nīþas, þe hīe ǣr drugon,
wesan, þenden ic weal*de* wīdan rīces,
1860 māþmas gemǣne, ma*n*ig ōþerne
gōdum gegrēttan ofer ganotes bæðˀ;
sceal hring-naca ofer *h*ea[*f*]u bringan
lāc ond luf-tācen. Ic þā *l*ēode wāt
gē wiðˀ fēond gē wiðˀ frēond fæste geworhte,
1865 ǣghwæs untǣle eal*de* wīsan."
  Ðā gīt him eorla hlēo inne gesealde,
mago Healfdenes māþmas twelfe,
hēt [*h*]ine mid þǣm lācum lēode swǣse
sēcean on gesyntum, snūde eft cuman.
1870 Gecyste þā cyning æþelum gōd,
þēoden Scyldinga ðegn betstan
ond be healse genam; hruron him tēaras,
blonden-feaxum. Him wæs bēga wēn,
ealdum infrōdum, ōþres swīðˀor,
1875 þæt h[*ī*]e seoððˀ*an* [*nā*] gesēon mōston,
mōdige on meþle. *Wæs* him se man tō þon lēof,
þæt hē þone *brēost*-wylm forberan ne mehte
ac him *on* hreþre hyge-bendum fæst

1857a MS. *ge* mænum: em. Eduard Sïevers, *PBB* 9 (1884), 40.

1862b MS. *h*ea þu: em. Kluge. The MS. reading "ofer heaþu" could mean "after the war"; cf. line 1781.

1868a MS. inne: em. Thorpe.

1875a MS. he seoððˀa.: Kemble (1835) saw the final "n." Em. and trans. from Grundtvig, Thorpe, Kluge, and Bugge. Alternatively, W. S. Mackie, *MLR* 34 (1939), 524, would keep "hē" and em. to "mōst[*e*]." Then trans. "that he (Hrothgar) would never again see the brave men in the assembly." Either emendation, to the singular or the plural, affects interpretation of Hrothgar's character. See Commentary, p. 347.

1876b MS. *.æs*: Thorkelin A *þæs* but Kemble saw *wæs*.

   if it pleased you to rule the land of your people.
   Your character pleases me better each moment,
   my dearest Beowulf. You have brought it to pass
1855 that peace-bond, friendship, shall tie our peoples,
   Geats and Spear-Danes, in common kinship,
   and strife shall sleep, malicious attacks
   which they weathered before; so long as I rule
   this broad kingdom we shall give treasures,
1860 and many shall greet each other with gifts
   across the gannet's bath. The ring-necked boat
   shall carry overseas gifts of friendship,
   the strongest tokens. I know our peoples
   will stand fast knitted toward friend and foe,
1865 blameless in everything, as in the old manner."
    Then still in the hall the shield-guard of nobles,
   kinsman to Healfdene, gave him twelve treasures,
   bade him go with gifts, seek his own dear people,
   journey safely, and come back quickly.
1870 Then the good king, of a noble race,
   great Scylding prince, held that best thane
   round the neck and kissed him; his tears ran down,
   streaked his gray beard. Wise in his age,
   he expected two things, but one the more strongly,
1875 that never again would they look on each other
   as in this brave meeting. That man was so dear
   that he could not withhold those deep tears;
   fixed in his heart by the bonds of thought,

æfter dēorum men   dyrne langað
1880 beorn wið blōde.   Him Bēowulf þanan,
      gūð-rinc gold-wlanc,   græs-moldan træd
      since hrēmig;   sǣ-genga bād
      āge[*n*]d-frēan,   sē *þe* on ancre rād.
      Þā wæs on gange   gi*fu* Hrōðgāres
1885 oft geæhted;   þæt wæs ān cyning,
      æghwæs orleahtre,   oþþæt hin*e* yldo benam
      mægenes wynnum,   sē þe oft manegum scōd.

XXVII   Cwōm þā tō flōde   fela-mōdigra,
      hæg-stealdra [*hēap*];   hring-net bæron,
1890 locene leoðo-syrcan.   Land-weard onfand
      eft-sīð eorla,   swā hē ær dyde;
      nō hē mid hearme   of hliðes nosan
      gæs[*tas*] grētte,   ac him tōgēanes rād,
      cwæð þæt wil-cuman   Wedera lēodum
1895 sca*þan* scīr-hame   tō scipe fōron.
      Þā wæs *on* sande   sǣ-gēap naca
      hladen here-*wǣ*dum,   hringed-stefna,
      mēarum ond māð*m*um;   mæst hlīfade
      ofer Hrōðgāres   *h*ord-gestrēonum.
1900 Hē þæm bāt-wearde   *bun*den golde
      swurd geseade,   þæt hē syð*þan* wæs
      on meodu-bence   māþm[*e*] þȳ weorþr[*a*],
      yrfe-lāfe.   Gewāt him on naca,
      *d*rēfan dēop wæter,   Dena land ofgeaf.
1905 Þā wæs be mæste   mere-hrægla sum,
      segl sāle fæst;   sund-wudu þunede;
      nō þær wēg-flotan   wind ofer ȳðum
      sīðes getwæfde;   sǣ-genga fōr,
      flēat fāmig-heals   forð ofer ȳðe,
1910 bunden-stefna   ofer brim-strēamas,
      þæt hīe Gēata clifu   ongitan meahton

1883a   MS. aged: em. Kemble.
1889a   No gap in MS.: conjectural restoration by Grein.
1893a   MS. gæs.....: restored by Grundtvig.
1902b   MS. maþma þy weorþre: em. Thorpe.
1903b   MS. nacan: em. Rieger.

a deep-felt longing   for the beloved man
1880 burned in his blood.   Then Beowulf left him,
a fighter gold-proud,   rejoicing in treasure,
marched over the turf.   Their long-ship waited,
ready for its captain,   rode at anchor.
As they traveled seaward,   the gifts of Hrothgar
1885 were often praised.   He was one king
blameless in everything,   till age took from him
the joy of his strength   —a thing that harms many.
XXVII   Then the young soldiers,   brave-hearted men,
came to the ocean,   the locked ring-shirts,
1890 their body-guards, clinking.   The coast-guard saw
the return of the nobles,   as before he had seen
their landing in armor.   No insults reached
the guests from the bluff,   but he rode toward them,
declared that the Weders   would surely welcome
1895 the return of that ship   with bright-armored men.
Wide, sea-worthy,   the ship on the beach
was laden with war-gear,   ring-prowed and tall,
with the treasure and horses.   The high mast towered
over Hrothgar's hoard-gold.   Then Beowulf gave
1900 a sword to the ship-guard,   bound with such gold
that later on the mead-bench   he was the more honored
by that fine treasure,   an heirloom of old.
The hero departed   in his swift-moving ship,
steered for blue water,   set Denmark behind.
1905 The mast was rigged   with the sea-wind's cloak,
great sail in its ropes;   the planking thundered.
No hindrance the wind   behind the crest-glider
as it boomed through the sea,   slid over water,
foamy-necked floater   winging on waves;
1910 its iron-bound prow   cut across currents
until they could see   the cliffs of Geatland,

cūþe næssas;   cēol up geþrang
lyft-geswenced,   on lande stōd.
Hraþe wæs æt holme   hȳð-weard geara,
1915 sē þe ǣr lang*e* tīd   lēofra manna
fūs æt faroðe   *feor* wlātode;
sǣlde tō sande   sīd-fæþme sc*ip*
oncer-bendum fæst,   þȳ lǣs hym ȳþ*a* ðrym
wudu wynsuman   forwrecan *meahte*.
1920 Hēt þā ūp beran   æþelinga gestrē*on*,
frætwe ond fǣt-gold;   næs him feor þan*on*
tō gesēcanne   sinces bryttan,
Higelāc Hrēþling,   þǣr æt hām wunað
selfa mid gesīðum   sǣ-wealle nēah.
1925   Bold w*æs* betlīc,   brego-rōf cyning,
hēa[*h on*] healle,   Hygd swīðe geong,
wīs, wel-þungen,   þēah ð*e* wintra lȳt
under burh-locan   gebide*n* hæbbe
Hǣreþes dohtor;   næs hīo hnāh swā þēah
1930 nē tō gnēað gifa   Gēata lēodum
māþm-gestrēona.   Mōdþrȳðo wæg,
fremu folces cwēn,   firen’ ondrysne.
Nǣnig þæt dorste   dēor genēþan
swǣsra gesīða,   nefne sin-frēa,
1935 þæt hire an dæges   ēagum starede;
ac him wæl-bende   *we*otode tealde,
hand-gewri*þ*ene;   hra*þe seo*þðan wæs
æfter mund-gripe   mēce geþinged,
þæt hit sceāden-mǣl   scȳran *mō*ste,
1940 cwealm-bealu cȳðan.   Ne bið swylc *cwēn*līc þēaw
idese tō efnanne,   þeah ðe *hī*o ǣnlicu sȳ,
þætte freoðu-webbe   fēores *on*sǣce
æfter lige-torne   lēofne mannan.

1918a MS. oncear bendum: em. Grundtvig.
1926a MS. hea halle: em. E. A. Kock, *Anglia* 42 (1918), 116.
1931b MS. mod þrȳðo wæg. Word division and translation follow G. V.
Smithers (1966). See Commentary, p. 349.
1939b Beginning with “mōste,” Scribe II takes over, starting a new MS.
line. See Backgrounds, p. 245.

familiar headlands;   thrust by the wind,
the deep keel drove   hard toward the beach.
There was the harbor-guard,   ready on the shore,
1915 who long had waited,   scanning the ocean
on watch for the men   coming from afar.
The broad-beamed ship   was moored to the beach
by strong anchor-ropes,   that the force of the waves
might not destroy   the handsome wood.
1920 The chief then ordered   the treasure unloaded,
gems, gold plate.   They had not far to go
to find their lord,   the giver of treasures,
Hygelac, Hrethel's son,   who dwelt at home,
in his hall with his thanes,   there near the sea-wall.
1925   His buildings were splendid,   the king a great ruler
mighty in hall,   and Hygd very young,
wise, and courteous,   although few winters
Hæreth's daughter   as yet had passed
within that stronghold.   Nor was she thereby
1930 the more close-fisted,   a niggard in gifts
to men of the Geats.   Modthrytho, however,
that mighty queen,   did terrible crimes.
None of the boldest   among the retainers
dared to approach her,   unless a great lord.
1935 Whoever looked into her eyes   in broad daylight
could count on the garrote,   the death-bonds prepared,
woven by hand,   an arrest, and thereafter
the charge quickly settled   with the edge of a sword;
the sharp shadow-pattern   would suddenly fall,
1940 make known its death-evil.   Not queenly
customs in a lady,   however beautiful—
to take the lives   of beloved men,
a woman, peace-weaver,   inventing false charges.

<pre>
          Hūru þæt onhōhsnod[e]   Hem[m]inges mæg;
1945 ealo-drincende   ōðer sædan,
          þæt hīo lēod-bealewa   læs gefremede,
          inwit-nīða,   syððan ærest wearð
          gyfen gold-hroden   geongum cempan,
          æðelum dīore,   syððan hīo Offan flet
1950 ofer fealone flōd   be fæder lāre
          sīðe gesōhte;   ðær hīo syððan well
          in gum-stōle,   gōde, mære,
          līf-gesceafta   lifigende brēac
          hīold hēah-lufan   wið hæleþa brego,
1955 ealles mon-cynnes   mīne gefræge
          þ[one] sēlestan   bī sæm twēonum,
          eormen-cynnes.   Forðām Offa wæs
          geofum ond gūðum   gār-cēne man,
          wīde geweorðod;   wīsdōme hēold
1960 ēðel sīnne;   þonon Ēom[ē]r wōc
          hæleðum tō helpe,   Hem[m]inges mæg,
          nefa Gārmundes,   nīða cræftig.
XXVIII   Gewāt him ðā se hearda   mid his hond-scole
          sylf æfter sande   sæ-wong tredan,
1965 wīde waroðas;   woruld-candel scān
          sigel sūðan fūs.   Hī sīð drugon,
          elne geēodon,   tō ðæs ðe eorla hlēo,
          bonan Ongenþēoes   burgum in innan,
          geongne gūð-cyning   gōdne gefrūnon
1970 hringas dælan.   Higelāce wæs
          sīð Bēowulfes   snūde gecȳðed,
          þæt ðær on worðig   wīgendra hlēo,
          lind-gestealla   lifigende cwōm,
          heaðo-lāces hāl   tō hofe gongan.
1975 Hraðe wæs gerȳmed,   swā se rīca bebēad,
          fēðe-gestum   flet innanweard.
</pre>

1944 MS. on hohsnod hem ninges: em. Thorpe and Kemble.
1956a MS. þæs: em. Thorpe.
1960b MS. geomor 'sad': em. Thorpe. The name of Offa's son is attested by Bede as Lat. *Eumer,* OE. Ēomǣr.
1961b MS. hem inges: em. Kemble.

The kinsman of Hemming   put a stop to all that.
1945   Men round the table   told more of the story,
said that she caused   less harm to the people,
malicious trouble,   once she was given,
adorned in gold,   to the young champion
of the highest nobility,   once she arrived
1950   on Offa's bright floor   over shining seas;
she made the journey   at her father's bidding.
There she used well   the days of her life,
famous for goodness   upon the high-seat,
kept noble love   toward the leader of heroes,
1955   the best chief,   as I have heard,
in all the world,   from sea to sea.
Therefore that Offa   was honored by nations,
spear-braving warrior,   received a multitude
of victories, gifts;   in wisdom he held
1960   his homeland long.   From him sprang Eomer,
comfort for heroes,   kinsman to Hemming,
grandson of Garmund,   strong man in battle.

XXVIII   Then the tested warrior   amid his men,
hand-picked comrades,   walked up the shore,
1965   the wide sea-beach;   the world-candle shone,
bright from the south.   They had survived the journey,
now went in quickly   to where they knew
that their protector,   killer of Ongentheow,
the good young war-king,   dealt out rings
1970   inside his sea-fort.   Hygelac was told
of Beowulf's return,   that there in his homestead
the defender of warriors,   his shield-companion,
came from the battle-sport   alive and unharmed,
walked through the yards   to his court in the hall.
1975   It was speedily cleared,   as the ruler ordered,
its benches made ready   for the men marching in.

Gesæt þā wið sylfne,   sē ðā sæcce genæs,
mæg wið mæge,   syððan man-dryhten
þurh hlēoðor-cwyde   holdne gegrētte
1980 mēaglum wordum.   Meodu-scencum hwearf
geond þæt [*heal*]-reced   Hæreðes dohtor,
lufode ðā lēode   lið-wǣge bær
hae[*leþ*]um tō handa.   Higelāc ongan
sīnne geseldan   in sele þām hēan
1985 fægre fricgean;   hyne fyrwet bræc,
hwylce Sǣ-Gēata   sīðas wǣron:
"Hū lomp ēow on lāde,   lēofa Bīowulf,
þā ðū fǣringa   feorr gehogodest
sæcce sēcean   ofer sealt wæter,
1990 hilde tō Hiorote?   Ac ðū Hrōðgāre
wī[*d*]-cūðne wēan   wihte gebēttest,
mǣrum ðēodne?   Ic ðæs mōd-ceare
sorh-wylmum sēað   sīðe ne truwode
lēofes mannes;   ic ðē lange bæd
1995 þæt ðū þone wæl-gǣst   wihte ne grētte,
lēte Sūð-Dene   sylfe geweorðan
gūðe wið Grendel.   Gode ic þanc secge,
þæs ðe ic ðē gesundne   gesēon mōste."
Bīowulf maðelode,   bearn Ecgðīoes:
2000 "Þæt is undyrne,   dryhten Hige[*lāc*],
[*mǣru*] gemēting   monegum fīra,
hwyl*c* [*orleg*]-hwīl   uncer Grendles
wearð on ðām wange,   þǣr hē worna fela

1981a MS. þæt reçed, with "síðe" added above line by same hand in different ink: em. Kemble. The MS. reading can be made to alliterate if "hwearf" is moved down from the previous line. Then 1981 becomes: hwearf geond þæt reced Hæreðes dohtor (thus von Schaubert's edition).

1983a MS. hæ[ð] nū, with "ð" erased but correction not completed. Em. Trautmann. The uncorrected MS. form could be dat. pl. for the "Hæðnas," a Norse tribe mentioned in *Widsið* 81. See Wrenn-Bolton, p. 296.

1991a MS. wið cuðne: em. Thorkelin.

2000b MS. hige...: em. Thorkelin when he revised Transcript B (Malone, *NC*, p. 77).

2001–2 Lost words at edge restored by Thorpe and by Samuel Moore, *JEGP* 18 (1919), 210.

      Then he sat down with him,   kinsman with kinsman,
he who survived   those terrible fights,
after he had loyally   greeted his sworn lord
1980 in formal speech,   with earnest words.
The daughter of Hæreth   went down the hall
pouring mead-cups,   was a friend to the men,
bore the strong drink   to the warriors' hands.
Then Hygelac began   to question with courtesy
1985 his comrade in hall.   Great curiosity
about their adventures   led him to words:
"How did you fare,   my beloved Beowulf,
upon your journey,   taken so suddenly,
seeking the strife   over salt water,
1990 battle at Heorot?   And did you better
the well-known grief   of Hrothgar the king?
Cares of the heart,   sorrow-surgings
boiled within me;   I did not trust
that venture's outcome.   Often I asked you
1995 not to attack   that murderous spirit,
but to let the South-Danes   test out Grendel
themselves in battle.   Great thanks to God
I now give here,   at your safe return."
      Beowulf replied,   Ecgtheow's son:
2000 "Our famous meeting,   my lord Hygelac,
is scarcely a secret   to much of mankind,
such crashing battle   Grendel and I
set dancing in hall,   where so many times

Sige-*Scyld*ingum   sorge gefremede,
2005   yrm*ð*e tō aldre;   ic ðæt eall gewræc,
swā *be*gylpan [*ne*] þearf   Grendeles māga
[*ǣnig*] ofer eorðan   ūht-hlem þone,
sē *ð*e lengest leofað   lāðan cynnes
[*fǣcne*] bifongen.   Ic ðǣr furðum cwōm
2010   tō ðām hring-sele   Hrōðgār grētan;
sōna mē se mǣra   mago Healfd*e*nes
syððan hē mōd-sefan   mīnne cūðe,
wið his sylfes sunu   setl getǣht*e*.
Weorod wæs on wynne,   ne seah ic wīdan feorh
2015   under heofones hwealf   heal-sittendra
medu-drēam māra*n*.   Hwīlum mǣru cwēn,
friðu-sibb folc*a*,   flet eall geond-hwearf,
bǣdde byre geonge;   oft hīo bēah-wriðan
secge [*sealde*],   ǣr hīe tō setle gēong.
2020   Hwīlum fo*r* [*d*]ugu*ð*e   dohtor Hrōðgāres
eorlum *on* *e*nde   ealu-wǣge bær,
þā ic Frēaware   *flet*-sittende
nemnan hȳrde,   þǣr hīo [*næ*]gled-sinc
hæleðum sealde.   Sīo gehāten [*wæs*]
2025   geong, gold-hroden,   gladum suna Frōdan;
[*h*]*a*fað þæs geworden   wine Scyldinga,
rī*ces* hyrde,   ond þæt rǣd talað
þæt hē mid ðȳ *wī*fe   wæl-fǣhða dæl,
sæcca gesette.   Oft *s*eldan hwǣr
2030   æfter lēod-hryre   lȳtle *hwī*le
bon-gār būgeð,   þēah sēo brȳd duge!

2006a   Addition by Grein.
2007a   MS. *en*.. in Thorkelin B only: restored by Kemble.
2009a   MS. .... First restored by Bugge as "fācne" (in crime), of which
"fæcne" is a variant spelling. Malone, *NC*, p. 77, explains the Thorkelin A
and B readings *fæ* and *fer* as interpretations of a damaged "æc" ligature.
2019a   Lost word at edge supplied by Thorpe.
2020a   MS. .*ugu*ðe from Thorkelin B: restored by Grundtvig.
2023b   MS. ..*gle*d sinc: restored by Grein.
2024b   MS. ...*se* in Thorkelin B only. Malone, *NC*, p. 78, suspects
reversal by B and would read .*es* which produces "wes" as a side-form of
"wæs." Recent editions supply "is" (Kluge).
2026a   MS. .*a*fa*ð*: restored by Kemble.

      he grieved the Scyldings,   humbled those victors,
2005 made life a misery.   I avenged all that
      so well that none,   no kinsman of Grendel
      wrapped in foul sin,   not any on earth
      who lives the longest   of the evil race,
      can boast of that dawn-clash.   I arrived and greeted
2010 Hrothgar in ring-hall;   the famous man,
      kinsman of Healfdene,   gave me a seat
      with his own sons   once he had learned
      my journey's purpose.   The gathering rejoiced;
      never have I seen,   in all my days
2015 under heaven's roof,   a greater mead-feast
      of noble retainers.   His famous queen,
      peace-weaver of nations,   walked through the hall,
      encouraged the striplings;   time and again
      before she was seated   she gave gold bracelets.
2020 At times his daughter   took vessels of mead
      to the veteran nobility   throughout the whole hall;
      I heard the men give her   the name Freawaru
      when she passed to those heroes   the gem-studded cup,
      She has been promised,   young, gold-laden,
2025 to the gracious Ingeld,   son of King Froda.
      The Scylding king   has brought this about,
      the guard of his kingdom,   accepts the opinion
      that with the young woman   he'll settle his share
      of the killings and feud.   But seldom anywhere,
2030 after a slaying,   will the death-spear rest,
      even for a while,   though the bride be good.

Mæg þæs þonne ofþyncan   ðēod[*ne*] Heaðobeardna
ond þegna gehwām   þāra lēoda,
þonne hē mid fǣmnan   on flett gǣð,
2035 *d*ryht-bearn Dena,   duguða biwenede;
on him gladiað   gomelra lāfe,
heard ond hring-mǣl   Heaðabear[*d*]na gestrēon,
þenden hīe ðām wǣpnum   wealdan mōston,
[XXIX] oððæt hīe forlǣddan   tō ðām lind-plegan
2040 swǣse gesīðas   ond hyra sylfra feorh.
Þonne cwið æt bēore   sē ðe bēah gesyhð,
eald æsc-wiga,   sē ðe eall ge[*man*]
gār-cwealm gumena   —him bið gri*m* [*se*]*fa*—
onginneð geōmor-mōd   geo*ng*[*um*] cempan
2045 þurh hreðra gehygd   *higes* cunnian,
wīg-bealu weccean,   ond þæt wo*rd* ācwyð:
'Meaht ðū, mīn wine,   mē*ce* gecnāwan,
þone þīn fæder   to gef*eohte* bær
under here-grīman   hinde*man* sīðe,
2050 dŷre īren,   þær hyne Dene slōgon,
wēoldon wæl-stōwe,   syððan Wiðergyld læg,
æfter hæleþa hry*re*,   hwate Scyldungas?
Nū hēr þāra b*a*nena   byre nāt-hwylces
frætwum hrēmig   on flet gǣð,
2055 morðres gyl*pe*[*ð*]   ond þone maðþum byreð,
þone þe ðū m*id* rihte   rǣdan sceoldest.'
Manað swā ond myndgað   mǣla gehwylce
sārum wordum   oððæt sǣl cymeð,
þæt se fǣmnan þegn   fore fæder dǣdum
2060 æfter billes bite   blōd-fāg swefeð,

2032b MS. ðeoden: em. Kemble.

2037b MS. heaða bearna: em. Thorpe.

2039 In MS. large capital "O" in *"oððæt"* indicates beginning of fitt, but there is no roman numeral. The numbering then skips XXX and continues with XXXI at 2144.

2042b Thorkelin B: ge..m, which Thorkelin later completed as "genam" (took, endured). Em. Thorpe.

2043b MS. gri*m*....*fa*: completed by Conybeare and Kemble.

2044b MS. geo*ng*..: restored by Kemble.

2055a MS. gyl*ped* from Thorkelin B: em. Kemble.

"The lord of the Heathobards   may well be dis-
                                                                pleased,
and each of his thanes,   his nation's retainers,
when the Danish attendant   walks in their hall
2035   beside his lady,   is honorably received.
On Danish belts   swing shining heirlooms,
sharp as of old,   the Heathobards' ring-treasures
for as long as they could   wield those weapons,
[XXIX]   till they finally led   into that shield-play
2040   their beloved companions   and their own lives.
Then at the beer-feast   an old fighter speaks,
who sees that ring-hilt,   remembers it all,
the spear-death of men   —has a fierce heart—
begins in cold sorrow   to search out a youngster
2045   in the depths of his heart,   to test his resolve,
strike blade-spark in kin,   and he says these words:
'Can you, my comrade,   now recognize the sword
which your father bore   in the final battle,
under grim war-mask   for the last time,
2050   that precious iron,   when the Danes killed him,
controlled the field,   when Withergyld fell
in our heroes' crash   at Scylding hands?
Now some son or other   of your father's killers
walks in this hall,   here, in his pride;
2055   exults in his finery,   boasts of his slayings,
carries that treasure   that is rightfully yours.'
He continually whets   the young man's mind
with cruel words,   until a day comes
when the lady's retainer,   for his father's killings,
2060   sleeps bloody-bearded,   hacked by a sword,

ealdres scyldig;   him se ōðer þonan
losað [*li*]*figende*,   con him land geare.
Þon*ne* bīoð [*āb*]rocene   on bā healfe
āð-sweorð eorla;   [*syþ*]ðan Ingelde
2065 weallað wæl-nīðas   ond hīm *wīf*-lufan
æfter cear-wælmum   cōlran *weor*ðað.
Þȳ ic Heaðobear[*d*]na   hyldo ne *telge*,
dryht-sibbe dæl   Denum unfǣcne,
frēondscipe fæstne.   Ic sceal forð *sprecan*,
2070 gēn ymbe Grendel,   þæt ðū geare *cunne*,
sinces brytta,   tō hwan syððan *wearð*
hond-rǣs hæleða.   Syððan heofones *gim*
glād ofer grundas,   gǣst yrre cwōm
*eat*ol, æfen-grom,   ūser nēosan,
2075 ðǣr wē *gesunde*   sæl weardodon.
Þǣr wæs Hondsciō   hild onsǣge,
feorh-bealu fǣgum;   *hē* fyrmest læg,
gyrded cempa;   him *Grendel* wearð,
mǣrum magu-þegne,   tō mūð-bonan,
2080 lēofes mannes   līc eall forswealg.
Nō ðȳ ǣr ūt ðā gēn   īdel-hende
bona blōdig-tōð   bealewa gemyndig
of ðām gold-sele   gongan wolde,
ac hē mægnes rōf   mīn costode,
2085 grāpode *gearo-f*olm.   Glōf *hangode*
sīd ond syllīc,   searo-bendum fæs*t*;
sīo wæs orðoncum   eall gegyrwed,
dēofles cræftum   ond dracan fellum,
Hē mec *þǣr* on innan   unsynnigne,
2090 dīor *dǣd*-fruma,   gedōn wolde
manigra sumne;   hyt ne mih*t*e swā,

2062a MS. ..*figende* from Thorkelin A: em. Heyne.
2063a MS. ..rocene: em. Kemble.
2064b MS. ...ðan: em. Kemble.
2067a MS. heaðo bearna: em. Thorpe.
2076b MS. hilde: em. Adolf Holtzmann, *Germania* 8 (1863), 496.
2079a MS. mǣrū magū þegne: em. Kemble.
2085a MS. *geareo*: em. Thorkelin.

his life forfeited.   The slayer will escape,
get away with his life,   he knows the country.
Then, on both sides,   broken like swords
the nobles' oath-swearing,   once deadly hate
2065 wells up in Ingeld;   in that hot passion
his love for the peace-weaver,   his wife, will cool.
So I count it little,   the Heathobards' loyalty,
friendship so firm,   peace-sharing with Danes,
think it less than the truth.   Now let me turn
2070 again to Grendel,   that you may know fully,
my treasure-giver,   how the hand-combat
came to an end.   Once heaven's jewel
had passed over earth,   the angry spirit,
dread night-terror,   came seeking us out
2075 where still unharmed   we kept guard in the hall.
Then was Hondscio   taken in battle,
fated for death,   the first to fall,
sword-belted warrior;   Grendel killed
that good young thane   and then he devoured
2080 his entire body,   swallowed him up.
No sooner for that   did he mean to depart
from the hall of gold   empty-handed,
bloody-toothed killer;   mighty and baleful,
he tested my strength;   his war-claw seized me.
2085 His glove hung down,   a huge pouch, magical,
strangely seamed.   It had been wrought
with cunning spells,   a devil's strength,
and hard dragon-skins.   The fierce evil-doer
wanted to stuff me   into it, guiltless,
2090 as one of many.   It was not to be so
that night, once I rose,   stood up in anger.

syððan ic on yrre upp-ri*h*t āstōd.
Tō lang ys tō reccenne, hū i*c* ðā*m* lēod-sceaðan
yfla gehwylces hon*d-lēan* forgeald

2095 þǣr ic, þēoden mīn, þīn*e* lēode
weorðode weorcum. Hē on weg losade,
lȳtle hwīle līf-wynna br*ēac*;
hwæþre him sīo swīðre swað*e wear*dade
hand on Hiorte, ond hē hēa*n* ðonan

2100 mōdes geōmor mere-gr*u*nd gefēoll.
Mē þone wæl-rǣs wine Scyldunga
fǣttan golde fela lē*ano*d*e*,
manegum māðmum, syððan me*r*gen cōm
ond wē tō symble geseten hæfdon.

2105 Þǣr wæs gidd ond glēo; gome*la Scilding*,
fela fric*gende*, feorran re*hte*;
hwīlu*m h*ilde-dēor hearpan wynne,
gome[n]-wudu grētte, hwīlum gyd āwræc
sōð *ond sā*rlīc, hwīlum syllīc spell

2110 rehte æfter r*i*hte rūm-heort cyning;
hwīlum eft *onga*n eldo gebunden
gomel gūð-wiga *giogu*ðe cwīðan,
hilde-strengo; hreðer *inn*e wēoll,
þonne hē wintrum frōd worn *gem*unde.

2115 Swā wē þǣr inne andlangne *dæg*
nīode nāman, oððæt niht becwōm
ōðe*r* tō yldum. Þā wæs eft hraðe
gearo *gyr*n-wræce Grendeles mōdor,
sīðode *sor*h-full; sunu dēað fornam,

2092b MS. upp ri*hte* in Thorkelin A (thus an adverb), but the "e" is gone in the later Transcript B, followed in most editions as a silent emendation. The "e" is an authentic reading according to Malone, *NC*, p. 80, but the meter is improved without it.

2093b MS. hu*iedā* in Thorkelin A with "e" misread for "c," and "d" for "ð." First deduced by Grundtvig.

2094b Usually em. "ondlēan" (payment, requital) but see line 1541 and Commentary, p. 336.

2097b MS. br*æc* in Thorkelin A, where Scribe II's "ea" is transcribed as "æ" five other times. Restored by Kemble.

2108a MS. go *mel* from Thorkelin A and B: em. Grundtvig.

It is too long to tell   how I gave that enemy
full hand-payment,   return for all evils
that nation had suffered,   but there, my king,
2095 I won for your people   some honor through deeds.
He fled down the path,   remained alive
for a little while,   yet his right hand stayed
behind at Heorot,   guarded a trail
quite plain to see—   in pain he fled,
2100 sick to the heart,   died on the mere-bottom.
     "For that hard struggle   the Scyldings' friend
gave plated gold,   reward enough,
many jeweled weapons,   when morning came
and all were gathered   in the great feast-hall.
2105 There was song and story: an aged Scylding,
widely learned,   told of the old days;
at times the fighter   struck the harp to joy,
sung against chant-wood,   or made a lay
both true and sorrowful;   the great-hearted king
2110 fittingly told   a marvelous tale;
then again in his turn,   wrapped in his age,
the old warrior   lamented his youth,
his lost war-strength;   his heart moved within him
as, wise in winters,   he remembered it all.
2115 And so in that hall   we enjoyed our ease
the whole long day   until another night
returned to men.   Grendel's mother
swiftly made ready   to take her revenge,
an unhappy journey.   Her son had died

2120 wīg-hete *Wed*ra.   Wīf unhȳre
  hyre bearn gewræc, *beorn* ācwealde
  ellenlīce; þǣr wæs Æschere,
  frōdan fyrn-witan, feorh ūðgenge.
  Nōðer hȳ hine ne mōston, syððan *m*ergen cwōm
2125 dēað-wērigne, Denia *lēo*de
  bronde forbærnan, *n*ē on bǣl hladan
  lēofne mannan; *h*īo þæt līc ætbær
  fēondes fæð[*mum*] [*un*]der firgen-strēam.
  Þæt wæs Hrōðgā*r*[*e*] hrēowa tornost,
2130 þāra þe lēod-fruman lange begēate.
  Þā se ðēoden *mec* ðīne līfe
  healsode hrēoh-mōd *þæt ic* on holma geþring
  eorlscipe efnd*e* ealdre genēðde,
  mǣrðo fremed*e*; h*ē* mē mēde gehēt.
2135 Ic ðā ðæs wælm*es*, þ*ē* is wīde cūð
  grim[*n*]e gryrelīc*ne* grund-hyrde fond.
  Þǣr unc hwīl*e* wæs hand gemǣne;
  holm heolfre wēoll, ond ic hēafde becearf
  in ðām [*gūð*]-s*ele* Grendeles mōdor
2140 ēacnum ecgum; unsōfte þonan
  feorh oðferede. Næs ic fǣge þā gȳt,
  ac mē eorla hl*ēo* eft gesealde
  māðma menigeo, mag*a* Healfdenes.
XXXI "Swā se ðēod-kyning þēawum lyfde;
2145 nealles ic ðām lēanum forloren hæfde,
  mægnes mēde, ac h*ē* mē [*māðma*]s geaf,
  sunu Healfdenes, on [*mīn*]*n*e sylfes dōm;
  ðā ic ð*ē*, beorn-*c*yning, bringan wylle,
  ēstum geȳwan. Gēn is eall æt ð*ē*
2150 lissa gelong; *ic* lȳt hafo
  hēafod-māga, nefne, Hygelāc, ðec."

2128 MS. fæðrungu. according to Malone, *NC*, p. 81: em. Grein and
Kemble.
2129a Lost letter restored by Grundtvig.
2136a MS. grimme: em. Thorpe.
2139a No gap in MS.: conjectural restoration by Thorpe.
2146–47 Words lost at edge restored by Kemble.

2120 in battle with the Weders.   The monstrous woman
avenged her son,   snatched and killed
one man boldly.   There Æschere died,
wise old counselor,   in her fierce attack.
Nor had they the chance,   the men of Denmark,
2125 when morning returned,   to burn his body,
to lay on the pyre   the beloved man:
she had carried him off   in a fiend's embrace,
took his body beneath   the mountain stream.
This, for Hrothgar,   was the worst assault,
2130 the greatest sorrow   of all he'd endured.
In his angry grief   the king implored me
by your life, Hygelac,   to show my courage
in the press of waters,   put life in danger,
that I might work fame;   he promised full reward.
2135 It is now known afar   that under the waves
I found the keeper   of the terrible deep.
Down there, for long,   we fought hand to hand;
the mere seethed in blood,   and I cut off the head
of Grendel's mother   in that deep [war]-hall
2140 with her own great edge.   With no small trouble
I returned with my life,   not doomed at that time;
and the nobles' protector,   kinsman of Healfdene,
gave me once more   many treasures.

XXXI   "That nation's king   thus kept to good custom;
2145 indeed, I have hardly   lost all that booty,
reward for strength—   the son of Healfdene
gave me [treasures]   at my own choice,
which I wish, great king,   to bring to you,
to show my good will.   All my joys
2150 still depend on you: I have few relatives,
and no chief kinsman   except you, Hygelac."

Hēt ðā in beran   eafor-*hēa*fod-segn,
heaðo-stēapne helm,   *hā*re byrnan,
gūð-sweord geatolīc,   *gyd* æfter wræc:
2155 "Mē ðis hilde-sceorp   *H*rōðgār sealde,
snotra fengel;   .sume *w*orde hēt,
þæt ic his ærest ðē   ēst gesægde;
*c*wæð þæt hyt hæfde   Hiorogār cyning,
*lē*od Scyldunga,   lange hwīle.
2160 Nō ðȳ *æ*r suna sīnum   syllan wolde,
hwatum *H*eorowearde,   þēah hē him hold wǣre,
brēost-gewǣdu.   Brūc ealles well!"
Hȳrde ic þæt þām frætwum   fēower mēaras,
lungre, gelīce   lāst weardode,
2165 æppel-fealuwe;   hē him ēst getēah
mēara ond māðma.   Swā sceal mǣg dōn,
nealles inwit-net   ōð*rum* bregdon
dyrnum cræfte,   dēað rē*n*[*ian*]
hond-gesteal*l*an.   Hygelāce wæs,
2170 *nī*ð*a* heardum,   nefa swȳðe hold
ond geh*wæðer* oðrum   hrōþra gemyndig.
Hȳrde ic þæt hē ðone heals-bēah   Hygde *ge*sealde,
wrǣtlīcne wundur-*māððum*,   ðone þe him Wealhðēo
                                                    geaf,
ðēod[*nes*] dohtor,   þrīo wicg somod
2175 swanco*r* ond sadol-beorht;   hyre syðð*an* wæs
æfter bēah-ðēge   br[*ē*]ost geweorðod.
   Swā *beal*dode   bearn Ecgðēowes,
guma gūð*um* cūð,   gōdum dædum,
drēah æfter dōm*e*,   nealles druncne slōg
2180 heorð-gen*ēa*tas;   næs him hrēoh sefa,
ac hē ma*n*-cynnes   mǣste cræfte,
gin-fæsta*n* gife,   þe him God sealde,
hēold hilde-dēor.   Hēan wæs lange
swā hyne Gēa*ta* bearn   gōdne ne tealdon,
2185 nē hyne on medo-bence   micles wyrð*n*e

2168b MS. *ren*...: em. Kemble.
2174a MS. ðeo*d*..: restored by Kemble.
2176b MS. *b*rost: em. Thorpe.

He ordered brought in   the boar's-head standard,
high-crowned helmet,   great iron shirt,
ornamented war-sword,   then said this speech:

2155 "All this battle-gear   Hrothgar gave me,
wise and generous;   he asked especially
that I first tell you   the history of his gift.
He said King Heorogar,   the Scyldings' leader,
had owned it long.   No sooner for that

2160 did he make it a gift   to brave Heoroweard,
the iron chest-guard   for his own son,
loyal though he was.   Enjoy it all well!"
Then, as I've heard,   four swift horses,
exactly matching,   followed that treasure,

2165 apple-dark steeds.   With good heart he gave
both treasure and horses.   So ought a kinsman
always act,   never weave nets
of evil in secret,   prepare the death
of close companions.   With war-bold Hygelac

2170 his nephew kept faith,   his man ever loyal,
and each always worked   for the other's welfare.
I also have heard   that he gave Queen Hygd
the golden necklace,   that Wealhtheow gave him,
wondrous treasure-ring,   and three sleek horses

2175 under gold saddles.   After that gold-giving
the shining necklace   adorned her breast.

        Thus Ecgtheow's son   had shown great courage,
famous in battles,   renowned for good deeds,
walked in glory;   by no means killed

2180 comrades in drink;   had no savage mind:
brave and battle-ready,   he guarded the gift
that God had given him,   the greatest strength
that man ever had.   Yet his youth had been miserable,
when he long seemed sluggish   to the Geatish court;

2185 they thought him no good;   he got little honor,

drihten We[*d*]e[*r*]a   gedōn wolde;
swȳðe [*wēn*]don   þæt hē slēac wǣre,
æðeling un*from*.   Edwenden cwōm
tīr-ēadigum *men*n   torna gehwylces.

2190   Hēt ðā eorla *hl*ēo   in gefetian,
heaðo-rōf cyning,   *Hrē*ðles lāfe,
golde gegyrede;   næs *mid* Gēatum ðā
sinc-māðþum sēlra   *on* sweordes hād;
þæt hē on Bīowulfes   *be*arm ālegde,

2195   ond him gesealde   seofan þūsendo,
bold ond brego-stōl.   Him wæs *bā*m samod
on ðām lēod-scipe   *lo*nd gecynde,
eard, ēðel-riht,   ōðrum *sw*īðor,
sīde rīce,   þām ðǣr sēlra wæs.

2200   *E*ft þæt geīode   ufaran dōgrum
hilde-*hlæ*mmum,   syððan Hygelāc læg,
ond Hear[*dr*]ēde   hilde-mēceas
under bord-*h*rēoðan   tō bōnan wurdon,
ðā hyne gesōhtan   on sige-þēode

2205   hearde hild-frecan,   Heaðo-Scylfingas,
nīða genǣgdan   nefan Hererīces:
syððan Bēowulfe   brāde rīce
on hand ge*hwearf*.   Hē gehēold tela
fīftig wintra   —*wæs* ðā frōd cyning,

2210   eald ēþel-[*w*]eard—   oððæt ān ongan
deorcum nihtum   draca *rīcs*[*ī*]*an*,
sē ðe on hēa*um hofe*   hord beweo*tode*,
stān-beorh stēa[*p*]ne;   stīg under *læg*
eldum uncūð;   þǣr on innan gīong

2186a   MS. ...*hten* wereda, with *drihten* from Thorkelin B: em. Cosijn.
2187a   MS. ...*d*on: restored by Grein.
2202a   MS. hearede: em. Grundtvig.
2205a   MS. hilde frecan: em. Grundtvig (for meter).
2207a   "Bēowulfe" begins folio 182ʳ which is badly faded and often illegible. Experts disagree on which portions of this page have been freshened up by a later scribe.
2210a   MS. eþel peard: read thus by Malone, *NC*, p. 84.
2211b   MS. rics an from Thorkelin A: em. Kemble.
2213a   MS. stearne: em. Malone, *NC*, p. 84.

no gifts on the mead-bench   from the lord of the
Weders.
They all were convinced   he was slow, or lazy,
a coward of a noble.   A change came to him,
shining in victory,   worth all those cares.

2190   Then the battle-bold Hygelac,   protector of nobles,
had them bring out   the heirloom of Hrethel,
covered with gold;   at that time in Geatland
there was no greater treasure   in the form of a sword;
he laid that blade   on Beowulf's lap

2195   and gave him lands,   seven thousand hides,
a hall, and gift-throne.   Both of them together
had inherited land   within that nation,
the native right   to hold the homeland,
but the higher in rank   ruled the kingdom.

2200   It came to pass   in later days—
after crash of battles,   when Hygelac had fallen
and swords cut down   Heardred his son
under the shield-wall   where Battle-Scylfings,
hardened war-makers,   had sought him out,

2205   flushed in his victory,   violently swung
on Hereric's nephew—   after that dark time,
the kingdom passed   into Beowulf's hands.
He ruled it well   for fifty winters—
by then an old king,   aged guardian

2210   of the precious homeland—   until a certain one,
a dragon, began to rule   in the dark nights,
the guard of a hoard   in a high barrow-hall,
towering stone-mound;   the entrance beneath it
lay unknown to men.   Some man or other

2215   *niða* nāt-*hwylc,*   *sē* [*þe*] *nēh gefēng*
       hæðnum *horde,*   hond ....
      since fāhne.   *Hē þæt* syððan [*wræc*],
      þēah ðe hē slǣpende   besyre[*de wur*]*de*
      þēofes cræfte;   *þæt sīe ðīod on*[*fan*]*d,*
2220   *bū*-folc beorna,   þæt hē gebolge*n* wæs.

XXXII   Nealles mid gewe[*a*]ldum   wyrm-hord ā[*b*]rǣ[*c*],
      sylfes willum,   sē ðe him *sāre ge*sceōd,
      ac for þrēa-nēdlan   þ[*ēow*] nāt-*hwylces*
      hæleða bearna   hete-sweng*eas* flēoh,
2225   *ærn*[*e*]s þear*fa,*   ond ðǣr inne *f*eal[*h*],
      secg syn-*b*ysig;   sōna [*in*]w[*l*]āt[*o*]de,
      þæt [*gehðo*] ðām gyst*e*   [*gryr*]e-br[*ð*]g[*a*] stōd;
      hwæðre [*earm*]-sce*ap*en   ....

2215b MS. *se..neh gefeng* from readings by Sedgefield and Malone under ultraviolet light. Conjectural restoration by Sedgefield.

2217b Four or five illegible letters follow "syððan." Conjectural restoration by Sedgefield. Klaeber's alternative is to place the "ne" in the b-line and supply "bemǎð" (concealed) instead of "wræc."

2218 MS. *þ..hð. h.*, confirmed by Thorkelin B. In the second half-line, only *de* was legible to Zupitza. Restoration by Kluge.

2219b MS. *on...d*: restored by Grein.

2221 MS. ge weoldū: em. Zupitza, disputed by Malone, *NC*, p. 85. MS. wyrm horda cræft: em. Kaluza.

2223b MS. *þ...*: restored as *þ*[*ēow*] 'slave' by Grundtvig (accepted by Malone) and as *þ*[*egn*] 'retainer' by Kemble (accepted by Zupitza). The social status of the thief may affect interpretation.

2225 MS. *ærn*.s: thus read and restored by Zupitza. MS. *f*eal with "f" altered from "w" (Malone, *NC*, p. 85), emended by Grein from Thorkelin A and B weall.

2226b MS. mwatide is meaningless. Em. by Thorpe, followed by Chambers and von Schaubert. A more conservative alternative offered by Ettmüller and Heyne is "in [þ]ā tīde" (in that time). Upon the assumption that the reading was inaccurately freshened up, Dobbie conjectured an original "onfunde" (he discovered); see *MLN* 67 (1952), 242–45. The context is insufficient for confident emendation.

2227 Conjectural restoration by Malone, *NC*, p. 85, for the first illegible space, about five letters long; "gryre" conjectured by Grein from MS. ....*e* br.g.

2228a Conjectural restoration of..a four-letter space by Kemble.

2215 crept inside it,   reached out toward
     the heathen treasure,   took in his hand
     . . . adorned with treasure.   He [avenged] that later,
     though he'd been tricked   while lying asleep
     by the cunning thief: the people soon knew,
2220 all house-dwellers,   that the dragon was angry.
XXXII   Not deliberately,   for his own desires,
     did he injure the dragon,   break into his hoard,
     but in desperate trouble   this [slave] of nobles,
     I know not who,   fled angry blows,
2225 homeless, roofless,   entered that place,
     a sin-troubled man.   When he looked inside,
     [fear] and terror   rose in that guest.
     But the [frightful] shape   . . . .

.... sceap*en*
2230 ...... þā *hyne* se fǣ[r] begeat
sinc-fæt [*sōhte*].   Þǣr wæs swylcra fela
in ðām eorð-[*hū*]*se*   ǣr-gestrēona,
swā hȳ on geār-da*gum*   gumena nāt-hwylc,
eormen-lāfe   *æþe*lan cynnes,
2235 þanc-hycgende   þǣr geh*ȳd*de,
dēore māðmas.   Ealle hīe dēað *for*nam
ǣrran mǣlum,   ond s[*e*] ān ðā gēn
*lēod*a duguðe,   sē ðǣr lengest hwearf,
weard wine-geōmor,   [*w*]ēnde þæs ylcan
2240 *þæt hē* lȳtel fæc   long-gestrēona
brūcan *m*ōste.   Beorh eall-gearo
wunode on wonge   *wæt*er-ȳðum nēah,
nīwe be næsse   nearo-*cræf*tum fæst.
Þǣr on innon bær   eorl-*gest*rēona
2245 hringa hyrde   hord-wyrðne *dǣl*,
fættan goldes,   fēa worda cwæð:
"Heald þū nū, hrūse,   nū hæleð ne m[*ō*]stan,
eorla ǣhte!   Hwæt, hyt ǣr on ðē
gōde begēaton.   *G*ūð-dēað fornam,
2250 [*f*]eorh-beal[*o*] frēcne   fȳra gehwylcne
lēoda mīnra,   þā[*r*]a ðe þis [*līf*] ofgeaf,
gesāwon sele-drēam[*as*].   Nāh hwā sweord wege

2230b MS. fæs, with very small superscript "fær" or "er" added in much later hand (Malone, *NC*, p. 85).

2231a An illegible five-letter space, restored by Grein and newly supported by Robert P. Creed, *PQ* 35 (1956), 206–8. Cf. line 2300.

2232a MS. eorð/ .. *se*: restored by Zupitza.

2237b MS. si: em. Kemble.

2239b MS. rende (so Sedgefield and Malone); Zupitza saw "rihde" freshened up over an original "wende." The original "c" of "ylcan" was later altered to "d."

2245b MS. hord, with "o" later altered to "a."

2247b MS. mæstan, with an original "o" under the "æ" (Zupitza).

2250 MS. reorh bealc: em. Zupitza and Malone. MS. fyrena: em. Thorpe.

2251b MS. þana / ðe þis ofgeaf: em. Kemble.

2252a Two illegible letters at end of fol. 182ᵛ restored by Bugge. An alternative restoration by Holthausen is to leave "sele-drēam" singular and to add "Ic" to the start of the b-line.

. . . .
2230 . . . . . .   when fear overcame him
       [he seized] the treasure-cup.   There were many like it,
       ancient treasures,   within that earth-hall,
       where someone had hidden,   in the early days,
       the immense legacy   of a noble race,
2235 their precious belongings,   buried by a grieving,
       thoughtful man.   Death swept them off
       in those distant times,   and the one man left
       of the nation's war-troop   who survived the longest,
       mourning his friends,   knew his fate,
2240 that a short time only   would he enjoy
       the heaped treasures.   The waiting barrow
       stood high in the fields   near the breaking waves,
       new-built on the headland,   its entrance hidden.
       That keeper of rings   carried down into it
2245 the goods worth burial,   nobles' treasures,
       plated gold,   spoke few words:
       "Hold now, earth,   now that heroes may not,
       the treasure of princes.   From you long ago
       good men took it.   Death in battle,
2250 awful life-loss,   took every man,
       all of my people,   who gave up this [life],
       who knew hall-joys.   Now I have none

oððe fe[*ormie*]   fæted wǣge,
drync-fæt dēore;   dug[*uð*] ellor s[*c*]ōc.
2255 Sceal se hearda helm   [*hyr*]sted golde
fǣtum befeallen;   feormynd swefað,
þā ðe beado-grīman   bȳwan sceoldon;
gē swylce sēo here-pād,   sīo æt hilde gebād
ofer borda gebræc   bite īrena,
2260 brosnað æfter beorne;   ne mæg byrnan hring
æfter wīg-*fru*man   wīde fēran
hæleðum be healfe.   Næs hearpan wyn,
gomen glēo-bēame*s*,   nē gōd hafoc
geond sæl swingeð,   nē se swifta mearh
2265 burh-stede bēateð.   Bea*lo*-cwealm hafað
fela feorh-cynna   forð onsended!"
Swā giōmor-mōd   giohðo mænde,
ān æfter eallum;   unblīðe hwe[*arf*]
dæges ond nihtes,   oððæt dēaðes wylm
2270 hr*ā*n æt heortan.   Hord-wynne fond
eald ūh*t*-sceaða   opene standan,
sē ðe byrnende   biorgas sēceð,
nacod nīð-draca,   niht*es* flēogeð
fȳre befangen;   hyne fold-būend
2275 [*swīðe ondrǣ*]da[*ð*].   Hē gesēcean sceall
[*ho*]r[*d on h*]rūsan,   þær hē hæðen gold
warað *win*trum frōd;   ne byð him wihte ðȳ sēl.
Sw*ā* se ðēod-sceaða   þrēo hund wintra
*h*ēold on hrūsa[*n*]   hord-ærna sum
2280 ēacen-*cr*æftig,   oððæt hyne ān ābealch
mon on mōde;   man-dryhtne bær
fǣted *w*æge,   frioðo-wǣre bæd
hlāford sīnne.   Ð*ā* wæs hord rāsod,
onboren bēaga *h*ord,   bēne getīðad

2253a MS. fe.....: restored by Grein.
2254b MS. dug..: restored by Kemble. MS. seoc: em. Grein.
2255b MS. ...sted: restored by Grundtvig.
2268b MS. hwe.r.: em. Grein.
2275a Only "da" legible in MS. Restoration by Zupitza.
2276a MS. ...r. / .. .*r*usan: restorations by Zupitza, Grein, Grundtvig.
2279a MS. hrusam: em. Thorkelin.

who might carry sword,   [polish] the cup,
gold-plated vessel;   the company is gone.
2255 The hardened helmet   now must lose
its golden plates;   the stewards sleep on
who were meant to burnish   each battle-mask;
so too the war-coat   that withstood in battle
the bite of iron   across shield-clashings;
2260 it decays like its warrior.   Rusted, the chain-shirt
cannot follow   close by the war-leader,
far beside heroes.   No harp-joy,
play of song-wood—   no good hawk
swings through the hall,   nor the swift roan
2265 stamps in the courtyard.   An evil death
has swept away   many living men."
   Thus in his grief   he mourned aloud,
alone, for them all;   in constant sorrow
both day and night   till the tide of death
2270 reached his heart.   The old dawn-scorcher
then found the hoard   in the open barrow,
that hateful burner   who seeks the dead-mounds,
smooth flame-snake,   flies through the dark
wrapped round in fires;   earth-dwellers
2275 [fear him greatly.]   It is his to seek out
[treasure] in the earth,   where he guards for ages
heathen gold;   gains nothing by it.
   Three hundred years   that harm to the people
held one of its hoards,   dwelt in the earth,
2280 mighty in powers,   until a lone man
kindled its fury;   he took to his master
the gold-plated flagon,   asked guarantees
of peace from his lord.   The hoard had been pilfered,
its treasure lessened,   and pardon granted

2285 fēasceaftum men.   Frēa scēawode
     fīra fyrn-geweorc   *f*orman sīðe.
     Þā se wyrm onwōc,   wrōht wæs genīwad;
     stonc ðā æfter stāne,   stearc-heort onfand
     fēondes fōt-lāst;   hē tō forð gestōp
2290 dyrnan cræfte,   dracan hēafde nēah.
     Swā mæg unfæge   ēaðe gedīgan
     wēan ond wræ̆c-sīð,   sē ðe Waldendes
     hyldo gehealdeþ.   Hord-weard sōhte
     georne æfter grunde,   wolde guman findan,
2295 þone þe him on sweofote   sāre getēode;
     hāt ond hrēoh-mōd   hlǣw oft ymbe-hwearf
     ealn*e* *ūtan*weardne,   nē ðǣr ænig mon
     on *þære* wēstenne;   hwæðre [*wīges*] gefeh,
     bea[dwe] weorces;   hwīlum on beorh æthwe*arf*
2300 sinc-fæt sōhte.   Hē þæt sōna onf*and*
     ðæt hæfde gumena sum   goldes gefandod,
     hēah-gestrēona.   Hord-wea*r*d onbād
     earfoðlīce,   oðð*æt* æfen c*wōm*;
     wæs ðā gebolgen   beorges hyrde
2305 wolde [*s*]e lāða   līge forgyldan
     drin*c*-fæt dȳre.   Þā wæs dæg sceacen
     *wyr*me on willan;   nō on wealle læ[*n*]g
     *bī*dan wolde,   ac mid bæle fōr,
     fȳre gefȳsed.   Wæs se fruma egeslīc
2310 lēodum on lande,   swā hyt lungre wearð
     on hyra sinc-gifan   sāre geendod.
XXXIII   Ðā se gæst ongan   glēdum spīwan,

2296b   MS. hlaewū: em. Kemble.
2298b   MS. hilde: em. Trautmann.
2299a   MS. be*a*. The em. follows Malone, *NC*, p. 88, who argues that
Scribe II wrote "bead," skipping one "we" in a copy text that read "beadwe
weorces."
2305a   MS. fela ða: em. Bugge.
2307b   MS. læg: em. Cosijn. The MS. reading can be retained simply by
placing a comma at the end of the line (thus von Schaubert's edition). Then
the translation would go: "he did not remain inside the wall, he would not
wait."

2285   the miserable man;   his lord looked upon
       the gold of the ancients   for the first time.
       By then, also,   the dragon had wakened
       and with it new strife.   It slithered and sniffed
       along the stone walls,   found a footprint.
2290   Cleverly, in secret,   the outlaw had stepped
       past the dragon's head.   Thus, when the Ruler's
       favor holds good,   an undoomed man
       may easily survive   dangers in exile.
       The dragon searched the ground,   wanted to find
2295   the man who had sorely   harmed him in sleep.
       Fierce-hearted, hot,   round the outside
       of the mound he turned;   but there was no man
       in that wilderness.   He rejoiced in the thought
       of flame-work, [a fight];   returned now and then
2300   into the barrow-cave,   looked for his cup.
       Then he saw that someone   had disturbed his gold,
       high treasures.   The hoard-keeper waited,
       miserable, impatient,   till evening came.
       By then the barrow-snake   was swollen with rage,
2305   wanted revenge   for that precious cup,
       a payment by fire.   The day was over
       and the dragon rejoiced,   could no longer lie
       coiled within walls   but flew out in fire,
       with shooting flames.   The onset was horrible
2310   for the folk of the land,   as was its ending
       soon to be hard   for their ring-giving lord.

XXXIII   The visitor began   to spew fire-flakes,

           beorht hofu bærnan;   bryne-lēoma stōd
           eldum on andan;   nō ðǣr āht cwices
2315   lāð lyft-floga   lǣfan *wolde*.
           Wæs þæs wyrmes wīg   wīde gesȳne,
           *ne*aro-fāges nīð   nēan ond feorran,
           hū *se* gūð-sceaða   Gēata lēode
           hatode ond hȳn*de*;   *h*ord eft gescēat,
2320   dryht-sele dyrn*ne*   ǣr dæges hwīle.
           Hæfde land-wara   *lī*ge befangen,
           bǣle ond bronde;   beorges *g*etruwode,
           wīges ond wealles;   him sēo wēn *g*elēah.
              Þā wæs Bīowulfe   brōga gecȳðed
2325   snūde tō sōðe,   þæt his sylfes h[*ā*]m,
           bolda sēlest,   bryne-wylmum mealt,
           gif-stōl Gēata.   Þæt ðām gōdan wæs
           hrēow *o*n hreðre,   hyge-sorge mǣst;
           wēnde *se* wīsa   þæt hē Wealdende
2330   ofer ealde riht,   ēcean Dryhtne,
           bitre gebulge;   *b*rēost innan wēoll
           þēostrum geþoncum,   swā him geþȳwe ne wæs.
           Hæfde līg-draca   lēoda fæsten,
           ēa-lond ūtan,   eorð-weard ðone
2335   glēdum forgrunden;   him ðæs gūð-kyning,
           Wedera þīoden,   wrǣce leornode.
           Heht him þā gewyrcean   wīgendra hlēo
           eall-īrenne,   eorla dryhten,
           wīg-bord wrǣtlīc;   wisse hē gearwe
2340   þæt him holt-wudu   he[*lpan*] ne meahte,
           lind wið līge.   Sceold*e* [*lī*]þend-daga
           æþeling ǣr-gōd   ende gebīdan,
           worulde līfes,   ond se wyrm somod,
           þēah ðe hord-welan   hēolde lan*ge*.
2345   Oferhogode ðā   *h*ringa fengel,

2325b   MS. him: em. Grundtvig.
2340b   MS. he....: restored by Thorkelin.
2341b   MS. sceold*e* .. / þend daga (letter-spaces at MS. line-end from
Thorkelin B): restoration by Malone, *NC*, p. 89. Usually emended as "læn-
daga" (loaned days) following Grundtvig.

burn the bright halls;   the glow rose high,
a horror everywhere.   The fiery terror
2315 left nothing alive   wherever it flew.
Throughout the night sky   the burnings were visible,
cruelest warfare,   known near and far;
the Geatish people   saw how the burner
had raided and hurt them.   He flew back to the hoard,
2320 the mysterious hall,   just before day.
His flames had set fire   to men and their houses;
he trusted his barrow,   its deep walls,
his strength in fire;   his trust was to fail.
    Then to Beowulf   the disaster was told,
2325 soon made plain,   for his own home was burned,
finest of buildings,   the hall in fire-waves,
gift-throne of Geats.   To the good king
it was great anguish,   pain deep in mind.
The wise man believed   he had angered God,
2330 the Eternal Ruler,   very bitterly,
had broken the old law;   his breast welled
with dark thoughts   strange to his mind.
The dragon had razed   the land along the sea,
the people's stronghold,   their fort near the shore.
2335 For that the war-king,   guard of the Weders,
planned a revenge.   The shielder of warriors,
lord of his men,   commanded them fashion
a wonderful battle-shield   entirely covered
with strongest iron;   he knew well enough
2340 that linden-wood   could not [help] him
against such flames.   The king, long good,
was to reach the end   of his seafaring days,
his life in this world,   together with the serpent,
though long it had ruled   the wealth of the hoard.
2345   Then the ring-giver   scorned to approach

þæt hē þone wīd-flogan   weorode gesōhte,
sīdan herge;   nō hē him þā sæcce ondrēd,
nē him þæs wyrmes wīg   for wiht dyde,
eafoð ond ellen,   forðon hē ǣr fela
2350   nearo nēðende   nīða gedīg*de*,
hilde-hlemma,   syððan hē Hrōðgā*res*,
sigor-ēadig secg,   sele fælsode
ond æt gūð*e* forgrāp   Grendeles mǣgum
lāðan cynnes.   Nō þæt lǣsest wæs
2355   hond-ge*mōt*[a],   þǣr mon Hygelāc slōh,
syððan Gēata cyning   gūðe rǣsum,
frēa-wine folc*a*   Frēs-londum on,
Hrēðles eafora   hiora-dryncum swealt,
bille gebēate*n*.   Þonan Bīowulf cōm
2360   sylfes cræfte,   sund-nytte drēah;
hæfde him on earm*e*   [*eorla*] þrītig[*ra*]
hilde-geatwa,   þā hē tō ho*l*me [*st*]āg;
nealles Hetware   hrēmge þorf[*t*]*on*
fēðe-wīges,   þe him foran ongēan
2365   *l*inde bǣron;   lȳt eft becwōm
fram þām *h*ild-frecan   hāmes nīosan.
Ofer*s*wam ðā sioleða bigong   sunu Ecgðēowes,
*ea*rm ān-haga   eft tō lēodum;
þǣr him *H*ygd gebēad   hord ond rīce,
2370   bēagas ond brego-*s*tōl;   bearne ne truwode,
þæt hē wið æl-fylcum   ēþel-stōlas
healdan cūðe,   ðā wæs *H*ygelāc dēad.
Nō ðȳ ǣr fēasceafte   *f*indan meahton
æt ðām æðelinge   ǣnige ðinga,
2375   þæt hē Heardrēde   hlāford w*ǣ*re,
oððe þone cynedōm   cīosan wol*d*e;
hwæðre hē hi[*ne*] on folce   frēond-lārum hēold,

2347b   MS. þā: em. Thorkelin.
2355a   MS. hond gemot: em. Kemble.
2361–62   The MS. leaf begins: ... XXX hilde geat wa þahe to ho*l*me
..ag: em. and trans. follow Fred C. Robinson, *SP* 62 (1965), 12.
2363b   MS. þorf. with "on" from Thorkelin B: restored by Kemble.
2377a   MS. hī: em. Thorpe.

the dragon with troops,   with a full army;
he did not fear   a fight with the serpent;
its strength and fire   seemed nothing at all
to the strong old king,   since he had endured
2350 much violence before,   taken great risks
in the smash of battles,   after he had cleansed
Hrothgar's hall,   rich in his victories,
crushed out Grendel   and his kin in battle,
a hateful race.   Nor was it the least
2355 hand-to-hand combat   where Hygelac lay,
when the Geatish king,   in the fierce battle-rush
far off in Frisia,   the friend of his people,
Hrethel's son,   died from sword-drinks,
struck down and slain.   Beowulf escaped
2360 by his own strength,   did hard sea-duty;
he held in his arms   the battle-outfits
of thirty [warriors]   when he turned to the sea:
No need to boast   about that foot-fight
among the Hetware   who bore shields against him;
2365 few returned   to seek their homes
after facing the brave,   the daring man.
Across gray seas   Ecgtheow's son,
alone and lonely,   swam to his homeland.
There Hygd offered   treasure and kingdom,
2370 rings and the high-seat;   she did not believe
her son could hold   their native land
against the foreigners   now that Hygelac was dead.
No sooner for that,   through any counsel,
could the wretched nobles   convince the hero
2375 to be Heardred's lord;   he would not take
the royal power.   Still he supported him
among his people   with friendly wisdom,

   ēstum mid āre, oððæt hē yldra wearð,
   Weder-Gēatum wēold. Hyne wrǣc-mæcgas
2380 ofer sǣ sōhtan, suna Ōhteres;
   hæfdon hȳ forhealden helm Scylfinga,
   þone sēlestan sǣ-cyninga,
   þāra ðe in Swīo-rīce sinc brytnade,
   mǣrne *þēoden.* Him þæt tō mearce wearð;
2385 hē *þǣr* [*f*]or feorme feorh-wunde hlēat,
   sw*eor*des swengum, sunu Hygelāces,
   ond *him* eft gewāt Ongenðīoes bearn
   hā*mes* nīosan, syððan Heardrēd læg,
   lēt ðone brego-stōl Bīowulf healdan
2390 Gēatum wealdan; þæt wæs gōd cyning.
XXXIIII Sē ðæs lēod-hryres lēan gemunde
   uferan dōgrum, Eadgilse wearð,
   fēasceaftum frēond; folce gestēpte
   ofe*r* sǣ sīde sunu Ōhteres,
2395 wigum ond wǣpnum; hē gewrǣc syððan
   cealdum cear-sīðum, cyning eald*r*e binēat.
   Swā hē nīða *ge*hwane genesen hæfde,
   slīðra geslyh*ta,* sunu Ecgðīowes,
   ellen-weorca, oð ðone ānne dæg,
2400 þē hē wið þām wyrme gewegan sceolde.
   Gewāt þā twelfa sum, torne gebolgen,
   dryhten Gēata dracan scēawia*n.*
   Hæfde þā gefrūnen, hwanan sīo fǣhð ārās,
   bealo-nīð biorna; him tō bearme *cwōm*
2405 māðþum-fæt mǣre þurh ðæs me*ldan* hond.
   Sē wæs on ðām ðrēate þreottēoð*a* secg,
   sē ðæs orleges ōr onstealde,
   hæft *hyge*-giōmor, sceolde hēan ðonon
   wong *wīsian.* Hē ofer willan gīong,
2410 tō ðæs ðe hē eorð-sele ānne wisse,
   hlǣw under *hrū*san holm-wylme nēh,
   ȳð-gewinne; sē wæs innan full

2383a MS. þara ðe / ðe: em. Kemble.
 2385a MS. orfeorme: em. Hermann Möller, *Das altenglischen Volksepos*
(Kiel: Lipsius & Tischer, 1883), p. 111.

kept him in honor,   until he grew older,
could rule the Geats.   Then outcasts came,
2380 seeking him out,   Ohthere's sons,
across the sea;   had rebelled against Onela,
lord of the Scylfings,   best of the sea-kings,
of those who gave treasure   in Swedish lands,
a famous prince.   That was the end
2385 for Hygelac's son,   when his hospitality
later earned him   a death-wound by sword,
and Ongentheow's son   turned about
once Heardred lay dead,   returned to his home,
let Beowulf hold   the royal chair
2390 and rule the Geats.   He was a good king.
XXXIIII   He later found a way   to pay back the conquest
of the Geatish people;   was a friend to Eadgils,
supported in his exile   the son of Ohthere,
sent him an army,   good troops and weapons,
2395 across the sea.   The Swede made his journey,
cold in his cares,   took the king's life.
And so he survived,   the son of Ecgtheow,
every encounter,   each awful conflict,
heroic battles,   till that one day
2400 when he had to fight   against the worm.
Angered to the heart,   the king of the Geats,
one among twelve,   went to find the dragon.
He had heard by then   how the feud began,
fiery destruction;   the jeweled cup
2405 had been laid in his lap   by the thief's hand.
He was thirteenth   in the troop of men
who had been first,   the cause of disaster,
an abject captive;   he sadly showed
the trail to that shore.   Against his will
2410 he led them to where   he knew a cave,
a certain barrow,   between cliff and beach,
near the crash of waves.   Inside, it was heaped

wrǣtta ond wīra.   Weard unhīore,
gearo gūð-freca   gold-māðmas hēold,
2415 eald under eorðan;   næs þæt ȳðe cēap
tō gegangenne   gumena ænigum.

    Gesæt ðā on næsse   nīð-heard cyning
þenden hǣlo ābēad   heorð-genēatum,
gold-*wi*ne Gēata.   Him wæs geōmor sefa
2420 wǣfre ond wæl-fūs,   wyrd ungemete nēah,
sē ðone gomelan   grētan sceolde,
sēcean sāwle hord,   sundur gedǣlan
līf wið līce;   nō þon lange wæs
feorh æþelinges   flǣsce bewunden.

2425   Bīowulf maþelade,   bearn Ecgðēowes:
"Fela ic on giogoðe   gūð-rǣsa genæs,
orleg-hwīla;   ic þæt eall gemon.
Ic wæs *s*yfan-wintre,   þā mec sin*ca bal*dor,
frēa-wine folca   æt mīnum fæ*der* genam.
2430 Hēold mec ond hæfde   Hrēðel cyn*ing*,
geaf mē sinc ond symbel,   sibbe gemund*e*;
næs ic him tō līfe   lāðra ōwihte
beorn *in* burgum   þonne his bearna hwylc,
Herebe*ald* ond Hæðcyn,   oððe Hygelāc mīn.
2435 Wæs þām yldestan   ungedēfelīce
mǣges dǣdum   morþor-bed strēd,
syððan hyne Hæðcyn   of horn-bogan,
his frēa-wine   flāne geswencte,
miste mercelses   ond his mǣg of*s*cēt,
2440 brōðor ōðerne,   blōdigan gāre.
Þæt *wæs* feoh-lēas gefeoht,   fyrenum gesyngad,
hreðre hyge-mēðe;   sceolde hwæðre swā þēah
æðeling unwrecen   ealdres linnan.

    "Swā bið geōmorlīc   gomelum ceorle
2445 tō gebīdanne,   þæt his byre rīde
giong on galgan;   þonne h*ē* gyd wrece,
sārigne sang,   þonne his sunu hangað
hrefne tō hrōðre   ond hē him help[*e*] ne mæg,
eald ond infrōd,   ænige gefremm*an*.

2448b MS. helpa*n*: em. Kemble.

with delicate gold-work.   The terrible guard,
ready for combat,   protected those riches
2415 ancient in the earth;   no easy bargain
for any man   to try to acquire them.
  The war-brave king   sat down on the cliff,
and wished good luck   to the men of his hearth,
the Geatish ring-giver.   His spirit was sad,
2420 restless, death-ripe;   immeasurably near
the fate that was coming   to the old man,
to seek out his soul,   parting the two,
his life from the body.   Not much longer
would Beowulf's life   be wrapped in his flesh.
2425 And now he spoke out,   Ecgtheow's son:
"Many times in my youth   I faced battle-rushes,
saw many wars;   I remember it all.
I was seven years old   when the treasure-giver,
gold-friend of Geats,   took me from my father.
2430 King Hrethel kept   and fostered me well,
kept kin in mind,   gave jewel and feast.
In no way was I,   a man of his stronghold,
more hateful to him   than his own sons,
Herebeald, Hæthcyn,   or Hygelac my lord.
2435 For the eldest brother   a death-bed was strewn,
undeservedly,   by his kinsman's error:
Hæthcyn shot him,   his brother, his leader,
with an arrow from his bow   curved and horn-tipped;
missed his mark   and struck his brother,
2440 one son's blood   on the other's shaft.
There was no way to pay   for a death so wrong,
blinding the heart,   yet still the prince
had lost his life,   lay unavenged.
  "So it is bitter   for an old man
2445 to have seen his son   go riding high,
young on the gallows;   then may he tell
a true sorrow-song,   when his son swings,
a joy to the raven,   and old and wise
and sad, he cannot   help him at all.

2450 Symble bið gemyndgad morna gehwylce
  *ea*foran ellor-sīð, ōðres ne gȳmeð
  tō gebīdanne burgum in innan
  yrfe-weardas, þonne se ān hafað
  þurh dēaðes nȳd dǣda gefondad.
2455 Gesyhð sorh-cearig on his suna būre
  wīn-sele wēstne, windge reste
  rēote berofene; rīdend swefað,
  hæleð in hoðman; nis þǣr hearpan swēg,
  gomen in geardum, swylce ðǣr iū wǣron.

XXXV �
2460 ⎰ "Gewīteð þonne on sealman, sorh-lēoð gæleð,
  ān æfter ānum; þūhte him eall tō rūm,
  wongas ond wīc-stede. Swā Wedra helm
  æfter Herebealde heortan sorge
  wea*lle*nde wæg; wihte ne meahte
2465 on ðām feorh-bonan fæghðe gebētan;
  nō ðȳ ǣr hē þone heaðo-rinc hatian ne meahte
  lāðum dǣdum, þēah him lēof ne wæs.
  Hē ða mid þǣre sorhge, [*sīo*] þe him sār[*e*] belamp,
  gum-drēam ofgeaf, Godes lēoht gecēas;
2470 eaferum lǣfde, swā dēð ēadig mon,
  lond ond lēod-byrig, þā hē of līfe gewāt.

  "Þā *wæs* synn ond sacu Swēona ond Gēata
  ofer [*wīd*] wæter wrōht gemǣne,
  here-nīð hear*da*, syððan Hrēðel swealt,
2475 oððe him Ongenðēowes eaferan wǣran
  frome, fyrd-hwate; frēode ne woldon
  ofer heafo healdan, ac ymb Hrēosna-beorh
  eat*olne* inwit-scear oft gefremedon.

2464a MS. weal / ..*n*de with Thorkelin A and B weal linde probably in
error; Conybeare (1826) attested an "e" after the second "l." See Dobbie,
p. 244, for analysis of the misreading.

2468b MS. þe hī sio sar: this looks corrupt since "sār" (grief) is regularly
neuter. Em. by Sedgefield, on the analogy of line 2222b, as the best of many
suggestions, including retaining the MS. form as feminine (Chambers, von
Schaubert).

2473a Lost word at edge of MS. Thorkelin A rid: restoration by
Grundtvig.

2478b MS. oft ge ge fremedon: em. Thorkelin.

2450   Always, each morning,   he remembers well
          his son's passing;   he does not care
          to wait for another   guardian of heirlooms
          to grow in his homestead,   when the first has had
          such a deadly fill   of violent deeds.

2455   Miserable, he looks   upon his son's dwelling,
          deserted wine-hall,   wind-swept bedding,
          emptied of joy.   The rider sleeps,
          warrior in grave;   no harp music,
          no games in the courtyard,   as once before.

XXXV   "Then he goes to his bed,   sings his cares over,
2460   alone, for the other;   all seems too open,
          the fields and house.   Thus the Weder-king
          carried in his heart   overflowing grief
          for Herebeald;   he could not ever

2465   settle the feud   against the slayer,
          no sooner could hate   his warrior son,
          do hostile deeds,   though he did not love him.
          Because of this sorrow   that hurt him so,
          he left man's joy,   chose God's light,

2470   gave to his sons,   as a good man does,
          the land and strongholds   when he went forth.
              "Then war returned   to Swedes and Geats,
          a common hatred   across [wide] water,
          fierce battle-rage   once Hrethel died

2475   and Ongentheow's sons   made bolder threats;
          proud, war-keen,   they wanted no peace
          kept over water,   but at Sorrow Hill
          made gruesome ambush,   malicious slaughter.

Þæt mæg-wine   mīne gewrǣcan,
2480 fǣhðe ond fyrene,   swā hyt gefrǣge wæs,
þēah ðe ōðer his   ealdre gebohte,
heardan cēape;   Hæðcynne wearð,
Gēata dryhtne,   gūð onsǣge.
Þā ic on morgne gefrægn   mǣg ōðerne
2485 billes ecgum   on bonan stǣlan,
þǣr Ongenþēow   Eofores nīosað;
gūð-helm tōglād,   gomela Scylfing
hrēas [*heoro*]-blāc;   hond gemunde
fǣhðo genōge,   feorh-sweng ne of*t*ēah.
2490   "Ic him þā māðmas,   þē hē mē sealde,
geald æt gūðe,   swā mē gifeðe wæs,
lēohtan sweorde;   hē mē lond forgeaf,
eard, ēðel-wy*n*.   Næs him ǣnig þearf
þæt hē tō Gifðum   oððe tō Gār-Denum
2495 oððe in Swīo-rīce   sēcean þurfe
*wyrs*an wīg-frecan,   weorðe gecȳpa*n*;
symle ic him on fēðan   beforan wolde,
āna on orde,   ond swā tō aldre sceall
sæcce fremman,   þenden þis sweord þolað,
2500 þæt mec ǣr ond sīð   oft gelǣste,
syððan ic for dugeðum   *Dæg*hrefne wearð
tō hand-bonan,   Hūga *ce*mpan.
Nalles hē ðā frætwe   Frēs-cyning[*e*],
*br*ēost-weorðunge   bringan mōste,
2505 ac in c[*a*]mp[*e*] gecrong   cumbles hyrde,
æþeling on elne;   ne wæs ecg bona,
ac him hilde-grāp   heortan wylmas,
bān-hūs gebræc.   Nū sceall billes ecg,
hond ond heard sweord   ymb hord wīgan."
2510   Bēowulf maðelode,   bēot-wordum spræc
nīehstan sīðe: "*I*c genēðde fela
gūða on geogoðe;   gȳt ic wylle,

2488a   No gap in MS.: conjectural restoration by Grein.
2503b   MS. fres cyning: em. Grundtvig.
2505a   MS. incempan: cm. Kemble.

My kinsmen and leaders   avenged that well,
2480 both feud and outrage,   as was often told,
though the older one   paid with his life,
no easy purchase: Hæthcyn fell,
the lord in battle,   Geatish leader.
The next morning,   as I have heard it,
2485 the third brother   brought full vengeance
back to the slayer   with keen edges,
once Ongentheow   sought out Eofor:
his helmet broken,   the old Scylfing
crashed down, sword-pale;   the hand could recall
enough of the quarrel,   did not withhold the blow.
2490   "I earned those treasures   that Hygelac gave me,
paid him with battle   as fate allowed me,
with glittering sword;   he had given me land,
my native home.   He had no need
2495 to go to the Gifthas,   to Swedes or Spear-Danes
for some worse fighter   to buy with gifts.
Always I walked   before him on foot,
his man at the point,   and so, life-long,
shall I do battle,   while this sword serves,
2500 which then and now   has held up well
ever since the time,   in front of the hosts,
I slew Dæghrefn,   the champion of the Hugas,
with my bare hands.   He never brought back
his breast-ornament   to the Frisian king:
2505 the standard-bearer   fell in combat,
a prince, in valor;   no edge killed him—
my hand-grip crushed   his beating heart,
his life's bone-house.   Now the edge of the sword,
hand and hard blade,   must fight for the treasure."
2510   Beowulf spoke,   made his battle-vows
for the last time: "Often I dared
many battles in youth;   I wish even now,

froð folces weard,   fǣhðe sēcan,
mærðu fremman,   gif mec se mān-sceaða
2515   of eorð-sele   ūt gesēceð!"
Gegrētte ðā   gumena gehwylcne,
hwate helm-berend   hindeman sīðe,
swǣse gesīðas: "Nolde ic sweord beran,
wǣpen tō wyrme,   gif ic wyste hū
2520   wið ðam āglǣcean   ell*es* meahte
gylpe wiðgrīpan,   swā ic giō wið Grendle dyde;
ac ic ðǣr heaðu-fȳres   hā*tes* wēne,
[*o*]reðes ond attres;   forðon ic mē on hafu
bord ond byrnan.   Nelle ic beorges weard
2525   oferflēon fōtes trem,   ac unc [*furður*] sc*eal*
weorðan æt wealle,   swā unc wyrd getēoð,
Metod manna gehwæs.   Ic eom on mōd*e* from,
þæt ic wið þone gūð-flogan   gylp of*er*sitte.
Gebīde gē on beorge,   byrnum werede,
2530   secgas on searwum,   hwæðer sēl mæge
æfter wæl-rǣse   wunde gedȳgan
uncer twēga.   Nis þæt ēower sīð,
nē gemet mannes,   ne*fne* mīn ānes,
[*þæ*]t hē wið āglǣcan   eofoðo dǣle
2535   eorlscype efne.   Ic mid elne sceall
gold gegangan,   oððe gūð nimeð,
feorh-bealu frēcne,   frēan ēowerne!"
    Ārās ðā bī ronde   rōf ōretta,
heard under helm*e*,   hioro-sercean bær
2540   under stān-cleofu,   strengo getruwode
ānes mannes;   ne bið swylc earges sīð!
Geseah ðā be wealle,   sē ðe worna fela,

2514a MS. mærdū: em. Bugge.

2523a MS. reðes 7 hattres: em. Grein and Grundtvig respectively. Of special interest since it resembles hendiadys in classical rhetoric. For further discussion and references, see A. S. Cook, *MLN* 40 (1925), 137–142, and R. D. Stevick, *MLQ* 20 (1959), 339–343.

2525b No gap in MS: conjectural restoration by Klaeber.

2533b MS. nefne from Thorkelin B only.

2534a MS. wat: em. Grundtvig.

    an old folk-guard,   to seek a quarrel,
    do a great deed,   if the evil-doer
2515 will come to me   out of his earth-hall!"
    He then addressed   his faithful men,
    brave in their helmets,   for the last time:
    "I would not carry   sword or weapons
    against the serpent   if I knew how else
2520 to grapple proudly,   wrestle the monster,
    as I did with Grendel;   but here I expect
    the heat of war-flames,   his poisonous breath,
    and so I am dressed   in shield and armor.
    Not one foot   will I retreat
2525 from the barrow-keeper,   but here by the wall
    it must go between us   as fate decides,
    the Lord, for each man.   My heart is bold,
    I forego boasting   against this war-flyer.
    Wait on the barrow   safe in your mail,
2530 men in your armor,   to see which of us
    shall better survive   the wounds dealt out
    in the rush of battle.   It is not your business,
    nor fitting for any,   except me alone,
    to test out his strength   against this monster,
2535 do a hero's deed.   I must succeed,
    win gold by courage,   or battle seize me,
    final life-hurt   take your lord away!"
      The famous champion   stood up with his shield,
    brave behind helmet,   in hard war-shirt,
2540 went under stone-cliff,   trusted the strength
    of a single man;   hardly the coward's way!
    Then he who survived,   good in his virtues,

      gum-cystum gōd,   gūða *ged*īgde,
      hilde-hlemma,   þonne hnitan fēðan,
2545 *sto*[*n*]dan stān-bogan,   strēam ūt þonan
      brecan of beorge;   wæs þǣre burnan wælm
      heaðo-fȳrum hāt;   ne meahte horde nēah
      unbyrnende   ǣnige hwīle
      dēop gedȳgan   for dracan lēge.
2550 Lēt ðā of brēostum,   ðā hē gebolgen wæs,
      Weder-Gēata lēod   word ūt faran,
      stearc-heort styrmde;   stefn in becōm
      heaðo-torht hlynnan   under hārne stān.
      Hete wæs onhrēred,   hord-weard oncnīow
2555 mannes reorde;   næs ðǣr māra fyrst
      frēode tō friclan.   From ǣrest cwōm
      oruð āglǣcean   ūt of stāne,
      hāt hilde-swāt;   hrūse dynede.
      Biorn under beorge   bord-rand onswāf
2560 wið ðām gryre-gieste,   Gēata dryhten;
      ðā wæs hring-bogan   heorte gefȳsed
      sæcce tō sēceanne.   Sweord ǣr gebrǣd
      gōd gūð-cyning,   gomele lāfe,
      ecgum ung*l*eaw;   ǣghwæðrum wæs
2565 bealo-hycgendra   *brō*ga fram ōðrum.
      Stīð-mōd gestōd   *wið* stēapne rond
      winia bealdor,   ðā se wyr*m* gebēah
      snūde tōsomne;   hē on searwum bād.
      Gewāt ðā byrnende   gebogan scrīða*n*,
2570 tō gescipe scyndan.   Scyld wēl gebearg
      līfe ond līce   lǣssan hwīle
      mǣrum þēodne   þon*n*e his myne sōhte;
      ðǣr hē þȳ fyrste,   for*m*an dōgore,
      wealdan mōste,   swā him wyrd ne gescrāf
2575 hrēð æt hilde.   Hond u*p* abrǣd
      Gēata dryhten,   gryre-fāhne slō*h*
      incge-lāfe,   þæt sīo ecg gewāc,

in manly customs,   who endured many wars,
the din of battle   when foot-troops clashed,
2545 saw a stone arch   by the barrow-wall,
and a stream flowing out,   its waters afire
with angry flames;   he could not get through,
enter the passage,   without being burned,
come near the hoard   for the dragon's flames.
2550 Then the king of the Geats,   angry as he was,
let a word rise up,   fly out from his breast,
a strong-hearted bellow;   his voice clanged,
war-bright echo,   under gray stone.
Hate rose up: the dragon had heard
2555 the voice of a man;   there was no more time
to ask for a peace.   First came his breath,
a flickering fire,   out from the stone,
hot battle-hiss;   the earth shook.
Down by the barrow   the lord of the Geats
2560 swung his shield   toward the strange terror;
coiled and scaly,   its heart was bent
on seeking battle.   The good war-king
had already drawn   his heirloom sword,
an edge not dull.   The sight of the other
2565 brought fear to each   of those destroyers.
The brave man braced   against his shield,
lord of his troop,   as the angry serpent
coiled itself up;   in armor he waited.
Then coiling in flames   it came slithering forth,
2570 rushed to its fate.   The shield protected
the famous king   in life and limb
a shorter time   than he had hoped;
for the first time,   on his final day,
he managed as he could   when fate did not give him
2575 glory in battle.   The Geatish king
swung up his hand,   slashed the glittering horror
with his heirloom sword,   so that the edge broke,

brūn on bāne,   bāt unswīðor
þonne his ðīod-cyning   þe*arfe* hæfde,
2580 bysigum gebǣded.   Þā wæs beorges weard
æfter heaðu-swenge   on hrēoum mōde,
wearp wæl-fȳre;   wīde sprungon
hilde-lēoman.   Hrēð-sigora ne gealp
gold-wine Gēata;   gūð-bill geswāc,
2585 nacod æt nīð*e*,   swā hyt nō sceolde,
īren ǣr-gōd.   Ne wæs þæt ēðe sīð,
þæt se mǣra   maga Ecgðēowes
grund-wong þone   ofgyfan wolde;
sceolde [*ofer*] willan   wīc eardian
2590 elles hwergen,   swā *sceal* æghwylc mon
ālǣtan lǣn-da*gas*.   Næs ðā long tō ðon
þæt ðā āglǣcean   hȳ eft gemētton.
Hyrte hyne hord-weard   —hreðer ǣðme wēoll—
nīwan stefne;   nearo ðrōwode,
2595 fȳre befongen,   sē ðe ǣr folce wēold.
Nealles him on hēape   hand-gesteallan,
æðelinga bearn   ymbe gestōdon
hilde-cystum,   ac hȳ on holt bugon,
ealdre burgan.   Hiora in ānum wēoll
2600 sefa wið sorgum;   sibb ǣfre ne mæg
wiht onwendan   þām ðe wēl þenceð.
XXXVI   *W*īglāf wæs hāten,   Wēoxstānes sunu,
lēof*l*īc lind-wiga,   lēod Scylfinga,
mæg Ælfheres;   geseah his mon-dryhten
2605 under here-grīman   hāt þrowian.
Gemunde ðā ðā āre   þe hē him ǣr forgeaf,
wīc-stede weligne   Wǣgmundinga,
folc-rihta gehwylc,   swā his fæder āhte;
ne mihte ðā forhabban,   hond rond gefēng,
2610 geolwe linde;   gomel swyrd getēah,
þæt wæs mid eldum   Ēanmundes lāf,

2589a No gap in MS.: conjectural restoration by Rieger.
2596b MS. heand gesteallan: em. Kemble.

           bright on bone-scales,   bit less deeply
           than its great ruler   needed in danger,
2580 hard pressed in battle.   After that war-stroke
           the barrow-guard   grew more savage,
           spewed deadly fire;   those war-flames leapt
           and danced about;   the Geatish gold-friend
           did not boast then   about his victories.
2585 His naked war-sword   had failed in need,
           as it never should have,   his land's best blade.
           It was no easy journey   when Ecgtheow's son,
           renowned and brave, had to leave the field,
           make his dwelling   in another place,
2590 as each man must,   give up loaned time.
           Not long after,   the terrible fighters
           closed once more.   The hoard-guard took heart,
           his belly swelled   with fierce new hissing.
           Enveloped in flames,   he who earlier
2595 had ruled his people   felt keen pain.
           But not at all   did the sons of nobles,
           hand-picked comrades,   his troop stand round him
           with battle-courage: they fled to the wood
           to save their lives.   Only one
2600 felt shame and sorrow.   Nothing can ever
           hold back kinship   in a right-thinking man.
XXXVI   He was called Wiglaf,   Weohstan's son,
           a worthy shield-bearer,   Scylfing prince,
           kinsman of Ælfhere;   saw his liege-lord
2605 tortured by the heat   behind his battle-mask.
           He remembered the honors   that he gave him before,
           the rich homestead   of the Wægmunding clan,
           the shares of common-land   that his father had held,
           and he could not hold back.   His hand seized the shield,
2610 yellow linden-wood;   he drew his sword,
           known to men   as Eanmund's heirloom,

suna Ōhtere[*s*].   Þām æt sæcce wearð,
wræcca[*n*] wine-lēasum,   Wēohstān bana
mēces ec*gum*,   ond his māgum ætbær
2615 brūn-fāgne helm,   hringde byrnan,
eald-sweord etonisc.   Þæt him Onela forgeaf,
his gædelinges   gūð-gewædu,
fyrd-searo fūslīc;   nō ymbe ðā fæhðe spræc,
þēah ðe hē his brōðor bearn   ābredwade.
2620 Hē frætwe gehēold   fela missēra,
bill ond byrnan,   oððæt his byre mihte
eorlscipe efnan   swā his ær-fæder;
geaf him ðā mid Gēatum   gūð-gewæda
æghwæs unrīm,   þā hē of ealdre gewāt,
2625 frōd on forð-weg.   Þā wæs forma sīð
geongan cempan   þæt hē gūðe ræs
mid his frēo-dryhtne   fremman sceolde.
Ne gemealt him se mōd-sefa,   nē his mæges lāf
gewāc æt wīge;   þ[æt] se wyrm onfand
2630 syððan hīe tōgædre   gegān hæfdon.
Wīglāf maðelode,   word-rihta fela
sægde gesīðum—   him wæs sefa geōmor:
"Ic ðæt *mæl* geman   þær wē medu þēgun
þon*ne* wē gehēton   ūssum hlāforde
2635 in bīor-sele,   ðe ūs ðās bēagas geaf,
þæt wē him ðā gūð-getāwa   gyldan woldon,
gif him þyslicu   þearf gelumpe,
helmas ond heard sweord.   Ðē hē ūsic on herge gecēas
tō ðyssum sīð-fate   sylfes willum,
2640 onmunde ūsic mærða,   ond mē þās māðmas geaf,
þe hē ūsic gār-wīgend   gōde tealde,
hwate helm-berend,   þēah ðe hlāford ūs
þis ellen-weorc   āna āðōhte

2612a MS. ohtere: em. Grundtvig.
2613 MS. *wræcca* from Thorkelin A: em. Ettmüller. MS. weohstanes: em. Grundtvig.
2628b MS. mægenes: em. Ettmüller.
2629b MS. þa: em. Thorpe.

son of Ohthere.   Weohstan had slain
that friendless exile   by sword-edge in battle,
had brought to the uncle   the jeweled helm,
2615 linked mail-shirt,   the ancient sword
fashioned by giants.   Onela gave him
the polished gear   of his dead nephew,
said no words   to start up a feud,
though he had killed   his brother's son.
2620 Weohstan held them   for many winters,
the mail-shirt and sword,   till his son was ready
to show as much courage   as his graying father.
He gave him then   —they lived among the Geats—
a great deal of armor   when he went from life,
2625 an old man's journey.   This was the first time
that the young warrior   had met the battle-charge,
was to withstand it   beside his lord.
His resolve did not melt,   nor his father's gift
fail him at combat,   as the fire-snake found out
2630 once they had clashed,   met in battle.
      Wiglaf spoke   in fitting words
to his armored companions—   was grieved to the heart:
"I recall the time,   when taking the mead
in the great hall,   we promised our chief
2635 who gave us these rings,   these very armlets,
that we would repay him   for these war-helmets,
tempered edges,   if he ever needed us.
For that he chose us   from all his forces,
chose as he pleased   his men for this journey.
2640 He thought us war-worthy   —and gave me these gifts—
because he believed   we would be spear-men
good in a battle,   eager in helmets;
though he had planned,   our chief in his courage,

tō gefremmanne,   folces hyrde,
2645 forðām hē manna mǣst   mǣrða gefremede,
dǣda dollīcra.   Nū is sē dæg cumen
þæt ūre *man*-dryhten   mægenes behōfað,
gōdra gūð-rinca;   wutun gongan tō,
helpan hild-fruman,   þenden hyt sȳ,
2650 glēd-egesa grim!   God wāt on mec
þæt mē is micle lēofre   þæt mīnne līc-haman
mid mīnne gold-gyfan   glēd fæðmie.
Ne þynceð mē gerysne   þæt wē rondas beren
eft tō earde,   nemne wē ǣror mægen
2655 fāne gefyllan,   *f*eorh ealgian
Wedra ðēodnes.   Ic wāt gear*e*,
þæt nǣron eald-gewyrht,   þæt hē āna scyle
Gē*ata* duguðe   gnorn þrōwian,
gesīgan æt sæcce;   ūrum sceal sweord ond helm,
2660 byrne ond b[*ea*]du-scrūd   bām gemǣne."
Wōd þā þurh þone wæl-rēc,   wīg-*hea*folan bær
frēan on fultum,   fēa worda *cwæð*:
"Lēofa Bīowulf,   lǣst eall tela,
swā ðū on *g*eoguð-fēore   geāra gecwǣde,
2665 þæt ðū ne ālǣte   be ðē lifigendum
dōm gedrēosan;   scealt nū dǣdum rōf,
æðeling ān-hȳdig,   ealle mægene
feorh ealgian;   ic ðē ful-lǣstu."
Æfter ðām wordum   wyrm yrre cwōm,
2670 atol inwit-*gæst*,   ōðre sīðe,
fȳr-wylmum fāh,   fīonda nīo*sian*
lāðra manna.   Līg ȳðum fōr,
born bord *wið* rond;   byrne ne meahte
geongum gār-wigan   gēoce gefremman;
2675 ac se maga geonga   und*er* his mǣges scyld

2660a MS. byrdu scrud: em. Ettmüller.
2671b Thorkelin A mosum, B niosnan: restoration deduced by Grundtvig.
2672–73 Several different word-divisions are possible here, such as: līg-
ȳðum forborn / bord wið rond[*e*]. The present arrangement is adapted from
R. Willard, *MLN* 76 (1961), 290–93.

> to do this deed   alone, as folk-guard,
> 2645 because of all men   he had done most,
> won daring fame.   The time is at hand
> when our generous lord   could use the strength
> of good soldiers.   Let us go to him now,
> help our war-leader   through this heat,
> 2650 fire-horror.   As for me, God knows
> I would much rather   the fire seize my body
> beside my gold-giver,   lord and friend.
> It is hardly right   that we should bear shields
> back to our homes   unless we can first
> 2655 kill off this monster,   save the life
> of the king of the Weders.   I know for a truth
> that the worth of his deeds   is not so poor
> that alone among Geats   he should suffer,
> fall in combat.   Now sword and helmet,
> 2660 mail-shirt, war-gear,   must be ours together."
> Then he rushed in   through deadly fumes,
> brought his helmet   to the aid of his lord,
> said only this: "Beowulf, my leader,
> do everything well,   as you said, when young,
> 2665 you'd never permit   your good name to fail
> alive, brave-minded;   deed-famed prince,
> now you must guard   your life with strength,
> use all your might;   I will help you!"
> After those words   the dragon charged
> 2670 again, angry,   a shimmering form
> in malignant coils,   surged out in flames,
> sought hated men.   The fire came in waves,
> the shield burned to the boss.   Mail-shirt offered
> the untried warrior   no protection,
> 2675 but the young man   bravely went in

elne geēode,   þā his āgen [*wæs*]
glēdum forgrunden.   Þā gēn gūð-cyning
m[*ǣrða*] gemunde,   mægen-strengo slōh
hilde-bille,   *þæt* hyt on heafolan stōd
2680 nīþe genȳded;   Nægli*n*g forbærst,
geswāc æt sæcce   sweord Bīowulfes,
gomol ond græg-mǣl.   Him þæt gifeðe ne wæs,
þæt him īrenna   ecge mihton
helpan æt hilde;   wæs sīo hond tō strong
2685 sē ðe mēca gehwane,   *mī*ne gefrǣge,
swenge ofersōhte,   þonne hē tō *sæ*cce bær
wǣpen wundum heard;   næs him *w*ihte ðē sēl.
      Þā wæs þēod-sceaða   þriddan sīðe,
frēcne fȳr-draca   fǣhða gemyndig,
2690 rǣsde on ðone rōfan,   þā him rūm āgeald;
hāt ond heaðo-grim,   heals ealne ymbefēng
biteran bānum;   hē geblōdegod wearð
sāwul-drīore;   swāt ȳðum wēoll.
XXXVII   Ðā ic æt þearfe [*gefrægn*]   þēod-cyninges
2695 andlongne eorl   ellen cȳðan,
cræft ond cēnðu,   swā him gecynde wæs.
Ne hēdde hē þæs heafolan,   ac sīo hand gebarn
mōdiges mannes,   þǣr hē his mǣges healp
þæt hē þone nīð-gæst   nīoðor hwēne slōh,
2700 secg on searwum,   þæt ðæt sweord gedēaf
fāh ond fǣted,   þæt ðæt fȳr ongon
sweðrian syððan.   Þā gēn sylf cyning
gewēold his gewitte,   wæll-seaxe gebrǣd,
biter ond beadu-scearp,   þæt hē on byrnan wæg;
2705 forwrāt Wedra helm   wyrm on middan.
Fēond gefyldan   —ferh ellen wræc—
ond hī hyne þā bēgen   ābroten hæfdon,
sib-æðelingas.   Swylc sceolde secg wesan,
þegn æt ðearfe!   Þæt ðām þēodne wæs

2676b Conjectural restoration by Grundtvig for word lost at edge.
2678a MS. m.....: conjectural restoration by Grundtvig.
2694a No gap in MS.: addition by Kemble.
2698b MS. mægenes: em. Kemble.

      to his kinsman's shield,   showed quick courage
      when his own [was] destroyed   by the fiery breath.
      Then the war-king   recalled [his past glories,]
      with huge strength   swung his blade so hard
2680 that it caught in the head;   Nægling snapped,
      Beowulf's sword   shattered in battle,
      old and gleaming.   It was not his fate
      that edges of iron   might help him in combat.
      That hand was too strong,   as I have heard,
2685 that broke in its swing   every weapon,
      wound-hardened sword,   that he carried to battle;
      he was no better off   for all his strength.

        Then the land-burner,   vicious fire-dragon,
      made a third rush   at those brave men,
2690 found his chance,   pouring hot flames,
      caught and pierced him   right through the neck
      with his sharp fangs;   all bloodied he was,
      dark life-blood;   it flowed out in waves.
XXXVII   Then as I [have heard],   at the great king's need
2695 the upright prince   showed courage beside him,
      strength and daring,   as was his nature.
      He did not mind the head: the brave man's hand
      was burned to a crisp   when he helped his kinsman—
      a warrior in armor,   Wiglaf struck
2700 that strange opponent   a little lower down,
      so that the sword plunged in,   bright with ornaments,
      and afterward the fire   began to die out.
      The king could still manage,   was not yet faint,
      and drew his belt-knife,   sharpened by battle,
      which he wore on his mail-shirt;   the protector of
                                   the Weders
2705 finished the dragon   with a stroke down the belly.
      They had killed their foe   —courage took his life—
      both of the nobles,   kinsmen together,
      had destroyed the dragon.   So a man should be,
      a thane at need!   For the great king

2710 sīðas[t] sige-hwīle   sylfes dǣdum
    worlde geweorces.   Ðā sīo wund ongon,
    þe him se eorð-draca   ǣr geworhte,
    swelan ond swellan;   hē þæt sōna onfand
    þæt him on brēostum   bealo-nīðe wēoll
2715 attor on innan.   Ðā se æðeling gīong
    þæt hē bī wealle,   wīs-hycgende,
    gesæt on sesse;   seah on enta geweorc,
    hū ðā stān-bcgan   stapulum fæste
    ēce eorð-reced   innan healde.
2720 Hyne þā mid handa   heoro-drēorigne
    þēoden mǣrne,   þegn ungemete till
    wine-dryhten his   wætere gelafede,
    hilde-sædne,   ond his hel[m] onspēon.
    Bīowulf maþelode—   hē ofer benne spræc,
2725 wunde wæl-blēate;   wisse hē gearwe
    þæt hē dæg-hwīla   gedrogen hæfde,
    eorðan wyn[ne];   ðā wæs eall sceacen
    dōgor-gerīmes,   dēað ungemete nēah:
    "Nū ic suna mīnum   syllan wolde
2730 gūð-gewǣdu,   þær mē gifeðe swā
    ǣnig yrfe-weard   æfter wurde,
    līce gelenge.   Ic ðās lēode hēold
    fīftig wintra;   næs sē folc-cyning,
    ymbe-sittendra   ǣnig ðāra,
2735 þē mec gūð-winum   grētan dorste,
    egesan ðēon.   Ic on earde bād
    mǣl-gesceafta,   hēold mīn tela,
    ne sōhte searo-nīðas,   nē mē swōr fela
    āða on unriht.   Ic ðæs ealles mæg,
2740 feorh-bennum sēoc,   gefēan habban;
    forðām mē wītan ne ðearf   Waldend fīra

2710a   MS. siðas: em. Grein.
2714b   Nothing now left in MS. after "beal," but Thorkelin A bealomð,
B bealo niði where the second "i" answered to the downstroke of an "e."
Restored thus by Malone, *NC*, p. 96.
2723b   MS. hel. with Thorkelin A helo, B heb: em. Grein.
2727a   MS. wyn..: restored by Thorkelin.

2710 it was the last time   he gained victory,
his last work in the world.   Then the deep gash
the earth-dragon made,   the wound began
to burn and swell;   he soon understood
that something deadly   seethed in his breast,

2715 some poison within.   So Beowulf went,
wise-minded lord,   to sit on a seat
opposite that earth-wall;   he saw how the arches,
giants' stone-work,   held up the earth-cave
by pillars inside,   solid forever.

2720 Then his loyal thane,   immeasurably good,
took water in his hand,   bathed the bloodied one,
the famous king,   his liege, dear friend,
weak in his wound,   and unstrapped his helmet.
     Then Beowulf spoke,   despite the gash,

2725 the gaping wound   —he knew for certain
he had finished his days,   his joy in the world,
that his time was over,   death very near:
"Now I would want   to give to my son

2730 these war-garments,   had it been granted
that I have a guardian   born from my body
for this inheritance.   I ruled this people
for fifty winters,   and there was no ruler
of surrounding nations,   not any, who dared

2735 meet me with armies,   seek out a battle,
make any onslaught,   terror, oppression,
upon Geatish men.   At home I awaited
what the years brought me,   held my own well,
sought no intrigue;   not often I swore

2740 deceitful oaths!   Sick with my death-wound
I can take joy   in all these things;

      morðor-bealo māga,   þonne mīn sceaceð
      līf of līce.   Nū ðū lungre geong
      hord scēawian   under hārne stān,
2745 Wīglāf lēofa,   nū se wyrm ligeð,
      swefeð sāre wund,   *since* berēafod.
      Bīo nū on ofoste,   þæt ic ǣr-welan,
      gold-æht ongite,   gearo scēawige
      swegle searo-gimmas,   þæt ic ðȳ sēft mæge
2750 æfter māððum-welan   *mīn* ālǣtan,
      līf ond lēodscipe,   þone ic longe hēold."
XXXVIII   Ðā ic snūde gefrægn   sunu Wīhstānes
      æfter word-cwydum   wundum dryhtne
      hȳran heaðo-sīocum,   hring-net beran,
2755 brogdne beadu-sercean   u[n]der beorges hrōf.
      Geseah ðā sige-hrēðig,   þā hē bī sesse gēong,
      mago-þegn mōd*ig*   māððum-sigla fealo
      gold glitinian   grunde getenge,
      wundur on wealle,   ond þæs wyrmes denn
2760 ealdes ūht-flogan   orcas stondan,
      fyrn-manna fatu,   feormend-lēase,
      hyrstum behrorene.   Þǣr wæs helm monig,
      eald ond ōmig,   earm-bēaga fela,
      searwum gesǣled.   Sinc ēaðe mæg,
2765 gold on gr*und*[e],   gum-cynnes gehwone
      oferhīgian,   hȳde sē ðe wylle!
      Swylce hē siomian geseah   segn eall-gylden
      hēah ofer horde,   hond-wundra mǣst,
      gelocen leoðo-cræftum;   of ðām lēoma stōd,
2770 þæt hē þone grund-wong   ongitan mea*hte,*
      wrǣ[*t*]e giondwlītan.   Næs ðæs wyrmes þǣr
      onsȳn ǣnig,   ac hyne ecg fornam.
      Ðā ic *on* hlǣwe gefrægn   hord rēafian,

2755b MS. urder: em. Thorkelin.
2765a MS. grund: em. Grundtvig.
2769b MS. leoman: em. Kemble.
    2771a MS. wræce: em. Thorpe and universally accepted since OE. "t"
looks much like "c." But the MS. form, meaning "vengeance, punishment,"

> the Ruler of men   need not blame me
> for murder of kin,   once life is gone,
> has left my body.   Now you go quickly,
> find the treasure   under gray stones,
2745 beloved Wiglaf,   now that the dragon
> sleeps in his wounds,   cut off from gold.
> Go now in haste,   that I may see
> the golden goods,   have one full look
> at the brilliant gems,   that by its wealth
2750 I may more easily   give up my life
> and the dear kingdom   that I have ruled long."

XXXVIII   Then, as I have heard,   Weohstan's son,
> hearing the words   of his wounded ruler,
> quickly obeyed him,   took his link-shirt,
2755 ringed battle-webbing,   under the barrow's roof.
> Once past the seat,   the victorious thane
> —brave young kinsman—   saw red gold, jewels,
> glittering treasure   lying on the ground,
> wondrous wall-hangings;   in the den of the serpent,
2760 the old dawn-flier,   stood golden beakers,
> an ancient service,   untended, unpolished,
> its garnets broken.   Helmets lay heaped,
> old and rusted,   and scores of arm-rings
> skillfully twisted.   How easily jewels,
2765 gold in the earth,   can overcome anyone,
> hide it who will—   heed it who can!
> There he also saw   a golden standard
> hanging over the hoard,   intricate weaving
> of wondrous skill;   a light came from it
2770 by which he could see   the whole treasure-floor,
> gaze on the jewels.   There was no more sign
> of the dragon, now dead.   Then, as I've heard,
> alone in the barrow,   he rifled the hoard,

---

makes curious sense: "so that he might see that floor, look upon that vengeance." See also note to line 3060.

eald ent*a* geweorc   ānne mannan,
2775   him on bearm hl[*a*]*don*   bunan ond discas
sylfes dōme;   segn ēac genō*m*,
bēacna beorhtost.   Bill ǣr gescōd
—ecg wæs īren—   eald-hlāfordes
þām ðāra māðma   mund-bora wæs
2780   longe hwīle,   līg-egesan wæg
hātne for horde,   hioro-weallende
middel-nihtum,   oðþæt hē morðre swealt.

Ār wæs on ofoste,   eft-sīðes georn,
frætwum gefyrðred;   hyne fyrwet bræc,
2785   hwæðer collen-ferð   cwicne gemētte
in ðām wong-stede   Wedra þēoden
ellen-sīocne,   þǣr hē hine ǣr forlēt.
Hē ðā *m*id þām māðmum   mǣrne þīoden,
dryhten sīnne,   drīorigne fand,
2790   ealdres æt ende;   hē hine eft ongon
wæteres weorpan,   oðþæt *w*ordes ord
brēost-hord þurhbræc.   [*Bēowulf maþelode,*]
gomel on gio[*h*]ðe,   gold scēawode:
"Ic ðāra frætwa   Frēan ealles ðanc,
2795   Wuldur-cyninge,   wordum *secg*e,
ēcum Dryhtne,   þe ic hēr on starie,
þæs ðe ic *m*ōste   mīnum lēodum
ǣr swylt-dæge   swylc ge*strȳ*nan.
Nū ic on māðma hord   mīne be*b*ohte
2800   frōde feorh-lege,   fremmað gēna
*lē*oda þearfe;   ne mæg ic hēr leng wesan.
Hātað *h*eaðo-mǣre   hlǣw gewyrcean,
beorhtne æfter bæle   æt brimes nosan;
sē scel tō gemyndum   mīnum lēodum
2805   hēah hlīfian   on Hrones-næsse,
þæt hit sǣ-līðend   syððan hātan

2775a   MS. hlo*don* from Thorkelin B: em. Grein.
2792b   Lack of alliteration indicates the loss of a half-line. Conjectural restoration by Sedgefield.
2793a   MS. giogoðe: em. Grein.
2799b   MS. minne: em. Ettmüller.

old work of giants,   loaded an armful
2775 of gold cups and dishes,   chose as he pleased,
took the standard too,   the brightest emblem.
Already the short-sword   of his aged leader,
its edge strong iron,   had wounded the guardian,
keeper of treasure   from time out of mind,
2780 who kept fire-terror   in front of the hoard,
waves of flame,   surging on air
in the dead of night,   until he died in slaughter.
     Now Wiglaf hurried,   eager to return,
to bring back the jewels.   Curiosity
2785 urged him on,   whether he'd find
his lord still alive   where he had left him
lying in the open,   his strength gone.
Then, with the treasure,   he came out to find
his lord, the great king,   bleeding still,
2790 at the end of his life.   Again he began
to sprinkle him with water,   until the point of a word
broke through his breast-hoard: [Beowulf spoke,]
old in his grief,   as he saw the gold:
"I give thanks aloud   to the Lord of all,
2795 King of glories,   eternal Ruler,
for the bright treasures   I can see here,
that I might have gained   such gifts as these
for the sake of my people   before I died.
Now that I have given   my old life-span
2800 for this heap of treasures,   you are to watch
the country's needs.   I can stay no longer.
Order a bright mound   made by the brave,
after the pyre,   at the sea's edge;
let it rise high   on Whale's Cliff,
2805 a memorial to my people,   that ever after
sailors will call it   'Beowulf's barrow'

218   *Beowulf*

Bīowulfes biorh,   ðā ðe brentingas
ofer flōda genipu   feorran drīfað."
     Dyde him of healse   hring gyldenne
2810 þīoden þrīst-hȳdig,   þegne gesealde,
geongum gār-wigan,   gold-fāhne helm,
bēah ond byrnan,   hēt hyne brūcan well:
"Þū eart ende-lāf   ūsses cynnes,
Wǣgmundinga;   ealle wyrd fors[w]ēo[p]
2815 mīne māgas   tō metod-sceafte,
eorlas on elne;   ic him æfter sceal."
Þæt wæs þām gomelan   gingæste word
brēost-gehygdum,   ǣr hē bǣl cure,
hāte heaðo-wylmas;   him of h[re]ðre gewāt
2820 sāwol sēcean   sōð-fæstra dōm.
[XXXIX] Ðā wæs gegongen   gum[an] unfrōdum
earfoðlīce,   þæt hē on eorðan geseah
þone lēofestan   līfes æt ende,
blēate gebǣran.   Bona swylce læg,
2825 egeslīc eorð-draca,   ealdre berēafod,
bealwe gebǣded.   Bēah-hordum leng
wyrm wōh-bogen   wealdan ne mōste,
ac him īrenna   ecga fornāmon,
hearde, heaðo-scearde,   homera lāfe,
2830 þæt se wīd-floga   wundum stille
hrēas on hrūsan   hord-ærne nēah.
Nalles æfter lyfte   lācende hwearf
middel-nihtum,   māðm-ǣhta wlonc
ansȳn ȳwde,   ac hē eorðan gefēoll

2814b MS. for / speof, with the second word-element squeezed in before a large hole in the parchment. Emended by Kemble on the model of line 477. Wrenn (1st ed.) would read MS. for / speon, with "n" written on a partly erased "f." This would yield "forspēon" (has lured). Malone and Zupitza read only an abnormally placed final "f" before the hole (*NC*, p. 98).

2819b MS. hwæðre: em. Kemble (followed by Dobbie). The MS. form, meaning "however," also makes sense. If not a scribal error, it may point up the contrast between the body's death and the soul's immortality: see Richard L. Hoffman, *JEGP* 64 (1965), 664–65 (followed by Bolton).

2821 No number in MS. but the large capital of "Ðā" indicates a new fitt. MS. gumū: em. Heyne.

when the steep ships drive   out on the sea,
on the darkness of waters,   from lands far away."
　　From round his throat   he took the golden collar,
2810 brave-hearted king,   and gave to his thane,
the young spear-fighter,   his gold-plated helmet,
rings, mail-shirt,   bade use them well:
"You are the last   man of our tribe,
the race of Wægmundings;   fate has swept
2815 all my kinsmen   to their final doom,
undaunted nobles.   I must follow them."
That was the last word   of the old man
from the thoughts of his heart   before he chose
the high battle-flames;   out from his breast
2820 his soul went to seek   the doom of the just.
[XXXIX]　　It had come to pass   for the young warrior
that he saw the man   dearest in his life
lying dead on the ground   in his terrible wound.
His killer lay there,   huge earth-dragon,
2825 robbed of his life,   dead from blows.
Never again   would the coiled serpent
guard a treasure,   but the edges of iron
had taken him down,   hard, battle-notched,
forged under hammers,   so that the wide-flyer,
2830 stilled by wounds,   had come aground
beside the hoard-cave.   No more to whirl
through the midnight air,   breathing out flames,
proud in his treasure,   show his blazing form
high in the dark: he fell to the earth

Beowulf

2835 for ðæs hild-fruman hond-geweorce.
  Hūru þæt on lande lȳt manna ðāh,
  mægen-āgendra, mīne gefrǣge,
  þēah ðe hē dǣda gehwæs dyrstig wǣre,
  þæt hē wið attor-sceaðan oreðe gerǣsde,
2840 oððe hring-sele hondum styrede,
  gif hē wæccende weard onfunde
  būon on beorge. Bīowulfe wearð
  dryht-māðma dǣl dēaðe forgolden;
  hæfde æghwæð[er] ende gefēred
2845 lǣnan līfes. Næs ðā lang tō ðon,
  þæt ðā hild-latan holt ofgēfan,
  tȳdre trēow-logan, tȳne ætsomne,
  ðā ne dorston ǣr dareðum lācan
  on hyra man-dryhtnes miclan þearfe;
2850 ac hȳ scamiende scyldas bǣran,
  gūð-gewǣdu, þǣr se gomela læg;
  wlītan on Wīlāf. Hē gewērgad sæt,
  fēðe-cempa, frēan eaxlum nēah,
  wehte hyne wætre, him wiht ne spēo[w].
2855 Ne meahte hē on eorðan, ðēah hē ūðe wēl,
  on ðām frum-gāre feorh gehealdan,
  nē ðæs Wealdendes wiht oncirran;
  wolde dōm *Go*des dǣdum rǣdan
  gumena gehwylcum sw*ā* hē nū gēn dēð.
2860 Þā wæs æt ðām geong[*an*] grim andswar*u*
  ēð-begēte þām ðe ǣr his elne forlēas.
  Wīglāf maðelode, Wēohstānes sunu,
  sec[*g*] sārig-ferð— seah on unlēofe:
  "Þæt, lā, mæg secgan, sē ðe wyle sōð specan,
2865 þæt se mon-dryhten, sē ēow ðā māðmas geaf,
  ēored-geatwe, þe gē þǣr on standað,

2844a MS. æghwæðre: em. Kemble.
2854b MS. speop: em. Thorkelin.
2860a MS. geongū: em. A. J. Barnouw, *Textkritische Untersuchungen*
(Leiden: Brill, 1902), p. 36.
2863a MS. sec: em. Thorkelin. Wrenn-Bolton retains MS. form as "sēc,"
a by-form of "sēoc" (ill, weak, sad).

2835 by the handiwork of the great war-leader.
   Indeed, it is said there is hardly a man
   among the great heroes anywhere on earth,
   though he were valorous in every deed,
   who might succeed in a brave war-rush
   against such a fiery poison-breather,
2840 or run his hands through heaps in the ring-hall,
   if he discovered the guard in the barrow
   awake and watchful. That mass of treasure
   came to Beowulf only by death;
2845 both man and dragon had ended their time.
   Not long after, the battle-late troop,
   faith-breaking cowards, gave up their forest;
   the ten had not dared to join in the spear-play
   when their sworn lord had greatest need.
2850 Deep in their shame they carried their shields,
   iron war-shirts, to where Beowulf lay,
   looked at Wiglaf. Heart-weary, he bent,
   the brave champion, beside his lord's shoulder,
   still washed him with water, though it did no good.
2855 He could not, in the world, much as he wished,
   keep any life in the old spear-leader
   nor change the course of the Ruler's will.
   The judgment of God then ruled the deeds
   of every man, as He still does now.
2860 Then a hard answer was easily given
   by the young retainer to those without courage.
   Wiglaf spoke out, the son of Weohstan,
   a man sore-hearted, looked at the faithless ones:
   "Easily enough can a man who speaks truth
2865 say that the lord who gave you those ornaments,
   that fine war-gear you stand in there,

þonne hē on ealu-bence   oft gesealde
heal-sittendum   helm ond byrnan,
þēoden his þegnum,   swylce hē þrȳdlīcost
2870 ōwer feor oðða nēah   findan meahte,
þæt hē gēnunga   gūð-gewǣdu
wrāðe forwurpe,   ðā hyne wīg beget.
Nealles folc-cyning   fyrd-geste*allum*
gylpan þorfte;   hwæðre him God ūðe,
2875 sigor*a* Waldend,   þæt hē hyne sylfne gewræc,
āna mid ecge,   þā him wæs elnes þearf.
Ic him līf-wraðe   lȳtle meahte
ætgifan æt gūðe,   ond ongan swā þēah
ofer mīn gemet   mǣges helpan;
2880 symle wæs þȳ sǣmra,   þonne ic sweorde drep
ferhð-genīðlan,   fȳr unswīðor
wēoll of gewitte.   [*W*]ergendra tō lȳt
þrong ymbe þēoden,   þā hyne sīo þrāg *b*ecwōm.
[*N*]ū sceal sinc-þego   ond swyrd-*gifu*,
2885 eall ēðel-wyn   ēowrum cynne,
lufen ālicgean;   lond-rihtes mōt
þǣre mǣg-burge   monna ǣghwylc
īdel hweorfan,   syððan æðelingas
feorran gefricgean   flēam ēowerne,
2890 dōm-lēasan dǣd.   Dēað bið sēlla
eorla gehwylcum   þonne edwīt-līf."
XL   Heht ðā þæt heaðo-weorc   tō hagan bīodan
up ofer ecg-clif,   þǣr þæt eorl-weorod
morgen-longne dæg   mōd-giōmor sæt,
2895 bord-hæbbende,   bēga on wēnum,
ende-dōgores   ond eft-cymes
lēofes monnes.   Lȳt swīgode
nīwra spella,   sē ðe næs gerād,
ac hē sōðlīce   sægde ofer ealle:
2900 "Nū is wil-geofa   Wedra lēoda,
dryhten Gēata   dēað-bedde fæst,
wunað wæl-reste   wyrmes dǣdum;

2882b MS. fergendra: em. Grundtvig.
2884a MS. hu: em. Kemble.

when often he gave   to his hall-men, retainers,
sitting on mead-planks,   his own thanes—
when the king gave out   chest-guard and helmet,
the most splendid goods   he could find anywhere,
2870 near or far—   that he threw them away,
utterly, terribly,   once war came upon him.
The king of our land   had no need to boast
about armed comrades.   However, God granted,
2875 Ruler of victories,   that he avenge himself,
alone, with his sword,   when courage was needed.
Small life-shield   could I give at battle,
and yet for all that,   I still began,
beyond my strength,   to help my kinsman.
2880 Ever the slower   those deadly coils
once I stabbed with my sword;   a weaker fire
poured from his head.   Too few defenders
pressed round the king   when his worst time came.
Now all treasure,   giving and receiving,
2885 all home-joys,   ownership, comfort,
shall cease for your kin;   deprived of their rights
each man of your families   will have to be exiled,
once nobles afar   hear of your flight,
2890 a deed of no glory.   Death is better
for any warrior   than a shameful life!"
XL   Then he commanded   that the battle's outcome
be told at the palings   beyond the cliff-edge,
where noble counselors   had sat in dejection
2895 the whole forenoon,   their shields close at hand,
expecting either   the return of their lord
or his final day.   The messenger who came,
rode up the bluff,   was not long silent
about the news,   but truly enough
told the whole story   in the hearing of all:
2900 "Now is the giver   of the Weders' joys,
lord of the Geats,   laid in his death-bed;
he lies slaughtered   by the dragon's thrust.

him on efn ligeð   ealdor-gewinna
siex-bennum sēoc;   sweorde ne meahte
2905 on ðām āglǣcean   ǣnige þinga
wunde gewyrcean.   Wīglāf siteð
ofer Bīowulfe,   byre Wīhstānes,
eorl ofer ōðrum   unlifigendum,
healdeð hige-mǣðum   *hēafod*-wearde,
2910 lēofes ond lāðes.   Nū *ys lēodum* wēn
orleg-hwīle,   syððan under[ne]
Froncu*m* ond Frȳsum   fyll cyninges
wīde weorðeð.   Wæs sīo wrōht scepen
heard wið Hūgas,   syððan Higelāc cwōm
2915 faran flot-herge   on Frēsna land,
þǣr hyne Hetware   hilde genǣgdon,
elne geēodon   mid ofer-mægene,
þæt se byrn-wiga   būgan sceolde,
fēoll on fēðan;   nalles frætwe geof
2920 ealdor dugoðe.   Ūs wæs ā syððan
Merewīoingas   milts ungyfeðe.
Nē ic te Swē*o*-ðēode   sibbe oððe trēowe
wihte ne wēne,   ac wæs wīde cūð,
þætte Ongenðīo   ealdre besnyðede
2925 Hæðce*n* Hrēþling   wið Hrefna-wudu,
þā for on*mēd*lan   ǣrest gesōhton
Gēata lēode   Gūð-Sci*l*fingas.
Sōna him se frōda   fæder Ōhthere*s*,
eald ond eges-full   ondslyht āgeaf,
2930 ābrēot brim-wīsan,   brȳd āheorde,
gomela[*n*] iō-mēowl*an*   golde berofene,
Onelan mōdor   ond Ōhtheres;
ond ðā folgode   feorh-genīðlan,
oððæt hī oðēodo*n*   earfoðlīce

2911b MS. under: em. Grein.
2916b MS. gehnægdon: em. Grein. The MS. form, retained by von
Schaubert, can represent either "genægan" (attack, assail) or "gehnægan" (to
humble, vanquish).
2929b MS. hond slyht: em. Grein.
2931a MS. gomela: em. Grein.

Beside him his killer   is also stretched,
dead from knife-wounds;   with his strong sword
2905 he could not cleave,   cut into that monster,
not wound him at all.   Wiglaf sits there,
the son of Weohstan,   watches over Beowulf,
one noble over the other;   beside the lifeless
he keeps the head-watch,   weary to his heart,
2910 guards both the dead,   the loved and the hated.
Now the people   may well expect
a time of war,   when the death of our king
is known, no secret,   to Franks and Frisians.
That feud was forged   against the Hugas
2915 when Hygelac landed   his fleet in Frisia,
against the Hetware—   they gave him a battle,
pressed forward quickly   with the greater strength,
till the mailed warrior   had to bow down;
he fell in the ranks;   gave no rings then,
2920 the prince to his troop.   Ever since then
the Merovingian   has shown us no kindness.
Nor do I expect   from the Swedish people
much peace or friendship: it was known afar
that Ongentheow   chopped off the life
2925 of Hæthcyn, Hrethel's son,   near Ravenswood,
when in their pride   the Geatish people
first sought out   the Battle-Scylfings.
The father of Ohthere,   old in his war-craft,
cunning and terrible,   soon struck back,
2930 cut down the fleet-king,   rescued his wife,
the aged queen   bereft of her gold,
the mother of Onela,   of Ohthere too,
and then hunted down   his sworn enemies,
until they escaped   with their lives, barely,

2935   in Hrefnes-holt   hlāford-lēase.
         Besæt ðā sin-herge   swēorda lāfe
         wundum wērge;   *wēan oft* ge*h*ēt
         earmre *t*eohhe   on*dlonge* niht,
         cwæð hē on mergenne   mēces ecgum
2940   gētan wolde,   sum' on galg-trēowu[*m*]
         [*fuglum*] tō gamene.   Frōfor eft gelamp
         sārig-mōdum   somod ǣr-dæge,
         syððan hīe Hygelāces   horn ond bȳman,
         gealdor ongēaton,   þā se gōda cōm
2945   lēoda dugoðe   on lāst faran.
XLI   "Wæs sīo swāt-swaðu   Sw[ē]ona ond Gēata,
         wæl-rǣs weora   wīde gesȳne,
         hū ðā folc mid him   fǣhðe tōwehton.
         Gewāt him ðā se gōda   mid his gædelingum,
2950   frōd fela-geōmor   fæsten sēcean,
         eorl Ongenþīo   ufor oncirde;
         hæfde Hygelāces   *hil*de gefrūnen,
         wlonces wīg-cræft;   wiðres *n*e truwode
         þæt hē sǣ-mannum   onsacan mihte,
2955   heaðo-līðendum,   hord forstandan,
         bearn ond brȳde;   bēah eft þonan
         eald under eorð-weall.   Þā wæs ǣht boden
         Swēona lēodum;   segn Hygelāce[*s*]
         freoðo-wong þone   for[ð] oferēodon,
2960   syððan Hrēðlingas   tō hagan þrungon.
         Þǣr wearð Ongenðīow   ecgum sweord[*a*]
         blonden-fexa   on bid wrecen,

2940b MS. galg treowu: em. Kemble.
2941a No gap in MS.: conjectural restoration by Thorpe.
2946b MS. swona: em. Thorkelin.
2958–59 MS. hige lace: em. Kemble. MS. ford: em. Thorkelin. If
"Higelāce" is to be kept unemended, then Chambers offers the best treatment:
take "boden" (offered) as having a double subject, place the semicolon after
"Higelāce," and translate "then pursuit was offered to the people of the
Swedes, [and] a [captured] banner to Hygelac." Then the subject of the
following "oferēodon" is an understood "they."
2961b MS. sweordū: em. Kemble.

2935 up into Ravenswood,   their king dead behind them.
     With a large force   he then surrounded
     the sword's survivors,   wound-weary men,
     and the whole night long   he threatened more trouble
     to the hapless soldiers,   said that his blades
2940 would cut them open   when morning came,
     that some would swing   on the gallows-tree
     as sport [for the birds].   But help came at dawn
     to the heartsick men: they heard the sound
     of Hygelac's war-horn,   where the valiant prince
2945 came down the path   with his own picked troop.
XLI   "That bloody trail   of Swedes and Geats,
     swathe of the killed,   was known afar,
     how the two tribes   stirred up the feud.
     Then Ongentheow,   together with kinsmen,
2950 wise in age,   foresaw a sad fight,
     so turned away   to find a stronghold,
     sought higher ground,   had heard stories
     of Hygelac's strength,   proud war-skill,
     did not trust his force   to hold the Geats,
2955 the seafaring soldiers,   to defend his treasure,
     his sons and wife,   against battle-sailors.
     So he retreated,   old, to his earth-works.
     Pursuit was offered   to the Swedish men;
     Hygelac's banners   overran that field
2960 once the men of Hrethel   attacked the encampment.
     Gray-haired Ongentheow   was brought to bay
     in a bristle of swords;   the Swedish king

þæt se þēod-cyning   ðafian sceolde
Eafores ānne dōm.   Hyne yrringa
2965 Wulf Wonrēding   wæpne geræhte,
þæt him for swenge   swāt ǣdrum sprong
forð under fexe.   Næs hē forht swā ðēh,
gomela Scilfing,   ac forgeald hraðe
wyrsan wrixle   wæl-helm þone,
2970 syððan ðēod-cyning   þyder oncirde.
Ne meahte se snella   sunu Wonrēdes
ealdum ceorle   ondslyht giofan,
ac hē him on hēafde   helm ǣr gescer,
þæt hē blōde fāh   būgan sceolde,
2975 fēoll on foldan;   næs hē fǣge þā gīt,
ac hē hyne gewyrpte,   þēah ðe him wund hrine.
Lēt se hearda   Higelāces þegn
brād[n]e mēce,   þā his brōðor læg,
eald-sweord eotonisc   entiscne helm
2980 brecan ofer bord-weal;   ðā gebēah cyning,
folces hyrde,   wæs in feorh dropen.
Ðā wǣron monige,   þe his mæg wriðon,
ricone ārǣrdon,   ðā him gerȳmed wearð,
þæt hīe wæl-stōwe   wealdan mōston.
2985 Þenden rēafode   rinc ōðerne,
nam on Ongenðīo   īren-byrnan,
heard swyrd hilted   ond his helm somod;
hāres hyrste   Higelāce bær.
H[ē ðām] frætwum fēng   ond him fægre gehēt
2990 lēana [fore] lēodum   ond gelǣst[e] swā;
geald þone gūð-rǣs   Gēata dryhten,
Hrēðles eafora,   þā hē tō hām becōm,
Iofore ond Wulfe   mid ofer-māðmum,
sealde hiora gehwæðrum   hund þūsenda

2972b   MS. hond slyht: em. Kemble.
2978a   MS. brade: em. Thorpe.
2989a   MS. h....: restored by Grundtvig.
    2990   Room for four or five letters at lower right-hand corner of leaf;
conjectural restoration by Heyne. MS. gelæsta: em. Kemble.

had to submit   to Eofor's judgment.
Angrily, Wulf   the son of Wonred

2965   swung out his weapon,   so that blood spurted
from under the hair,   a glancing stroke.
But it brought no fear   to the old Scylfing;
he quickly returned   a better blow
for that bloody stroke,   a worse exchange

2970   as he wheeled upon him.   No answering blow
could the son of Wonred   offer in return;
the old man had carved   so deep in his helmet
that, covered all over   in a mask of blood,

2975   he went down headlong   —still not doomed,
though the wound ran freely,   but later recovered.
Then the fierce warrior,   Hygelac's thane,
as his brother lay there,   swung his broad sword,
old blade of giants,   broke through the shield-wall,

2980   let it crash down   on the great iron helmet.
The king fell over,   shepherd of his people,
dropped at last,   his old life gone.
Then there were many   who bandaged the brother,
stood him up quickly   once there was room
and they could control   that bloody field.

2985   And then one warrior   plundered the other,
took from Ongentheow   his iron link-coat,
the hilted sword,   and his helmet too,
and carried to Hygelac   the gray-beard's weapons.
He received them well,   promised reward

2990   once they were home,   and fulfilled it thus:
the king of the Geats,   the son of Hrethel,
once they returned   to the land of their people,
paid Wulf and Eofor   with immense treasure—
one hundred thousand   in land and rings.

2995   landes ond locenra bēaga   —ne ðorfte him ðā lēan
                                           oðwītan
      mon on middan-gearde—   syðða[n] hīe ðā mærða
                                        geslōgon;
      ond ðā Iofore forgeaf   āngan dohtor,
      hām-weorðunge   hyldo tō wedde.
      "Þæt ys sīo fæhðo   ond se fēondscipe,
3000   wæl-nīð wera,   ðæs ðe ic [wēn] hafo,
      þē ūs sēceað tō   Swēona lēoda,
      syððan hīe gefricgeað   frēan ūserne
      ealdor-lēasne,   þone ðe ær gehēold
      wið hettendum   hord *ond* rīce
3005   æfter hæleða hryre,   hwate Scildingas,
      folc-rēd fremede,   oððe furður gēn
      eorlscipe efnde.   [Nū] is ofost betost,
      þæt wē þēod-cyning   þær scēawian
      ond þone gebringan,   þe ūs bēagas geaf,
3010   on ād-fære.   Ne scel ānes hwæt
      meltan mid þām mōdigan,   ac þær is *m*āðma hord,
      gold unrīme,   grimme gecēa[po]d,
      ond nū æt sīðestan   sylfes fēore
      bēagas [geboh]te;   þā sceall brond fretan,
3015   æled þeccean,   nalles eorl wegan
      māððum tō gemyndum,   nē mægð scȳne
      habban on healse   hring-weorðunge,
      ac sceal geōmor-mōd,   golde berēafod,
      oft, nalles æne,   elland tredan,
3020   nū se here-wīsa   hleahtor ālegde,
      gamen ond glēo-drēam.   Forðon sceall gār wesan
      monig morgen-ceald   mundum bewunden,
      hæfen on handa,   nalles hearpan swēg

2996b   MS. syðða: em. Grundtvig.
3000b   No gap in MS.: conjectural restoration by Kemble.
3005b   The "hwate Scildingas" would be the Danes unless an emendation
is in order. See Commentary, p. 373.
3007b   MS. me: em. Kemble.
3012b   MS. gecea..*d*: restored by Kemble.
3014a   MS. .....te: restored by Grundtvig.

2995 No man on earth   had cause to reproach him
     since they had earned   their glory in battle.
     And he gave to Eofor   his only daughter,
     a grace in the home,   a pledge of friendship.
     "That is the feud,   the hatred of tribes,
3000 war-lust of men,   for which I [expect]
     the Swedish people   will seek us out
     in a new battle,   after they have heard
     that our lord is lifeless,   he who once held
     the hoard and kingdom   against all enemies
3005 after the death   of the brave Scyldings,
     worked in courage   for the good of the nation.
     Let us make haste   to look upon him [now],
     the king of our people   there on the ground,
     and bear him home   who gave us rings,
3010 to the ways of his pyre.   No small token
     shall melt with that heart,   but the whole hoard,
     uncounted treasure   purchased with valor,
     and now at the last   [bought] with his life.
     The fire shall eat them,   flames unweave
3015 the precious metals;   no brooch-jewels
     to be worn in memory,   or maiden's throat
     honored by gold,   but, sad in mind,
     nobles bereft   of rings and giver
     each must wander   no short time
3020 in the lands of exile,   now that our king
     has laid down laughter,   every joy.
     The spear must be seized,   morning-cold,
     hefted in hand,   on many dark dawns;

wīgend weccean,   ac se wonna hrefn
3025 fūs ofer fǣgum   fela reordian,
earne secgan,   hū him æt ǣte spēow,
þenden hē wið wulf   wæl rēafode."
Swā se secg hwata   secggende wæs
lāðra spella;   hē ne lēag fela
3030 wyrda nē weorda.   Weorod eall ārās,
ēodon unblīðe   under Earna-næs,
wollen-tēare,   wundur scēawian.
Fundon ðā on sande   sāwul-lēasne
hlim-bed healdan,   þone þe him hringas geaf
3035 ǣrran mǣlum;   þā wæs ende-dæg
gōdum gegongen,   þæt se gūð-cyning,
Wedra þēoden,   wundor-dēaðe swealt.
Ǣr hī þǣr gesēgan   syllīcran wiht,
wyrm on wonge   wiðer-ræhtes þǣr,
3040 lāðne licgean;   wæs se lēg-draca
grymlīc gry[re-fāh],   glēdum beswǣled.
Sē wæs fīftiges   fōt-gemearces
lang on legere;   lyft-wynne hēold
nihtes hwīlum,   nyðer eft gewāt
3045 dennes nīosian;   wæs ðā dēaðe fæst,
hæfde eorð-scrafa   ende genyttod.
Him big stōdan   bunan ond orcas,
discas lāgon   ond dȳre swyrd,
ōmige, þurhetone,   swā hīe wið eorðan fæðm
3050 þūsend wintra   þǣr eardodon.
Þonne wæs þæt yrfe   ēacen-cræftig,
iū-monna gold,   galdre bewunden,
þæt ðām hring-sele   hrīnan ne mōste
gumena ænig,   nefne God sylfa,
3055 sigora Sōð-cyning,   sealde þām ðe hē wolde
—hē is manna gehyld—   hord openian,
efne swā hwylcum manna,   swā him gemet ðūhte.
XLII   Þā wæs gesȳne,   þæt se sīð ne ðāh
þām ðe unrihte   inne gehȳdde

_____

3041a MS. gry..... Thorkelin could read "gryre." Restoration by Bugge.

no harp music   will wake the warriors,
3025 but the black raven   above doomed men
shall tell the eagle   how he fared at meat
when with the wolf   he stripped the bodies."
    Thus the brave man   told grievous news,
was hardly wrong   in his words or prophecies.
3030 The company rose,   went down unhappily
under Eagles' Cliff   to look with tears
at the awesome sight.   On the sand they found,
at his hard rest,   with life-soul gone,
the man who had given them   their rings many times.
3035 Then the last day   of the good man had come,
when the battle-leader,   king of the Weders,
died that wonderful death.   Before, they had seen
that stranger thing,   the huge worm lying
stretched on the sand   in front of his enemy.
3040 The terrible armor   of the shining dragon
was scorched by his flames.   In length he measured
fifty foot-paces.   Once he controlled
the air in joys,   had ridden on the wind
throughout the night,   then flew back down
3045 to seek his den.   Now he lay there,
stiff in death,   found no more caves.
Beside him were piled   pitchers and flagons,
dishes in heaps,   and well-wrought swords
eaten by rust,   just as they had lain
3050 in the deeps of the earth   for a thousand years.
In those days,   mighty in its powers,
the gold of the ancients   was wrapped in a spell,
so that no man   might touch that ring-hall
unless the Lord,   Truth-king of victories,
3055 —man's true shield—   should give permission
to whom He wished   to open the hoard,
to whatever man   seemed fit to Him.
XLII   Then it was clear   that it had not profited
the one who wrongly   had hidden away

3060 wræ[*t*]e under wealle.   Weard ǣr ofslōh
　　 fēara sumne;　　 þā sīo fǣhð gewearð
　　 gewrecen wrāðlīce.　　 Wundur hwār þonne
　　 eorl ellen-rōf　　 ende gefēre
　　 līf-gesceafta,　　 þonne leng ne mæg
3065 mon mid his [*mā*]gum　　 medu-seld būan.
　　 Swā wæs Bīowulfe,　　 þā hē biorges weard
　　 sōhte, searo-nīðas;　　 seolfa ne cūðe
　　 þurh hwæt his worulde gedǣl　　 weorðan sceolde.
　　 Swā hit oð dōmes dæg　　 dīope benemdon
3070 þēodnas mǣre,　　 þā ðæt þǣr dydon,
　　 þæt se secg wǣre　　 synnum scildig,
　　 hergum geheaðerod,　　 hell-bendum fǣst,
　　 wommum gewītnad,　　 sē ðone wong str[*u*]de;
　　 næs hē gold-hwǣte　　 gearwor hæfde
3075 āgendes ēst　　 ǣr gescēawod.
　　　 Wīglāf maðelode,　　 Wīhstānes sunu:
　　 "Oft sceall eorl monig　　 ānes willan
　　 wrǣc ādrēog[*an*],　　 swā ūs geworden is.
　　 Ne meahton wē gelǣran　　 lēofne þēoden,
3080 rīces hyrde　　 rǣd ǣnigne,
　　 þæt hē ne grētte　　 gold-weard þone,
　　 lēte hyne licgean　　 þǣr hē longe wæs,
　　 wīcum wunian　　 oð woruld-ende;
　　 hēold on hēah-gesceap.　　 Hord ys gescēawod,
3085 grimme gegongen;　　 wæs þæt gifeðe tō swīð,
　　 þe ðone [*þēod-cyning*]　　 þyder ontyhte.

3060a　MS. wræce: em. Thorpe. See also line 2771. Else von Schaubert
retains the MS. form and gives "gehȳdde" the meaning of "performed." Her
translation would run: "the act had not profited him who had performed
unlawful vengeance under the wall," i.e., the dragon (see her edition, Kom-
mentar, pp. 167–68, and Glossar, p. 129).
3065a　MS. ..gū: restored by Kemble.
3073b　MS. strade: em. Grundtvig.
3074–75　Perhaps the most obscure two lines in the poem, yet often
crucial in interpretation. Treated here as a half-ironic remark. The "he" is
Beowulf. See Commentary, p. 374, and A. J. Bliss in Bibliography, p. 385.
3078a　MS. adreogeð: em. Kemble.
3086a　No gap in MS.: conjectural restoration by Grein.

3060   the glittering jewels   under the wall.
        First the hoard-guard   had slain a man
        unlike other men,   and then that quarrel
        was fiercely avenged.   It is a mystery where
        a courageous man   will meet his fated end,
3065   no longer dwell   in the mead-hall with [kinsmen].
        So it was for Beowulf   when he sought combat,
        deadly barrow-guard;   he did not know
        how his parting from life   might come about.
        The princes of old   had sunk the treasure
3070   so deep with spells,   buried till Doomsday,
        that he who plundered   the floor of treasures
        would be guilty of sin,   tortured by evils,
        bound in hell-chains   at devils' shrines.
        None the more readily   had he earlier seen
3075   the gold-bestowing   kindness of the owner.
            Wiglaf addressed them,   Weohstan's son:
        "Often many earls   must suffer misery
        through the will of one,   as we do now.
        We could not persuade   our beloved leader,
3080   our kingdom's shepherd,   by any counsel,
        not to attack   that gold-keeper,
        to let him lie   where long he had lain,
        dwelling in his cave   till the end of the world.
        He held to his fate.   The hoard has been opened
3085   at terrible cost.   That fate was too strong
        that drew [the king   of our people] toward it.

Ic wæs þær inne   ond þæt eall geondseh,
recedes geatwa,   þā mē gerȳmed wæs,
nealles swæslīce   sīð ālȳfed
3090 inn under eorð-weall.   Ic on ofoste gefēng
micle mid mundum   mægen-byrðenne
hord-gestrēona,   hider ūt ætbær
cyninge mīnum.   Cwico wæs þā gēna,
wīs ond gewittig;   worn eall gespræc
3095 gomol on gehðo   ond ēowic grētan hēt,
bæd þæt gē geworhton   æfter wines dædum
in bæl-stede   beorh þone hēan,
micelne ond mærne,   swā hē manna wæs
wīgend weorð-fullost   wīde geond eorðan,
3100 þenden hē burh-welan   brūcan mōste.
Uton nū efstan   ōðre [*sīðe*]
sēon ond sēcean   searo-[*gimma*] geþræc,
wundur under wealle;   ic ēow wīsige,
þæt gē genōge   nēon scēawiað
3105 bēagas ond brād gold.   Sīe sīo bær gearo,
ædre geæfned,   þonne wē ūt cymen,
ond þonne geferian   frēan ūserne,
lēofne mannan,   þær hē longe sceal
on ðæs Waldendes   wære geþolian."
3110   Hēt ðā gebēodan   byre Wīhstānes,
hæle hilde-dīor,   hæleða monegum,
bold-āgendra,   þæt hīe bæl-wudu
feorran feredon,   folc-āgende,
gōdum tōgēnes: "Nū sceal glēd fretan,
3115 —weaxan wonna lēg—   wigena strengel,
þone ðe oft gebād   īsern-scūre,
þonne stræla storm   strengum gebæded
scōc ofer scild-weall,   sceft nytt*e he*old.
fæ[ð]er-gearwum fūs,   flāne fullēode."
3120   Hūru se snotra   sunu Wīhstānes

3101b No gap in MS.: restoration by Grundtvig.
3102b No gap in MS.: addition by Bugge.
3119a MS. fæder gearwū: em. Thorkelin.

I went inside   and looked all around,
saw the room's treasure,   when the way was clear;
not at all gently   was a journey allowed
3090 under that earth-work.   I quickly seized
a huge load of treasure,   rich hoard-goods
piled in my arms,   carried them out,
back to my king.   He was still living then,
had his wits about him.   He spoke of many things,
3095 old in his sorrow,   bade me address you,
ordered that you build him   a burial mound
on the site of his pyre,   high and famous,
for your friend's deeds,   since he was the best,
the worthiest warrior   throughout the world,
3100 as long as he enjoyed   the wealth of his stronghold.
Let us hurry now,   make a second [journey]
to see the hoard,   bright-[gemmed] gold,
the marvel in the cave.   I shall lead you,
that you may examine   the rings close at hand,
3105 see enough broad gold.   Prepare the bier,
make it ready quickly   when we come out again;
then carry our lord,   our beloved man,
to where he must dwell   long in God's keeping."

3110   The son of Weohstan,   sound in battle,
the brave man ordered   that they announce
to all warriors,   owners of dwellings,
that men of property   from near and far
were to bring timber   for the king's pyre:
"The fire must gnaw   —the flames growing dark—
3115 this prince of warriors   who often withstood
the rains of iron,   hard battle-hail,
when arrow-storms,   string-sent, rattled
loud upon the shield-wall,   shafts did duty,
swift in their feathers,   well served by barbs."
3120   And then the wise man,   son of Weohstan,

ācīgde of corðre   cyniges þegnas
syfone [æt]s[om]ne,   þā sēlestan,
ēode eahta sum   under inwit-hrōf
ʍilde-rinc[a];   sum on handa bær
3125   æled-lēoman,   sē ðe on orde gēong.
Næs ðā on hlytme,   hwā þæt hord strude,
syððan orwearde,   ænigne dæl,
secgas gesēgon   on sele wunian,
læne licgan;   lȳt ænig mearn
3130   þæt hī ofostlīc[e]   ūt geferedon
dȳre māðmas;   drācan ēc scufun,
wyrm ofer weall-clif,   lēton wēg niman,
flōd fæðmian   frætwa hyrde.
Ƿ[ā] wæs wunden gold   on wæn hladen,
3135   æghwæs unrīm,   æþeling boren,
hār hilde-[rinc]   tō Hrones-næsse.
XLIII   Him ðā gegiredan   Gēata lēode
ād on eorðan   unwāclīcne,
helm[um] behongen,   hilde-bordum,
3140   beorhtum byrnum,   swā hē bēna wæs;
ālegdon ðā tōmiddes   mærne þēoden
hæleð hīofende,   hlāford lēofne.
Ongunnon þā on beorge   bæl-fȳra mæst
wīgend weccan;   wud[u]-rēc āstāh
3145   sweart ofer swi[o]ðole;   swōgende lē[c],
wōpe bewunden;   wind-blond gelæg

3121b   "cyniges" begins fol. 201, the last leaf of the poem. It is badly
torn and the verso is hopelessly faded in many places. Even with the help
of ultraviolet light, paleographers remain uncertain about many readings.
3122a   MS. syfone .. s..ne (as read by Malone, *NC*, p. 103): restored
by Grein.
3124a   MS. ʍilde rinc: em. Ettmüller.
3130a   MS. ofostlic from Thorkelin B: em. Ettmüller.
3134a   MS. has abbreviation for "þæt":. em. Thorkelin.
3135b   MS. æþelinge: em. Kemble.
3136a   "hilde" is followed by an erasure of three letters; restoration by
Ettmüller.
3139a   MS. helm: em. Grein.
3144b   MS. wud..ec Thorkelin A wud rec: restored by Kemble.
3145a   MS. swicðole: em. Karl Bouterwek, *ZDA* 11 (1859), 82 ff.

       chose from the council   the best men there,
       seven king's thanes   in a [gathered] band.
       The eight of them went   down in the barrow,
       beneath the evil roof.   He who led them
3125 held a torch,   firelight in hand.
       No lots were drawn   over that hoard
       once the men saw   how every part of it
       lay unguarded   throughout the hall,
       gold wasting away.   Little they mourned
3130 that hasty plunder   of the precious goods,
       but carried them out,   then pushed the dragon
       over the cliff-wall,   gave to the waves
       the hoard-keeper,   let the sea take him.
       Then the twisted gold   was loaded on a cart,
3135 incredible wealth,   and the noble [warrior],
       the gray-haired king,   was carried to Whale's Cliff.

XLIII   The Geatish people   then built a pyre
       on that high ground,   no mean thing,
       hung with helmets,   strong battle-boards,
3140 bright coats of mail,   as he had requested,
       and then they laid   high in the center
       their famous king,   their beloved lord,
       the warriors weeping.   Then on that headland
       the great fire was wakened.   The wood-smoke
                                climbed up,
3145 black above flames;   the roaring one danced,
       encircled by wailing;   the wind died away

3145–46 There is now a hole between "le" and the final "e" of "wōpe."
Thorkelin A and B read "let wope," emended by Bugge to "lēc" (played,
danced, flew up). Most editions assume, as here, that A and B misread "c"
as "t" but they also assume "lēc" is a phonetic error and emend it to "lēg"
(fire). It is then an easy variation on "swioðole." Malone, *NC*, p. 104, would
retain the MS. form as a verb, taking "swōgende lēt" as "the roaring one
(i.e., the fire) declined," parallel to 3146b.

oðþæt hē ðā bān-hūs   gebrocen hæfde,
hāt on hreðre.   Higum unrōte
mōd-ceare mǣndon,   mon-dryhtnes *cw*[*e*]*alm*;
3150 *swylce* giōmor-gyd   [*Ge*]at[*isc*] mēowle
[*Bīowulfe brægd*,]   bunden-heor*de*,
[*so*]*ng* sorg-cearig.   [*Sǣde*] geneahhe
þæt hīo hyre [*here-geon*]gas   hearde *ond*[*r*]*ē*de
*wæl-f*ylla wo[*r*]n,   *were*u*de*s egesan,
3155 hy[*n*]ðo *ond hæft-n*ȳd.   Heofon rēce *swealg*.
Geworhton ðā   Wedra lēode
hl*ǣ*w on *hō*e,   sē *wæs* hēah ond brād,
*wē*g-līðendum   wīde *ge*sȳne,
ond be*tim*bredon   on tȳn dagum
3160 beadu-rōfes bēcn;   bronda lā*fe*
wealle beworht*on*,   swā hyt weorðlīcost
fore-*s*notre men   findan mihton.
Hī on beorg dydon   bēg ond siglu,
eall swylce hyrsta,   swylce on horde ǣr
3165 nīð-hēdige men   genumen hæfdon;

3149b   Thorkelin A cw aln, B ...lm: restored by Kemble.

3150b   MS. .*eat*...: restoration by Pope.

3151   A rip has destroyed the first half-line; the conjecture—and it is only that—is by Malone, *NC*, p. 105. For the second half-line A. H. Smith's ultraviolet examination gives us the "b" and Thorkelin B the "de."

3152   MS. ..*ng* sorg (by Smith's ultraviolet photograph): restored by Bugge. For MS. ..*lð*e Thorkelin A and B read "sealde." The "l" and "d" are now doubtful; Pope and Davis thought they could see them as "i" and "d." Emendation by Bugge, now seconded by Pope (2nd ed.). Malone accepted the Thorkelin readings as accurate (*NC*, p. 105) and would translate, "It would happen often that she would dread cruel invasions."

3153   MS. ...*g.n*gas in Malone's conflation of the different expert examinations: conjectural restoration by W. S. Mackie, *MLR* 36 (1941), 98. MS. *ond*.e*de*: restored by Bugge.

3154a   MS. wonn: em. Bugge.

3155   MS. hyðo 7 *h.f.*nyd by Smith's ultraviolet photograph and confirmed by Pope in 1964: restored and emended by Bugge. Nothing now visible after "rēce"; Thorkelin A and B sealg. Malone and Zupitza could piece together a vision of the "w" first suggested by Ettmüller.

3157a   "hl*ǣ*w" from Pope and Davis, "hō*e*" from Smith's Plate VI.

3159a   MS. be*ti*. / bredon with the "m" as deduced by Malone, *NC*, p. 107.

      until the fire   had broken that bone-house,
      had burned to the heart.   Sad and despairing,
      the warriors grieved   for the death of their lord.
3150 In the same fashion   a Geatish woman,
      her hair bound up,   [wove] a grief-song,
      the lament [for Beowulf.]   Over and over
      [she said] that she feared   [the attacks of raiders],
      many slaughters,   the terror of troops,
3155 shame and captivity.   Heaven swallowed the smoke.
      Then the men of the Weders   built on that cliff
      a memorial barrow   that was high and broad,
      to be seen far off   by ocean travelers,
      and it took ten days   to build that monument
3160 to the famous man.   The remains of the pyre
      they buried in walls   as splendidly worked
      as men wise in skill   knew how to fashion.
      Within this barrow   they placed jeweled rings,
      all the ornaments   the brave-minded men
3165 had earlier taken   away from the hoard;

       forlēton eorla gestrēon   *eor*ðan healdan,
       gold on grēote,   þǣr hit nū gēn lifað
       *el*dum swā unnyt,   swā hy[*t ǣr*]or wæs.
       Þā ymbe hlǣw rioda*n*   hilde-dēore,
3170 æþelinga *bearn,*   ealra twelf[*e*],
       woldon [*care*] *cw*īðan,   *k*yning mǣnan,
       word-gy*d* wrecan   ond ymb *we*[*r*] *sprec*an:
       eahtodan *eor*lscipe   ond his ellen-weorc
       duguðum dēmdon.   Swā hit *ged*[*ēfe*] bið
3175 þæt mon his wine-dryhten   wordum *h*erge,
       ferhðum frēo*ge*,   þonne hē forð scile
       of *līc*-haman   [*lǣded*] weorðan.
       Swā begnornodon   Gēata lēode
       hlāfordes [*hr*]yre,   heorð-genēa*t*as;
3180 cwǣdon þæt hē wǣre   wyruld-cyni*ng*[*a*],
       *man*num mildust   ond *mon-ðwǣr*ust,
       lēodum līðost   ond lof-geornost.

3168b MS. hy. ..or, from Malone, *NC*, pp. 107–8: restoration by Kemble.
3170b MS. twelfa: em. Ettmüller.
3171a The MS. has room here for about four letters, hence Klaeber's restoration.
3172b MS. *w*.. with *e* from Thorkelin B: restored by Grein.
3174b MS. *gd*... from Malone, *NC*, p. 108: expanded and restored by Kemble.
3177b The MS. and ultraviolet photographs produce nothing for this word. Conjectural restoration by Holthausen. Alternatives proposed by Kemble and Malone are "lǣne" (transitory) and "līfes" (of life).
3179a MS. ...yre: restored by Thorpe.
3180b MS. wyruldcyni*ng*: em. Kemble.
3181 MS. .*annū*, Thorkelin B supplying the "m." MS. is torn from "ond" to "ust" Thorkelin A and B read "mondrærust" in evident error, corrected by Grundtvig.

they gave to the earth   for its final keeping
the treasure of princes,   gold in the ground,
where it lies even now,   as useless to men
as it was before.   Then round the barrow
twelve nobles rode,   war-brave princes.

3170 They wanted to mourn   their king in their [grief],
to weave a lay   and speak about the man:
they honored his nobility   and deeds of courage,
their friend's great prowess.   So it is [fitting]

3175 that a man speak praise   of his beloved lord,
love him in spirit,   when he must be [led]
forth from his life,   the body's home.
Thus did the Weders   mourn in words
the fall of their lord,   his hearth-companions.

3180 They said that he was,   of the kings in this world,
the kindest to his men,   the most courteous man,
the best to his people,   and most eager for fame.

ROYAL GENEALOGIES

I. *The Danes (Scyldings)*

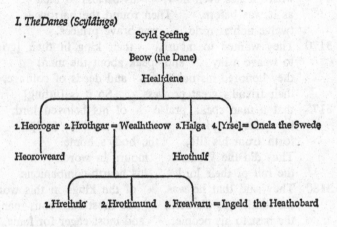

Scyld Scefing

Beow (the Dane)

Healfdene

1. Heorogar   2. Hrothgar = Wealhtheow   3. Halga   4. [Yrse] = Onela the Swede

Heoroweard

Hrothulf

1. Hrethric   2. Hrothmund   3. Freawaru = Ingeld the Heathobard

II. *The Geats (Weders)*

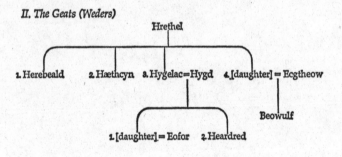

Hrethel

1. Herebeald   2. Hæthcyn   3. Hygelac = Hygd   4. [daughter] = Ecgtheow

Beowulf

1. [daughter] = Eofor   2. Heardred

III. *The Swedes (Scylfings)*

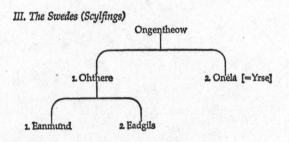

Ongentheow

1. Ohthere   2. Onela [= Yrse]

1. Eanmund   2. Eadgils

Backgrounds

History of the Manuscript

Beowulf survives only in one manuscript codex, British Museum MS. Cotton Vitellius A. XV., which contains five different works in Old English: *The Passion of St. Christopher, The Wonders of the East, Alexander's Letter to Aristotle* (all in prose), *Beowulf,* and the poetic fragment *Judith.* The manuscript was written by two scribes around A.D. 1000 in late West Saxon, the literary dialect of the period. Scribe I copied the three prose pieces and the first 1,939 lines of *Beowulf.* Scribe II, who had a more old-fashioned hand, copied the rest of *Beowulf* and *Judith.* Currently there are 116 leaves in the codex; *Beowulf* fills 70 of them, and we are extremely lucky to have the complete poem. The beginning of *St. Christopher* and the bulk of *Judith* were already lost in 1563 when Lawrence Nowell, Dean of Lichfield and an early Anglo-Saxonist, put his name and date on the first surviving leaf. Nowell was probably responsible for the preservation of the manuscript after Henry VIII's dissolution of the monasteries. Its earlier history is unknown. In Elizabethan times it passed into the great library of Sir Robert Cotton, the antiquary, from which comes its British Museum designation. Sir Robert catalogued his books according to the busts of Roman emperors that stood over each of his bookcases, and in this instance the emperor was Vitellius. Under the bust of Nero lay the great Middle English poems *Pearl* and *Sir Gawain and the Green Knight,* in MS. Cotton Nero A. X.

In 1731 a fire swept through the Cottonian library, damaging many books and scorching the *Beowulf* codex. In 1786–87, after the manuscript had been deposited in the British Museum, the Ice-

245

lander Grímur Jónsson Thorkelin made two transcriptions of the poem for what was to be the first edition, in 1815. To make Transcript A, Thorkelin employed an unidentified copyist who knew no Old English and copied quite mechanically. Transcript B was made by Thorkelin himself, who had a knowledge of the language, although, like his copyist, he made errors of transcription. Today these two transcripts, errors and all, are invaluable for determining letters and words which have since crumbled away. *Beowulf* suffered the worst damage of the five pieces in the codex, and the fire scorched the edges of the leaves containing the last two thousand lines more severely than the earlier portion. The most damaged leaves today are those containing lines 1685–2339 and the last leaf. The damage is not only from fire; letters have also faded to the point of illegibility, apparently from wear. At some earlier date, we may assume, the last leaf of *Beowulf* was for a period of time the final leaf in the codex. Perhaps, too, Beowulf's tragic third fight with the dragon was more frequently read than his earlier adventures, since folio 182, where this adventure begins, is quite worn out. In the nineteenth century the manuscript was rebound to prevent further deterioration.

Beowulf is untitled in the manuscript and was named by early editors. Cotton Vitellius A. XV. is small in size—roughly five by eight inches—and unpretentious in execution. The capital letters are poorly made, and the illustration accompanying *The Wonders of the East* are crude. As the product of a scriptorium, the codex is no more than journeyman work of the Benedictine revival and does not compare with the three other manuscript books in which the bulk of Old English poetry is preserved.

Beowulf probably was not widely known in its own day, since Beowulf's adventures are not mentioned in any other Anglo-Saxon source. It is likely, in fact, that in the last part of the Old English period (A.D. 850–1100) it was understood mainly as a fabulous monster-story. The first three pieces in the codex all tell of strange and marvelous monsters. St. Christopher, for instance, was not only a giant, as in his *Passion*; in the eleventh-century MS. Otho B. X., now lost, he appeared as one of the Cynocephali, or dog-headed cannibals, who are also mentioned in *The Wonders of the East* and *Alexander's Letter*. In *Beowulf* Grendel and his mother could also be regarded as giant cannibals. Perhaps we owe the initial preservation of the poem to someone who wanted to collect stories about monsters, or more generally about "the marvelous," a term which could also include the slaying of the tyrant Holofernes by the demure Judith. If this were so, then the collection was probably not made until the second half of the tenth century, and it is possible that all five works were first assembled in the *Beowulf* codex.

Date and Location of Origin

Theories abound, but scholars do not know by whom, how, when, or where *Beowulf* was composed. The linguistic evidence shows that all five pieces in the *Beowulf* codex had a previous manuscript history. *Beowulf* itself is likely to have had a relatively long descent through a chain of copies, perhaps over two hundred years, since some earlier non-West Saxon forms are embedded in the language of the surviving manuscript. However, dating by archaic forms is trickly, since they may have been part of the conventional poetic diction of the late Old English period. In themselves, such forms do not prove that the whole poem is an early composition. We also need external evidence. The poem mentions that Beowulf's liege lord, Hygelac of the Geats, was killed in a raid on the Frisians. This is the one indisputable historical fact in the poem. It is corroborated by the historian Gregory of Tours (d. 594), who dates the death of Hygelac, Latinized to Chlochilaichus, as circa 521.

This date sets an absolute earlier limit. However, the history of the Anglo-Saxon settlement of England, which only began in the fifth century A.D., suggests that the earliest likely date would be sometime in the age of the Venerable Bede, who lived A.D. 673–735. The latest possible date for the poem is usually set in the 790s, when the Vikings sacked the monasteries at Lindisfarne and Jarrow, or in the 830s, when the Danes first began to overrun England in earnest. The argument for this later limit is, in essence, that during the ninth-century Danish invasions no Anglo-Saxon could have composed a poem sympathetic to the Danes. But this patriotic view of human, and poetic, nature is perhaps too simple. With the nation in turmoil, a man might have had any number of reasons to write about the transient glory of Danish kings in the far past, not the least being the barbarity of the present invaders. Another line of argument used for an early date is that the allusions to sixth-century Scandinavian heroes, whom the poet apparently expected his audience to recognize easily, give us solid internal evidence for placing the poem at a time when these stories were still vivid in the memory of the early Angles and Saxons. However, the rate at which such lore died out in England is quite unknown. The pervasive Christian atmosphere of the poem is often urged as a criterion for dating, be it early or late, but the exact nature of the Christianity in *Beowulf* is still a matter of debate. We are left with a broad range of possible dates—anywhere from A.D. 650 to 850.

There is an equally wide range of possible places of origin. It was formerly thought on linguistic grounds that the poem had to come from the Anglian area, either Northumbria or Mercia. However, in the 1940s Kenneth Sisam demonstrated that the tests for the dialect origins of earlier Old English verse are often inconclusive and that we are probably dealing with a general Old English poetic dialect, artificially combining archaic and regional forms. We are free to place Beowulf anywhere in Anglo-Saxon England that we can find plausible historical circumstances. If we opt for the brilliant age of Bede, then the court of the scholar-king Aldfrith of Northumbria (d. 705) would suit admirably. If we look to the eighth century, the court of Offa of Mercia (A.D. 757–96) is especially attractive. Offa was the greatest English king of this period, important enough to quarrel with Charlemagne, and a ruler who could afford to build the sixty-mile-long earthwork known as Offa's Dyke, to mark his Welsh border. The story of his earlier Continental namesake, Offa, King of Angeln in the fourth century, is told in *Beowulf* 1931–62, in one of the few really puzzling digressions in the poem. Possibly it was meant as a compliment to a royal patron.

A high level of Anglo-Saxon culture also existed in seventh-century East Anglia, as we can see from the magnificent royal ship-burial discovered in 1939 at Sutton Hoo, Suffolk. This treasure-burial is sufficiently like the burials of Scyld and Beowulf to suggest that possibly the poem was composed in the East Anglian royal palace of the Wuffing dynasty at nearby Rendlesham, within living memory of the ship-burial, which is dated to A.D. 625–55. The mound at Sutton Hoo contained some grave-goods that link it with the royal burials at Uppsala, Sweden. With surprising exactness, *Beowulf* describes goods not merely of Anglo-Saxon times, but also Swedish goods of the presumed date of the historical events in the poem, A.D. 500–600. Was it through the early East Anglian court that the detailed knowledge of Scandinavian tribal history in *Beowulf* became available in England? The genealogy of the East Angles names one Wehha as the first king to rule over them in England. His son was Wuffa, from whom the dynasty took its name, the Wuffingas. These names correspond roughly to Weohstan, Wiglaf, and the Wylfingas in *Beowulf*. It is conceivable that the Geats (in Swedish, the "Gauts") who lived near Uppsala, migrated to Anglia under the leadership of Weohstan or Wiglaf, bringing with them Swedish heirlooms that were later buried at Sutton Hoo. Perhaps they left Gautland after a disastrous defeat by the Swedes, as prophesied at the end of *Beowulf*. That the poem was composed under such circumstances makes a tantalizing hypothesis, but, alas, it cannot be definitely proven.

Aristocratic culture was not confined to royal courts, and *Beowulf* may have been composed in a monastery instead. From the middle of the seventh century on, the Anglo-Saxon aristocracy frequently entered monasteries, where they usually became powerful political leaders in the ecclesiastical sphere. Members of their entourages frequently went with them. Very likely the heroism and the Christianity of *Beowulf* would have appeared two aspects of the same thing to the first audience of the poem, whether they heard it in the cloister or the mead-hall. In either case, the noble audience would have heard it recited aloud before a group, instead of perusing it silently in the study. Oral delivery of literary works, from memory or manuscript, was the customary mode of "publication" throughout the Middle Ages. In addition, heroic poetry had the important function of reinforcing the ideals and shared values of the community of listeners.

Composition and Authorship

These points raise the question of how *Beowulf* was composed. Is it the work of one man? If so, did he write it or did he compose it orally, harp in hand, chanting a traditional song, extempore, like the old bards in the poem itself? After all, its first words are *"Listen! We have heard* of the glory of the Spear-Danes." We know that its elevated, highly traditional language comes ultimately from oral poetry, which had a common pool of formulaic diction available for extempore performances of known tales. The bard would use familiar themes and phrases in his improvisation much as jazz musicians today combine riffs, tags, and other musical formulas when they improvise upon a tune. It is likely that the Homeric epics were composed this way, and up to the 1930s it remained a living art in rural Yugoslavia, where Milman Parry collected many of the chants of the *guslars* and first formulated his theory of oral-formulaic composition to explain certain peculiarities of Homeric diction.

The origin of the diction and style of *Beowulf,* however, is not necessarily the origin of the poem itself. Later Old English poets who translated Latin texts into poetry such as the OE. *Phoenix* used this oral diction although they obviously had to read while they wrote. On the other hand, *Widsith,* one of the earliest Old English poems, a memory catalogue of rulers and tribes chanted by a fictional poet named Widsith, "the far-traveled one," is just as obviously oral in origin. In fact, it is probably a composite poem that grew in the resinging over the centuries. The mere presence of formulaic diction, then, is not enough to prove that *Beowulf* was composed aloud by a trained bard any more than the intricacy of some of its poetic effects is proof that it was written by a cleric-poet familiar with Vergil's *Aeneid.* A moment's glance at *Paradise Lost,* composed orally by the blind Milton, makes it clear that the question of compositional method cannot be decided on the evidence of the diction alone.

In the case of *Beowulf,* both theories of composition, the oral and the written, have had their vociferous spokesmen, because it is a crucial matter for informed criticism of the poem. Oral-formulaic poems are governed by different literary conventions than written works. They are not necessarily inferior productions, or mere folk poetry—the *Iliad* proves this—but they use a different poetic grammar and must be approached with different expectations. As in the case of the Yugoslavian *guslars,* the oral poet in his purest form is illiterate, and he thinks his poetic thoughts in metrical formulas and fixed narrative themes. This is no inconsiderable art in itself. He is a performer, not a writer, and he may sing badly or well, depending on the deftness with which he can use the traditional language. But he has no conception of a fixed text, since he thinks in metrical formulas. He will keep the sequence of events in a poem fairly stable from one performance to the next, but he never sings the same poem *exactly* the same way twice. This variation in language deprives literary critics of one of their favorite objects of study: close-knit verbal effects occurring in the final draft of a text. Scholars who believe *Beowulf* was composed orally are still at work trying to set up an alternative critical approach.

We may not have to choose between the two hypotheses in their extreme forms. It is possible that *Beowulf* was first written down during an oral bard's dictation, when he had the chance to ponder and resay many phrases that would go unrevised in an ordinary performance. It the text came into being this way, it might present not a final draft, but the poet's idea of a "best text." Dictation has been suggested as the reason for the extraordinary length of the *Iliad* and *Odyssey*. Whatever the actual case, we do not know it. It is enough that the Homeric poems and *Beowulf* are the products of oral poetic tradition. The lover of narrative poetry will then look for, and will even relish, a certain looseness in composition. Not novelty, but the apt use of tradition will be prized. The slight inconsistencies and repetitions in the story of Beowulf are common features of traditional poetry and are not to be judged harshly. Perhaps we might also imagine that the poem was delivered in three sittings, one fight per night, a thousand lines each, which would account for some of the recapitulations. After such traditional features are allowed for, we can read and talk about *Beowulf* as we would any other long poem.

It cannot be definitely proved that one man gave *Beowulf* the form in which we know it today. But there is no reason not to think so. For many readers the literary experience of the poem itself, the way it hangs together in the mind, will be sufficient evidence that it is the product of one man's imagination. However, there was a time when as many as six different authors could be discerned in the text (by Karl Müllenhof, in 1889). Even today, Francis P. Magoun, Jr., who first applied the oral-formulaic theory of composition to Old English poetry, has divided *Beowulf* into three originally separate lays. Under this theory, the poem would come into being when the three songs concerning the three fights were first joined together, but even after the creation of this "ur-*Beowulf*," the digressive narratives woven around the three fights would continue to be added by different singers over a period of time. The final singer who gave us our single text could then be credited only for his choice of words and his emphasis within episodes, but not for the choice of subject matter or the poem's over-all structure. So runs this theory. But it brings us no closer to the historical truth of the matter. Even if *Beowulf* were highly uneven in literary quality, which it assuredly is not, multiple authorship would still be questionable, since it could have been composed by a single poet of uneven talent. We are free to suppose that a single man was responsible for the beauties (and occasional awkwardnesses) of the poem's structure, the inclusion of the interlaced narratives, and the conception of individual episodes. What we may *not* suppose is that he invented these stories out of thin air. Most of them are attested in our sources, though often in altered form. If, for the sake of convenience, we choose to assume a single mind behind our text and we refer to him as "the *Beowulf* poet," we should not forget that in an important sense he was only one member in a long chain of poetic storytellers. It is unlikely that he thought of himself as highly original. Like all Old English poets, he was content to exercise his individual talent within the limits of his poetic tradition. The delights and surprises of his stately, vigorous style come not from innovation so much as from his superlative use of inherited poetic techniques. In this sense *Beowulf* is not the product of a single mind, but of a tradition transformed from within.

Sources and Traditions of the Poem

The character of Beowulf was probably the poet's own creation. He appears unknown outside the poem, while virtually every other character is found in early legends. Beowulf's name does not alliterate, as was the convention, with his father's Ecgtheow, or his tribe's, the Wægmundings. If the poet did not invent him, he probably chose an obscure figure from folklore, a man strong as a bear—hence *Bēo-wulf* 'bee-wolf'—and placed him in a realistic historical setting where he could act with the dignity befitting a Germanic hero.

The fairy-tale quality of Beowulf's three monster-killings indicates a folktale source for the central plot. A widespread tale of the type named variously "Strong John," "The Bear's Son," or "The Three Stolen Princesses" (Aarne-Thompson Folktale-Type #301) lies behind the episodes of Grendel and his mother, but in precisely what form we shall never know. The German scholar Friedrich Panzer collected two hundred variants of this tale-type in the late nineteenth century. His analysis showed that Part I of *Beowulf* has its closest affinities with the "Sandhaugar Episode" in the Old Icelandic *Grettis saga* (dated c. 1300). Other stories in Old Norse that echo the details of Beowulf's heroic efforts in Denmark are *Samsons saga* and the story of Bothvarr Bjarki ("Little Bear") in *Hrolfs saga Kraka*. These and other medieval analogues are conveniently collected in *Beowulf and Its Analogues*, translated by G. N. Garmonsway and Jacqueline Simpson. The episode in the story of Grettir the Strong is strikingly akin to Beowulf's first two fights and is worth summary:

A farmstead called Sandhaugar has twice been raided at Christmas-time and each time a man has disappeared, leaving only traces of blood. When Grettir hears of this, he visits the farm, in disguise since he is an outlaw. When the mistress of the house leaves for church on Christmas Eve, Grettir stays behind to watch for whatever it is that haunts the farm. He barricades himself in the main hall, and lies down in his bed in his clothes. Near midnight he is attacked by a huge she-troll, or giantess, with a trough in one hand and a great knife in the other. She rushes at Grettir, who jumps up to attack her, and they fight long and hard in the hall, destroying most of the interior. When she drags Grettir out of the farmhouse, the framework of the outer door is torn off and carried away on their shoulders. They reach the edge of a deep gorge, with a waterfall and river below. Grettir finally wrestles himself free from her bear-hug and manages to cut off her right arm with his knife. She falls down into the waterfall. Grettir is very weary, and returns to the farm quite black and blue.

Later on, the priest of the parish, who doubts the truth of Grettir's story, goes with him to the gorge. There is a cave behind the waterfall, high up under the overhanging cliff. It is sixty feet from the top to the pool below. Grettir rigs a rope, which he leaves the priest to guard. Then he dives under the waterfall and reaches the cave. Inside, a great fire is burning and a giant is sitting beside it. He jumps up and lunges at Grettir with a wooden-hafted pike called a "hafted short-sword" (ON. *hepti-sax*). Grettir strikes back with his own short-sword and cuts the shaft in two. The giant reaches for a sword hanging on the wall of the cave and, as he does, Grettir eviscerates him. The priest on the cliff above sees some of the giant's gore in the rushing water and concludes that Grettir has been killed. Instead of holding the rope, he runs home. Grettir gives the giant one blow after another until he is dead. Then he kindles a light and explores the cave, where he finds treasure and the bones of the two men who were killed. Bringing the bones in a bag, he swims to the rope, which he is forced to climb hand over hand since the priest is not there to pull him up.

Later on he accuses the priest of faithlessness, and the priest admits
he should have waited longer. After that there is no more trouble from
trolls at Sandhaugar. (Chaps. 64–66)

There are many similarities here to Beowulf's battles with the
Grendel tribe. The conclusion to be drawn is not that the later
Grettis saga derives from *Beowulf,* or *Beowulf* from some earlier
version of the Grettir story, but that they both go back independently
to a common original.

The source of the dragon fight in Part II is less clear. G. V.
Smithers has recently made an interesting argument that Part II was,
at an earlier stage in its history, a variant of the story pattern found
in Part I. Other scholars have thought that the poet found Parts I
and II already joined, since Beowulf demonstrates his bearlike
strength by hugging a Frisian warrior to death (2501 ff.) and refers
back to his conquest of Grendel in lines 2518 ff. However, a dragon
fight is not the usual conclusion to the type of folktale behind Part I.
(The tale type is outlined in *B & A,* pp. 331–32.) The idea of a
dragon fight was readily available in popular story and the poet may
have been the first and last to apply it to the hero Beowulf. The
futility of the hero's death distinguishes our poem from other dragon
stories, and the whole artistic conception of Part II appears to be
original with the poet. In fact, no exact parallel to Part II exists in
early literature, even when the search is narrowed to a dragon fight
where the hero dies protecting mankind, as Thor does in Norse
mythology, or where the dragon is formerly a man, like Fafnir in the
Poetic Edda and the *Vǫlsunga saga.*

Nonetheless, it is possible that the poet was influenced by some
early version of the Norse myth of Ragnarǫk, the Downfall of the
Gods, in which Thor fights the cosmic serpent wrapped round the
World-Tree Yggdrasill. An apocalyptic sense of a whole world pass-
ing away is always near the surface in Part II. The Norse story of
the death of Baldr, accidentally killed by his brother Hǫthr, may
have provided a pattern for the tragic death of the Geatish prince
Here*beald*, accidentally killed by his brother *Hæth*cyn at archery
(2435 ff.). Another resemblance in name elements is the allusion
in 1197 ff. to Hama, who carried off the *Brōsinga mēn* 'the necklace
of the Brosings' to a shining city. In Norse myth the necklace of the
goddess Freyja is the *Brísinga men*, and in one adventure it is carried

off by the god *Heim*dallr (cf. Hama), who fought over it with Loki. Perhaps the poet drew on Norse myths, diminishing their stature to fit his Christian heroic world, to achieve a larger symbolism. The building of Heorot, which follows a paraphrase of Genesis, was surely intended by the poet as a creation myth by which the poem's landscape comes into being. Since the Christian Doomsday would not be suitable for a secular story, a Norse myth of the Apocalypse in which Thor fought a dragon may have influenced the poet's sense of an ending.

Another possible source for Beowulf's dragon fight may lie within the poem itself: the lay of Sigemund (875 ff.) tells how that hero kills a dragon and carries off his treasure. Sigemund has a nephew, Fitela, as Beowulf has Wiglaf, but Sigemund kills his dragon without aid. While Sigemund acquires gold and glory, Beowulf dies and his treasure is buried with him, "as useless to men as it was before" (3168). The poet uses the Sigemund story to foreshadow Beowulf's final conflict and to contrast with its grimmer glory. It might be source enough. Or he could have invented the Sigemund story, since it is the only known dragon-killing by that doughty hero in the rich early sources of the Nibelung legend. Although more an artistic device than a source, it does suggest the poet had knowledge of the Nibelung stories. The most famous dragon story among them concerns Sigurth, son of Sigmundr in Old Norse, later to become the Siegfried of the *Nibelungenlied*. The dragon slain by Sigurth is Fafnir, who was originally a giant's son. Once he has acquired the gold of the Nibelungs by nefarious means, he makes his dwelling in a burial mound and turns into a dragon to guard his hoard. To kill him, Sigurth digs a pit in the path that Fafnir follows when going to drink and then stabs him from below. Before Fafnir dies, he informs Sigurth that the treasure is cursed and will bring about his death. Not only the fatal curse (cf. 3069 ff.) but also the transformation of man into dragon may be echoed in *Beowulf*. This is especially likely if the Last Survivor, who so movingly speaks an elegy for his tribe when he buries the treasure (2247–66), was in some earlier version a troll who lived in a burial mound. This speculation would place the dragon in the same class of supernatural beings as Grendel, who at one point carries a huge glove made of dragon-skins. (See further Smithers, *The Making of "Beowulf."*)

Grendel's nature is, of course, diabolical from a Christian point of view: he is a member of the race of Cain, from whom all misshapen and unnatural beings were spawned, such as ogres and elves. He is a creature dwelling in the outer darkness, a giant, a cannibal. When he crawls off to die, he is said to join the rout of devils in Hell. However, he also appears to have roots in Scandinavian folklore. In Old Norse literature, monsters of his type make their appearance chiefly as *draugar*, or animated corpses. They are ordinary folk who have been buried upright in cairns, according to Norse custom, but if they harbor a grievance after death they will refuse to stay put and will roam about at night wreaking aimless vengeance. They are articulate and usually angry, in contrast to the silent zombies of Haiti. A *draugr* is supernaturally strong and invulnerable (being already dead) and will often have a mother called a *ketta*, or "she-cat," who is even more monstrous than he. Grendel, then, appears to be a blend of the *draugr* figure and a devilish monster from the world of Christian folklore.

The nature of the *Beowulf* dragon is something else again. One would like to say, "Dragons will be dragons," and be done with it. No serpent in Western literature means well. But whether we should also understand the dragon as a Christian symbol for the general evil in the world, or as the Devil who appears as serpent and Leviathan in the Bible, has been a matter of considerable controversy. The dragon's nature is important to any interpretation of the overriding moral purpose of the poem. As a creature from the natural history of the Middle Ages, he is mainly a dragon of the native Anglo-Saxon type: fire-breathing, a night-flyer, and the guardian of a hoard within a burial mound. The Cotton *Maxims*, a group of early gnomic sayings, declare that "it is the dragon's place to dwell in a barrow, ancient, proud in treasure." The Anglo-Saxon Chronicle for A.D. 793 describes terrifying portents that preceded a famine in Northumbria: great flashes of lightning were seen "and fiery dragons flying through the air." The poet invented many loaded terms to calumniate the horrible Grendel, but he names the dragon mainly by his actions, as "old night-flyer" or "harm-doer." Perhaps he saw him as a natural disaster, tragic yet unavoidable, like a plague or famine.

On the other hand, the poet was clearly a Christian, and he may well have been a learned man. The early and highly popular allegorized natural history called the *Physiologus* (later the *Bestiary*), of which a fragment survives in Old English, treats Draco as venomous, the largest of all serpents and a symbol for Our Ancient Enemy. The *Beowulf* dragon is sufficiently snakelike, both in his appearance and behavior, to qualify as a Christian symbol. If we assume that the poet knew and used such patristic writers as Aldhelm or Gregory the Great, then he might well have regarded the dragon as a flame-breathing symbol for the Devil himself, guarding a hoard of gold that infects men with greed and pride and so leads to death and damnation. But this is a large assumption, since the poet does not "cue in" such an allegorical meaning. A final judgment on the dragon's nature as an adversary will therefore have to rest not on traditional concepts but on how the reader interprets Beowulf's last battle.

In whatever form the poet found the sources for his main plot, he worked consciously to develop them. He amplified a simple story line to suit his purposes, as in the eloquent treatment of the faithful Wiglaf, or the elaborate interlacing of historical elements with the dragon fight, a technique similar to Shakespeare's double plots. The main story of *Beowulf* has been called "a fairy-tale with all the magic removed" (Shippey, *N & Q*). This effect is achieved mainly by the surrounding references to historical tribes and stories of their heroes. We know from the references in *Beowulf* itself that shorter heroic lays about these tribes' exploits were already in existence. The poet could probably depend upon his audience for a quick and appreciative recollection of such poetry when he chose to allude to these traditional stories. They did not have to be about Anglo-Saxons. Knowledge of the Danes, Swedes, Geats, and other northern peoples apparently lay deep in the memory of Anglo-Saxon audiences. Once we allow for the confusions wrought by time, the references in *Beowulf* fit well with other accounts of the early legendary history of these peoples, such as Saxo Grammaticus' *Gesta Danorum*. Hrothgar's hall, Heorot, may even have actually existed at Lejre, a village near Roskilde, Denmark. The poet drew on stable oral traditions of geographical locations, royal genealogies, and large events such as wars and migrations. These legendary facts authenticated the monster-plot by placing it in the known world of the past.

The stories of Scyld, Finn, Ingeld, and others are attested in Anglo-Saxon or Scandinavian sources, although we cannot be sure that every hero existed in history. Northern heroic legend—*Beowulf* included—has a way of moving toward the archetypal in its depiction of characters and their conflicts. The tragedy of broken pledges between Hengest the Dane and Finn, the king of the Frisians, as well as the strife between Ingeld the Heathobard and his father-in-law, King Hrothgar, were favorite subjects in Germanic story because they dramatized the conflict between the ideals of loyalty and vengeance. The poet was free to use such well-known heroic legends selectively to develop his themes. In addition, the *Beowulf* poet was also capable of adapting legendary or mythical material, perhaps only half-remembered, so as to achieve special tonal effects. For instance, the burial of the mythical Scyld, which begins the poem, pairs with Beowulf's burial at the end. Its somber brilliance hangs over Beowulf's early victories like an augmented chord. (The background of individual legends is found in the Commentary.)

While the oral traditions behind *Beowulf* are Germanic and pagan, its written traditions are Romano-Christian. The Bible provides not only the cosmos of the Creation and its Maker, but also the story of Cain and Abel, which the poet treats as a metaphor for the world of Germanic feud. "There were giants in the earth in those days," says Genesis 6:4, and their destruction by the Flood is retold in *Beowulf* (1688 ff.). Giants of Grendel's species may also have descended from biblical apocrypha such as the Book of Enoch. The apocryphal *Vision of St. Paul* contains a frightening picture of Hell which seems to be the source for details in the description of Grendel's mere. Some scholars also hear echoes from the New Testament or the Church Fathers. This is a difficult matter to judge, since the diction of the poem is already pervasively Christian. Such words as *heaven, hell, devil,* and *soul* appear part of the poet's natural vocabulary. It is plain that the Christian tradition behind *Beowulf* was not limited to written works. The poet seems to know the orally composed Christian poetry of Cædmon, and he is familiar with the art of preaching, which he practices in Hrothgar's sermon (1700 ff.). The poet moves between secular and doctrinal concerns with a freedom that shows he was comfortably settled in Christian Latin traditions. He can bemoan the Danes' reversion to heathenism in the tones of the sternest moralist (175–88), but later on he depicts Hrothgar as possessing the piety of an Abraham when he thanks God for deliverance. He seems to have used St. Paul's notion of "natural law" for his concept of the world of heroic antiquity. His pagans are noble monotheists but there is no overt mention of Christ the Redeemer or His Passion—not even when Hrothgar uses Christian symbolism to warn Beowulf against the sin of pride. This deliberate avoidance is perhaps the most significant feature of the poet's use of Christian tradition. Apparently he wanted his audience to imagine their forebears as though they were figures from a Germanic Old Testament.

On the whole, we may say that the Germanic and Christian traditions are fused in *Beowulf* as they were in Anglo-Saxon society. It is bootless to try to untangle the proportions of their influence upon the poet's diction or his conceptions of character and epic tragedy. It is possible that he also knew classical writers such as Ovid and Vergil. The *Aeneid*, in particular, offers parallel sentiments and phrases, and was known and used by Bede. However, *Beowulf* is not an epic in the classical sense, and its similarities to the *Aeneid*, and more remotely to the *Odyssey*, are best regarded as independent expressions of the heroic world-view.

Heroic and Social Codes in the Poem

The Angles, Saxons, and Jutes came to England from the area just below Denmark during the first great wave of Germanic migrations in the fifth century, which also saw the fall of Rome. (The second wave was to be the Viking expansion from Denmark and Norway, to as far south as Sicily, in the ninth and tenth centuries.) These "Engels" (hence "English") brought with them the social pattern of a people on the move, organized principally around individual chieftains and their faithful bands of followers. They were first invited across the Channel, Bede tells us, in A.D. 449 by Vortigern, king of the Britons, to help him repel the Picts and Scots. They found victory so easy and the land so fertile that they moved over in force, subjugating the Britons as well. As they slowly settled into a more stable society, they passed on no legends of their victories in England that we know of, but they preserved memories of heroes from their Continental homeland through an oral poetry now almost wholly lost.

Even more important for classical Old English poetry, they kept alive the ancient Germanic heroic code by which they had lived and died and which made them, in one historian's happy phrase, "an aristocracy of the brave." It is very close to the code described in

A.D. 98 by Tacitus in his *Germania*, a taciturn little treatise that sets
barbarian virtue against Roman decadence. The chieftain of the
comitatus, or small war band, is surrounded by noble warriors, his
comites 'companions,' who have sworn to defend him with their
lives. He, in turn, is unstintingly liberal in giving them gifts and
weapons. In Old English, he is their *dryhten* 'lord' and they are his
gedryht 'troop,' a word with the same root. They are divided into
two groups, the *duguð*, or 'doughty' experienced men, and the
geogoð, or untried 'youths.' Their virtues were those of reckless and
absolute personal courage, loyalty to one's chief; and, on the chief's
part, generosity and protection. The aim was glory—the fame of "a
good name" after death.

In Old English heroic poetry, the chief was often called "the gold-
giver," but this lacked the pejorative sense that Tacitus managed to
create. Rather, it indicated the Germanic custom of taking the sym-
bolic measure of a man's worth by the amount of gold he could win
through valor. Thus the chief, by his large-handed generosity, was
asserting his confidence in his man's daring and courage in combats
to come; and his follower, by accepting the chief's gift, was vowing
an equally perfect fidelity. Tacitus quite rightly emphasized the
bloody-minded ferocity behind the *comitatus* oath, but it was still a
noble bond between men and not very far from what we now call
brotherly love. In Old English religious poetry, it was readily assimi-
lated to the scheme of Christ as the Supreme Chief and the disciples
as His *comitatus*. Because of the absolute devotion the "gold-giver"
inspired in his followers, this fusion of concepts could be used in
religious poetry without the least impropriety. It follows also that if
a man was for some reason exiled from his lord and homeland, his
resulting misery was irremediable. Under such a code, in such a
world, to be exiled was to be without protection by lord or kindred,
without friends, means of livelihood, or the respect and trust of
others. In the magnificent meditative poems *The Wanderer* and *The
Seafarer*, this theme of exile becomes an underlying metaphor that
expresses the Christian view of man alone in a desolate world,
searching, as St. Paul puts it, for "our heavenly home." In both
secular and religious Old English poetry it meant everything to have
a lord.

The very first generalization in *Beowulf* sets forth the interde-
pendence in the *comitatus* bond from the leader's point of view:

So ought a young man,   in his father's household,
treasure up the future   by his goods and goodness,
by splendid bestowals,   that later in life
his chosen men   stand by him in turn,
his retainers serve him   when war comes.
By such generosity   any man prospers. (20–25)

The slightly contractual flavor of this maxim is quite in keeping with actual examples from Anglo-Saxon history. When the dragon attacks Beowulf, Wiglaf's impassioned outcry to the cowardly troop illustrates the proper devotion of a retainer. It is anything but "blind loyalty."

While Wiglaf is the ideal retainer, the heroic view of this relationship was not confined to poetry, as can be seen from the story of Lilla in Bede's *Ecclesiastical History*. During the reign of King Edwin of Northumbria, an assassin named Eumer was sent into that province by Cuichelm, king of the West Saxons. He carried a poisoned dagger with him for his task, and on Easter he was admitted to the king's presence. While he was delivering a supposed message, he suddenly rose, drew the dagger from under his clothes and attacked the king. Lilla, the king's counselor and best friend, having no shield to protect the king, threw himself in the way. The dagger went quite through his body, mortally wounding him, and even wounded the king (who later recovered). The assassin was immediately attacked but killed a second of the king's men before being slain.

Besides an immediate self-sacrifice like Lilla's, the Anglo-Saxon's devotion to his lord could produce complex tragic situations. In A.D. 786 the Anglo-Saxon Chronicle recorded the finale of a brutal and long-lasting feud, in which one Cyneheard sought out Cynewulf, king of the West Saxons, who thirty years before had usurped the kingdom from Cyneheard's brother Sigebryht. Cyneheard kills Cynewulf in a surprise attack while the latter is visiting a mistress. The small group of retainers the king had brought with him rush to the woman's quarters when they hear the uproar and engage the slayer Cyneheard and his band of men. Although the king's retainers are badly outnumbered and their lord is already dead, they fight until every one of them is killed (except for one Welsh hostage), even though Cyneheard tries to bribe them and then offers safe passage to those of his kinsmen among them. The next morning the main body of the king's thanes ride up to find Cyneheard and his men barricaded inside the house. Once again, some of the rebels inside are kinsmen of the king's warriors. Cyneheard "then offered them payment and lands according to their own judgment if they would grant him the [rule of the] kingdom. And they [the men inside] said that kinsmen of theirs [i.e., of those outside] were with them and would not leave them. And they [outside] replied that no kinsman of theirs was dearer to them than their lord and they would never follow his killer." The attackers then offer safe exit to their kinsmen, but their kinsmen refuse it just as the king's retainers refused Cyneheard the night before, and, indeed, because they had done so: "They said that they cared no more for that than did your comrades who were slain with the king." All but one die fighting, in consequence. Their tragic pride could not be helped in a day when one's good name meant more than life itself. They simply could not stand to be known as less brave, less honorable, than their opponents, and they would have fully understood Wiglaf's veiled suggestion to the cowardly troop after the dragon fight: "Death is better than a life of shame."

In the story of Cynewulf and Cyneheard we see this ethic of loyalty overcoming an equally strong obligation in Anglo-Saxon society: the duty to one's kindred. The conflict between these two obligations, which also informs the Finnsburh Episode in *Beowulf*, is doubtless the reason the Chronicle story was so well remembered. Throughout the Anglo-Saxon period, as in some Latin countries today, a man's kin were his strongest support in everyday affairs. If a man was killed, it was the duty of his kinsmen, however remotely related, to avenge him in kind. Naturally, this system led to long-standing, self-propelling vendettas. They might lie dormant for a generation or two and then erupt in a new rash of slayings.

While blood for blood was the most satisfying form of repaying the wrongs done one's kin, an equally respectable and more customary method was a money payment called the *wer-gild* 'man-payment.' This could be accepted by the kindred of the slain man without loss of face because each man's life had a set money value according to his standing in society. A nobleman or *eorl* was a "man of twelve hundred" shillings (a shilling then being worth vastly more than the modern shilling). The ordinary free man, the *ceorl* (later deteriorating to "churl"), was "a man of two hundred." A slave had no wergild, being only a chattel, and his cost to his owner, usually one pound, was all that had to be paid if he were damaged beyond repair. The Church equated a priest with a noble thane in the scale of wergilds, and a man's monastery assumed the role of his kindred after he took orders. Any compensation would be paid to his monastery. The Church understood, and at times condoned, the unwritten law of blood for blood among the laity, but early it took the position that the wergild was preferable, for practical as well as moral reasons. The scale of payment for priests perhaps reflects the fact that many powerful *æþelingas* 'princes, nobles' entered the Church.

One of the most moving scenes of grief in *Beowulf* is the hero's recollection of the case of King Hrethel, Hygelac's father (2435–70), whose eldest son Herebeald was killed accidentally by an arrow shot by his brother Hæthcyn. Hrethel's unappeasable sorrow lay mainly in the fact that this death had to go unpaid and unavenged, since it had occurred within the kindred. The poet has Beowulf liken it to the sorrow and loss of honor, indeed the loss of any meaning to life, felt by an old *ceorl* when he sees his son hanged as a criminal and can expect no compensation since it is a legal death. Hrethel eventually dies of a broken heart. In both cases, we also see the misery of a father's childlessness in a world where inheritance and patronymics figure importantly. The reactions of the old fathers are quite different from the usual responses to such tragedies today and they illustrate the central position of kinship obligations in Anglo-Saxon life.

Not all was dark in Anglo-Saxon life. The poetry frequently depicts the occupations of the happy company of warriors: riding, drinking wine, listening to the harp of the bard. And in the extended description of court life in Hrothgar's hall, we encounter more directly the high decorum of noble behavior, expressed in what were, for Germanic life, elaborate courtesies. There we also see the emphasis, as in Homeric epic, on open hospitality to guests and, above all, the joyous cameraderie the *gedryht* felt when feasting in their lord's hall. The traditional songs of the bard, chanted to the accompaniment of his harp, are so placed in these descriptions that they seem the natural climax of the happy tumult, an outpouring of the company's feelings of harmony by their most articulate spokesman.

We must expect some exaggeration and simplification in any picture of the past. In reality, Anglo-Saxon *æþelingas* did not spend all their time either in the mead-hall or in battle. They did have wives and families. Women in this aristocratic society, as in our poem, had all the dignity and standing they commanded in Tacitus' day: "they believe that there resides in women an element of holiness and prophecy, and so they do not scorn to ask their advice or lightly disregard their replies" (*Germania,* chap. 8).[1] A good example is Queen Wealhtheow's dignified, poignant plea to Hrothgar about his sons' succession to the throne (1169–87). Wealhtheow and the other female characters have genuine status at court, as did noblewomen in real life. Sometimes they were "peace-weavers," given in diplomatic marriage to an enemy tribe, which could lead to tragic situations, as in the cases of Finn's queen, Hildeburh, and Hrothgar's daughter, Freawaru. Noblewomen in Anglo-Saxon society, as in the poem, possessed their own goods. There are important Anglo-Saxon queens in history from the seventh century on, some of whom played power politics, others who became abbesses of great foundations, and any number of lesser noblewomen who are named in land charters. On the whole, women probably had an even larger role in the day-to-day life of the *eorl* class than they do in *Beowulf*, where the poet uses them mainly to create an impression of splendid civility and heroic pathos.

There are other differences between the world of *Beowulf* and the world of its audience. A noble of rank had his lands to look after, farmed by peasants called *gebūras,* in a tenure system resembling the later English manorial scheme. The nobleman was responsible for everyone in his household and had the serious duties of keeping peace in the neighborhood and attending public assemblies called "folkmoots" where legal cases were decided. If he was a particularly important man, he might have additional duties at court or be appointed the king's officer for his area. He would frequently be involved in litigation himself, not so much concerning wergilds as movable property and land rights. In addition, such a thane might well be literate and associate frequently with important churchmen of his region. Ealdorman Æthelweard, for instance, the patron of Bishop Ælfric, vigorously promoted literary activity in the tenth-century Benedictine revival and also found time to write a Latin *Chronicle* himself. The

---

[1] Quotation from *Tacitus on Britain and Germany*, trans. H. Mattingly (Baltimore: Penguin, 1948), p. 107.

story is told that King Alfred's mother offered a volume of English poetry to whichever of her sons learned to read it first. These examples suggest a life-style among the nobility that differed considerably from what we find in *Beowulf*.

Archaeology and Poetic Realism

Considering the omission of mundane details and the changes of viewpoint necessary for the poem's vision of the heroic past, it is remarkable that the elaborate descriptions of the weapons, armor, long-ships, halls, and funeral practices correspond closely to seventh-century archaeological finds in England and Scandinavia. For some artifacts that have been found in royal burial sites, it is as though the poet had described them at first hand. It is difficult to pronounce on the fact that no description in the poem corresponds to an artifact from later than the 600s. This could mean that the author lived in the 600s and created his poetic world out of the sumptuous regal objects of the time or that he lived later and was deliberately looking backward in time, from perhaps the late eighth century, and recreating a vanished glory. Much of the earlier paraphernalia would still exist, passed on from generation to generation. One of the highest terms of praise for a sword, for instance, is "an ancient heirloom, the work of giants." This hyperbole meant the sword had been "pattern-welded," perhaps by Celto-Roman smiths on the Rhine in the 500s, from a higher grade of iron than was used in later times. The old swords were better made, less likely to splinter in battle, and in a warrior culture they had virtually the status of cult objects. The complicated gold chasing on hilt, pommel, and scabbard of some of the remaining specimens shows the lavish care these weapons received. Kings usually retained their own goldsmiths and, as in *Beowulf*, the gift of a sword or helmet was an event for everyone in the hall to observe and marvel over. Even the hall Heorot corresponds closely to the long house in the *villa regia* recently excavated at Old Yeavering, in Northumberland, which is likely to have been a royal mead-hall.

Many of the artifacts found at Sutton Hoo were already old when they were buried and take us even further back, within a century of the historical King Hygelac's fatal expedition against the Frisians in A.D. 521. The remains of a small lyre were found there, and experiment with a replica of this instrument may yield information about possible conditions of harp-and-voice performances of oral poetry. A scrupulous long-term study of the Sutton Hoo treasure, led by R. L. S. Bruce-Mitford of the British Museum, has already clarified a number of hard passages in the poem. As far as we can tell from Sutton Hoo and other archaeological finds, the *Beowulf* poet seems never to exaggerate or invent in his descriptions of royal accouterments. His epithets often show an exact knowledge of how such objects were made. Apparently the heroic trappings of the poem— swords, helmets, corselets—are described as though drawn from real life. To Anglo-Saxon noblemen, of course, they would have been anything but trappings: they were the visible symbols of a man's worth.

Anglo-Saxon Rulers

Although no commoner receives extended attention in the poem, heroic obligations to one's lord were felt by *eorl* and *ceorl* alike in real life. It was a faithful swineherd, for instance, who first avenged the death of Cynewulf's ealdorman by killing King Sigebryht in A.D. 755. That event illustrates how easily this cohesive bond transcended class distinctions and also suggests the relatively small size of the early Anglo-Saxon kingdoms, whose population numbered only in tens of thousands. The kings exercised a high degree of direct, personal control, and as the *Chronicle* story reveals, either they exercised it fully or other strong nobles would try to step into their place. Legitimacy, especially in the early days of the Anglo-Saxon settlement, was based mainly on strength, and even a strong body of kinsmen was not a sure guarantee of a peaceful succession, since an ambitious chief might lurk among them, waiting his chance. It has been pointed out that in Bede's *Ecclesiastical History* as well as in *Beowulf* the pivot of strife was usually a contest between uncle (father's brother) and nephew. The dynastic struggle described in *Beowulf* between the Swedish king Onela and his nephews Eanmund and Eadgils, and the future treachery of the Danish prince Hrothulf, Hrothgar's nephew, read like scenarios for the bloody struggle mentioned by Bede between King Hlothere of Kent and his nephew Eadric (Bk. IV, chap. 26) or the story of the gracious and saintly

Oswin, murdered in A.D. 651 at the command of his treacherous cousin Oswy (III, 14).

Such abominations were not the norm, but nonetheless the world of the Anglo-Saxons was turbulent enough that both *Beowulf* and Bede, and undoubtedly the common man, set great store on true virtue in kings. Peace was difficult enough to keep in any case, during the seventh and ninth centuries especially. A king of however small an area, if he were strong, just, and wise enough to keep war from breaking out, was a treasure beyond gold. Thus, when Beowulf dies, it is poetically appropriate that the Geats do not use the dragon's treasure to buy peace from their enemies, but bury it with Beowulf in honor of their priceless king. They act from one of the deepest pieties in the heroic life, and one that was not too distant from actuality. King Edwin of Northumbria ruled so well, Bede writes, that "the proverb still runs that a woman could carry her new-born babe across the island from sea to sea without any fear of harm. And such was the king's concern for the welfare of his people, that in a number of places where he had noticed clear springs adjacent to the highway, he ordered posts to be erected with brass bowls hanging from them, so that travellers could drink and refresh themselves. And so great was the people's affection for him, and so great the awe in which he was held, that no one presumed to use these bowls for any other purpose. The king's dignity was highly respected throughout his realm, and whether in battle or on a peaceful progress through city, town, and countryside in the company of his thanes, the royal standard was always borne before him" (II, 16).[2] A similar standard is given Beowulf by Hrothgar in recognition of his victory and his pre-eminent suitability for kingship (1020–21). A more important parallel with Edwin is that Beowulf, once he is king, keeps the Geats safe from enemy attack for fifty years (Edwin ruled for seventeen). Beowulf is much beloved by his people, and when he dies, chaos again breaks loose, as it did for the Northumbrians after Edwin was slain. At the end of the poem, the mourners' insistence on Beowulf's fairness and kindness quite overburdens his heroic epitaph.

---

[2] Bede, *A History of the English Church and People,* trans. Leo Sherley-Price (Baltimore: Penguin, 1955), pp. 129–30.

> They said that he was, of the kings in this world,
> the kindest to his men, the most courteous man,
> the best to his people, and most eager for fame. (3180–82)

Fame, "the Last Infirmity of Noble Mind"

A man's good name on others' lips—in Old English *lof* 'fame,
praise,' or *dōm*, loosely 'the good judgment of others,' related to the
verb 'deem'—was the final goal of the heroic life. It is no accident
that the last word of the poem should be *lof-geornost* 'most eager for
fame. The Old English version of Bede's history (I, 34) uses a
similar epithet for Edwin's powerful predecessor Æthelfrith: *se
gylp-geornesta* 'the most eager for glory,' translating *gloriae cupidis-
simus*. Beowulf's epitaph sounds a bit like Edwin and Æthelfrith com-
bined, and to some critics it has seemed an uneasy combination, since
Beowulf has sometimes been viewed as lacking one of the four cardi-
nal virtues needed for perfect kingship. His wisdom and strength—
sapientia et fortitudo—are self-evident throughout, and Beowulf him-
self recalls with satisfaction that he has always acted with justice,
justitia. However, in his heroic quest for an immortal name he may
have lacked *temperantia*—prudence, self-control, temperance. It may
be that when he resolves to fight the dragon alone, thereby reducing
his chances for success and jeopardizing his people, he shows an
excess of heroic pride. In the middle of the poem Hrothgar delivers
a sermon to Beowulf on this very subject. But no one can ever have
enough prudence in an uncertain world, and Beowulf has the courage,
the greatness of heart, to endure whatever doom is to be his. It is a
heroic poem, after all. So one argument might run. Yet it is also
elegiac, and the same poem that sets before us a hero possessing all
the necessary ferocity to kill monsters also depicts him as a king
who feels Christian guilt: Beowulf's first thought when the dragon
begins his depredations is that he has somehow offended God. Was
he too proud then? The late Professor G. N. Garmonsway pointed
out that often in literature the concept of heroism hinges upon a
certain excess, the attempt to outdo not only others, but also one-
self. To Wiglaf's sorrowful criticism,

> Often many earls must suffer misery
> through the will of one, as we do now (3077–78),

Garmonsway replied that "the comitatus failed to perceive that man does not live by common sense alone" (*Franciplegius*, p. 142). Whether Beowulf is an ideal king or flawed by his heroic quest for fame remains a question that disturbs every full interpretation of the poem's philosophy.

"Wyrd" and *Natural Christianity*

Perhaps the instability of Anglo-Saxon aristocratic life was built into the social system. To achieve a place in such a world, a nobleman had to rely on his own personal strength, which is always an ambiguous force for others' good. At the same time, he was extraordinarily dependent on the faithfulness of others—his thanes and kinsmen. In addition, there were even darker shadows. The Anglo-Saxons believed that life was a struggle against insuperable odds and that a man's *wyrd* or 'lot' would be what it would be. But it is hard for us today to utter their *che sarà, sarà* in the right tone of voice. Even in early pagan days, they do not seem to have believed in a supernatural conception of Destiny. *Wyrd* originally meant simply "what happens" and later was used by King Alfred in his translation of Boethius as a term for "what comes to pass" under the *fore-þanc* 'forethought' of God's Providence. There was no active malevolent force in the pagans' universe, as there is in Hardy's gloomy Wessex novels. Indeed, in pre-Christian times they do not seem to have had highly developed beliefs in a personal afterlife. Perhaps it was precisely because they lacked such beliefs, because life was potentially meaningless, that they looked to the heroic notion of personal fame to find the strength to resist *wyrd*. The Anglo-Saxons had an incomparable sense of the transience and pointlessness of mortal life. Only a man's name lived on, and then only in the mouths of others, usually the poets. This is one reason for the great value they assigned traditional lore right up through the Norman Conquest.

The early Anglo-Saxons' fatalistic outlook and sense of mortality made them exceptionally ready for Christianity. Its arrival in England is nowhere better described than in Bede's account of the conversion of Edwin and his Northumbrian nobles in A.D. 627 by Bishop Paulinus (II, 13). The king's counselors are asked their opinion about the new faith Paulinus has preached to them, and Coifi, the high priest of their pagan cult (probably devoted to Woden, Thor,

and Tiw, the Germanic Mars), declares boldly that he is ready to
try Christianity because the old religion has shown no efficacy. For
his own part, it has not advanced him in honor or in the king's
favor, though he has shown it great devotion. He speaks as a thane
who has not yet won sufficient *lof*. Then another member of the *witan*
or 'council' speaks, in justifiably the most famous simile in Old
English literature:

> "Your Majesty, when we compare the present life of man with that
> time of which we have no knowledge, it seems to me like the swift
> flight of a lone sparrow through the banqueting-hall where you sit
> in the winter months to dine with your thanes and counsellors. Inside
> there is a comforting fire to warm the room; outside, the wintry storms
> of snow and rain are raging. This sparrow flies swifly in through one
> door of the hall, and out through another. While he is inside, he is
> safe from the winter storms; but after a few moments of comfort, he
> vanishes from sight into the darkness whence he came. Similarly, man
> appears on earth for a little while, but we know nothing of what went
> before this life and what follows. Therefore if this new teaching can
> reveal any more certain knowledge, it seems only right that we should
> follow it." [8]

This simile of the sparrow is of a piece with a major leit-motif in
Beowulf: līf is lǣne 'life is transitory.' The hall-joys in the poem are
as short, if as warmly lighted, as the sparrow's flight from door to
door. In a dark and meaningless world, this simile is instantly con-
vincing as the truth. In it, we can recognize the metaphysical bias of
Beowulf, and we can understand why it is not a happy, confident
poem, vigorously exercising a soldier's faith like the *Song of Roland.*
To the degree that *Beowulf* is a Christian poem, the subject is not
simply heroism but our own mortality.

The new faith was eagerly seized, but, as the French say, English-
men take their pleasures sadly. In embracing Christianity the early
Anglo-Saxons did not find a joyous new life so much as solemn
security, a sense of the real foundations of the world. *Cædmon's
Hymn,* the earliest religious poem in Old English and orally com-
posed in the old heroic diction, praises God the Maker, the estab-

---

[8] Ibid., pp. 124–25.

lisher of all things, more than the Christ who died for our salvation or His Divine Love:

> Now let us praise   the Guardian of Heaven,
> the powers of the Ruler,   his creative Thought,
> the works of the Glory-Father,   for He established,
> the eternal Lord,   all beginnings.
> First he built,   for the sons of men,
> the roof of Heaven,   holy Maker;
> then middle-earth   mankind's Guard,
> the eternal Lord,   afterwards adorned,
> the fields of men,   our God Almighty.

The Song of Creation in *Beowulf* (90–99) touches much the same point, that God gives stability and order to the world. A paraphrase of Genesis like *Cædmon's Hymn,* the Song follows so quickly upon the description of the building of Heorot that the great hall becomes an emblem for God's world itself. This meaning is strengthened by the introduction of Evil incarnate in the person of Grendel, who listens in pain to the bard singing of God's beautiful and good creation. Immediately he resolves to attack the hall in the night, and in another few lines the joy, music, and feasting in Heorot have been reduced to the brevity of a swallow's flight through the hall. Such a world can hardly do without its heroes or a ground plan of the cosmos.

This may give some indication of how Christian learning appears in *Beowulf*. It is part of the furniture of the poet's mind and it provides him with a traditional and highly developed symbolism of good and evil, light and dark; but he uses explicit Christian ideas sparingly, selectively, to create a special kind of poetic world in which native Germanic wisdom and Christian beliefs exist in harmony. We must remember that, even to a contemporary, *Beowulf* was already set in the past. The concept of "our ancestors" meant the pre-Christian Continental tribes, and they appear in the poem much as the Anglo-Saxons at the time of the Conversion do in Bede, perhaps even more as Old Testament figures appeared to medieval Christians. The characters are still pagans but they deserve our respect, as all ancestors do. They are good men, who know God by nature, and who act and speak accordingly. Their God is a rather impersonal Creator, Providence, and ultimate Judge. He is more God the Father than the Son or Holy Spirit. He is frequently thanked and praised, especially by Hrothgar, the most pious of all the characters, who regards Beowulf as a deliverer sent expressly by God. The poet himself mentions God's destruction of the wicked by the Flood as well as the story of Cain. The allusions to biblical stories are drawn only from Genesis, and there is no mention of Christ or events in the New Testament. This omission must be deliberate, because familiar mention of the Devil, many traditional epithets for God, and occasionally the imagery—e.g., the sun as "the bright beacon of God"—all indicate an implicit acceptance of the Christian order of things throughout the poem. Several phrases also point to a belief in a life after death in which God will judge a man according to his deeds.

Very likely, in all these matters, the poet was governed by considerations of artistic propriety. He had the task of presenting the older heathen world sympathetically to Christian nobles. The problem was not to give older pagan materials a "Christian coloring," in F. A. Blackburn's phrase of 1897,[4] but to keep a too-obvious Christianity from marring the poem's conception of the past as a blend of Germanic and Christian beliefs (thus Larry D. Benson, "The Pagan Coloring"). So the poet did not dwell on Christian teachings that his characters could not have known, but concentrated instead on those features of the old Germanic life that still lived on in the amalgamated beliefs of his audience.

Beowulf, for instance, trusts in his own strength as much as in God's grace (OE. *ār*), and in the fights with Grendel and his mother the poet's own view, clearly stated, is that Beowulf wins through both these causes working together (967–68, 1056–57, 1270–74, 1553–56). God's will is an important factor in both battles. The poet troubles to point this out, but the triumphant champion simply acknowledges it in passing. To his mind, the important values are courage and strength. Yet, when the dragon's ravages begin, Beowulf's first thought is that somehow he has transgressed "against the old law" (2330). As far as scholars can determine, this phrase refers to "natural law," the idea that a rational knowledge of the

---

[4] See *ABC*, pp. 1–21.

Creator was obtainable through his works alone, and that this knowledge created a body of moral obligations for all men, whether or not the Gospel had yet reached them. Charles Donahue has shown it is likely that this idea, which originated with St. Paul in Romans 1:19–21 and 2:14–15, reached Anglo-Saxon England through Celtic influence.

The Old Testament flavor of *Beowulf* is better explained by this view of the pre-Christian past than by St. Augustine of Hippo's notion that all pagans were damned without baptism, even though Augustine's doctrines were widely accepted by early Anglo-Saxon churchmen. Limbo, to which virtuous pagans were consigned, was not created till St. Anselm's arguments in the twelfth century. We do hear some Anglo-Saxon voices clamoring with an Augustinian strictness against Germanic pagan practices, and even against poetry that had pagans as its subject. "What has Ingeld to do with Christ?" writes Alcuin in a famous letter to the monks at Lindisfarne, who apparently were listening to heroic lays in the refectory: "The King of Heaven wants no fellowship at all with pagan and damned kings!" However, the monks had become lax in other matters, too, and elsewhere Alcuin does not regard pagan literature as totally without value. The *Beowulf* poet, who was not interested in clerical reform, takes a condemnatory tone only toward the heathen rites to which the Danes turn for help from Grendel. Otherwise he admires the good characters in the poem exactly as their virtues deserve. In real life, the typical Anglo-Saxon attitude was to revile the hellish rites of the heathen but otherwise to cherish their good character and morals. We find this attitude in Bede and in the letters of the eighth-century Anglo-Saxon missionaries to the Continent. Beowulf is praised as a just and merciful king at the end of the poem in terms that apply whether we see him as an imitation of Christ or simply as a good king. Morality was time-transcendent. The poet made natural man as Christian as he could without introducing doctrinal matters.

The Perspective of Christian Stoicism

The way fate operates in *Beowulf* is another illustration of the easy blending of Christian and Germanic ideas in the poem. The cause of all things is ultimately Providence. Yet man, and notably Beowulf, has free will—his actions directly affect the course of events in his life. There is a fatalistic atmosphere surrounding Beowulf's death, but it is created by means other than the simple idea of fate. In his first two fights, we learn that God's blessing has directly aided Beowulf's undertakings. Yet Beowulf must also use his own will power. The poet was anything but a predestinarian. We can see this in his adaptation of the details of his folktale source, at the point where Beowulf has almost lost the battle with Grendel's dam (1556 ff.). The sword Hrunting has failed him. Suddenly he sees a huge sword hanging on the wall. With it he is able to chop through the monster's neck and immediately "a light shone out from within [the hall] just as from the skies shines the candle of heaven." This simile cannot be mere chance. What was probably a simple motif of a magical sword in the older folktale has been transformed by the poet into white magic. The bright light sanctifies Beowulf's victory, symbolizing the triumph of good over evil. The sword itself is destroyed in the process, its blade melting away in "battle-icicles" from the poisonous blood of the monster. Only the golden hilt remains, engraved with the legend of how God destroyed the race of giants in the Flood. This sequence suggests that Beowulf wins his underwater victory as an agent of Providence and in a manner that somehow resembles the cleansing of the earth by the Flood. Yet it is equally significant that this Christian symbolism comes only *after* Bewulf's triumphant feat. Even within the poet's religious perspective, the hero's actions, performed on his own, are of the first importance. God helps those who help themselves.

The admiration of brave men and their deeds, however, did not mean that the heathen past could finally be regarded as a triumphant time. The characters in the poem, even though they believe in a Creator, still live in a tragic world that lacks the New Dispensation. That is, they must do without the confident hope of true Christians, and that is the most excruciating quality of their heroism. They are doomed even before they begin, and as we watch the stirring pageant of their actions we must inevitably be moved to pity as well as admiration. A serious and learned Anglo-Saxon Christian, when he looked at the poem's emphasis on earthly fame and rewards, on man's desperately courageous mortality, might even have seen an implicitly stated argument about the limitations of the heroic life, the brevity of its achievements, and the need for a transcendent faith.

If there is an argument for faith in *Beowulf*, it is rather like the one demonstrated by Boethius in his dialogue *The Consolation of Philosophy,* translated into Old English by King Alfred and one of the best known literary works of the Middle Ages. Without ever once mentioning the name of Christ or using explicitly Christian doctrine, Boethius undertook to show, to the satisfaction of the strictest classical logician, that sound reasoning can explain the evil and disorder in the world. His argument was intended to lead his readers to a knowledge of Providence and the harmonious order in all creation, and to a justification of man's free will against the arguments of predestination. Boethius phrased his demonstration in the most urgent terms: imprisoned in Rome by Theodoric for political activity in A.D. 525 and soon to be executed, he created a dialogue between himself and Lady Philosophy, who appears in a vision to console him in his cell. The dialogue was a major synthesis of Christian ideas and traditional classical thought and was immensely influential during the next thousand years. Boethius, knowing that he must be a writer first and a teacher afterward, alternated his *metra,* his poems, with the prose dialogue of his highly personal argument with Lady Philosophy. The result touches chords of feeling quite as strongly as it compels logical agreement.

"By indirections, to find directions out" has always been an artistic approach of great force, and it was not neglected even in the Dark Ages. The Boethian method of self-consolation by appealing to the senses and affections as well as the intellect is adopted in the OE. *Wanderer,* a Christian's meditation on the dismal fortunes of an exile who stands as a type of all mankind. The maxims of traditional wisdom in *Beowulf* often sound like the Wanderer's reflections or the sayings in Alfred's Boethius. They form a commentary on the whole cycle of contrasts in the poem. For instance, after stating that Grendel's fate was determined by wise God and Beowulf's courage, the poet goes on to say:

> The Lord then ruled
> all the race of men,   as He still does now.
> Therefore understanding   is always best,
> the spirit's forethought.   Much love, much hate,
> must he endure   who thinks to live long
> here in this world,   in our days of strife. (1057–62)

This expresses a native pessimism and stoicism in the face of adversity, but even more a reliance on the reason, the highest human faculty in Christian psychology. We cannot tell what God has stored up in the future for us; we must bear the reversals of fortune precisely because God rules mankind (hence the word *forþan* 'therefore'). If we stay long in this uncertain world, we will experience many vicissitudes. This attitude of alert resignation, the solemn-cheerful acceptance of one's lot, provides a metaphysical counterpoise to the violent actions of the story which dramatize Beowulf's heroic assertions of the will. The actions are evaluated by the poet and Hrothgar in terms of a man's *wēn* 'expectation' and its *edwenden* 'reversal.' Hrothgar never expected to be delivered from Grendel. Once delivered, he did not expect Grendel's dam. Old Beowulf had no thought of future disaster, being so strong a king, until one day the dragon appeared.

Hrothgar's Sermon and Patristic Learning

In his speech on the dangers of a noble warrior's pride, Hrothgar returns to the topic of "uncertain fortune." Instead of using the classical image of the wheel of fortune as Boethius did, the poet makes Hrothgar draw on common patristic metaphors that appear elsewhere in Old English sermons. The guardian of the prosperous warrior's soul, i.e., his reason, will sleep if he thinks too well of himself and forgets his ultimate end. Then, in this slumber of pride, the devil will be able to approach him, and will shoot the arrows of sin under his helmet. He will not be able to protect himself and will grow the greedier and eventually meet a bad end. The metaphor of spiritual armor comes from St. Paul (Ephesians 6:13–17), and this brief allegorical exemplum brings Hrothgar's speech closer to the language of surviving Old English sermons than any other speech in the poem. Yet it is only one part of an extremely powerful argument in which Hrothgar also uses the vicissitudes of his own fortunes as an example and makes his strongest appeal not to specifically Christian notions but to the inescapability of death for even the most famous warrior. We feel an intense Christian morality shaping the language, but the dramatic force of the whole speech remains at the level of a personal admonition to Beowulf, couched in poetic terms.

Hrothgar's sermon is a long speech, placed in a commanding position in the poem. It crowns Beowulf's adventures in Denmark by cautioning him about the future. For these reasons, it raises questions of interpretation that affect our whole view of the poem. Beowulf himself is as silent as the poet and makes no answer to Hrothgar's warning. Do we dare conclude then that Beowulf succumbs to pride in the dragon fight? Does he set too great a value on earthly goods in seeking the dragon's hoard? The poem raises these questions in the minds of some (not all) readers without answering them directly. Critics have had to look for implicit answers in the poem's construction, which can be regarded as both intricate and simple. In their search they have also continually felt the force of another insistent query: How Christian *is* the poem? *Beowulf* discloses such different aspects of imaginative reality that we can answer "very" or "not very" depending on which features we choose to emphasize: the heroic action or the reflective language, the beginning of the poem or the end, the main fights or the digressive episodes. Even two of the most astute modern scholars, Anglo-Saxonists of the first rank, can come to opposite conclusions: Dorothy Whitelock in *The Audience of Beowulf* demonstrates the case for "very Christian," while Kenneth Sisam in *The Structure of Beowulf* concludes "not very." The choice of words in their titles, "audience" vs. "structure," indicates their two different types of evidence and argument. It also points up the fact that "How Christian is *Beowulf*?" is essentially a historical question, posed in terms that will not yield a plain answer based solely on the text. "Christianity" is a large and pliable concept at any point in history where we might conceivably locate the poem, and *Beowulf* like all good poetry is a work of multiple meanings. While Christian allegory in the Dark Ages was usually more explicit than *Beowulf*, to an especially learned listener the poem may well have offered implicit typologies, as did the patristic interpretations of Scripture. In another equally alert Christian, it may have awakened, instead, a complex piety toward the heroes of the good old days. We can only guess at what the poet, for his own part, intended as the outer frame of intellectual reference for the moral ideas in the poem.

Commentary

Scyld Scefing (4–52)

"Shield, the son of Sheaf" or perhaps "Shield with a sheaf" was the eponymous founder of the Danish royal dynasty, the *Scyldingas* 'descendants of Scyld.' Perhaps faintly reminiscent of an earlier vegetation deity, he comes to the Danes as a child in a boat. Neither he nor his son Beow, who appears in lines 18 and 53 as Beowulf probably because of scribal error, are historical figures. They reappear at an entirely mythical level in the later and often fictitious Anglo-Saxon royal genealogies, as does Sceaf. In the poem Scyld's great deeds save the Danes in a disastrous, leaderless time—the common noun *scyld* also means "protection"—and he prefigures the glory of the Scylding line. His mysterious arrival and departure over water is a widespread motif in folktale and myth (cf. the Perseus legend).

The sense of mystery in Scyld's arrival and rise to power is enhanced by the distant focus of the brief narrative. It almost sounds like an epigraph. The first verse-paragraph about Scyld also foreshadows the Geatish Beowulf's own rise to fame in Denmark, up through the end of Part I. In youth Scyld was wretched and Beowulf inglorious (lines 2183–88); both possess great strength and courage; both come over water to aid the Danes in distress; the poet says that Scyld, and Hrothgar says that Beowulf, was sent by God. But there is no one-to-one correspondence: Scyld fights no monsters and he is more the good king than the heroic thane.

The second paragraph about Scyld introduces a contrast within this parallel, although we cannot see it until we come full circle to Beowulf's burial at the end of the poem. The motif of a king's burial

overarches the whole poem, to be changed in meaning by the inter-
vening story. Beowulf's burial follows the Germanic practices of
cremation and barrow building, while Scyld's being set adrift in his
boat is a poetic adaptation of a royal ship-burial like those found
at Sutton Hoo and Oseburg, in southern Norway. Unlike the realistic
rites of Beowulf's funeral, where the lamentations of the mourners are
prominent, Scyld's rites remain part of his myth. The poet wished to
keep Scyld's memory alive, his mystery intact, and so he returns
him to his own story. The scene may remind readers of the death
of King Arthur. Though the heroic calm surrounding Beowulf's death
is itself mysterious, there are contrasts between the meanings of the
two funerals. Scyld restored the Danish kingdom, and his passing is
glorious, as are his progeny. But Beowulf's death brings an end to
leadership and royal lineage. The Geats can only look forward to
catastrophes similar to the "sinful distress" the Danes experienced
before the coming of Scyld. That peculiar term (fyren-ðearfe 14) is
an allusion to the bad Danish king Heremod and his outrageous
slaughter of his own retainers and subsequent abandonment of his
people (see lines 901 ff., 1709 ff.). In the later genealogies, Scyld
is the son of Heremod, but in *Beowulf* Scyld founds a new dynasty.
See further G. V. Smithers, *English and Germanic Studies* 4
(1951–52), 65–67.

This allusion raises the question of how far to press the comparison
between prologue and epilogue. The difference between the moral
character of Beowulf and Heremod is virtually absolute, yet in both
cases the nation is left leaderless. Is this a parallel or a contrast?
The ethical axiom in lines 20–25—king's generosity=retainers' fi-
delity—is also relevant to Beowulf's death, since his troop flies in
fear of the dragon. This thematic contrast will be even stronger if
we retain the MS. reading "Beowulf" (the Dane) for Scyld's son.

Two textual notes: In lines 5–6, to deprive Germanic warriors of
their mead-benches means to conquer them and take over the hall
where their lord gives them rings. Wrenn's edition emends *eorl* 6 to
Eorl[e], the tribe of the *Eruli* (Lat. *Heruli*), described by Procopius
as the most ferocious nation in Denmark c. A.D. 250–400. Whoever
in history first exacted tribute from the Danish islands, as Scyld does
in lines 9–11, would have had to terrify the terrible Eruli. If this is an
historical reference, then, it is hyperbole. But it is unlikely that the
name of an individual tribe would appear in this quasi-mythical

context. A scribal error seems more plausible.

In line 33 *īsig* 'icy' suggests that the time of Scyld's sea burial is winter, when voyages were not usually made by the living (thus Hoops, *Kommentar*, p. 13). It seems more a metaphor for death and grief than a reference to the season. In his study of Old English poetic diction, E. G. Stanley suggests it may mean no more than *winter-ceald* 'winter-cold,' a term generally evocative of sorrow. See *Anglia* 73 (1955), 440–41. Another possible connotation of *īsig* is "baleful, ill-omened"; see Vivian Salmon, "Some Connotations of *Cold* in Old and Middle English," *MLN* 74 (1959), 314–32. In a close Christian reading *īsig* might further suggest the icy hole at the top of the world in the early Northern conception of Hell. For this, see "Grendel's Mere," below, and Paul Salmon, "The Site of Lucifer's Throne," *Anglia* 81 (1963), 118–23. Albert Cook suggests that the ice is too literal to be a metaphor for death; he hears it as merely a tonal portent, like the heavy, abrupt rhythm of the whole line (*The Classic Line* [Bloomington: Indiana University Press, 1966], p. 18).

The Danish Royal Line (59–63)

The three sons of Healfdene, 'Half-Dane,' listed in order of birth, are mentioned in Scandinavian sources as well. Heorogar had a son, Heoroward, but upon Heorogar's apparently early death, the second brother Hrothgar took the throne. Heorogar may have intended this: line 2158 ff. say he bestowed his mail-shirt upon his brother instead of his son—probably because Heoroward was still a child. The third brother, Halga the Good, is not mentioned again in the poem and is said in the Scandinavian sources to have died early. Halga's son Hrothulf is raised by Hrothgar and Queen Wealhtheow. Hrothulf is mentioned in connection with his uncle Hrothgar in the problem passages at 1017 and 1163 ff. The ironic hints there suggests that sometime in the future he will treacherously slay his first cousin Hrethric (Hrothgar's son) to gain the kingship.

The restoration and translation of line 62 assume a minimal skip in the text. From the lines preceding this loss, one would expect the name of Healfdene's fourth child. From the word *cwēn* 'queen' and line 63 it must be a woman. *Heaþo-Scilfingas* is a name for the Swedes, whose kings were of the Scylfing dynasty, and its *-as* ending

is a variant genitive singular. Thus, "the Battle-Scylfing's" specifies
whose queen she was. Onela (ON. *Áli*), mentioned again in lines
2616, 2932, is the only Scylfing king whose name, in this case,
Onelan, fits the MS. *elan*. His wife's name was *Yrsa* in Old Norse
(OE. *Yrse*, Lat. *Ursula*). The connection looks obvious. However,
Kemp Malone has argued that the name of any daughter of Healfdene
must begin with an alliterating *h*, and that therefore Yrse cannot be
his true daughter. He suggests, as the most plausible explanation, that
Yrse was first married to Halga, who then died; that she then mar-
ried Onela; and that tradition subsequently mistook Healfdene's
daughter-in-law for his own daughter (Malone, *Studies in Heroic
Legend*, pp. 124–141). H. C. Matthes, in *Anglia* 71 165–80, agrees
that Yrse cannot be Healfdene's daughter and suggests the loss in
line 62 is greater than a few words. He thinks a whole passage has
been dropped, containing information about Heorogar's reign and
Hrothgar's succession to the throne. There might be two names in-
volved here: Yrse's, as it may be restored from the sense of 62b–63,
and the name of the fourth child of Healfdene, mentioned right after
Halga at the start of the lost passage. The scribe's eye might have
skipped down the page from *hȳrde ic þæt* to another repetition of this
common formulaic expression. Matthes suggests that the fourth
child was a son, possibly the figure Heremod. If this were so, it would
call for a critical re-evaluation of the poet's use of Heremod.

The Building of Heorot and the Creation Song (67–101)

The royal seat of the Danes from earliest times was Leire, on the
island of Zealand, nowadays a village surrounded by ancient grave
mounds. To the Anglo-Saxons, the name of the hall, Heorot, 'hart,'
was symbolic of kingship. For instance, a bronze stag is fitted to
the top of the royal whetstone-scepter found at Sutton Hoo. The
gables of Heorot may have been like horns curving upward at the
ends of the ridgepole and associated with the hall's symbolic name.
The nearest analogy to Heorot's roof may be twelfth-century Nor-
wegian stave churches. See especially the plates of the Borglund and
Urnes churches in Anders Bugge, *Norwegian Stave Churches* (Oslo:
Dreyer, 1953). The analogy is not entirely clear: the stave churches
are thought to have been modeled on pagan temples, but at Anglo-
Saxon Yeavering the temple is separate from the king's great hall.

Possibly the name "Heorot" is meant to give a semidivine meaning
to the hall and its king. The precise extent of sacral kingship among
the Anglo-Saxons is debatable. See E. O. G. Turville-Petre, "The
Divine Kings," *Myth and Religion of the North: The Religion of
Ancient Scandinavia* (New York: Holt, Rinehart and Winston,
1964), pp. 190–95; William A. Chaney, *The Cult of Kingship in
Anglo-Saxon England* (Manchester: Manchester University Press,
1970); J. M. Wallace-Hadrill, *Early Germanic Kingship in England
and on the Continent* (London: Oxford University Press, 1971).

The building of the royal hall surpasses Hrothgar's other kingly
actions. In lines 80–81 it is also the setting in which he fulfills his
promise of gift-giving, a visible sign that as a Germanic lord he
rules his men righteously. The hall with its many decorations of
gold (308, 715, 926) is created in part to express this ideal of a
happy society. Hard upon this situation comes the allusion in 81–85,
an example of the foreshadowed contrasts by which the poet cre-
ates his ironic perspective. We can fill out the allusion from *Widsith*
45–49, where we learn that Heorot is later attacked by the son-in-
law of Hrothgar, Ingeld the Heathobard. Unlike *Beowulf, Widsith*
says that in this attack the Heathobards were repulsed by Hrothgar
and his nephew Hrothulf. This does not preclude the burning of the
hall. The feud began when the Danes killed Froda, Ingeld's father.
The later attack will break a peace pledge made when Hrothgar
gives his daughter Freawaru in marriage to Ingeld. This broken loy-
alty is emphasized metrically by the contrast, across the caesura, of
the stressed words *ecg-hete* 'sword-hate' and *aþum-swerian* 'between
father and son-in-law.' That the feud will break up the pact is fore-
seen by Beowulf in his report to Hygelac.

The song of Creation, patterned after Genesis 1:16 ff. and sung
by Hrothgar's *scop* in lines 90–98, is metaphorically connected with
the building of Heorot. Paul Beekman Taylor has pointed out that
the two actions of building associate Hrothgar with God, and Heorot
with Earth. The image of the hall as the world endures long after
the song and banquet have ended because the later descriptions of
Heorot re-echo the Creation Song. Professor Taylor also suggests
further analogies between the burning of Heorot and the fires of
Doomsday and between Grendel and Satan. There is also a pagan
analogy in the early Norse poem the *Völuspá,* offering these
correspondences: Heorot—Asgard—Earth; Hrothgar—Odin—God/

Adam; Grendel—Loki—Satan; Beowulf—Thor—Christ. The correspondence between the Old English and Norse is pointed: (1) in Snorri Sturluson's later account, Asgard even contains Gimli, a hall with a roof of gold, like Heorot; (2) Beowulf dies fighting the dragon, while Thor dies fighting the Midgarth serpent (which lies, biting its tail, in the deep sea encircling Middle-Earth). The point of these equations is not to reduce three stories to one allegorical abstract, but to show that, for the themes of creation and destruction, the *Beowulf* poet would have found a basic story structure in both pagan and Christian myth. His symbolic conception of Heorot seems to come from that fruitful field where Christian and pagan traditions overlap. See Taylor, *TSL* 11 (1966), 119–130.

This does not mean that Hrothgar's actions should be evaluated as though he were truly godlike. Since he is a man in a heroic story, another meaning of the construction of Heorot might be the very opposite, as Professor Martin Bickman has argued in an unpublished paper: "Like the Tower of Babel, Heorot is built by peoples from all over . . . in both cases, the builders are at first unaware of the vanity of their effort, that there are factors operating completely beyond their control, forces that dwarf the will and power of mortals. The juxtaposition of the building of Heorot and the Creation song is meant to accentuate the differences, not the similarities, between the two events." However we judge it, the passage as a whole shows us the poet's combination of the long and the short view into a cyclical vision of history. Heorot somehow symbolizes all of human society—its noble aspirations and its desperate instabilities. Its golden roof is a dominant image in the poem, emphasized not only by its luminous magnificence, juxtaposed to its future burning, but also then transformed into Creation itself, the goodness of which is metaphysically obnoxious to the demonic Grendel.

The Race of Cain (104–114)

The story of a race of demonic monsters and giants descended from Cain comes from a tradition established by the apocryphal *Book of Enoch* and early Jewish and Christian interpretations of Genesis 6:4, "There were giants in the earth in those days, and also afterward, when the sons of God [i.e., of Seth and Enos] had relations with the daughters of men, who bore children to them." Early commentators traced the descent of Cain's unnatural sin through some of the separate stories in Genesis. Thus the "daughters of men" in Genesis 6:2 were interpreted as Cain's descendants mentioned in Genesis 6:4, and their progeny were identified as the giants. These giants were taken to be wicked and were used to explain the following verses, Genesis 6:5–8, in which God, appalled at man's evil, decides on the Flood. From this traditional connection, presumably, came the legend that God vanquished the giants with the Flood, which is the "payment" alluded to in line 114b. Robert E. Kaske has recently shown that the term "giants" had figurative force as "enemies" in Old Norse poetry and as "proud, arrogant men" in Gregory the Great's commentaries on Scripture. Professor Kaske points out that the Frisians were also known for their large stature in later times. There seems no bar, then, to reading "giants" throughout the Finnsburh Episode, and probably the reader is meant to bear in mind some of the Biblical associations awakened here when he later comes to the Episode. See Kaske, "The *Eotenas* in *Beowulf*," in *OEP*, pp. 285–310.

In line 112 the *eotenas* 'etens' (ON. *jötnar*) were giants, sometimes man-eating, as in Wyclif's witty remark against transubstantiation: "No man is an etene to fede him þus bodili of Crist" (*Selected Works*, II, iii). The *ylfe* 'elves' are evil here, but *ælf-scīene* 'bright as an elf or fairy' occurs elsewhere in Old English, and the elves appear to have been both beautiful and evil, as they are in later English and Norse tradition. The *orc-nēas* 'hell-corpses' or 'evil spirits of the dead' (Wrenn) were the Anglo-Saxon equivalent of zombies. They may have lived in barrow graves like their Old Norse counterparts, the *draugar*. For more details, see Hoops, *Beowulfstudien,* pp. 17–20, and on the *draugar*, N. K. Chadwick, "Norse Ghosts," *Folklore,* 57 (1946), 50–66, 106–27.

The wickedness of Cain and the begetting of monsters were thought to live on after the Flood in the line of Ham, one of Noah's three sons (often spelled Cham or Cam). From his line, too, came the gods of the heathen, who were as devilish to the Christians as the monsters spawned by Cain. The scribe's original *cames* 107 and his *camp* 1261 reflect the blending of Cain and Cam in the monster legend. This blending can be seen again when *Cham* appears twice for *Cain* in a discussion by Alcuin (A.D. 735–804) in *Interrogationes et Responsiones in Genesin,* 96. See Oliver F. Emerson, "Legends of Cain, especially in Old and Middle English," *PMLA* 21 (1906), 831–929, esp. 878–929.

It is difficult to ascertain the degree of Christianity that a knowledge of this legend might imply. The origin of the race of Cain is described again in 1260 ff., the giants and the Flood in 1689 ff. Dorothy Whitelock argued that the poet was composing for Christians who were fully converted. He could throw out allusions to biblical events without troubling to be explicit about them. The allusion in line 114, Professor Whitelock thinks, would have been cryptic to a newly converted audience. See her *Audience,* p. 51. On the other hand, it must be granted that 114 is the only line where an aspect of the legend is not set forth in an expository, somewhat explanatory manner. It seems impossible to decide whether the accounts of the Cain-Abel story fulfilled the poetic pleasure of encountering the familiar or the equal delight of hearing something new. Kenneth Sisam points out that Cædmon began with the Creation, not with the Passion, and he also notes that in the eighth century Bishop Daniel of Winchester advised the missionary Boniface to convince heathens by discussing subjects more akin to Genesis than to the Gospels. Sisam rightly emphasizes that Genesis was a crucial part of Christian teaching to laymen. He concludes that the poem discloses a relatively elementary stage of Christianity. See his *Structure,* p. 76. Both arguments should be read in full; neither resolves the question.

The Initial Viewpoint on Grendel (115–163)

In line 119, the words *swefan* 'to sleep' and *symble* 'feast' are bound across the caesura to *sorge* 'sorrow' by stress and alliteration, so that the emphasis of the meter itself falls upon the steep contrast in the narrative. The antithesis here, as in 129 and 130, incarnates in the verse structure the physical irony of Grendel's presence in Heorot. In other passages such collocations have diverse ironic purposes. Some critics, following Tolkien, relate these devices within the smaller structural unit of the line to the larger contrast in the structure of the total narrative, between Beowulf's youth and age, his rise and fall. The darkness just before dawn (line 126) was conventionally the time of greatest misery, sorrow, or terror. The convention probably arose because battles usually began then, but its emotive range is not limited to battle scenes (see 2450). By extension, "morning" in OE. poetry has the connotation "sorrowful." See further E. G. Stanley, *Anglia,* 73 (1955), 434–35.

Emphasis is built up in 133 ff. through absolute statements and the repeated "too." The open and unqualified assertion of 133b–34a will be repeated almost verbatim with a new meaning in 191–92. Absolute assertion is half the technique here; ironic understatement plays a strong counterpoint against it. This alternation of urgent emphasis and calm withdrawal creates a viewpoint close to the Danes' but at the poet's own distance. He seems to care little at this point about providing a visual picture of the locale or carnage, but is careful to establish a special tone of voice. This emphatic passage helps prepare the central irony of Beowulf's first fight, the complete reversal of Grendel's expectations once they grapple.

In 138–43 there may be an implied criticism of the Danes: if it was easy to find men who slept elsewhere, then who was courageous enough to stay? Yet any criticism heard must be carefully weighed, since the poet's strategy also creates the sense that this is such a great persecution that everyone must flee. The slight shifts here in tone, and possibly in viewpoint, have not yet been compared by critics to the larger shifts in narrative viewpoint during Beowulf's three main battles. The latter have been described by R. M. Lumiansky, "The Dramatic Audience in *Beowulf,*" *JEGP,* 51 (1952), 545–50, and Charles Moorman, "Suspense and Foreknowledge in *Beowulf,*" *CE* 15 (1954), 379–83, esp. 382–83.

"Hall-thane" for Grendel is ironic in several ways. As a thane he should serve Hrothgar loyally, hold fast friendship; as the one who now serves the hall at night, he is in fact its master; as a hall-keeper he fails badly, once Beowulf arrives. Perhaps we may see the poet looking ahead to the Grendel fight again as he sets up the irony, shameful to the Danes, of Grendel as the "retainer" of their hall. He calls Beowulf a hall-thane in 719. His verbal imagination seems to have been sparked by this aspect of the story, and elsewhere in the first half of the poem he uses similar compounds coined from words for "hall" and "man (with a duty)", e.g., 249, 770.

A bit later (154–58), the grimly comic irony of the legal language has a double edge. The poet starts from the notion that Grendel should pay the Danes wergild for the men he kills. The

Danes should like to expect this, of course, but he won't even cease killing, much less pay up. But how *should* a creature from the darkness be expected to pay mankind? It is possible, further, that here we are meant to chuckle at the expense of the Danes. Their hopes for negotiation may not seem very real once couched in the negative and used to define the very hopelessness of their situation. But ironic language often partly asserts as it partly negates, and their hopes may have more than a figurative existence. The Danes will seem the more foolish if one reads this passage as leading toward 175–188. Whether it should be read thus is open to argument.

Klaeber pointed out that "dark death-shadow" (160) is an epithet for the Devil in the OE. *Christ I*, 257. Line 164, literally "the enemy of mankind," is a common OE. expression for the Devil. Do these phrases mean Grendel is the Devil incarnate or perhaps a symbol for him? Opinion varies, depending on one's view of the patterns of significance in the whole poem, but it is indisputable that the poet applies the words for demons more lavishly to Grendel than to Grendel's mother and the dragon. It seems fair to say that he is devilish, and about the Devil's business, though this may not necessarily entail his standing only for the Evil One. He is also a monster, a solitary *ān-gengea* 'an alone-goer," and an outlaw at feud with man. Unlike true devils he has corporeality and can be caught and killed. Further discussion in J. R. R. Tolkien, "Appendix: (a) Grendel's Titles," in *ABC*, pp. 88–91; E. G. Stanley, "Beowulf," in *C & B*, pp. 104–08.

Grendel and the Throne (168–169)

Because of the abrupt change of subject and the ambiguous reference of several words, lines 168–69 have been often discussed and are still somewhat problematical. Tolkien held them to be an inauthentic scribal retouching (*ABC*, p. 96, n. 34), while Wrenn suggested they are an out-of-place reference to Cain and should follow line 110. The ambiguous words offer the following alternatives: *hē*—Grendel or Hrothgar? *gif-stōl* 'throne'—God's or Hrothgar's? *grētan*—'approach' or 'attack'? *his*—God's or Hrothgar's? *myne*—'mind,' 'purpose,' 'love,' or 'gratitude'? Obviously, a wide variety of sentences can be composed from these different possibilities. Most scholars today accept the lines as authentic and in place and treat *hē* as Grendel and *his myne* as "God's love" or "God's purpose."

There is no unanimity about whose the *gif-stōl* is. I assign it to Hrothgar by an argument from cultural history, not philology. There is plentiful evidence that kings in early Christian Europe were invested with divinely approved powers. Robert M. Estrich, *JEGP* 43 (1944), 384–89, showed that one major symbol of a king such as Hrothgar was his high seat. There is some reason to believe that the seat of the gift-throne might actually have been a chest in which the king's treasure was kept. (Were this the case, *māþðum* 169 might be the treasure itself, rather than the gold-adorned chair.) Such a symbol might well have had a taboo on it, to which lines 168–69 might refer. This taboo keeping Grendel away would come either from God or from the king's *mana*, his spiritual power, which would ultimately derive from God. This interpretation, while not beyond dispute, has been reinforced with further evidence by William A. Chaney, *PMLA* 77 (1962), 513–20, and Margaret Pepperdene, *JRSAI* 85 (1955), 188–92. Miss Pepperdene observes that the limit set upon Grendel's powers is a promise of hope. God has not abandoned the Danes completely; compare the leaderless time before Scyld's arrival. She sees the lines as a subtle stroke, revealing the secret design of Providence to the poet's audience but not to the Danes.

The Backsliding of the Danes (175–188)

This account of the Danes' heathen rites and, more especially, the following moralizing comments, have been thought to conflict with the view of the Danes' apparently Christian beliefs elsewhere in the poem—as in the song of Creation above, Hrothgar's thanks to God at 381 ff., and his sermon to Beowulf at 1724 ff. The questions raised may be classed under three general heads: (1) the poet's artistic intentions at this point; (2) whether the passage is genuine or a later scribal addition; and (3) how best to regard the religious attitudes of the Danes in the poem as a whole. The last question turns, once again, into the question of the cultural setting and how far we ought to apply the possibilities available in Christian Latin literary culture when we examine the poem's ideas and events.

(1) Most commentators agree that the poet intended a contrast between the godly song of Creation in the Danes' days of bliss and this hopeless, damning heathenism in time of despair. This connection might be said to have its stylistic proof in the way the poet brings praise of the names of God into his description of the Danes (180–83). He shows how to praise the Creator even as he shows them not doing so. Klaeber pointed out that the Danes' behavior is very similar to the backsliding of Anglo-Saxons under duress, a phenomenon which continued in isolated instances through the end of the Anglo-Saxon period. It is even possible there was some topical reference in the passage now lost to us. The poet's intention in terms of his story is much clearer: the passage marks the nadir of the Danes' fortunes and the hero is introduced shortly afterwards.

(2) The homiletic tone of 180b–188 has led Tolkien and others to question their authenticity (as in *ABC,* pp. 101–3). Truly, though intoned at a high pitch, it is not a high moment, but tends toward pious ejaculation. Tolkien's principal argument was that the lines did not fit the rest of the poem. They sounded wrong. This judgment by one of the most sensitive readers of *Beowulf* is not lightly dismissed. However, it is open to the countersuggestion that the lines are authentic and bad. Sometimes, Horace said, even good Homer could nod. It is also true that early medieval works rarely show an Aristotelian unity in which all parts fit the whole. But these arguments do not refute Tolkien's; in the absence of external evidence, the grounds for either authenticity or interpolation are both necessarily subjective. Probably it is best to follow Wrenn in his cautious inclusion. Without some guideline external to the poem, we should not reject a passage on the grounds of tone alone. Hrothgar's sermon is in the same homiletic mode.

(3) The poet knew his characters were heathens, yet Hrothgar is a noble monotheist, and Beowulf trusts as much in God as in his great strength. Norman Eliason has remarked that lines 175–88 offer an implicit signal that the poet meant his Christianization of pagan times and peoples to be understood as a fictional device; see *Anglia* 71 (1953), 445. If so, what are the artistic uses of this temporal setting? Tolkien, taking the poem as an elegy on mortality, held the view that its language is "partly re-paganized" to create a view of the heroic society of the past at once "heathen, noble, and hopeless." A. G. Brodeur has a different formulation: the chief characters are

in fact pagan, in spirit Christian. The poet admits the paganism of
the Danes here only to ignore it and henceforth treats them as
Christians. It is "hardly likely that he consciously attempted to
archaize"—"the Christianity of his own time forbade." See Brodeur,
pp. 216–19.

Brodeur thinks that the poet treated the Danes as pagans who sin
only from ignorance, not intent, and that lines 183b–188 "at once
set forth true Christian doctrine and express the poet's feeling that
it is a great pity that good men, with the best intentions" can damn
themselves through ignorance (p. 205). Coming at the question from
a more historical point of view, Larry D. Benson holds that the poet
placed the passage early in the poem precisely "to engage his audi-
ence's sympathy for his characters by emphasizing their very pagan-
ism." Benson claims that the dominant attitude of eighth-century
Christian Englishmen toward the ancient Germanic pagans, and
toward the pagans on the Continent who were the object of con-
temporary missionary work, was "one of interest, sympathy, and
occasionally even admiration." Thus he hears a "tone of compassion"
in the passage. However, this type of rhetorical contrast (*Wā biđ . . .
Wēl biđ . . .*) is usually a stern warning in OE. homilies, and I am
not sure I can hear "compassion" or "pity" in 183–88. In any case,
Benson's reconstruction of a tradition of sympathetic Anglo-Saxon
Christian attitudes toward Germanic pagans deserves the fullest at-
tention. See his "The Pagan Coloring of Beowulf," in *OEP*, pp.
193–213.

The *gāst-bona* 'soul-slayer' in line 177 is probably Woden, since
his was the principal aristocratic warrior cult in both Scandinavia
and England, and its survival into Christian times would insure this
application of a devilish epithet. However, Tiw (or Tyr), an earlier
war god whose name survives in "Tuesday," would be equally pos-
sible. See further H. R. Ellis Davidson. "The Germanic War Gods."
Gods and Myths, pp. 54–61. For either god, the known rites involved
the blood sacrifice of animals and, on great occasions, human beings.

The Geats (195)

The Geats lived in southwestern Sweden between the west coast
and Lake Väner, in the valley of the Göta River. In Old Icelandic
they are *Gautar*, in Old Swedish, *Gotar*. Before this etymological

equation was firmly established by R. W. Chambers, they had been thought of as Jutes. Not any more. That Hygelac was one of their kings is attested by the eighth-century *Liber Monstrorum* (*Book of Monsters*), where he is called King Huiglaucus of the Getae and is distinguished for his amazing size. According to this Latin source written in England, his gigantic bones are preserved as a prodigy on an island at the mouth of the Rhine, where he was slain by the Franks. Gregory of Tours and the anonymous author of the *Gesta Francorum* (c. 727) both confirm the fact that he made a raid on the Franks in which he was killed c. A.D. 521. However, both these Frankish sources refer to Hygelac (Latinized as Chlochilaicus) as a Dane. *Beowulf* therefore offers important corroboration of the English conception of his historical identity as a Geat or Gaut.

The death of the historical Hygelac (Hugleikr, in Scandinavian sources) probably weakened the Geatish nation seriously, though our poem says the legendary Beowulf then ruled the nation for fifty years in strength and prosperity. After the Geats' defeat by the Swedes, predicted by the Messenger at the end of *Beowulf*, they disappear from history and legend. It has been argued that, after the final overthrow of the Geatish kingdom and its absorption by the Swedes, certain exiled Geats with Danish connections settled in East Anglia and established the Wuffing dynasty, which may have included Wiglaf among its forebears. See J. N. O'Loughlin in "Sutton Hoo—The Evidence of the Documents," *Medieval Archaeology* 8 (1964), 1–19. If true, this would explain why an Anglo-Saxon poet knows so much about this minor Swedish tribe. For arguments that the historical Geats survived in Sweden long after the mid-500s, see R. T. Farrell, *Beowulf, Swedes and Geats* (London: Viking Society for Northern Research, University College London, 1972), pp. 29–43.

But it may be that the Geats of *Beowulf* are not really very historical. Jane Acomb Leake in her recent *The Geats of Beowulf: A Study in the Geographical Mythology of the Middle Ages* (Madison: University of Wisconsin Press, 1967) shows that in the ancient world the Latin *Getae* was often a name for the Goths, who were also supposed to be related to the monstrous Gog and Magog. Over the centuries, map makers confusedly drew together the Baltic and upper Greece, so that Denmark and Thrace, home of the mythical Getae, became contiguous. In one written tradition the Getae are mon-

strously large, hairy, and located in Scandinavia. Mrs. Leake shows
how this Latin tradition, originally Mediterranean, was absorbed into
the North in the late Dark Ages and she points out that some Anglo-
Latin writers confused *Getae* and *Geatas*. She goes on to claim that
the Geats of *Beowulf* are really the Getae of the mythical Latin
tradition.

The basis for her claim is that the poem is "a work of art, not
history, in which free play of the imagination, not adherence to fact,
played the basic role." To support this premise, she has to argue
that "the 'Geats' never existed as an historical tribe" and that the
Hygelac of the poem is "a king in the realm of make-believe" (pp.
125 ff.). She sees the use of the well-attested raid on the Frisians
c. 521 as merely giving historical verisimilitude to an otherwise fan-
tastic story. This seems a bit extreme. Simply because the mythical
Getae exist—and Mrs. Leake's book is invaluable for discovering
and tracing their history—it does not necessarily follow that the
Geats of *Beowulf* are *not* the Gautar. It might be possible that the
poet's idea of the Geats depends on both the historical Gautar and
the mythical, monstrous Getae. Other conceptions in *Beowulf* are
blended.

The Foamy-Necked Floater (218)

The translation takes *hringed-stefna* 'the ring-necked one' 32 as a
ship roughly like the Oseberg ship, built about A.D. 800, which was
used for the burial of a Viking queen. This vessel has interlace
carvings on its prow and stern whose stems each rise to a beautiful
scroll. Either the scroll or the carved frieze of stylized animal forms
might suggest the term "ringed." It seems reasonable to assume the
poem described ships contemporary with its presumed date of com-
position, A.D. 700–800, and not the earlier keelless ships of Sutton
Hoo (c. 620) or ships used during the poem's action in the 500s.
See Charles Green, *Sutton Hoo: The Excavation of a Royal Ship-
Burial* (New York: Barnes and Noble, 1963), pp. 48 ff.; A. W.
Brøgger and Haakon Shetelig, *The Viking Ships: Their Ancestry and
Evolution* (Oslo: Dreyer, 1953). The Swedish and English remains
of ships built for nobles suggest that the ships in *Beowulf* can be
imagined as single-masted sailing vessels roughly eighty feet long

and six feet deep amidships, with a beam of about seventeen feet. They would have had thwarts and rowlocks and the general appearance of a Viking ship, but less ornate.

The hull of Beowulf's ship is described as *wudu bundenne* 'bound wood' 216. This suits the ships preserved to us: their ribs were lashed to a hull made of overlapping horizontal planks held together by iron rivets. Caulked with resin (cf. line 295), this "bound wood" was apparently extremely supple, which may give a realistic force to the kenning "wave-rider" 198. A modern anecdote will illustrate: when Captain Magnus Andersen sailed an exact replica of the Gokstad Viking ship across the Atlantic in 1893 (Bergen, Norway, to Newfoundland in twenty-eight days), he reported that in a heavy sea the bottom of the hull would rise and fall as much as three quarters of an inch, while the gunwales would twist out of line as much as six inches. The hull remained both watertight and elastic (Brøgger and Shetelig, p. 142).

The language that describes Beowulf's ship, "the foamy-necked floater, most like a bird" 218, is both a kenning and a simile, and it may have been deliberately selected to go with *swan-rād* 'the swan's riding place' 201. The kennings for sea images in *Beowulf* are superbly adapted to their contexts: "Just as *hron* ['whale' 10] suggested vast sovereign sway, *swan* is suggestive of easy grace, swiftness and speed."—Adrien Bonjour, *Twelve Papers*, p. 117. The word element *rād* means "road" only in the sense of "mooring" as in Hampton Roads. It almost suggests "pasture" and, in *hron-rād*, Scyld's own domain. See Caroline Brady, "The Old English Nominal Compounds in -*rād*," *PMLA* 67 (1952), 538–71.

The foamy-necked floater beaches upon a crux at 224a. Agreement about the lexical meaning of *ēoletes*, probably a compound, may never be reached, although its contextual meaning is clear enough. Many emendations have been offered but none has held the day. In recent years there has been a discernible rush to divide the unemended form as *eo* + *letes*, but even this may be only a fad: *eol* + *etes* also yields interesting etymologies. A sampling of some guesses will show the fascination this Circe of a word has had for unwary philologists: "sea journey," "foreign journey," "confluence of waters," "elk's pasture" (with "elk" figurative for "ship"), "boar-carrying," "horse-abandoning."

The Coast-Guard's Challenge (229–300)

This is the first of Beowulf's three encounters with the Danes in which we see the impact of his character upon others. So much critical attention has focused on Unferth's "flyting" against Beowulf that this quiet crescendo of three meetings in three different settings—on the coast, at the hall-door, and before Hrothgar's throne—has not had its due. The stages of this triple landing in Denmark rise both in courtly formality and heroic tone; each meeting is developed by a similar pattern of exchanged speeches.

Margaret Pepperdene has recently given a sensitive reading of the small dramatic revelations of character between Beowulf and the coast-guard in *ES* 47 (1966), 409–19. The coast-guard is at once sturdily formal and yet flushed with curiosity. There is a delightfully comic aspect to the situation when he tells the Geats to explain their presence in Denmark and then goes on talking himself. Behind his tactless bluster lie anxiety, a desire for company, and a puppyish admiration of their noble leader. In his embarrassed volubility he insults them as spies and orders them about. In his reply at 287 ff. he is almost stupidly wooden as he apologetically recites the duties of intelligence. By contrast, Beowulf's speech at 260 ff. reveals his quick insight into the coast-guard's flustered, dogged state of mind. He comes through as quietly amused, magnanimous, and easy with himself and his undertaking. He shows self-control and kindness in dealing with the coast-guard's embarrassment.

There are always more refractions of attitudes in a dramatic situation created through poetic language than one can ever name. Another reader, returning to the text after Pepperdene's perceptions, might notice countervailing attitudes. Though it is not an overriding quality, Beowulf shows an aggressive sureness in defining the plight of the Danes and his heroic mission. His self-confidence verges on rudeness. He does not waste on the soldier coast-guard the more courtly phrases with which he addresses the prince Wulfgar, and his ironies in 269 ff. turn both toward and away from kindliness. Then comes the modulation in tone of voice that any serious reflection about the future must bring, and in 280 ff. the hero's arrogance (if it is even so much as that) gives way to awe and uncertainty. This counterpoise to Pepperdene's reading does not exhaust the human music of the passage.

Commentary 295

Shields and Mail-Shirts (245, 321 ff., and elsewhere)

The coast-guard calls Beowulf and his men *"lind*-carriers" in line 245. This refers to the wood used in Anglo-Saxon shields, from the linden or lime tree. Its soft white wood was light enough to give maneuverability to the circular shields, whose diameters varied from twelve to thirty-three inches. The shields were made from two or more layers of narrow strips of wood, laid with their grains at right angles. These strips, having a total thickness of not more than a half inch, were fastened with metal or leather binding round the rim, and the front was sometimes covered with leather. In the center of the shield was an iron boss, usually conical or hemispherical; the hand-grip was on the back of the shield, directly behind the boss. Very little of the wood and leather have remained in the surviving shield remnants, so that this reconstructed picture depends on archaeologists' inferences. From MS. illustrations and other evidence, it appears that some of the shields were curved, and in at least one case almost conical, with a depth of twenty inches. See David Wilson, *The Anglo-Saxons* (Harmondsworth: Penguin, 1971), pp. 115–18, and R. Ewart Oakeshott, *The Archaeology of Weapons* (New York: Praeger, 1960), pp. 120–22.

Later, at line 326, the shields are called *regn-heard*. This word probably means "magically hard," with the first element meaning "divine or magical power" (cf. ON. *regin* 'god'). Wrenn in his second edition (p. 81) contended that this meaning of *regn* had been lost by the time of *Beowulf*, when it meant only "rain." If so, it is possible that we are dealing with a compressed metaphor: "hardened by a rain (of spears and arrows)." However, Klaeber translated the compound as "wondrously strong," and Hilda R. Ellis Davidson, in the course of explaining *scūr-heard* 'shower-hard' 1033, calls the postulated semantic loss unlikely. See her *The Sword in Anglo-Saxon England* (London: Oxford University Press, 1962), p. 133, n. 2. Surely some of the poetic vocabulary was already archaic at the time of composition, but here the idea of magic seems probable, especially when we compare the fittings of the Sutton Hoo shield. The dragon and eagle ornaments of gilt bronze on the face of the shield and the twelve gilt bronze-and-gesso dragon heads, each about two inches long, set at equal distances around the rim are best interpreted as magically protective symbols. The boss itself is ornamented in part with zoomorphic designs and dragon heads. This brings up the question of *rondas* in line 326: "rims" or "bosses"? The ON. cognate clearly means "rim," but the context of *rond* in *Beowulf* 2673 requires "boss." For 326, it is easy to imagine a smith magically tempering the boss and inlaying it with figures, but the more prominent appearance of the dragons' heads round the Sutton Hoo shield rim, which would usually deflect the enemy's sword, has led to the translation "rims."

Ring-mailed shirts, also called corselets or byrnies, have been preserved mainly in Danish peat-bog burials which date from the third to the fifth centuries, and hence well before *Beowulf*. The remains of a mail-shirt were found at Sutton Hoo, but it was not so skillfully made as the Continental finds and we might speculate that this side of English metalwork was in decline while Anglo-Saxon goldsmiths were reaching the height of their ornamental art. The poet might not necessarily be describing contemporary or English war-garments, since the Danish bog finds are the closest analogy to his description. One complete shirt is described as three feet long, with short sleeves and a V-neck. The rings of two of the best shirts were only one eighth and one quarter of an inch in diameter, respectively, so that as many as twenty thousand iron rings would have gone into making one byrnie. Each ring was riveted or welded shut as it was interlinked, thus forming a net (cf. line 406). This heavy mesh would undoubtedly be worn over a leather jerkin. Sometimes the rivets were bronze, which would give a gleaming double luster to the whole mail-coat. See Oakeshott, *The Archaeology of Weapons*, pp. 90, 96; Wilson, *The Anglo-Saxons*, pp. 125–26; Haakon Shetelig, Hjalmar Falk, trans. E. V. Gordon, *Scandinavian Archaeology* (Oxford: Clarendon Press, 1937), p. 403.

In an important article, "Beowulf's Armor," in *ELH* 32 (1965), 416–19, Professor George Clark notes that from Beowulf's departure from Sweden until his speech in Heorot there is an increase in the detail and significance of the armor imagery. In lines 321–30 its surface brilliance seems virtually metaphorical. *Īren-þrēat* 'the troop clad in iron' 330, when heard as part of the alliterative line, seems to refer as well to the bristling stack of spears; the soldiers' martial valor is expressed by the sharp visualization of their gear. Their equipment is all in order, ready for a response to violence and disorder. Perhaps the style of description also suggests the pointless dangers of the heroic life as well as bright deliverance for Heorot. Clark argues convincingly that, throughout the poem, arms and armor symbolize the ambiguities at the heart of the heroic vision.

Magical Helmets (303–306)

Lines 303–6 are much discussed. The boar was apparently a figure of defensive magic, being an animal of desperate courage and also a cult object sacred to the god Freyr; Mrs. Davidson suggests that perhaps the earliest form of this protection in Sweden were actual boar masks (*Gods and Myths*, p. 99). The "boar-helmets" of the poem are supported by archaeological finds: a boar figure of gilded bronze, three inches long, with garnet eyes, is fixed atop the crest of the Anglo-Saxon helmet found in 1848 at Benty Grange, Derbyshire, while gilt boars' heads make up the ends of the eyebrows of the visor of the Sutton Hoo helmet (possibly of Swedish origin). Right behind these small heads the cheek guards are attached. Such analogies help determine the meaning of otherwise impenetrable grammatical ambiguity. Only recently have the possible meanings of the lines been resolved into any truly likely readings, and it remains to be seen if any current reading will stand up under later scholarship.

My literal rendering would be: "Boar-figures shone over cheek-guards, adorned with gold; shining and fire-hardened, the war-spirit in battle-masks held life-protection." This interpretation depends largely on A. T. Hatto, "Snakes-swords and Boar-helms in *Beowulf*," *ES* 38 (1957), 145–60, especially p. 159 where he connects the two meanings of *grīma*, 'visor' and 'mask, specter.' The MS. form *grummon* is taken as originally this noun in the dative plural, *grimmum*, with late *-on* for *-um* and a minim error giving *u* for *i*. An alternative translation based on the interpretation argued in Wrenn's edition: "Boar-shapes shone over cheek-guards: gold-adorned, shining and fire-hardened, it (the boar-shape) kept life-guard; the war-hearts (i.e., warriors) raged (or were excited)." Here *grummon* is taken as the preterite plural of the verb *grimman*, *guþ-mod* is given a different meaning, and the sentence is divided and parsed differently. These are only two readings among many, and neither is wholly satisfactory. Other possibilities include treating *ferh-wearde* as two words, *ferh* 'life' as *fearh* 'pig', and *gūþ-mōd* 'war-minded' as an adjective.

Beowulf's First Heroic Boast (405–455)

Heroic confidence permits a remarkable variety of tones in this fifty-line speech: from the first proud salutation—almost a whoop of self-proclamation—through the circumlocutory courtesies of 425 ff., to the grim ironic humor of "No need then . . ." (more dogged, facing a more real danger than the translation conveys). Beowulf has a feeling for the imagination of disaster, yet is entirely free of self-pity. This combination of qualities is a token of his youthful humanity. The plurality of the dramatic effects depends in part on the poet's taking exceptional advantage of the stock "turns" of a hero's speech. Among these conventional themes surviving today are the directions for the disposal of the body and armor. They appear in transmuted form, for example, in "The St. James Infirmary Blues."

The Scandinavian custom of covering a dead man's head with a cloth lies behind 446a. The grim humor of that passage may perhaps extend to *lices feorme* 451a. The usual interpretive translation is "(my) body's burial (or removal)," which I follow. Martin Puhvel, *ELN* 1 (1964), 159–63, finds the evidence for this "slight and inconclusive" and argues for *feorm* in its ordinary literal meaning "food, sustenance." If so, then: "You need not worry then about feeding my body." This irony would refer both to Grendel's dining habits and the Danes' role as hosts.

According to some sources, *niceras* 'nickers' 422a were no more than hippopotamuses or walruses. But the major meaning seems to have been "water demons," which survives today in "nixie," i.e., "water-sprite". In later traditions, nickers and their cognates were shape changers, often taking the form of a horse. In *Beowulf* they seem to be sea devils that have a large animal-like shape.

Hrothgar's Reply and Ecgtheow's Exile (456–490)

No emendation of 457a is wholly convincing, partly because any suggestion must rest on the larger interpretation of Hrothgar's character in this speech. In accepting Trautmann's emendation, I take the view that Hrothgar is showing a proud restraint in his welcome. Although earlier, in private, the king had expressed great hopes of a savior, here face to face he notices first, and at length, that Beowulf is fulfilling his father's obligation toward him. One might extend Hoops's paraphrase (*Kommentar*, p. 72) to indicate Hrothgar's attitude: "You come to help us. As a matter of fact (and of face-saving irony), your father once came to ask my help. He prospered by my aid." As his speech continues, the old king comes to see Beowulf's heroic task as no easier to achieve than his own shame has been to bear. And the untested hero is not accepted wholeheartedly, as the Unferth episode soon shows. This current of meaning in the speech should be noticed since Hrothgar's confidence in Beowulf and his glad welcome of a God-send are more obvious. Both these tones spring from Hrothgar's aristocratic nature.

The name of Beowulf's father, *Ecg-þēow*, is a compound of "sword" and "servant." It probably does not have significance beyond its general warlike sound. See G. T. Gillespie, "The Significance of Personal Names in German Heroic Poetry," in *Mediaeval German Studies Presented to Frederick Norman* (London: University of London Institute of Germanic Studies, 1965), pp. 16–21. The man Ecgtheow slew, *Heatho-lāf*, is mentioned only here. His name means "war-remnant" or "battle-legacy." The Wylfings have been connected with the Wulfings (Lat. *Vulgares*) of *Widsith* 29, who lived near the mouth of the Oder River on the South Baltic coast (the northern part of modern East Germany). Hrothgar's queen, Wealhtheow, is called "lady of the Helmings" in line 620, and a king named *Helm* 'protector' ruled the Wulfings according to *Widsith* 29. These names are closely enough connected that Wealhtheow may have been born a Wylfing princess. If so, Hrothgar's ties by marriage would have made it easier for him to compose the feud between Ecgtheow and the Wylfings.

Who, exactly, "could not keep him [Ecgtheow] for fear of war"? Was it his own people? Or was Ecgtheow a Geat? The answer lies behind the corrupt MS. *gara cyn* 'the race of spears' 461. Some see Wylfings there; most see Geats. There is no decisive external evidence. This edition follows the arguments of Joseph Tuso for the emendation [*w*]*ara-cyn* first suggested by the early editor Benjamin Thorpe. The compound is taken to refer to the Wylfings and to mean "the people of the shore" or "the guardian people."

In most of the poem, Ecgtheow is not so much a character as a patronymic epithet. The main purpose of the stock phrase "son of Ecgtheow" is to indicate a set of relationships. Beowulf's father would be remembered simultaneously in his other kinship definitions: a son-in-law to King Hrethel the Geat, a brother-in-law to Prince Hygelac, and a man who in exile took oaths of allegiance to the Danish king (472b). This would place Beowulf neatly and clearly in a known world of tribal histories.

Unferth (499–528 and later)

In the *Odyssey*, Bk. VIII, Odysseus refuses to join in the games of the Phaeacians and the courtier Euryalus deliberately insults him, saying he is no athlete. Odysseus replies quite as rudely, throws the discus a greater distance than anyone else, then boasts of his prowess and tells of his past life. His host, King Alcinous, accepts his angry behavior and reproves Euryalus, who then plays up and gives Odysseus a sword. This is parallel to Unferth's initial quarrelsomeness, to Beowulf's reply and its reception by Hrothgar, and to Unferth's friendly gift of the sword Hrunting when Beowulf is about to dive into the mere (1455–70a, 1487 ff.). The rude challenge by a retainer is a motif of heroic poetry that solves the literary problem of demonstrating the disruptive, self-assertive side of the hero's character while at the same time showing his courtesy and restraint. For similar "testing" scenes in the *Aeneid* and Old Norse literature, see Klaeber, p. 149.

Unferth may be the poet's own invention. Certainly in this exchange and his later about-face he is primarily a foil to Beowulf. However, he also appears in another context, sitting at the feet of Hrothgar and his nephew Hrothulf in a passage (1163–68) that appears to allude to future treachery. In this context, possibly a traditional one, Unferth is called *þyle* (ON. *þulr*), probably meaning "official spokesman," though the term is vague. Proposed meanings have varied from "jester" and "court poet" to "pagan priest." Norman Eliason has argued that in his role as *þyle* it was proper for Unferth to engage Beowulf in a "flyting" or slanging match. See "The Þyle and Scop in *Beowulf*," *Speculum* 38 (1963), 276–84, where Eliason exonerates Unferth from an active role in fomenting

Hrothulf's supposed revolt. Other scholars see *Unferð þyle* as a type of "the wicked counselor" common in Germanic story.

Unferth's name might mean "Mar-peace" or "Strife" if derived from *un* + *frið*, and the poet may have thought of him as an abstract personification, according to Morton W. Bloomfield in *ABC*, pp. 155–64. Bloomfield also points to possible allegorical abstractions in the names of other characters: *Won-rēd* 'Void-of-counsel' 2971 and *Hygd* 'Thought' 2172. The most exact etymology, to my mind, has been advanced by Fred C. Robinson, who takes *un-ferð* as 'un-wit, folly.' Rather than "strife," the OE. connotation of *Unferð* might be "Nonsense." Robinson tries to resolve the dual nature of this character—both a silly court jester and a more somber, sinister figure—toward the idea of a pusillanimous buffoon. See Robinson's article in *Pope Studies*, pp. 127–31. But perhaps Unferth's character should remain a blended conception in the reader's mind, half silly and half sinister.

Beowulf's Reply to Unferth (530–606)

This passage contains extraordinary poetic figures and reveals a wide range of feeling in Beowulf. At first, he is coolly amused and dismissive of Unferth. Then during his account of the swim he is nonchalant and boasting, while the story itself casually reveals his natural generosity. He finishes with an angry rebuke of Unferth that is filled with ironic scorn. The qualities of character that come through are proof positive that he is a true Germanic hero. Not only can his imagination entertain the possibility of terrible disaster, as in his first speech to Hrothgar; he also has a natural bias toward success that permits him a dimension of blithe ironic humor in 560 ff.

In his swimming adventure, as in all but the last of his life, Beowulf is able to conquer the unexpected through his strength and courage. His heroism is emphasized by the shift from the dual person (*wit*, *unc* 'we two,' 'us two') to the isolated *mē* that is buffeted by the waves and monsters. The malevolent personification of the storm in 546–48 and the desolate imagery of the exile theme create a metaphorical adversary greater than the simple idea of "hostile nature." It is as if, instead of using the sparrow simile, the counselor had said to King Edwin, "Sire, the life of man seems to me as though two boys went out swimming on a fine day for a dare, and the sea rose up in a storm, nature turned destructive, and demonic forces from the deep came up under them and tried to drag them down . . ." Or one may think of the closing of *Moby-Dick*.

There is a thematic connection between the language of feasting that Beowulf uses to describe killing the monsters with his sword (560–67) and the language of the Grendel episode. References to feasting appear more frequently in the first eight hundred lines than anywhere else. The juxtaposition of scenes of feasting and battle can even be called the structural principle of the first third of the poem. Generally speaking, each of these two types of scene is described in language that contains some hint of the other. In the feasting scenes, man's diminished awareness when he is happy, the fact that you can't think long on sorrow when you are joyful, makes the poet think of a sudden attack or future malice. Conversely, Grendel's terrifying carnage (730–45) is described as though it were a hall feast and he an exultant retainer. A moment later Beowulf reverses all that.

Here, as well, the sea monsters intend to feast (*þēgon*) on Beowulf, but like a good retainer he served (*þēnode*) them with his sword, "as was only fitting." He "knows the noble custom" (cf. Wulfgar, 359b) of this metaphorical occasion. The situation is grim, but Beowulf's witty treatment of it is nonchalant and gay—there is something ludicrous about lumbering sea-beasts seeking their places around the table as though they were a heroic troop in the hall. The word *fylle* 562a is literally 'feast,' but the translation follows the analogy of *hioro-dryncum* 'sword-drinks' 2358. See further James L. Rosier, "The Uses of Association: Hands and Feasts in *Beowulf*," *PMLA* 78 (1963), 8–14.

The appearance of daylight, "God's bright beacon," and the calming of the waves following Beowulf's slaying of the monsters—by sword, under water—are like a précis of his fight with Grendel's mother, where his personified mail-shirt again acts like a staunch retainer. The same motifs occur, in the same order. The poet may have used set groupings of conventional motifs when composing such passages. For this hypothesis, see Donald K. Fry, *Neophilologus* 52 (1968), 48–54, and *Speculum* 44 (1969), 35–45, and David K. Crowne, *NM* 61 (1960), 362–72. Here the religious epithet for the sun does not imply actual supernatural aid, as does the light simile in 1570–72a. But it may suggest Creation's benign regard for the

hero who endures. The bright morning light also returns with moral
force following Beowulf's defeat of Grendel (917–18). The idea in
572–73 of *wyrd* sparing the courageous man is repeated in substance
in 2291–93a, where it is *Waldend*, God as 'the Ruler,' who favors
the *unfæge* 'the undoomed man.' On this blended conception of
destiny, see "Backgrounds," above.

Like Unferth at the end of his speech, Beowulf returns to the
matter of Grendel with an ad hominem attack. Both speeches are
comparisons predicting the outcome of the fight from Beowulf's past
deeds. This symmetry lends an orderliness to their quarrel and high-
lights the contrast of Beowulf's confident conclusion. The comparison
of heroes and antiheroes is one of the poet's constant concerns.
While Unferth may have some good qualities—here a keen mind
and *mōd micel* 'great courage' in 1167—he still is deeply flawed.
Beowulf knows this and emphasizes it. For killing his brother,
Unferth will suffer in Hell (Robinson would read "hall"). The con-
demnation may be made in the poet's voice, not Beowulf's, and it
can be regarded as an unfortunate lapse into religious cliché. The
problem is similar to lines 176–88. But it should be remembered that
when Beowulf looks back over his life at the end of the poem, one
of his major satisfactions is that he broke no bonds of kinship or
friendship. Further, when the poet several times compares him to
Heremod, it is to point up Beowulf's peaceableness and good faith
as opposed to Heremod's wild killing of his comrades. Any brother-
slayer is, like Grendel, a descendant of Cain.

In closing his speech, Beowulf shows a witty sobriety in alluding
to the earlier Dutch courage of the Danes who will "walk bravely
to mead" once the new day comes. Line 605 could be omitted with-
out loss of sense. Why then is it there? The poet uses its two stock
phrases for an ironic emphasis in the boast—the "new day" of
Beowulf's deed will dawn on the Danes, "the sons of men"—and for
the Christian overtones of such terms. The word *swegl-wered* 606
may echo the praise of God in Psalm 103:2, "robed in light as with
a cloak." The curious *sūþan* 'from the south' further associates God's
favor with the sun shining on Beowulf's deed, since it is the antithesis
of the frozen Hell located in the far north. See T. M. Pearce,
"Beowulf and the Southern Sun," *American Notes and Queries* 4
(1966), 67–68.

Queen Wealhtheow (612)

After such a masterful speech, Hrothgar rejoices in Beowulf's evident powers, and the focus shifts to the courtly, aristocratic behavior of the Danes in the person of Queen Wealhtheow. She is intelligent, gracious, of splendid bearing: a true queen in any court. Her name was probably not invented by the poet. The first element, *Wealh*, is usually explained as "Celtic, British" or by extension "foreign"; *þēow* can mean "slave," "captive," or "servant." E. V. Gordon constructed an etymology for the first element that would permit the translation "chosen servant." See *MÆ* 4 (1935), 169–75.

Noblewomen appear frequently in Germanic story and Anglo-Saxon history; they enjoyed a position of respect and frequently one of independence and equality. *Maxims I* (also known as the *Exeter Book Gnomes*), lines 84b to 92, state the qualities a lady should possess: "A woman shall prosper, beloved among her people, shall be cheerful, keep counsel, shall be generous with horses and treasure; at the mead-taking she shall always, everywhere, first greet the lord of nobles before the troop of retainers, place the first cup promptly in her lord's hand; and she shall know good counsel in housekeeping, for their mutual benefit." Wealhtheow meets this ideal in every respect. The epithet "attired in gold," occurring three times in this passage, emphasizes her great worthiness. This description is linked to a series of epithets for Hrothgar which emphasize his role as the beloved protector of his people, victorious in his task (*gūð-rōf* 608a, *sige-rōf* 619b). Unlike "Victory-Scyldings" in Beowulf's speech, these epithets are not ironic, but illustrate the ideal of peaceful kingship that Wealhtheow's courtesy serves.

By offering the cup to Beowulf with the same courtesy she first offered it to the king, Wealhtheow expresses the Danes' complete trust in him as their protector, while at the same time the order of offering shows that the king still comes first. In accepting the cup, Beowulf accepts a symbol of the obligation to help Hrothgar. In his next speech he makes clear that from the outset he has freely accepted the choice of success or death in Heorot. The contrast between the warrior lusting for battle and the gentle, high-born lady is summed up in the alliterating words of 629; yet his boast is ceremonious, too. Even in his fierce resolve, he can be as ceremonious as she. This paradox is created in the passage preceding his speech by the poet's care for the details of ceremony, the language he lavishes on king, queen, and cup, and the measured pace of his lines. Without this setting, Beowulf's speech would be rant.

The Preparations for Battle (671–709)

Beowulf's disarming himself can be understood several ways. It was probably a feature of the underlying "Bear's Son" folktale that the hero wrestled the monster barehanded. Beowulf's physical strength is tremendous—"he was the strongest man alive" 195. And from his viewpoint as a retainer in 435–37, it makes the odds greater so he can gain more fame. But here he sees it as a matter of chivalry: poor Grendel is not warrior enough to know how to use weapons. Further, Beowulf's courage is emphasized by his ignorance of Grendel's immunity to weapons. See Joseph L. Baird, *N & Q* 14 (1967), 6–8. In addition, Beowulf intends to go naked against a creature weaponed by his evil nature. His vulnerability becomes a kind of innocence that confronts the armed malevolence of the monster. See George Clark, *ELH* 32 (1965), 422.

Beowulf wisely refrains from predicting the outcome, leaving the decision to God. In this he differs significantly from the expectant Grendel and from his men who despair in 691 ff. "On whichever hand" 686a is a conventional expression deliberately selected for the context of the coming fight. One of these "hands" has the grip of thirty men and God's favor behind it, and we may feel a certain reassurance in the poet's associative word pattern.

"The cheek-bolster received the noble's face" 688. This periphrasis emphasizes the fact that no boar-helmet now guards his face (cf. 303–6). Then, inconsistently, the Geats, who can despair of living through the night, fall fast asleep. But the poem was meant to be heard aloud, and the two events are combined for the immediate effect of increasing a listening audience's fear.

The Geats' grim thoughts are followed by the poet's frank antici-pation of the happy outcome and his reflection on God's limitless power (696–702a). This shift of focus dramatizes the idea of man's fallibility in a providential world. Yet, to complicate matters, the note of reassurance shifts again to an evocation of terror as Grendel begins his walk (702b–4). Then the poet intimates that Grendel, too, will find his expectations reversed, that the men can't be harmed against God's will (705–9). These rapid shifts in mood and view-point set up a "design for terror" (Brodeur's phrase) while removing crude suspense. They free us from what C. S. Lewis called "narrative lust," an exclusive interest in what happens next, so that we may concentrate on a double perspective that will continue through the whole fight. Up close to the action, as we hear the ominous sound of *cōm* 'he came' 702b, to be repeated twice more, we feel as much in the dark as the Geats. The anticipations, however, invite us to abstract ourselves and consider the ironic fate that overtakes both men and monsters unawares. The harsh sonorities of Grendel's ap-proach thrill along our nerves, yet all the time we know whom fate is going to strike.

Among the characters, only Beowulf shows an appreciation of the uncertain future as he remains awake and watchful. *Ac* 'but' 708a is additive (translated as "and"), and suggests that his righteous anger in 709 is an instrument of God's will. The "men" to whom "it was known" that the Geats would be safe when God so wished (705 ff.) are puzzling. It would be odd if "men" included the Geats, the Danes, or Beowulf. The phrase may be an afterthought to motivate the sleep of the Geats. Most likely these "men" are the generality of men who share the poet's Christian perspective.

Grendel's Approach to Heorot (702–727)

This is one of the finest passages in all of Old English poetry and must be read aloud to be appreciated. The threefold repetition of *cōm* 'came' is hair-raising: Death is on the march. The several stages of this action are an extended form of variation and reveal the poet's ability to expand and transcend the poetic conventions of his day.

Beginning in 702b and including *Wōd* 714a, there are four stages, each beginning with a forceful verb of motion and following the same rhetorical pattern: first there is a statement, in highly evocative language, of Grendel's fearsome motion and his position in relation to Heorot and then a comment on the circumstances of this final visit. At each new stage there is a sudden advance in Grendel's position, as though a movie camera were moving from a long shot toward a close-up. And with each new *cōm*, Grendel *sounds* larger than before. This dramatic effect is increased in 715 by switching the verb from the viewpoint of those he approaches (*cuman* 'to come') to his own forward motion (*wadan* 'to move, stride'). Then, as he enters the hall, we see him at close range from Beowulf's point of view. The light from his eyes is enough. See further Alain Renoir, "Point of View and Design for Terror," *NM* 63 (1962), 154–67; Brodeur, pp. 88–92; S. B. Greenfield, "Grendel's Approach to Heorot: Syntax and Poetry," in *OEP*, pp. 275–84.

Great Expectations (712–790)

The compound *mān-scaða* 'evil harmer' 712a, 737b, appears in connection with harming one "of the race of men." With a short *a* in *man*, the compound would mean "man-harmer" and perhaps also "a harmer who is a man." Grendel is not only a devilish embodiment of evil, he is also often called a "man" or "warrior"; he lives exiled from the joys of men; and the poet treats him ironically as a hapless retainer. One source of Grendel's power as a terrifying figure is this interconnection in the poet's language, by which he seems half human without losing his supernatural attributes. See Joseph L. Baird, "Grendel the Exile," *NM* 67 (1966), 375–81.

Grendel is most "human" in his logical but erroneous expectations. The triple use of *mynte* 'thought, planned, intended' at 712a, 731a, and 762a is a sophistication like the *cōm* triad. It gives poetic order to the most highly wrought dramatic irony of the episode, the contrast between Grendel's plans and the actual event. The poet spends many more lines on anticipations of Grendel's reversal and descriptions of his state of mind than on the action of the fight, which is very simple. The ironic anticipations increase the rhythm of terror by giving us brief releases from tension so as to increase each new shock. Grendel's last visit to Heorot dramatizes the classical Germanic idea of the hubris of heedless expectation (OE. *wēn*). See the excellent discussion by Richard N. Ringler, *"Him sēo wēn gelēah*: The Design for Irony in Grendel's Last Visit to Heorot," *Speculum* 41 (1966), 49–67.

One measure of the excellence of the poetry in Fitt XI is the poet's ability to bring together the two designs, for terror and for irony, so that the action has several dimensions at once. It seems his vision of the scene grew as he let his verbal imagination play with ironic vocabulary and epithets and with echo words like *fæste, dæg, aldor* and *ǣr*. His poetic poise can be illustrated by 716–19, where the litotes of the first sentence still terrifies by its grimly understated remembrance of Grendel's nightly visits even as it is transformed, in the second sentence, into the ironic fate in store for him. On the echo word see Ringler and John O. Beaty, *PMLA* 49 (1934), 365–73.

Beowulf's "Dereliction" (736–745a)

Why does Beowulf allow Grendel to kill and eat his companion? (Later at 2076 we learn his name was *Hond-sciōh* 'Hand-shoe,' i.e., 'Glove.') W. W. Lawrence believed that in the original folktale the younger hero had to wait until his older companions had fought and failed, but Klaeber and Chambers saw this as a spot where the poet did not fully assimilate his sources. Arthur Brodeur offers an aesthetic justification: all this terror must find a victim immediately, lest it become unreal (p. 93).

A. K. Moore, in *MLN* 68 (1953), 165–69, also thinks Lawrence's explanation is not compelling. Citing Tacitus, Moore claims that the Germanic chieftain was under no obligation to lead an attack; he acts in the general, not the particular, interest. Beowulf, because he alone is the hero, is obligated for the good of all to find out how best to grapple with the monster. Moore's point is developed further by T. M. Pearce, in *TSL* 11 (1966), 169–76, who compares Odysseus's due deliberation, and due loss of men, in conquering the Cyclops. In his view, it required great valor for Beowulf to refrain from helping Hondscioh.

All these explanations seem equal in cogency. Brodeur's may be the most attractive to readers fascinated by the vividness of the killing and devouring in lines 740–45.

The Wrestling Match (745b–819a)

The beginning of the struggle between Beowulf and Grendel remains unclear in its physical details, though the rhythm and speed of the reversal are perfectly plain. As Grendel seized Beowulf—or is it "started to seize"?—the hero either "received him with hostile intent" (Klaeber), or "perceived his hostile intent" (Wrenn), or "received the hostile-thinking-one." *Onfēng hraþe / inwit-þancum* 748–49 has to be twisted a bit to fit any of these readings. The important point is that Beowulf has been ready for him all along. Whether Grendel actually seizes him first is questionable. Wrenn (2nd ed., p. 198) takes *nam* 'seized' and *rǣhte ongēan* 'reached toward' as progressive or continuous tenses: Grendel was only in the act of doing these things. Ringler (pp. 56–57) believes this interpretation, which increases the ironic suspense, is further supported by 1266–69 and *grāpode gearo-folm* 'groped ready-handed' 2085b. He concludes that there is no evidence that Grendel actually laid hold of Beowulf. However, because Wrenn's interpretation seems to strain the verbs and because the whole passage is quite paratactic, I have supposed in the rather loose translation that "seized" followed by "reached toward" is simply another example of the excitement of telling a story aloud. The poet tones down his dramatic *nam* clause with the variation, "reached out with his open hand" (*mid folme*). Most commentators think Grendel does the reaching, but the lines can be repunctuated so that "the warrior in bed reached toward the fiend [or enemy] with his open palm"; thus F. G. Cassidy, *MLN* 50(1935), 88–89. *Ond wið earm gesæt* can mean that Beowulf "sat up [pushed himself up] on his arm" or "sat up against [Grendel's] arm" thus driving it back. There is no sure solution to this difficult phrase. See further Wrenn-Bolton, pp. 125–26.

Perhaps the problems in this passage come mainly from readers expecting a blow-by-blow description. Yet Donald K. Fry, in *MP* 67 (1970), 364–66, argues for coherent visual details throughout the fight. As Grendel reaches for Beowulf with his right hand, the hostile-thinking hero (*inwit-þancum*) quickly grabs the outstretched arm and leans his weight up behind it, twisting it behind Grendel's back. Beowulf then stands up behind Grendel, twisting the arm in a hammer lock and squeezing Grendel's fingers with his free left hand until they burst. The monster tries to turn clockwise out of Beowulf's grip, but the hero turns faster, keeping in position. He realizes that Grendel will eventually slip the hammer lock, and so rips off the arm by twisting it sharply upwards. *Voilà!* But surely the modern canon of verisimilitude can be pressed too far. Perhaps the destructive force of Beowulf's grip comes not from a hammerlock but simply from "the strength of thirty men."

"Ealu-scerwen" (769) and Dramatic Irony

The Danes hear only a terrific clamor, as from a thunderous drinking party. (The poet chose his noise words from the vocabulary of hall-joys.) This shift of viewpoint lets the reader stand halfway between the Danes' bitter fear and Beowulf's conquering might. See further R. M. Lumiansky, "The Dramatic Audience in *Beowulf*," *JEGP* 51 (1952), 545–50. The general sense of the unique word *ealu-scerwen* has long been known from its context to be "terror" or possibly "disorder." Still, probably more has been written about its possible meanings than any other word in Old English. The scholarly editions of *Beowulf* must be consulted in full for even a brief summary. Do countless articles bespeak an insoluble problem? I feel comfortable basing my translation on E. B. Irving, Jr.'s interpretation in *"Ealuscerwen:* Wild Party at Heorot," *TSL* 11 (1966), 161–68, supported by the extensive evidence of G. V. Smithers, "Five Notes on Old English Texts," *EGS* (now *Eng. Philol. Studies*) 4 (1951–52), 67–75. This view treats the word as an ironic "ale-sharing" or "ale-pouring" at the expense of the Danes. They are the absent hosts, in a heroic society that puts a premium on generous hospitality. *Cēn* 'brave' 768b they may be, but they only know that something beyond their ken is being served up inside their hall. The poet's wry amusement here is also directed at Grendel. If the Danes are the hosts, he is the "guest," now kept against his will. Beowulf makes this connection himself in 967–72 by apologizing to Hrothgar for being unable to detain (all of) Grendel. Some alternative meanings for *ealu-scerwen*: "dispensing (or depriving) of good fortune," "depriving of ale," "dispensing of bitter drink." On the last, see Carleton Brown, *"Poculum Mortis* in Old English," *Speculum* 15 (1940), 389–99.

There is an anticipation of the destruction of Heorot by fire in the Heathobard feud, in lines 781–82 (cf. 82 ff.). The introduction of this allusion into the middle of the fight with Grendel shows the delicate poise of the poet's mind when considering the force of fate and the transience of the world. Joyous relief is about to come to the Danes, though at this moment their hair stands on end. Yet the poet sees beyond even this contrast into the cylical nature of human conflict and its tragic futility. See further Brodeur, pp. 220 ff., and Bonjour, *Twelve Papers*, pp. 11–28.

The wail of "God's adversary" in the hall seems a virtual parody of the scop's Creation Song in lines 90–94. Just as Grendel heard a melodious song of God's goodness in a hall built, like the earth itself, for man's use, so now the ordinary inhabitants of that hall hear the unearthly scream of a tortured devil while the building is destroyed inside. This parody—perhaps it is only a return to the cluster of themes used for the Building of Heorot—is not simply an ironic view of the reversed situation: it is an acknowledgment of the terrifying power of evil, even in defeat. These thematic echoes, and even Grendel's "song," are also meant as praise of Beowulf's heroism. The verse-paragraph closes very deliberately with a formulaic repetition from lines 196–97, one of the first and most characteristic descriptions of the hero. The whole passage gains an epic distance.

Grendel's Arm (833–836 and 984–990)

Grendel's arm is a "token" both of Beowulf's feat and the Danes' suffering. I take "arm and axle" (i.e., shoulder) at 835a as an explanatory variation on *hond*; most translations take "hand, arm, and shoulder" as a series. It is not so quite straightforward, I think; 835a allows for a slight gasp of surprise. From 926 and 983 it seems that Beowulf places the arm outside the hall-door, up under the gabled roof. Thus in 836 the juxtaposition of Grendel's claw and the high roof makes a striking image, reinforced by the alliteration and the connotation of "wide, spacious" in *gēapne*. The juxtaposed image is repeated in 926–27 and (in looser form) in 983–1002a. When rounded off by the reflections on mortality at 1002 ff., this repetition seems almost to hint at an unnamed relationship between these two emblems, the one symbolizing a beneficent king's rule restored by a thane's courage, the other the destructive cannibalistic force of evil.

The picture of the talon here and at 984–90 reveals the full extent of the mysterious horror Beowulf has conquered, and it is the most visible evidence we are to receive of the force in his famous hand-grip. The translation of the second passage follows Wrenn's evidence for *egl* as 'spike' (2nd ed., p. 245). Other editors, including Klaeber and Dobbie, emend to *egl*[*u*] 'loathsome,' with elided final vowel. Then 987a reads "hateful, monstrous," modifying *hand-sporu*. C. J. E. Ball, *Archiv* 201 (1964), 43–46, suggests the emendation *egl*[*a*] *heoru* 'terrible sword' and would translate, "At the tip, each and every one of the nails was just like a steel weapon, the hand-spears of the heathen creature, the terrible sword of the warrior."

Fitt XIII: The Poetry of Praise (837–924)

Having made a brief statement of Beowulf's triumph (825 ff.), the poet now moves into a complex dramatization of the joy and gratitude felt on all sides. The superbly orchestrated activities here will provide an appropriate setting for Hrothgar's formal speech in 928 ff., but this setting is more interesting poetically. The modulations of tone are delightful, from the joyous irony of 841–42 to the harsh vision of the lake boiling with blood, and the solemn slam of *þǣr him hel onfēng* 852b.

The feeling of exultant "crowing" comes alive through the verse, though there is little attention to dramatic verisimilitude. The treatment is atemporal and unified mainly by pace and theme. There is an implicit contrast between two kinds of traveling—Grendel's difficult trip to the mere and the Danes' blithe return to Heorot. The very actions of the Danes grow in exuberance, from first walking warily round the tracks, to impromptu horse-racing and, finally, to the scop breaking into controlled song. The mode of this shifting, kaleidoscopic energy is not strict narration, but the celebration of Beowulf's worth.

The so-called "Sigemund-Heremod digression" is really the central panel in the tapestry (the poet himself speaks of "weaving words" in 874a). From the author's own practice as well as his description of the scop, it is clear that he thought a just poetry of praise depended on three things: (1) a knowledge of the old heroic lore; (2) the ability to make true alliterative meters; and (3) most importantly, the ability to compare deeds wisely. He uses the Danish scop's song to vault into a new, timeless realm where he and the scop speak together with the voice of history. From this vantage, he compares the great thane with the rulers of nations, by contrastive allusions to the bad king Heremod. At the same time, by significant omissions from the Sigemund story and the mention of a dragon, he can silently take the measure of heroic achievement without destructive irony.

The familiar formulas of extent at 857 ff. ("far and wide") should not be dismissed as a momentary relaxation of attention. Rather, the poet slides into hyperbole in order to imitate, to dramatize exactly

how the "many often spoke." The naïve emphasis in this new voice
is as genuine as the twangy assertions of American schoolboys dis-
cussing Mickey Mantle. The verbal gesture captures the feeling of
the speaker's arm sweeping out to include "the whole world." Yet
he recovers his balance in 860–61 through the slowing effect of the
syntax and larger consonant clusters. A drum roll of *r*'s and re-
newed metrical pomp replace the boyish enthusiasm, and Beowulf
again seems worthy of a kingdom. The formula "between the two
seas" probably refers to the Baltic and the Atlantic. The four formu-
las are in order of increasing scope.

The sentence at 862–63, especially its last phrase repeating that
Hrothgar "was a good king," may seem ironic to readers who re-
flect on a Germanic warrior's lofty personal pride and concern for
his good name. Yet Hrothgar is always "good"—and not merely by
conventional epithet, but because he is gracious and generous. He
may be old and weak, but he had sense enough not to deny Beowulf's
help out of pride. In fact, the dangers of pride are the main theme
of his sermon later on. It could be said that Denmark has been
saved partly by the king's wise consent, and I think the lines are
as sincere as any genuine afterthought. The poet may also want the
last half-line, repeating the epithet for Scyld from line 11, to hang
in the air like a leitmotif of deliverance as he enters this "digression"
about a warrior and a king.

The Improvisation by the Danish Scop (867b–874a)

This passage is the fullest direct account of a poet at work in OE.
literature and corroborates our knowledge of Germanic verse tech-
nique. Perhaps it is most valuable as a glimpse of the author's under-
standing of his own literary history: here a scop of the heroic age
improvises by putting old and new matter together in "truly bound"
(i.e., correctly alliterating) verses. *Hwīlum* and *eft* do not tell us how
much time the scop needs, nor can we confidently infer the *Beowulf*
poet's own method of composition from this account. But evidently
he felt that his counterpart of an earlier day would compose aloud
in formulaic diction. The translation is expanded for clarity's sake
and takes interpretive liberty with *wrixlan* 874a, which is usually
assumed to refer simply to the technique of variation. It can also
mean "to exchange" words (as in 366) and possibly refers to the

weaving together of the three subjects.

I follow Hoops, *Beowulfstudien,* pp. 52 ff., in seeing only one lay and not three in succession (on Beowulf, Sigemund, Heremod) as does Klaeber. This judgment rests on a conception of the poet's art and on his gradual shift from indirect to direct discourse, rather than on any explicit statement in the text. The poet does not report Beowulf's exploit again, but gives his full attention to the scop's laudatory comparison and contrast of Sigemund and Heremod. Most critics today believe that the audience already knew these stories, just as they knew Beowulf's, and that the poet meant his allusions to emphasize themes relevant to Beowulf. If so, then the poet also sees beyond the Danish scop's comparison of Sigemund, to Beowulf's death in the dragon fight. The interpretive problem here is to keep the poet's double vision of heroism and mortality in balance without a clear historical knowledge of his intentions. Further reading: Robert E. Kaske, "The Sigemund-Heremod and Hama-Hygelac Passages in *Beowulf,*" *PMLA* 74 (1959), 489–94.

The Sigemund Matter (874b–897)

The first part of the Sigemund passage alludes to the great tale of revenge later immortalized in the ON. *Vǫlsunga saga* (c. 1200), chaps. 2–8. There we read that Sigmundr, the eldest son of King Vǫlsungr of Hunaland, has a twin sister, Signý, who is married against her will to King Siggeirr of Gautland. (OE. *Wælsing* 877 = ON. *Vǫlsung.*) At the wedding feast Odin appears as a gray-cloaked, one-eyed stranger; he plunges a sword into a tree trunk and offers to give it to whichever man can draw it out. As in the story of Arthur and Excalibur, only Sigmundr can draw it, and King Siggeirr is publicly shamed. Later he invites the Vǫlsungs to a feast, treacherously kills King Vǫlsungr, and takes his ten sons prisoner. His wife Signý asks they be set in stocks out in the woods, rather than be slain outright. One by one they are killed and eaten by an old she-wolf, until on the tenth night only Sigmundr is left. Signý sends a servant to him with a handful of honey to smear on his face and mouth. The wolf licks his face clean and stretches her tongue into his mouth. He bites into her tongue and she pulls away so hard that the stocks split open, but he holds on till her tongue is torn out by the roots and she dies. Some men say this she-wolf was King Siggeirr's mother who had changed her shape by witchcraft.

Now Sigmundr is free and lives secretly in the forest. Signý bears King Siggeirr two sons, and when each turns ten years old she sends them into the forest to help Sigmundr gain revenge. But neither passes tests of valor, and she bids Sigmundr kill them, which he does. Then Signý exchanges shapes with a witch, goes into the forest, and asks Sigmundr for shelter overnight. He gives the old woman lodging, and as they are sitting down to eat she appears young and fair. He takes her to bed for three nights and then she returns home to her true shape. In due time she bears their child, Sinfjǫtli (OE. *Fitela*). When he is almost ten, she makes sure he is ready to visit Sigmundr by stitching his kirtle to his arms. The sons of Siggeirr had screamed at this, but Sinfjǫtli does not flinch, even when she strips the kirtle off him "so that the skin came away with the sleeves. She said he would find it painful. 'Such pain seems little enough to a Vǫlsung,' said he." Sinfjǫtli joins Sigmundr and passes the test the others failed: Sigmundr leaves him to make bread for supper from a bag of meal containing a large poisonous snake. When he returns, the bread is made. Sigmundr asks him if he found anything in the meal. Sinfjǫtli admits he had a suspicion there was something alive, "but whatever it was, I've kneaded it in with the rest."

All the time they are together in the forest, Sigmundr thinks Sinfjǫtli is King Siggeirr's son and only a Vǫlsung on his mother's side. For a time they range far and wide killing men for their wealth. One day they come upon two men alseep, with wolfskins hanging above them. The heroes put on the skins and cannot get out of them again, for they are under a magical spell which allows the wearers human form only once every ten days. They even speak in the language of wolves. "Wolf" is a name for an outlaw in both ON. and OE., and the two live up to it, with more killing, and very nearly do not get out of the wolfskins alive. Once free, they burn the skins and destroy the spell. Finally they come to Siggeirr's homestead to take revenge. They are discovered in the entrance hall by the king's two young children, who tell their father. Signý, overhearing, takes them out and bids Sigmundr kill them. He refuses to harm her children, but Sinfjǫtli kills them both and throws their bodies down in front of Siggeir. After a valiant fight the two Vǫlsungs are overpowered and imprisoned in a stone burial mound, to starve to death. Just as the mound is being closed, Signý smuggles Sigmundr's sword down to them. With so good a sword they saw their way out through the stones and return to set fire to the hall. Sigmundr bids Signý come out before the blaze rises higher. Then, in one of the great speeches of Germanic revenge tragedy, she refuses, revealing Sinfjǫtli's parentage and all she has done. "Indeed, I have done so much in order that this vengeance should come about, that it is not fitting that I should live, on any terms. Gladly will I now die with King Siggeirr, unwillingly though I married him." She kisses them both and walks into the flames where she meets her death with Siggeirr and all his men. (Quotations from *B&A,* pp. 257, 258, 262.)

We know that at least part of this tale was known in Anglo-Saxon England, from a stone carving dated A.D. 950–1050 in the Old Minster, Winchester, which shows a wolf thrusting its tongue into the mouth of a prostrate bound man. See *Antiquaries Journal* 46:2 (1966), 329–32. The text of *Beowulf* itself may also offer corroboration. The stock phrase *fǣhðe ond fyrena* 'feuds and crimes' 879a appears to refer to the killings for wealth, though it is possible that these are the wrongs done Sigemund. Line 878 seems to point to the more magical adventures, for instance, their living as wolves. The word *nefa* 'nephew' 881a (Lat. *nepos*) had been a euphemism for a bastard son since the early days of the Church when a fallible bishop might foster several "nephews." It probably hints at the true relation between Sigemund and Fitela. The introductory *wēl-hwylc* 874b, though translated with the force of "virtually all," is literally "almost all" the adventures of Sigemund and thus may refer to the more repugnant aspects of the Vǫlsung story omitted by the scop. These verbal clues are circumstantial, and there is no allusion to the moving events at the center of the revenge story. Hence Klaeber is very cautious and says we have no positive evidence that the Anglo-Saxons knew a story with the Sigmundr-Signý motif. On the other hand, if we grant the Danish scop a sense of propriety, it only makes sense, when praising Beowulf, to omit the incest and revenge motifs. Above all else, the scop's allusive comparison emphasizes Sigemund's solitary courage. Probably the idea of slaying a "tribe of giants" was introduced to increase the parallel with Beowulf (since Grendel is a giant in stature and lineage) and the contrast with Heremod, who perishes among giants.

The second part of the Sigemund story, the dragon-slaying, appears only in *Beowulf*, and is too simple and widespread a type to trace accurately. It has been argued that this was originally the exploit of Sigurðr, the son of Sigmundr in ON. story (and later the Siegfried of the *Nibelungenlied* and Wagnerian romance), except that here the deed has been transferred from son to father. But scholars find it equally plausible that Sigemund's adventure is his own, and was transferred later to his more famous son. (See W. W. Lawrence, p. 321.) If this is so, then the fatal curse on the treasure that Sigurðr won from the dragon Fafnir, which Wrenn treats as the most significant parallel in the story, may not have been known to the audience of *Beowulf*. If the Anglo-Saxon audience already knew the story of Beowulf, it would be enough to mention any dragon-fight to create a tragic anticipation in the midst of heroic praise.

The Contrast of Heremod (901–915)

The stingy and murderous King Heremod, of the Danish line that preceded Scyld's dynasty, is also mentioned by Hrothgar in 1709–24. The poet alludes to him indirectly at 14–16 and 2177–83, where he again serves as a contrast to Beowulf. In Hrothgar's sermon, however, he stands as a warning to Beowulf against the misuse of great personal strength to the injury of the people. The features emphasized in Heremod's story are clear enough, but some of the details remain obscure, because our only sure source of information are the allusions in *Beowulf*. The parallels between Heremod and the tyrant Lotherus in Saxo Grammaticus that once led to a reconstructed story (accepted by Klaeber and Lawrence) are now regarded as too vague to stand up. See Kemp Malone, *Studies in Heroic Legend*, pp. 179–80.

The names Heremod and Sigemund are paired in a context of praise in an ON. poem of uncertain date, the *Hyndluljóð* (collected in the *Flateyjarbók*, c. 1375). Freyja praises Odin's generosity, saying, "To Hermóðr he gave a helm and corselet, / And to Sigmundr a sword of his own" (strophe 2). Possibly there was a traditional association of the two names that influenced our poet, and perhaps the name *Here-mōd* 'Battle-heart' was not invented for *Beowulf*, despite its aptness. Together with names like *Hyge-lāc* 'Instability of thought' and *Hygd* 'Thought,' its meaning may be taken as part of an abstract moral design woven through the poem, but these names probably are better understood as emblematic of the characters' traditional qualities than as signs of a hidden allegory.

Heremod's *sīð* 908 might be his "journey" into exile (1714 ff.) or more generally his "fate" or "conduct." Klaeber explained the "sorrow-wellings" that "lamed [disabled] him too long" (904–5) by saying that Heremod was unhappy for the greater part of his life and called this a touch of "sentimental softness." However, *tō lange* 'too long' 905a is probably litotes for "always," and in view of the forceful verb "lamed," *sorh-wylmas* is likely to refer to the vicious moods we hear of later. Heroic poetry, generally speaking, has a relatively small vocabulary for psychological states of mind, and I take the phrasing at 904–5 to fit the emphatically unsoft phrases before and after. N. F. Blake goes even further and puts *sorh-wylmas* with the "giants" of 902: since this compound is twice used for the fires of Hell in the OE. poem *Guthlac* and since we know from *Beowulf* 112–14 that the giants are a devilish brood which live in Hell, lines 902b–5a may allude to Heremod's actual damnation. *On fēonda geweald* 903a should then be translated as "into the power of devils." See *JEGP* 61 (1962), 278–87.

It was once thought, on the strength of some late and confused versions of Danish legends, that *mid eotenum* 902 might mean "among the Jutes." This now seems unlikely both from the grammatical form and the slightness of similarity. They are giants and may be taken as Grendel's relatives. Or the reference may be a figurative description of warlike enemies. See Kaske, in *OEP,* p. 298.

Line 915b is literally "sin invaded him [Heremod]." Sin was often conceived by early Christians as an active external force—cf. Hrothgar's metaphor of the arrows of sin piercing the soul's armor in 1744–46. The sudden shift in the blind pronoun references in the Old English, which often proves confusing the first time through, shows the poet's confidence that his audience will regard the contrast between Heremod and Beowulf as absolute, unmistakable. Heremod would appear to be a clear antitype of Beowulf. However, John Leyerle believes that Beowulf has behaved in such a manner at the Danish court that it leads the scop to allude to Heremod and that 915b might conceivably refer to Beowulf. He claims that "this half-line, like the entire performance of the scop, is ambiguous." See *MÆ* 34 (1965), 101.

Thanksgiving, Reply, Gift-Giving (925–1049)

Hrothgar's ceremonious speech begins as a psalm of praise to the Lord. In retrospect, he now attains a Boethian wisdom about Divine Providence and human short-sightedness. The repetition of *wēnan* and *wīde feorh* within five lines (933, 937) recalls the poet's emphasis on Grendel's heedless *wēn*. Beowulf now has reversed the Danes' despairing expectations as well. Hrothgar treats him as an agent of Providence and his strength as God-given. Lines 946 ff. are not a legal adoption, which Queen Wealhtheow warns against in 1175 ff., but a special and lasting bond of gratitude, as Hrothgar's following magnanimous speech indicates.

Beowulf's reply shows a judicious mixture of heroic pride and youthful courtesy. He begins with an apology both boastful and deferential and continues with the triumphantly laborious irony of Grendel as the guest he welcomed. At the same time, the energy of his language shows the enormous effort that was required to put the devil in his place.

The metaphor of binding Grendel on his "death-bed" will enhance the special use of the sleep-after-feast theme some lines later (1002–8). This theme occurs after Heorot is speedily rebuilt and preparations for the present feast are completed. Some editions start a new paragraph with the second half of 1008. Yet the shift from the gnomic lines about the feast in Heorot is not really a change of subject, since the poet ends his reflections with the metaphor of human life as a feast (cf. the famous sparrow simile in Bede). He has so placed his brief meditation that it not only reflects Grendel's fate but also presses forward against the present joy in the hall. To cross the caesura of 1008 is to gain a profound feeling for the brevity of the splendid civility in the Danish court.

The description of the helmet given to Beowulf is an expanded form of variation. The poet might have gone into equal detail about any of the four gifts without tiring his audience. Why does he select this gift? Why not the royal standard (relating Beowulf to kingship) or the sword and byrnie (such gear is important in the coming fight with Grendel's mother)? The expansion is in the direction of the meaning, "Hrothgar gave Beowulf protection in war." Certainly this would be Hrothgar's desire, though he must now protect by kingly gifts rather than by personal strength. But why such an emphasis on actual battle? Because it thrusts the earlier and later conflicts into this moment of peace and thanksgiving. The treasure-giving passage is closed by the poet's own reflections on the need to beware the future (1057 ff.). These weapons are used in wars between men, and thus this gift-giving forms part of the larger context of the Finnsburh Episode.

Hrothgar is called "Lord of the Ingwines" at 1044. *Ingwine* 'friends of Ing' or 'members of the cult of Ing' is an older name for the Danes, originally the same as the *Ingvaeones* in Tacitus. Literally *eodor* means 'protector' and is used in this sense only twice more in the poem, in the phrase *eodor Scyldinga* (428, 663). A much more common word, *ealdor* 'prince,' would fit the sense and meter equally well. Both uses of *eodor* seem determined, however, by the royal formality of the occasion. In addition, this passage of feasting and gift-giving is liberally sprinkled with epithets selected to emphasize Hrothgar's greatness as "the son of Healfdene." There may be an irony here, or at least a porosity in this language, since it leads into the Finnsburh Episode, which is a moral disaster.

Hrothulf's Future Treachery (1014b–1019 and 1163–1165)

Lines 1017–19 hint that there will be future treachery by Hrothulf. Their placement suggests a genuine allusion. It comes soon after the musings on mortality and is followed by the bloody tragedy of treachery and revenge in the Finnsburh Episode. The poet again alludes to Hrothulf right after the Episode, as if to point up the unwitting aptness of its story, ostensibly told as a Danish triumph. Leaving other considerations aside, these passages seem *poetically* connected so as to make Wealtheow a tragic figure comparable to Hildeburh in the Episode. Seen in the large view, the brightly lit harmony in Heorot becomes a terrifyingly fragile thing. This interpretation depends on the reader's recognition of a common type of literary subtlety: implication. In both references to Hrothulf, the hint about the future comes in a temporal adverb: "*at that time,* there was no treachery"; "there was *still* peace between them" (1164). As a literary meaning, a nuance, it seems very clear. There is a comparable passage in *Widsith* 45–49, which is probably earlier than *Beowulf,* where a temporal adverb is again applied to the amity between Hrothulf and Hrothgar:

Hrōþwulf ond Hrōðgār   hēoldon lengest
sibbe ætsomne,   suhtor-fædran,
siþþan hȳ forwrǣcon   Wicinga cynn
ond Ingeldes   ord forbigdan,
forhēowan æt Heorote   Heaðobeardna þrym.

Hrothulf and Hrothgar   for the longest time
held kinship together,   nephew and uncle,
once they drove back   the race of the Vikings,
pushed to the dirt   Ingeld's spear,
cut down at Heorot   the Heathobard army.

The same dark hint may be present in "longest."

However, *Beowulf* scholars have been unwilling to trust literary
inferences by themselves and have looked for supporting external
evidence. The likelihood that after Hrothgar died Hrothulf deposed
and slew his son Hrethric has been treated as historically verifiable
through a complicated conflation of various Scandinavian authorities.
See Chambers, p. 26. This reconstruction is tricky, to say the least.
It rests on the correction of a genealogy in the twelfth-century
Langfeðgatal and a brief statement of Saxo Grammaticus that one
Roricus (OE. Hrethric), a miserly gift-giver, was slain by Rolfo
(Hrothulf) the righteous. Saxo's account comes in his paraphrase of
the *Bjarkamál*, an early poem now lost. This account would repre-
sent an actual event with a reversal of the good and bad personages
during later transmission. For an even more complicated hypotheti-
cal reconstruction, in which Hrothulf kills Hrothgar as well, see
Kemp Malone, "Hrethric," *PMLA* 42 (1923), 268–312, discussed
by Chambers, p. 447–49.

Recently, and with salubrious effect, Kenneth Sisam has cast a
cold eye on these proceedings, asserting that in all sources, early
and late, Hrothulf is an admirable character (*Structure,* pp. 35–39,
80–82). This is indisputably true of the later legendary king with
the same name, Rolf Kraki (Rolfo). It is possible, after all, that
Widsith 45–46 simply refers to an alliance of unparalleled length
and peacefulness. Sisam treats the temporal words in the *Beowulf*
passages as simple references to a bygone time. He would translate
þenden 1019 as "in the age of heroes" or "in the great days of
Heorot" and *þā gȳt* 'still' 1164 as "when Beowulf visited Heorot."

He sees the general purpose of the great feast scene as the rehabilitation of the reputation of the Danes, tarnished by their lack of champions against Grendel. Sisam disallows any parallel between Hildeburh and Wealhtheow. The rejoicing after the scop's recitation is a contrast not with Hrothulf's future treachery but with the attack of Grendel's mother.

Sisam's bluff skepticism is very healthy. But the poem itself is a respectable early source. There could easily have been an early story about a Hrothulf who was a contrast to his father Halga the Good, and this story could be alluded to only in *Beowulf*. The problem lies in how to treat the allusion as a source: Do we read it at face value or do we allow for an artful irony? I would resolve the question by assuming that both readings are combined in a double perspective upon Hrothulf: the Danes' view, limited to their present knowledge, and the poet's knowledge of future events.

The Finnsburh Episode (1068–1159b)

Lines 1056–62 give equal weight to Beowulf's courage and God's power in changing the course of events. The *fore-þanc* 'forethought' and *andgit* 'understanding' necessary in God's world might be interpreted as the rational soul, by which even a non-Christian can reason his way to God's Providence, as in Boethius. The vicissitudes of fortune and the need to look beyond them are also present in these reflections. But the passage is not from a homily, and the lines need no special twist to be coherent with the philosophical design in Grendel's defeat. They comment on the qualities that Grendel lacked and Beowulf possesses. We may also wonder, just for a moment, whether Beowulf, now at the height of success, still possesses *fore-þanc*. The lines are also obliquely directed at the instability of the Danish peace, a theme to be explored by the Finnsburh Episode immediately following. There is "much that is dear, much hateful" in the divided loyalties of the Episode itself. Or should the "days of strife" (*win-dagum*) be translated instead as "days of wine" (*wīn-*)? It would then echo the connection between feasting and mortality in 1008. We will not overpraise the poet if we see all these meanings simultaneously. The further into this design, the greater the pressure of meaning that each passage exerts on others.

The poet treats the Finnsburh story with remarkable imaginative freedom. Yet the Episode has always been notorious for its obscurity and a dense hedge of surrounding scholarly discussion. Several impenetrable passages occur at the exact points where all hypothetical reconstructions must (very gingerly) be grounded. This has created a permanent field day for quandary lovers. However, the general outline of the story is clear as it stands. If we do not attempt a speculative reconstruction, three basic difficulties remain: (1) keeping the action and characters clearly identified; (2) interpreting the motives of the principal characters, especially Hengest; (3) seeing how this story-within-a-story fits the larger design of the whole poem. These problems are due to the highly allusive, recollective style of narration.

(1) *What Happens.* Fortunately, we also possess *The Finnsburh Fragment,* forty-seven lines from near the beginning of a short heroic lay by a different poet. It exists today only in the transcription made by George Hickes in his *Thesaurus* of 1705, from a single MS. leaf that was later lost. Unlike the highly selective Episode in *Beowulf,* the *Fragment* is a straightforward, formalized account of a single battle scene and excellent poetry in its own right. It fills out the story almost to the point where it begins in *Beowulf* and also clarifies the roles of the participants. It is conveniently edited, with full commentary, in Klaeber's edition of *Beowulf,* and a new edition of both the Episode and the *Fragment* by Donald K. Fry has now appeared (London: Methuen, 1974). A poetic translation—in fact, probably the best rendering of any OE. poem into Modern English poetry—has been made by Richmond Lattimore in his *Poems from Three Decades* (New York: Scribners, 1972), pp. 215–16.

By conflating the two accounts we get a story with fairly good continuity, even though a number of important circumstances remain unknown. Some sixty men of the Half-Danes, a subgroup of the Danes, led by their young lord Hnæf, have been visiting King Finn of Frisia in his stronghold, or *burh.* (Perhaps this was a fortified palisade near the sea; from lines 1125–27 it seems located some distance from his royal seat, or *hēa-burh.*) Finn is married to Hnæf's sister, Hildeburh, who has borne him a son or sons. As is usual, the three noble in-laws are also identified by their patronymics: Finn is Folcwalda's son, while Hnæf and Hildeburh are the children of Hoc. From *trēowe* 'faith' or 'pledge' 1072, we might conjecture that Hildeburh had been given in marriage to settle an earlier feud between the Danes and Frisians. Such a settlement—not a very effective one, it seems—will later be offered by Hrothgar (see 2020 ff.) and it may have been a common Danish policy. However, the actual circumstances of Hildeburh's marriage are not stated. We see her only as the *Beowulf* poet presents her: an innocent victim, caught in the middle, suffering helplessly as she loses brother, son, and husband.

One night, for reasons that are never specified, some of the Frisians make a surprise attack on the hall where the Half-Danes are sleeping. The *Fragment* begins just as this attack gets under way. From the Danish point of view, it is unmitigated treachery, especially since the Half-Danes were guests of Finn. It is not clear who exactly the attackers are. The word *eotenas* 'giants' is probably a general name for the Frisians, but it may indicate a band of Jutes in Finn's retinue. Whether or not Finn instigated the attack is equally obscure. One line of argument, held by Chambers and Brodeur, sees no treacherous intent on his part throughout the story. Rather, the surprise attack is due to unruly members of his retinue, while Finn himself drawn into the fighting only reluctantly and seeks to end the feud by offering generous terms. His blameless character then becomes a major factor in the Danes' later moral dilemma. But this is only one line of conjecture. The feud is, after all, associated with Finn's name, and in line 1112 he is explicitly called the *bana* 'slayer' of Hnæf (though this does not necessarily mean he planned treachery for his guests).

Most of the *Fragment* is devoted to the battle at the two doors of the hall, in which the Danes defend themselves for five days without losing a man, while many of the Frisians are slain (like the Episode in *Beowulf*, the *Fragment* has a patriotic Danish slant). One door is held by three heroes who figure importantly in later events: Guthlaf, Ordlaf (called Oslaf in the Episode), "and Hengest himself." The *Fragment* breaks off but the story is continued in *Beowulf*. Subsequently, as we learn from the opening of the Episode, both Hnæf and his unnamed nephew, the son of Finn and Hildeburh, are killed. The Danes continue to fight, led by Hengest, Hnæf's chief retainer. Finn loses so many men that he cannot dislodge the remaining Danes from their defensive position (it is not clear if they are still in the hall). Apparently—though this too is an arguable point—both sides have fought to exhaustion.

To bring this stand-off to an end, one side, identified only as "they" (*hig* 1085), offers terms to the other. The Frisians are usually assumed to make the peace offer, on the grounds that the sentence up to this point has emphasized their plight and that Finn later swears to fair and generous terms. For the Danes, to accept their enemy as their overlord is a shameful thing, but they have no choice. "It was an *impasse*; an irreconcilable conflict between human endurance and the ethics of a rigid code. So the Danes finally accepted Finn's terms" (Lawrence, p. 116). However, this is only an assumption. Long ago, Sophus Bugge (cited at the end of this section) suggested, instead, that it is Hengest, already planning future vengeance for his slain lord, who compels the Frisians to settle. The emphatic variations in 1080–85 could easily imply superior Danish strength. In this case, "they" (1085) would be the Danes. Even if the Danes were not decisively stronger, Hengest would still be in a position of moral strength: if the Frisians turned away from their fruitless seige, they would lose face forever.

The settlement entails the surviving Danes becoming Finn's retainers, "out of necessity" (1103), since they now have no ring-giver. This phrase does not necessarily imply coercion on Finn's part. It can simply mean "in the nature of things": they are forced to follow him since they must have sustenance and protection through the winter in enemy territory. This Danish side of the peace compact is described very briefly—it is more assumed than described, really—and the fact that they follow the slayer of their own lord Hnæf is mentioned as tactfully as possible. For his part, Finn swears solemnly to Hengest that he will treat them with all honor, that they will have equal place with the Frisians in a new hall, that they will receive as many gifts as his Frisian retainers, and that "the sword will settle" any affronts to Danish self-respect. The Frisians are not to taunt them by mentioning past events.

These extraordinary terms are spelled out in detail because the dramatic audience that hears the story is Hrothgar's Danish court, and it would require the most exceptional circumstances for any honorable retainer to follow the slayer of his lord. As Beowulf himself says in 1384–85, "It is better for every man to avenge his friend than to mourn overmuch." To pledge fealty to Finn instead of killing him could only have seemed a shameful expedient. Yet the Danes could not die gloriously in battle and thus avoid the harder job of facing ethical choices, because Finn could not press the fight

to an end. Whether the terms be Hengest's or Finn's, the conditions
of the settlement, as told in *Beowulf*, are bent backwards in favor of
the Danes—the more so if we recall that they have killed Finn's own
son. The terrible, moving thing about this revenge ethic is that,
even so, the Danes still feel placed in an intolerable position.

(2) *Hengest*. The modern reader may not feel quite so cheerful
as the audience in Hrothgar's hall about the final bloody vindication
of Danish honor. Is it a just and triumphant retribution, or only one
more sad pledge breaking? The Episode is told in such a way that it
seems to be both, and the reader can see beyond the Danish view-
point to the tragic tension in the Danes' conflicting moral obligations.
In fact, many critics have held this conflict to be the nub of Hengest's
tragic dilemma. In the words of H. M. Ayres, whose interpretation
has had a decisive influence on modern readings of Hengest, he is
"torn between his oath to Finn and his duty to the dead Hnæf."
See *JEGP* 16 (1917), 282–95. However, the significance of this con-
flict depends entirely on how permanent both sides regarded the
pledge to Finn—and that remains unknown. We can argue that it
was a binding oath, since this was the norm, especially in poetic
story. Or we can say that the circumstances were most unusual
and take the plausible view that Hengest regarded an oath sworn
to an enemy under compulsion as a brittle thing (Lawrence, p. 123).
It is very hard to decide between these two views. The *Beowulf*
poet himself does not seem concerned with dramatizing the difficulty
of Hengest's choice. (His suffering during the winter of enforced
inaction is another matter.) Once spring comes, the poet's emphasis
is all on the "dreadful thoroughness" of the Danish revenge (Law-
rence's phrase). Perhaps the senselessness and inevitability of it
were tragedy enough.

The next step in the story seems to be, if we follow one interpre-
tation of 1107–8a, that Hengest swears his oath of fealty and Finn
pays *wergild* for Hnæf. An alternative and more frequent interpreta-
tion is to emend *āð* 'oath' to *ā[d]* 'pyre' so that the lines mean "the
pyre was made ready" with treasures piled up from Finn's hoard, as
in the funerals of Scyld and Beowulf. Combinations of these two
conjectures are also possible, such as "[Hengest] took his oath, and
the treasure from Finn's hoard was piled up [for the pyre]." It has
also been suggested that "the oath was performed" 1107a means
that Finn, having earlier pledged his word, now takes an oath in a

formal ceremony. Again, there is no firm textual basis for preferring one interpretation above another. It is clear only that the characters engage in some kind of formal, and probably mutual, activity at this point. The bodies are laid on the pyre under the direction of the doubly bereaved Hildeburh, who sings a dirge for her dead. After the funeral blaze has ended, the warriors return to their homes in Frisia, and Hengest and his men live with Finn through the winter. Hengest thinks frequently of his homeland—he is called a *wrecca,* or 'exile,' in 1137—but the winter weather forces him to stay till spring.

Then he "hastened from the court" (*fundode . . . of geardum* 1137–38). This is the ordinary meaning of the verb *fundian,* but usually a twist is put on it to fit the following phrase, from which it could be inferred that he did not actually leave: "he thought rather of vengeance than sea-journey." This remains an equivocal phrase. It needn't mean he does not depart. He could easily be thinking bloody thoughts while sailing to Denmark. We gain only further perplexity from another mention of a "sea-journey" in 1149, "after which" or "about which" (*æfter* can have either sense), Guthlaf and Oslaf speak their woes. Was this the first journey to Frisia under Hnæf, or a spring voyage by Hengest, or a second journey that Guthlaf and Oslaf have made to Denmark for reinforcements? And to whom do they speak? The verb *mǣnan* can be understood as "relate," "complain," or "upbraid," so that in lines 1148–50 they could be (a) enlisting Danes in Denmark, or (b) egging Hengest on (in Denmark or Frisia), or (c) baiting Finn just before attacking him. Too much can be made of these unanswerables. The possibilities are so open that Professor Ayres suggested that perhaps no one travels anywhere in the spring.

The details of the Danish revenge were obviously the best known part of the story, since they are so very casually mentioned. If we knew them, they might clarify the poet's intentions in his treatment of Hengest. As it is, his part in the vengeance on Finn is left unstated. We are told only that "Hengest did not refuse the universal custom" (*worold-rǣdenne*) when Hunlaf's son (*Hunlāfing*) laid a sword in his lap. Hunlaf was probably a brother of Guthlaf and Oslaf who fell at Finnsburh, since ON. forms of their three names appear together in a list of Danish princes in the *Skjǫldunga saga* (c. A.D. 1200). The sword, called "battle-flame" either as a kenning or proper name, is "well known among the 'giants' [Frisians]"—i.e., it had killed many of them at Finnsburh. The "world-wide custom" is vengeance; the compound can also be translated as "universal duty," "law of the world," or "the obligation that the world imposes." The action of Hunlaf's son, usually symbolizing a Germanic thane's pledge of fealty to his lord, thus becomes a vow that he will join Hengest in seeing that the duty of vengeance is carried out. There is the heaviest sort of ironic understatement, then, in saying that Hengest "did not refuse" the usual practice. But what role he takes in the final slaughter and return of Hildeburh is left untold.

Dramatic though Hengest's situation is, it is probably best not to regard his story as a drama at all. In most dramatic writing the action reveals character, but all that we see of Hengest is his inaction during the winter. It is indeed tragic that he has pledged his word yet cannot refrain from vengeance, but the poet does not directly dramatize it as a conflict tearing at his heart. We see only his numbness, expressed mainly in poetic terms. Lines 1126–45, which Brodeur called "the analysis of Hengest's inner conflict," are a simple narrative sequence thickly studded with associative images: Hengest winters unhappily, a homesick exile, "entirely unlucky" or "quite without choice" *(eal unhlitme)*, unable to travel because of winter. When spring permits voyaging, he thinks mainly of revenge and does not refuse Hunlafing's sword. This is the sum of the stated action. We can infer what we please, and if we assume a situation of "inner conflict," then Hengest's frustration is objectified in the image of the stormy, ice-locked sea. The imagery in 1130–37 is a special type of metaphor in OE. poetry: an extension of the factual into the symbolic. See further Irving, *Reading,* p. 172, and E. G. Stanley, *Anglia* 73 (1955), 439. It does not reflect his inward state with *dramatic* precision, because the imagery of winter weather is part of the traditional OE. poetic theme of exile and characterizes the misery of all lordless retainers. Hengest's individual plight is generalized by this use of typical language; the traditional association clothes him with dignity and pathos. The "argument" of this imagery of exile forms an ironic paradox: Hengest stays with his lord (Finn), though he is exiled from his lord (Hnæf). This is not so much the analysis of a divided heart as an expression of his deep grief and shame.

The associative language in the description of spring carries an even greater flux of poetic meanings. Spring came finally "as it still does today" (1134), and this formula is a deliberate echo of the poet's reflection (1057 ff.) that God then ruled the whole race of men, as he still does today. The poet remarks that the seasons keep their order forever, which in this context seems a reference to Providential order. Then the weather is called "glory-bright." This compound, *wuldor-torhtan*, would suggest nothing more than the increase in Danish glory when Finn is killed, except that *wuldor* 'glory' also means 'heaven' and is frequently used in epithets for God. Thus the arrival of spring symbolizes Hengest's exultant release and renewed strength in a special context: the orderly change of seasons is associated with God's rule and gives a quasi-divine sanction to Hengest's deliverance that makes his case comparable to the Danes' heaven-sent deliverance from Grendel. This is, after all, a Danish tale told at Beowulf's victory banquet.

(3) *Thematic Design*. The shaping power of the poet's language can be seen in the extremely elliptical denouement. Once this righteous "sword-evil" is released upon Finn (1146 ff.), it is swift and terrible in its rhythms and impersonality. The subject is no longer Hengest, nor even the fact that the vengeance is his. Rather, its brutal efficiency is ticked off in a casual series of phrases at the end of which Queen Hildeburh is carried away, unnamed, like a piece of booty herself. A dehumanized agent brings about the destined action: "The restless spirit could not be restrained in the breast" (1150–51). This free-standing phrase can mean "the soul left the body," i.e., Finn was killed, or "the anger *(mōd)* of the Danes burst out in action." The poet has so placed the phrase that the undefined "spirit" *(mōd)* seems an impersonal agent acting of its own accord.

Personification of the inhuman forces in the feud occurs earlier when "war carried off" almost all of Finn's thanes (1080) and again in the magnificent description of the funeral pyre: after a series of gruesomely exact images of the burning corpses, the fire becomes a "greedy spirit" that consumes the best men of both tribes. This insatiable force blazes up again in the name of Hunlafing's sword, "Battle-Flame." Although it is given only a few vivid lines, the pyre has an especially memorable impact because it is paired with the austere pathos of Hildeburh's suffering. The initial statement of her situation is clinched by one of the steepest, most reserved examples of understatement anywhere in the poem: "she was a sad

lady" 1075. The poet does not delay in making an absolute con-
trast: her happiest moments in life had been here under Frisian
skies, where now her kinsmen on both sides have killed each other.
Then we see her at the pyre, her profound grief stated only by
her formal role as the dirge singer (see Commentary below on
3110–82). Nothing is said of her third bereavement at the end of the
Episode. She is returned to Denmark, her world indiscriminately and
totally destroyed by the feud.

As the scop ends the Finnsburh tale, Danish merriment breaks
out in Hrothgar's hall. Queen Wealhtheow comes forward to advise
the king to be sure to bequeath the kingdom to his sons, deserving
though Beowulf may be. Kinship comes first. She expresses con-
fidence that their sons will be supported by his nephew Hrothulf,
who sits in honor with Hrothgar. Yet when Hrothulf's treachery
comes to pass, Wealhtheow will find herself in a pathetic situation
strikingly like Hildeburh's—a desolated, useless "peace-weaver." It
is too close an analogy to be unintentional. There is a deliberate
juxtaposition of themes between the Finn Episode and the setting in
which it is heard. Frisian treachery opens the Episode, while
Hrothulf's treachery is touched on before and after. The strong inti-
mation of his future bad faith is in fact part of the introduction to
Wealhtheow's speech. The juxtaposition of this dark hint against
her speech makes Wealhtheow seem isolated even amid the celebra-
tion. She becomes a tragic figure by implication.

This is the larger artistic reason the poet has emphasized Hilde-
burh's tragic situation. He is rarely interested *only* in the pathos
(or heroism) of a single individual's situation. Though he may treat
it with intense particularity, he will usually link it to other passages,
to define some aspect of the heroic world of the poem. Thus
Hildeburh's plight connects up with still another too-apt analogy:
Freawaru, Queen Wealhtheow's daughter, will later be given in mar-
riage to Ingeld of the Heathobards to help settle a feud, and Beowulf
foresees that this peace-weaving will be to no avail, that she too
will suffer. It almost seems as though the peaceful days of the Danes
are limited to the time of Beowulf's visit. As a matter of fact, while
the tale of Finn is told in the apparent security of the well-lighted
hall, Grendel's mother is about to strike back at the Danes, carry-
ing on her own sort of feud. The overarching theme of "the pre-
carious peace of the Danes" is to Part I what the Swedish-Geatish

feud will be to Part II. Similarly, in the larger structure of the poem, the Finnsburh Episode will be balanced by the prophetic speech of the Messenger some eighteen hundred lines later.

Further interpretations of the Episode: Sophus Bugge, *PBB* 12 (1887), 20–36; Kemp Malone, *JEGP* 25 (1926), 157–72; *ELH* 10 (1943), 257–84; Ritchie Girvan, *PBA* 26 (1940), 327–60; A. G. Brodeur, *University of California Publications in English* 14 (1943), 31–39; Donald K. Fry, *ChR* 9 (1974), 1–14.

Wealhtheow's Gift of the Great Collar (1160–1231)

The introduction to Wealhtheow's first speech here creates a sharp dramatic irony. The Finnsburh Episode has just ended. Her confident expectation of Hrothulf's fidelity is undercut by lines 1163–65 and the presence of Unferth, whom the poet remembers again as the killer of his own kin. From the later perspective of Part II, we may find a special poignancy in the queen's insistence that Hrothgar not treat Beowulf as one of his own sons: had he tried to settle the kingdom upon him, Beowulf might well have acted as he does later in Geatland—protecting the king's son but refusing to take the crown while a legitimate heir is alive. As it is, there will be future kin-killing in Denmark. This likelihood becomes a poetic certainty as Wealhtheow glowingly expresses her faith in the power of gifts. The ideal troth between a leader and his men (cf. lines 20–25) will be broken yet again, as it has just been broken in the Finnsburh Episode. The listening Danes seem to know nothing of this tragic cycle, but see only the bright victory that concludes the bloody story. There is a similiar contradictory value, both a bright and dark side at once, in the great gold collar that Wealhtheow now gives to Beowulf. It symbolizes both the magnificent splendor and the uselessness of fame and wealth. The description of the collar brings to the surface the ironies that the poet sees in the very idea of possession.

The necklace of the Brosings, to which the poet compares the collar, is linked to a story of the Goths. In the thirteenth-century ON. *Þidreks saga af Bern (The Saga of Dietrich of Bern)*, the fierce warrior Heimir (OE. Hama) takes sides with Þidrekr when he quarrels with his uncle King Erminrekr (OE. Eormanric). This king was the historical Ermanaric, king of the fourth-century East Goths. In the saga, Heimir is forced to flee the wrath of Erminrekr, and later the outlaw enters a monastery to make atonement for his sins. In doing so, he gives the monks all his wealth and armor. But there is no mention of a necklace, which, in the *Beowulf* version, Hama appears to have stolen from Eormanric. Perhaps two legends are already conflated here in the poem, since the closest parallel to the necklace itself is the ON. "necklace of the Brísings," made by fire dwarfs for the goddess Freyja and stolen from her by Loki. If we dare rely on the later saga for information, perhaps "the bright city" 1199 is the monastery. At the very least, to "choose eternal reward" is to become Christian and also, in this context, to give up worldly goods. It may also be a periphrasis for "to die."

The comparison of Hama's necklace to the fate of the great gold collar-ring is a pointed one. The poet spends ten or more lines (1202–14a) describing how Hygelac wore it into his last battle— in Frisia, the locale of the Finnsburh Episode. Hama gave away (or, alternately, preserved through his wisdom) a necklace comparable to the one Hygelac wears on a plundering raid. Hygelac acts *for wlenco* 'out of pride,' while Hama "chose eternal counsel [reward]." At the end of these lines, the poet shifts abruptly back to Beowulf: "the hall received the noise" (1214b literally). Presumably this refers to applause ringing out as Beowulf receives the gifts, and it may rightly remind the reader of the rhythmic close of the Heremod passage at line 915, which incarnates the contrast between Heremod and Beowulf in the verse form itself.

The two digressions, of Sigemund-Heremod and Hama-Hygelac, bracket Beowulf's newly won fame and treasure. Parallels: (1) both deal with pairs of heroes; (2) in each digression the first hero is legendary; (3) the second hero is a more realistic leader who meets a bad end through a character flaw. Both episodes offer implicit contrasts to Beowulf and provide contexts for evaluating his heroic act and the psychology behind it. The results of Hygelac's rash action: "Dead Geats filled the field" 1213–14a. This provides the context for the "noise" of 1214b. Perhaps there is a sense here that the applause for Beowulf is premature. After another five hundred lines, Hrothgar will warn Beowulf against two typical character flaws, avarice and pride (see esp. 1748–61), and will tell him to "choose the better course, eternal gains" (*ēce rǣdas* 1760). In the Hama context this same phrase, in 1201b, catches up an echo from the Finnsburh Episode: the *worold-rǣdenne* 1142 or "world-wide custom" of blood revenge which Hengest did not disdain. Through such echoes, feuding and the booty connected with it are lexically opposed to heavenly gain.

Later on, when Beowulf gives the great collar to Hygd, Hygelac's queen, at 2170 ff., the poet says that Beowulf never slew anyone in drink nor had a rough unruly mind (like Heremod and Hygelac). Rather, Beowulf controlled his *gin-fæste gife* 'ample gift' 2182a of enormous strength and used it well. This phrase is the same (but for one pen-stroke) as his "gem-fast gift" of strength in *gim-fæste gife* 1271a. Perhaps the two formulas are identical and we should emend. A patristic reading might connect this "gem," Beowulf's gift of strength, to the parable of the talents and jewel imagery that explained it. In any case, we are invited to make an ethical judgment in this extended and slightly opaque comparison to Hama and Hygelac. It raises the delicate question of whether Beowulf achieves the temperate rationality urged in Hrothgar's sermon or whether he shares some part of the arrogance with which Hygelac takes the great collar to his unhappy end.

The episode of the collar is also designed to show the present in terms of the future. Gifts cannot control the future. The pattern of *wyrd* is unknown to men and cannot be woven into a stable, predictable peace (cf. 1233–35). Yet Wealhtheow, the "peace-weaver," proclaims at the end of her second speech to Beowulf that "here each noble is true to the other, hearts are kind and loyal to their lord." She is wrong, and not only because of Hrothulf's future treachery. Little does anyone at Hrothgar's court know that this very night Grendel's mother will attack. The idea is given further poetic force by the theme of feasting and wine drinking, followed by sleep— and, for Æschere, followed by death. (The musical theme of "sleep after feast" has already been sounded for Grendel, and for all men, in 1002–8.) The startling renewal of Grendel's "feud" recapitulates the meaning of gnomic lines 1059–62 that introduced the human feuds of the Finnsburh episode: anyone who thinks to live long in this world must endure many reversals. In the course of two hundred lines this theme of unexpected disaster has played over the heads of Hnæf, Hildeburh, Hengest, Finn, Wealhtheow, and Hygelac (the latter two by anticipation). Now it comes home to the main plot. Beowulf's response at 1384 ff., so briskly undespairing, shows us the philosophical dimensions of his nerve.

Further reading: Irving, *Reading,* pp. 137–45; Kaske, *PMLA* 74 (1959), 489–94; E. G. Stanley, in *Brodeur Studies,* pp. 136–51.

Grendel's Mere (1357–1441a)

The depiction of the mere is the more remarkable because it is a conceptual landscape made fearsomely realistic by the poetry. The scenery generally follows the pattern of the waterfall and cave in Chapter 66 of *Grettis saga,* summarized above in "Sources and Traditions," page 253. Another parallel frequently urged is the *Aeneid,* VI, 237–42, which describes a vaporous black lake near a deep cave. However, Alain Renoir has recently shown that the two artistic treatments are dissimilar. The *Aeneid* passage is still, unreal, impersonal, while Grendel's mere is humanized and in motion. See Renoir's "The Terror of the Dark Waters: A Note on Virgilian and Beowulfian Techniques" in *The Learned and the Lewed,* ed. Larry D. Benson, *Harvard Studies in English* 5 (1974), 147–60.

The closest parallel is from the vision of Hell in Sermon 17 of the tenth-century *Blickling Homilies,* ed. Richard Morris, EETS, Old Series, no. 73 (London, 1880), pp. 209–11. This scene is based on the apocryphal *Vision of St. Paul,* where the saint visits Hell under the protection of St. Michael. The Blickling sermon concludes with this vision in order to illustrate how St. Michael acts as God's minister. The similarities to the mere are italicized:

> But now let us ask the archangel St. Michael and the nine orders of holy angels that they be a help to us against hell-fiends. They were the holy ones that receive men's souls. Thus St. Paul was looking toward the northern part of this middle-earth, *where all the waters go down under,* and there he saw a *hoary stone over that water,* and north of that stone *the woods had grown very frosty, and there were dark mists,* and *under that stone was the dwelling of nickers* and outlawed creatures [OE. *wearga*]. And he saw that on that cliff many black souls were hanging on the *icy trees* with their hands bound, and the devils in the likeness of nickers were seizing them *as does the greedy wolf,* and *the water was black underneath the cliff.* And between the cliff and the water there was [the distance of] twelve miles, and when the branches broke off then those souls that were hanging on the branches plunged downward, and the nickers seized them. These, then,

were the souls of those who here in this world had sinned unrighteously and would not repent of it before their life's end. But let us now earnestly ask St. Michael that he lead our souls into bliss, where they may rejoice in eternity without end. Amen.   (my translation)

These remarkable verbal parallels in the later sermon suggest that the Blickling homilist may have known *Beowulf* (the frosty trees are not found in the early versions of the *Vision of St. Paul*). More importantly, such details show that the landscape of the mere symbolizes Hell. It is a Garden of Evil, in which one of the race of Cain dwells, freezing in sin. The stag that avoids these dark waters is probably based on Psalm 42: "As the hart pants after the running streams, so my soul cries aloud to Thee, O God." The hart would rather die than hide his head in the mere, just as any rational soul would prefer death to eternal damnation. The hart is also a symbol of royalty (cf. "Heorot" and the stag atop the scepter at Sutton Hoo) and thus may pre-figure the royal soul that faces moral dangers in Hrothgar's sermon. It is, after all, Hrothgar who describes the mere first and most frighteningly. Lines 1409–11 in the poet's own voice also echo the journey of the Israelites across the desert out of Egypt in Exodus 13:18–20. The *enge ān-paðas, uncūð gelād* 'narrow one-paths, an unknown way' 1410 is a formula repeated in the OE. poem *Exodus*, line 58. Both Beowulf's *sīð* 'journey' and the journey of the Israelites lead to a happy conclusion after deep difficulties are braved. Thus Beowulf is risking his soul as well as his life when he enters the mere.

Probably the description should not be pushed harder than this. The poet troubled himself to make the scene realistic as well. The emphasis on the sea creatures recalls the Breca episode, to add credibility to Beowulf's dive. The horn is blown to flush out the nickers from their hiding places, as in a real hunt. The harsh war sound, twice ringing out over the weird lake, also announces the great supernatural battle to come. See Laurel Braswell, "The Horn at Grendel's Mere," *NM* 74 (1973), 466–572.

For a more strenuous derivation of the symbolic meanings of the mere, based on scriptural typology, see D. W. Robertson, Jr., "The Doctrine of Charity in Mediaeval Literary Gardens," in *ABC,* esp. pp. 183–88.

Hands and Heads (1304, 1343, 1417, 1541, and later)

The alliterative patterns that led Rieger to emend *hand-lēan* at
1541 and 2094 are equivocal. The MS. reading "hand-reward" makes
more poetic sense than the emendation "reward, requital." Textual
and metrical arguments for the MS. readings are given by Richard
W. Bevis, *ELN* 2 (1965), 165–68. General arguments for the poetic
design of such verbal associations are offered by James L. Rosier,
PMLA 78 (1963), 8–14, and *MÆ* 37 (1968), 137–41. The context
for the similar *hondslyht* at 2929 and 2972 is quite different: it is
Hygelac's battle with Ongentheow, in which swords, not hands, figure
prominently. These later *hand-* compounds lack any surrounding *h*-
alliteration and are better emended to *ondslyht* 'onslaught,' which
the scribe presumably aspirated as in *Hunferð* for *Unferð*.

The larger context for the "hand-payments" is the feud and the
loyalty to one's group that keeps it alive. It is a shame, the poet says,
that those "on both sides," the Danes and the Geats, could not make
a good exchange for the hand and arm of Grendel (1304 ff.). Instead,
they bought it with the lives of their friends. If taken to the limits of
its literal meaning, this would be a sickening irony. But the design
of verbal associations has a different effect. The pattern of grace
notes traced by the repetition of *hand, heafod, hafelan,* and *helm*
prolongs the thematic significance of the Finnsburh Episode. We
now see Beowulf directly implicated in the Danes' feud by his slaying
of Grendel. Hrothgar even speaks of Beowulf's second combat as a
"feud" (1380). The feud theme explains the disregard for the sex
of Grendel's mother in 1392 where Beowulf refers to his quarry as
"he" and "Grendel's kinsman." It also accounts for the strange epithet
"man of the Scyldings" (1563), technically quite inaccurate since
Beowulf is a Geat. Because he is fighting for the Danes, the poet
considers him a member of their feud-group. For a different inter-
pretation, see John R. Byers, Jr., *MP* 66 (1968), 45–47.

There is an implicit analogy between the human body and the
body of men that make up the feud-group. As Hrothgar is the head
of Denmark, so Æschere was his right-hand man. Hrothgar may be
addressing the subgroup of Æschere's own men when he refers to
the now-dead "hand that served your joys" in 1343–44, or he may
be using this larger analogy to the body. The focus on Æschere's
gift-giving hand may also remind us, by contrast, of the death-giving
hand of Grendel, now stolen back by Grendel's mother. See further

L. Whitbread, *RES* 25 (1949), 340. Thus Grendel's mother gives Beowulf "hand-payment," and she seizes him the same way he will later give Dæghrefn a chest-crushing death hug in Frisia (2501 ff.). This, too, is a purposeful equivalence. The hero has the strength of thirty men in his hand-grip. The poet could see the moral ambiguity of conquering a monster by monstrous strength. And in fact, in Beowulf's second fight, strength alone does not suffice.

The verbal network continues throughout this passage. When Hrothgar describes the hart dying on the bank of the mere rather than diving in "to save his head," the word choice is again thematic: the poet is anticipating the shocking discovery, in the same location, of Æschere's bodiless head (1417–21). The "head" association extends into subsequent events, too, as when Beowulf beheads Grendel and his mother. Another strand in the fabric is the word *helm* 'helmet,' figuratively "protection, cover." Heads are protected by helmets, which are emphasized when the company prepares to take its rest in Heorot on the night that Grendel's mother attacks. Helmets are emphasized again when Beowulf dons his armor at 1441 ff. Figurative uses of this word element are woven into the description of the mere (*oferhelmað* 1364) and Beowulf's ardent reply to Hrothgar (*helm* 1392).

This sort of verbal consciousness-raising is meant to make us aware of the unceasing struggle between different feuding groups, the (literally) dismembering effect it has upon them, and the lack of protection afforded by this concept of human interaction. By contrast, Beowulf's armor is strongly personified in 1441 ff. Idealized by this poetic figure, it becomes his loyal war-band of accouterments which, like Wiglaf in the battle with the dragon, will not fail him at need. However, all ordinary swords do fail under his furious strength. Only the discovery of the magical sword in the mere-hall, and God's help, will enable him to slay Grendel's mother. The untrustworthiness of swords is related to the Germanic anxiety about personal honor. One's manhood is forever open to challenge in this feuding society, as we can hear in the tone of unease beneath the praise of Unferth's sword which Beowulf takes on his dive (1465 ff., 1523 ff.).

The Fight with Grendel's Mother (1495–1605a)

Literally lines 1495a–96 read: "then it was the time of [a] day

before he could find the bottom." This means either that it took
Beowulf a whole day to reach bottom, which would suit the Danes
leaving the cliff later on at the ninth hour (the medieval "nones,"
or 3:00 P.M.); or else it can mean that it was now daytime, daylight,
when he reached bottom (cf. line 2320). The latter explanation as-
sumes that Beowulf is not capable of superhuman feats such as
holding his breath for the space of a day. See further S. O. Andrew,
Postscript on "Beowulf" (London: Cambridge University Press,
1948), p. 99, and Fred C. Robinson, "Elements of the Marvelous
in the Characterization of Beowulf," in *Pope Studies*, pp. 119–23.
The trouble with this interpretation is that if one insists on realism,
then it would still be dark when the troop of men have to track
Grendel's mother through the wood, find Æschere's head on the
cliff, and see well enough for one Geat to shoot a sea beast with an
arrow. We may accept the idea that the poet is merely referring to
full daylight if we are also willing to assume that absolute chronolog-
ical consistency is not to be found in this sort of poetry.

This is a convenient solution to 1495 but it raises a more general
problem: What assumptions should we make about the nature of this
part of the narrative? Does it tell of a Christian marvel or a realistic
deed? Professor Robinson explicitly assumes that Beowulf is a man,
not a good monster from folklore. He is superior to other men, but
not to his environment. I am inclined to go along with the conception
of Beowulf as "only human," even though he has the strength of
thirty men and fights supernatural adversaries. But the puzzle re-
mains why this episode should be closed off by a second reference to
the time of day: "Then came the ninth hour of the day" 1600a. This
is an almost unavoidable biblical echo. It is the same hour that
Christ, abandoned by all but a faithful few, died on the cross (see
Luke 23:44–46).

This detail and others have led some critics to see a parallel be-
tween this episode and Christ's death, the Harrowing of Hell, and the
Resurrection. The complex of ideas that moves from the Harrowing
to the story of the Deluge, which will shortly be retold in 1688b–93,
parallels a sequence of themes in the rites of baptism in the early
Church. The significance of this parallel has been urged at length by
Allen Cabaniss, "*Beowulf* and the Liturgy," in *ABC*, pp. 224 ff.
Under this view, the Danes who lose faith in the hero and depart,
thinking him dead, not only foreshadow the troop of deserters in the

dragon fight, they also symbolize "the disbelieving heathen" (cf. their earlier backsliding into pagan rites, under the pressure of Grendel's attacks).

However, beyond the startling echo of the Passion in the "ninth hour" reference, I cannot see the Christianity of this episode as especially liturgical. This is action poetry; Beowulf engages in heroic combat. It is possible to see very real Christian overtones here without turning the scene into something it is not. For instance, as Beowulf swims upward the poet says that the waters are now "cleansed" (1620). The verb applies with equal but indistinct force to the rites of baptism and exorcism: even today, a short exorcism is included in the Catholic sacrament of baptism. The verb is even less applicable to the loosing of the souls of the unbaptised from Hell by Christ's Harrowing. It does apply directly, however, to the awful waters of the hellish black lake. Now that the monsters have given up their loaned days of life, their lake turns calm. It is understandable that the poet focuses closely on such details, since Beowulf finds himself in such strange straits. But even the most Christian details, such as the miraculous light that bursts forth after his victory, matter mainly because the outcome of the action interests us intensely.

As we follow the action of the fight, we can see that a number of motifs from the Grendel fight are being replayed. The eerie light from Grendel's eyes "most like to fire" (727) reappears as the weird firelight of the mere-cave. It is the bright light which is conventional in the "arrival" theme in OE. poetry and influences the poet's choice of "battle-flame" for Beowulf's sword at 1523. Beowulf now discovers, on his first *sīð* to this "hall," what Grendel discovered on his final trip to Heorot: an angry and wakeful watchman, or, in this case, watchwoman. Later, Beowulf and his men will return marching joyously to Heorot upon the same verb, *Cōm þā* 1623, 1644, by which Grendel slid toward his dark fate the night before. With something of the triumphant verbal playfulness with which he earlier described Grendel, Beowulf will afterwards refer to the two monsters as "guardians of the house" (1666). These parallels first emphasize the reversal of fortune that Beowulf encounters as a "hall-guest" (1545) of the mere-wife, and they make his dilemma appear more hopeless than it would be as unadorned narrative. Then, after his second victory, the verbal parallels with the first fight reassure the audience that the race of Cain has been well and truly requited.

When the moment of victory comes at 1563–69, it is swift and brutal, and the inner truth of what it actually feels like to kill someone is first stated baldly as a combination of fury and despair. Then, hard upon Beowulf's bloody rejoicing (1569), the poet allows himself to become infected with feud-rage. He retells the Grendel feud with renewed irony while carrying Beowulf through the trophy-carving episode (1570–90). To take Grendel's head for Æschere's is a raw, primitive version of "an eye for an eye." Beowulf has already decapitated the sea witch, but his rage is unabated. The picture of the mutilation is unflinching: "The corpse spread wide open after he cut into it."

The psychology of the moment may be disquieting to the modern reader. But the emotions of battle are not the only source of Beowulf's power. He would have been done for, had not God and his loyal mail-shirt helped him, and God judged the fight in his favor "after he stood up again." The syntactical arrangement of 1550–56 binds these three causes together neatly, inseparably. If we want to think that the hero's own effort of will matters the more, since it comes first in the time sequence, we have to recognize that the poet put it last in the grammatical sequence. He also modified God's decision with *ȳðelīce* 'easily.' However, that "easily" is itself bound by alliteration to the heroic *eft* of "after he stood up *again*." The poet thus makes it impossible to give a simple explanation for Beowulf's success.

The light that next shines out from the cave "even as from heaven comes the shining light of God's candle" (1571–72a) may have its ultimate source in the beam of heavenly light shining down upon St. Anthony after he has successfully resisted the attack of devils in a tomb in the desert. At this point in his biography, a work well known in Anglo-Saxon times, the saint calls out, "Where were you, good Jesus, where were you?" A voice replies, "Anthony, I was right here, but I waited to see you in action. And now, because you held out valiantly and did not surrender, I will always be your helper and I will make you renowned everywhere." The sudden appearance of a light at the point when the causes of a heroic triumph are explained is only one of a series of detailed likenesses between the *Vita Antonii* and *Beowulf* that Margaret Goldsmith has set forth in her book *The Mode and Meaning of "Beowulf"* (London: Athlone Press, 1970), pp. 257–68. The Antonian model of saints' lives was a frequent literary source for Old English and Anglo-Latin heroic stories, and perhaps it was used here. The quotation is paraphrased from Evagrius' Latin translation of Athanasius' fourth-century life of St. Anthony; see esp. *PG*, vol. 26, columns 849–59.

Another explanation of the light—but not of the simile—is offered by Martin Puhvel, who takes the "light" (1570a) as the giant-sword itself, luminescent and supernatural. See his "The Deicidal Other-world Weapon in Celtic and Germanic Mythic Tradition," *Folklore* 83 (1972), 215–16. I think the light is more specifically Christian, on the basis of the candle-sun simile and its nearness to the simile of the Father unbinding the frost when the giant-sword melts a few lines later. Similes are so rare in *Beowulf* that I believe the occurrence of these two so close together must be significant.

The Giant-Sword and Other Swords (1605b–1615, 1677–1698a, and elsewhere)

The action of lines 1605–22 encloses the simile of the giant-sword melting away in "battle-icicles" (a unique compound in Old English). The sword melts in a manner "most like to ice" when God the Father unbinds the frost in spring. The passage moves from the sad thoughts of the Geats to the cleansing of the lake. The simile itself moves from the supernatural mere-hall to the normal natural world, from battle-icicles to the Father unloosing the bonds of frost in spring. The true God keeps control of time and seasons, the poet says, to complete his meaning. The process of change (and by extension *edwenden* 'surprising reversal') is controlled by God. To use the etymological root of *Metod*, "he is the true Measurer" 1611b. For an excellent discussion of the simile in relation to the whole episode, see Irving, *Reading*, p. 125.

There is also a possibility that the simile alludes to the patristic conception of evil as ice. St. Augustine's commentary on Psalm 125:4 offers an interesting parallel: "How therefore do sins bind us? Even as the ice binds the water, so that it does not flow. Thus we too are frozen by our icy sins. However, when the warm spring wind blows, then the ice melts and the streams are full. . . . Thus we are frozen in captivity, chained by our sins. But when the wind of the Holy Spirit blows upon us, our sins are forgiven, and we are released from the ice of wickedness." (Freely rendered from *PL* 37, cols. 1663–64.) In 1929 E. A. Kock suggested taking *wǣl-rāpas* 1610a with a short *ǽ* as "quelling chains." The patristic linking of ice-sin-death would encourage a double meaning in these deadly "water-bonds." See further Thomas D. Hill, "The Tropological Context of Heat and Cold Imagery in Anglo-Saxon Poetry," *NM* 69 (1968), 522–32. For the melting of the sword itself, Celtic analogies are again offered by Martin Puhvel in *ELN* 7 (1969), 81–84.

In any case, if we are to see God's hand in Beowulf's victory, we must be willing, it appears, to see him working invisibly. If we apply the simile to its actual reference point, God melts the sword like ice *by* the evil blood of the sinful monsters. This is a gentle paradox. We may also recall that it is at exactly the same point in the order of the year, when the bonds of ice melt, that Hengest began his revenge in the Finnsburh Episode. There is no simile in the Finnsburh passage but the spring imagery is highly figurative. New killing comes as the ice melts, and the ice melts following God's order "as it still does now" (1134b). The resemblance between the two passages is equivocal. Does it mean that feud-killing follows God's plan? Or perhaps only that it occurs, ironically, *within* God's plan?

As Hrothgar regards the hilt in 1687 ff., the poet looks away from the present action of the poem to the biblical fate of the race of Cain, slain by the Flood. Aesthetic distance is much increased here, and the shift of viewpoint enhances our sense that human life is a series of recapitulations. The enormous head of Grendel goes quite unregarded. Instead, the focus is on the story of the giants' feud with God engraved upon the hilt. Seeing the hilt leads Hrothgar directly to admonish Beowulf not to become another Heremod. Why does Hrothgar do this? As God's victorious agent in the Grendel feud, conquering amid waters as God conquered through the Flood, Beowulf might easily forget that "God rules everything" (1727). Thus the hilt functions as an integrating device, tying together the bloody battle in the mere-hall, God's presence in biblical history and less obviously behind the present victory, and Hrothgar's reflections on the inner dangers of the moral life of any hero. As a symbol, the golden hilt illuminates the passages both before and after it with the idea of the ever-present danger of falling into sin through feud. The poet has led up to Hrothgar's sermon with more theological images and similes than anywhere else in the poem. For a brief discussion of the sermon itself, see the final section of "Backgrounds" above.

The descriptions of the giant-sword and other swords in the poem employ terms that were once very difficult, but thanks to recent scholarship they are much clarified. The standard work is Hilda R. Ellis Davidson, *The Sword in Anglo-Saxon England* (Oxford: Clarendon Press, 1962), which draws on archaeological and literary sources to describe how swords were made and used and includes an account of the successful modern forging of a "pattern-welded" sword in the Anglo-Saxon manner. This forging process involves the weaving and welding together of a bundle of some sixteen slender iron rods to make a single blade. It produces the complex ringlike pattern on the flat of the blade earlier thought to be false damascening. It also accounts for the poetic images of rings, weaving (*brogden-mǣl* 1667), snakes, and poison twigs (*āter-tānum fāh* 1459). Unferth's sword Hrunting is described by this last phrase, which derives from several associations: (a) the sword as a deadly serpent in battle; (b) the use of acid (poison) in manufacturing swords; (c) the agency of Woden, god of war, in watching over the smithy. (In the OE. poem *The Nine Herbs Charm*, Woden is said to take nine "glory twigs" and slay an adder so that it flies into nine pieces.) For arguments that the phrase at 1459 applies instead to the gleaming hilt, see A. T. Hatto, *ES* 38 (1957), 147–60, 257–59, and W. P. Lehmann, *University of North Carolina Studies in Germanic Languages and Literatures,* No. 58, ed. W. Arndt et al. (Chapel Hill: University of North Carolina Press, 1967), pp. 221–32.

Other work processes—hammering, filing, tempering, reheating—account for such poetic terms as "the terrible survivor of files" and "shower-hard" (1032 ff.). Hrunting is said to be "hardened in the blood of battle," a metaphor derived from the quenching of the glowing blade in liquid during tempering. Anglo-Saxon swords were often inscribed with the name of the maker, and their pommels ornately decorated with inlaid gold. Sometimes rings were attached to the pommels. This may be the meaning of the term *fetel-hilt* 1563, used for the giant-sword; alternatively, the word may mean a fastening which secured the sword to its scabbard. There is enough room on surviving sword hilts for an inscription such as Hrothgar reads. It need only have been the first words of a verse from Genesis.

The Blithe-hearted Raven (1801–1802) and Its Larger Context

"Swift, swift, you dragons of the night, that dawning / May bare the raven's eye!" exclaims Iachimo in Shakespeare's *Cymbeline* (II. ii. 48–49). Earlier folklore confirms the raven of 1801–2 as a traditional harbinger of morning. He was the herald of a prehistoric sun deity, a bird of good omen, companion of Cuchulain and Woden, and more. See Kathryn Hume, *MP* 67 (1969), 60–63, and Martin Puhvel, *ELN* 10 (1973), 243–47. Here the raven is an explicit symbol of joy, and his presence enhances the joy of the assembled company in Heorot. Having heard Hrothgar's sermon, which ends with the promise of further treasure-giving in the morning, Beowulf is glad at heart and goes quickly to his place at the feast (1785–86). Everyone in Heorot is happy. Their safety is newly and, as it seems, permanently secure.

However, the raven is also traditionally associated with the wolf and eagle in the Old English poetic theme of the carrion-eating Beasts of Battle. This theme is used deftly and imaginatively by the poet in 3020–27, where it is adjusted perfectly to its context. It is hard to imagine that the poet who also used the ominous *oððæt ān ongan* 'until one began' to introduce both Grendel and the dragon (100b, 2210b) would say *oððæt hrefn blaca* 'until the black raven' here without intending to awaken a sense of impending carnage. Thus the interpretive problem here is the conflict between the two traditional associations of the raven—joy versus foreboding. If the solution is to choose one over the other, we are likely to do violence to the poem's subtlety and complexity.

Therefore we might seek a wider prospect. The idea of "conflicting meanings" could be a short definition of literary irony. J. R. R. Tolkien's famous 1936 article "*Beowulf*:The Monsters and the Critics" demonstrated that it is the genius of the entire poem to place "rise" against "fall" in the most sharply significant way. Throughout *Beowulf* the major structural principle is ironic contrast between parallel situations—be they situations of action or of language. If we read the lines on the raven in their larger context, we find that the blithe-hearted bird has a significant place in a pattern of verbal echoes and thematic contrasts with other episodes.

Of course, the joyful raven might only be hyperbole: Beowulf has now so purified Heorot that the very raven sings to welcome a new dawn, a new era. But it is more likely that the poet wants to replay the fearsome night scene from the Grendel episode, in order to create an opposite meaning through an echo effect. There is ample evidence for this reading. Night is now like a protecting helmet (*niht-helm* 1789) instead of a time of fear. The phrase "all the men rose" 1790b happily repeats the eerie formula of line 651, where the Danish troop rose to leave the hall to Beowulf and his men. Again, the hall towers in the darkness, gold-bright (compare 1799–1801 with 714–16). However, the emphatic and memorable verb, *þā cōm*, that brought Grendel stalking up to the hall now brings heaven's brightness instead (1802b). The idea of a contrast is continued if we accept Sievers' restoration of line 1803a, "light after shadow."

For all this, the passage still has a hasty pace which seems slightly off balance. The Geats are eager to leave as soon as they can get through the stock cycle of events—feasting, sleeping, waking, gift-giving. Closer associations may explain the unsettling pace. The "guest" that "sleeps within" in 1800b is thematically related to the sleeping guardian of the arrogant man in the immediately preceding context of Hrothgar's sermon: he dwelled continually at feast— *wunaδ hē on wiste* 1735a—and knew nothing of death. Now it is Beowulf who "sleeps after feasting." This is the same theme that gave philosophical order to man's ignorance of the future in the two fights with the Grendel tribe. Men do not know what to expect (*wēnan*) or how to foresee fate: this idea is ingrained in the poem. So, to Hrothgar, came *gyrne æfter gomene* 'sorrow after joy' 1775a, as he himself emphasizes at the end of his sermon. And thus the guest sleeps after feasting until the raven wakes him. This pell-mell sequence of themes implies that the pattern of the warrior's life is an unending cycle of hall-joy followed by battle-sorrow. The weary Beowulf appears content with it, does not look beyond it. Time enough tomorrow to be up and doing. In fact, he says nothing in reply to Hrothgar's warning. He is properly more interested in receiving treasures from Hrothgar than in the dangers of pride or the dangers of self-analysis.

It is a pity that Beowulf does not reply. No matter how brief or formal a speech, it would help resolve the much-debated question of the state of his soul. At least the reader would know that Beowulf had *heard*. Perhaps his lack of response is meant to be a correlative to the impact of Hrothgar's sermon upon the reader. Its rhetorical power can have the effect of lulling the listener, of drawing the unwary reader into the situation of the Danes just before Grendel's

mother attacked. The organ tone—all stops pulled out—in which
Hrothgar thunders home his point about the inescapability of death,
is rhetorical, not dramatic. It invites a pleasant shudder. If the hearer
does not make an act of moral renewal in response, he may find his
own musings really rather comfortable. Yes, death *is* inevitable and
will level us all, even the hero. Why, look at old Hrothgar himself—
why, look even at me! There is something near self-congratulation
in Hrothgar's rhetorical strategy. The speech ends with equal natural-
ness: help comes to Hrothgar from God, treasure will come to
Beowulf from Hrothgar, and the raven of foreboding is blithe. The
reader has been pulled into a philosophical trap that Boethius knew
well, and how excellently so—since it would have little point unless
the reader's consideration of his own future *was* comfortable, self-
satisfied. Either we respond with moral and poetic alertness to the
fact of our own deaths, so strenuously asserted at 1761–68, or else
we begin, ourselves, to act out that part of Hrothgar's exemplum
where "the guardian of the soul" sleeps. While we are lulled, the
guardian of Denmark also sleeps, happy for the nonce but with new
battles soon to come.

The sensation of instability that I have tried to search out here is
balanced by the bright spectacle of the morning's gift-giving. The
raven passage also expresses the poet's abundant sense of Beowulf's
generosity. He sleeps "large-hearted" 1799a, to be wakened by the
raven "blithe-hearted" 1802a. The first gift dealt out that morning
is given by Beowulf: he returns the sword Hrunting to Unferth and
he "did not blame its edges," though it was useless to him in the
mere-hall. He was, the poet then says, a *mōdig secg* 1812b—a brave,
proud man, courageous, noble, magnanimous in spirit. In this con-
text, *mōdig* touches all these associations. Beowulf's next speech
declares his eagerness to return to his own lord Hygelac and shows
him to be loyal and courteous in equal measure. If he was earlier
silent in response to Hrothgar's sermon, exulting in victory and
treasure, here he is, by nature it seems, generous and peace seeking.
First he declines to humiliate Unferth, and later he gives a gold-
bound sword to the Danish coast guard, increasing his status at court.
During his speech he is elaborately deferential toward young Prince
Hrethric, vows that the Geats will aid him should the need ever arise,
and repledges his own strength in Hrothgar's service. If Beowulf in
Denmark has been strong and impetuous—and what monster-slaying

hero is not?—here he also appears intelligent, foresighted, protective, generous with his strength and fame, and interested in permanent ties of friendship and peace between the Geats and Danes. Hrothgar himself sees Beowulf this way in his farewell speech. The more he sees of the young hero, the more he likes him, and Hrothgar's interpretation of his character is that even as a young man he has wisdom enough to be a good king.

Hrothgar's Tears (1866–1887)

It can be argued that Hrothgar perceives Beowulf's parting speech as a point-for-point enactment of the virtues necessary to protect him from the dangers noted in the sermon. It is difficult to know whether we are meant to go beyond the old king's viewpoint during his closing speech at 1841–65. I myself see no clues in the poet's artistry there that might invite us to rate Beowulf less highly than Hrothgar does. But when we encounter Hrothgar's tears, we are clearly meant to look beyond him as a dramatic character. He is not the bearer of the whole meaning of this subsequent passage. The references by Beowulf and Hrothgar to "earlier strife" at 1828 and 1857–58 will have gently reminded us that the Danes may well need Beowulf's help again, from monstrous human enemies. Hrothgar cannot know, as the audience of the poem does, that war will soon come again from the Heathobards, despite the marriage of his daughter to their king. Nor can he surmise, as the audience can, that his nephew Hrothulf will treacherously usurp the Danish throne from his son Hrethric.

This privileged knowledge of ours creates a larger narrative context curiously disjoint with the moment of feeling as it is presented. Hrothgar finds that he loves Beowulf more deeply than he realized. Perhaps the reader must be a father or mother and have seen a child depart for far places (summer camp, the army, college) before the depth of Hrothgar's pang can be known. The fullness of these feelings lies beyond the agile imagination of youth. Perhaps, too, one must have sustained the losses of middle life to understand the poet's violent psychological language in 1876–80, so passionately sympathetic to the father's loss of his surrogate son. The alignment of such feelings with our story-bound sense of the larger context of future wars and betrayal should be, at the least, unsettling. It asks us to widen our conception of the pattern of feelings in the heroic life. To apprehend the moment fully, we must admit an unfamiliar intimacy into the midst of a formalizing parting. We are not to put aside our ironic foreknowledge, but to see the homely, touching way in which the future, whatever it brings, does not matter to men who would be of the same blood.

It seems the *Beowulf* poet felt that a rupture in the father-son relationship was particularly pathetic. He returns to it again in the stories that Beowulf later tells of Hrethel and the old man with the hanged son. Beowulf's own kin-feelings deepen from this point on. Witness the end of his report to Hygelac, his remarks about his foster-father Hrethel, his lack of heirs (2813–16), and his final words. There is a parallel, then, not immediately apparent, between Hrothgar's tears and the kin-sadness that the aged Beowulf will feel in Part II. Perhaps the desire to make this parallel accounts for the violent energy with which the poet says that a deep-felt longing burned in Hrothgar's blood. It almost seems as though the language of erotic poetry were being misapplied to a father's love for a son. But, as the young hero marches away, treading the turf gold-proud, the poet immediately raises his viewpoint to an Olympian height: Hrothgar was "a king blameless in everything until age took his strength from him." This phraseology opens the possibility that the poet meant to imply that it is weak, unmanly, for the elderly to feel such emotional bonds so strongly. Or is old age simply an unavoidable harm in human life? Almost too much is going on in the passage. It can also be read completely in abstractions: "Aged wisdom weeps for the departing strength of youth." This, however, would be *Beowulf* as written by John Bunyan.

An alternative translation of the lines describing Hrothgar's feelings has recently been offered by Thomas L. Wright, *MP* 65 (1967), 39–44. Working from several philological arguments, Wright claims it is uncertain that the text originally said that Hrothgar did not expect to see Beowulf again. He would translate 1878–80a as "for in his heart he held him fast, in the custom that belongs to dear men, as a warrior of the same blood." This is an attractive resolution of the strangely dense psychological language, but at the cost of contorting a number of familiar formulas.

The Hygd-Modthrytho Comparison (1925–1976)

Splendidly crisp sea-breezes brighten the passage that takes Beowulf home to Geatland. Perhaps no other poet in the English language has had such a precise command of the evocative details of ocean sailing. The brief scene springs instantly to life. Less readily enjoyed, or even understood, are the lines beginning with MS. *mod þryðo wæg* at 1931b ff. The story soon unfolds of a terrible queen whose evil deeds are in sharp contrast to young Queen Hygd's graces. This second queen's character improves after the legendary King Offa takes her to wife. This may seem an early version of *The Taming of the Shrew*. In any case, fierce queens were commonplace in Germanic legend, and as material for a narrative perhaps there is nothing strange about this story. However, its abrupt introduction and relevance to Beowulf's story have long been questioned.

The first problem here is how to read 1931b: are there two words or three, and do they contain a proper name? If there is no name, then there may be a silent omission in the MS. It is agreed by most modern commentators that *þryðo* cannot easily be a free-standing proper name here, but for arguments to justify the reading *mōd Þrȳðo wæg* 'Thrytho carried arrogance' (i.e., was proud), see Elsie von Schaubert's edition, Kommentar, pp. 114–15. Wrenn in his revised edition and Sisam, *RES* 22 (1946), 266, took the view that *mōd-þryðo* was a single compound word, "pride, arrogance, violence of character," and that the name of the queen who "waged" *mōd-þrȳðo* also contained the element *þrȳð*, and thus the scribe's eye skipped from one to the other, omitting a passage.

A queen's name containing the *þrȳð-* element is known from the thirteenth-century Latin *Lives of the Two Offas*. This is a confusing document that bears some explaining. The first Offa of the title was the fourth-century king of the Continental Angles. His innocent wife is an early prototype of Constance in Chaucer's *Man of Law's Tale* and she does not concern us. Offa II was the great king of Mercia during the eighth century (ruled 757–96) who built Offa's Dyke to mark his Welsh border—a sixty-mile-long earthwork still visible today. The eldest son of Charlemagne sought (unsuccessfully) the hand of his daughter in marriage, and there are letters between Charlemagne and Offa II which speak of exchanges of gifts in a pact of friendship. Offa II, who also introduced the penny to English coinage, was the most powerful Anglo-Saxon king before Alfred the Great. By the end of his reign, his overlordship included all lands south of the Humber. So much is history. In the *Lives of the Two Offas*, which is essentially a romance, Offa II is said to marry a relative of Charlemagne who had arrived in England after being set adrift in a boat for having committed terrible crimes. Her name, "Quendrida, id est regina Drida," was falsely etymologized from OE. *Cyneðryð*. This was, in fact, the name of Offa II's queen, which appears on his coinage. It is not known whether the historical queen had any bad habits. In the *Lives*, however, she arranges the murder of St. Ethelbert (whom the historical Offa II had ordered beheaded) and of others, including her husband. Eventually she meets a bad end. Now, in *Beowulf*, a character like this one is made out to be the queen of Offa I, the Angle. This earlier king's own boundary-making abilities are celebrated in the early OE. poem *Widsið*, 35–44, where he is said to keep peace all around him, by the sword, and to have drawn his boundary line along the river Eider. After he has been celebrated, the *Widsið* poet moves next to Hrothulf and Hrothgar and their successful resistance to the attack of Ingeld. This has an enticing similarity to the sequence of topics in *Beowulf*: the next piece of extended narrative will be Beowulf's own prediction of Ingeld's attack. Possibly both poets felt that these two legendary episodes belonged together.

The *Beowulf* narrative will resemble the *Lives of the Two Offas* only if we transfer the bad queen from the later Offa to the earlier. However, there is another analogue. The story of Hermuthruda in Book IV of Saxo Grammaticus' history is closer to *Beowulf* than either of the two Offa stories as they stand. The two simple plots in Saxo and *Beowulf* are essentially the same. In addition, Hermuthruda also has a *þrýð*- element in her Latinized name: *-thruda*. If her story was told in *Beowulf* as Modthrytho's, then we do not need to assume a scribal omission. The present text follows arguments along these lines advanced by G. V. Smithers, "Four Cruces in *Beowulf*," *Studies in Language and Literature in Honour of Margaret Schlauch*, ed. M. Brahmer et al. (Warsaw: Panstowe Wydawnictwo Naukowe, 1966), pp. 413–30.

It may still be objected that we do not know a Modthrytho from any source other than *Beowulf*. This is not to say that we cannot accept *Beowulf* itself as evidence, but that firm corroboration is lacking. We could allow "Thryth" to stand as a simplex if we emended, with Schücking and Chambers, to *mōd Þrȳð[e ne] wæg*, with the meaning that Hygd "did not show the pride of Thryth." Finally, in a remarkably inventive argument, Norman E. Eliason has recently disposed of Thryth altogether. He argues that the wife of Offa in *Beowulf* was actually Hygd herself at an earlier time. Then she was widowed and later married Hygelac. See Eliason's article in *Franciplegius*, pp. 124–28.

The relevance of comparing Modthrytho to Hygd is not far to seek, once it is granted that relevance can be found at all. Margaret Goldsmith treats the story of Modthrytho's rehabilitation as an example of inordinate self-love yielding before lawful love. Her beauty has led her to arrogance, but subjugation to the proper (medieval) duties of womanhood brings her back into God's order. She thus is the female counterpart of Heremod, who also misused the gifts God had given him. See Goldsmith, pp. 253–54. These ideas were certainly in the air at whatever date we set the poem, but I think this definition of the theme is slightly abstract and out of context. Better sense is made of the passage by Robert Kaske in his "Hygelac and Hygd," *Brodeur Studies,* pp. 200–6. Kaske starts from the possibility of name play in the pairing of *Hyge-lāc* 'lack of thought' (or 'instability of mind') with *Hygd* 'mind, thought.' Kaske then views this royal couple in terms of the dual theme of *sapientia et fortitudo*, wisdom and strength. Hygd, both in her conduct and her name, is meant as an implicit contrast to Hygelac. Offa is explicitly characterized as ideally wise and strong. (I might add that this is emphasized so much that some critics have thought it may be a topical allusion to the actual Offa II of Mercia, through his earlier namesake. If so, the poem might have originated at his court. See further Whitelock, *Audience*, pp. 58–64.) The point of the contrast between Offa the Angle and Hygelac is this: while a strong and wise king can bring a vicious queen under control, a wise queen can do little about her lord's lack of wisdom or his misuse of strength. See Kaske's further remarks in *Critical Approaches*, pp. 20–21.

This line of interpretation is the best explanation so far of the poet's treatment of Hygd and the placement of the digression on Offa's queen. Hygd's wise courtesy catches up the theme of "the peace-weaving queen" from the depiction of Wealhtheow in Denmark. This theme will be touched on again almost immediately when

Beowulf mentions the marriage of Freawaru to settle a feud. The contrast drawn between Hygd and Offa's discourteous queen slowly evolves into extended praise of Offa as king, ending with a genealogical flourish. To complete the contrast, our minds naturally move to Hygd's king, and, of course, Hygelac does not "in wisdom hold his homeland long" like Offa, but seeks a feud in Frisia. In his single speech in the poem (1987–98), Hygelac asks about Beowulf's recent dangers in "the very platitudes of cautious anxiety" (Kaske's phrase). This is a touching human irony, since he is soon to fall through his own recklessness. It is Hygelac upon whom the faithful young Beowulf depends entirely (2146b–51).

The abrupt entry into the Modthrytho story is really no more obscure than the exit from the comparison at 915b—"But sin invaded him [Heremod]"—or the shift at 1214 from the slaughter fields of Frisia to applause for Beowulf. In all three cases, the contrast falls athwart the caesura, the most salient feature of the line. Throughout the poem, the poet seeks to bring unlike elements into meaningful juxtaposition, and the piercing change from Hygd to Modthrytho was meant originally, I believe, to be forceful, not forced.

The closing of this episode offers another kind of evidence that it is meant to join together the dark stresses in both Danish and Geatish society. After the poet has told of Offa, he turns back to Beowulf and sends him marching over the sand while "the world-candle shone, bright sun [or gem] from the south." Again possibly a patristic symbol, this is less disputably the bright light obligatory in the poetic theme of "a hero's arrival on a beach." The poet has delayed completing the expected pattern of images in this theme until he has landed his comparison upon the Geatish shore as well. A contemporary audience would have heard this digression not as narrative for its own sake, but as part of the whole episode of Beowulf's arrival in Geatland. By delaying its completion, the poet can weave the theme of "good and bad rulers" into the theme of "arrival." This fits perfectly with Hrothgar's earlier notion that Beowulf would make a good king for Geatland and the later moment when Hygd shows her wisdom by offering him the kingdom. On the arrival theme, see David K. Crowne, *NM* 61 (1960), 362–72, and Donald K. Fry, *NM* 68 (1967), 168–84.

Beowulf's Report to Hygelac (2000–2151)

Beowulf's long speech to Hygelac has been important to criticism for two contrary reasons. First, it is Beowulf's own perception of events in Denmark, given out in free form without the constraints of chronological sequence. Secondly, it feels awkward. Its second half, especially, seems no more than a lame recapitulation. The most succinct proponent of this second view is Kenneth Sisam, *Structure*, pp. 44–50. For the first view, see Morton W. Bloomfield's review of Sisam in *Speculum* 41 (1966), 370–71. One way of shifting the ground of discussion about the artistic worth of this recapitulation is to claim that *Beowulf* was composed orally and that this retelling of the fight against the Grendel family is subject to the special processes of "resinging." For a debate on this matter, see Francis P. Magoun, Jr., *Arv* 14 (1958), 95–101, and Charles Witke, *NM* 67 (1966), 113–17.

The general reader's interest in the new details offered about Grendel will focus mainly on his *glōf* 'glove, pouch' made of dragon-skins and his etymologically related victim *Hondsciōh*. Compare Ger. *Handschuh* 'hand-shoe,' i.e., 'glove.' The poet's imaginative collocation of such verbal similarities is satisfying, but, after two thousand lines, not exactly news. These details have only the durable interest of lore.

The news that Beowulf first elects to tell has a more truly poetic interest. He utters a sad truth at 2029–31: seldom, if anywhere, does the death-spear rest long, even though the bride who is given to keep peace is among the best. Beowulf's imagination seizes upon the inevitable consequence of the uneasy compact that Hrothgar has made by giving his daughter Freawaru to Ingeld. The avenger of Hondscioh and Æschere can readily foresee how Heathobard warriors will be affronted by the sight of their own heirlooms in Danish hands. The cruel egging-on that Beowulf attributes to a nameless old warrior is matched by the well-known character Starcatherus in Saxo Grammaticus' later retelling of the Ingeld story. Saxo's character spends many Latin stanzas railing against young Ingeld's sloth in avenging his sire, until finally Ingeld, goaded by the old counselor, leaps up and slays his hosts, the sons of the Saxon king Swerting. The motif is the same in Saxo but there it is extended into rodomontade. To be sure, in *Beowulf* it is not Ingeld himself who kills

Freawaru's retainer, but the imagined situation is at once more plausible and more concisely realized than in Saxo. (For a contrary view, see Klaeber's edition of *Beowulf*, p. 203.) Probably the *Beowulf* poet, like Saxo, knew an entire version of the episode. Likely enough, his audience knew it as well. Once we grant this, we must concede that even the dullest contemporary would understand the poet's point that Beowulf can clearly foresee the future of the feud between the Danes and Heathobards (lit. "War-Beards").

Now, how much Beowulf's foreknowledge of a story that listeners already know may be said to prove his sagacity, fitness to govern, or good character is a point that only a lesser Solomon among literary critics might wish to judge. It is more important to acknowledge that it is a rousing passage. It provides us with a very human though not very admirable psychology to explain the cyclical eruption of feuds throughout the poem. Thematically the passage is closely related to the remorseless revenging in the Finnsburh Episode. I suspect—*pace* Bloomfield and other close readers of Beowulf's own viewpoint here—that the imagined account of renewed hostilities is not meant to shed new light upon his character nor to provide an occasion to fault it. It is, first and foremost, a dramatic rendering of future events. Beowulf's voice here is not distinguished from that other prophetic voice in the poem, the poet's. The melding of their two perspectives at this point is comparable to the moment when the nameless Messenger prophesies the downfall of the Geats at the hands of the Swedes (2900–3027). Beowulf's troop fled into the wood instead of facing the dragon, yet the Messenger—by anyone's logic—must be one of that troop since he is not Wiglaf. However, he foretells a moving epic prophecy that does not come specifically from the perspective of a cowardly man soon to be exiled. His perspective, like Wiglaf's, depends instead upon the death of Beowulf and the fact that the feud-ridden Geats are now leaderless. In Beowulf's report we see a similar focus on cause and result, delivered in a similarly *un*self-characterizing voice.

Transitions (2163–2209)

The poet was definitely thinking about characterization, however, in the evaluative retrospect he offers at 2166 ff. "Thus shall a man do," we read, "never set malice-nets for his kinsmen." Instead, he should keep faith. Thus did the kinsman of Hygelac, in unsaid but obvious contrast to Heremod. The beginning of the sentence recalls the first moral axiom of the poem at lines 20–25. Whatever we may say or leave unsaid about the Beowulf who will seek the dragon's treasure, here he is the shining example of fidelity. Hygelac could possess no greater good than his faithful nephew. The negatives that guard Beowulf's virtue in 2167 ff. and 2179 ff. have been understood by some critics, however, as ambiguous denials. It may be a slightly sophistical argument to say he is not wholly good because the poet so emphatically says he was not a faithless murderer. First, this negative assertion could be litotes, grossly understating the hero's obvious virtues. Secondly, it probably is an implied contrast to Heremod and, one might add, to most of the other kings in the poem except Offa and Hrothgar. Thirdly, after each negation comes an *ac* 'but, rather' or else a heavily contrastive caesural pause followed by a positive. These tandem poetic devices assert Beowulf's fidelity and his proper use of his God-given talent of enormous strength. Yet I would certainly have to admit, on the other side of the question, that negatives, no matter how roundly restated as positives, are by their nature faint praise. The poet could surely have broken through his lexical-metrical habit of *ne*-plus-*ac* had he wished to present a brightly one-sided evaluation of Beowulf's heroism.

Beowulf's "inglorious youth" (2183b–89), as it is infelicitously called by critics, exemplifies the idea of *edwendan* 'reversal' one more time before the dragon comes. It also shows the poet's rather flat-footed management of the telescopic perspective. He is better when com-posing, putting disparate things together, than when he takes a long panoramic view down across the years. This would be one view of the obvious seams in the poem's fabric throughout the transition between Parts I and II. A contrary reading might run something like this: in seven lines (2200–6), the poet works in three references to *hild* 'battle' and entirely resets the tone for the historical events which will so significantly surround the dragon fight. The giving of great treasures (including the ill-fated neck-ring), Beowulf's canine loyalty to his rash young leader, Hygelac's disaster in Frisia, his son's equally unhappy end, Beowulf's subsequent strength as a king—all these come upon the reader like pebbles on a rooftop. It is a clatter of undeveloped events that will gain in clarity as Beowulf retells them. The alacrity of the narrative at this point, its very speediness, *is* the poet's world-view.

I find it easy, frankly, to sit on the fence while reading these transitional lines. They have much narrative purpose, since they announce the principal themes of Part II before the dragon appears, but the poetry of the poem is better elsewhere.

"Who Robbed the Dragon? 'I,' Said the ——?" (2214b–2231a)

It is a wonderful irony that the passage which could most clarify the metaphysical structure of *Beowulf* is most nearly obliterated in the MS. and, as far as anyone knows, sheerly through wear and tear. If the last third of the poem saw more use than Part I in the monastic refectory, we can only guess what its use was. The "thief" or "servant" of 2223b and the precious cup of 2231a may bear some resemblance to the craven servant in the biblical parable of the talents, as may the Last Survivor who buries the hoard. The dragon may signify Malice, and this initial episode may have been understood in patristic terms. Or it could all be very ordinary, no more than the taboo violation common in folktales. Readers may remain forever tantalized, but they will never know the full truth of the matter. The single clear note is *oðð*æ*t* ā*n ongan* 'until one began' 2210b. To linger longer over the other mysteries of the corrupt text is to play the Sibyl without a message.

The Meanings of the Hoard

The meanings of the hoard are contextual and ambiguous. And they are presented like an extended variation. That is, the essential aspects of the situation that the poet wishes us to see have been distributed into distinct groupings of significance (thus Joan Blomfield). These meanings are spread out through Part II. We first see the hoard as the occasion for vengeance, when the thief robs it. The dragon had ruled it long, just as Beowulf had long ruled his kingdom, until a new feud erupts. Their equivalence as adversaries is governed partly by this parity of the two rulers—gold-keeper and gold-giver—and partly by their equal fates. Then, in the Lay of the Last Survivor (see below), the hoard is presented differently: as an emblem of mortal joy, of the transience of earthly glory, of a past now lost to us. It is only after the dragon fight, when both Beowulf

and the dragon lie dead, that the curse on the hoard is offered in a
third context, to provide a (superfluous?) explanation for the strife
and death.

The extent to which the hoard mirrors the avarice of the men who
look upon it varies with each context. It seems a possible stimulus
for greed in Beowulf's final death secene. Yet elsewhere in the poem
gold is a good. Fitt XXXII (2221–311), which introduces the hoard
as a field of force in the poem, shows a determinedly ironic under-
mining in its metrical linkings. It is as though the wrong words have
been stressed, in order to lead us to a skeptical assay of the heroic
values attached to the gold. "Treasure" is paired by stress with
"death" in 2236, the "hoard of heathens" is twice mentioned (2216,
2276), and the fitt ends with the metrical linking of *sinc* and *sār*,
'treasure' and 'grief.' The ultimate uselessness of the hoard is, plainly,
to be the supreme irony. This is emphasized by the poet's "elaborately
equivocal use of familiar formulas," in Randolph Quirk's phrase. See
his essay in *EENS*, esp. pp. 165–71. Against this view should be set
Stanley Greenfield's argument that the hoard has so many meanings
in the poem, and such contrary ones, that it can have no overriding
signification. Instead, it presents us, as we move from context to
context, with an unresolved tension of meanings that is itself aestheti-
cally effective. See his essay in *Pope Studies*, pp. 107–17.

The Lay of the Last Survivor (2247–2266)

In an earlier folk version, the Last Survivor may have entered
the mound alive with his treasure and have turned into a dragon at
death. See Smithers, *The Making of "Beowulf,"* p. 11. But questions
of his original identity do not occupy an appreciative reader at this
point. This impressive, moving elegy speaks first to our sense of
human loss. The verse is audibly enriched by many "beauties," as
an eighteenth-century critic might have called them, such as the
matched verbs, urgent in their rhythms, and the ornamental internal
rhymes. A richly imagined grief gives shape to this precise evocation.
The final portion also compares closely with the passage in Hrothgar's
sermon that directly confronts Beowulf with his own death
(1757–68). Both are built up by formal, highly connected repetitions
that lead to a final assertion of death's reality. The personification of

armor matters as much as elsewhere in the poem and helps create
the sense that the Last Survivor is somehow the leader of the noble
race that finishes here. The emphasis on *ān* 'one, alone' will recur
when Beowulf goes alone to meet the dragon. The poetic gesture
of committing to the earth all that heroes may no longer hold will
be repeated when the Geats rebury the hoard in Beowulf's barrow,
"where it lies even now, as useless to men as it was before"
(3167–68).

While the elegy has a virtuoso intensity and can easily be read as
a set piece, it acts as an integral part of *Beowulf* because of these
parallels and also because of the early repetition of the formula
fǣted wǣge 'gold-plated cup' in 2253b and 2282a. This invites the
conclusion that the thief stole the same cup mentioned by the Last
Survivor when he entrusts the treasure to the earth. (The formulaic
usage will not permit absolute certainty, however.) The burial elegy
is also the first of many deflections away from straight chronological
narration in Part II. Up to this speech, the narrative has told of the
depredation of the hoard and has aligned it with the end of Beowulf's
rule. Now the viewpoint becomes retrospective and remains so for
the rest of the poem. Past, present, and future become intertwined,
and the grief of the Last Survivor will be renewed and extended until
it includes Beowulf's grief and the reader's as well.

It is not merely the loss of the Good Company, as in the dissolu-
tion of Malory's Round Table, nor the overwhelming inevitability
of death and its flattening force as a personal truth—though these
meanings are increasingly apparent. More, it is the loss of the heroic
past, the grief inherent in Time itself, that leads the poet to find
tears in these dead and buried things. *Ubi sunt qui ante nos fuerunt*?
Where are those who went before us? This is a hallowed motif in
medieval literature and can be traced from early Latin homilies
through the OE. *Wanderer* to Villon's "Where are the snows of
yesteryear?" In the hands of Latin and Old English homilists, the
ubi sunt motif usually reinforced the idea of the vanity of worldly
things. Caesar is dead, Pompey is dead—where are the kings of this
world now? And in what King can man place his faith? In *Beowulf*,
the religious implications are less evident. The imaginative pressure
behind the Lay is more like the sparrow simile in Bede's account
of the Conversion of Northumbria. To show that man cannot hold
the present securely against the uncertainties of *wyrd*, the poet will

now develop the themes of Hygelac's Frisian raid and the compli-
cated feuds of the Swedish-Geatish wars. His perspective on the past
will be as something supremely valuable but already irrevocably lost,
as it is here. The Lay is crucial in establishing this new key for the
still, sad music of the poem.

Narrative Method in Part II

All suspense in Part II has been deliberately removed. We know
only too well what will happen next. No sooner does the dragon
settle down upon the barrow-gold than we learn that he will "gain
nothing by it" (2277). The same phrase will be applied to Beowulf
at 2687, when the sword Nægling fails him in the second rush against
the dragon. Similarly, we are told far in advance that both the hero
and the dragon will meet their end-day in the fight. With the final
outcome anticipated by the poet's early intrusions (2310–11, 2323b,
2341–44), there is a collapse of sequential time into cyclical time.
The past is continually overlapping into the present as the reader
goes between the dragon fight and its complex elegiac setting drawn
from the Geats' past. The ebb and flow of time-boundaries may be
confusing at first, but this tidal method enlarges the significance of
the relationship between setting and action in a unique way. A new
and timeless world comes into being during the poet's telling and
retelling. It gives a hypostatized continuity to the lost past and the
lost present. The slow waves of narrative advance in the dragon
fight are balanced against the increasing regression toward darkness
in the interspersed memories of battles, particularly with the fierce
old Swedish king Ongentheow.

The internal (present) and external (past) actions of Part II are
told over in a dreamlike "montage" fashion. The reader traverses the
two sorts of scene with an unaccustomed ease; the scene-changes no
longer seem like juxtapositions. Thus the very methods of "telling
over" and "going between" come to have a poetic meaning. They
tell us that memory is the limit of human foreknowing. Understand
history though we may, we are tragically doomed to repeat it. There
is no escape from the bloody heroic past, which is, at the same time,
lost to us. It is basically an elegiac style and in a sense not really a
storytelling style at all. (I say this with some temerity, since the
actual battle with the dragon, or the scene in lines 2961–81 where

Ongentheow is cut down, bearded with his own blood, are filled with as much primitive narrative delight as the Grendel fight at its best.) The design of Part II creates cruelly *obvious* ironies; in this it differs sharply from the dark inklings and portents of Part I. And the recitation of Part II goes far more swiftly than the first two thousand lines. In the poet's hands, the verses swell up and flatten out with astonishing ease. The poet created a great deal of elbow room by anticipating the outcome, yet in his asides he says rather less than many critics have wished he had. The speed with which he develops the full sadness of Beowulf's final triumph becomes, itself, an emblem of the transience of the heroic life. It is no wonder there are conflicting cues about the hero and the hoard in the received text.

Part II also has many intentional resemblances to Part I, particularly to the Grendel fight. Beowulf himself recalls his success against Grendel, and the reader recalls Hrothgar's gift-stool, which Grendel could not touch, when Beowulf's gift-stool is burned by the dragon (2326–27). Formulas that were earlier associated with Grendel occur again at 2300, 2303, and 2321 ff. Like Grendel, the dragon pursues his feud against mankind only after dark. The reader will readily see other similarities as well. Generally, this structural *déjà vu* gives the feeling that this combat will be like Beowulf's earlier exploits, only this time he will fail.

As in the adventures in Denmark, there are three main figures in the center: the old king, the young retainer, and the monstrous adversary. There is a sense in which the hoard takes the place of the dragon in this static figure grouping. Even after the dragon dies, the hoard remains a challenging adversary. For a far-ranging discussion of such figure groupings in heroic and epic narrative, see Thomas H. Greene, "The Norms of Epic," *CL* 13 (1961), 193–207.

Beowulf's First Reaction (2324–2332)

Dark thoughts do not become a hero, yet after the dragon's attack Beowulf's first conclusion is that he has "offended the Ruler, bitterly angered the eternal Lord, against the old law." It is easy to make too much of this, just as it is easy to overemphasize the verbal link between *ofer-hygd* 'pride' at 1740 and 1760 with lines 2345–46, "then the prince of rings scorned *(oferhogode)* to seek the far-flyer with a troop of men." In fairness, it should be pointed out that, while a man may feel guilt, he is not therefore guilty of an actual offense. On the other hand, the poet need not have attributed such feelings to the hero, need not have raised the question in this oblique, studied way. Perhaps the two most certain meanings of the *ofer ealde riht* passage (2327–32) are the implicit comparison of Beowulf, his hall now burned to the ground, to Hrothgar facing sudden reversal of fortune, "greatest of mind-sorrows"; and the humanizing effect of the irony that notices how unusual these "dark breast-thoughts" are for the aged hero.

They are surely guilt feelings. Beowulf will soon utter dark words enough when he rehearses his part in Geatish history. In that long speech, seated before the barrow, he will remember a blameless life. Here, before he moves to revenge himself upon the dragon-king (2335–36), he is unsettled. It is probable that by the "old law" the poet intended St. Paul's conception of the natural moral law which rational deists could discover on their own, without the help of Christian revelation. See further Charles Donahue, *Traditio* 7 (1949–51), 263–77.

The Chronology of Geatish History in Part II (See also the Royal Genealogies on p. 244.)

(Passage B)

Hæthcyn the Geat accidentally kills his elder brother Herebeald. Their father, King Hrethel, dies of grief.

Ongentheow's sons attack the Geats at Sorrow Hill (Geatland).

(Passage C)

In retaliation, Hæthcyn attacks Ongentheow in Sweden, but is killed by him at Ravenswood. There Hygelac's men Wulf and Eofor kill Ongentheow. Hygelac's forces sweep the field.

(Passage A)

Hygelac is killed on his expedition to Frisia. Beowulf escapes.

After young Heardred, the son of Hygelac, becomes
king, he harbors two of Ongentheow's grandsons,
Eanmund and Eadgils, the sons of Ohthere.

Their uncle Onela, the Swedish king, attacks his two
nephews in Geatland and kills their protector Hear-
dred. It is probably at this point that Weohstan, Wig-
laf's father, kills Eanmund on behalf of Onela. (See
lines 2609–19.) Onela allows Beowulf to rule the
Geats.

Later Eadgils returns to Sweden, with arms and men
supplied by Beowulf, and kills his uncle Onela.

Beowulf now rules the Geats in peace for a long
time. The death of Eanmund the Swede remains un-
avenged.

Later, after Beowulf's death, Eanmund's brother Ead-
gils will probably seek revenge against Wiglaf, the
son of Eanmund's killer.

The events of this bloody chronicle are told in three main pas-
sages: Passage A (2349–2400), Beowulf's survival in Frisia and
Heardred's later fall. Passage B (2425–2515), Beowulf's memories
of Hrethel and, more briefly, of Ravenswood and Frisia. Passage C
(2910–3000), the Messenger's speech telling the story of the battle
of Ravenswood and predicting future war. However, the passages are
not in chronological order. The events in Passage B occur first in
time, followed by the Ravenswood episode in Passage C, and finally
the more recent deaths of Hygelac and Heardred in Passage A.
In the telling, we first encounter, in Passage A, what is most recent
and next, in Passage B, go back in time to what is most remote.
Finally, in Passage C, the future doom of the Geats is aligned with
a battle that occurred a generation earlier. Historical time is thus
broken apart and reassembled in the poem's own mosaic of mean-
ings. Further, the viewpoint and theme of these three passages differ
in each case. Passage A gives the poet's viewpoint on the theme of
survival; Passage B, Beowulf's viewpoint on revenge and heroic
reward; Passage C, the Messenger's (and the poet's) view of the
dark future that lies beyond heroism. For an excellent discussion

of the poet's artistic uses of this history, see Stanley B. Greenfield, *Neophilologus* 47 (1963), 211–17.

Beowulf's Survival in Frisia (2345–2400)

There is an abrupt shift in narrative perspective at *forðon* 'because' 2349b, which may interest readers who wish to charge Beowulf with overweening pride. The dragon seemed as nothing to Beowulf *because* he had survived so many battle-crashes, especially the fall of his lord Hygelac. This passage begins a long pause in the main action—roughly two hundred lines—in which the past is examined. Not until 2562 will the actual dragon fight get underway.

The poet has shifted his focus pointedly, to a period of time after the destruction of Grendel and his mother. By the litotes of "not the least of hand-meetings" (2354–55) we are to understand that Beowulf's exploits during Hygelac's raid were the most famous deeds he performed during the interval between Grendel and the dragon. But what is famous about the defeat of the Geats in Frisia? (A question balanced in Part I by: What is famous about the Danes' victory in Frisia against Finn?) Moreover, this interval begins with the death of Hygelac and includes the death of his son Heardred. It is the time span between the fall of one Geatish king and another. The foolishness of Hygelac's Frisian raid is thus given pride of place in the skein of Geatish history interwoven with the dragon fight. Its prominence is increased by Beowulf's association with his lord Hygelac everywhere in the poem. Here the Frisian raid appears almost as an archetype for the Geatish battles told later, and perhaps also for their causes.

Beowulf is characterized as an *earm ān-haga* 'a wretched solitary' 2368, a formulaic phrase from exile poetry like *The Wanderer*. His lord is dead, and he is alone on the sea, far from home. Loneliness may also be part of the theme of swimming or sea voyage; compare the "no lonelier man" than Beowulf (577b) during his swimming contest with Breca. In both episodes, the word *ān* 'one' is given marked emphasis. We have already heard *ān* applied twice to the Last Survivor (2237b, 2268a), to the dragon (2210b), and at the close of this passage Beowulf is said to have survived "until that one day" (*ānne* 2399b) that he must meet that other snaky One. The "earth-hall" of the dragon is "a certain one" (2410) as well, and at 2533 Beowulf declares that this heroic venture is "his alone" *(ānes)*. The singular *ān* rings out all through this part of the poem not only to sound the elegiac note but also to define Beowulf as the exceptional man. The hero, by nature, is set apart from other men. Beowulf is also something more: he is the last hero.

The emphasis on *ān* is clear in the text. The actual details of Beowulf's retreat from Frisia are more cloudy. The Roman numeral XXX in the MS., usually taken to modify "battle-outfits" in 2361b–62a, is possibly a lost fitt number inadvertently inserted in the middle of Fitt XXXIII. Possibly *oferswām* 'swam across' 2367a should not be taken literally. These uncertainties have led Fred C. Robinson to a newly cautious translation: "From there [i.e., from the battle] came Beowulf by means of his own physical strength— undertook a journey on the sea. He had held battle-gear on his arm when he moved toward the sea . . . Then, alone and wretched, the son of Ecgtheow crossed the expanse of ocean, returning to his own people." *(Pope Studies,* p. 126.) See also Karl P. Wentersdorf, *SP* 68 (1971), 395–415. I prefer Robinson's earlier interpretation in *SP* 62 (1965), 1–16, which I adopt in the translation, because of the contrast to the Hetware (Frisians) immediately following: Beowulf performs incredible feats even in defeat, while the winners have nothing to boast about.

Beowulf survives Hygelac's poor judgment (though Hygelac does not) and shows his own wisdom in refusing to take the throne instead of Hygelac's son, as Queen Hygd offers. Then he must survive anew the poor judgment of Heardred, who harbors the Swedish princes Eadgils and Eanmund against their powerful uncle Onela. The upshot of that ill-considered hospitality is that Onela invades Geatland and kills Heardred, but Eadgils escapes to slay Onela later in Sweden, with support sent by Beowulf. (For the earlier death of Eanmund see the note below on Wiglaf's sword, 2599 ff.) These events place Beowulf in a peculiar position. It is not Hygd but the conquering Onela who gives Beowulf the Geatish throne. This would not appease any self-respecting hero's sense of honor, and Beowulf promotes warfare between Eadgils and Onela. In so doing, he carries on the feud which has already cost the lives of two Geatish kings, Hæthcyn and Heardred. With Onela's death, Heardred is avenged. But now of course the Swedes must avenge Onela. The cycle of feuding seems endless. Does his part in it make Beowulf a good king or does it lay him open to criticism? A king must be a strong fighter ready to protect his people, yet he should also promote peace and not act like Hygelac. Recent interpretations have developed this dilemma at length. The poet probably meant to nudge his audience's judgment toward the problematic, but the most noticeable quality of this passage (2379–400) is its rapidity as poetry. Be it perfect or flawed, Beowulf's kingship is transitory—*lǣne*. It lasts only "until that one day" when he must fight the worm.

A textual point oddly related to the question of kingship: "that was a good king" 2390b. This is a prime example of the free-floating half-line, grammatically unconnected to its surroundings. It could be that Onela is good, since he lets Beowulf rule the Geats; most critics have thought so. The half-line concludes a sentence that started at 2386 with Onela as the main subject. Yet Beowulf is a good king too, and elsewhere in the poem there are sudden shifts of reference across the caesura. Perhaps Beowulf is to be contrasted with Onela. Unlike Onela, who twice invaded Geatland, Beowulf makes no feuding raids as a king. But we have no grammatical way of knowing this was intended. When the diction is as fully formulaic as this half-line, Old English poetic style will often lack particularity of reference. When the poet is not particular, the reader cannot be.

Beowulf's Meditation in Old Age (2425–2537)

"For God's sake, let us sit upon the ground, / And tell sad stories of the death of kings." These words of Shakespeare's *Richard II*, with their youthful self-pity subtracted, might be applied to Beowulf as he sits on the cliff above the dragon's barrow. The tone of his speech is set by a phrase Hrothgar might have uttered: *ic þæt eall gemon* 'I remember it all' 2427b. It has the packed force of multiple feelings. The way we are supposed to hear it is modified by the poet's scene-setting, which heavily emphasizes Beowulf's inescapable *wyrd,* the doom that is coming "to seek out the treasure of [his] soul, to separate the life from the body." This is a language of spirituality, of last things. The first element of the variation is probably meant to recall Hrothgar's sermon. It is a verbal parallel to the fact that Beowulf is seeking the treasure of the dragon. *Wyrd* is to Beowulf as Beowulf is to the dragon. The theme of "seeking" returns musically at the end of Beowulf's speeches before battle: he

seeks gold or death (2535–36). In his heroic boasts at 2510 ff.,
he also seeks a feud with the dragon (2513) and, as everywhere in
his life, he seeks fame, the enduring glory of a good name. He wants
to be, once again, the Grendel-conquerer of his youth. All the while,
as the poet's insistent interruptions at 2510 and 2516 tell us, death
seeks him. This irony does not make us wiser than the hero.

Interestingly, the perspective created by the scene-setting
(2419–25) at first looks like Beowulf's own thoughts, because *wyrd*
is syntactically a variation on his "sad mind." It is as though Beowulf
knew that his mysterious fate sits beside him before battle, though
in fact the poet does not say he knows. I suspect the poet wanted
to blur the focus for a moment, to allow the impersonal voice of epic
to merge with the old king's voice of memory.

Beowulf redreams the past: his happy fostering by Hrethel and
that father's unpayable grief. The story of one brother accidentally
killing another strikes us today as merely pathetic, and it takes an
active historical imagination to reconstruct the feelings of shame
and profound loss of face, of a mind-wearying injustice in the bosom
of the family. Yet this is an innocent wrong. We hear the paradox
at its most unendurable in the weird quietude of the long vowels in
line 2440: *brōðor ōðerne,   blōdigan gāre.*

The extended simile that follows, of the old man mourning his
son on the gallows, is one of the most remarkable passages in
Beowulf. Whether we see its poetic depth as part of Beowulf's char-
acter or we treat it as an immediate local effect undertaken by the
poet mainly for thematic reasons, we will conclude that it is perfectly
fitted to the case of Hrethel, Beowulf himself, and the rest of the
poem, especially the Lay of the Last Survivor. The connection with
the last is clear from the pun in "the riders sleep" (2457), which
could also be "the rider sleeps," since singular and plural forms are
mixed. It is both the former warriors and the dead gallows-rider
who "sleep." Together with the absence of the harp, of joy in the
courtyards, this takes us back to the Lay. Like the Last Survivor, the
old father mourns alone—*ān* once again (compare 2461 with
2268)—and both of them pass away from grief-wellings in the heart.

This parallel heightens the elegiac tone of the simile. All is past,
nothing is as it once was. So Beowulf might speak to himself, and
something of this tone comes out in his final speech to Wiglaf
(2813–16). But Beowulf has also made this simile to explain the

death of Hrethel, and its aptness turns on the fact that the nameless old father cannot avenge a death that has occurred as a criminal execution. See further Dorothy Whitelock, *MÆ* 8 (1939), 198–204. Part of Hrethel's sorrow is that he cannot engage in right conduct and prosecute a feud. Foreknowing the outcome of the dragon fight, we realize that it, too, will result in unavengeable deaths and that there is no human justice that can redress the loss of the hero.

The simile juxtaposes the old man upon Beowulf's memory of his sorrowing foster-father, producing the effect that both Hrethel and Beowulf have grown old in grief. Then Hrethel dies in a conventional phrase—"he chose God's light"—and Beowulf's dream of his familial past turns into the nightmare of history. He has kept faith and *sibb* 'peace, friendship, kinship' throughout his life, but he has lost his dear foster-father and also his three foster-brothers: Herebeald, Hæthcyn, and "Hygelac mine." The heroic mourner now gives way to the epic historian. Beowulf remembers with crisp righteousness the vengeful killings at Ravenswood, and he recalls those exploits in the dignified ironies of impersonal violence. "The hand could remember enough of the feud, did not withhold the death-blow" (2488–89).

Then, in a sudden, perfect change, Beowulf is moved to remember, with the deepest satisfaction, how he repaid at battle the gifts Hygelac gave him. Even as his voice swells with pride, we may notice that he has presented the deaths of the Geatish dynasty in historical order—first Herebeald, then Hrethel, then Hæthcyn at Ravenswood, and now finally Hygelac's fall in Frisia. The continuity of Beowulf's loyalty is so great that it tends to destroy historical time, and the verb tenses shift between past and present in 2493 ff. Hygelac died in Frisia, but that is not so much a grief to Beowulf as it is a call to new achievement now. He thinks of how well and truly he crushed the life out of "Day-Raven" the Frisian champion (cf. the note on the morning raven at 1800–2); how he, Beowulf, never lost glory as Hygelac's retainer. His sword (which will fail him now) was always doughty in the service of that king.

Against the many losses that he can remember, Beowulf has set what he sees as his gains, that part of himself that has survived the crash of history. It is his good name as a man of strength, courage, and loyalty. In weighing up the past, Beowulf has made a remarkable recovery from the moment when his death-ripe spirit began to brood

on Hrethel's grief. As a dramatic monologue, his speech has acted
out the psychology of a hero. Probably nowhere else in the poem
are we closer to the poet's own understanding of Beowulf's char-
acter. The speech as a whole discloses a greater range of feelings
than at any time earlier and it increases our awe at Beowulf's en-
durance. At the same time we have been brought full circle in the
larger temporal design of Part II. Beowulf's recollections have car-
ried him from age seven up through the fall of Hygelac, the very
point in the history of human feuds where the poet stopped earlier.

The *brēost-weorðunge* 'breast-ornament' 2504a that the dead
Dæghrefn fails to bring to the Frisian king has been identified by
some critics as the famous neck-ring that passed from Wealhtheow
to Beowulf to Hygelac. This is certainly possible since the poet is
careless about over-all consistency in small details. However, such
ornament was usual for Germanic warriors like Dæghrefn and there
is no allusive modifier to refer us definitely to the great neck-ring.
More likely the compound word was chosen to go with Dæghrefn's
crushed chest. The strength of hand that could perform that deed
is the subject of Beowulf's following boasts. They are appropriate to
the occasion, even required as an epic convention, and yet how
heavily the weight of history, of *fæhðe* 'feud,' presses on the first
boast (2511–15). He would seek a feud with the dragon. So in
youth, now in age. And will he crush him as he did Dæghrefn? He
wishes he could grapple the monster as he did Grendel, and he
swears that he will not retreat one foot's pace. He resolves to fight
alone, without his troop. This has been understood variously by
critics: as a tactical maneuver (Sisam); as *ofer-mōd*, the excessive
pride of a hero (Tolkien); and as a form of heroic courage which
we cannot grasp (Garmonsway). All three explanations seem true
in some degree. The aura of rash pride comes as an after-image of
the battle with Dæghrefn, while Beowulf's heroic resolve comes from
the texture of the speech itself. Further reading: John C. Pope,
"Beowulf's Old Age," *Meritt Studies* (1970), pp. 55–64; John Nor-
ton, "Tolkien, Beowulf, and the Poet: A Problem in Point of View,"
ES 48 (1967), 527–29.

Wiglaf, His Sword and Lineage (2599b–2668)

In one man at least (*in ānum* 2600), *sibb* 'kinship' did not fail.

The cowardly retainers flee to the wood, an artistic convenience that leaves the stage bare for the final drama between the three main figures. As this point there is a long pause of sixty-five lines, in which Wiglaf's character is developed. By the contrast of his right action to the troop's, we are reminded of the first moral axiom of the poem (lines 20–25): a leader should give gifts, so that later in his old age his men will stand by him when war comes. Generosity creates loyalty. Together these form the heroic bond between men. If Wiglaf did not already exist in legend (something we don't know), the poet would have had to invent him, in order to dramatize the values at stake. The fight involves more than the dragon, and it is no accident that Beowulf and Wiglaf kill him *together*. Their relationship—depicted with stark, almost sentimental formality (see 2663–68)—is essential to the meaning of their struggle. The reader is entirely justified if he has the intuition that they somehow have become father and son by the end.

This inner action is offset not only by the cowardly troop (which functions as a dramatic audience, like the Danes earlier), but also by the history of Wiglaf's sword, which he has from his father Weohstan. Apparently Weohstan was by blood both a Swede (Scylfing) and a Geat (Wægmunding). He is represented as having killed Eanmund on behalf of that luckless prince's own uncle Onela. This slaying may have occurred when Onela attacked his exiled nephews in Geatland and slew Heardred, or it may have occurred at another time and place; the poem is not specific on this point. Weohstan is said to have been living among the Geats when he died and left Wiglaf his legacy of armor. Klaeber (p. xliv) assumed that once Eadgils returned to Sweden and killed Onela, Weohstan could no longer live there safely with the slain man's brother now on the throne. So he moved to Geatland and settled in the rich homestead of the Wægmundings. This conjecture fits the scant details of the text.

As soon as Wiglaf draws his sword, originally plundered from Eanmund by Weohstan, it calls to mind the history of this feud. This is the same poetic method by which the magical giant-sword from the mere gained its significance. Both swords are memorials of old conflicts, and both appear when Beowulf's own weapons have failed him. They are symbols of the historical context in which Beowulf fights; in the fights against the Grendel tribe, the context is biblical as well. Both swords raise Cain.

So much time is devoted to the history of Wiglaf's sword because, once Beowulf is dead, Eadgils will want to avenge his brother's death and will seek out the killer's son, Wiglaf. This intimation of future bloodshed is built up at the very moment when Wiglaf feels the bonds of kinship and loyal retainership most strongly. A cruel irony, and a noble one. See further Bonjour, *Digressions,* pp. 38–39.

The Final Scene of the Dragon Fight (2669–2820)

Death for Beowulf is now "immeasurably near," as Wiglaf has been "immeasurably good." Compare *ungemete* 'immeasurably' at 2721 and 2728. Yet it will take almost four hundred lines more to organize the meanings of this death, before the poem can come to its final rest on *lof-geornost* 'most eager for fame.' From the dragon's third rush until the end, there will be a musical series of repeated themes, like the coda at the end of a symphony. Some are large-scale connections that reach far back into the poem, such as the glum comment about Beowulf's sword-breaking strength: *næs him wiht ðē sēl* 'he was no better off for it' 2687. This same phrase was applied earlier to the dragon's guarding the gold at 2277. Now in the third rush neither fares the better. Other repetitions come more quickly, as when Wiglaf's desire for immolation with his lord nearly comes true when his hand is burned up (2697). He keeps faith in the final conflict, and "so should a man be, a thane at need!" The poet's open, heartfelt approval here is matched by his exclamation a little earlier after Beowulf's concluding boast in 2540–41: "he trusted in the strength of one *(ānes)* man—such is not a coward's way!" These comments by the poet himself have a gnomic weight, typifying and elevating the characters and directly celebrating their heroism.

Then, speaking with difficulty across his throat-wound, Beowulf reviews his life and finds it free of the sins of Heremod: he murdered no kinsmen, swore no false oaths, plotted against none. Like Scyld Scefing, he was strong enough to hold the homeland in peace. No one dared attack Geatland while Beowulf was king. Therefore he can face God with a clear conscience (2733–43). Thus far into the scene we are asked to contemplate only the sad nobility of a fine heroism that has reached its final limit. But now things take a curious turn: Fetch the treasure, Wiglaf, that by looking upon it I might more easily give up my life (2743–51). This slight deflection from Christian heaven-mindedness is newly pathetic when read in the original. Already we feel how paltry the treasure is in comparison to the old king's beloved land. There is a further swerve into direct criticism— or so it seems—when the poet exclaims a few lines later, "How easily may jewels, gold in the earth, overcome anyone, hide it who will—heed it who can!" (2764–66). This gnomic exclamation can be fitted into two contradictory contexts. First the positive context: the moralistic remark occurs when Wiglaf looks upon the treasure and it is not applied to Beowulf's motives or fate. Later the poet will have Beowulf say—albeit with terrific dramatic irony since the treasure will never be used—that he thanks God that he has gained such a treasure for his people (2794 ff.) When Beowulf dies, his soul goes to seek the judgment of the just (2820). Beowulf's character at death, his moral status in the eyes of God, seems above criticism.

Why then does the poet view the hoard with such a critical eye? The negative context: Beowulf did no criminal wrongs as a king. While we might hear this as a deeply felt understatement of his goodness, it can also imply the absence of positive virtues. The light from the golden banner-standard in the barrow is comparable to the strange supernatural light in the mere-cave. By the light of the standard, Wiglaf looks upon that *wræce* 'vengeance' in the MS. form of 2771a, usually emended to *wræ[t]e* 'treasure.' That is, he "looks upon that vengeance" which they have inflicted upon the dragon by depriving him of his gold. This is the hollow triumph of the feuding ethic, and the gold is its sole and temporary reward. "How easily may a man be overcome by gold in the ground!" With the barrow's "roof" (2755) singled out for notice and the "wonders on the walls," which are probably tapestries, the prospect before Wiglaf also recalls that greatest of mead-halls, Heorot. If the Building of Heorot had something in it of the Tower of Babel, then perhaps the warning exclamation here applies to all men, no matter how heroic or good. Next Wiglaf, "one man alone" (2774), takes that "brightest beacon" to his lord. Poetically, this may mean that he is symbolizing the acquisitive streak in his lord Beowulf, "most eager for fame," and in heroic society generally. The context then swings from negative back to positive as we encounter Beowulf's gratitude to God for this favor.

Voices of Lament (2821–3027)

Three dismal celebrations of victory follow Beowulf's death. First the poet tells over the results of the battle in a labored, exhausted manner as though he had been through the battle himself (2821–45). Then Wiglaf rises from his "heroic Pietà" (Irving's fine phrase) to deliver his denunciation of the cowardly troop. The image of Wiglaf uselessly bathing his dead lord's brow is a revealing picture of a mental state. Still he could not change the course of events ruled by God, says the poet with grim metaphysical satisfaction. Wiglaf's grief and the hopeless acceptance of circumstance required inside the world of the poem (though a Christian audience would have a higher hope) are then expressed by Wiglaf's fully spoken moral indignation. This is the truest form of his grief. The very long first sentence of his speech is a masterful imitation of a man gargling in rage. The next sentence brilliantly organizes his feelings toward both his lord and the wretched troop. He finishes by formally proclaiming their ignominious fate. Their breaking of the *comitatus* bond is described here in terms of feud obligations and personal dishonor, rather than as an affective or moral bond. Not only the cowards in the troop, but also all their kinsmen, will be deprived of their rights and exiled. But no one could call Wiglaf vicious in the face of the magnitude of the event. He is entirely justified.

Then we hear a third voice responding to Beowulf's death. The poet speaks in the epic voice of the nameless Messenger who addressed the Geatish council, which is waiting as Beowulf's men did beside the mere. The council makes yet another dramatic audience, this time bearing witness to an action that will occur in the future. At the end of the speech the members even arise like the Danes: *Weorod eall ārās* 'the company all arose' 3030. Only now they go to view their dead lord. The Messenger's speech extends the skein of consequences in Beowulf's death to its utmost, and after his speech the theme of "looking upon the hoard" will return a second time like a refrain. The Messenger reviews the feuds with the Swedes and the Frisians ("the Merovingian" of 2921) and concludes with a prophecy that parallels Beowulf's dramatic preview of Ingeld's attack upon the Danes. His speech sounds many themes from the Lay of the Last Survivor, only now applied to the Geats' coming exile and slavery. The air darkens around these lines as they close with the theme of the Beasts of Battle, the carrion-feeding wolf, eagle, and raven. For a comparison of this use of the theme with its other appearances in OE. poetry, see Bonjour, *Twelve Papers*, pp. 135–49.

During the description of the battle at Ravenswood, there may be a faint echo of the dragon in the language applied to Ongentheow in 2956–57. Two young thugs of Hygelac—Wolf and Boar are their names in Old English—kill the old *folces hyrde* 'guardian of the people' and he goes down with almost as resounding a crash as the dragon. Whenever a superior force overcomes a war leader, as when the force of the Hetware overcame Hygelac (2913–20), the fall is heavy. The Messenger's speech also carries on the theme of "exchange." Earlier it was Beowulf's life for the treasure, a dear bargain, and now the ebb and flow of battle and the "worse exchange" of blows (2969) continue that metaphor. This swirling violence of the Swedish-Geatish battle comes to be a human metaphor for *wyrd* itself. The unstable circumstances of warrior life become the tragic destiny that all men in this world must expect. Along with this always expected slaughter of men (cf. 2999–3000), the Messenger has emphasized the theme of tremendous material reward for killing. And no man, he says, in a phrase that is neither praise nor blame, could reproach Hygelac for his inordinate reward to these two animal-named killers, since they had done great deeds in battle. The combination of these themes, though not conveyed to us in an ironic tone, may further convince the morally sensitive reader of the futility of buying glory or gold through battle-deeds.

A textual note: the Messenger refers to Beowulf as "he who long held the hoard and kingdom after the fall of heroes, the brave Scyldings." This allusion to the *hwate Scildingas* 'brave Scyldings' 3005–6 remains an unsolved puzzle. It could refer to the Danes during the time of Grendel's prosecution or to later events such as the Heathobard attack or Hrothulf's treachery. Or it could be an error for *Scil[f]ingas* 'the Swedes,' referring to the fall of Eanmund, Onela, or Ongentheow. The word *hwate* is sufficiently formulaic to be applied even to enemies in heroic poetry. A third possibility is that it is a more garbled error that just happens to make sense. Then

it would need more extensive emendation, such as Hoops's *scild-*
[w]ig[an]. We can only conjecture what effect the allusion was meant
to have. For a digest of some of the more indefatigable conjecturers'
arguments, see Wrenn-Bolton, pp. 205–6.

"To Look upon the Wonder" (3028–3109, esp. 3074–3075)

The Geats go to look upon the two immobile hulks, each a lord
of the earth in his way. Here the dragon is described as a perfectly
possible natural animal. His body can be measured (fifty feet long),
and its scales are scorched. The dragon is real and is the more a
"wonder" for it. But the treasure beside him now becomes magical,
mythical. The thousand years it has lain in the earth may be a
reference to Doomsday and the loosing of the giant Gog and Magog
upon the world in Revelations 20:7–8. The heathen spell upon the
gold—no man may touch it unless God so wills—is an inversion of
lines 168–69 where Grendel may not touch Hrothgar's gift-throne.
The "malice-roof" (3123) of the barrow may recall the gold roof
of Heorot and may allude to a patristic interpretation of the biblical
verse. See Carl T. Berkhout, *PLL* 9 (1973), 428–31. The poet is
working hard in this passage to modify and complicate our under-
standing of the hoard.

His description of the magic spell links Christian history with his
praise of Beowulf, the one man God thought fit to open the hoard.
The wrongful burying of the treasure (another biblical allusion?)
did not profit him who hid it. Its guardian killed men and was slain
in revenge. Then the perspective lengthens, and a new mystery is
considered: the unknown moment when any courageous man will
meet the end of life's journey, will give up the life of kinsmen in
the mead-hall (3062–65). In the following *swā-* clause Beowulf
is cited as an example. Previously, the hero's conduct has been
the departure point for the poet's examples: as Beowulf does, thus
should a man do. But now the process is reversed, and the poet's
comment creates a sudden new aesthetic distance. For a moment,
Beowulf's life is like the sparrow's flight through the lighted hall in
Bede. He could not know, himself, how he would meet his end.
Death is always a surprise, as Hrothgar said in his sermon.

What happens next is a major crux in *Beowulf*. In lines themselves
incantatory, with another *swā* 'thus' and another reference to Dooms-

day, the poet chants an ambiguous exoneration of Beowulf from the damnations of the treasure charm. His final "nonetheless" remark at 3074–75 has been interpreted so many different ways that the notes to Dobbie's edition require three compact pages of small print to outline the alternatives. Surely before the century is out someone will have written an entire book on the textual criticism of these two lines. I have followed Wrenn and Stanley in the general outlines of my interpretation in the text and translation. This keeps to the meanings that are possible without emendation. Even so, large areas of nuance remain unspecified: *gearwor* = more (or too) readily, eagerly, fully, clearly; *ēst* = bounty, prosperity, kindness, generosity, munificence. One literal rendering under this interpretation: "By no means more eagerly had he [Beowulf] previously examined the owner's bounty (prosperity) as expressed by gold." This construes *gold-hwate* with *āgendes ēst*. But two alternative translations of the same construction are "the treasure abounding in gold" (Smithers, Wrenn) and "the gold-bestowing munificence of the owner" (Stanley). Then, if we emend slightly to *gold-hwat* and construe it instead with *hē*, it might mean "gold-greedy." In another view, the "he" might be the hypothetical plunderer of the preceding line, and *āgendes* 'the owner's, the ruler's' might be a reference to God. One might also emend *næs hē* to *næ[fn]e* 'unless' and translate "unless the Possessor's favor were first shown the more clearly to him who desired the gold" (Donaldson's translation of Klaeber's text). Or one might translate "not before had he [Beowulf] beheld more fully the gold-abounding grace *(ēst)* of the Lord" (Chambers).

Most of these interpretations will have a direct bearing upon the poet's conception of Beowulf's moral relationship to the hoard. Is he damned under its curse? The poet has just said that God can protect man in this situation (3054–57), yet here the sense could be that the true force of the curse was not known till Beowulf died from it. See further Stanley, *Brodeur Studies,* p. 145. The real literary problem in the lines, if they are left unemended, is that they are an instance of litotes, ironic understatement. Our comprehension of any litotes is, by the nature of the device, mainly a matter of ear. Each reader must decide for himself how far to take whatever irony he hears and against what unstated standard the irony makes its measurements.

I have allowed my ear to be guided by the other contexts of the hoard. Of course conflicting echoes are heard, but rather than ending in complete befuddlement, I am moved to leave open the question of Beowulf's salvation or damnation. Who could in conscience make the significance of the whole poem turn upon one dark spot of smeared sense? Instead, I focus mainly on the cruel "kindness" of the hoard's owner (i.e., the dragon); his "gold-giving" has been destructive, useless. This strong irony is uttered in a moment of mystery, surrounded by a demonic unknown. The larger theme of 3058–74 is the acceptance of the inescapable. Beowulf has been the unwitting victim of his unknowable fate. Perhaps his very unwittingness leaves open the possibility that he is not utterly damned by the curse. Perhaps our seeing his fate now, in this longer perspective, is a tacit condemnation. Faced with a true wonder, we are balked from a conclusion, are left wondering.

This is only how I resolve the crux, however. Not everyone stands in wonder, and one of the most notable critics of the poem, J. R. R. Tolkien, goes so far as to stand aghast. He took the opening of Wiglaf's following speech to apply to Beowulf: "Often many must suffer through the will of one, as has happened to us" (3077–78). Of this remark, Tolkien says: "There could be no more pungent criticism in a few words of 'chivalry' in one of responsibility" (*E & S,* 1953, p. 18). Recently his interpretation has been much amplified, especially by John Leyerle (see Introduction). On the other side, the late G. N. Garmonsway understood Wiglaf's remark as a failure to perceive that Beowulf acted by a transcendent standard of conduct. He could not be a hero otherwise. Man does not live by common sense alone, Garmonsway aptly observed, and if there was a fatal necessity in Beowulf's insistence that he fight the dragon alone, still every hero must make as good a death as he can, and who is to call Beowulf's aspirations selfish? See further Garmonsway's article, "Anglo-Saxon Heroic Attitudes," in *Franciplegius,* pp. 139–46.

We cannot avoid the dilemma of these two conflicting readings with the philological dodge that *ānes willan* 3077a means "for the sake of one" instead of "through the will of one." Nor can we justifiably claim that the "one" is really the thief or the Last Survivor or the dragon. The lines following the bell-like *ān* are too exclusively focused on Beowulf's rash leap toward glory. Yet we should not be led by this passage into easy accusations of Beowulf. It is the critic's responsibility to utter whatever judgment he makes about Beowulf in the same tone of voice that Wiglaf achieves here. If there are the imprecations of a despairing grief in his tone, there is also a tinge of rueful admiration: "He *would* fight the dragon." But I still have not got it just right. It is a special tone, carried throughout the speech by a special sad-yet-easy sentence structure. Moreover, by Wiglaf's recounting the death scene to the Geats, the poet keeps it alive and present in our imaginations, resaying it one more time from the bravest viewpoint now left in the poem. At its conclusion we see that there is no doubt in Wiglaf's mind that Beowulf is quite good enough to dwell long in God's protection (3105–9). This, however, is no protection from the larger ironies of the whole poem.

The Final Rituals (3110–3182)

There is a movement toward restoring the social order in Wiglaf's "Now let us go see the hoard, look upon the marvel in the cave" and the preparations for Beowulf's burial. The pyre and barrow, described with such realistic detail, fully suit what is known of pagan practices in Sweden and England in the sixth and seventh centuries. The nameless Geatish woman who sings the prophetic lament at the cremation is also a figure from tradition (cf. Hildeburh at Hnæf's pyre in the Finnsburh Episode). Perhaps no other picture in the poem is so sharply focused, so brilliantly visualized, as the final Fitt XLIII.

The roaring fire is personified as a dancer, if the emendation of 3145 by Sophus Bugge is correct. Throughout the poem, fire has been personified as a greedy devourer, and hence it is akin to the Beasts of Battle. Here it is "awakened" and then takes its proper place in the ritual as a roaring warrior doing a funeral dance. Cult dances, though not at funerals, are well attested for seventh-century England. There is a warrior dancing with two spears on a buckle from Finglesham, Kent, and similar scenes on the Sutton Hoo helmet. The pagan element in Beowulf's cremation is strong without being explicitly cultic. The ascension of the smoke from the pyre directly toward heaven is a sign of good favor for the hero in the afterlife. For parallel crematory customs and beliefs among Scandinavian peoples, see H. M. Smyser's article in *Franciplegius* and P. B. Taylor, *Archiv* 201 (1965), 349–51, and *PQ* 42 (1963), 257–59.

The meaning of another personification—"Heaven swallowed the

smoke"—is taken by Professor Taylor as a sign of Beowulf's state
of grace, on the analogy of Odin's funeral in Snorri Sturluson. How-
ever, two features of the text in *Beowulf* complicate this view. First,
"the wind-mix subsides" favorably in the middle of the moaning and
roaring "until he [the fire] had broken through that bone-house."
This last kenning recalls the burning of another house, Heorot.
Secondly, heaven swallows the smoke (an odd verb, in any case,
much like the fire's "eating" in 3114) as a half-line conclusion that
rounds off the Geatish woman's prediction of future slavery and
humiliation. At the very least, the phrase has a double meaning,
positive for Beowulf and negative for the survivors.

The action of the whole episode has the rhythmic motion of a
chant. The finale recalls the burial of Scyld. Perhaps the strongest
verbal reminiscence is when the Geats "gave to the waves the guar-
dian of treasures, let the sea take him" (3133). Were this said of
Scyld, the *frætwa hyrde* 'guardian of treasures' would be a gold-
giving king. Thus the dignified language of the earlier ritual rings out
over the summary disposal of the dragon's bulk. The poet is seeking
to create an all-encompassing set of rituals in his language, by which
to end his own performance. This can be heard in the nuances re-
calling the Lay of the Last Survivor when the hoard is reburied.
Again, when Wiglaf orders the Geats to make preparations for the
funeral, the poet shifts into the historical present in lines 3114–19.
Traditionally these lines are assigned to Wiglaf, although there is no
formulaic introduction of the speaker (So-and-so *maðelode,* Such-
and-such's son). Perhaps we do better to assume that the poet him-
self makes a bold intrusion here to renew the prophetic force of the
Messenger's speech. This preview of Beowulf's cremation is mainly
devoted to how he survived earlier battles, safe in his armor. Now
the armor, which has played a symbolic role throughout the poem,
will burn with him who was the armor of the Geats against all shafts
of fortune. This feels like the closing of a piece of music.

The theme of "looking upon the hoard" is also brought to a close
with an ironical hint about *wyrd*: no one drew lots (*hlytme*) over
that plunder. Its lot and Beowulf's have already been decided. The
reburial of the hoard in Beowulf's barrow, "as useless to men as it
was before," is another ritual, with several meanings. One, it reiter-
ates the vanity of earthly wishes and the irony of the final fight with
the dragon. Two, it is a ritual acting-out of the Geats' grief for their

beloved leader. Three, the hoard is now Beowulf's, his alone, hard-earned like his fame. Thus to place it with him is to act from the deepest sense of fittingness, to honor him appropriately. Some critics have wondered why the Geats do not use the treasure to buy peace from the Swedes and Franks in the future. This misses all the poetry of the act. The reburial occurs during the description of the noble barrow on the headland. The barrow and the hoard are fused in a double image that immediately becomes song: the final mourning and panegyric.

The final dozen lines focus on the fact of death, not on what will happen after death. The twelve riders in the final ritual undertake to praise Beowulf while mourning him. The two emotions of admiration and of grief, often experienced in poignant tension by the bereaved, are drawn together by an increasingly formal movement (notice the internal rhyme at 3172) till they meet in the final epitaph. "Thus mourned the Geats . . . " and the Geats recede into the past as the poet utters their, and his, final words about Beowulf. Lines 3180–82 read like a gravestone inscription. In fact they have much in common with classical epitaphs and the formulaic conclusions of saints' lives. The first three adjectives are, literally, "the *kindest* to men" "the most *humane* (or *courteous*)," and "the *gentlest* to his people." Obviously they are the positives that confirm Beowulf's earlier negatives, "I slew no kindred, sought no enemies, swore no false oaths" (2736 ff.). He was a calm, strong and guileless king, and these words sum up the elegiac feelings of the nation that has lost him. However, the fourth adjective, *lof-geornost* 'most eager for fame,' is poised in gentle tension with the three less loaded adjectives. It is no shame for a hero to seek glory. For the poem to come to rest finally on *lof-geornost* is perhaps to acknowledge that ideal. On the other hand, through the whole poem we have been invited to look beyond earthly fame as the highest good. Does "most eager" imply "too eager"? By ending upon this word, the poet firmly balances his two perspectives on Beowulf.

Afterword to the 2006 Edition

I am very gratified that over the years this book has found a wide and varied audience, from high school students to Ph.D. candidates as well as the general reader interested in poetry. I believe that its longevity is due to my putting the original Old English poem on display in a fairly comprehensible fashion, even though there are places where I would now refine my facing translation or expand the commentary.

Increasingly in the last decade colleagues who regularly use this book have asked me if I would ever consider updating it. I have brooded over what an "update" could possibly mean for a book that is already selective and is aimed at making *Beowulf* available as poetry to those who have not studied Old English before. Certainly it cannot mean a full account, nor even a cursory survey, of the many developments in the study of the poem over the last quarter century. At the same time, some of those developments do bear upon the literary interpretation of the poem. Moreover, new research tools have come into being, the ongoing *Dictionary of Old English* (*DOE*) chief among them, that give us a more accurate understanding of words and concepts in Old English. Recent editions and re-examinations of the MS. have led me to change my mind about the best way to render particular lines. In addition, a number of difficult passages remain in dispute.

The first section below is a digest of what I regard as the most important work on topics that affect my interpretation and translation of the poem. This section is highly selective and has no pretensions to complete coverage. All the different areas of *Beowulf* study, past and present, are already thoroughly discussed in the now indispensable *A Beowulf Handbook,* eds. Bjork and Niles (to

380

1994), and Andy Orchard's *A Critical Companion to "Beowulf"* (to 2002), both of which contain exhaustive bibliographies. For an annotated bibliography from 1979 to 1990, see Hasenfratz, *Beowulf Scholarship*. For reviews of research published since 2002, see the *Beowulf* section of "The Year's Work in Old English Studies" appearing annually in the *Old English Newsletter* (*OEN*).

In the second section below I briefly discuss the choices that editors must make in punctuating and emending the sole surviving MS. of the poem, and then list the specific points in the original text where I would now choose a different reading or where I regard the meaning as still uncertain.

All new references in this Afterword, cited here by author or short title, are listed in full in Section IV of the Bibliography. The *DOE* and *OEN* appear under Healey and Liuzza, respectively.

I.

Scholars still "do not know by whom, how, when, or where *Beowulf* was composed" (p. 247 above), but the range of suggested possibilities has expanded, and scholarship on the subject has flourished mightily. The articles in the 1981 Colin Chase volume (p. 410 below) made many scholars consider the possibility of dating the poem to the Danish invasions of the ninth and tenth centuries. On paleographical grounds, in that volume and his own book of the same year, Kevin Kiernan even advanced a theory that the composition of the poem is as late as the production of the MS. itself (ca. A.D. 1020, in his view). For objections to Kiernan's theory, see R. D. Fulk in *PQ* for 1982, among others. On different paleographical grounds, Michael Lapidge recently posited an archetype of the surviving MS. dated to no later than A.D. 750 (see *ASE* 29), while Fulk's analysis of the poem's meter and phonology suggested initial composition by no later than 725 if originally Mercian, or 825 if originally Northumbrian (see his *History*, § 420). On the other hand, the earlier groundbreaking work of Ashley Crandall Amos convinced many of us that there are few, if any, safe linguistic grounds for dating Old English poems. Writing in 1997 not only about its date, but also the poem's provenance, author, and audiences, Robert E. Bjork and Anita Obermeier noted a trend for scholars to prefer a later date and possibly a southern locale, but they concluded that we have arrived only "at a cautious and necessary incertitude" (*Handbook,* p. 33). This remains true today. (Further discussion by Liuzza in Baker, Howe in Chase 1997 rpt., Fulk in *ASE* 32, Cronan in *ASE* 33, and Newton, *The Origins of "Beowulf."*)

I still hold the same views about "Composition and Authorship" (pp. 249–52 above) without any substantial change of opinion about the oral vs. written controversy. Even if we accept the idea that the extant text is the product of many re-singings by more than one scop, we still can decide to take our unique MS. copy as what we choose to experience as the poem. It could even be argued that, since we live in our own writing-bound culture, we can only have a literary experience of this one text recorded in writing, to which most readers respond as if to a unified sensibility, though not provably a single "author." Nevertheless, the study of *Beowulf* as traditional oral poetry has seen great advances since the 1970s, particularly in the work of John Miles Foley and John D. Niles. Equally valuable is Katherine O'Brien O'Keeffe's *Visible Song,* a pioneering description of what she calls "transitional literacy." The late Edward B. Irving, Jr.'s, *Rereading "Beowulf"* is perhaps the best recent volume of literary criticism based upon the notion of oral composition; his close readings often transcend the controversy. Andy Orchard has conveniently charted the repeated formulas in the poem for the light they might throw "on the poem's structure or the poet's compositional technique (or both)": see his *Companion,* Appendices II and III.

As for the prosody of the poem, I continue to feel confident that a careful perusal and enthusiastic application of the Guide to Reading Aloud (pp. 29–38 above) will, with a little coaching or listening to a tape, give the reader everything necessary for voicing *Beowulf* aloud as poetry, that is, as formed speech that obeys its own artistic rules. Yet it is important to note that the intensive analysis of Beowulfian prosody, and of Old English meter generally, has gone far beyond the systems of scansion described in my Guide. I would call particular attention to the works by Cable, Creed, Fulk, Hutcheson, Kendall, and Russom. I also acknowledge an important omission in not having mentioned in the Guide the central work of A. J. Bliss. All these works are perhaps only for specialists, but any one of them can improve the ear of a reciting reader.

It is a truism of literary study that we do not read a text without supplying some sort of context for it. And we choose the contexts in which we understand it on the basis of our own often unexamined assumptions. Today Anglo-Saxon studies as a field has gained a sharp self-consciousness about its own assumptions. In *The Search for Anglo-Saxon Paganism,* E. G. Stanley described the attitudes of the nineteenth-century Continental scholars who invented this academic subject, while Carl T. Berkhout and others have described in detail the careers of English Renaissance antiquaries, including Lawrence Nowell, the first known possessor of the *Beowulf* manuscript. The most searching examination of the ways we have constructed our contexts, and the motives behind them, has come from Allen J. Frantzen. His book *Desire for Origins* makes it crystal clear that the contexts for the study of *Beowulf* do not exist on their own somewhere in the past, waiting to be discovered by modern scholars, but rather that we invent and apply them as our predilections lead us. Over the years, critics' views of the poem have been shaped (not always consciously) by religious, political, and nationalistic motivations.

There are many critical approaches to *Beowulf,* using different contexts. Some apply distinctly modern theoretical concepts and do not bear upon my reading of the poem. Interesting examples of deconstructionist and feminist approaches may be found in Gillian Overing's *Language, Sign, and Gender in "Beowulf,"* while James W. Earl uses what he calls "psychoanalytic anthropology" in his *Thinking About "Beowulf."* Other critics have approached the poem in the context of Anglo-Saxon cultural history; see particularly Nicholas Howe, *Migration and Mythmaking,* and Craig R. Davis, *Demise of Germanic Legend.* Still others have examined the world of the poem from the viewpoint of anthropology, as does John M. Hill in *The Cultural World.* See further his chapter on "Social Milieu" in the *Handbook.*

The great majority of literary studies take the poem itself as providing most of its own contexts, though sometimes those contexts are linked with other poetic or historical texts. The critical topics are of course quite various. A sampling might include diction, variation, formulas, macrostructure, microstructure, unity, episodes and digressions, myths, historical analogues, literary analogues, allegory, and symbolism. These and other topics are treated extensively

in different chapters of the *Handbook*. I have already had my say in
my Introduction, Background, and Commentary about what I con-
sider the most important literary features of the poem. Recent col-
lections of literary criticism of *Beowulf* include those edited by
Baker, Donoghue, Fulk, and Howe. The best short book-length
treatment of the poem remains George Clark's 1990 *Beowulf* in
Twayne's English Authors series.

The historical contexts possible for the poem are continually
being enriched in one way or another. Students of literature were
grateful indeed when three distinguished Anglo-Saxon historians
brought out *The Anglo-Saxons* in 1982 (listed under Campbell in
Section IV of the Bibliography), an up-to-date and integrated
overview of Anglo-Saxon political and social history. Although we
do not know in which century, or in which Anglo-Saxon kingdom
or monastery, the poem should be located, the more that we can
know about the period, the better. The literary history of the entire
period has been treated by Greenfield and Calder, and most re-
cently by Fulk and Cain. Students will also find useful introduc-
tions to Old English literature in Donoghue's book of that name,
and in the collections edited by Godden and Lapidge, and by Li-
uzza. Two collections that focus on current critical approaches are
edited by Aertsen and Bremmer, and by O'Brien O'Keeffe.

One historical context for the poem that has developed consider-
ably in recent years has been archaeology. In 1977 the Sutton Hoo
ship-burial and the great hall at Yeavering dominated our percep-
tion of the relationship between the poem and material reality. Sut-
ton Hoo remained the determining context for the goods and burial
customs mentioned in *Beowulf* all during the time that scholars be-
lieved the poem had to have an early date. (See further Roberta
Frank, "The Odd Couple.") But British medieval archaeology has
developed at a rapid rate since the 1970s, and there have been no-
table new Anglo-Saxon and Viking discoveries. Comparisons with
archaeological finds elsewhere in Northern Europe have also
proven fruitful. Catherine M. Hills sketched archaeological devel-
opments to 1992 in her chapter in the *Handbook* and concluded, in-
terestingly enough, that the Anglo-Saxon evidence found up to that
point was "at least partly compatible with a later date of composi-
tion than that usually suggested by reference to Sutton Hoo" (her
p. 310). For work subsequent to 1992, see the "Archaeology" sec-
tion in "The Year's Work in Old English Studies" in *OEN*.

Then there is the perennial double question of the nature of the hero and the metaphysical design in which the poem places him. Analyses of both Beowulf's character and the poet's viewpoint on the story have proceeded apace in the last few decades without any final resolution, and none is likely to occur soon. Most interpretations of the poem's design and purpose have usually been bound up with assumptions about its presumed historical circumstance. Even if we did not have to make unprovable assumptions about an historical context, any consensus in criticism would probably continue to be thwarted by the poem's elliptical and ironic strategies of both style and design. The poet rarely commits himself to a single judgment on the actions of his characters, offering instead competing perspectives and oblique analogies.

Recent scholarship has refined the meanings of what too often are undefined blanket terms in the criticism of *Beowulf,* "Christian" and "pagan," so much so that I would no longer dare to say, as I do on p. 259 above, that the Germanic and Christian traditions are as fused in *Beowulf* as they were in Anglo-Saxon society. Such a statement assumes too symmetrical an analogy between literature and life. Moreover, while there may have been different kinds of fusion in various periods and social strata, critics of the poem continue to disagree on whether the Germanic past of the story is fused with, or at odds with, the evident Christianity of the poet.

We can describe with confidence the Christian concepts in the poem (see pp. 258–60, 268–77 above, and Orchard, *Companion,* pp. 130–68), but the precise type of "Christianity" enjoyed by the poet and his audience will depend on which century we choose to place the poem. In an important reappraisal of seventh- and eighth-century sources, the late Patrick Wormald (p. 414 below) showed that our modern understanding of the Conversion had been skewed by an overreliance on a single source, the Venerable Bede, and his persuasive picture of a wholesale exchange of one set of values for another. Wormald demonstrated that both secular poetry and ecclesiastical prose were products of an aristocratic society, and argued that this "warrior nobility" had successfully assimilated the new faith while retaining many of its earlier values (his p. 57). If we choose to date the poem later in the period, it is probably equally unwise to think of a monolithic Anglo-Saxon world-view, particularly in the Danelaw: Judith Jesch has recently described the evidence for a "light pagan colouring" that continued for several generations among Anglo-Scandinavians in northern England during the tenth and eleventh centuries. For that period, she urges that we abandon "our strictly dichotomous and antithetical view of paganism and Christianity" ("Scandinavians and 'Cultural Paganism' in Late Anglo-Saxon England," in Cavill, pp. 55–68; quotes on p. 67).

In his chapter on this topic in the *Handbook,* Edward B. Irving, Jr., usefully discusses the three different meanings "pagan" has had in *Beowulf* criticism: literal, vestigial, and ethical (his pp. 177–80). As for the Christianity of the poem itself, he finds it "distinctly limited" and "tailored to the dimensions of heroic poetry" (his p. 186; see further his essay in *ASE* 13). Irving's view assumes that the poem belongs to a single genre, heroic poetry. However, as has been said many times, *Beowulf* is a poem that is over before it begins; it anticipates its end in its beginning. Its "pastness" and its elegiac elements are undeniable. The poet's view of his noble characters and their actions in the past may well be critical while at the same time admiring (pp. 27, 377, 379 above). The most influential presentation in the last twenty years of this binocular view of the poem has been Fred C. Robinson's elegant little book, *"Beowulf" and the Appositive Style* (p. 414 below), which takes the position of E. G. Stanley's article on the "Hæthenra Hyht" (p. 408 below) and extends it through a masterful presentation of the poet's deployment of appositions of several kinds: lexical, grammatical, and narrative. These characteristics of the poem's style create a kind of openness of meaning, since apposition does not state the precise relationship between the two things apposed (for the parallelism and parataxis of grammatical apposition, see pp. 8–9 above).

Robinson argues that the poet intended these different kinds of apposition to be controlled equivocations by which his audience would understand, for instance, both Christian and pre-Christian meanings of words like "metod" or "god" at the same time. (This view underlies the decision not to capitalize such words for God in Mitchell and Robinson's edition of *Beowulf.*) While I agree with Robinson that the poem often combines tones of admiration and regret, I demur on this one point about lexical appositions. I do not think that phrases like "ēce Dryhten" ("eternal Lord"), which occurs twice in *Cædmon's Hymn* as well as many times in *Beowulf,* are actually "ambiguous poetic words" that "hold in suspension two apposed word meanings" (his p. 31). We don't have clear external evidence that Anglo-Saxons could hear a specifically "pre-Christian" or "pagan" meaning in a word like "Metod" ("Ruler, Measurer"). Robinson's lexical argument is ultimately driven by the subject matter of the poem: "It is quite simply the dramatic setting of the poem that activates the non-Christian meanings of words" (p. 49). I can certainly agree that, in Hrothgar's "sermon" to Beowulf, for instance, the deliberate omission of any reference to salvation creates a sense of benighted mortality, but it is hard to imagine that Hrothgar's metaphor of spiritual armor had no Christian associations for an Anglo-Saxon audience in any period.

Paul Cavill has convincingly shown that "for the Christian ideas he chooses to use, the poet employs mostly the standard words and images that were current in the range of Old English poetry now extant." He suggests that "the Christianity of the poem is much more ordinary and less idiosyncratic than has been asserted in recent years" ("Christianity and Theology in *Beowulf*," Cavill, pp. 15–39; quotes on p. 39). That the characters speak in this standard Christian language does not invalidate Robinson's sense of a forever-lost Germanic "then" as seen from a Christian "now." Indeed, his elaboration of the other types of apposition in the poem is authoritative, and his treatment of the poem's style is deeply engaging. Robinson's view of appositions provided the basis for my 1992 article on "Lyric Time in *Beowulf*," in which I explore how the poem's patterns of sonorities reinforce its contrast between human time and God's existence outside of time.

All in all, my interpretation of the poem has not changed substantially over the years, although I have learned a great deal from subsequent *Beowulf* scholarship and criticism. I am pleased to see my sense of the poem's deliberate indeterminacy (pp. 27–28 above) confirmed by John D. Niles's emphasis on the poem's multiplicity, which, taken with our newly "self-reflective criticism," leads him to "cast doubt on anyone's claim to have the power to name *the* meaning of *Beowulf*" (*Handbook*, p. 9). Recently, in fact, Johann Köberl published an entire book titled *The Indeterminacy of "Beowulf."* I agree wholeheartedly with Nicholas Howe that "we should also entertain the possibility that there was never a single, commonly accepted reading in Anglo-Saxon England of the poem we call *Beowulf*. Instead, as is typical of complex texts, we should accept the likelihood that for as long as people knew the poem in Old English there may have been different, possibly contradictory readings of the poem—even among those who lived at the same time and in the same place. . . . Our sense of the past and its poetry should honour the same possibilities for subtlety, contingency, and contradiction we admit in our time" (Chase rpt., p. 220).

II.

Recent scholarly work on the Old English text has led me to re-examine my editorial choices: to emend, not to emend, or to accept a conjecture. I believe most of them remain justifiable, but new examinations of the MS., especially by Kevin Kiernan and R. D. Fulk, and new arguments for alternative readings have led me to make a number of small changes as well as several substantive reinterpretations.

I have gone back over my text in the light of the subsequent editions of Nickel et al., Mitchell and Robinson, George Jack, and Kiernan et al., and the work of such textual scholars as Fulk and Alfred Bammesberger. I am especially grateful to Professor Fulk for his generosity in sharing with me a number of his forthcoming articles prior to their publication. I have also reviewed Birte Kelly's lists in *ASE* 11 and 12 of conjectures and emendations in earlier editions, and I have made extensive use of the digitally enhanced facsimile of the MS. in the *Electronic Beowulf*. The new fourth edition of Klaeber, edited by Bjork, Fulk, and Niles, was not yet available when this Afterword went to press.

On the issue of punctuation, I am in a sense fortunate that the following notes are limited to comments on my original edition as it stands. If I were given the opportunity to punctuate the Old English text anew, I would be at a loss about how to proceed confidently. There is no longer any such thing as "the naked text" in literary studies today. Scholars have recently emphasized the extraordinary degree to which any edition digests for the reader a great deal of the data that confront the editor, who necessarily omits some features and subjectively emphasizes others. For *Beowulf* this has been demonstrated engagingly by James W. Earl in "The Raw and the Cooked." Punctuation is by its nature a form of editorial intervention and interpretation (Where does one sentence end and another start?), but the application of modern punctuation to Old English poetry can be especially misleading because of the parallelism and parataxis of its style. Punctuation is a particular problem in sequences in which one phrase seems to go equally well with those that precede and follow it. A good example of this is the conjectural reconstruction in my note below to lines 2228–30, where the punctuation of my translation is deliberately left open, to show the grammatical ambiguity in Old English. Mitchell and Robinson discuss this and related problems in their edition, pp. 172–75, and Mitchell and Susan Irvine have recently tried out a new system of representing Old English syntax in "*Beowulf" Repunctuated*.

In one respect, I definitely now know that, if I could, I would change my presentation of the Old English text (p. 42 above) so that it followed George Jack's practice of indicating with square brackets all emendations by omission. For example, at 2296b the MS. reads "hlæwū" (= hlæwum). All editions emend silently to "hlæw," but Jack prints it as "hlæ[w]," which I think is far preferable.

I also have modified my stance toward emendation so that it is more in line with current thinking. Fulk, "Textual Criticism," *Handbook*, pp. 35–53, has traced the trends in editing *Beowulf* from the too-free conjectural emendations against which Sisam and Robinson argued (p. 43 above) to the subsequent ultraconservative method of preserving the MS. readings if at all possible. In 1977 I retained a number of MS. readings, often concurring with Wrenn-Bolton. However, at many hard spots I also followed what consensus I could find in the modern editorial tradition. Today I acknowledge the criticism of Raymond P. Tripp, Jr., "On 'Post-Editorial' Editions," who takes me and other editors to task for accepting traditional decisions too readily and not trying to find new solutions to problem passages. In addition, I was still under the spell of Klaeber's edition even as I resisted it, and did not often question his glossary, the magisterial influence of which has been well emphasized by Robinson, "*Beowulf* in the Twentieth Century" (see also Fulk, *Handbook*, p. 51).

Some of my changes below reflect our new skepticism about "the received text" of the mid-twentieth century. There is, moreover, a growing and healthy trend toward seeing the production of the *Beowulf* manuscript as a composite enterprise by several people (perhaps more than the two scribes), probably layered over time, with a component of oral performance somewhere behind its formulas and structural patterns. Such a "text," if that is the right word, undoubtedly played a much different role in its culture than the MS. text does in ours today. But that does not mean that we cannot try to reconstruct something like the likeliest exemplar of the surviving copy. (For a contrary view, see A. N. Doane, "*Beowulf* and Scribal Performance," in Amodio and O'Brien O'Keeffe, pp. 62–63). The *Beowulf* scribes made identifiable errors in the mechanics of copying: confusion of similar letterforms, eye-skips, dittography, and metathesis. Even Kiernan, the most conservative edition that I have examined, recognizes these types of errors.

I still incline toward the conservation of MS. forms when possible. However, lately the sense that the MS. is a record (albeit often a faint one) of living practices has led some scholars to decry a knee-jerk editorial conservatism. They believe that there is a place for well-grounded emendations in the edited text. Such emendations must take into consideration the full range of Old English philology, paleography, literary style and structure, and such cultural contexts as we can determine with certainty. One has to be broadly eclectic to find the most cogent grounds in each case, since those grounds will vary from passage to passage (see further Fulk, "Some Emendations," forthcoming). Even then, such judgments, no matter how balanced or sound one feels them to be, will be subjective to some degree, as E. Talbot Donaldson wittily demonstrated in "On the Psychology of Editors."

Case by case, in the notes below I have been conservative when possible and conjectural when necessary. I continue to rank highly the editorial choices that enhance what I conceive to be the literary style of the poem. At times I prefer fluency and syntactic continuity to awkward MS. readings. I have not hesitated to accept what I consider reasonable conjectures when it is clear to me that a word or words have been lost. I have tried to make the poem as continuously readable as the damaged MS. will permit, while at the same time refining my earlier representation of the Old English text whenever I can.

"Kiernan" stands for the *Electronic Beowulf* and "M&R" for Mitchell and Robinson's edition of *Beowulf*. "Em." stands either for "emend" or "emendation(s)."

18a, 53b: Conservative editions retain the puzzling MS. readings "Beowulf" for the name of Scyld's son in the Danish line (pp. 278–79 above). While it is likely enough that the scribe misunderstood an original "Beow" or "Beawa" in his exemplar (see Jack, pp. 10–11, his note to 53b, and Bruce, *Scyld and Scef*), still he wrote this word very legibly, twice, and it is possible that he knew of an earlier Danish Beowulf. So I retract the em. "[*Bēow*]" and, along with other modern editions including Jack and M&R, now keep the MS. reading. The puzzle remains.

47b: Now, following Kiernan, I read with no change of sense "*gy*[*l*]denne."

159a: Because the word "āg-lǣca" is applied chiefly to Grendel and the dragon, it seemed reasonable to me to translate it usually as "monster," but I was overly influenced by Klaeber's glossary. The word occasionally also refers to Beowulf. The *DOE* now lists as its primary meaning "awesome opponent, ferocious fighter." Newly discussed by Jane Roberts, "Hrothgar's 'admirable courage,'" in Amodio and O'Brien O'Keeffe, pp. 241–46, with references to prior scholarship.

168–69: An alternative resolution of this notorious crux (discussed on pp. 287–88) is Robinson's translation in which he takes "grētan," "mōste," and "for" in different but well-attested senses: "By no means was he [Grendel] compelled by God to show respect for the throne, that precious thing, nor did he feel love for it." (The last phrase could also still be translated "nor know His love.") See his "Why Is Grendel's Not Greeting the *Gifstol* a *Wræc Micel*?" in Korhammer, pp. 257–62; quote on p. 262.

229–300: I partially disavow my earlier reading of the tones in the coast-guard's challenge (p. 294). While clearly there is tension in his speeches, it is better not to see his stiffness as comical. My interpretation, while it was great fun to write, is too modern a conception of the dramatic situation, especially for his reply at 287b–89, where Bammesberger, *Linguistic Notes,* pp. 84–86 (followed by Jack and M&R), takes "gescād" as "meaning" instead of "distinction," which then gives the translation: "A keen-witted shield-bearer who thinks rightly must know the meaning of both words and deeds." In an epic context such a declaration is not "almost stupidly wooden," a phrase I now retract.

304a: Better to emend for obvious sense: "hlēor-ber[g]an."

389b–90a: A good example of changing editorial philosophies over the years. Grein's conjecture, which I used, restores lost alliteration, but is not in the actual poem. Jack and M&R leave the two half-lines blank, which I now think is preferable. Kiernan prints the text consecutively with no indication of any loss. There is a similar loss, of only a half-line, at 403b.

404b: Literally, "so that he stood inside," if MS. "hēoðe," meaning "interior," is retained. But the word has no known cognates and the em. "heo[r]ðe" is preferable, as Fulk demonstrates in "Six Cruces," pp. 354–55. Trans. "till he stood on the hearth."

414a: With Jack, M&R, and earlier editors, it is better to assume an omitted crossbar and em. "hādor" to "ha[ð]or," a rare poetical word. Translate "under the restraint (or confinement) of heaven (or the sky)." This is an instance in which the authority of Klaeber's glossary has impeded a likely reading. Fulk, "Some Lexical Problems," explains how the em. improves meter and matches Old Norse cognates.

431b–32a: M&R do not emend to "[ond]" as I and others do, but treat the two half-lines of the MS. reading as vocative address first to the Geats and then to the Danes. This would foreground Beowulf's intention to cleanse Heorot "āna" ("alone"), but it seems an unlikely construction, given that he is already in the midst of asking Hrothgar for a favor.

443b: Kiernan clearly shows "o," not "a": read "Gēotena" with same meaning.

445a: An alternative word division accepted by many is "mægen-hrēð manna," which avoids the question of whether the unusual name *Hrēð-menn* identifies the Danes or the Geats. The alternative also gives better alliterative weight to the half-line. Trans. "the great glory of men," or "the glorious host of men" as does Fulk in "Six Cruces," pp. 356–58.

457a: An alternative restoration, first offered by Grundtvig, is "F[*or w*]ere-fyhtum"; M&R gloss this hypothetical noun as a "fight arising from uncompensated murder" and Wrenn-Bolton as "defensive warfare." The word is unattested, but adds only three letters to make sense of the MS. Trautman's em., which I follow, adds more letters but is a well-attested word. Both restorations make sense in context and restore the "w" needed for alliteration.

461b: The em. I have followed makes sense in context and only changes one letter, but Grundtvig's em. "[*Wede*]ra" ("of the Geats") is widely accepted, since it is a frequent name in the poem and makes sense in context.

499a and ff.: The interpretations of Unferth by Bloomfield and Robinson (p. 301 above) have been challenged half a dozen times over the years, but both his character and his name remain in dispute. The "un-" may be an intensifier rather than a negative element. The MS. spelling of "Hun-" has been claimed to be authentic on various grounds, often as a genuine Germanic name-element. However, editions and criticism continue to print the name as "Unferth." Representative discussions: Roberts, "Old English *Un-*"; Fulk, "Unferth and His Name."

578a: Other editions regularize MS. "hwaþere" to "hw[*æ*]þere," correcting the scribe's minor spelling error. I now do so too.

581a: M&R would keep MS. "wudu" ("wood") and trans. this half-line as "the tossing ship." I follow the em. of most editions to "w[*a*]du" ("waves"). In their note to this passage M&R appear to assume that Breca and Beowulf were rowing throughout this episode, but at 553b ff. Beowulf is pulled to the bottom by a seamonster. M&R also think "Finna land" 580b cannot be modern Finland, which would be "preposterously remote." Like many others, however, I regard the passage as an account of Beowulf's marvelous exploits. Whether the contest began by swimming or rowing depends on how one takes "on sund rēon" 512b, the difficulties of which are discussed by Fulk, "Afloat in Semantic Space."

600a: MS. "sendeþ" is preferable to the em. "s[nē]deþ" ("devours"), which I accepted, assuming metathesis. Usually "on-" is prefixed to "sendan" when it means "send to death," a reading that Fulk neatly obtains simply by a new word division, "swefeþ, ondsendeþ." The "ond" for "on" is either a variant spelling, or it may have arisen from the scribe seeing "ond onsendeþ" in his exemplar. See Fulk, "Some Emendations," forthcoming.

646b: Roberts (cited above in note to 159a) takes "āhlǣcan" here to refer to Beowulf, translating 646a–47 as "He knew that battle at that high hall was assigned to this awesome combatant" (her p. 245).

747b–48a: For the erasure before "rǣhte ongēan" I would now supply the pronoun "[*him*]" following Robinson, *PBA* 94, pp. 55–57, and Fulk, "Some Contested Readings," p. 194. The sense remains the same, but even with this extra object pronoun it is grammatically ambiguous. Literally, "the foe reached toward him with his hand." My trans. takes the foe ("fēond") to be Grendel.

875a: This is an excellent example of editorial subjectivity. The MS. "Sigemunde" is defensible as a paratactic parallel with "ellendǣdum" 876a, both dependent on "fram," as in my translation. Von Schaubert, Wrenn-Bolton, and Nickel keep the MS. reading. However, Klaeber, Jack, and M&R em. to "Sigemunde[*s*]" because "the construction seems slightly awkward" (Jack) and possibly the scribe dropped a final "s" before "secgan" 875b. On the other hand, Kiernan shows a large space between "Sigemunde" and "secgan," and parataxis is an essential feature of the poem's grammatical style.

980b: It now seems perversely ascetic of me to have kept MS. "Eclafes" for a likely "Ec[*g*]lafes."

984b–87a: "Almost certainly some [emendations] are needed" (Wrenn-Bolton) for this difficult passage, but "it is not indisputably defective in sense, grammar, alliteration, or meter" (Fulk, "Some Lexical Problems"). I do not have full confidence in the emendations that have been made to improve the sense accepted by Jack and M&R. My trans. follows Wrenn-Bolton's reading of the unemended MS.

1079b: If, instead of the em. "hē[o]" ("she"), we take the MS. "hē" and begin a new sentence at this half-line (thus the edition of Donald K. Fry, p. 411 below, Nickel, and Jack), then the reference is to Finn and his loss of worldly joy. The MS. certainly makes sense as is, but I persist in emending to the feminine pronoun because it is more poignant and better suits the futile role of the "peace-weaver" in the larger thematic design of the poem. See further pp. 329–30 above.

1130a: I would now emend to "þēah þe hē [ne] meahte." It is likely that the scribe, having written the "he," skipped a "ne" as he looked at the three minims beginning "meahte."

1372a: A better conjecture, with the same sense as "[hȳdan]," is "[helan]," which assumes the scribe made an eye-skip while copying the string of similar letters "hafelanhelan." Thus Gerritsen, "Emending *Beowulf*," p. 452.

1375b: Fulk, "Some Lexical Problems," argues on etymological grounds for Sedgefield's em. of "drysmaþ" to "[ð]rysmaþ." He points out that *drysmian* "grow dark" is not otherwise attested, unlike *ðrysmian* "suffocate," which makes good sense. My translation followed Wrenn's acceptance of Sedgefield, but in the OE. text I printed "d" in error. It is likely the scribe missed the crossbar on the "ð," a common copying error, as I can now attest.

1382a: Earlier scholarship took "wundini" to be an archaic form by which the poem could be dated to the seventh century, hence the MS. reading has been much discussed. I originally retained it, following Wrenn, so as not to emend possible evidence out of existence. However, the bulk of opinion now is that such an archaic form could never have survived centuries of copying and that the reading may in fact be "wun / dmi" (see textual note, p. 128 above), which is accepted by Kiernan in his note to the electronic facsimile of folio 163v, although I see "dini" there. He emends to "wund[*un*]golde" as a compound noun, which is reasonable enough. Most modern editors emend to "wund[*num*] golde" on the assumption that in the exemplar the four minim strokes of "nu" had a tilde over the last two, abbreviating an "m." Further discussion in Jack, at line 1382, and Fulk, "Contested Readings," pp. 195–96.

1537a: E. G. Stanley has proposed emending to "Gefēng þā be [*f*]eax[*e*]" ("Seized then by the hair"), partly for alliterative stress and partly by analogy with an actionable insult found in Anglo-Saxon law. See his "Did Beowulf Commit 'Feaxfeng' against Grendel's Mother?" *N&Q*, n.s.23 [vol. 221] (1976), 339–40.

1545a: "Ofsæt," which I and others have translated as "sat upon," I now reluctantly revise to "set upon" or "pressed down upon," following Robinson's demonstration that under "ofsittan" in the Old English Corpus of the *DOE* there are no entries with the meaning "sit upon." See his "Did Grendel's Mother Sit on Beowulf?" in Godden, Gray, and Hoad, pp. 1–7.

1546a: I would now supply "[*ond*]" for meter and read "brād [*ond*] brūn-ecg." It is very easy to omit the one-stroke OE. abbreviation "7" for "ond."

1809b: My trans. assumes that MS. "lēanes" ("reward, gift") is a scribal metathesis for "l[*ǣ*]nes" ("loan"), to which I would now emend the OE. text.

1855–65: In *PBA* 94, pp. 60–61, Robinson suggested that the earlier strife mentioned here may be echoed in a passage in Saxo Grammaticus in which the Geats were conquered by the son of Scyld (see also the note in M&R). This seems quite possible. Moreover, the passage as a whole traces out a familiar thematic design: past hostilities ended, peace newly pledged by gifts, and a future unity "toward friend and foe" (1864a). Still, questions remain. If the passage alludes to "lore about earlier hostilities between Danes and Geatas" which later generated the reference in Saxo, does it matter that in our poem the son of Scyld is Beowulf the Dane (lines

18, 56)? Also, the language is sufficiently general that the "malicious attacks / which they weathered before" could be enemy attacks against both of the two tribes, instead of conflict between them.

1862b: Accepting Robinson's interpretation of the passage makes the MS. reading "ofer heaþu" ("after the war") at least as likely as Kluge's em. "ofer hea[ƒ]u" ("across the sea").

1903b: Here I translated the MS. reading, but emended the OE. text, as every edition does, to "Gewāt him on naca" for meter (with "on" stressed). The trans. should have read, "The ship went forth."

1931b–32: This remains a problem passage (see pp. 349–52 above). One drawback to the interpretation I originally followed is that it assigns an adjective of praise, "fremu" ("excellent"), to the bad queen, though perhaps the word simply anticipates her later reform. Another problem is that, if it is a name and the subject of the sentence, then "Mōd-þrȳðo" should not end in "-o."

Recently Robinson in *PBA* 94, pp. 53–55, followed by M&R, has revived a solution proposed by Kemp Malone, "Hygd," *MLN* 56 (1941), 356–58. He divides "mōd" from the name "þrȳðo," identifies Hygd as the "fremu folces cwēn" and the subject of the sentence, and translates, "The excellent queen of the people weighed the arrogance of Thryth." The bad queen's name would then mean "force, physical power," in contrast to "Hygd" ("thought, reflection"). This solution is attractive in its coherence, but it has two drawbacks. It requires a negative meaning of "arrogance" for "mōd," which always has the sense of "mind, heart, spirit" when standing alone in *Beowulf*, although in ecclesiastical texts it can mean "pride, arrogance, power, violence." This reading also takes "wæg" ("weighed") in the figurative sense of "considered," a meaning not attested elsewhere in OE. for the verb "wegan" ("carry, wear, bear, have, move"). M&R cite the *DOE* s. v. "ā-wegan," 2.c. "consider, ponder," which may be a sufficient analogy, but there are only three citations under that figurative sense. Ideally, one would like firmer evidence that "wegan" itself means "consider."

These drawbacks and half a dozen parallels in other OE. poems have led R. D. Fulk in "The Name of Offa's Queen" to see no name at all in 1931b but a formulaic expression, "mōd-þrȳðo wæg" (lit. "carried arrogance," i.e., behaved arrogantly). Sisam first noted these parallels in 1946 (p. 349 above), the closest of which is "hige-þrȳðe wæg" ("bore arrogance") in *Genesis A*, line 2240b. They always occur in the second half-line and certainly seem formulaic. Seeing only a weak analogy between this bad queen and Cynethryth in the *Lives of the Two Offas,* Fulk (p. 622) develops a casual remark by E. A. Kock in *Anglia* 44 (1920), p. 103: her name "may just as well have been *Fremu.*" The *DOE* gives only scant evidence for this word as an adjective meaning "excellent, brave," and Fulk prefers to derive it from a well-attested noun, "fremu" ("advantage, benefit"). He treats the half-line as a proper name followed by an epithet,"Fremu, folces cwēn," and translates the lines as "It was with arrogance that Fremu, a princess of the people, acted, with terrible wickedness" (Fulk, p. 628). There is no barrier to this interpretation of "fremu," but I see no compelling reason to accept it, either. The confusion of names at a later date does not vitiate the *Lives of the Two Offas* as a loose analogue, and it remains likely that some form of a "þrȳð" name lies behind the extant text.

If we accept the Malone-Robinson interpretation, I would alter it slightly by giving "mōd" its more usual meaning of "mind, spirit, heart," and by taking "fremu" as a strong adjective with the same root and meaning as "fremfull" in the *DOE,* "kind, benign." I would then translate: "The kind queen of the people [Hygd] weighed the spirit of Thryth, [her] terrible crime." The parallel object phrase in 1932b sufficiently darkens its appositive, "mōd," and the alliteration on "f" stresses the contrast between "kind" and "crime."

If, on the other hand, one is persuaded by the many parallel formulas adduced by Sisam and Fulk or is unconvinced of a figurative meaning for "wæg," then 1931b is most likely to mean "behaved arrogantly." What would come next, if one does not take "fremu" as a proper name, is anybody's guess. I would now vote for the scribe making an eye-skip, of unknowable length, between two occurrences of "þrȳð." Fulk notes that a gap in the text was first suggested by Grundtvig in 1820.

1956a: Instead of Thorpe's em., read MS. "þæs" following Robinson, *PBA* 94, p. 54.

2024b: I am now disinclined to follow Malone in relying solely on Thorkelin B and, with other editions, instead add conjectural "[*is*]" at the line end.

2186a: M&R retain MS. "wereda"; the half-line then reads, "the lord of hosts." The more usual em., which I have adopted and translated, assumes metathesis of "Wedera."

2207–52: These lines occur on folio 179, the status of which has been the subject of much dispute since Kiernan's book appeared in 1981. The notes below supplement my brief discussion on p. 356 above.

2223b: As I mention in the textual note (p. 180) to the conjectural restoration "*þ*[*ēow*]" ("slave"), the social status of the thief can be important to interpretation. See further Andersson, "The Thief," and Frederick M. Biggs, "*Beowulf* and some fictions," pp. 61–69. The letter "þ" is now much clearer in Kiernan than in Zupitza or Malone, where it looked like "b"; Kiernan in the note in his facsimile thinks "*þ*[*ēof*]" ("thief") is "the most likely restoration" and regards his perception of the partial "f" as "fairly convincing." Fulk, "Some Contested Readings," pp. 214–15, sees no room for a fourth letter on the MS. line and proposes "*þ*[*ēo*]" as a rare spelling of "*þ*[*ēow*]."

2226b: For MS. "mwatide" I followed von Schaubert in accepting Thorpe's conjecture of "[*in*]w[*l*]āt[*o*]de" ("looked inside"), but I now favor either Dobbie's "[*onfun*]de" ("discovered") or Ettmüller's "[*in*] [*þ*]ā tīde" ("at that time"), which Fulk prefers, although he calls it "disappointingly banal." Fulk would translate the passage as "and the guilty man penetrated therein straightway at that time, so that terror arose for the visitor" ("Some Contested Readings," p. 217).

2228–30: In *"Beowulf" and the "Beowulf" Manuscript,* Kiernan argues that the illegibility of the last MS. line at the bottom of folio 182r and the top line and a half of 182v is due to the erasure and rewriting by Scribe II of repeated lines. Kiernan regards the entire leaf of folio 182, both recto and verso, as a palimpsest and sees

Scribe II as actually revising the beginning of the final part of the poem. He conjectures that, after erasing both sides of the folio, the scribe wrote upon the vellum while it was still damp, and then saw the need to correct himself by rubbing out certain words of his new text, leaving gaps "uniquely discolored and napped" (p. 229), which he never finished filling in. Although not all Beowulfians agree with every element of Kiernan's overall interpretation of the MS., most accept his important discovery that here there is an erased dittograph between the two occurrences of the word "sceapen."

I initially translated "[*earm*]-sc*ea*pen" far too loosely, guessing at a reference to the dragon. Literally, this restoration means "[the] wretchedly made/created [one]," and is more likely to refer to the thief. Fulk's own examination of the MS. has suggested enough clues for him to conjecture "[*ealdre nēþde*]" ("risked [his] life") for line 2228b. This would then be the line repeated and erased at the top of folio 182v. This repetition seems quite likely, as does Fulk's conjectural restoration of the following half-line, 2230a, "[*forht on ferhðe*]" ("afraid in spirit"). See Fulk, "Some Contested Readings," pp. 218–220.

Without the repetition, the two lines (2228 and 2230) would then read continuously. I would translate them and the next half-line: "Nevertheless, the wretched creature risked his life, afraid in spirit, then [or when] fear seized him, he sought [i.e., took] the treasure-cup."

2232a: Kiernan and Fulk both read "eorð-*se*[*le*]" with the same meaning as "eorð-[*hū*]*se*," namely "earth-hall."

2253a: Grein conjectured "fe[*ormie*]" ("polish") and Kiernan "f[*æ*]g[*rie*]" ("decorate"), but along with M&R and Jack I now accept "f[*orð bere*]" ("bear forth") as proposed by Gerritsen, "Emending *Beowulf*," pp. 448–50, and supported by Fulk, "Some Contested Readings," p. 198.

2276a: Zupitza's conjecture "[*ho*]r[*d*]" ("hoard") was accepted by Malone and subsequent editions. Kiernan reads "[*hearm*]?" ("harm") with ultraviolet light and fiber-optic backlighting, which nearly matches Thorkelin B's "bearn" but does not make much sense. Grein, followed by Fulk, "Some Contested Readings,"

p. 198, proposed "[*hea*]r[*h*]" ("altar, temple"), but that is a highly loaded word in the criticism of the poem. I do not want to turn the barrow into a pagan temple on the basis of a conjectural restoration. It is enough that the "hoard" itself is "heathen gold."

2405b: I translated this half-line as "by the thief's hand," but the noun "melda" is more precisely "a reporter, informer" or else "a betrayer," whom I still take to be the thief.

2525b–27a: My text and translation treat "fate" and "God" here as parallel subjects, but they need not be. Fulk, "Some Emendations" (forthcoming), takes "wyrd" ("fate") 2526b as a direct object of "getēoð" ("allots, decides") and, preferring Bugge's conjecture "[*feohte*]" ("the fight") in 2525a, translates as, "The fight will turn out for us just as God confers fate upon us." Jack's edition construes the passage similarly, translating "as the Creator of every man allots our destiny to us." This analysis of the grammar was first proposed by B. J. Timmer, *ES* 40 (1959), 49–52.

2564a: In translating "an edge not dull," I used Bugge's emendation, accepted by most editors, "un[*s*]lāw," but in error I printed the MS. reading in my OE. text, "ungl*e*aw," which in fact means "dull, unwise." Perhaps it is a better choice if it anticipates the failure of the sword a few lines later, but the likelihood of a "g" miswritten for "s" in the understated expression "an edge unslow" is increased by the placement of words on the MS. lines: "god" and "guð" stand on the next line up directly over "gl*e*aw." Correct my OE. text to read "un[*s*]lāw."

2965a: In Kiernan's ultraviolet image, the "d" of Wulf's patronym is clearly a "ð," so my OE. text should now read "Wonrē[*d*]ing," emended to agree with 2971b.

3066–73: These lines together with 3074–75 are discussed on pp. 374–77 above, which should be read with pp. 356–57. I treat the clause beginning "Swā wæs Bīowulfe" 3066a ("So it was for Beowulf") as an example of the preceding generalization, and then start a new sentence with the next "Swā" clause at 3069a, taken as another "Thus" statement illustrating the limits of human foreknowledge. However, the two "Swā" clauses could also be taken as a pair of correlative conjunctions making up one continuous sentence: "So it was for Beowulf . . . just as the princes of old had solemnly sworn it, that he who plundered the treasure would be guilty of sin. . . ." A. J. Bliss (p. 409 below) argues for this interpretation, treating Beowulf as in effect the plunderer, guilty of the sins of arrogance and avarice, and hence damned. Bliss aligns his overall view with those of Leyerle and Stanley (pp. 19–20, 26 above).

It is not clear from the text that "se secg" ("the man") in 3071 is necessarily a stand-in for Beowulf, although it is true that the pair of clauses can be construed in these two ways. I prefer not to use the ambiguous grammar either to indict or to exonerate the hero. See further Bruce Mitchell, "*Beowulf,* Lines 3074–75"; Jonathan S. Myerov, "Lines 3074–3075 in *Beowulf*"; and Frederick M. Biggs, "*Beowulf* and Some Fictions," pp. 66–68.

3074–75: These remain "the most obscure two lines in the poem" (p. 234 above) and continue to be crucial to interpretations of Beowulf's moral and metaphysical relationship to the hoard. As I say on p. 376, I am unwilling to base an entire interpretation of the hero on two poorly understood lines. I stand by my views there, and my translation of the lines, because nothing more convincing has yet come along.

To give only examples that do not emend: Bliss translates the lines as, "In the past he [Beowulf] had seen and understood the gold-bestowing favour of God much less clearly than he did now" (his p. 59). M&R translate: "Previously he (Beowulf) had not at all seen the gold-bestowing favour of God more clearly (i.e., God had never given Beowulf a greater treasure than this one)." Even this statement remains ambiguous. As Jack points out, it could mean either, "Only now did Beowulf fully perceive the magnificence of the hoard won from the dragon," or "Only now did Beowulf fully recognize that earthly treasure is bestowed by God alone." And either of those extensions of meaning needs to be understood at least somewhat ironically, given the context of Beowulf's imminent death.

Recently John Tanke, interpreting "gold-hwæte" as "gold-luck," sees the curse "as a protective spell laid upon a sacrificial treasure" resulting only in death, not damnation. He translates the lines as, "He had by no means more readily foreseen good luck with gold, the Owner's favor" ("Beowulf, Gold-Luck," p. 358). Along similar

lines, Fulk understands "gold-hwæte" as a curse on the gold and
suggests that the lines "mean Beowulf by no means had sought out
(or contemplated?) a curse on the gold, rather the owner's (God's?)
favor" ("Six Cruces," p. 363).

3121–82: These lines occur on folio 201, the last leaf of the poem,
and most of them have been restored in part either by "a late hand"
(Zupitza, p. 144) or by Scribe II (Westphalen, cited on p. 42 above,
his pp. 30–32). Gerritsen, "Have with you to Lexington," suggests
the restorer may have been Laurence Nowell. Kiernan believes the
restorer was Scribe II working some ten years after he originally
copied the poem. The folio "was apparently at one time an outside
cover"; its verso is soiled, faded, and especially hard to read (quote
from Fulk, "Some Contested Readings," p. 201).

3171b: For what I printed as "*k*yning," Kiernan's facsimile shows
"scyning," the MS. reading adopted by M&R, who emend to
"[*ond*] cyning" (first proposed by Sievers). Fulk, "Some Contested
Readings," pp. 205–07, discerns traces of the OE. ampersand "7"
and argues on both paleographical and metrical grounds that "we
should assume that *7 cyning* has been retouched as *kyning* (p. 206).
I now follow the emendation "[*ond*] cyning."

3181a: Both Kiernan and Fulk ("Some Contested Readings,"
p. 208) in their separate examinations of the MS. see "*manna*," not
Malone's "*mannum*."

3182b: On p. 379 above I wrote that the last word of the poem,
"lof-geornost" ("most eager for fame"), is "poised in gentle ten-
sion" with the previous three superlative adjectives. That tension is
increased if one emphasizes the negative meaning of the word at-
tested in ecclesiastical contexts, as do Stanley, "Hæthenra Hyht"
(p. 408 below), and Robinson, *Appositive Style*, pp. 80–82. The
tension is considerably lessened in other scholars' interpretations
of the lexical and comparative evidence; for some, the last word
is an unalloyed positive. See further Mary P. Richards, "A Re-
examination"; Roberta Frank, "Old Norse Memorial Eulogies,"
and her "Skaldic Verse" in Chase (p. 410 below), pp. 123–39; and
George Clark, "*Beowulf*: The Last Word."

Bibliography

I. Further Language Study

See suggested texts for learning Old English cited on p. 38.

II. Useful Bibliographies

Chambers, R. W. *Beowulf: An Introduction*. 3rd ed., with supplement by C. L. Wrenn. London: Cambridge University Press, 1959. [Contains an annotated bibliography classified by subject up to 1958.]

Fry, Donald K. *Beowulf and the Fight at Finnsburh: A Bibliography*. Charlottesville: University of Virginia Press, 1969. [A listing by author to July 1967. Entries are indexed by subject and line reference.]

MLA International Bibliography. Published annually by the Modern Language Association of America. [Vol I. lists work on *Beowulf* and other Old English subjects.]

Robinson, Fred C. *Old English Literature: A Select Bibliography*. Toronto: University of Toronto Press, 1970. [Lists basic works in Old English literature, language, and culture. Annotated and cross-referenced.]

III. Works Frequently Cited or Consulted in the Introduction and Commentary

Baum, Paull F. "The Meter of *Beowulf*," *MP* 46 (1948–49), 73–91, 145–162.*

Benson, Larry F. "The Literary Character of Anglo-Saxon Formulaic Poetry," *PMLA* 81 (1966), 334–41.

---

* For explanation of abbreviated citations, see following section.

——. "The Alliterative *Morte Arthure* and Medieval Tragedy," *TSL* 11 (1966), 75–87.

——. "The Pagan Coloring of *Beowulf*," in *OEP*, pp. 193–213.

——. "The Originality of *Beowulf*," in *The Interpretation of Narrative: Theory and Practice*, ed. Morton W. Bloomfield (Cambridge, Mass.: Harvard University Press, 1970), pp. 1–43.

Bessinger, Jess B., Jr., and Robert P. Creed, eds. *Franciplegius: Medieval and Linguistic Studies in Honor of Francis Peabody Magoun, Jr.* New York: New York University Press, 1965.

Blomfield, Joan. "The Style and Structure of *Beowulf*," *RES* 14 (1938), 396–403.

Bonjour, Adrien. *The Digressions in "Beowulf."* Oxford: Blackwell, 1950.

——. *Twelve "Beowulf" Papers, 1940–60.* Neuchâtel: Librarie E. Droz, 1962.

Brodeur, Arthur G. *The Art of Beowulf.* Berkeley: University of California Press, 1959.

Brown, Arthur, and Peter Foote, eds. *Early English and Norse Studies Presented to Hugh Smith in Honour of his Sixtieth Birthday.* London: Methuen, 1963.

Burlin, Robert B., and Edward B. Irving, Jr., eds. *Old English Studies in Honour of John C. Pope.* Toronto and Buffalo: University of Toronto Press, 1974.

Carrigan, Eamon. "Structure and Thematic Development in *Beowulf*," *Proceedings of the Royal Irish Academy* 66 (1967), 1–51.

Chadwick, Nora Kershaw. "The Monsters and Beowulf," in *The Anglo-Saxons: Studies in Some Aspects of Their History and Culture Presented to Bruce Dickins*, ed. Peter Clemoes (London: Bowes and Bowes, 1959), pp. 171–203.

Chambers, R. W. *Beowulf: An Introduction.* 3rd ed., with supplement by C. L. Wrenn. London: Cambridge University Press, 1959.

Creed, Robert P. "On the Possibility of Criticizing Old English Poetry," *Texas Studies in Language and Literature* 3 (1961), 97–106.

——, ed. *Old English Poetry: Fifteen Essays.* Providence: Brown University Press, 1967.

Curschmann, Michael. "Oral Poetry in Mediaeval English, French and German Literature: Some Notes on Recent Research," *Speculum* 42 (1967), 36–52.

Davidson, Hilda R. Ellis. *Gods and Myths of Northern Europe.* Baltimore: Penguin, 1964.

Dobbie, Elliott van Kirk, ed. *Beowulf and Judith.* The Anglo-Saxon Poetic Records, IV. New York: Columbia University Press, 1953.

Donahue, Charles. "*Beowulf*, Ireland and the Natural Good," *Traditio* 7 (1949–51), 263–77.

————. "*Beowulf* and Christian Tradition: A Reconsideration from a Celtic Stance," *Traditio* 21 (1965), 55–116.

Dronke, Ursula. "Beowulf and Ragnarök," *Saga-Book of the Viking Society for Northern Research* 17 (1969), 302–25.

Evans, J. M. "*Genesis B* and Its Background," *RES* 14 (1963), 1–16, 113–23.

Gardner, John. "Fulgentius's *Espositio Vergiliana Continentia* and the Plan of *Beowulf*," *PLL* 6 (1970), 227–62.

Garmonsway, G. N. "Anglo-Saxon Heroic Attitudes," in *Franciplegius*, pp. 139–46.

————, and Jacqueline Simpson, trans. *Beowulf and Its Analogues*. With a section on "Archaeology and Beowulf" by Hilda R. Ellis Davidson. New York: E. P. Dutton, 1971.

Goldsmith, Margaret E. *The Mode and Meaning of "Beowulf."* London: Athlone Press, 1970.

Greenfield, Stanley B., ed. *Studies in Old English Literature in Honor of Arthur G. Brodeur.* Eugene: University of Oregon Press, 1963.

————. "'Gifstol' and Goldhoard in *Beowulf*," in *Pope Studies*, pp. 107–17.

Hoops, Johannes. *Beowulfstudien.* Heidelberg: C. Winter, 1932.

————. *Kommentar zum "Beowulf."* Heidelberg: C. Winter, 1932.

Heusler, Andreas. *Deutsche Versgeschichte mit Einschluss des altenglischen und altnordischen Stabreimverses.* 2 vols. Berlin and Leipzig: W. de Gruyter, 1925–27.

Irving, Edward B., Jr. *A Reading of Beowulf.* New Haven and London: Yale University Press, 1968.

Jones, Gwyn. *Kings, Beasts and Heroes.* London and New York: Oxford University Press, 1972.

Kahrl, Stanley, "Feuds in *Beowulf*: A Tragic Necessity?" *MP* 69 (1972), 189–98.

Kaske, Robert E. "*Sapientia et Fortitudo* as the Controlling Theme of *Beowulf*," *SP* 55 (1958), 423–57, reprinted in *ABC*, pp. 269–310.

————. "*Beowulf*," in *Critical Approaches*, pp. 3–40.

————. "*Beowulf* and the Book of Enoch," *Speculum* 46 (1971), 421–31.

Klaeber, Frederick, ed. *Beowulf and the Fight at Finnsburg.* 3rd ed. Boston: D. C. Heath, 1950.

Lawrence, William W. *Beowulf and Epic Tradition.* Cambridge, Mass.: Harvard University Press, 1928.

Leyerle, John. "Beowulf the Hero and King," *MÆ* 34 (1965), 89–102.

————. "The Interlace Structure of *Beowulf*," *UTQ* 37 (1967), 1–17.

Lord, Albert B. *The Singer of Tales.* Cambridge, Mass.: Harvard University Press, 1960.

Lumiansky, Robert M., and Herschel Baker, eds. *Critical Approaches to Six Major English Works: "Beowulf" Through "Paradise Lost."* Philadelphia: University of Pennsylvania Press, 1968.

Magoun, Francis P., Jr. "The Oral-Formulaic Character of Anglo-Saxon Narrative Poetry," *Speculum* 28 (1953), 446–67.

———. "Beowulf and King Hygelac in the Netherlands," *ES* 35 (1954), 193–204.

———. "*Béowulf A*: A Folk-Variant," *Arv* 14 (1958), 95–101.

———. "*Béowulf B*: A Folk-Poem on Beowulf's Death," in *EENS*, pp. 127–40.

Malone, Kemp, ed. *The Thorkelin Transcripts*. Early English Manuscripts in Facsimile, I. Copenhagen, Baltimore, and London: Rosenkilde and Bagger, 1951.

———. *Studies in Heroic Legend and Current Speech*, ed. Stefán Einarsson and Norman E. Eliason. Copenhagen: Rosenkilde and Bagger, 1959.

———, ed. *The Nowell Codex*. Early English Manuscripts in Facsimile, XII. Copenhagen, Baltimore, and London: Rosenkilde and Bagger, 1963.

Mandel, Jerome. "Contrast in Old English Poetry," *ChR* 6 (1971), 1–13.

Nicholson, Lewis E., ed. *An Anthology of Beowulf Criticism*. Notre Dame, Ind.: University of Notre Dame Press, 1963.

———. "The Literal Meaning and Symbolic Structure of *Beowulf*," *Classica et Mediaevalia* 25 (1964), 151–201.

Notopoulos, James A. "Studies in Early Greek Oral Poetry," *Harvard Studies in Classical Philology* 68 (1964), 1–77.

Pope, John C. *The Rhythm of Beowulf*. 2nd ed. New Haven: Yale University Press, 1966.

Quirk, Randolph. "Poetic Language and Old English Metre," in *EENS*, pp. 150–71.

Rollinson, Philip B. "The Influence of Christian Doctrine and Exegesis on Old English Poetry: An Estimate of the Current State of Scholarship," *Anglo-Saxon England* 2 (1973), 217–84.

Rosier, James L., ed. *Philological Essays: Studies in Old and Middle English Literature in Honour of Herbert Dean Meritt*. The Hague: Mouton, 1970.

Schücking, Levin L. "Das Königsideal im *Beowulf*," *MHRA Bulletin* 3 (1929), 143–54; repr. and trans. as "The Ideal of Kingship in *Beowulf*," in *ABC*, pp. 35–49.

Shepherd, Geoffrey. "Scriptural Poetry," in *C & B*, pp. 1–36.

Shippey, T. A. "The Fairy-Tale Structure of *Beowulf*," *N & Q* 16 (1969), 2–11.

———. *Old English Verse*. London: Hutchinson University Library, 1972.

Sievers, Eduard. *Altgermanische Metrik*. Halle: Max Niemeyer, 1893.

Sisam, Kenneth. *Studies in the History of Old English Literature*. London: Oxford University Press, 1953.

———. *The Structure of "Beowulf."* London: Oxford University Press, 1965.

Smithers, G. V. *The Making of "Beowulf."* Durham, Eng.: University of Durham Press, 1961.

Stanley, Eric G. "Old English Poetic Diction and the Interpretation of the *Wanderer*, the *Seafarer*, and the *Penitent's Prayer*," *Anglia* 73 (1955), 413–66.

———. "Hæthenra Hyht in *Beowulf*," in *Brodeur Studies*, pp. 136–51.

———, ed. *Continuations and Beginnings: Studies in Old English Literature*. London: Nelson, 1966.

———. "*Beowulf*," in *C & B*, pp. 104–41.

Storms, Gotfrid. "The Figure of Beowulf in the O. E. Epic," *ES* 40 (1959), 3–13.

———. "The Significance of Hygelac's Raid," *Nottingham Mediaeval Studies* 14 (1970), 3–26.

Taylor, Paul B., and Peter H. Salus, "The Compilation of Cotton Vitellius A. XV," *NM* 69 (1968), 199–204.

Tolkien, J. R. R. "*Beowulf*: The Monsters and the Critics," *PBA* 22 (1936), 245–95; repr. in *ABC*, pp. 51–103.

———. "The Homecoming of Beorhtnoth Beorhthelm's Son," *E & S* 6 (1953), 1–18.

von Schaubert, Else, ed. *Beowulf*. 18th ed. [Originally ed. M. Heyne, revised by L. L. Schücking.] 3 vols. Paderborn: F. Schöningh, 1963.

Watts, Ann Chalmers. *The Lyre and the Harp: A Comparative Reconsideration of Oral Tradition in Homer and Old English Epic Poetry*. New Haven and London: Yale University Press, 1969.

Whitelock, Dorothy. *The Audience of "Beowulf."* Oxford: Clarendon Press, 1951.

———. *The Beginnings of English Society*. The Pelican History of England, vol. 2. Baltimore: Penguin, 1952.

Whitesell, J. Edwin. "Intentional Ambiguities in *Beowulf*," *TSL* 11 (1966), 145–49.

Wrenn, Charles Leslie, ed. *Beowulf with the Finnesburg Fragment*. 2nd ed. London: Harrap, 1958.

———, ed. *Beowulf with the Finnesburg Fragment*. 3rd ed. Revised by W. F. Bolton. London: Harrap, 1973.

Zupitza, Julius, ed. *Beowulf (Facsimile)*. 2nd ed., with new collotype photographs, introduction by Norman Davis. Early English Text Society, No. 245. London: Oxford University Press, 1959.

IV. Selected Additional Works (to 2006)

Aertsen, Henk, and Rolph H. Bremmer, Jr., eds. *Companion to Old English Poetry.* Amsterdam: VU University Press, 1994.

Amodio, Mark C., and Katherine O'Brien O'Keeffe, eds. *Unlocking the Wordhoard: Anglo-Saxon Studies in Memory of Edward B. Irving, Jr.* Toronto: University of Toronto Press, 2003.

Amos, Ashley Crandall. *Linguistic Means of Determining the Dates of Old English Literary Texts.* Cambridge, MA: Medieval Academy of America, 1981.

Andersson, Theodore M. "The Thief in *Beowulf*," *Speculum* 59 (1984), 493–508.

Baker, Peter S., ed. *Beowulf: Basic Readings.* New York and London: Garland Publishing, 1995; rpt. in 1997 as *The Beowulf Reader.*

Bammesberger, Alfred. *Linguistic Notes on Old English Poetic Texts,* Anglistische Forschungen 189. Heidelberg: Carl Winter Universitätsverlag, 1986.

Berkhout, Carl T., and Milton McC. Gatch, eds. *Anglo-Saxon Scholarship: The First Three Centuries.* Boston: G.K. Hall, 1982.

———. "Laurence Nowell (1530–ca. 1570)," in *Medieval Scholarship: Biographical Studies on the Formation of a Discipline,* Vol. 2: *Literature and Philology,* eds. Damico, Helen, Donald Fennema, and Karmen Lenz (New York and London: Garland, 1998), pp. 3–17.

———. "*Beowulf* 2200-08: Mind the Gap," *ANQ: A quarterly journal of short articles, notes, and reviews* 15:2 (2002), 51–58.

Bessinger, Jess B., Jr., and Robert F. Yeager, eds. *Approaches to Teaching "Beowulf."* New York: The Modern Language Association of America, 1983.

Biggs, Frederick M. "*Beowulf* and some fictions of the Geatish succession," *ASE* 32 (2003), 55–79.

Bjork, Robert E., and John D. Niles, eds. *A Beowulf Handbook.* Lincoln: University of Nebraska Press, 1997.

Bliss, A. J. "*Beowulf,* Lines 3074–75," in *J. R. R. Tolkien, Scholar and Storyteller: Essays in Memoriam,* eds. Mary Salu and Robert T. Farrell (Ithaca and London: Cornell University Press, 1979), pp. 41–63.

———. *The Metre of Beowulf.* Oxford: Blackwell, 1958; rev. ed. 1967.

———. *An Introduction to Old English Metre.* Oxford: Blackwell, 1962.

Brown, Alan K. "The Firedrake in *Beowulf*," *Neophilologus* 64 (1980), 439–460.

Bruce, Alexander M. *Scyld and Scef: Expanding the Analogues.* New York and London: Routledge, 2002.

Cable, Thomas. *The Meter and Melody of Beowulf.* Urbana: University of Illinois Press, 1974.

Calder, Daniel G., ed. *Old English Poetry: Essays on Style.* Berkeley: University of California Press, 1979.

Campbell, James, Eric John, Patrick Wormald, with P. V. Addyman et al. *The Anglo-Saxons.* Ithaca: Cornell University Press, 1982.

Cavill, Paul, ed. *The Christian Tradition in Anglo-Saxon England: Approaches to Current Scholarship and Teaching.* Cambridge: D. S. Brewer, 2004.

Chase, Colin, ed. *The Dating of "Beowulf."* Toronto Old English Series, No. 6. Toronto and Buffalo: University of Toronto Press, 1981; rpt. 1997.

Chickering, Howell. "Lyric Time in *Beowulf,*" *JEGP* 91 (1992), 489–509.

Clark, George. *Beowulf,* Twayne's English Authors Series 477. Boston: Twayne, 1990.

———. "*Beowulf*: The Last Word," in *Old English and New: Studies in Language and Linguistics in Honor of Frederic G. Cassidy,* eds. Hall, Joan H., Nick Doane, and Dick Ringler (New York and London: Garland Publishing, 1992), pp. 15–30.

Creed, Robert P. *Reconstructing the Rhythm of "Beowulf."* Columbia: University of Missouri Press, 1990.

Cronan, Dennis. "Poetic words, conservatism, and the dating of Old English poetry," *ASE* 33 (2004), pp. 23–50.

Davis, Craig R. *"Beowulf" and the Demise of Germanic Legend in England.* New York and London: Garland, 1996.

Donaldson, E. Talbot. "The Psychology of Editors of Middle English Texts," *English Studies Today* 4 (1966), 45–62.

Donoghue, Daniel, ed. *Beowulf: A Verse Translation* [by Seamus Heaney], Norton Critical Edition. New York and London: W. W. Norton & Co., 2002. Contains background materials and critical essays.

———. *Old English Literature: A Short Introduction.* Oxford: Blackwell, 2004.

Earl, James W. *Thinking About "Beowulf."* Stanford: Stanford University Press, 1994.

———. "*Beowulf*: The Raw and the Cooked," *OEN* 31:3 (1998), 16–27.

Foley, John Miles. *Traditional Oral Epic: The Odyssey, Beowulf, and the Serbo-Croatian Return Song.* Berkeley and Los Angeles: University of California Press, 1990.

———, ed., with J. Chris Womack and Whitney A. Womack. *De Gustibus: Essays for Alain Renoir.* New York and London: Garland, 1992.

Frank, Roberta. "Old Norse Memorial Eulogies and the Ending of *Beowulf,*" in *The Early Middle Ages,* ed. William H. Snyder, ACTA 6 (Binghamton:

Center for Medieval Studies, SUNY Binghamton, 1982 for 1979), pp. 1–19.

———. "*Beowulf* and Sutton Hoo: The Odd Couple," in *Voyage to the Other World: The Legacy of Sutton Hoo,* eds. Kendall, Calvin B., and Peter S. Wells (Minneapolis: University of Minnesota Press, 1992), pp. 47–64.

Frantzen, Allen J. *Desire for Origins: New Language, Old English, and Teaching the Tradition.* New Brunswick: Rutgers University Press, 1990.

Fry, Donald K., ed. *Finnsburh: Fragment and Episode.* London: Methuen, 1974.

Fulk, R. D. "Dating *Beowulf* to the Viking Age," *PQ* 61 (1982), 341–57.

———. "Unferth and His Name," *MP* 85 (1987), 113–27.

———, ed. *Interpretations of "Beowulf": A Critical Anthology.* Bloomington: Indiana University Press, 1991.

———. *A History of Old English Meter.* Philadelphia: University of Pennsylvania Press, 1992.

———, and Christopher M. Cain, with Rachel S. Anderson. *A History of Old English Literature.* Oxford: Blackwell, 2003.

———. "On argumentation in Old English philology, with particular reference to the editing and dating of *Beowulf,*" *ASE* 32 (2003), 1–26.

———. "The Name of Offa's Queen: *Beowulf* 1931–2," *Anglia* 122:4 (2004), 614–39.

———. "Some Contested Readings in the *Beowulf* Manuscript" *RES,* n. s. 56 (2005), 192–223.

———. "Six Cruces in *Beowulf* (Lines 31, 83, 404, 445, 1198, and 3074–5)," in *Latin Learning and English Lore: Studies in Anglo-Saxon Literature for Michael Lapidge,* Vol. I, eds. Katherine O'Brien O'Keeffe and Andy Orchard (Toronto: University of Toronto Press, 2005), pp. 349–67.

———. "Afloat in Semantic Space: Old English *sund* and the Nature of Beowulf's Exploit with Breca," forthcoming in *JEGP.*

———. "Some Lexical Problems in the Interpretation and Textual Criticism of *Beowulf* (Verses 414a, 845b, 986a, 1320a, 1375a)," forthcoming in *SN.*

———. "Some Emendations and Non-Emendations in *Beowulf* (Verses 600a, 976a, 1585b, 1663b, 1740a, 2525b, 2771a, and 3060a)," forthcoming in *SP.*

Gerritsen, Johan. "Emending *Beowulf* 2253—Some Matters of Principle, With a supplement on 389–90, 1372 & 240," *Neophilologus* 73 (1989), 448–53.

———. "Have with you to Lexington! The *Beowulf* Manuscript and *Beowulf,*" in *In Other Words: Transcultural Studies in Philology, Translation, and Lexicology presented to Hans Heinrich Meier on the occasion of his sixty-fifth Birthday,* eds. J. Lachlan Mackenzie and Richard Todd (Dordrecht: Foris Publications, 1989), pp. 15–34.

Godden, Malcolm, and Michael Lapidge, eds. *The Cambridge Companion to Old English Literature.* Cambridge: Cambridge University Press, 1991.

————, Douglas Gray, and Terry Hoad. *From Anglo-Saxon to Early Middle English: Studies Presented to E. G. Stanley.* Oxford: Clarendon Press, 1994.

Greenfield, Stanley B. "The Authenticating Voice in *Beowulf*," *ASE* 5 (1976), 51–62.

————, and Fred C. Robinson. *A Bibliography of Publications on Old English Literature to the end of 1972.* Toronto and Buffalo: University of Toronto Press, 1980.

————, and Daniel Calder, with Michael Lapidge. *A New Critical History of Old English Literature.* New York: New York University Press, 1986.

Hasenfratz, Robert J. *Beowulf Scholarship: An Annotated Bibliography, 1979–1990.* New York and London: Garland, 1993.

Healey, Antonette di Paolo, ed., et al. *Dictionary of Old English.* Toronto: Pontifical Institute of Mediaeval Studies, 1997– . Fascicles A through F are currently available on CD-ROM from <http://www.doe.utoronto.ca/pub/fasc-a-f.html>

Hill, John M. *The Cultural World in Beowulf.* Toronto: University of Toronto Press, 1995.

Howe, Nicholas. *Migration and Mythmaking in Anglo-Saxon England.* New Haven: Yale University Press, 1989.

————. "The Uses of Uncertainty: On the Dating of *Beowulf*," Afterword to the 1997 rpt. of Chase, pp. 213–20.

————, ed. *Beowulf: A Prose Translation* [by E. Talbot Donaldson], Norton Critical Edition. New York: W. W. Norton & Co., 2002. Contains background material and critical essays.

Hutcheson, B. R. *Old English Poetic Metre.* London: D. S. Brewer, 1995.

Irving, Edward B., Jr. "The Nature of Christianity in *Beowulf*," *ASE* 13 (1984), 7–21.

————. *Rereading "Beowulf."* Philadelphia: University of Pennsylvania Press, 1989.

Jack, George, ed. *Beowulf: A Student Edition,* rev. ed. Oxford: Clarendon Press, 1995.

Kelly, Birte. "The formative stages of *Beowulf* textual scholarship: part I," *ASE* 11 (1982), 239–75.

————. "The formative stages of *Beowulf* textual scholarship: part II," *ASE* 12 (1983), 253–79.

Kendall, Calvin B. *The Metrical Grammar of Beowulf.* Cambridge: Cambridge University Press, 1991.

Kiernan, Kevin S. *"Beowulf" and the "Beowulf" Manuscript.* New Brunswick, N.J.: Rutgers University Press, 1981.

————, ed., with Andrew Prescott, Elizabeth Solopova, David French, Linda Cantara, Michael Ellis and Cheng Jinn Yuan. *Electronic Beowulf,* 2 CD-ROMs. London and Ann Arbor: The British Library and the University of Michigan Press, 1999.

Köberl, Johann. *The Indeterminacy of "Beowulf."* Lanham, MD: University Press of America, 2002.

Korhammer, Michael, with Karl Reichl and Hans Sauer, eds. *Words, Texts and Manuscripts: Studies in Anglo-Saxon Culture Presented to Helmut Gneuss on the Occasion of His Sixty-Fifth Birthday.* Cambridge: D. S. Brewer, 1992.

Liuzza, Roy Michael, ed., et al. *Old English Newsletter.* Kalamazoo: Medieval Institute and Rawlinson Center for Anglo-Saxon Studies, 1967– . Available online at <http://www.oenewsletter.org/OEN> which also contains a searchable database for the annual *OEN* bibliography from 1972 to the present.

———. "On the Dating of *Beowulf,*" in Baker, *Beowulf: Basic Readings,* pp. 281–302.

———, ed. *Old English Literature: Critical Essays.* New Haven: Yale University Press, 2002.

Mitchell, Bruce. "*Beowulf,* Lines 3074–75: The Damnation of Beowulf?" *Poetica* (Tokyo) 13 (1982), 15–26; rpt. in his *On Old English: Selected Papers* (Oxford: Blackwell, 1988), pp. 30–40.

———, and Fred C. Robinson, eds. *Beowulf: An Edition with Relevant Shorter Texts.* Oxford: Blackwell, 1998.

———, and Susan Irvine. "*Beowulf*" *Repunctuated,* OEN Subsidia 29. Kalamazoo: Medieval Institute and Rawlinson Center for Anglo-Saxon Studies, 2000.

Myerov, Jonathan S. "Lines 3074–3075 in *Beowulf*: Movement into Knowing," *Anglia* 118:4 (2000), 531–55.

Newton, Sam. *The Origins of Beowulf and the Pre-Viking Kingdom of East Anglia.* Cambridge: D. S. Brewer, 1993.

Nicholson, Lewis E., and Dolores Warwick Frese, eds. *Anglo-Saxon Poetry: Essays in Appreciation for John C. McGalliard.* Notre Dame and London: University of Notre Dame Press, 1975.

Nickel, G., ed., with J. Klegraf, W. Kühlwein, D. Nehls, and R. Zimmerman. "*Beowulf*" *und die kleineren Denkmäler der altenglischen Heldensage "Waldere" und "Finnsburg."* 3 vols. Heidelberg: Carl Winter Universitätsverlag, 1976–82.

Niles, John D., ed. *Old English Literature in Context: Ten Essays.* Totowa, N.J.: Rowman and Littlefield, 1980.

———. *Beowulf: The Poem and Its Tradition.* Cambridge, MA: Harvard University Press, 1983.

———. *Homo Narrans: The Poetics and Anthropology of Oral Literature.* Philadelphia: University of Pennsylvania Press, 1999.

———. "Toward an Anglo-Saxon Oral Poetics," in Foley et al., *De Gustibus,* pp. 359–77.

O'Brien O'Keeffe, Katherine. *Visible Song: Transitional Literacy in Old English Verse.* Cambridge: Cambridge University Press, 1990.

————, ed. *Reading Old English Texts*. Cambridge: Cambridge University Press, 1997.

Orchard, Andy. *A Critical Companion to "Beowulf."* Cambridge: D. S. Brewer, 2003.

Overing, Gillian R. *Language, Sign, and Gender in Beowulf*. Carbondale: Southern Illinois University Press, 1990.

Richards, Mary P. "A Re-examination of *Beowulf* 3180–3182," *ELN* 10 (1973), 165–67.

Roberts, Jane. "Old English *Un-* 'Very' and Unferth," *ES* 61 (1980), 289–92.

Robinson, Fred C. *"Beowulf" and the Appositive Style*. Knoxville: University of Tennessee Press, 1985.

————. *"Beowulf* in the Twentieth Century," *PBA* 94 (1997), 45–62.

Russom, Geoffrey R. *Old English Meter and Linguistic Theory*. Cambridge: Cambridge University Press, 1987.

————. *"Beowulf" and Old Germanic Metre*. Cambridge: Cambridge University Press, 1998.

Short, Douglas D. *"Beowulf" Scholarship: An Annotated Bibliography*. New York and London: Garland, 1980.

Stanley, Eric G. *The Search for Anglo-Saxon Paganism*. Cambridge: D. S. Brewer, 1975.

Tanke, John. "Beowulf, Gold-Luck, and God's Will," *SP* 99:4 (2002), 356–79.

Tripp, Raymond P., Jr. "On 'Post-Editorial' Editions of *Beowulf*," *In Geardagum* 3 (1979), 18–25.

Wormald, Patrick. "Bede, *Beowulf* and the Conversion of the Anglo-Saxon Aristocracy," in *Bede and Anglo-Saxon England*, ed. Robert T. Farrell. Oxford: British Archaeological Reports, 46 (1978), pp. 32–95.

Abbreviations

This list includes abbreviations of periodicals, series, and books in the Introduction, Commentary, and Bibliography. NOTE: Further abbreviations used in the textual notes are listed on p. 44.

ABC
    Lewis E. Nicholson, ed. *An Anthology of Beowulf Criticism.* Notre Dame, Ind.: University of Notre Dame Press, 1963.
Archiv
    Archiv für das Studium der Neueren Sprachen and Literaturen
Arv
    Arv: Journal of Scandinavian Folklore
ASE
    Anglo-Saxon England (1972–). Published annually by Cambridge University Press.
B & A
    G. N. Garmonsway and Jacqueline Simpson, trans. *Beowulf and its Analogues,* with a section on "Archaeology and Beowulf," by Hilda R. Ellis Davidson. New York: E. P. Dutton, 1971.
Bonjour, *Digressions*
    Adrien Bonjour. *The Digressions in "Beowulf."* Oxford: Blackwell, 1950.
Bonjour, *Twelve Papers*
    Adrien Bonjour. *Twelve "Beowulf" Papers, 1940–60.* Neuchâtel: E. Droz, 1962.

Brodeur
    Arthur G. Brodeur. *The Art of Beowulf.* Berkeley: University of California
        Press, 1959.
Brodeur Studies
    Stanley B. Greenfield, ed. *Studies in Old English Literature in Honor of
        Arthur G. Brodeur.* Eugene: University of Oregon Press, 1963.
C & B
    Eric G. Stanley, ed. *Continuations and Beginnings: Studies in Old English
        Literature.* London: Nelson, 1966.
CE
    College English
Chambers
    R. W. Chambers. *Beowulf: An Introduction.* 3rd ed., with supplement by
        C. L. Wrenn. London: Cambridge University Press, 1959.
ChR
    The Chaucer Review
CL
    Comparative Literature
Critical Approaches
    Robert M. Lumiansky and Herschel Baker, eds. *Critical Approaches to Six
        Major English Works: "Beowulf" Through "Paradise Lost."* Philadel-
        phia: University of Pennsylvania Press, 1968.
Davidson, *Gods and Myths*
    Hilda R. Ellis Davidson. *Gods and Myths of Northern Europe.* Baltimore:
        Penguin, 1964.
Dobbie
    Elliott Van Kirk Dobbie, ed. *Beowulf and Judith.* The Anglo-Saxon Poetic
        Records, IV. New York: Columbia University Press, 1953.
DOE
    Dictionary of Old English. See under Healey et al., Section IV of Bibliog-
        raphy.
E & S
    Essays and Studies
EENS
    Arthur Brown and Peter Foote, eds. *Early English and Norse Studies Pre-
        sented to Hugh Smith in Honour of his Sixtieth Birthday.* London:
        Methuen, 1963.
EETS
    Early English Text Society
EGS
    English and Germanic Studies
ELH
    ELH (formerly *Journal of English Literary History*)

ELN
   English Language Notes
ES
   English Studies
ESt
   Englische Studien
Franciplegius
   Jess B. Bessinger, Jr., and Robert P. Creed, eds. *Franciplegius: Medieval and Linguistic Studies In Honor of Francis Peabody Magoun, Jr.* New York: New York University Press, 1965.
Goldsmith
   Margaret E. Goldsmith. *The Mode and Meaning of "Beowulf."* London: Athlone Press, 1970.
Irving, *Reading*
   Edward B. Irving, Jr. *A Reading of Beowulf.* New Haven and London: Yale University Press, 1968.
JEGP
   Journal of English and Germanic Philology
JRSAI
   Journal of the Royal Society of Antiquaries of Ireland
Klaeber
   Frederick Klaeber, ed. *Beowulf and the Fight at Finnsburg.* 3rd ed. Boston: D. C. Heath, 1950.
Lawrence
   William W. Lawrence. *Beowulf and Epic Tradition.* Cambridge, Mass.: Harvard University Press, 1928.
MÆ
   Medium Ævum
Malone, *NC*
   Kemp Malone, ed. *The Nowell Codex.* Early English Manuscripts in Facsimile, XII. Copenhagen, Baltimore, and London: Rosenkilde and Bagger, 1963.
Malone, *Studies in Heroic Legend*
   Kemp Malone. *Studies in Heroic Legend and Current Speech,* ed. Stefán Einarsson and Norman E. Eliason. Copenhagen: Rosenkilde and Bagger, 1959.
Meritt Studies
   James L. Rosier, ed. *Philological Essays: Studies in Old and Middle English Language and Literature in Honour of Herbert Dean Meritt.* The Hague: Mouton, 1970.
MLN
   Modern Language Notes
MLQ
   Modern Language Quarterly

MLR
  Modern Language Review
MP
  Modern Philology
N & Q
  Notes and Queries
NM
  Neuphilologische Mitteilungen
OEN
  Old English Newsletter. See under Liuzza et al., Section IV of Bibliography.
OEP
  Robert P. Creed, ed. *Old English Poetry: Fifteen Essays.* Providence: Brown University Press, 1967.
PBA
  Proceedings of the British Academy
PBB
  Paul und Brauns Beiträge zur Geschichte der deutschen Sprache und Literatur
PG
  Patrologiae cursus completus, Series Graeca
PL
  Patrologiae cursus completus, Series Latina
PLL
  Papers on Language and Literature
PMLA
  PMLA (Publications of the Modern Language Association of America)
Pope Studies
  Robert B. Burlin and Edward B. Irving, Jr., eds. *Old English Studies in Honour of John C. Pope.* Toronto and Buffalo: University of Toronto Press, 1974.
PQ
  Philological Quarterly
RES
  Review of English Studies
Sisam, *Structure*
  Kenneth Sisam. *The Structure of "Beowulf."* London: Oxford University Press, 1965.
Sisam, *Studies*
  Kenneth Sisam. *Studies in the History of Old English Literature.* London: Oxford University Press, 1953.
SN
  Studia Neophilologica
SP
  Studies in Philology

TSL
   Tennessee Studies in Literature
UTQ
   University of Toronto Quarterly
Whitelock, *Audience*
   Dorothy Whitelock. *The Audience of "Beowulf."* Oxford: Clarendon Press, 1951
Wrenn
   Charles Leslie Wrenn, ed. *Beowulf with the Finnesburg Fragment.* 2nd ed. London: Harrap, 1958.
Wrenn-Bolton
   Charles Leslie Wrenn, ed. *Beowulf with the Finnesburg Fragment.* 3rd ed. Revised by W. F. Bolton. London: Harrap, 1973.
ZDA
   Zeitschrift für Deutsches Altertum und Deutsche Literatur
ZDP
   Zeitschrift für Deutsche Philologie

Glosses to Select Passages

1. Scyld Scefing (1–52)
2. The Song of Creation (86–114)
3. The Fight with Grendel (710–836)
4. The Description of the Mere (1345–96)
5. The Lay of the Last Survivor (2231b–77)
6. Wiglaf's Speeches Before Battle (2631–68)
7. Beowulf's Last Words (2792b–2820)
8. Beowulf's Memorial (3156–82)

For students with an elementary knowledge of Old English grammar who wish to translate from the original, these eight passages are glossed below. The glosses generally exclude proper names and basic recognition vocabulary such as pronouns and direct cognates. Recurrent words are not reglossed every time. Grammatical information is given as needed to help with translation. Selected points of grammar are keyed to the paradigms and explanatory sections in Sweet's *Primer* (Sw) and Mitchell and Robinson's *Guide* (MR) cited below. Nouns and adjectives are listed as nominative singulars, verbs as infinitives; it is assumed students will know case endings and principal parts of verbs. When more than one grammatical gender is possible for a noun, all are indicated, as in "*reced* mn." Whether an adjective is strong or weak is not usually indicated in the glosses since it depends on its function in the sentence. First and second personal pronouns are declined like strong adjectives. The demonstrative pronoun *þæt* disregards the gender of its predicate nouns in lines 11b, 716b, and 1372b (see MR 187.2.c). Parentheses in Old English words indicate variant spellings. Strong verb classes are indicated by Roman numerals (I, II), weak verb classes by Arabic numerals (1, 2). An asterisk precedes unrecorded infinitives (**sculan, *mōtan*). Other abbreviations:

acc.	accusative	nom.	nominative
adj.	adjective	part.	participle
adv.	adverb	pl.	plural

anom.	anomalous	poss.	possessive
cf.	compare	prep.	preposition
cj.	conjunction	pres.	present
compar.	comparative	pret.	preterite
dat.	dative	pret.-pres.	preterite-present
dem.	demonstrative	pron.	pronoun
f.	feminine	reflex.	reflexive
ff.	following	rel.	relative
gen.	genitive	sing.	singular
indecl.	indeclinable	st.	strong
indef.	indefinite	subj.	subjunctive
inf.	infinitive	superl.	superlative
instr.	instrumental	trans.	translate
interj.	interjection	var.	variant
m.	masculine	vb.	verb
n.	neuter	wk.	weak

The introductory grammar-readers abbreviated as Sw and MR are: Henry Sweet, *Anglo-Saxon Primer,* revised by Norman Davis, 9th ed. (Oxford: Clarendon Press, 1953); Bruce Mitchell and Fred C. Robinson, *A Guide to Old English: Revised with Texts and Glossary* (Oxford: Basil Blackwell, 1982, distributed in North America by University of Toronto Press). For further work in the original, a convenient dictionary is John R. Clark Hall, *A Concise Anglo-Saxon Dictionary*, edited with supplement by Herbert D. Meritt, 4th ed. (Cambridge: Cambridge University Press, 1962). Also useful to students is Stephen A. Barney, with the assistance of Ellen Wertheimer and David Stevens, *Word-Hoard: An Introduction to Old English Vocabulary* (New Haven and London: Yale University Press, 1977).

I wish to acknowledge the invaluable aid of Professor Mary Blockley of Smith College, who enthusiastically collaborated in the preparation of these glosses.

1. Scyld Scefing (1–52)

1 *hwæt* interj. 'lo, truly, indeed, listen'.   *Gār-Dene* m. 'Spear-Dane'   *geār-dæg* m. 'day of yore'

2 *þēod-cyning* m. 'tribal king'   *þrym* m. 'glory'   *gefrignan* III 'hear of' Sw 64, MR 102

3 *hū* cj. 'how'   *þā* pl. dem. pron. 'those'   *æþeling* n. 'prince, noble'   *ellen* n. '(works of) valor, courage'   *fremman* 1 'do, perform' Sw 71, MR 116

4 *sceaþa* m. 'warrior, harmer' (cf. Mod. Eng. adj. 'scathing')
   þrēat m. 'troop'

5 *monegum* dat. pl. of *manig* adj. 'many'   *mægþ* f. 'tribe'
   meodo-setl n. 'mead-bench'   *oftēon* II 'deny, deprive' with dat.
   of person and gen. of thing

6 *egsian* 2 'terrify'   *eorl* m. 'nobleman' see also p. 279   *syððan*
   cj. 'since'   *ǣrest* adv. 'first'   *weorðan* III 'become' Sw 64c,
   MR 202–203

7 *fēasceaft* adj. 'destitute, helpless'   *findan* III 'find'   *þæs* dem.
   pron., gen. sing. n. 'for that' Sw 47, MR 16   *frōfor* f. 'help,
   comfort'; here *frōfre* can be gen. sing. or acc. sing. Sw 6(6)c, MR
   50   *gebīdan* VI 'experience, live to see'

8 *wēaxan* I 'wax, grow'   *wolcen* n. 'cloud, sky'   *weorð-mynd*
   fmn. 'honor, glory'   *þēon* I 'prosper'

9 *oðþæt* cj. 'until'   *ǣghwylc* pron. 'each'   *ymbsittan* V
   'surround' pres. part. declined as adj. 'surrounding (ones),
   neighbors' MR 204.1

10 *ofer* prep. 'across, over'   *hron-rād* f. 'whale's riding-place,
   ocean'   *hȳran* 1 'hear, obey'   **sculan* pret.-pres. vb. 'must'
   Sw 77, MR 130, 210

11 *gombe* f. 'tribute'   *gyldan* III 'yield, pay'   *gōd* adj. 'good'
   cyning m. 'king'

12 *ðǣm* dat. sing. pron. 'to him'   *eafera* m. 'offspring, son'
   æfter adv. 'afterwards'   *cennan* 1 'bring forth, bear'

13 *geong* adj. 'young'   *geard* m. 'yard, dwelling'   *sendan* 1
   'send' Sw 70–71, MR 121

14 *folc* n. 'people, nation, folk'   *tō* prep. 'for, as'   *frōfor* see
   line 7   *fyren-ðearfe* f. 'wicked distress' see also p. 279
   ongitan V 'understand, perceive'

15 *þæt* rel. pron. 'that, which'   *ǣr* adv. 'formerly'   *drēogan* II
   'endure, suffer'   *aldor-lēas* adj. 'lordless'

16 *lange* adv. 'long'   *hwīl* f. 'time, while'   *him* dat. sing., the
   eafera of line 12   *þæs* as in line 7   *Līf-frēa* m. 'Life-lord'

17 *wuldor* n. 'glory, heaven'   *Wealdend* m. 'Wielder, Ruler'
   worold-ār f. 'worldly honor'   *forgifan* V 'give'

18 *brēme* adj. 'famous'   *blǣd* m. 'fame, renown'   *wīde* adv.
   'widely'   *springan* III 'spring, spread'

19 *eafera* see line 12   *Scede-land* n. 'southern Scandinavia'   *in*
   'in' prep. ff. noun Sw 96, MR 213

20 *swā* adv. 'thus'   *sceal* from **sculan* 'must, ought' see line 10
   geong adj. 'young'   *guma* m. 'man'   *gōd* n. 'good' (of
   persons or things)   *gewyrcan* 1 'perform, achieve'

21   *from* adj. 'bold, splendid'   *feoh-gift* f. 'costly gift, dispensing of treasure'   *on* prep. 'in'   *fæder* m. 'father' Sw 23, MR 60.2 *bearm* m. 'bosom, possession'

22   *þæt* cj. 'so that'   *yldo* f. 'old age'   *eft* adv. 'again, thereafter' *gewunian* 2 'remain with'

23   *wil-gesīþ* m. 'dear companion'   *wīg* n. 'war'   *cuman* IV 'come'

24   *lēod* m. 'man' (*lēode* pl. 'people')   *gelæstan* 1 'serve, stand beside'   *lof-dǣd* f. 'praiseworthy deed'   *sceal* as in line 20

25   *mǣgþ* see line 5   *gehwǣre* adv. 'everywhere'   *man(n)* m. 'man' used here as indef. pron. 'anyone'   *geþēon* I 'prosper'

26   *him* reflex. dat. Sw 87(1), MR 191.5   *gewītan* I 'go, depart' (trans. with inf. *fēran*)   *gescæp-hwīl* f. 'fated time'

27   *fela-hrōr* adj. as noun 'very strong (one)'   *fēran* 1 'go, travel' *Frēa* m. 'Lord' cf. line 16   *wǣr* f. 'protection'

28   *þā* adv. 'then'   *ætberan* IV 'carry, bear'   *brim* n. 'sea' *faroð* mn. 'current'

29   *swǣs* adj. 'intimate, favorite'   *gesīð* m. 'comrade, retainer' cf. line 23   *swā* cj. 'as'   *selfa* reflex. pron., wk. nom. sing. m. 'himself'   *biddan* V 'ask'

30   *þenden* cj. 'while, as long as'   *word* n. 'word'   *wealdan* VII 'wield, rule, possess' with dat. obj.   *wine* m. 'friend, lord'

31   *lēof* adj. 'dear'   *land-fruma* m. 'ruler of the land'   *lange* see line 16   *āgan* pret.-pres. vb. 'own, possess' with implied obj. Sw 77, MR 130

32   *þǣr* adv. 'there'   *hȳð* f. 'harbor'   *standan* III 'stand' *hringed-stefna* m. 'ringed or curved prow' (part for whole)

33   *īsig* adj. 'icy' see also p. 280   *ūt-fūs* adj. 'ready to set out' *æþeling* see line 3   *fær* n. 'ship'

34   *ālecgan* 1 'lay down'   *þā* adv. 'there'   *lēof* adj. 'beloved' *þēoden* m. 'chief, king'

35   *bēag* m. 'ring'   *brytta* m. 'giver, dispenser'   *bearm* m. 'middle' cf. line 21   *scip* n. 'ship'

36   *mǣre* adj. 'famous'   *mæst* m. 'mast'   *māð(ð)um* var. of *mādm* m. 'treasure'   *fela* indecl. adj. or noun 'much, many' with gen. obj. here and line 37

37   *of* prep. 'from'   *feor-weg* m. 'distant path'   *frætwe* f. pl. 'ornaments'   *lǣdan* 1 'carry, bring'

38   *hȳran* 1 'hear of' with acc. obj. (but with dat. obj. in line 10 for the sense 'listen to, obey')   *cȳmlīcor* compar. adv. 'more beautifully'   *cēol* m. 'ship'   *gegyrwan* 1 'equip, adorn'; trans. the inf. as passive Sw 95, MR 161

39 *hilde-wǣpen* n. 'battle weapon'   *heaðo-wǣd* f. 'battle dress, armor'

40 *bill* n. 'sword'   *byrne* f. 'mail coat, byrnie'   *him* poss. dat. Sw 87(1), MR 191.2   *bearm* see lines 21, 35   *licgan* V 'lie'

41 *mādm* see line 36   *mænigo* indecl. f. noun 'multitude'   *mid* 'with' prep. ff. pron.   *scoldon* from *sculan (see line 10)

42 *flōd* m. 'flood, tide'   *ǣht* f. 'possession, power' (from vb. *āgan* 'own, possess' see line 31)   *feor* adv. 'far'   *gewītan* I 'go, depart'

43 *nalæs* var. of *nealles* adv. 'not at all'   *lǣssa* adj. 'lesser' compar. of *lȳtel* 'little' Sw 33, MR 76   *lāc* n. 'gift'   *tēon* 2 'provide' (*tēodan* pret. 3rd pl.)

44 *þēod-gestrēon* n. 'treasure of the people'   *þon* var. of *þonne* adv. cj. 'than' MR 168   *dōn* anom. vb. 'do' Sw 81, MR 128

45 *þe* indecl. rel. particle 'who, which, that' Sw 50, MR 162   *æt* prep. 'at, in'   *frum-sceaft* f. 'origin, beginning'   *forð* adv. 'forth, away'   *onsendan* 1 'send away'

46 *ǣnne* var. of *ānne* acc. sing. m. of wk. adj. *āna* 'alone'   *ofer* prep. 'over, across'   *ȳð* acc. pl. f. 'wave' Sw 17, MR 48 *umbor-wesende* adj. 'being a child' (*umbor* n. 'infant' plus pres. part. of *bēon, wesan* 'to be')

47 *gȳt* adv. 'yet, still'   *him* 'for him' or else poss. dat. with *hēafod* in line 48   *āsettan* 1 'place, set'   *segn* mn. 'banner, standard' *gelden* var. of *gylden* adj. 'golden'

48 *hēah* adj. 'high'   *hēafod* n. 'head'   *lǣtan* VII 'let'   *holm* m. 'sea'   *beran* IV 'bear' with unexpressed obj.

49 *gifan* V 'give' with unexpressed obj.   *on* prep. 'to'   *gār-secg* m. 'encircling ocean'   *him* poss. dat. pl.   *geōmor* adj. 'sad, mournful'   *sefa* m. 'mind, heart' (sing. with pl. sense)

50 *murnende* pres. part. of *murnan* III 'mourn' as adj. 'mourning' *mōd* n. 'heart, mind'   *cunnan* pret.-pres. vb. 'know, know how to' Sw 77, MR 130

51 *secgan* 3 'say' Sw 74, MR 126   *sōð* n. 'truth' hence *tō sōðe* 'in truth, as a fact'   *sele-rǣdende* m. pl. 'hall-counselor'

52 *hæleð* m. 'warrior, hero' (unchanged in the nom. acc. pl.) *heofon* m. 'heaven'   *hwā* pron. 'who, what' Sw 49, MR 20 *hlæst* m. 'load, freight'   *onfōn* VII 'receive' with dat. obj. Sw 68, MR 103.5

2. The Song of Creation (86–114)

86 *þā* adv. 'then'   *ellen-gǣst* m. 'strong spirit, demon' *earfoðlīce* adv. 'wretchedly, with difficulty'

87 *þrǣg* f. 'time'   *þolian* 2 'endure, suffer'   *sē þe* dem. pron.
    with indecl. rel. particle: 'he who, who' Sw 50, MR 162.4
    þýstru f. 'darkness'   *bīdan* I 'wait, dwell'

88 *þæt* cj. 'for that, because'   *dōgor* mn. 'day'   *gehwā* pron.
    'each' dat. with gen. pl.   *drēam* m. 'joy, rejoicing'   *gehȳran*
    1 'hear'

89 *hlūd* adj. 'loud'   *heall* f. 'hall'   *þǣr* adv. 'there'   *hearpe* f.
    'harp'   *swēg* m. 'sound, music'

90 *swutol* adj. 'clear'   *sang* m. 'song'   *scop* m. 'poet, singer' see
    p. 4   *secgan* 3 'say'   *sē þe* see line 87   *cūþe* pret. sing. of
    cunnan pret.-pres. vb. 'know, know how to' Sw 77, MR 130

91 *frumsceaft* f. 'creation, origin'   *fīras* m. pl. 'men'   *feorran*
    adv. 'from far back (in time)'   *reccan* 1 'tell, narrate'

92 *cweðan* V 'say'   *Ælmihtiga* wk. adj. as noun 'the Almighty'
    eorðe f. 'earth'   *wyrcan* 1 'work, make'

93 *wlite-beorht* adj. 'bright shining'   *wang* m. 'plain'   *swā* cj.
    'as' with force of rel. pron., hence trans. as 'which'   *wæter* n.
    'water'   *bebūgan* II 'encompass, surround'

94 *gesettan* 1 'set'   *sige-hrēþig* adj. 'victorious, triumphant'
    sunne f. 'sun'   *mōna* m. 'moon'; both these gen. sing. nouns
    depend on *lēoman* in line 95

95 *lēoma* m. 'light' here acc. pl.   *tō* prep. 'for, as'   *lēoht* n.
    'light'   *land-būend* m. 'land-dweller'

96 *gefrætwian* 2 'adorn, decorate'   *folde* f. 'earth'   *scēat* m.
    'region'

97 *leomum* dat. pl. of *lim* n. 'limb, branch'   *lēaf* n. 'leaf'   *līf* n.
    'life'   *ēac* adv. 'also'   *gescyppan* VI 'create'

98 *cynn* n. 'race, people'   *gehwylc* pron. 'each' with gen. pl.   *þe*
    indecl. rel. particle 'that, which'   *cwic* adj. 'living'   *hweorfan*
    III 'turn, move'

99 *swā* adv. 'thus'   *ðā* pl. dem. pron.   *driht-guma* m. 'retainer,
    warrior'   *drēam* see line 88   *libban* 3 'live' Sw 74, MR 126

100 *ēadiglīce* adv. 'blessedly, happily' (contrast line 86b)   *oððæt* cj.
    'until'   *ān* adj. as noun 'one' Sw 39, MR 83   *onginnan* III
    'begin'

101 *fyren* f. 'crime, sin'   *fremman* 1 'do, perform'   *fēond* m.
    'enemy, devil' (cf. Mod. Eng. 'fiend')   *on* prep. 'in'   *helle* f.
    'hell'

102 *grimma* wk. adj. 'grim, fierce' Sw 28, MR 64   *gǣst* m. 'spirit'
    hāten past. part. of *hātan* VII 'name, call'

103 *mǣre* adj. 'famous' hence 'notorious, well known' or perhaps
    mǣre f. 'incubus, night monster' (see gloss to line 762) in
    apposition to *mearc-stapa* m. 'border walker'   *mōr* m. 'moor,
    wasteland'   *healdan* VII 'hold, control'

104   *fen* n. 'fen, marsh'   *fæsten* n. 'stronghold, fastness'   *fīfel-cynn* n. 'race of giants'   *eard* m. 'dwelling place, land'

105   *won-sǣlī* adj. 'unhappy, unblessed'   *wer* m. 'man'   *weardian* 2 'guard, occupy'   *hwīl* f. 'a while, period of time'

106   *siþðan* cj. 'since (the time)'   *Scyppend* m. 'the Creator' *forscrīfan* I 'condemn, proscribe' with dat. obj.   *habban* 3 'have'

107   *in* prep. 'among, with, in'   *cynn* n. 'race, tribe'   *cwealm* m. 'murder, killing'   *gewrecan* V 'avenge'

108   *ēce* adj. 'eternal'   *Drihten* m. 'the Lord'   *þæs þe* cj. 'after, because'   *slēan* VI 'slay, strike down'

109   *gefēon* V 'rejoice' with gen. or dat. obj.; its subject *hē* is Cain *fǣhð(o)* f. 'feud, enmity'   *ac* cj. 'but'   *feor* adv. 'far' *forwrecan* V 'drive away, banish'; its subject *hē* is God

110   *Metod* m. 'Measurer of fate' hence 'God'   *for þȳ* cj. 'because of'   *mān* n. 'crime'   *man-cynn* n. 'mankind' with ff. stressed prep.   *fram* 'from' Sw 96, MR 213

111   *þanon* var. of *þonan* adv. 'then, from him'   *untȳdre* m. 'evil brood'   *eall* adj. 'all'   *onwæcnan* VI 'awake, be born'

112   *eoten* m. 'giant, monster'   *ylfe* m. pl. 'elves'   *orc-nēas* m. pl. 'evil spirits of the dead'

113   *swylce* adv. 'likewise, also'   *gīgant* m. 'giant'   *þā* rel. pron. 'that, who'   *wið* prep. 'against'   *winnan* III 'fight'

114   *lang* adj. 'long'   *þrāg* f. 'time'   *him* dat. pl.   *ðæs* gen. pron. 'for that'   *lēan* n. 'reward, requital'   *forgyldan* III 'pay back'

3. The Fight with Grendel (710–836)

710   *þā* adv. 'then'   *cuman* IV 'come' (trans. with inf. *gangan*; see also p. 306)   *of* prep. 'from'   *mōr* m. 'moor'   *mist-hliþ* n. 'misty hill'

711   *gongan* var. of *gangan* VII 'go, walk' (trans. the inf. as a pres. part.)   *yrre* n. 'anger, ire'   *beran* IV 'bear'

712   *myntan* 1 'intend'   *mān-scaða* m. 'evil harmer' (see also p. 307) *cynn* n. 'race'

713   *sum* adj. 'a certain (one)'   *besyrwan* 1 'trick, trap'   *sele* m. 'hall'   *hēah* adj. 'high' Sw 29(b), 100, MR 72

714   *wadan* VI 'advance, go'   *wolcen* n. 'cloud, sky' (cf. line 8) *tō þæs þe* cj. 'until, to the point where' Sw 96, MR 169   *wīn-reced* mn. 'wine-hall'

715   *gold-sele* see line 713   *guma* m. 'man'   *gearwe* adv. 'readily, surely' here superl. Sw 35, MR 135   *witan* pret.-pres. vb. 'know, recognize' Sw 76, MR 130

716 *fǣt* n. 'gold plate'   *fāg*, var. *fāh* adj. 'decorated'   *forma* adj.
'first'   *sīð* m. 'journey, undertaking'

717 *hām* m. 'home'   *sēcan* 1 'seek' Sw 72, MR 122

718 *nǣfre* adj. 'never' (*ne* + *ǣfre* 'ever')   *aldor-dæg* m. 'day of life'
ǣr adv. 'before'   *siþðan* adv. 'since'

719 *heard* adj. 'hard' here compar. Sw 31, MR 74 (modifies both
objects of *fand*)   *hǣlo* f. 'luck'   *heal-ðegn* m. 'hall-retainer'
findan III 'find' Sw 64, MR 102

720 *reced* mn. 'hall' cf. line 714   *rinc* m. 'warrior'   *sīðian* 2
'journey' (trans. the inf. as a pres. part. after *cōm* MR 205.1)

721 *drēam* m. 'joy'   *bedǣlan* 1 'deprive'   *duru* f. 'door'   *sōna*
adv. 'at once, immediately'   *onirnan* III 'give way, burst open'

722 *fȳr-bend* f. 'fire-bond' (i.e., forged in fire; see lines 774–75)   *fæst*
adj. 'fast, firm'   *syþðan* cj. 'after, as soon as'   *folm* f. 'hand'
gehrīnan I 'reach, touch' with *hire* as direct obj.

723 *onbregdan* III 'rip open'   *bealo-hȳdig* adj. as noun 'evil-minded,
hostile (one)'   *þā . . . ðā* 'then . . . when' Sw 99, MR 150–53
gebelgan III 'enrage, swell with anger'

724 *reced* see line 720   *mūþa* m. 'mouth'   *raþe* adv. 'quickly'
þon var. of *þȳ* dem. pron. with *æfter,* as instr. of time Sw 47, 88,
MR 16, 192

725 *fāg* see line 716   *flōr* m. 'floor'   *fēond* m. 'enemy' (cf. Mod.
Eng. 'fiend')   *treddian* 2 'tread, step'

726 *ēode* pret. of anom. vb. *gān* 'go' Sw 80, MR 128   *yrre-mōd* adj.
as noun 'angry-minded (one)'   *him* poss. dat. Sw 87(1), MR
191.2   *of* prep. 'from'   *ēage* n. 'eye'   *standan* VI 'stand'

727 *līg* m. 'fire'   *gelīcost* superl. adj. 'most like'   *lēoht* n. 'light'
unfǣger adj. 'unlovely' (litotes for 'horrible'; see p. 9)

728 *gesēon* V 'see, behold'   *rinc* m. 'warrior'   *manig* adj. 'many'
with gen. pl. noun

729 *swefan* V 'sleep'   *sibbe-gedriht* f. 'troop of kinsmen'   *samod*
ætgædere adv. 'all together'

730 *mago-rinc* m. 'kinsman-warrior'   *hēap* m. 'band'   *þā* adv.
'then'   *mōd* n. 'heart, mind'   *āhliehhan* VI 'laugh, exult'

731 *myntan* 1 'intend' as in line 712   *gedǣlan* 1 'separate, divide'
ǣr þon adv. with instr. pron. 'before'   *dæg* m. 'day'   *cwōme*
var. of *cōme* pret. 3rd sing. subj. of *cuman* IV 'come'

732 *atol* adj. 'terrible'   *āglǣca* m. 'monster'   *ān* st. adj. 'one' Sw
39, MR 83   *gehwylc* pron. 'each'

733 *līf* n. 'life'   *wið* prep. 'from'   *līc* n. 'body'   *þā* cj. 'since,
when'   *ālimpan* III 'befall'

734 *wist-fyllo* f. 'fill of feasting'   *wēn* f. 'expectation'   *wyrd* n.
'fate' (see also p. 269)   *þā* adv. 'then'   *gēn* adv. 'yet'

735 *mā* compar. adv. as indecl. noun 'more' Sw 37 **mōtan* pret.-
pres. vb. 'may, be allowed to' Sw 77, MR 130, 208

736 *ðicgean* var. of *ðicgan* V 'eat, partake of' *ofer* prep. 'over, on'
but here, of time, 'beyond, after' *niht* f. 'night' *þrȳð-swȳð*
adj. as noun 'very strong (one)' *behealdan* VII 'behold, watch'

737 *mæg* m. 'kinsman' *mān-scaða* see line 712 and p. 307

738 *under* prep. 'under' but here 'in, with' *fǣr-gripe* m. 'fearful
grip, sudden attack' *gefaran* VI 'go, proceed, act' *willan*
anom. vb. 'wish, intend' Sw 79, MR 129, 211

739 *nē* cj. 'nor' *þæt* dem. pron., neut. acc. 'it' as general reference
āglǣca see line 732 *yldan* 1 'delay' *þencan* 1 'think' Sw 72,
MR 122

740 *ac* cj. 'but' *gefōn* VII 'seize' *hraðe* adv. 'quickly' (cf. line
724) *forman sīðe* see line 716

741 *slǣpan* 1 'sleep' *rinc* see lines 720, 728 *slītan* I 'tear, rip'
unwearnum dat. pl. as adv. 'without hindrance'

742 *bītan* I 'bite' *bān-loca* m. 'bone-locker' i.e., 'muscle' *blōd*
n. 'blood' *ēder* f. 'vein' *drincan* III 'drink'

743 *syn-snǣd* f. 'huge morsel' or 'sinful morsel' *swelgan* III
'swallow' *sōna* see line 721 *habban* 3 'have' Sw 74,
MR 126

744 *unlyfigend* adj. as noun 'unliving (one)' *eal* adj. as acc. sing. n.
noun 'all' *feormian* 2 'eat, consume'

745 *fōt* m. 'foot' Sw 22, MR 58 *folm* f. 'hand' cf. line 722 *forð*
adv. 'forward, onward' *nēar* compar. of adv. *nēah* 'nigh, near'
ætsteppan VI 'step forward'

746 *niman* IV 'snatch, seize' *þā* adv. 'then' *mid* prep. with dat.
'with' *hand* f. 'hand' Sw 19, MR 61 *hige-þīhtig* adj. as noun
'strong in spirit, determined'

747 *ræst* f. 'resting place, bed' *rǣcan* 1 'reach' *ongēan* adv. or
prep. 'against, toward' with 'him' understood; see pp. 308–309

748 *fēond* m. 'enemy' cf. line 725 *folm* f. 'hand' as in lines 722 and
745 (perhaps 'open hand' here) *onfōn* VII 'receive, perceive'
hraþe adv. 'quickly'

749 *inwit-þanc* m. 'hostile intent' *wið* prep. 'against' *earm* m.
'arm' *gesittan* V 'sit down' but here 'sit up' (see p. 309)

750 *sōna* see lines 721, 743 *þæt* pron. 'that' in anticipation of the ff.
þæt clause; Sw 99, MR 148 *onfindan* III 'find out, discover'
fyren f. 'crime, sin' *hyrde* m. 'keeper, shepherd'

751 *mētan* 1 'meet' *middan-geard* m. 'middle dwelling, world of
men'

752 *eorþe* f. 'earth' *scēat* m. 'corner, region' gen. pl. as adv. of
place Sw 86, MR 190.5 *elra* compar. adj. 'other, any other'

753   *mund-gripe* m. 'hand-grip'   *māra* compar. adj. 'greater'   *mōd*
      n. 'heart, mind' cf. line 730   *weorðan* III 'become'

754   *forht* adj. 'afraid'   *ferhð* mn. 'spirit'   *nō þȳ ǣr* adv. cj. with
      instr. pron. 'none the sooner'   *fram* adv. 'from (there), away'
      magan pret.-pres. vb. 'can, be able to' Sw 75, MR 130, with vb. of
      motion understood

755   *hyge* m. 'mind, heart' cf. line 746   *him* poss. dat., cf. line 726
      hin-fūs adj. 'eager to leave' cf. line 30   *willan* anom. vb. 'wish,
      want' cf. line 738   *heolster* m. 'hiding place'   *flēon* II 'flee'

756   *sēcan* 1 'seek'   *dēofol* mn. 'devil'   *gedræg* n. 'company,
      gathering'   *drohtoð* m. 'way of life'

757   *swylce* cj. 'such as'   *ealder-dæg* m. 'day of life' cf. line 718
      gemētan 1 'meet, find' cf. line 751

758   *gemunan* pret.-pres. vb. 'remember'   *gōda* wk. adj. as noun
      'good (man)'   *mæg* m. 'kinsman' cf. line 737

759   *ǣfen-sprǣc* f. 'evening speech'   *uplang* adv. 'upright'
      āstandan VI 'stand up'

760   *fæste* adv. 'fast, firmly'   *wiðfōn* VII 'seize, lay hold of'
      finger m. 'finger'   *berstan* III 'burst, break'

761   *eoten* m. 'giant'   *ūtweard* adj. '(moving) outward'   *eorl* m.
      'nobleman'   *furþur* adv. 'further'   *steppan* VI 'step'

762   *myntan* see lines 712, 731   *mǣra* wk. adj. 'famous (one)' here
      ironic (cf. line 36); possibly *mǣre* f. 'incubus, night monster' (see
      N. Kiessling, *MP* 65 [1968], 191–201)   *þǣr* cj. 'if'   *magan*
      pret.-pres. vb. 'can, be able' see line 754   *swā* adv. 'thus, so'

763   *wīdre* compar. adj. as adv. 'farther'   *gewindan* III 'go, turn'
      weg m. 'way'   *þanon* var. of *þonan* adv. 'thence, from there'

764   *flēon* II 'flee' as in line 755   *on* prep. 'to, into'   *fen-hopu* n.
      'fen-retreat'   *witan* pret.-pres. vb. 'know, realize' cf. line 715,
      Sw 76, MR 130   *geweald* n. 'power, control'

765   *gram* adj. as noun 'wrathful, hostile (one)'   *grāp* f. 'grasp'
      gēocor adj. 'grievous'   *sīð* m. 'journey, undertaking' cf. line 716

766   *hearm-scaþa* m. 'harmful enemy'   *ātēon* II 'take (a journey)'

767   *dryht-sele* m. 'noble hall, retainers' hall'   *dynnan* 1 'resound,
      make a din'   *weorðan* III 'become, happen, come to pass'

768   *ceaster-būend* m. 'town-dweller'   *cēne* adj. as noun 'bold, keen
      (one)'   *gehwylc* pron. 'each'

769   *eorl* m. 'nobleman' cf. line 761   *ealu-scerwen* f. 'ale-pouring'
      see p. 310 and trans. on p. 93   *yrre* adj. 'angry' cf. 726
      bēgen adj. as noun 'both' Sw 39, MR 84

770   *rēþe* adj. 'fierce, cruel'   *ren-weard* m. 'house-guardian'
      reced mn. 'hall'   *hlynsian* 2 'resound'

771 *wundor* n. 'wonder, marvel'   *micel* adj. 'great'   *wīn-sele* m.
     'wine-hall'

772 *wiðhabban* 3 'withstand' Sw 74, MR 126   *heaðo-dēor* adj. as
     noun 'battle-brave (one)'   *hrūse* f. 'earth'   *feallan* VII 'fall'

773 *fæger* adj. 'fair, lovely'   *fold-bold* n. 'earth-dwelling, building'
     þæs dem. pron., adv. gen. 'so, to such a degree'   *fæste* adv.
     'firmly'

774 *innan* adv. 'inside'   *ūtan* adv. 'outside'   *īren-bend* f. 'iron
     band' cf. line 722

775 *searo-þanc* m. 'ingenuity, skill'   *besmiþian* 2 'fasten with
     smith's work'   *syll* f. 'floor'   *ābūgan* II 'bend away'

776 *medu-benc* f. 'mead-bench' cf. line 5   *monig* adj. 'many' (sing.
     for pl. sense 'many a mead-bench')   *mīne* poss. pron. as instr.
     gefrǣge n. 'reported information' (thus *mīne gefrǣge* 'as I have
     heard tell')

777 *regnian* 2 'adorn'   *þǣr* cj. 'where, when'   *gram* see line 765
     winnan III 'struggle, fight'

778 *þæs* obj. of vb., anticipating ff. *þæt* clause   *wēnan* 1 'expect'
     with gen. obj.   *wita* m. 'wise man'

779 *hit* acc. pron. (neuter used loosely for the hall despite *sele* m. in
     lines 771–773)   *ā* adv. 'ever'   *gemet* n. 'measure, power,
     manner' (thus *mid gemete* 'by ordinary means')   *ǣnig* pron.
     'any' with gen. pl.

780 *betlīc* adj. 'splendid'   *bān-fāg* adj. 'adorned with bone'
     (antlers?)   *tōbrecan* IV 'break to pieces'   *magan* pret.-pres.
     vb. 'can, be able'

781 *list* mf. 'skill, cunning'   *tōlūcan* II 'unlock'   *nymþe* cj.
     'unless'   *līg* m. 'fire' cf. line 727   *fæþm* m. 'embrace, power'
     (for the allusion see lines 82–85 and pp. 282, 310)

782 *swelgan* III 'swallow' pret. subj. with obj. understood   *swaþul*
     mn. 'flame, heat'   *swēg* m. 'sound'   *āstīgan* I 'step up,
     mount'

783 *nīwe* adj. 'new, surprising'   *geneahhe* adv. 'sufficiently'
     standan VI 'stand'

784 *atelīc* adj. 'horrible' (cf. *atol* 732)   *egesa* m. 'fear, terror'
     ānra gehwylcum 'in each of the ones' cf. line 732b

785 *þāra þe* 'of those that' taken with *ānra* 784   *of* prep. 'on, from'
     weal(l) m. 'wall'   *wōp* m. 'wail, weeping' see p. 311
     gehȳran 1 'hear'

786 *gryre-lēoð* n. 'terror-song, horrible song'   *galan* VI 'sing'
     andsaca m. 'enemy' (an obj. of *gehȳrdon* while subject of *galan*,
     i.e., 'heard him to sing . . .')

787 *sige-lēas* adj. 'victory-less'   *sang* m. 'song'   *sār* n. 'wound,
     sore'   *wānigean* 2 'bewail'

788 *hel(l)* f. 'hell'   *hæft* m. 'captive, slave' (*hæfton* acc. sing.)
     healdan VII 'hold'

789 *mægen* n. 'might, strength'   *strang* adj. 'strong'; here superl.

790 *dæg* m. 'day' sing. with pl. sense (lines 789–790 echo 196–197; see
     p. 311)

791 *nolde* = *ne* + *wolde*, pret. sing. of *willan* anom. vb. 'will, want,
     wish' Sw 79, MR 129   *eorl* m. 'noble, warrior'   *hlēo* mn.
     'protector'   *ǣnige þinga* 'by any means, in any way' gen. pl. of
     þing n. 'thing, reason, deed' used as adv. Sw 86, MR 190.5

792 *cwealm-cuma* m. 'murderous visitor, killer guest'   *cwic* adj.
     'alive'   *forlǣtan* VII 'leave, let go'

793 *nē* cj. 'nor'   *līf-dæg* m. 'life-day, day of life'   *lēode* m. pl.
     'people, nation'   *ǣnig* st. adj. as noun 'any'

794 *nytt* adj. 'useful'   *tellan* 1 'reckon, consider' Sw 72, MR 122
     þǣr adv. 'there, then'   *genehost* superl. of *geneahhe* adv.
     'enough, sufficiently'; trans. with *eorl* as 'more than enough'
     bregdan III 'draw, swing'

795 *eorl* m. 'noble, warrior' sing. with collective force   *eald* adj.
     'old'   *lāf* f. 'heirloom' i.e., sword

796 *frēa-drihten* m. 'noble lord'   *feorh* mn. 'life'   *ealgian* 2
     'protect'

797 *mǣre* adj. 'famous'   *þēoden* m. 'lord, chief'   *þǣr* cj. 'if,
     wherever'   *magan* pret.-pres. vb. 'can, be able' with vb. 'to do'
     or 'to protect' understood   *swā* adv. 'so, thus' (line 797b echoes
     762b)

798 *þæt* dem. pron. 'it' anticipating lines 801b–805a   *witan* pret.-
     pres. vb. 'know'   *þā* cj. 'when'   *gewin* n. 'fight'   *drēogan*
     II 'engage in, perform'

799 *heard-hicgende* adj. 'brave-minded'   *hilde-mecg* m. 'warrior'

800 *healf* f. 'side'   *gehwā* pron. 'each'   *hēawan* VII 'hew, cut'
     þencan 1 'think, intend' Sw 72, MR 122

801 *sāwol* f. 'soul' (Grendel's)   *sēcan* 1 'seek, reach'   *syn-scaða*
     m. 'evil-doer, sinful harmer'

802 *ǣnig* adj. 'any'; trans. with *cyst* and negative vb.   *ofer* prep.
     'upon'   *eorþe* f. 'earth'   *īren* n. 'iron (sword)'; here gen. pl.
     cyst f. 'the best, choicest'

803 *gūð-bill* n. 'war-sword'   *nān* pron. 'none'   *grētan* 1
     'approach, reach, touch'   *nolde* see line 791

804 *sige-wǣpen* n. 'victory weapon'   *forswerian* VI 'bespell' with
     dat. objects   *habban* 3 'have'

805 *ecg* f. 'edge'   *gehwylc* pron. declined as st. adj. 'each, every'
*sculan pret.-pres. vb. 'must'; trans. with infinitives in lines 807
and 808   *aldor-gedāl* n. 'separation from life'

806 see line 790

807 *earmlīc* adj. 'wretched'   *wurðan* var. of *weorðan* II 'become'
ellor-gāst m. 'spirit from elsewhere'

808 *fēond* m. 'enemy'   *geweald* n. 'power, control'   *feor* adv.
'far'   *sīðian* 2 'journey'

809 *þā* adv. 'then'   *þæt* dem. pron. anticipates the *þæt* clause in
lines 812 ff.   *onfindan* III 'find out, discover'   *fela* indecl.
noun 'many' with gen. in lines 810 and 811   *ǣror* compar. adv.
'earlier'

810 *mōd* n. 'heart, mind'   *myrðu* f. 'affliction, injury'   *mann* m.
'man, human'   *cynn* n. 'race, kind'

811 *fyren* f. 'crime, sin'   *gefremman* 1 'do, perform'   *fāg* var. of
fāh adj. 'hostile, at feud' with vb. 'to be' understood (contrast the
meaning of 'decorated' in lines 716 and 725; *fāh/fāg* can also mean
'(blood-)stained' as in lines 420, 934, 1631)

812 *him* poss. dat. Sw 87(1), MR 191   *līc-homa* m. 'body-covering'
lǣstan 1 'serve, avail, last'

813 *mōdega* wk. adj., var. of *mōdig* 'spirited, brave'   *mǣg* m.
'kinsman'

814 *hæfde* see line 804   *hond* f. 'hand' dat. sing. Sw 19, MR 61
gehwæþer pron. 'either (one)'   *ōðer* adj. as noun 'the other'

815 *lifigende* pres. part. of *libban* 3 'live'; trans. as 'while living'
lāð adj. 'hateful'   *līc-sār* n. 'body wound'   *gebīdan* I
'experience, suffer'

816 *atol* adj. 'terrible'   *ǣglǣca* m. 'monster'   *him* poss. dat.
on prep. 'in'   *eaxl* f. 'shoulder'   *weorðan* III 'become'

817 *syn-dolh* n. 'great wound, evil wound'   *sweotol* adj. 'clear,
evident'   *seonu* f. 'sinew'   *onspringan* III 'spring apart, tear
apart'

818 *berstan* III 'burst, break'   *bān-loca* m. 'bone-locker' i.e.,
'muscle' cf. line 742   *weorðan* III 'become'

819 *gūð-hrēð* n. 'battle glory'   *gyfeþe* adj. 'given, granted'
*sculan pret.-pres. vb. 'must'; trans. with infinitives in lines 820
and 821   *þonan* adv. 'thence, from there'

820 *feorh-sēoc* adj. 'life-sick, mortally ill'   *flēon* II 'flee'   *fen-hlið*
n. 'fen cliff, marshy bank'

821 *sēcean* var. of *sēcan* 1 'seek'   *wyn-lēas* adj. 'joyless'   *wīc* n.
'dwelling'   *witan* pret.-pres. vb. 'know'   *þē* instr. dem. pron.
'by means of that' i.e., the wound   *geornor* compar. adv. 'the
more surely' from *georne* adv. 'readily, certainly, eagerly'

822 *aldor* var. of *ealdor* n. 'life'   *ende* m. 'end'   *gegangan* VII 'reach, arrive at'

823 *dōgor* n. 'day'   *dæg-rīm* n. 'number of days' parallel subject with *ende*   *Denum eallum* poss. dat.

824 *æfter* prep. 'on account of, along with'   *wæl-ræs* m. 'slaughter rush, deadly fight'   *willa* m. 'desire, wish'   *gelimpan* III 'happen, come to pass' here past part.

825 *gefælsian* 2 'cleanse'   *ǣr* adv. 'previously'   *feorran* adv. 'from far away'   *cuman* IV 'come'

826 *snotor* adj. 'wise'   *swȳð-ferhð* adj. 'strong-minded'   *sele* m. 'hall'

827 *generian* 2 'save'   *wið* prep. 'against'   *nīð* m. 'hostility, violence'   *niht-weorc* n. 'night work'   *gefēon* V 'rejoice' with gen. or dat. object

828 *ellen-mærþu* f. 'fame gained through courage, heroic deed'

829 *Gēat-mecga* gen. pl. of *Gēat-mæcg* m. 'Geatish kinsman'   *lēod* m. 'man'   *gilp* n. 'boast'   *gelæstan* 1 'perform, fulfill'

830 *swylce* adv. 'likewise, also'   *oncȳþð* f. 'grief, distress'   *eall* adj. 'all'   *gebētan* 1 'make better, remedy'

831 *inwid-sorg* var. of *inwit-sorh* f. 'evil sorrow'   *þē* indecl. rel. particle 'which, that'   *drēogan* II 'endure, suffer'

832 *þrēa-nȳd* f. 'terrible necessity, oppressive need'   *þolian* 2 'suffer, endure'

833 *torn* n. 'distress'   *unlȳtel* adj. 'not small' (litotes; see p. 9)   *tācen* n. 'token, sign'   *sweotol* see line 817

834 *syþðan* cj. 'once, from the time when'   *hilde-dēor* adj. as noun 'battle-brave (one)'   *hond* f. 'hand' (Grendel's)   *ālecgan* 1 'lay down, place'

835 *earm* m. 'arm'   *eaxl* f. 'shoulder'   *þǣr* adv. 'there'   *eal* adv. 'all'   *geador* adv. 'together'

836 *grāp* f. 'grip, claw'   *gēap* adj. 'curved, vaulted, spacious'   *hrōf* m. 'roof'

4. The Description of the Mere (1345–96)

1345 *þæt* pron. 'that' anticipating the ff. *þæt* clause   *land-būend* m. pl. 'land-dwellers'   *lēode* m. pl. 'people'

1346 *sele-rǣdend* m. 'hall-counselor'   *secgan* 3 'say, tell'   *hȳran* 1 'hear'

1347 *sēon* V 'see'   *swylc* dem. pron. 'such'   *twēgen* m. adj. 'two' Sw 39, MR 84

1348 *micel* adj. 'great, large'   *mearc-stapa* m. 'border walker,

wanderer on the frontier'   *mōr* m. 'moor'   *healdan* VII
'hold'; trans. the inf. as pres. part.

1349 *ellor-gǣst* m. 'spirit from elsewhere'   *ðǣra* var. of *ðāra* gen. pl.
pron.   *ōðer* adj. 'another, one of two, the second' here
correlative with line 1351: trans. 'one . . . the other'

1350 *þæs þe* gen. pron. as adv. 'so far as, to the extent that'
gewislīcost superl. adv. 'most clearly'   *gewitan* pret.-pres. vb.
'know, perceive' Sw 76, MR 130   *magan* pret.-pres. vb. 'can,
be able'

1351 *ides* f. 'woman, lady'   *onlīcnæs* f. 'likeness'   *ōðer* see line
1349   *earm-sceapen* adj. 'miserable, wretchedly made' (from
scieppan VI 'create, make, shape')

1352 *wer* m. 'man'   *wæstm* m. 'stature, form'   *wrǣc-lāst* m. 'path
of exile'   *tredan* V 'tread, walk'

1353 *næfne* var. of *nefne* cj. 'except'   *māra* compar. adj. 'greater,
larger' (from *micel* 'great' Sw 33, MR 76)   *ǣnig* adj. 'any'
ōðer adj. 'other'

1354 *geār-dæg* m. 'day of yore'   *nemman* 1 'name, call'

1355 *fold-būende* m. pl. 'earth dweller'   *nō* adv. 'not at all'   *hīe*
can be either the *fold-būende* or the monsters   *fæder* m. 'father'
acc. sing. Sw 23, MR 60.2   *cunnan* pret.-pres. vb. 'know' Sw
77, MR 130, 209

1356 *hwæþer* cj. 'whether'   *him* dat. sing. or pl.; trans. 'for him, for
them'   *ǣnig* adj. as noun 'any' ('father' understood)   *ǣr* adv.
'formerly'   *ācennan* 1 'beget, bear'

1357 *dyrne* adj. 'secret, hidden'   *gāst* m. 'spirit'; trans. the gen. pl.
as 'among'   *dȳgel* adj. 'secret, mysterious'   *lond* var. of *land*
n. 'land'

1358 *warian* 2 'guard, occupy'   *wulf-hleoþu* acc. pl. of *wulf-hliþ* n.
'wolf-slope'   *windig* adj. 'windy'   *næs(s)* m. 'headland, bluff'

1359 *frēcne* adj. 'dangerous'   *fen-gelād* n. 'fen-path'   *ðǣr* cj.
'where'   *fyrgen-strēam* m. 'mountain stream'

1360 *næss* see 1358   *genip* n. 'darkness, mist'   *niþer* adv.
'downward' (cf. Mod. Eng. 'nether')   *gewītan* I 'go, travel'

1361 *flōd* m. 'flood, tide'   *folde* f. 'earth, ground'   *nis = ne + is*
Sw 97, MR 184.4   *feor* adv. 'far'   *heonon* adv. 'hence, from
here'

1362 *mīl-gemearc* n. 'mile-measurement'; trans. the gen. as 'by'
mere m. 'mere, lake, pool'   *standan* VI 'stand'

1363 *hangian* 2 'hang'   *hrinde* adj. 'frost-covered'   *bearu* m.
'grove, wood'

1364 *wudu* m. 'wood, tree(s)'   *wyrt* f. 'root'   *fæst* adj. 'fast'
wæter n. acc. 'water'   *oferhelmian* 2 'overhang, overshadow'

1365 *þǣr* adv. 'there'   *magan* pret.-pres. vb. 'can, be able' with
      understood subject *man* 'one'   *niht* f. 'night'   *gehwā* pron.
      'each'   *nīð-wundor* n. 'evil portent'   *sēon* V 'see'

1366 *fȳr* n. 'fire'   *flōd* see line 1361   *nō* see line 1355   *þæs* gen.
      pron. as adv. 'to such a degree, so'   *frōd* adj. as noun 'old,
      wise (one)'   *libban* 3 'live' Sw 74, MR 126

1367 *guma* m. 'man'   *bearn* n. 'child, son'   *grund* m. 'ground,
      bottom'   *witan* pret.-pres. vb. 'know, ascertain'; here pres.
      subj.

1368 *ðēah þe* cj. 'although'   *hǣð-stapa* m. 'heath-walker' i.e., stag
      hund m. 'hound, dog'   *swencan* 1 'press, afflict'

1369 *heorot* m. 'hart, stag'   *horn* m. 'horn'   *trum* adj. 'strong'
      holt-wudu m. 'forest'   *sēcan* 1 'seek'; here pres. subj.

1370 *feorran* adv. 'from afar'   *geflȳman* 1 'put to flight'   *ǣr* adv.
      'sooner' with correlative cj. *ǣr* in line 1371   *feorh* mn. 'life'
      sellan 1 'give, give up'

1371 *aldor* var. of *ealdor* n. 'life'   *ōfer* m. 'bank, shore'   *ǣr* cj.
      'before'   *willan* anom. vb. 'will' (Sw 79, 92, MR 129, 211) with
      vb. of motion understood from *in* prep. 'in' (cf. Mod. Eng. 'the cat
      wants out')

1372 *hafela* m. 'head'   *hȳdan* 1 'hide, preserve'   *nis* see line 1361
      hēoru adj. 'pleasant'   *stōw* f. 'place'

1373 *þonon* var. of *þonan* adv. 'thence, from there'   *ȳð-geblond* n.
      'the mix (or toss) of waves'   *āstīgan* I 'climb, ascend'

1374 *won* adj. 'dark, black'   *tō* prep. 'to'   *wolcen* n. 'cloud, sky'
      (cf. lines 8 and 714)   *wind* m. 'wind'   *styrian* 1 'stir up'

1375 *lāð* adj. 'hostile, hateful'   *gewidre* n. 'weather, storm'   *oðþæt*
      cj. 'until'   *lyft* fmn. 'air, sky' (cf. Mod. Eng. 'aloft')
      drysmian var. of *ðrysmian 2 'grow dark, become suffocating'

1376 *rodor* m. 'sky, heaven'   *rēotan* II 'weep'   *nū* adv. 'now'
      rǣd m. 'counsel, help'   *gelang* adj. 'at hand'

1377 *eft* adv. 'again'   *æt* prep. 'at'   *ān* adj. 'alone'   *eard* m.
      'region, dwelling place'   *gīt* var. of *gȳt* adv. 'yet, still'
      cunnan pret.-pres. vb. 'know' Sw 77, MR 130 (*const* var. of *canst*)

1378 *frēcne* see line 1359   *stōw* see line 1372   *ðǣr* adv. 'where'
      findan III 'find'   *magan* pret.-pres. vb. 'can, be able'

1379 *fela-sinnig* adj. 'very sinful'   *secg* m. 'man, warrior'   *sēcan*
      see line 1369   *gif* cj. 'if'   *durran pret.-pres. vb. 'dare'

1380 *þā* dem. pron., not adv.   *fǣhð* f. 'revenge, feud, battle'   *fēoh*
      n. 'property, riches' here dat. sing. (cf. Mod. Eng. 'fee')
      lēanian 2 'reward, repay'; pres. indicative as future tense

1381 *eald-gestrēon* n. 'ancient treasure'   *ǣr* adv. 'formerly'   *dōn*
      anom. vb. 'do' Sw 80, MR 128

1382 *wundini* instr. sing. of past part. *wunden,* from *windan* III 'twist, wind'; trans. 'twisted into rings'   *gold* n. 'gold'   *gyf* see line 1379   *on weg* adv. 'away' (*weg* m. 'way')   *cuman* IV 'come' Sw 65, MR 103.2, 109

1383 *maþelian* 2 'make a speech'   *bearn* n. 'son'

1384 *sorgian* 2 'sorrow, grieve'   *snotor* adj. 'wise'   *guma* m. 'man'   *sēlre* n. nom. sing. of *sēlra* wk. adj. 'better' (compar. of *gōd* 'good' Sw 33, MR 76)   *bið* 3rd person pres. sing. of *bēon* anom. vb. 'to be'; here impersonal with dat. pron.   *ǣghwā* pron. 'every one'

1385 *frēond* n. 'friend'   *wrecan* V 'avenge'   *þonne* cj. 'than' *fela* indecl. adv. 'much'   *murnan* III 'mourn'

1386 *ūre* gen. pl. personal pron.; trans. 'of us'   *ǣghwylc* pron. 'each (one)'   **sculan* pret.-pres. vb. 'must' Sw 77, MR 130, 210 *ende* m. 'end'   *gebīdan* I 'await, experience'

1387 *worold* f. 'world'   *līf* n. 'life'   *wyrcan* 1 'work, strive to gain' with gen. object   **mōtan* pret.-pres. vb. 'may, be allowed' Sw 77, MR 130, 208

1388 *dōm* m. 'favorable judgment, glory, repute'   *ǣr* prep. 'before' *dēaþ* m. 'death'   *driht-guma* m. 'warrior, retainer'

1389 *unlifigend* adj. 'unliving, dead'   *æfter* adv. 'afterwards' *sēlest* adj. 'best' superl. of *gōd*; cf. line 1384

1390 *ārīsan* I 'arise'   *rīce* n. 'kingdom'   *weard* m. 'guardian' *uton* var. of *wutun* (from 1st person pl. subj. of *wītan* I 'go') used as imperative with ff. inf.; trans. 'let us'   *hraþe* adv. 'quickly' *fēran* 1 'go'

1391 *māge* f. 'kinswoman'   *gang* m. 'going, track'   *scēawi(g)an* 2 'look upon, examine'

1392 *hit* n. pron. of general reference   *gehātan* VII 'promise'   *nō* adv. 'not at all'   *on* prep. 'into'   *helm* m. 'protection, cover' *losian* 2 'escape, be lost'

1393 *nē* cj. 'nor'   *folde* see line 1361   *fæþm* m. 'bosom, embrace' *fyrgen-holt* n. 'mountain forest'

1394 *gyfen* var. of *geofon* mn. 'sea, ocean'   *grund* see line 1367 *gān* anom. vb. 'go' Sw 80, MR 128; here pres. subj.   *þǣr* cj. 'where, wherever'   *willan* anom. vb. 'will, wish, want' Sw 79, MR 129

1395 *dōgor* n. 'day'   *geþyld* f. 'patience'   *habban* 3 'have' Sw 74, MR 126; here sing. imperative

1396 *wēa* m. 'woe, trouble'   *gehwylc* pron. 'each'; trans. gen. as 'for' *swā* cj. 'as'   *wēnan* 1 'expect'   *tō* prep. 'from' with preceding dat. object

5. The Lay of the Last Survivor (2231b–77)

2231 **þǣr** adv. 'there'   **swylc** pron. 'such'   **fela** indecl. noun 'many'

2232 **eorð-hūs** n. 'earth-house'   **ǣr-gestrēon** n. 'ancient treasure'

2233 **swā** cj. 'just as'   **hȳ** var. of *hīe* acc. pl. pron.   **geār-dæg** m. 'day of yore'   **guma** m. 'man'   **nāt-hwylc** pron. 'someone' (from *ne wāt hwylc* 'I know not which')

2234 **eormen-lāf** f. 'immense legacy'   **æþele** adj. 'noble'   **cynn** n. 'people'

2235 **þanc-hycgende** adj. 'thoughtful'   **gehȳdan** 1 'hide'

2236 **dēor** adj. 'precious'   **māð(ð)um** m. 'treasure'   **eall** adj. 'all'   **hīe** acc. pl. pron. referring to *cynn*   **dēað** m. 'death'   **forniman** IV 'take away, destroy'

2237 **ǣrra** compar. adj. 'earlier'   **mǣl** n. 'time'   **ān** adj. as noun 'one'   **ðā** adv. 'then'   **gēn** adv. 'still, yet'

2238 **lēode** m. pl. 'people, nation'   **duguð** f. 'troop (of tried warriors)'; see p. 260   **lengest** superl. adv. 'long'   **hweorfan** III 'roam, move about'

2239 **weard** m. 'guardian'   **wine-geōmor** adj. 'mourning for friends'   **wēnan** 1 'expect' with gen. object   **ylca** pron. 'the same'

2240 **lȳtel** adj. 'little'   **fæc** n. 'period, space of time'   **long-gestrēon** n. 'long-kept treasure'

2241 **brūcan** II 'enjoy, use' with gen. object   ***mōtan** pret.-pres. vb. 'may, be allowed' Sw 77, MR 130   **beorh** var. of *beorg* m. 'barrow, mound'   **eall-gearo** adj. 'all ready'

2242 **wunian** 2 'dwell, be situated'   **wong** m. 'plain'   **wæter-yð** f. 'water wave, surf'   **nēah** prep. 'near' with dat.

2243 **nīwe** adj. 'new'   **be** prep. 'by, beside'   **næs(s)** m. 'headland, bluff'   **nearo-cræft** m. 'skill in enclosing'(?)   **fæst** adj. 'fast, firm' with vb. 'made' understood

2244 **on innan** adv. phrase 'into'   **beran** IV 'bear, carry'   **eorl-gestrēon** n. 'treasure of nobles'; depends on *dǣl*

2245 **hring** m. 'ring' gen. pl.; depends on *hyrde* m. 'guardian, keeper'   **hord-wyrðe** adj. 'worthy of a hoard'   **dǣl** m. 'part, portion'

2246 **fǣttan** wk. gen. sing. of *fǣted* adj. 'plated, decorated'   **gold** n. 'gold'; depends on *dǣl*   **fēa** adj. 'few' with gen. pl. of *word* n. 'word'   **cweðan** V 'speak, say'

2247 **healdan** VII 'hold'   **hrūse** f. 'earth'   **hæleð** m. pl. 'heroes'   ***mōtan** pret.-pres. vb. 'may, be allowed to' Sw 77, MR 130, 208

2248 **eorl** m. 'prince'   **ǣht** f. 'property, power'   **hwæt** interj. 'lo, truly'   **hyt** var. of *hit* pron. 'it'   **on** prep. 'from, in'

2249 *gōde* pl. adj. as noun 'good (men)'   *begitan* V 'get, obtain'
       gūð-dēað m. 'war-death'   *forniman* IV 'take away, destroy'
2250 *feorh-bealo* n. 'life-bale, threat to life'   *frēcne* adj. 'dangerous,
       fearful'   *fȳras* var. of *fīras* m. pl. 'men'   *gehwylc* pron.
       'each'
2251 *lēod* m. 'man, member of tribe' (*lēode* pl. 'people' cf. line 24)
       mīn poss. pron.   *ðe* indecl. rel. particle 'that' (sing. with *ofgeaf*
       but pl. with *gesāwon*)   *līf* n. 'life'   *ofgifan* V 'give up, leave'
2252 *gesēon* V 'see, look upon'   *sele-drēam* m. 'hall-joy'   *nāh* =
       ne + *āh*, from pret.-pres. vb. *āgan* 'have, possess'   *hwā* indef.
       pron. 'anyone'   *sweord* n. 'sword'   *wegan* V 'carry, wear'
       (subj. mood)
2253 *oððe* cj. 'or'   *feormian* 2 'clean, polish'   *fǣted* adj. 'plated,
       decorated'   *wǣge* n. 'cup' see also p. 358
2254 *drync-fǣt* n. 'drinking vessel'   *dēor* adj. 'dear, precious'
       duguð f. 'troop of experienced retainers' cf. line 2238   *ellor*
       adv. 'elsewhere'   *scacan* VI 'depart'
2255 *sculan pret.-pres. vb. 'must' (with inf. *wesan* 'to be' understood)
       Sw 77, MR 146, 210   *hearda* wk. adj. 'hard'   *helm* m.
       'helmet'   *hyrsted* adj. 'adorned' (past part. of *hyrstan* 1 'adorn')
2256 *fǣt* n. '(gold) plate'   *befeallan* VII 'deprive of, bereave of' (past
       part.)   *feormynd* m. pl. 'polishers' (pres. part. of *feormian* 2
       'clean, polish' cf. line 2253)   *swefan* V 'sleep (in death)'
2257 *þā* pron. 'those'   *ðe* indecl. rel. particle 'who, that'   *beado-
       grīma* m. 'war-mask, helmet'   *bȳwan* 1 'polish, prepare'
       sceoldon from *sculan 'must, ought' see line 2255
2258 *gē* cj. 'and'   *swylce* adv. 'likewise'   *here-pād* f. 'war-cloak,
       mail-coat'   *hild* f. 'war'   *gebīdan* I 'endure, experience'
2259 *ofer* prep. 'over, across'   *bord* n. 'shield'   *gebræc* n.
       'breaking, crashing'   *bite* m. 'bite'   *īren* n. 'iron (sword)';
       here gen. pl.
2260 *brosian* 2 'crumble, decay'   *æfter* prep. 'after'   *beorn* m.
       'man, warrior'   *magan* pret.-pres. vb. 'can'   *byrne* f. 'mail-
       coat'   *hring* m. 'ring, ring-mail'
2261 *æfter* prep. 'beside, along with'   *wīg-fruma* m. 'war-leader'
       wīde adv. 'far, widely'   *fēran* 1 'go, travel, follow'
2262 *hæleð* m. 'hero, warrior'; here poss. dat. pl.   *be* prep. 'by'
       healf f. 'side'   *næs* adv. 'not at all, by no means' with vb. 'to
       be' understood   *hearpe* f. 'harp'   *wyn* f. 'joy'
2263 *gomen* n. 'play, sport'   *glēo-bēam* m. 'music-wood, harp'   *nē*
       cj. 'nor'   *hafoc* m. 'hawk'
2264 *geond* prep. 'throughout'   *sæl* n. 'hall' (cf. *sele*)   *swingan* III
       'swing, beat'   *swifta* wk. adj. 'swift'   *mearh* m. 'horse'

2265   *burh-stēde* m. 'fortress courtyard'   *bēatan* VII 'beat, stamp'
       bealo-cwealm m. 'evil death, baleful killing'   *habban* 3 'have'
       (uncontracted 3rd sing. pres.) Sw 74, MR 126

2266   *fela* indecl. adj. 'many' (with gen. pl.)   *feorh-cynn* n. 'race of
       the living'   *forð* adv. 'forth, away'   *onsendan* 1 'send away'

2267   *swā* adv. 'thus, so'   *giōmor-mōd* adj. as noun 'sad at heart'
       giohðo f. 'sorrow'   *mænan* 1 'lament, speak of'

2268   *ān* adj. as noun 'one'   *æfter* prep. 'for' with dat.   *eall* m. 'all'
       unblīðe adj. 'unhappy'   *hweorfan* III 'turn, go, roam' cf. line
       2238

2269   *dæg* m. 'day' and *niht* f. 'night' are adverbial gen. Sw 86, MR
       190.5   *oððæt* cj. 'until'   *dēað* m. 'death'   *wylm* 'welling,
       flood'

2270   *hrīnan* I 'touch, reach'   *æt* prep. 'to'   *heorte* f. 'heart'
       hord-wynn f. 'hoard-joy, delightful treasure'   *fond* var. of *fand*,
       from *findan* II 'find'

2271   *eald* adj. 'old'   *ūht-sceaða* m. 'dawn harmer, attacker at night'
       open adj. 'open'   *standan* III 'stand'; trans. the inf. as pres.
       part.

2272   *byrnan* III 'burn'; here pres. part. as adj. with *sē ðe* 'he who'
       biorg var. of *beorg* m. 'barrow, mound'   *sēcan* 1 'seek'

2273   *nacod* adj. 'naked, smooth, (scaly?)'   *nīð-draca* m. 'hostile
       dragon'   *nihtes* see line 2269   *flēogan* II 'fly'

2274   *fȳr* n. 'fire'   *befangen* past part. of *befōn* VII 'encircle,
       surround'   *fold-būend* m. pl. 'earth-dweller'

2275   *swīðe* adv. 'greatly'   *ondrǣdan* VII 'dread, fear'   *gesēcean* 1
       'seek'   **sculan* pret.-pres. vb. 'must'

2276   *hord* n. '(a) hoard' or 'treasure' generally   *on* prep. 'in'
       hrūse see line 2247   *þǣr* cj. 'where'   *hǣðen* adj. 'heathen'
       gold n. 'gold'

2277   *warian* 2 'guard'   *winter* m. 'winter, year'   *frōd* adj. 'old,
       wise'   *byð* 3rd person pres. sing. of *bēon* anom. vb. 'to be';
       here impersonal with dat. pron.   *wihte* dat. sing. of *wiht* f.
       'anything' used as adv. with *ne*; trans. 'not at all'   *ðȳ* instr.
       dem. pron. 'thereby, by means of that'   *sēl* compar. adv.
       'better'

6. Wiglaf's Speeches Before Battle (2631–68)

2631   *maðelian* 2 'make a speech'   *word-riht* n. 'word about what is
       right'   *fela* indecl. adj. as noun 'many' with gen. pl.

2632   *secgan* 3 'say, speak'   *gesīð* m. 'companion'   *him* poss. dat.
sefa m. 'mind, heart'   *geōmor* adj. 'sad, troubled'

2633   *mǣl* n. 'time, occasion'   *gemunan* pret.-pres. vb. 'remember'
þǣr cj. 'where, when'   *medu* m. 'mead' Sw 19, MR 61
þicgan V 'partake of'

2634   *þonne* cj. 'when'   *gehātan* VII 'promise'   *ūssum* dat. sing. of
ūre poss. pron. declined as st. adj.   *hlāford* m. 'lord'

2635   *bīor-sele* m. 'beer hall, banquet hall'   *ðe* indecl. rel. particle
'who, that'   *ðās* acc. pl. of *þes* dem. pron. 'this'   *bēag* m.
'ring, collar, bracelet'   *gifan* V 'give'

2636   *ðā* pl. dem. pron.   *gūð-getāwa* f. pl. 'war gear'   *gyldan* III
'pay, repay'   *willan* anom. vb. 'will, want, intend' Sw 79, MR
129, 211

2637   *gif* cj. 'if'   *þyslicu* st. f. adj. 'such'   *þearf* f. 'need'
gelumpe sing. pret. subj. of *gelimpan* III 'happen, befall' with dat.
object

2638   *helm* m. 'helmet'   *heard* adj. 'hard'   *sweord* n. 'sword'
ðē var. of *þȳ* instr. dem. pron. 'on this account, for this reason';
correlative with *þē* in line 2641   *ūsic* var. of *ūs* acc. pl. pron.
on prep. 'from'   *herge* var. of *here* m. 'army'; here dat. sing.
gecēosan II 'choose'

2639   *tō* prep. 'for'   *sīð-fæt* m. 'expedition'   *sylf* pron. 'self'; trans.
the gen. as 'his own'   *willa* m. 'desire, wish'

2640   *onmunan* pret.-pres. vb. 'consider worthy (of)' with acc. of person
and gen. of thing   *ūsic* see line 2638   *mǣrðo* f. 'glory, great
deed'; here gen. pl.   *mē* pron., with the sense 'to me as well as
you'   *þās* see line 2635   *māð(ð)um* m. 'treasure'   *gifan* see
line 2635

2641   *þē* instr. dem. pron. 'because'; see line 2638   *gār-wīgend* m. pl.
'spear-warriors'   *gōd* adj. 'good'   *tellan* 1 'consider, reckon'

2642   *hwate* pl. adj. 'bold, brave'   *helm-berend* m. pl. 'helmet
bearers, warriors'   *þēah ðe* cj. 'although'   *hlāford* m. 'lord'
ūs personal pron., poss. dat.

2643   *ellen-weorc* n. 'brave deed, work of courage'   *āna* wk. adj.
'alone, only'   *āþencan* 1 'think, intend' Sw 72, MR 122

2644   *gefremman* 1 'perform, accomplish'; here an inflected inf. Sw 90,
MR 205.2   *folc* n. 'people, nation'   *hyrde* m. 'guardian,
shepherd'

2645   *forðām* cj. 'because'   *mann* m. 'man'; trans. the gen. pl. as
'among men' Sw 86, MR 190.4   *mǣst* superl. adj. as noun 'the
most, the greatest' with the ff. gen. pl.   *mǣrðo* see line 2640
gefremman see line 2644

2646 *dǣd* f. 'deed'   *dollīc* adj. 'daring, rash'   *nū* adv. 'now'
      dæg m. 'day'   *cuman* IV 'come'

2647 *ūre* poss. pron. 'our'   *man-dryhten* m. 'liege lord'   *mægen* n.
      'strength, might'   *behōfian* 2 'require, have need' with gen.
      object

2648 *gōd* adj. 'good'   *gūð-rinc* m. 'battle warrior'   *wutun* (from 1st
      person pl. subj. of *wītan* I 'go') used as imperative with ff.
      infinitives; trans. 'let us'   *gongan* var. of *gangan* VII 'go'   *tō*
      metrically stressed prep. with unexpressed noun, used as adv.
      when ff. vb.; trans. 'to that place, to him'

2649 *helpan* III 'help'   *hild-fruma* m. 'war leader'   *þenden* cj.
      'while, as long as'   *hyt(t)* f. 'heat'   *sȳ* var. of *sīe* sing. pres.
      subj. of *bēon* anom. vb. 'to be' Sw 78, MR 127

2650 *glēd-egesa* m. 'fire terror'   *grim* adj. 'grim, fierce, terrible'
      God m. 'God'   *witan* pret.-pres. vb. 'know'   *on* prep. 'about,
      concerning'   *mec* var. of *mē* sing. acc. pron.

2651 *þæt* cj. 'that'   *mē* dat. pron. with impersonal vb. 'to be'
      micle adv. 'much'   *lēofre* compar. adj. 'dearer' Sw 31, MR 74
      mīn poss. pron. declined as st. adj.   *līc-hama* m. 'body
      covering, body'

2652 *mid* prep. 'with'   *gold-gyfa* m. 'gold giver, lord'   *glēd* f. 'fire,
      flame'   *fæðmie* pres. sing. subj. of *fæðmian* 2 'embrace, seize'

2653 *þyncan* 1 'seem, appear' impersonal vb. with dat. pron.
      gerysne adj. 'proper, fitting'   *rond* m. 'shield'   *beran* IV
      'bear'

2654 *eft* adv. 'again, back'   *eard* m. 'homeland'   *nemne* var. of
      nefne cj. 'unless'   *ǣror* compar. adv. 'earlier, beforehand'
      mægen var. of *magon* 1st person pres. pl. of *magan* pret.-pres. vb.
      'can, be able'

2655 *fāne* var. of *fāhne* acc. sing. of *fāh* adj. as noun 'the hostile one'
      gefyllan 1 'fell, kill'   *feorh* mn. 'life'   *ealgian* 2 'protect'

2656 *þēoden* m. 'lord'   *witan* see line 2650   *gear(w)e* adv. 'surely,
      certainly'

2657 *þæt* cj. 'that'   *nǣron* = *ne* + *wǣron* 3rd person pret. pl. of
      bēon anom. vb. 'to be'   *eald-gewyrht* n. pl. 'service or reward
      for earlier deeds'   *þæt* cj. 'that, such that'   *āna* see line 2643
      **sculan* pret.-pres. vb. 'must' here pres. sing. subj.

2658 *duguð* f. 'band of tried retainers'; trans. the gen. as 'among'
      gnorn mn. 'sorrow, affliction'   *þrōwian* 2 'suffer, endure'

2659 *gesīgan* I 'sink, fall'   *æt* prep. 'at, in'   *sæc(c)* f. 'battle'
      ūrum dat. sing. of *ūre* poss. pron. 'our'; trans. as 'of us' (i.e.,
      Wiglaf and Beowulf) with *bām* in line 2660   **sculan* pret.-pres.

vb. 'must'; trans. with *gemæne* in line 2660   *sweord* n. 'sword'
helm m. 'helmet'

2660 *byrne* f. 'mail coat'   *beadu-scrūd* n. 'battle clothing'   *bām*
dat. of *bēgen* adj. as noun 'both' Sw 39, MR 84; trans. as 'by the
both'   *gemæne* adj. 'shared' with vb. 'to be' understood

2661 *wādan* VI 'go, move, advance'   *þā* adv. 'then'   *þurh* prep.
'through'   *wæl-rēc* m. 'slaughter smoke, deadly reek'   *wīg-
heafola* m. 'war-head' hence 'helmet'   *beran* see line 2653

2662 *frēa* m. 'lord'   *on* prep. 'in'   *fultum* m. 'help, support'
fēa acc. pl. adj. 'few' with gen.   *word* n. 'word'   *cweðan* V
'speak'

2663 *lēofa* adj. 'dear, beloved'   *læstan* 1 'do, perform' sing.
imperative with acc. object   *eall* st. adj. as n. acc. noun 'all'
tela adv. 'well, rightly'

2664 *swā* cj. 'as'   *geoguð-fēorh* mn. 'time of youth'   *geāra* adv.
'long ago'   *gecweðan* V 'speak, say'

2665 *ālǣtan* VII 'allow'   *be* prep. 'concerning' with pron. object *ðē*
lifigende pres. part. of *libban* 3 'live' declined as st. adj.; trans. as
'while living'

2666 *dōm* m. 'glory, repute'   *gedrēosan* II 'decline, fall away'
*sculan pret.-pres. vb. 'must' 2nd person pres. sing.   *nū* adv.
'now'   *dǣd* f. 'deed'   *rōf* adj. 'famous, brave'

2667 *æðeling* m. 'prince, nobleman'   *ān-hȳdig* adj. 'resolute, single-
minded'   *eall* adj. 'all'   *mægen* n. 'strength, might'

2668 *feorh ealgian* see line 2655   *ful-lǣstu* var. of 1st person pres.
sing. of *ful-lǣstan* 1 'help, support to the full'

7. Beowulf's Last Words (2792b–2820)

2792 *maþelian* 2 'make a speech'

2793 *gomel* var. of *gamol* adj. (perhaps adj. as noun) 'old'   *on* prep.
'in'   *giohðo* f. 'grief, sorrow'   *gold* n. 'gold'   *scēawian* 2
'look upon, behold'

2794 *frætwe* f. pl. 'treasure, ornaments'; trans. the gen. pl. as 'for'
Frēa m. 'the Lord'   *eall* adj. as noun 'all (things)'; trans. with
Frēan   *þanc* m. 'thanks'

2795 *Wuldur-cyning* m. 'King of glory'   *word* n. 'word'   *secgan* 3
'say, speak'

2796 *ēce* adj. 'eternal'   *Dryhten* m. 'Lord'   *þe* indecl. rel. particle
'which'   *hēr* adv. 'here'   *on* prep. 'upon'   *starian* 2 'look,
gaze'

2797 *þæs þe* cj. 'because' (depends on *þanc* in line 2794)   **mōtan*
pret.-pres. vb. 'may, be allowed' Sw 77, MR 130   *mīn* poss.
pron.   *lēode* m. pl. 'people'

2798 *ǣr* adv. 'before'   *swylt-dæg* m. 'death day'   *swylc* adj. as
noun 'such (things)'   *gestrȳnan* 1 'acquire'

2799 *nū* adv. 'now'   *on* prep. 'for'   *māð(ð)um* m. 'treasure'
hord n. 'hoard'   *mīne* goes with *feorh-legu*   *bebycgan* 1 'sell,
exchange'

2800 *frōd* adj. 'old, wise'   *feorh-legu* f. 'life span, allotted portion of
life'   *fremman* 1 'act, serve, attend to' here pres. pl. imperative
gēna adv. 'still, yet'

2801 *lēode* see line 2797   *þearf* f. 'need'   *magan* pret.-pres. vb.
'can, be able'   *hēr* see line 2796   *leng* compar. adv. 'longer'
wesan anom. vb. 'to be'

2802 *hātan* VII 'command, order' pres. pl. imperative   *heaðo-mǣre*
st. pl. adj. as noun '(those) famous in battle'   *hlǣw* m. 'mound,
barrow'   *gewyrcean* 1 'make, work'

2803 *beorht* adj. 'bright'   *æfter* prep. 'after, on account of'   *bǣl* n.
'pyre, fire'   *brim* n. 'sea'   *nose* f. 'promontory, headland'

2804 *scel* var. of *sceal*, from **sculan* pret.-pres. vb. 'ought, must' here
possibly future tense 'shall' Sw 92, MR 210   *tō* prep. 'for, as'
gemynd f. 'memorial, reminder'   *mīnum lēodum* see line 2797

2805 *hēah* adj. 'high'   *hlīfian* 2 'stand high, tower'   *Hrones-næss*
m. 'Whale's Cliff'

2806 *þæt* cj. 'that, so that'   *hit* refers to the *hlǣw* disregarding gender
sǣ-līðend m. pl. 'seafarers'   *syððan* adv. 'afterwards'   *hātan*
VII 'name, call' here pres. subj. pl. with future sense

2807 *biorh* var. of *beorg* m. 'barrow'   *ðā ðe* cj. 'when'   *brenting*
m. 'tall ship'

2808 *flōd* m. 'flood, sea'   *genip* n. 'darkness'   *feorran* adv. 'from
afar'   *drīfan* I 'drive'

2809 *dōn* anom. vb. 'do, put, take'   *him* poss. dat.   *of* prep. 'off,
from'   *heals* m. 'neck'   *hring* m. 'ring'   *gylden* adj.
'golden'

2810 *þioden* var. of *þēoden* m. 'lord'   *þrīst-hȳdig* adj. 'bold-minded,
brave'   *þegn* m. 'retainer'   *gesellan* 1 'give'

2811 *geong* adj. 'young'   *gār-wiga* m. 'spear-warrior'   *gold-fāh*
adj. 'gold-adorned'   *helm* m. 'helmet'

2812 *bēah* var. of *bēag* m. 'ring, collar'   *byrne* f. 'mail-coat'
hātan VII 'command, bid'   *brūcan* II 'use' with understood
objects

2813 *ende-lāf* f. 'last survivor, final remnant'   *ūsses* gen. of *ūre* poss.
pron. 'our'   *cynn* n. 'race, kin'

2814 *ealle* adj. 'all' with *māgas* in line 2815   *wyrd* f. 'fate'
forswāpan VII 'sweep away'

2815 *mǣg* m. 'kinsman'   *metod-sceaft* f. 'appointed destiny, death'

2816 *eorl* m. 'noble, warrior'   *on* prep. 'in'   *ellen* n. 'courage,
valor'   *æfter* prep. 'after' ff. its pron.   **sculan* pret.-pres. vb.
'must' with vb. of motion understood

2817 *gomel* adj. as noun 'the old (man)' cf. line 2793; treat the dat. here
as poss.   *gingæst* superl. of *geong* adj. 'young'; trans. as 'last,
final'   *word* n. 'word'

2818 *brēost-gehygd* f. 'inner thought'   *ǣr* cj. 'before'   *bǣl* n. 'fire,
pyre' cf. line 2803   *cure* from *cēosan* II 'choose' Sw 63, MR
107; here pret. subj. sing.

2819 *hāt* adj. 'hot'   *heaðo-wylm* m. 'battle flame'   *him* poss. dat.
of prep. 'from'   *hreðer* n. 'heart, breast'   *gewītan* 1 'go,
depart'

2820 *sāwol* f. 'soul'   *sēcean* 1 'seek'   *sōð-fæst* adj. as noun '(one)
firm in truth, just'   *dōm* m. 'judgment, glory'

8. Beowulf's Memorial (3156–82)

3156 *gewyrcan* 1 'make, build' Sw 70, MR 116   *ðā* adv. 'then'
lēode m. pl. 'people'

3157 *hlǣw* m. 'mound, barrow'   *hōe* dat. sing. of *hōh* m. 'headland'
hēah adj. 'high'   *brād* adj. 'broad'

3158 *wēg-līðend* m. 'seafarer'   *wīde* adv. 'widely, from afar'
gesȳne adj. 'visible, seen' (from *sēon* V 'see')

3159 *betimbran* 1 'build'   *tȳn* 'ten' (uninflected)   *dæg* m. 'day'

3160 *beadu-rōf* adj. as noun '(the one) bold in battle'   *bēcn* var. of
bēacen n. 'monument, sign' (cf. Mod. Eng. 'beacon')   *brond* m.
'fire, flame'   *lāf* f. 'remnant, leavings' here acc. sing. or pl.

3161 *weal(l)* m. 'wall'   *bewyrcan* 1 'surround'   *swā* cj. 'as'   *hyt*
var. of *hit* pron.   *weorðlīcost* superl. adj. 'most splendidly'

3162 *fore-snotor* adj. 'very wise'   *findan* III 'find, devise'   *magan*
pret.-pres. vb. 'can, be able' Sw 77, MR 130

3163 *hī* var. of *hīe* pl. pron.   *beorg* m. 'barrow, mound'   *dōn*
anom. vb. 'do, place, put' Sw 80, MR 128   *bēg* var. of *bēag* m.
'ring, collar, bracelet'   *sigle* n. 'jewel, brooch'

3164 *eall* adj. 'all'   *swylce . . . swylce* correlative prons. 'such . . .
as'   *hyrst* f. 'ornament'   *on* prep. 'from'   *hord* n. 'hoard'
ǣr adv. 'before, previously'

3165 *nīð-hēdig* adj. 'hostile-minded'   *geniman* IV 'seize, take away'
habban 3 'have' Sw 74, MR 126, 200

3166 *forlǣtan* VII 'let, leave' Sw 68, MR 104   *eorl* m. 'noble'
      gestrēon n. 'treasure'   *eorðe* f. 'earth'   *healdan* VII 'hold'

3167 *grēot* n. 'sand, earth' (cf. Mod. Eng. 'grit')   *þǣr* cj. 'where'
      nū adj. 'now'   *gēn* adv. 'still'   *libban* 3 'live, exist' Sw 74,
      MR 126

3168 *elde* var. of *ylde* m. pl. 'men'   *swā . . . swā* correlative cjs.
      '(just) as . . . as'   *unnyt* adj. 'useless'   *hyt* var. of *hit* pron.
      ǣror compar. adv. 'earlier'

3169 *þā* adv. 'then'   *ymbe* prep. 'around'   *hlǣw* see line 3157
      riodan var. of *ridon* pret. pl. of *rīdan* I 'ride' Sw 61, MR 93
      hilde-dēor adj. as noun '(one) brave in battle'

3170 *æþeling* m. 'prince, noble'   *bearn* n. 'son'   *eal* adj. 'all';
      trans. gen. pl. as 'in all'   *twelfe* m. nom. 'twelve'

3171 *willan* anom. vb. 'want, wish' Sw 79, MR 129   *caru* var. of
      cearu f. 'care, grief'   *cwīðan* 1 'bewail, lament'   *kyning* m.
      'king'   *mǣnan* 1 'speak of'

3172 *word-gyd* n. 'lay, elegy'   *wrecan* V 'recite, utter'   *ymb* =
      ymbe see line 3169   *wer* m. 'man'   *sprecan* V 'speak'

3173 *eahtian* 2 'consider, praise' Sw 73, MR 124   *eorlscipe* m.
      'nobility'   *ellen-weorc* n. acc. pl. 'courageous deeds'

3174 *duguð* f. 'power, excellence' here dat. pl. as adv. 'powerfully'
      dēman 1 'judge favorably, praise'   *swā* adv. 'thus'   *gedēfe*
      adj. 'fitting'

3175 *mon* indef. pron. 'one' (felt as pl. in *ferhðum* in line 3176)
      wine-dryhten m. 'friend and lord'   *word* n. 'word'   *herian* 1
      'praise, honor' here subj. in the *þæt* clause Sw 94, MR 156

3176 *ferhð* mn. 'spirit'   *frēogan* 2 'love'   *þonne* cj. 'when'   *forð*
      adv. 'forth, away'   *scile* from **sculan* pret.-pres. vb. 'must' Sw
      77, MR 130, 210

3177 *of* prep. 'from'   *līc-hama* m. 'body covering, body'   *lǣdan* 1
      'lead'   *weorðan* III 'become'

3178 *swā* see line 3174   *begnornian* 2 'lament, bemoan'   *lēode* see
      line 3156

3179 *hlāford* m. 'lord'   *hryre* m. 'fall'   *heorð-genēat* m. 'hearth-
      companion, retainer'

3180 *cweðan* V 'speak, say'   *wǣre* pret. subj. of *wesan* 'to be' Sw
      78, MR 127   *wyruld-cyning* m. 'king in this world, earthly king';
      trans. the gen. pl. as 'among'

3181 *mann* m. 'man' Sw 22, MR 58   *milde* adj. 'mild, kind'   (*-ust*,
      -ost are superl. throughout lines 3181–82)   *mon-ðwǣre* adj.
      'gentle, peaceful'

3182 *lēode* m. pl. 'people'   *līðe* adj. 'gracious, kind'   *lof-georn* adj.
      'eager for praise, fame'